Preparing Teachers for a Changing World

What Teachers Should Learn and Be Able to Do

Sponsored by the National Academy of Education

Edited by
Linda Darling-Hammond
John Bransford

In Collaboration with
Pamela LePage
Karen Hammerness
Helen Duffy

JOSSEY-BASS
A Wiley Imprint
www.josseybass.com

Published by Jossey-Bass
A Wiley Imprint
989 Market Street, San Francisco, CA 94103-1741 www.josseybass.com

Library of Congress Cataloging-in-Publication Data:
Preparing teachers for a changing world : what teachers should learn and be able to do /
edited by Linda Darling-Hammond and John Bransford in collaboration with Pamela LePage,
Karen Hammerness, and Helen Duffy ; sponsored by the National Academy of Education.— 1st ed.
    p.   cm.
  Includes bibliographical references and index.
  ISBN 0-7879-7464-1 (alk. paper)
  1. Teachers—Training of—United States.   2. Follow-up in teacher training—United States.
3. Teachers—In-service training—United States.   I. Darling-Hammond, Linda, 1951–.
II. Bransford, John.   III. National Academy of Education.
  LB1715.P733 2005
  370'.7'1—dc22

                                                                                        2004026736

Printed in the United States of America
FIRST EDITION
HB Printing 10 9 8 7 6

The Jossey-Bass Education Series

CONTENTS

PREFACE

All professions at some point in their development have worked to achieve consensus about the key elements of a professional education curriculum: the building blocks of preparation for all entrants into the occupation. In medicine, this happened at the turn of the twentieth century following the release of the famous Flexner Report that critiqued the uneven quality of medical education. Efforts to create a common curriculum for legal education followed shortly thereafter. Fields like engineering and architecture turned to this work in the mid-1900s. Over the last two decades, the teaching profession has begun to codify the knowledge base for professional practice and standards for the work of practitioners.

Meanwhile, great strides have been made in our understanding of learning and the teaching practices that support it. Over the last two years, the National Academy of Education, through its Committee on Teacher Education (CTE), has been considering the implications for the curriculum of teacher education of what the field has learned about effective learning and teaching, as well as about the learning of teachers.

This volume is the result of the Committee's work. It outlines core concepts and strategies that should inform initial teacher preparation, whether it is delivered in traditional or nontraditional settings. It is intended primarily for those who are responsible for the preparation of teachers: deans and faculty members in university-based programs as well as district personnel and school-based faculty in cooperating schools or alternative programs. A shorter summary volume is aimed at policymakers as well as practitioners. A companion volume examines the curricular implications of knowledge for teaching reading, as an initial effort to instantiate these recommendations in a content field. The Committee chose reading for this initiative because there is already a substantial body of research about how students learn to read, and a growing consensus about professional practice in the teaching of early reading upon which teacher education curriculum could be built.

This work stands on the shoulders of many other efforts. In 1989, the American Association of Colleges for Teacher Education published a seminal effort, the *Knowledge Base for the Beginning Teacher*, and followed this up with the *Teacher Educator's Handbook* in 1996. The National Board for Professional Standards (NBPTS), established in 1987, built on research about learning and teaching in developing standards articulating what expert teachers should know and be able to do. Additionally, the Interstate New Teacher Assessment and Support Consortium (INTASC), a consortium of state education agencies, higher education institutions, and national educational organizations, developed model standards and assessments for licensing beginning teachers that rest on the same body of research. Together these efforts create a continuum of expectations from beginning teaching to accomplished levels of practice.

These standards have become widespread. They have been incorporated into the teacher education accreditation standards of the National Council for the Accreditation of Teacher Education, and, according to a recent survey, most teacher education institutions have used these national and state standards to ground the foundation for their program designs and for teacher education outcome measures (Salzman, Denner, & Harris, 2002).

This report's recommendations are informed by these professional standard-setting initiatives and by important research compilations, such as the National Research Council's 1999 Report, *How People Learn*, which provides a comprehensive overview about what is known in the area of learning; the several *Handbooks of Research on Teaching*, sponsored by the American Educational Research Association; and the *Handbooks of Research on Teacher Education*, sponsored by the Association of Teacher Educators. These compilations have helped to develop conceptual frameworks for synthesizing knowledge about learning, teaching, and the learning of teachers.

Although this report has benefited greatly from the work that has preceded it, it is different from these other efforts in two ways: first, it seeks to inform the curriculum for teacher education by considering how what we know about *student learning* and teaching should inform what teachers have the opportunity to learn. Second, it considers emerging evidence on *teacher learning* and teacher education to suggest some of the strategies that may help new teachers learn this material more effectively. This report does not develop new standards or lists of all the things that teachers should know. Instead it includes recommendations for how knowledge deemed essential for beginning teachers can be incorporated into the initial teacher education curriculum. The report does not try to cover all of the curriculum content that people may argue is desirable in preservice programs; rather, it focuses on content considered essential based on strong professional consensus and on research evidence. A major emphasis is on preparing teachers for future learning as professionals. This is reflected in the title of this volume: *Preparing Teachers for a Changing World.*

The recommendations in this volume were developed through professional and scholarly consensus based on research about learning, teaching, teacher learning, and teacher education. In addition to building on the experiences of the standards boards, professional organizations, and research groups to articulate the knowledge base, we also have drawn on the knowledge and experience of CTE members and have conducted reviews of research associated with children's learning, development, assessment, and other domain-specific areas, as well as on how teachers learn, as the basis for making recommendations about curriculum. We have examined teacher education programs and curriculum artifacts (syllabi, assignments, and assessments) and vetted these ideas with researchers and practitioners of teacher education.

Similar processes have been used in developing curriculum in other professional schools such as law and medicine. For example, to obtain the necessary information about what content belongs in a medical school curriculum, developers reviewed relevant literature, consulted experts, and collected information from academics and practitioners about current practices and problems (Kern, Thomas, Howard, & Bass, 1998; Mandin & Dauphinee, 2000). Like other professions, we have also drawn upon the experiences and curriculum conceptions of specific professional education programs. Because the contexts of teacher education are so varied, we have looked at a wider range of well-developed programs than did the legal profession in basing much of its long-standing core curriculum on that of Harvard's Law School (Harvard Law School, 1936; Lagemann, 1983) or the medical profession in basing much of its curriculum development on the model developed at Johns Hopkins in the early twentieth century (Miller, 1980; O'Malley, 1970; Lagemann, 1983). Since then, many law schools and medical schools across the country have been involved in curriculum development and evaluation efforts that also provide parallels to our work (University of Michigan Law School, 1959; Marston & Jones, 1992; Mandin, Harasym, Eagle, & Watanabe, 1995; Watson et al., 1998; Mandin & Dauphinee, 2000; Joughin & Gardiner, 1996).

The Committee on Teacher Education comprises a diverse group of researchers, as well as practicing teachers and teacher educators, whose expertise spans the learning sciences; developmental psychology; linguistics;

subject matter areas such as mathematics, English, science, and history; and teacher education. To inform and ground its work, the Committee has collaborated with eight cooperating universities: The City University of New York, Dillard University, Indiana State University, New York University, Stanford University, University of Georgia, University of Texas at El Paso, and Xavier University. Liaisons from each institution played a critical role in providing grounded feedback. As part of their responsibilities, they took the work of the Committee back to their universities and conducted focus group seminars providing feedback on (1) what new teachers need to know, (2) how teacher education programs can help candidates cultivate that knowledge, (3) how this knowledge relates to career-long professional development for teachers, and (4) how this information can be most useful in various teacher education contexts that must also take into account such complex factors as the licensing structures that govern the teaching profession and education regulations of many other kinds.

Our effort has been to produce a volume that can be used by those who are doing the work of teacher education as well as those who are designing policies to support this work. We hope this volume hastens the day anticipated by Lee Shulman when he suggested that, "Those who can, do, and those who understand, teach."

MEMBERS OF THE NATIONAL ACADEMY OF EDUCATION'S COMMITTEE ON TEACHER EDUCATION

Committee co-chairs:

John Bransford
University of Washington

Linda Darling-Hammond
Stanford University

Committee members:

James Banks
University of Washington

David Berliner
Arizona State University

James Comer
Yale University

Sharon Derry
University of Wisconsin–
Madison

Evelyn Jenkins-Gunn
Pelham Memorial High School

Pamela Grossman
Stanford University

Carol Lee
Northwestern University

Joan Baratz-Snowden
American Federation of Teachers

Marilyn Cochran-Smith
Boston College

Emily Feistrizer
National Center for Education
Information

Edmund Gordon
Teachers College, Columbia University

Cris Gutierrez
Los Angeles Unified School District

Frances Degen Horowitz
The City University of New York

Lucy Matos
New Visions for Public Schools

Luis Moll
University of Arizona

Anna Richert
Mills College

Frances Rust
New York University

Lorrie Shepard
University of Colorado,
Boulder

Catherine Snow
Harvard University

Kenneth Zeichner
University of Wisconsin–
Madison

Arturo Pacheco
University of Texas at El Paso

Kathy Rosebrock
Novato Unified School District

Alan Schoenfeld
University of California, Berkeley

Lee Shulman
Carnegie Foundation for the
Advancement of Teaching

Guadalupe Valdés
Stanford University

Staff: Helen Duffy, Karen Hammerness, Pamela LePage

ACKNOWLEDGMENTS

Like all community efforts, this work owes a great deal to many individuals and organizations. The Committee would like to recognize Joan Baratz Snowden of the American Federation of Teachers, who conceived the initial idea for this effort and developed a proposal to move it forward. Ellen Lagemann, then president of the National Academy of Education, worked to get the project launched, and Nel Noddings, her successor as president, provided ongoing support and assistance to bring it successfully to its conclusion.

Key staff members at the Academy, especially NAE directors Kerith Gardner and Amy Swauger, supported the committee's work in innumerable ways. In addition, the Committee was ably assisted by its own directors and staff, including Ed Miech, Pamela LePage, Karen Hammerness, and Helen Duffy, who kept the committee organized, arranged meetings, helped to develop the outlines of the volume, and pursued subcommittees, writers, reviewers, references until the work was complete.

All of the committee members contributed to the conceptualization of the volume and reviewed many drafts over a period of three years. In addition, a group of cooperating universities—representing large and small schools of education from both the public and private sectors—provided liaisons to the Committee who informed the committee's deliberations, took ideas back to their universities for discussion and testing, provided feedback to the committee from their colleagues, and reviewed and critiqued chapters in progress. We are grateful to these individuals and their universities for supporting their contributions: Nicholas Michelli from the City University of New York; Kassie Freeman from Dillard University; Diana Quatroche and Tom Dickinson from Indiana State University; Frances Rust from New York University; Linda Darling-Hammond from Stanford University; Michael Padilla from the University of Georgia; Arturo Pacheco from the University of Texas at El Paso; and Rosalind Hale from Xavier University.

The Committee is grateful to Robert Floden, Michael Fullan, Sonia Nieto, and Seymour Sarason for very helpful reviews, and to Maureen Hallinan, who skillfully served as moderator for the revision process on behalf of the Academy.

The work of the Committee was funded by the U.S. Department of Education, under grant number R215U000018, and by the Ford Foundation, under grant number 1030-0468. Project officers Thelma Leenhouts of the Department of Education and Joe Aguerreberre of the Ford Foundation offered insightful comments and suggestions that sharpened the focus of the work and improved its outcomes. While we are grateful for the support of these funders, the product of this work does not represent the policy of either agency, and readers should not assume endorsement by the federal government or the foundation.

Finally, we appreciate the efforts of the many other teachers and teacher educators who contributed to this work by reviewing aspects of the volume in progress, and, most importantly, who daily engage in the work of teaching and learning. We hope, most of all, that this contributes to their important work.

ABOUT THE AUTHORS

COMMITTEE COCHAIRS:

John Bransford

University of Washington

John D. Bransford joined the University of Washington in Seattle in 2003 where he holds the title of the James W. Mifflin University Professorship and Professor of Education. Prior to this he was Centennial Professor of Psychology and Education and codirector of the Learning Technology Center at Vanderbilt University. Early works by Bransford and his colleagues in the 1970s included research in the areas of human learning, memory, and problem solving, and helped shape the "cognitive revolution" in psychology. Author of seven books and hundreds of articles and presentations, Bransford is an internationally renowned scholar in cognition and technology. He and his colleagues have developed and tested innovative computer, videodisc, CD-ROM, and Internet programs including the Jasper Woodbury Problem Solving Series in Mathematics, The Scientists in Action Series, and the Little Planet Literacy Series— programs that have received many awards.

Linda Darling-Hammond

Stanford University

Linda Darling-Hammond is the Charles E. Ducommun Professor of Education at Stanford University, where she has served since 1998 as faculty sponsor for the Stanford Teacher Education Program and codirector of the Stanford Educational Leadership Institute. While serving as William F. Russell Professor at Teachers College, Columbia University, she was the founding executive director of the National Commission for Teaching and America's Future, the blue-ribbon panel whose 1996 report *What Matters Most: Teaching for America's Future* catalyzed major policy changes to improve the quality of teaching and teacher education. She is past president of the American Educational Research Association. Among her more than 200 publications are *Teaching as the Learning Profession* (coedited with Gary Sykes), recipient of the National Staff Development Council's Outstanding Book Award for 2000, and *The Right to Learn*, recipient of the American Educational Research Association's Outstanding Book Award for 1998.

COMMITTEE MEMBERS:

James Banks

University of Washington

James A. Banks is Russell F. Stark University Professor and director of the Center for Multicultural Education at the University of Washington, Seattle. He is a past president of the American Educational Research Association (AERA) and of the National Council for the Social Studies (NCSS). He is a specialist in social studies education and multicultural education. His books include the *Handbook of Research on Multicultural Education, Second Edition*. He is the editor of the Multicultural Education Series of books published by Teachers College Press. Banks is a member of the Board of Children, Youth and Families of the National Research Council and the Institute of Medicine of the National Academy of Sciences and the National Academy of Education. He received the Distinguished Career Research in Social Studies Award from the National Council for the Social Studies in 2001 and the Social Justice in Education Award from the American Educational Research Association in 2004.

Joan Baratz-Snowden

American Federation of Teachers

Joan Baratz-Snowden is director of educational issues at the American Federation of Teachers. Her work includes overseeing the department's assistance and services to members, and the dissemination to the public of AFT's policies on issues such as standards and assessments, reading, teacher quality, and redesigning schools to raise achievement. Prior to joining the AFT, Dr. Baratz-Snowden was vice president for education policy and reform and for assessment and research at the National Board for Professional Teaching Standards (NBPTS). There, her responsibilities included addressing policy issues related to creating a more effective school environment for teaching and learning and increasing the supply of high-quality entrants into the teaching profession. Dr. Baratz-Snowden also directed the Education Policy Research and Services Division at the Educational Testing Service, and her policy research has examined the impact and use of standardized testing in schools, colleges, and universities and the entrance to teaching and other professions.

David Berliner

Arizona State University

David C. Berliner is Regents Professor of Education at Arizona State University. He is a past president of the American Educational Research Association, the Division of Educational Psychology of the American Psychology Association, and a member of the National Academy of Education. He is coauthor with Nathaniel Gage of the text *Educational Psychology,* now in its sixth edition, and has authored or coauthored more than 150 books, journal articles, and scholarly chapters.

Marilyn Cochran-Smith

Boston College

Marilyn Cochran-Smith is professor of education and director of the doctoral program in curriculum and instruction at the Lynch School of Education at Boston College. She has been president of the American Educational Research Association (AREA), is the editor of *The Journal of Teacher Education,* and is coeditor of the Practitioner Inquiry Series published by Teachers College Press. She is cochair of AERA's consensus panel on Teacher Education and a member of the Advisory Board for the Carnegie Foundation's Academy for the Scholarship of Teaching and Learning. Among her award-winning publications is *Inside/Outside: Teacher Research and Knowledge.*

James Comer

Yale University

James Comer grew up in a low-income neighborhood in East Chicago and credits his parents with leaving no doubt about the importance of education. He obtained a B.A. from Indiana University, a degree in medicine from Howard University, a Master of Public Health from the University of Michigan, and psychiatry training at the Yale University School of Medicine's Child Study Center. He currently is the Maurice Falk Professor of Child Psychiatry at the Yale University Child Study Center and associate dean of Yale's School of Medicine. Dr. Comer has focused on child development as a way of improving schools. His efforts in support of the healthy development of young people are known internationally. Dr. Comer is perhaps best known for the founding of the School Development Program in 1968, which promotes the collaboration of parents, educators, and community to improve social, emotional, and academic outcomes for children. His concept of teamwork is improving the educational environment in more than 500 schools throughout America.

Frances Degen Horowitz

City University of New York

Frances Degen Horowitz, a nationally recognized educational leader and renowned developmental psychologist, is president of The Graduate Center of The City University of New York, one of the country's leading institutions of advanced study. In 2004, Dr. Horowitz was elected a Fellow of the American Academy of Arts and Sciences and she has held many leadership roles in educational organizations. Acclaimed for her research, particularly in infant behavior and development, she is the author of more than 120 articles, chapters, monographs, and books, and her lecturing and teaching have taken her to Israel, the People's Republic of China, and throughout Central and South America. Dr. Horowitz attended Antioch College, graduating in 1954 with a bachelor's degree in philosophy. She earned a master's degree in elementary education from Goucher College and worked as an elementary school teacher before receiving her Ph.D. in developmental psychology from the University of Iowa in 1959.

Sharon Derry

University of Wisconsin–Madison

Sharon Derry is Professor of Educational Psychology at the University of Wisconsin-Madison. She received her Ph.D. in Educational Psychology from the University of Illinois with specialties in both cognition and instruction and quantitative/evaluative methods. Derry is a Principal Investigator within the Wisconsin Center for Education Research and manages several federally funded research projects that investigate methods for enhancing teacher learning through innovative uses of new media and Internet technology. Derry's publications appear in the *American Educational Research Journal, Journal of Educational Psychology, Review of Educational Research, Educational Psychologist, International Journal of Human-Computer Studies, Journal of AI in Education*, and in numerous other journals, edited books, and conference proceedings. She has edited books on topics related to technology and new media in education and interdisciplinary collaboration in research. For distinction in research she has received several awards, including an early-career award from the American Psychological Association and a Vilas Associate award at the University of Wisconsin-Madison.

Emily Feistrizer

National Center for Education Information

Dr. C. Emily Feistritzer is president and chief executive officer of the National Center for Alternative Certification (NCAC) and resident and founder of the National Center of Education Information (NCEI), a private, non-partisan research organization in Washington, specializing in survey research and data analysis. In that capacity, Dr. Feistritzer has conducted several national and state studies that include surveys of teachers, school administrators, school board presidents, state departments of education, university colleges of education, local school districts, and individuals interested in becoming teachers. In that time, Dr. Feistritzer has authored books on education, including multiple editions of *Alternative Teacher Certification: A State by State Analysis* (2004); *The Making of a Teacher: A Report on Teacher Preparation in the U.S.* (1999); *Profile of Troops to Teachers* (1998); *Profile of Teachers in the U.S.* (1996, 1990 and 1986); *Who Wants to Teach?* (1992); and *Teacher Crisis: Myth or Reality?* (1986). She is also publisher and founder of Feistritzer Publications, which publishes independent newsletters, including *Teacher Education Reports,* a biweekly newsletter covering all aspects of the teaching profession.

Evelyn Jenkins-Gunn

Pelham Memorial High School

Evelyn Jenkins Gunn has recently retired after over thirty years of teaching English and journalism at Pelham Memorial High School in Pelham, NY. She is currently the Chair of the Board of Regents at John Carroll University. Gunn serves as a consultant and workshop leader, has presented at national and regional professional conferences, and is a Carnegie scholar and fellow at the Carnegie Academy for the Scholarship of Teaching and Learning. She is the recipient of numerous awards: the Outstanding Educator Award from *Scholastic Magazine,* the Education Award from the New Rochelle NAACP, the Outstanding Secondary Teacher Award from the Alliance of Young Writers, and the 2000 John Carroll University Alumni medal. She is certified by the National Board for Professional Teaching Standards and was one of six teachers featured on a one-hour PBS television show entitled "No Greater Calling."

Edmund Gordon

Teachers College, Columbia University

Edmund Gordon, Professor Emeritus of Psychology at Yale University and Richard March Hoe Professor of Psychology and Education Emeritus at Teachers College, created the Institute for Urban and Minority Education (IUME) at Teachers College in 1973. Dr. Gordon left Teachers College for Yale, where he was the John M. Musser Professor of Psychology, and he returned to Teachers College after his retirement in 1991. Since then he has served as advisor to the president, trustee, and acting dean before reassuming the directorship of IUME. Recently, IUME has initiated a series of research and outreach initiatives aimed at understanding the educational, psychological, and social development of urban and minority students. Along with the institute's current effort, Dr. Gordon envisions a host of future activities aimed at providing educational and economic opportunity to the Harlem community. Dr. Gordon focuses much of his energies on a research project on the correlates of high academic achievement to describe and document how high-achieving people from historically low-achieving populations are able to succeed as they do.

Pamela Grossman

Stanford University

Pam Grossman is a professor of English education in the School of Education at Stanford University. A teacher educator herself, she teaches prospective secondary English teachers in the Stanford Teacher Education Program. Her research interests include the content and processes of teacher education, the connection between professional knowledge and professional preparation in teaching and other professions, the teaching of English in secondary schools, and the role of subject matter in high school teaching. Her most recent research projects include a large-scale study of pathways into teaching in New York City schools (with Susanna Loeb, Don Boyd, Hamilton Lankford, and Jim Wyckoff) and a study of the teaching of practice in professional preparation programs for teaching, the clergy, and clinical psychology. She recently completed a term as vice-president of Division K—Teaching and Teacher Education—for the American Educational Research Association.

Cris Gutierrez

Los Angeles Unified School District

Cris Gutierrez is a teacher-scholar and a peace educator. For twenty-two years, Cris has worked with adolescents from diverse backgrounds as a teacher, coach, counselor, and advisor. She helps youth to think deeply and to act creatively and humanely. She empowers them to see academics as tools for understanding themselves, contributing to their communities and our democracy, and creating a nonviolent culture. Building on her high school social studies and English teaching at Thomas Jefferson High School's interdisciplinary academy, Humanitas, in South Los Angeles, Cris has cofounded the Los Angeles Small Schools Collective and coleads the design team for Civitas. Civitas is a small, noncharter public high school, a "compact school," expected to open in 2006, where learning, teaching, scholarship, and activism can converge. In Santa Monica, Cris seeks to live simply and works to abolish nuclear weapons and end war.

Carol Lee

Northwestern University

Carol D. Lee is associate professor of education and social policy in the Learning Sciences Program of the School of Education and Social Policy and of African-American Studies, Northwestern University. Her research addresses urban education, cultural supports for literacy, classroom discourse, and instructional design. Her research focuses on the design of curriculum to support literate problem solving in response to literature in ways that build on the cultural capital of students from ethnic and language minority groups. She is the author of *Signifying as a Scaffold for Literary Interpretation* and *Finding Their Blooming in the Midst of the Whirlwind,* and coeditor of *Vygotskian Perspectives on Literacy Research.* She worked as a teacher in elementary, high school, and the community college across twenty-one years. She is a founder of one private and one charter school. She is the past president of the National Conference on Research in Language and Literacy and has been active with the National Council of Teachers of English and the American Educational Research Association.

Lucy Matos

New Visions for Public Schools

Lucy Matos is the founder of the Ella Baker School, a pre-K through eighth grade elementary school housed in the Julia Richman Educational Complex. A thirty-year veteran of the New York City school system, Ms. Matos cofounded Central Park East 1 Elementary School with Deborah Meier and six teachers and later served as its director. These schools have served as a model for those involved in the national restructuring efforts. In addition to her work in elementary, middle, and high schools, Ms. Matos has taught and lectured on a wide range of topics including school governance, parent involvement, curriculum development, and the evolving role of Latina women in policy positions. Ms. Matos currently works as a mentor for first-year principals with New Visions and the New York Leadership Academy and as a leadership coach for the Knowledge Works Foundation. Ms. Matos currently serves on the Board of Starfish Theaterworks, whose primary work is training teachers through its "Guiding Voices" program and whose goal is to improve student literacy through writing and acting.

Luis Moll

University of Arizona

Luis Moll is professor in the Department of Language, Reading, and Culture, and associate dean of academic affairs, at the College of Education of the University of Arizona. His research focuses on sociocultural approaches to child development and education, literacy, and bilingual learning. His recent research is a longitudinal study of biliteracy development in children. In 1998, Moll was elected to membership in the National Academy of Education. His publications include: *Vygotsky and Education,* and *Funds of Knowledge: Theorizing Practices in Households, Communities, and Classrooms.*

Arturo Pacheco

University of Texas at El Paso

Arturo Pacheco is the director of the Center for Research on Education Reform at the University of Texas at El Paso (UTEP) and also the El Paso Electric Professor of Educational Research. He served on the faculty and as dean of the College of Education at the University of California at Santa Cruz and Stanford University. At UTEP, Pacheco led his university in a complete restructuring of its teacher education program into a clinical field-based model with his colleagues in a set of partnership schools. Pacheco also served on several national boards and reform efforts associated with teacher education reform, including the American Association of Colleges of Teacher Education, the National Board for Professional Teaching Standards, and the Education Trust. Pacheco is coauthor of *Centers of Pedagogy: New Structures for Educational Renewal* (2000), and a variety of articles and chapters on teacher education reform and higher education, including the 2000 AACTE Hunt Lecture, *Meeting the Challenge of High Quality Teacher Preparation: Why Higher Education Must Change* (2000).

Anna Richert

Mills College

Anna E. Richert is a professor of education at Mills College in Oakland, California, where she codirects the Teachers for Tomorrow's Schools Credential and MA programs. Her research interests focus on teacher learning at both the preservice and inservice levels. They include consideration of the conceptions of knowledge that guide teacher learning work, conditions that support it in schools and in teacher education institutions, and knowledge outcomes for novice and experienced teachers. In her current work on the pedagogy of teacher education she has been studying how various pedagogical strategies offer particular learning opportunities for novice teachers. She is engaged in a project at the Carnegie Foundation for the Advancement of Teaching investigating the potential of records of K–12 teaching practice as "texts" for teacher education. Given her belief that teacher learning must be at the heart of school reform, she is active in a variety of local and national school reform efforts as well.

Kathy Rosebrock

University of San Francisco and Novato Unified School District

Kathy Rosebrock is an assistant professor of teacher education at the University of San Francisco and the Beginning Teacher Support and Assessment (BTSA) coordinator for Novato Unified School District. She is a former elementary school teacher of thirty-three years and continues to work closely with elementary school students and teachers in San Francisco and Marin County. She serves as the coordinator of a California Reading Initiative Project and a School Reform Literacy Coach in San Francisco and Pittsburgh Unified School Districts, through the Bay Area Writing Project at University of California, Berkeley. National Board Certified in Early Childhood Education since 1996. Marin County Teacher of the Year of 2003.

Frances Rust

New York University

Frances Rust is professor in the Department of Teaching and Learning at New York University. She is the winner of the 1985 AERA Outstanding Dissertation Award, and the recipient of the Teachers College Outstanding Alumni Award (1998) and the Association of Teacher Educators 2001 Award for Distinguished Research in Teacher Education. Her research and teaching focus on teacher education and teachers' research. Her most recent books are *Taking Action Through Teacher Research*, which she edited with Ellen Meyers; *Guiding School Change: New Understandings of the Role and Work of Change Agents,* which she edited with Helen Friedus; and *What Matters Most: Improving Student Achievement*, a volume of teacher research coedited with Ellen Meyers as part of her work as advisor to the Teachers Network Policy Institute.

Alan Schoenfeld

University of California, Berkeley

Alan Schoenfeld is the Elizabeth and Edward Conner Professor of Education and affiliated professor of mathematics at the University of California at Berkeley. He is vice president of the National Academy of Education, a Fellow of the American Association for the Advancement of Science, and past president of the American Educational Research Association. Schoenfeld serves as a senior advisor to the Education and Human Resources Division of the National Science Foundation, and a senior content advisor to the What Works Clearinghouse. Schoenfeld's research is on thinking, teaching, and learning, with an emphasis on mathematics. His research has focused on the nature of mathematical problem solving, and on how to assess it; on teachers' decision making; on issues of equity; and on ways to bridge the gaps between educational research and practice. For fun, he serves as a volunteer in the Berkeley public schools.

Lorrie Shepard

University of Colorado, Boulder

Lorrie A. Shepard is professor of research and evaluation methodology and dean of the School of Education at the University of Colorado at Boulder. Her research focuses on psychometrics and the use and misuse of tests in educational settings. Technical topics include validity theory, standard setting, and statistical models for detecting test bias. Her studies evaluating test use have addressed the identification of learning disabilities, readiness screening for kindergarten, grade retention, teacher testing, and effects of high-stakes accountability testing. Books include *Flunking Grades: Research and Policies on Retention* (with M. L. Smith) and *Methods for Identifying Biased Test Items* (with G. Camilli). Her current interest is the use of classroom assessment to support teaching and learning.

Lee Shulman

The Carnegie Foundation for the Advancement of Teaching

Lee S. Shulman is the eighth president of The Carnegie Foundation for the Advancement of Teaching, a policy center with the mission "to do and perform all things necessary to encourage, uphold and dignify the profession of the teacher." Shulman became the first Charles E. Ducommun Professor of Education Emeritus and Professor of Psychology Emeritus (by courtesy) at Stanford University after being professor of educational psychology and medical education at Michigan State University. He is a past president of the American Educational Research Association (AERA) and the National Academy of Education and recently became a Fellow of the American Academy of Arts & Sciences. Shulman's research and writings have dealt with the study of teaching and teacher education, the growth of knowledge among preservice teachers, the assessment of teaching, and medical education, among other topics. His most recent studies emphasize the importance of "teaching as community property" and the central role of a "scholarship of teaching and learning" in supporting needed changes in the cultures of higher education.

Catherine Snow

Harvard University

Catherine E. Snow, Henry Lee Shattuck Professor at the Harvard Graduate School of Education, carries out research on first and second language acquisition, and literacy development in monolingual and bilingual children. She chaired the committee that produced the National Research Council Report *Preventing Reading Difficulties in Young Children* (1998), and the study group that produced *Reading for Understanding: Toward an R&D Program in Reading Comprehension* (2002). She is a former president of the American Educational Research Association and a member of the National Academy of Education. Her research focuses on the social-interactive origins of language and literacy skills, the ways in which oral language skills relate to literacy learning, the literacy development of English language learners, and implications of research on language and literacy development for teacher preparation.

Guadalupe Valdés

Stanford University

Guadalupe Valdés is the Bonnie Katz Tenenbaum Professor of Education at Stanford University. She also has a joint appointment as a professor of Spanish and Portuguese. Valdés works in the area of applied linguistics. Much of her work has focused on the English-Spanish bilingualism of Latinos in the United States and on discovering and describing how two languages are developed, used, and maintained by individuals who become bilingual in immigrant communities. Valdés' recent work includes two books entitled *Learning and Not Learning English* and *Expanding Definitions of Giftedness: Young Interpreters of Immigrant Background*. Two other books include *Bilingualism and Testing: A Special Case of Bias* and *Con Respeto: Bridging the Distance Between Culturally Diverse Families and Schools*.

Kenneth Zeichner

University of Wisconsin–Madison

Ken Zeichner is Hoefs-Bascom Professor of Teacher Education and associate dean of the School of Education at the University of Wisconsin–Madison. From 1985–95, he was a senior researcher at the National Center for Research on Teacher Education/Teacher Learning, Michigan State University. He was the recipient of the AACTE Margaret B. Lindsey award for distinguished research in teacher education in 2002 and the AACTE award for excellence in professional writing in 1982 and 1993. He has also served as cochair of the AERA panel on research in teacher education, vice president of AERA (Division K) from 1996–98, and as a member of AACTE's board of directors from 1997–2000. He has published widely on issues of teacher education in North and South America, Europe, and Australia and has been listed by Thomson ISI as one of the most cited researchers in the social sciences between 1981 and 1999.

COMMITTEE STAFF

Helen Duffy

Helen Duffy has served as the director of the Committee on Teacher Education since August 2003. Before joining the CTE, she earned her Ph.D. from UC Berkeley where she received a UC All-Campus Consortium On Research for Diversity (UC ACCORD) fellowship to study a University of California outreach effort called the High School Puente Project. She has taught English and composition at the high school and university levels and served as Academic Coordinator for UC Berkeley's English teacher education program. In addition to working for the CTE, she has been engaged in a three-year study of an elementary school literacy reform effort in California's Silicon Valley. Her research interests include preservice and inservice teacher education, school reforms that promote equity and access to higher education, and adolescent literacy.

Karen Hammerness

Karen Hammerness served as a research associate for the Committee on Teacher Education from February 2001 to August 2003 while she was a postdoctoral fellow with the Stanford University School of Education. Her research focuses upon the pedagogies and practices of teacher education as well as upon the experience and ideals of teachers. She is currently writing a book about teachers' vision called *Seeing Through Teachers' Eyes: The Role of Vision in Teachers' Lives and Work* to be published by Teachers College Press. She graduated from Stanford University with a Ph.D. in educational psychology.

Pamela LePage

Pamela LePage is an assistant professor of special education and the cocoordinator of the mild to moderate SPED program at San Francisco State University. Before working as the director of the Committee on Teacher Education at Stanford University from August 2001 to August 2003, she taught at George Mason University in an innovative and interdisciplinary master's program for practicing teachers. Dr. LePage earned a Ph.D. in special education from the University of California, Berkeley and San Francisco State after teaching in special education for eleven years. She has three published books, two of which include *Transforming Teacher Education: Lessons in Professional Development* and *Educational Controversies: Toward a Discourse of Reconciliation.*

OTHER CONTRIBUTORS

Hanife Akar

Hanife Akar is currently an assistant professor of curriculum and instruction at Middle East Technical University (METU). She received a B.A. in English Language Teaching from Anadolu University and started her teaching career on the faculty of Political Sciences, Ankara University. She then earned a Cambridge University Royal School of Arts diploma for Overseas Teachers of English as well as her M.S. and Ph.D. in Curriculum Development and Instruction from METU, Turkey. She has been a visiting research scholar in the Republic of Poland and at Stanford University's School of Education. In 2002 she received a Complementary Doctorate Award by the Turkish Science Academy (TUBA). Her research interests are in teacher education, classroom management, curriculum evaluation, and policy analysis. She speaks Turkish, Dutch, English, and German.

Kelly Lyn Beckett

Kelly L. Beckett has an M.S. in Natural Resources and Environmental Sciences from the University of Illinois at Urbana-Champaign, where she specialized in Environmental Education. She is currently a doctoral candidate in Learning Science at the University of Wisconsin-Madison and a fellow in the Spencer Doctoral Research Program. Her research focuses on technology-based learning environments for ecological and environmental thinking, and her current project, Ecology 2020, uses the professional practices and technologies of urban planners as a model for an after-school program in which middle and high school students learn urban ecology by creating comprehensive redevelopment plans for their neighborhoods.

George Bunch

George C. Bunch is assistant professor of education at the University of California, Santa Cruz. He recently completed a Ph.D. in educational linguistics at Stanford University, where he was awarded a Spencer Dissertation Fellowship and an AERA Dissertation Grant. His areas of interest include second language acquisition and bilingualism, the study of academic language, and the preparation of mainstream teachers for working with linguistically diverse students. Articles and chapters coauthored by him have appeared in *Issues in Teacher Education, TESOL Journal,* and the forthcoming volume *Content-based Language Instruction in K-12 Settings,* published by Teachers of English to Speakers of Other Languages (TESOL). He has taught teacher preparation courses at Stanford and UC Santa Cruz and is an experienced K–12 teacher of English as a second language and social studies.

Lou-Ellen Finn

Lou-Ellen Finn brings to her work thirty-five years of teaching experience in the area of middle school science. She has been a classroom teacher, team leader, and served as curriculum coordinator of a large, urban public school. After retiring from teaching, she worked as the professional development coordinator for the Center for Learning Technologies in Urban Schools at Northwestern University. In that role she supported teachers in their use of project-based, technology-rich middle school science units. Finn is currently part of a curriculum design team at Northwestern that is developing a three-year middle school science curriculum through a grant from the National Science Foundation with several other university partners. In addition to her work at Northwestern, she has published in teacher-based journals such as *Educational Leadership* and *Middle Ground.* She has also presented at the American Educational Research Association annual meeting and the National Science Teachers Association convention.

Miriam Gamoran-Sherin

Miriam Gamoran Sherin is associate professor of learning sciences in the School of Education and Social Policy at Northwestern University. Her interests include mathematics teaching and learning, teacher cognition, and the use of video for teacher learning. Recent articles appear in *Cognition and Instruction, Teaching and Teacher Education,* and the *Journal of Mathematics Teacher Education.* In 2001, Professor Sherin received a postdoctoral fellowship from the National Academy of Education and in 2002 she was awarded a Career Grant from the National Science Foundation. In April 2003, Sherin received the Kappa Delta Pi/American Educational Research Association Division K Award for early career achievements in research on teaching and teacher education.

Louis Gomez

Louis M. Gomez is Aon Professor of Learning Sciences and professor of computer science at Northwestern University and vice president of teaching and learning at Teachscape. Professor Gomez is one of the codirectors of the NSF-sponsored Center for Learning Technologies in Urban Schools, a partnership between Chicago Public Schools, Detroit Public Schools, University of Michigan, and Northwestern University. Professor Gomez's primary interest is in working with school communities to create curriculum, professional development, and other social arrangements that support school improvement through communities of practice both within and beyond school. Prior to joining the faculty at Northwestern, Professor Gomez was director of Human-Computer Systems Research at Bellcore in Morristown, New Jersey. In addition to NSF support, Professor Gomez's school improvement work has been supported by the MacArthur, Joyce, and Spencer Foundations. Professor Gomez also received a Spencer Mentor Award to support graduate student intellectual growth.

Jacqueline Griesdorn

Jacqueline M. Griesdorn is assistant research professor of learning sciences in the School of Education and Social Policy at Northwestern University. Her interests include teacher professional development, small schools reform, and experiential sampling methods (ESM). Professor Griesdorn received her doctoral degree in foundations, policy, and leadership from the Curry School of Education in Charlottesville, Virginia in 1999. Professor Griesdorn has spent eight years working directly with school personnel and district leaders planning and designing, implementing, and evaluating school change initiatives. For the past three years Professor Griesdorn has worked in partnership with faculty from eleven Chicago land universities, district administrators, and Chicago teachers to develop prototype professional development courses in mathematics and science for K–8 teachers.

Morva A. McDonald

Morva A. McDonald is an assistant professor of education in the department of Curriculum and Instruction at the University of Maryland, College Park. She recently completed her Ph.D. in Administration and Policy Analysis at Stanford University. Her areas of interest include teacher education and the preparation of teachers for diversity, students' opportunities to learn both in and out of school, and urban education. Her recent research, which is conducted with a team of researchers from Stanford University and SUNY-Albany, focuses on the different pathways to becoming a teacher in NYC and understanding the relationship between preservice preparation and student outcomes.

Nicholas Michelli

Nick Michelli is university dean for teacher education for The City University of New York in the central Office of Academic Affairs and professor in the University's Ph.D. program in urban education at CUNY's graduate center. He is professor and dean emeritus at Montclair State University. He is the coauthor of *Centers of Pedagogy: New Structures for Educational Renewal.* He is coauthor of the chapter on critical thinking and higher education in the 2001 edition of ASCD's *Developing Minds.* In addition, he is coauthor with Tina Jacobowitz of a book forthcoming on renewing teacher education, and coeditor with David Keiser of *Teacher Education for Democracy and Social Justice.* He is senior advisor and author for a new series of textbooks for future teachers to be published by McGraw-Hill with a focus on democracy, social justice, and critical thinking.

Peter Youngs

Peter Youngs is an assistant professor in the Department of Teacher Education at Michigan State University. His research interests focus on state and district policy related to teacher licensure, induction, professional development, and school reform. He has recently published articles in *Educational Researcher, Educational Policy, Educational Administration Quarterly,* and *Review of Educational Research.* Prior to joining the faculty at Michigan State, he served as research associate at Stanford University and associate director of Performance Assessment for California Teachers (PACT).

Karen Zumwalt

Karen K. Zumwalt is the Edward Evenden Professor of Education in the Department of Curriculum and Teaching, Teachers College, Columbia University. From 1995–2000, she served as dean of the College and vice president for Academic Affairs. Her writings and research have focused on curriculum and teacher education. Her chapter on the policy implications of research on teaching for teacher education won AERA's first Interpretive Scholarship Award in 1983. As a member of the AERA Panel on Teacher Education, she and Elizabeth Craig have just completed an extensive review of research describing the profile of teachers—demographic characteristics and indicators of quality—and its impact. She received her Ph.D. in curriculum and philosophy from the University of Chicago, after teaching in the Cleveland, Ohio and Glencoe, Illinois public schools. She received her initial teacher preparation at the Harvard Graduate School of Education, where she student taught in the Boston public schools.

CHAPTER ONE

Introduction

John Bransford, Linda Darling-Hammond, and Pamela LePage

To a music lover watching a concert from the audience, it would be easy to believe that a conductor has one of the easiest jobs in the world. There he stands, waving his arms in time with the music, and the orchestra produces glorious sounds, to all appearances quite spontaneously. Hidden from the audience—especially from the musical novice—are the conductor's abilities to read and interpret all of the parts at once, to play several instruments and understand the capacities of many more, to organize and coordinate the disparate parts, to motivate and communicate with all of the orchestra members. In the same way that conducting looks like hand-waving to the uninitiated, teaching looks simple from the perspective of students who see a person talking and listening, handing out papers, and giving assignments. Invisible in both of these performances are the many kinds of knowledge, unseen plans, and backstage moves—the skunkworks, if you will—that allow a teacher to purposefully move a group of students from one set of understandings and skills to quite another over the space of many months.

On a daily basis, teachers confront complex decisions that rely on many different kinds of knowledge and judgment and that can involve high-stakes outcomes for students' futures. To make good decisions, teachers must be aware of the many ways in which student learning can unfold in the context of development, learning differences, language and cultural influences, and individual temperaments, interests, and approaches to learning. In addition to foundational knowledge about these areas of learning and performance, teachers need to know how to take the steps necessary to gather additional information that will allow them to make more grounded judgments about what is going on and what strategies may be helpful. Above all, teachers need to keep what is best for the child at the center of their decision making. This sounds like a simple point, but it is a complex matter that has profound implications for what happens to and for many children in school.

The importance of preparing teachers to exercise trustworthy judgment based on a strong base of knowledge is increasingly important in contemporary society. Standards for learning are now higher than they have ever been before, as citizens and workers need greater knowledge and skill to survive and succeed. Education is increasingly important to the success of both individuals and nations, and growing evidence demonstrates that—among all educational resources—teachers' abilities are especially crucial contributors to students' learning (see, for example, Ferguson, 1991a; Rivkin, Hanushek, and Kain, 2000; Wright, Horn, and Sanders, 1997). Furthermore, the demands on teachers are increasing. Not only do teachers need to be able to keep order and provide useful information to students, they also need to be increasingly effective in enabling a diverse group of students to learn ever more complex material and to develop a wider range of skills. Whereas in previous decades teachers were expected to prepare only a small minority for the most ambitious intellectual work, they are now expected to prepare virtually all students for higher-order thinking and performance skills once reserved for only a few.

To meet the expectations they now face, teachers need a new kind of preparation—one that enables them to go beyond "covering the curriculum" to actually enable learning for students who learn in very different ways. Programs that prepare teachers need to consider the demands of today's schools in concert with the growing knowledge base about learning and teaching if they are to support teachers in meeting these expectations. This volume was developed in response to this challenge: to summarize what is understood about how people learn and what teaching strategies support high levels of learning and to examine what approaches to preparing teachers can help them acquire this body of knowledge and skills.

The goal of preparing teachers who are equipped to help all students achieve to their greatest potential raises a number important questions, for example:

1. What kinds of *knowledge* do effective teachers need to have about their subject matter and about the learning processes and development of their students?

2. What *skills* do teachers need in order to provide productive learning experiences for a diverse set of students, to offer informative feedback on students' ideas, and to critically evaluate their own teaching practices and improve them?

3. What professional *commitments* do teachers need to help every child succeed and to continue to develop their own knowledge and skills, both as individuals and as members of a collective profession?

We focus especially on preparation for new teachers—knowing full well that it takes many years of experience to develop sophisticated expertise. We understand that teachers continually construct new knowledge and skills in practice throughout their careers rather than acquiring a finite set of knowledge and skills in their totality before entering the classroom. The goal for preservice preparation, then, is to provide teachers with the core ideas and broad understanding of teaching and learning that give them traction on their later development. This perspective views teachers' capacity not as a fixed storehouse of facts and ideas but as "a source and creator of knowledge and skills needed for instruction" (Cohen and Ball, 1999, p. 6). An important goal of this volume is to help teachers become "adaptive experts" who are prepared for effective lifelong learning that allows them continuously to add to their knowledge and skills (see, for example, Hatano and Inagaki, 1986; Hatano and Oura, 2003). Later chapters explore in more detail the concept of adaptive expertise as it is applied to teaching.

In addition to preparing teachers to learn throughout their lifetimes, we seek to describe the initial understandings that teachers need to serve adequately the very *first* students they teach. We believe that these students, like all others, are entitled to sound instruction and cannot afford to lose a year of schooling to a teacher who is ineffective or learning by trial and error on the job. This is especially important since beginning teachers—and those who are unprepared—are disproportionately assigned to teach students in low-income, high-minority schools and students in lower track classes who most need skilled teachers in order to succeed (National Commission on Teaching and America's Future, 1996).

So beginning teachers need to have a command of critical ideas and skills and, equally important, the capacity to reflect on, evaluate, and learn from their teaching so that it continually improves. We believe this is more likely if the essential knowledge for beginning teachers can be "conceptually organized, represented and communicated in ways that encourage beginners to create deep understandings of teaching and learning" (Barnes, 1989, p. 17). Although we focus on the conceptual map that novices need to begin to navigate the classroom landscape, we hope that the information in this volume will also be useful to veteran teachers. One of our major goals is to suggest frameworks for helping teachers organize their knowledge and their thinking so that they can accelerate their learning throughout their careers.

This report does not speak exclusively to traditional programs of teacher education organized for undergraduate college students. Its recommendations are for initial preparation programs of all kinds, including alternative programs designed for midcareer recruits and others who prepare in postbaccalaureate programs based in universities or school districts. Although program qualities, and quality, vary widely across the many contemporary routes into teaching, these do not divide neatly across categories often used to describe them. Both so-called "traditional" and "nontraditional" programs can range from at best rudimentary to highly coherent and effective. Many programs that states have designated as "alternative" provide strong preparation that has the added advantage of connecting candidates to the districts that want and need to hire them (for examples, see National Commission on Teaching and America's Future, 1996, p. 93). Many "traditional" undergraduate programs also have found ways to provide strong preparation for teaching, sometimes within the usual four-year parameters and sometimes by adding an additional year of study and clinical training (for examples, see Koppich, 2000; Merseth and Koppich, 2000; Miller and Silvernail, 2000; Zeichner, 2000). Our focus is not on the format, length, or location of teacher education but on its substance: what prospective teachers need to learn and how they may best be enabled to learn it.

THE CONTEXT OF TEACHING

If improvement in education is the goal, it is not enough to prepare good teachers and send them out to schools. If teachers are to be effective, they must work in settings where they can use what they know—where, for example, they can come to know students and families well; work with other teachers to provide a coherent, well-grounded curriculum; evaluate and guide student progress using information-rich assessments; and use texts and materials that support thoughtful learning. Unfortunately, given the patchwork of policies, the plethora of competing decision makers, and the fragmented design of factory-model schools, these conditions are not present in many, perhaps most, U.S. schools.

Many analysts have noted that there is very little relationship between the organization of the typical American school and the demands of serious teaching and learning (Darling-Hammond, 1997; Elmore, 1996; Goodlad, 1984; Sarason, 1993; Sizer, 1984). Unlike schools in many other countries, U.S. schools are typically not organized to keep students with the same teachers for more than one year or to provide extended time for teachers to plan and study teaching together. Furthermore, the systems that U.S. schools sit within rarely provide coherent curriculum guidance that includes supports for teachers to develop sophisticated lessons and teaching strategies. And, unlike those who attend schools in most other industrialized countries, students and teachers in relatively few U.S. schools are guided by challenging assessments that require the presentation and defense of ideas and the production of work that demonstrates how they can inquire, assemble and evaluate evidence, reason, and problem solve. Finally, U.S. schools are struggling both to overcome the vestiges of societal and educational discrimination and to develop models of organization and methods of instruction that successfully provide access to challenging curriculum material to the full range of learners, rather than rationing such curriculum to a small subset of students.

Given these challenges of contemporary schooling, it would be naïve to suggest that merely producing more highly skilled teachers can, by itself, dramatically change the outcomes of education. We must attend simultaneously to both sides of the reform coin: better teachers and better systems. Schools will need to continue to change to create the conditions within which powerful teaching and learning can occur, and teachers will need to be prepared to be part of this change process.

Although the system changes that are needed go far beyond what individual teachers should be expected to effect, there are at least three ways in which teacher education is implicated in supporting needed systemic reforms. First, because working in professional learning communities is a key to changing school cultures, we argue that the teacher education curriculum should help teachers learn how to work on the improvement of practice as members of such collaborative communities (see for example, Fullan, 1993a; Lieberman, 1988; Louis and Kruse, 1995; McLaughlin and Talbert, 2001). Second, if prospective teachers are to support more equitable and powerful education for their students, they will need to develop a strong sense of moral purpose, and they will need to understand the change process in organizations so that they can be constructive contributors to school reform (Fullan, 1993b). Finally, teacher education programs need to consider how they can engage in partnerships with schools and districts that work to transform schooling and teaching in tandem. In this way, prospective teachers can be prepared for the schools they need in order to teach effectively, and they can learn firsthand how to work in and develop contexts that will support the learning of all of their students.

Beyond Cookie Cutters

Specifying what successful teachers need to know and be able to do is not a simple task. As is true with all professions, including medicine, the law, and the clergy, there is no single "cookie cutter" formula for being successful. There is no one right way to behave as a teacher. Some effective teachers are charismatic whereas others are more retiring. Some are emotional and some are reserved. Some have a stern demeanor whereas others are more nurturing. There are many different ways that successful professionals can vary and still be highly effective. Within this variation, however, there are common kinds of practices that draw on shared understanding of how to foster student learning. For example, a recent study of ninety-two highly effective elementary and middle school teachers found that they vary in their styles but have many teaching strategies in common. (See "Common Practices Among Highly Effective Teachers.")

Common Practices Among Highly Effective Teachers

With funding from The Lyndhurst Foundation, the Public Education Foundation has been studying ninety-two elementary and middle school teachers identified as highly effective in Hamilton County, Tennessee. The teachers all had three-year average student scores in the top 25 percent of all teachers in the county on the Tennessee Value Added Assessment System (TVAAS) or, if they did not have a three-year TVAAS history, were nominated as highly effective based on other appropriate measures. The teachers were interviewed, surveyed, and observed over the course of a year. Although the teachers differed in their ages, backgrounds, and personalities, the researchers found that the teachers "offered a remarkably similar picture" of effective teaching—one that reflects many of the elements of teaching we describe in this volume. For example:

- Expectations for the students were clearly stated and exemplars of previous year's assignments were shown to students as models of what to produce.
- Student work could be found everywhere: inside the classroom, out the door, and down the hall.
- The teachers did not stand still and lecture; they covered every part of the room and monitored every activity that took place.
- Multiple small group activities were often found, while the traditional arrangement of desks in rows was practically nonexistent.
- There were high levels of "instructional discourse": Students were encouraged to ask questions, discuss ideas, and comment on statements made by teachers and other students.
- The organization of the rooms and the lessons was clearly evident. Materials were easily accessible when needed, and no class time was wasted from lack of preparation.

Source: Pamala Carter, Teacher Quality Initiative, Chattanooga-Hamilton County Public Education Foundation. www.pefchattanooga.org/www/docs/2–110. Reprinted with permission.

In any profession there are key elements that define what it means to be a professional, starting with the ethical pledge that members of professions make to the welfare of all of their clients. Thus a central part of being a professional teacher is a commitment to help all students succeed. Educators who have made such commitments to help all students succeed have demonstrated that it is indeed possible to do so, even in areas like mathematics, physics, and computer science where inequalities are longstanding (see "Supporting Student Achievement in Calculus"). But it has taken a great deal of work for these teachers to be successful. And they needed more than a basic desire to succeed. They needed to have knowledge and skills and access to other professionals to be able to follow through with their commitments rather than simply to try and fail.

Supporting Student Achievement in Calculus

Uri Treisman's work in the Berkeley Mathematics Workshop and in the Emerging Scholars Program at the University of Texas at Austin is one example of a project that has helped underrepresented students succeed in college-level calculus. Based on a study that found a strong correlation between success in mathematics and participation in study groups, Treisman and his colleagues designed a program that reflects the belief that students, if given the necessary direction and support, can develop a collective understanding of complex mathematical concepts (Garland, 1993). In his early work at UC Berkeley, Treisman noted that Asian American, African American, and Latino students experienced different success rates in calculus, even though they were all highly motivated, had families who were supportive of their education, and were well prepared academically. Treisman found that the Asian Americans who experienced success in calculus formed informal study groups through which they developed a collaborative understanding of the problems they studied and made public their conceptual understanding of complex mathematics. However, in response to their encounters with hostile institutions, African American students tended to separate their academic and personal lives and to engage in coursework on their own.

In response to those findings, Treisman created student workshops including intensive supplementary instruction, the creation of community study groups, orientation to the university, and academic counseling that is tied to the study sessions. The workshops provide a safe place for students to make their understandings of mathematics public and challenge their mathematical knowledge with rigorous work on hard problems. According to Treisman, moving student support programs from admissions-mandated, all-purpose tutoring centers to academic departments "demarginalizes" academic support. Rather than seeing tutors the day before an exam, the workshop is an ongoing, central part of students' participation in the course and includes regular academic counseling. Academic counseling is a critical feature of the model, addressing some of the structural impediments to persistence.

More than 150 programs based on Treisman's model can now be found at institutions across the country. A study of the mathematics workshop model at California State Polytechnic University (Pomona) found that the workshop model greatly improved the performance of women and Latino science, mathematics, and engineering majors taking calculus (Bonsangue and Drew, 1996). Participants in the workshop earned a grade 0.6 points higher on average than their classmates who did not participate. Women achieved the highest grades among all ethnic and gender groups. Similar success has been found in the University of Texas at Austin's Emerging Scholars Program. Between 1988 and 1993, fewer than 33 percent of African American and Latino students not participating in this program earned an "A" or "B" in calculus, and only half of those with math SAT scores of 600 or more made such grades. In contrast, 90 percent of those participating in the Emerging Scholars Program earned an "A" or "B" in calculus.

Sources: May Garland, "The mathematics workshop model: An interview with Uri Treisman," *Journal of Developmental Education,* 16 no. 3 (Spring 1993), pp. 14–16, 18, 20, 22; Martin Vern Bonsangue and David Eli Drew, "Increasing minority students' success in calculus," *New Directions for Teaching and Learning,* 61 (Spring 1995), pp. 23–33.

Analyses of programs for teacher preparation indicate that there is a great deal of variability in the information taught to teachers and the methods for doing so (Goodlad, 1984; Howey and Zimpher, 1989; Zeichner, Melnick, and Gomez, 1996) as well as in graduates' feelings of preparedness for different aspects of teaching (Darling-Hammond, Chung, and Frelow, 2002). Our goal is to provide a common framework for curriculum content and pedagogies in teacher education—a framework that is useful for preparing teachers with the knowledge, skills, and commitments that will enable them to help all students succeed. We do not propose a single curriculum for all programs; nor do we offer inflexible guidelines for a uniform approach. Given the range of different institutions serving distinctive missions and diverse students in different contexts, one could not imagine a highly specific curriculum that is the same in every detail for each institution. However, given the state of current research and consensus in the field, we can outline a set of core ideas that are addressed by all programs in ways that are appropriate for their students. Similarly, it would be impossible to develop curriculum recommendations for every type of teacher, field, or context. Instead, we address important considerations that influence curriculum decisions across teaching levels, subject matter areas, and kinds of teaching settings. Finally, the report includes suggestions about pedagogies and assessment strategies in teacher education that appear to help prospective teachers develop the capacities and dispositions they need to teach diverse children effectively and to help develop schools that support this work.

Similar Quests in Other Professions

The quest that we are undertaking is similar to ones previously pursued in other professions such as medicine, law, and engineering. For example, in the early twentieth century, medical schools consisted of a number of ad hoc apprenticeship systems and some university courses with little agreement about what was important to teach doctors or how to do so. The medical profession began to see the need to set standards for its professional community and develop a consensus about certain aspects of medical education. The Flexner Report (Flexner & Pritchett, 1910), a study of medical schools in North America conducted by Abraham Flexner between 1908 and 1910, documented the inconsistencies among different schools and indicated the need for developing a strong consensus about good medical education. The report argued that, ultimately, effective medical education should be grounded in research and teaching in the sciences coupled with systematic clinical instruction in teaching hospitals. This represented a major change from much of the existing medical school training of the day.

In his introduction to the Flexner Report, Henry Pritchett, president of the Carnegie Foundation for the Advancement of Teaching, noted that, although there was a growing science of medicine, most doctors did not get access to this knowledge because of the great unevenness in the medical training they received. He observed that, "Very seldom, under existing conditions, does a patient receive the best aid which it is possible to give him in the present state of medicine . . . [because] a vast army of men is admitted to the practice of medicine who are untrained in sciences fundamental to the profession and quite without a sufficient experience with disease" (p. x). He attributed this problem to the failure of many universities to appreciate and incorporate advances in medical education into their curricula (p. xi). Medical education was transformed as a common set of curriculum ideas, was adopted and taken up by the accrediting bodies that approved all programs, and was incorporated into the requirements for licensing that were used to admit all candidates to practice.

Other fields like engineering, law, and architecture also worked to develop a consensus about professional education later in the twentieth century. As they did so, they considered what core content students should encounter and what intellectual capacities and dispositions they should develop in order to "think like a lawyer" or an engineer or a doctor and to meet the needs of their clients. New fields such as bioengineering are currently being formed and they, too, are in the process of trying to bring some consistency to the field and considering what effective beginning professionals need to know and be able to do to succeed (for examples, see Harris, Bransford, and Brophy, 2002; http://www. Whitaker.org).

Processes like those previously described have resulted in curricular conceptions that define major areas of understanding in various fields. Law students, for example, study torts, contracts, constitutional law, civil and criminal procedure, and so on, in law schools across the country (Margolis, Arnone, and Morgan, 2002). Medical students study anatomy, physiology, and biochemical sciences as well as immunology, pathology, and a number of specialties of practice. Most professions also use what have been referred to as signature pedagogies. In law school, students are expected to read and analyze cases, and they are introduced to the Socratic Method when answering questions and building arguments. In medical schools, case methods and clinical rounds are frequently used. Specific kinds of design projects are found in schools of engineering.

These shared understandings and practices in other professions evolved from a consensus about what professionals need to know and be able to do if they are to profit from profession-wide knowledge and if they are to have the diagnostic and strategic judgment to address the needs of those whom they serve. If teachers are to have access to the knowledge available to inform their practice, such consensus must become a reality for the teaching profession as well.

AN ORGANIZING FRAMEWORK

We noted in the Preface that this is not the first attempt to explore systematically the kinds of knowledge, skills, and commitments that should enable teachers to be effective. An important precursor to this book is a report produced in 1989 by the American Association of Colleges for Teacher Education (AACTE) titled *The Knowledge Base for the Beginning Teacher* (Reynolds, 1989). This book makes careful arguments for what teachers need to know and why. Now, fifteen years later, new evidence about teaching and learning has accumulated that augments its findings. In addition, four generations of *The Handbook of Research on Teaching* and three editions of *The Handbook of Research on Teacher Education* are joined by specialized volumes like the *Handbook of Research on Reading.* These efforts to collect and codify research have supported the development of standards for teaching through the National Board for Professional Teaching Standards, the thirty-state Interstate New Teacher Assessment and Support Consortium, and professional associations like the National Councils of Teachers of English and Mathematics. This volume builds on these prior efforts and takes on the new question of how this knowledge, combined with a growing base of knowledge about how *teachers* learn, can inform the curriculum of teacher education.

One important feature of the current report is the effort to organize discussion around a conceptual framework that can help people organize the vast amounts of information relevant to effective teaching and learning. The framework we use is illustrated in Figure 1.1. It highlights three general areas of knowledge, skills, and dispositions that are important for any teacher to acquire:

- Knowledge of **learners** and how they **learn and develop** within social contexts,
- Conceptions of **curriculum content and goals**: an understanding of the subject matter and skills to be taught in light of the social purposes of education, and
- An understanding of **teaching** in light of the content and learners to be taught, as informed by assessment and supported by classroom environments.

The framework is reminiscent of Dewey's notion, outlined in *The Child and the Curriculum,* that the needs of the child and the demands of the curriculum are mediated by teachers (Dewey, 1902). It is similar as well to Ball and Cohen's representation of instruction as the interactions of teachers, students, and content, in environments that influence all of these (Ball and Cohen, 1999). The framework provides a set of lenses on any teaching situation that teachers can use to reflect on and improve their practice.

These interactions between teachers, learners, and content are framed by two important conditions for practice: first, the fact that teaching is a profession with certain moral as well as technical expectations and, second, the fact that, in the United States, education must serve the purposes of a democracy. This latter condition means that schools assume the purpose of enabling young people to participate fully in political, civic, and economic life in our society. It also means that education, including teaching, is intended to support equitable access to what that society has to offer. As we discuss in this volume, these goals for edu-

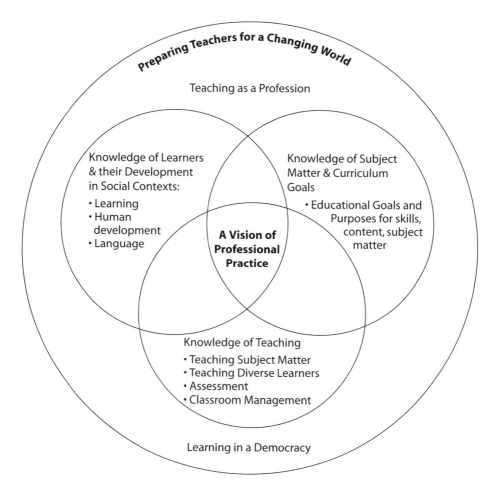

Figure 1.1 A Framework for Understanding Teaching and Learning

cation influence what teachers need to know and be able to do and what teacher education is expected to accomplish.

Teaching as a Profession That Serves Democratic Purposes

An especially important feature of Figure 1.1 is its emphasis on "teaching as a profession." It is important for teachers to understand their roles and responsibilities as professionals in schools that must prepare all students for equitable participation in a democratic society. Toward this end, it is helpful for them to see commonalities with members of other professional groups.

Characteristics of Professions. A useful source of information for examining the concept of "professionalism" comes from the Carnegie Foundation for the

Advancement of Teaching's Preparation for the Professions study, which is currently studying law, engineering, teaching, and the clergy. Drawing from various professions, Shulman (1998) has suggested that "six commonplaces" are shared by all professions. These are:

1. *Service to society*, implying an ethical and moral commitment to clients;
2. *A body of scholarly knowledge* that forms the basis of the entitlement to practice;
3. *Engagement in practical action*, hence the need to enact knowledge in practice;
4. *Uncertainty* caused by the different needs of clients and the non-routine nature of problems, hence the need to develop judgment in applying knowledge;
5. *The importance of experience* in developing practice, hence the need to learn by reflecting on one's practice and its outcomes; and
6. *The development of a professional community* that aggregates and shares knowledge and develops professional standards. (p. 516).

Source: Reprinted with permission. *The Elementary School Journal* Volume 98, Number 5. L. Shulman "Theory, practice and the education of professionals," pp. 511–526. ©1998 by The University of Chicago Press.

What teaching has in common with a range of other professions is that the work serves others and, because of its social importance, must do so responsibly. Thus, preparation must help teachers to both understand and move beyond their own personal knowledge and experiences to bring to bear a wider set of understandings on the problems of helping others learn. Although all professions have a body of scholarly knowledge and a social calling that form the basis of the entitlement to practice, the emphases and warrants for practice differ. Teaching can be viewed as a field that sits at the intersection of these other professional fields. Teachers might be viewed as similar to women and men of the cloth, as teaching has elements of a vocation or a calling, and it has strong connections to values and commitments. At the same time, although teaching may be a calling, it is not only a calling. There are systematic and principled aspects of effective teaching, and there is a base of verifiable evidence or knowledge that supports that work. In that sense, it is like engineering or medicine. Like these fields, there are aspects of teaching that are scientific, in the sense that research on practices and outcomes suggests some principles that can guide the judgments practitioners must make. At another level, teaching is a body of tradition and precedent and organized experience. In that sense, it resembles the law.

For the beneficiaries of the profession to be well served, teachers also need to be able to work with other colleagues in creating organizations that support learning. Unlike solo professionals such as architects and accountants who can, if they choose, hang out a shingle and practice their trade, the work of educators in schools is greater than the sum of the individual parts. As in clinics or hospitals where systems for providing good medical service must be created and norms of professional practice must be sustained, schools that provide healthy environments for learning and teaching require the common efforts of all of their members. Teachers must be able to function as members of a community of practitioners who share knowledge and commitments, who work together to create coherent curriculum and systems that support students, and collaborate in ways that advance their combined understanding and skill.

All of these features of professions are important because of the complexity of the work, which demands that professionals know a great deal about how to achieve their goals for clients in situations that are unpredictable and nonroutine, that they be able to enact what they understand in practice, and that they be able to continue to learn from their colleagues and their students about how to meet new challenges. Ultimately, Palmer (1998) sums it up nicely when he claims that good teachers must be truly present in the classroom, deeply engaged with their students and their subjects, and able to weave an intricate web of connections among themselves, their subjects, and their students, so that students can learn to weave a world for themselves.

The Social Importance of Teaching. The importance of developing a strong profession of teaching has been reinforced by recent research demonstrating how important teaching is to children's learning and life chances. Although conventional wisdom was based for many years on a conclusion widely attributed to the Coleman Report (Coleman and others, 1966)—that is, that schools make little difference beyond the influences of socioeconomic background—newer evidence based on different data and analytic methods suggests that schools do make a noticeable contribution to what children learn and that teachers are an important part of what matters (Ferguson, 1991a; Ferguson and Ladd, 1996; Greenwald, Hedges, and Laine, 1996; Strauss and Sawyer, 1986). For example, recent studies have found that a student's assigned teacher has a much stronger influence on how much she learns than other factors like class size and composition (see, for example, Sanders and Horn, 1994; Sanders and Rivers, 1996; Wright, Horn, and Sanders, 1997; Hanushek, Kain, and Rivkin, 1997). Students who are assigned to several highly effective teachers in a row have significantly greater gains in achievement than those who are assigned to less effective teachers; furthermore, the influence of each teacher has effects that spill over into later years (Sanders and Rivers, 1996). (See Figure 1.2.)

Several studies have found that differences in teacher qualifications across school districts can account for as much of the variation in student achievement as students' backgrounds or socioeconomic status. (See "How Teachers Matter.")

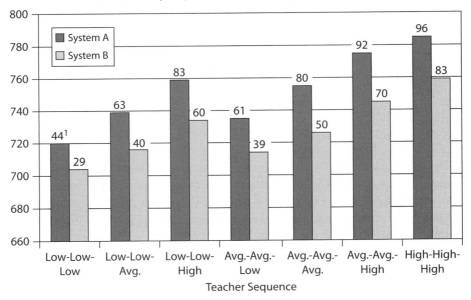

Figure 1.2 Cumulative Effects of Teacher Effectiveness

Source: Sanders & Rivers, 1996. Reprinted by permission of authors.

The authors of one of these studies emphasized the importance of investing in teachers as a means to support greater student success, especially for students who are educationally at risk:

> Of the inputs which are potentially policy-controllable (teacher quality, teacher numbers via the pupil-teacher ratio and capital stock), our analysis indicates quite clearly that improving the quality of teachers in the classroom will do more for students who are most educationally at risk, those prone to fail, than reducing the class size or improving the capital stock by any reasonable margin which would be available to policy makers. (Strauss and Sawyer, 1986, p. 47)

How Teachers Matter

Although many have assumed that students' backgrounds—such as income, parent education, and other family factors—are the major reasons for wide differences in student achievement, some studies have found that the quality of teachers can have an effect at least as large.

For example, in an analysis of nearly 900 Texas school districts, Ronald Ferguson (1991a) found that teachers' expertise—scores on a certification examination, master's degrees, and experience—accounted for more of the interdistrict variation in students' reading and mathematics achievement in grades one through eleven than student socioeconomic status. The effects were so strong and the variations in teacher expertise so great that, after controlling for socioeconomic status, the large disparities in achievement between black and white students were almost entirely accounted for by differences in the qualifications of their teachers. Ferguson also found that every additional dollar spent on more highly qualified teachers netted greater increases in student achievement than did less instructionally focused uses of school resources.

In a similar study in Alabama, Ferguson and Ladd (1996) found that, together, teachers' academic ability, education, and experience, when combined with class sizes, accounted for more of the predicted difference in student achievement gains in mathematics between districts scoring in the top and bottom quartiles than poverty, race, and parent education.

Still another study in North Carolina found that, after accounting for school and student background factors, teachers had a strikingly large effect on student achievement on the state competency tests: a 1 percent increase in teacher quality (as measured by National Teacher Examination scores) was associated with a 3 to 5 percent decline in the proportion of students failing the exam (Strauss and Sawyer, 1986). The authors of these studies concluded that thoughtful policymakers should pay more attention to investing in teacher quality as a way to improve student achievement.

Many kinds of teacher knowledge and experience appear to contribute to this effect, including teachers' (1) general academic and verbal ability, (2) subject matter knowledge, (3) knowledge about teaching and learning, (4) teaching experience, and (5) the set of qualifications measured by teacher certification, which typically includes the preceding factors and others (for reviews, see Darling-Hammond, 2000a; Wilson, Floden, and Ferrini-Mundy, 2001; Rice, 2003). There are, of course, many other attributes that matter for teaching, such as enthusiasm, perseverance, flexibility, and concern for children (see, for example, Schalock, 1979). And, as we discuss in the following sections, there are many specific teaching practices that influence student achievement that are related to what teachers have had an opportunity to learn (see, for example, Good and Brophy, 1994). In addition, the teaching context matters for teacher effectiveness, including such factors as class size, school size and organization, curriculum approaches, and opportunities for teacher collaboration (Howley, 1989; Lee, Bryk, and Smith, 1993; Lee and Smith, 1993, 1995; Newmann and Wehlage, 1995).

The findings that teacher knowledge matters are an important reason to treat teaching as a profession, so that, through strong professional education and widespread standards of practice, knowledge about effective learning and teaching is reliably made available to all practitioners. Being a professional involves understanding the social and legal obligations of one's job, including making decisions in the best interests of the client, based on profession-wide research and standards of practice. This commitment to practice based on what is known by the profession as a whole, rather than only one's own personal experience, is linked to the concept of "evidence-based practice," which requires of professionals that they be aware of the current knowledge base in their field. A true story included in the preface of the *Knowledge Base for the Beginning Teacher* explains this obligation well:

> A fascinating court case from the 1930s involv[ed] the *T.J. Hooper,* a tugboat. The *T.J. Hooper* and the ship it was guiding got into trouble in the Atlantic Ocean when a sudden storm blew up. The storm damaged the ship and caused injury and property loss to its clients, who promptly sued. At that time common practice among tugs was to get weather information via hand signals from shore. Although radio had been introduced it was not in common use. The *T.J. Hooper* did not use radio, but if it had, the tug master would have known of the danger and been able to take its client ship to shelter, thus avoiding damage to life, limb, and property. The case turned on the question of *T.J. Hooper's* responsibility: was adherence to common practice (e.g. hand signals) enough or did the situation demand "state of the art" (radio)? The courts ruled that, when important matters are at stake, the legal obligation is to use the state of the art. (Reynolds, 1989, p. ix, citing Gilhool, 1982)

State-of-the-art practice is typically reflected in professional standards for the kinds of evaluations professionals are expected to perform to figure out what is going on in a situation, the data they use to guide their decisions, and the kinds of strategies they then employ. These are not expected to be uniform across cases, but to be responsive to the specific needs of clients who differ in their needs and circumstances. The notion of evidence-based practice suggests that professionals be aware of what strategies are likely to be productive or unproductive for meeting particular goals, as well as what modifications are needed for certain situations. For example, although doctors routinely give vaccinations, they are expected not to do so in situations where their patients have certain allergies or have certain prior health conditions. Engineers may use certain standard protocols in designing particular kinds of buildings, but they are also expected to know how to vary those general approaches for steep inclines, earthquake-prone settings, or other special circumstances. A teacher may have a set of strategies for teaching reading to most 7-year-olds—strategies that are grounded in strong evidence about what is generally effective for the goals she is seeking—but she will need to know how to adapt these strategies for students with specific learning disabilities, those who are ready for more challenging tasks, or those who lack the prior linguistic knowledge or vocabulary anticipated by a particular approach.

The evidence base for professional practice includes both experimental studies of particular "treatments" or interventions and more naturalistic inquiries into how particular diseases progress, how earthquakes of various magnitudes affect different architectural and engineering design, or how children learn in different circumstances. Research by practitioners is also a source of evidence for practice. Careful observation and systematic collection of evidence can inform both one's own practice and that of others. In medicine, for example, single case studies of patients and observations of small samples of individuals appear in the professional literature on a regular basis to provide data about problems, treatments, or diseases that are being documented and explored. (See "Using Research and Clinical Experience to Develop a Professional Knowledge Base.")

Using Research and Clinical Experience to Develop a Professional Knowledge Base

As in other professions, medical researchers and practitioners recognize that mixed methods of research serve complementary purposes in building an evidence base for practice. For example, the January 2002 issue of the prestigious *New England Journal of Medicine* included studies of the progress of a sample of eight patients who received cardiac transplants (Quaini and others, 2002) and of fifty-three children infected with *E. coli* (Chandler and others, 2002). These nonexperimental studies, which built on careful observations by practitioners, provided information about the different trajectories of different patients with different health histories under different kinds of treatments. The same issue also included a large correlational study of 750,000 Norwegian women whose birth outcomes were examined using medical records that provided much grosser measures of their health histories (Skjaerven, Wilcox, and Lie, 2002). This descriptive study suggested trends to be followed up with more carefully controlled research studies. The usefulness of any of these studies is in their contribution to a larger body of work from which evidence can be triangulated. An evidence base requires the development of many converging clues to inform professional research, practice, and judgment.

It is important to note that, in all areas, clinical judgment still plays a major role that links with evidence-based research. As Brown (1999), a strong advocate for research-based medicine, warns new doctors: "Although the benefits of research-based practice to patients are logically and intuitively compelling, definitive evidence is lacking. It is logical to expect that methods that have been found to produce better patient outcomes in research studies produce better patient outcomes when incorporated into everyday practice. However there are reasons why this may not be so" (p. 9).

These reasons include, among other things, the fact that (1) studies tend to show that one treatment is better than another *on average*; however, results for a given patient may differ depending on many other factors; (2) research findings from one setting may not transfer to different settings and contexts; and (3) the profile of the research participants in any given study may be different than that of a particular patient a professional is working with. The professional's responsibility is to know both the literature and his or her patients well enough do what is in the best interests of that patient. Sometimes this means *not* applying the results of a single study if it does not apply to the case at hand, even if that study was well designed.

Other scholars agree that "Good doctors use both individual clinical expertise and the best available external evidence, and neither alone is enough. Without clinical expertise, practice risks becoming tyrannized by evidence, for even excellent external evidence may be inapplicable to, or inappropriate for, an individual patient. Without current best evidence, practice risks becoming rapidly out of date, to the detriment of patients" (Sackett, Rosenberg, Gray, Haynes, and Richardson, 1996, p. 71). These same doctors add that "Evidence-based medicine is not restricted to randomized trials and meta-analyses. It involves tracking down the best external evidence with which to answer our clinical questions" (Sackett and others, 1996, p. 72). Teachers need to be prepared both to seek out and use a range of current evidence about practice in their fields and to develop local knowledge about their own students as a basis for exercising professional judgment.

GOALS, CONTEXTS, AND EVIDENCE

It is especially important for teachers to understand that evidence about educational effectiveness must be evaluated with respect to a number of variables that can vary across teaching situations. This point is illustrated in a model developed by James Jenkins (see Figure 1.3). It helps educators see that the appropriateness of using particular types of teaching strategies depends on (1) the nature of the materials to be learned; (2) the nature of the skills, knowledge, and attitudes that learners bring to the situation; and (3) the goals of the learning situation and the assessments used to measure learning relative to these goals. One of the important points of the model is that a teaching strategy that works within one constellation of these variables may work very poorly when that overall constellation is changed. All the variables in the Jenkins model must be taken into account when analyzing evidence suggesting that a particular teaching strategy is "good" or "poor." We have adapted the model slightly to fit the current discussion.

Attempts to teach students about veins and arteries can be used to illustrate the interdependencies shown in the Jenkins framework. Imagine that the materials to be learned include a text, which states that arteries are thicker than veins and more elastic, and they carry blood rich in oxygen from the heart. Veins are smaller, less elastic, and carry blood back to the heart. What's the best way to help students learn this information? The Jenkins model helps us see how the answer to this question depends on who the students are, what we mean by "learning" in this context, and how we measure the learning that occurs.

If our goal were to ensure that students learn certain key facts about arteries, one strategy would be to use mnemonic techniques. For example, students might be taught to think about the sentence "Art(ery) was *thick* around the middle so he wore pants with an *elastic* waistband." The Jenkins framework reminds us that the ability to use this particular technique presupposes specific types of knowl-

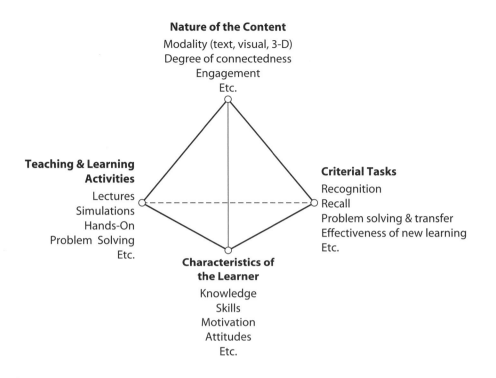

Nature of the Content
Modality (text, visual, 3-D)
Degree of connectedness
Engagement
Etc.

Teaching & Learning Activities
Lectures
Simulations
Hands-On
Problem Solving
Etc.

Criterial Tasks
Recognition
Recall
Problem solving & transfer
Effectiveness of new learning
Etc.

Characteristics of the Learner
Knowledge
Skills
Motivation
Attitudes
Etc.

Figure 1.3 Jenkins' Tetrahedral Model

Source: Permission granted by National Academies Press.

edge and skills on the part of the learners (for example, that they understand English, understand concepts such as elasticity, and so forth.). Given the availability of this knowledge, mnemonic techniques like the one noted earlier "work" for remembering factual content. If asked to state important characteristics of arteries (for example, thick, elastic), the preceding statement about Art(ery) could be helpful. A number of studies show that memory is enhanced when people are taught to use mnemonic techniques rather than simply left to their own devices.

Suppose that we change the goal from merely remembering factual content to learning with understanding. In the context of the Jenkins framework, this involves a change in learning goals and assessments of learning. Changes in goals typically require a change in teaching and learning strategies as well.

To learn with understanding, students need to understand *why* veins and arteries have certain characteristics. For example, arteries carry blood from the heart, blood that is pumped in spurts. This helps explain why they would need to be elastic (to handle the spurts). In addition, arterial blood needs to travel uphill (to the brain) as well as downhill, so the elasticity of the arteries provides an additional advantage. If they constrict behind each uphill spurt, they help the blood flow up.

Learning to understand relationships such as why arteries are elastic should facilitate subsequent transfer. For example, imagine that students are asked to design an artificial artery. Would it have to be elastic? Students who have only memorized that arteries are elastic have no grounded way to approach this problem. Students who have learned with understanding know the functions of elasticity and hence are freer to consider possibilities like a nonelastic artery that has one-way valves (Bransford and Stein, 1993).

This example illustrates how memorizing versus understanding represent different learning goals in the Jenkins framework, and how changes in these goals require different types of teaching strategies. The details of one's teaching strategies will also need to vary depending on the knowledge, skills, attitudes, and other characteristics that students bring to the learning task. For example, we noted earlier that some students (for example, those in the lower grades) may not know enough about pumping, spurts, and elasticity to learn with understanding if they are simply told about the functions of arteries. They may need special support such as dynamic simulations that display these properties. As a different kind of example, imagine that we want to include mnemonics along with understanding and one of the students in our class is overweight and named Art. Under these conditions, it would seem unwise to use the mnemonic sentence about Art(ery) that was suggested earlier.

Research examining whether "something worked" should take into consideration each of the perspectives of the Jenkins framework. For example, was the content taught something that is worth having students spend their time learning? What were the goals for learning, and were the assessments of learning consistent with the goals? Who was being taught and how might teaching strategies need to change for people with different sets of skills and knowledge? A sophisticated understanding of evidence and its implications for practice is important for effective teaching. The Jenkins framework helps highlight some key relationships that affect how particular teaching and learning strategies impact individuals' abilities to learn.

GOALS AND EVIDENCE FOR OUR RECOMMENDATIONS

The Jenkins framework is useful for exploring the learning both of students and of teachers who must learn to help them. Our first goal for this book is to suggest what is known about *students' learning and its implications for teachers' knowledge and skills.* We then explore how to help teachers acquire this knowledge in a way that allows them to be optimally effective. In essence, we ask:

- What kinds of experiences do children need in order to grow and learn, to develop the confidence and competence they need to succeed in life?

- What kinds of knowledge do teachers need to have in order to facilitate these experiences for children and youth?
- What kinds of experiences do teachers need to have in order to develop these kinds of knowledge?

The report focuses not on what current institutions generally deliver, but on what *students* need for their teachers to know if the teachers are to do a responsible job of guiding student learning.

The recommendations for teacher education discussed in this volume represent the considered judgments of a large number of experienced practitioners and scholars in the field of education. Whenever possible we refer to research studies to support our conclusions. But just as was the case in the early days of forging new medical, law, engineering, and bioengineering programs (and is still true in all these fields today), our evidence for preparing new teachers also comes from consensus among experienced practitioners and researchers.

In most professions, empirical research cannot directly link everything that practitioners learn in preparation programs to client outcomes. It would be difficult to find a research study that examines whether doctors who have taken a physiology course have better patient outcomes than those who have not. Similarly, it would be nice to have direct evidence that passing a course in biomechanics produces more successful bioengineering graduates, but it would be well nigh impossible to partial out the effects of a biomechanics course from the effects of other areas of learning on a complex set of practices. Although few would argue that bioengineers should not study biomechanics or that doctors should not study anatomy, the understanding they gain from these kinds of courses does not translate immediately into successful practice. Instead, understanding the principles of mechanics or the way the body is put together is made useful by connecting it to many other kinds of knowledge that together translate into actions and decisions.

Similar situations exist in education. It would be very helpful to have direct evidence that teachers are better at promoting learning if they understand concepts like Vygotsky's "zone of proximal development" (ZPD) (Vygotsky, 1978) or issues of transfer and how it is facilitated by certain approaches to teaching and assessment. But carefully controlled studies that attempt to link each discrete element of a curriculum to eventual outcomes would not likely be the most productive way to spend research funds. We are more likely to find that teachers who can use a concept like the zone of proximal development to figure out what a student knows and is ready to learn *and* who know how to organize a structured learning experience for that student pegged to his level of readiness are more successful. It is the combination of several kinds of knowledge with practical skills that sets professionals apart and that makes the influences of narrow elements of professional knowledge difficult to study. No single set of ideas is alone sufficient to produce the complex and changing array of judgments and activities that accomplished professionals demonstrate.

Even if we had direct evidence to guide all of the elements of a professional preparation program, fields change, and new insights and interpretations frequently replace old ones. We certainly see this in medicine: for example, in recent years we've heard that eggs are harmful to cholesterol levels and then that they are not; benefits were touted for hormone therapies and then some research found harmful effects, and so on. We expect our doctors to know enough to help us interpret these studies as they apply to our own health. In like fashion, among the major commitments and skills new teachers need to develop are the habits of mind to check continually the evidence base (both from their own practices and from the research literature) in order to evaluate their practices and work constantly to improve.

In addition to professional consensus, we have used four kinds of research evidence to support our recommendations. (See Figure 1.4.)

- The first is ***basic research on how people learn***, both generally and in specific areas like language, reading, or mathematics.
- The second kind of research looks at ***the influences of different conditions, including specific teaching strategies, on what and how people learn***.

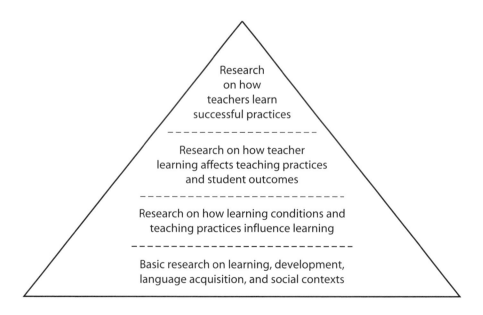

Figure 1.4 Research Bases Supporting Teacher Education Recommendations

- The third kind of research looks at *what kinds of teacher learning opportunities are associated with teaching practices that, in turn, influence student learning*.

- The fourth kind of research examines *how teachers learn* to engage in practices that successfully support student development and learning.

Although each of these kinds of research comprises distinctive lines of study, they build upon each other conceptually. What we know about how students learn ought to influence teaching practices, and what we know about effective teaching practices, as well as teacher learning, should influence teacher education. At this point in our history, it is fair to say that the areas of the segments shown in the triangle in Figure 1.4 also approximate the depth of these research bases. That is, there is a very large body of research on how people learn (the base of the triangle), and a substantial body of research on what conditions and teaching practices support productive student learning. There is a smaller body of research on the relationship between teachers' learning opportunities and what they do in the classroom as well as what their students learn, and a small, but growing body of research on how it is that teachers learn to engage in the kinds of practices that research suggests are most successful for students.

In the area of *basic research on learning*, for example, are studies that examine processes such as attention, pattern recognition, memory, and transfer. All of these processes are involved in any complex act, hence their relationships must also be understood. For example, there is an informative body of research that analyzes changes in cognitive processes as people develop expertise in particular areas (for example, physics, chess, electrical engineering). Novices often find new tasks to be highly attention-demanding. A great deal of effort is required for novices to function—in part because they have not yet developed the necessary pattern recognition and memory schemas that help them cope with complexity. In contrast, experts learn to recognize familiar patterns with great fluency and little effort, and they have acquired memory schemas that make it easier to remember information that they see, read, or hear (National Research Council, 2000).

Research on basic learning processes also demonstrates the difference between successfully storing information in memory and being able to retrieve and use it later on. Recognition memory puts the least demand on retrieval processes—hence we can often recognize the name of a person, book, or movie even thought we cannot generate it on our own. However, the ability to generate information without the help of recognition prompting is often extremely important, so learning theorists pay a great deal of attention to processes that support retrieval and use. Learning how ideas connect to one another and applying them to real-world problems enhances the probability that they will be remembered and usable later. Just as we saw with different approaches to learning about arteries, the kind of learning has a great deal to do with the uses to which information can be put. Similarly, the kinds of tests one chooses to assess learning need to be considered in the context of recognition versus generation. Multiple-choice tests are closer to recognition memory than they are to generative memory. Assessments that call for performance and application place more of an emphasis on generation and retrieval. An important issue for teachers to consider is whether recognition is sufficient, or whether students must learn to generate information when they operate in the world.

In addition to studies on basic processes of learning are studies that explore *how specific teaching practices foster certain kinds of learning*. A substantial body of research has found, for example, that students are better able to acquire complex skills when their teachers help them understand the underlying concepts and patterns that tie together the ideas they are studying; provide models for how to approach the task and reason through problems; provide scaffolds or structured steps that support the learning process; and coach students as they apply their knowledge to real-world tasks. In addition, students become more proficient when their teachers help them learn to evaluate and regulate their own learning (Anderson, 1989; Good and Brophy, 1994). Teachers who have learned to use these cognitive strategies have produced increased student learning of complex skills in the areas of reading (Duffy and Roehler, 1987; Palincsar and Brown, 1984; Palincsar, 1989), writing (Englert, 1989; Englert, Raphael, and Anderson, 1992), mathematical problem solving (Carpenter, Fennema, Peterson, Chiang, and Loef, 1989; Peterson, Fennema, and Carpenter, 1991; Wood and Sellers, 1996), and science (Otto and Schuck, 1983; Ruben and Norman, 1992), among others.

Clearly, an important warrant for recommendations about the teacher education curriculum is evidence about how students learn and how teaching can support this learning. Much of this research undergirds standards for student learning developed by subject area associations and standards for teacher performance developed by professional associations like the National Board for Professional Teaching Standards. Standards for beginning teachers based on this research have been developed by a group of more than thirty states that compose the Interstate New Teachers Assessment and Support Consortium and now appear in most states' licensing and program approval standards.

Teachers who understand how learning occurs are more able to both select and develop curriculum that supports rather than undermines the learning process. Ensuring that teachers have access to what is known about specific teaching strategies that foster more productive learning provides them with critically important tools for success. Having a sense of what teachers should know and be able to do, however, does not tell teacher educators all that they need to know to construct a set of learning experiences that will ensure these skills will be learned. In the limited amount of time available to prepare teachers, there are many questions and trade-offs that must be considered about what the most productive ways are to help people gain the understanding they need to enter the profession and become responsible teachers. We have a growing body of research to help inform these decisions, even though many questions must be answered in part through a combination of evidence, professional judgment, and consensus.

Research on the ***relationship between teacher education, teaching practices, and student achievement*** has looked at how various kinds of preparation relate to student learning. At the most general level, for example, a number of studies—conducted at the individual classroom, school, district, and state levels—have found that students' achievement is significantly related to whether their teachers are fully prepared or certified in the field they teach, after other teacher and student characteristics are controlled (see, for example, Betts, Rueben, and Danenberg, 2000; Darling-Hammond, 2000a; Ferguson, 1991a; Fetler, 1999; Fuller, 1998, 2000; Goe, 2002; Goldhaber and Brewer, 2000; Hawk, Coble, and Swanson, 1985; Strauss and Sawyer, 1986). Although these findings are broadly useful in suggesting that what teachers know influences what students learn, they do not provide much insight to guide specific teacher education curriculum decisions, because certification includes a wide array of general academic, subject area, and pedagogical requirements.

More helpful are studies that look at various aspects of teacher preparation. Some studies suggest that strong subject matter knowledge, usually measured as a major relevant to the field to be taught, such as mathematics or mathematics education, is associated with teacher effectiveness (Goldhaber and Brewer, 2000; Wenglinsky, 2002). Another study has suggested that master's degrees in relevant fields like mathematics or mathematics education contribute more to teacher effectiveness than master's degrees in fields not related to teachers' teaching fields (Goldhaber and Brewer, 1998).

Again, although helpful, this kind of research only scratches the surface of many important questions about what kinds of content knowledge teachers can benefit from and how they can best acquire it. For example, Liping Ma's research (1999) on how elementary teachers learn to teach mathematics in China—by revisiting the foundations of arithmetic, engaging in deep study of number concepts, and playing out their concrete applications to classroom pedagogy—poses an alternative to the common approach in the United States of accruing college-level mathematics courses that bear little relationship to the curriculum that will be taught.

Other studies have found that content methods courses are equally important elements of teachers' effectiveness. (See "Do Methods Courses Matter?") These studies suggest the importance of learning content-specific strategies for teaching. The fact that this research has documented effects for methods coursework within a content field suggests the potential importance of having sustained, in-depth opportunity for this kind of subject-specific study rather than a generic approach. In fact, the evidence that teachers appear to benefit from having taken a greater number of courses regarding methods of teaching in their content area also suggests that the tradition of offering only one subject area methods course in many preparation programs may be less than adequate. This is consistent with evidence that teachers often call for additional study of content-specific teaching methods both in preservice education and throughout their careers, wanting to explore in concrete ways the details of specific areas they are teaching—how to teach the theory of limits in calculus or the concept of place value in arithmetic, for example—rather than dealing with broad generalities (Ball and Cohen, 1999). This kind of finding is also consonant with evidence that professional development grounded in content-specific strategies can enhance teachers' effectiveness (Cohen and Hill, 2000).

Do Methods Courses Matter?

Using data on more than 2,800 students from the Longitudinal Study of American Youth (LSAY), David Monk (1994) found that the amount of college coursework mathematics and science teachers had taken in their content area and in subject-matter methods courses was positively related to student achievement gains. In mathematics, additional teaching methods courses had "more powerful effects than additional preparation in the content area" (p. 142). Similarly, Edward Begle (1979) found in his review of findings of the National Longitudinal Study of Mathematical Abilities that the number of credits a teacher had taken in mathematics methods courses was an even stronger correlate of student performance than was the number of credits a teacher had taken in mathematics courses. Goldhaber and Brewer (2000) found that, after teachers' content degrees in mathematics or mathematics education were taken into account, the additional effect of their full certification in the field—measuring the value added by pedagogical training—was a strong predictor of student achievement gains. The same trends were true to a somewhat smaller extent in science. All of these studies suggest that learning *how* to teach allows teachers to better use their knowledge of *what* to teach.

Some research has looked at how teacher preparation influences teachers' practices and student outcomes. For example, research as early as the 1960s found that teachers with greater methods training in science teaching were more likely to use laboratory techniques and discussions and to emphasize conceptual applications of ideas, whereas those with less education training placed more emphasis on memorization. Furthermore, teachers' coursework in science education was significantly related to students' achievement on tasks requiring problem solving and applications of science knowledge (Perkes, 1967). In a later review of sixty-five studies of science teaching, Druva and Anderson (1983) found that teachers' effectiveness, defined by both teachers' ratings and student achievement, was positively related to the teachers' course-taking background in both education and in science.

More recently, Wenglinsky (2002) examined the relationships between teachers' training, teaching practices, and student achievement using data from the National Assessment of Educational Progress (NAEP). After controlling for student characteristics and other school inputs, he found that eighth-grade students do better on the NAEP mathematics assessments when they have had teachers with a major or minor in mathematics or mathematics education, teachers who have had more preservice or inservice professional training in how to work with diverse student populations (training in cultural diversity, teaching limited English proficient students, and teaching students with special needs), and teachers who have had more training in how to develop higher-order thinking skills. They also did better when their teachers organized more hands-on learning (work with real-world problems and use of manipulatives) emphasizing higher-order thinking. Similarly, students do better on the NAEP science assessments when their teachers have majored in science or science education, have had more training in how to develop laboratory skills, and engage in more hands-on learning. In a path analysis, Wenglinsky concluded that teachers' preparation in content and pedagogy appeared to be associated with teaching practices, which in turn influence achievement. He also found that the combined effects of the teaching variables he studied—teachers' content background, professional learning opportunities, and specific practices—outweighed the effects of students' socioeconomic status on student achievement. This suggests that the equity goals we outlined at the beginning of this chapter are achievable if we can figure out how to ensure that more teachers have access to these kinds of knowledge.

Similarly, a research review from the National Reading Panel of the National Institute of Child Health and Human Development concluded that a set of identifiable teaching practices are strongly associated with improvements in children's reading achievement. These include the systematic teaching of phonemic awareness, guided repeated oral reading, direct and indirect vocabulary instruction with careful attention to readers' needs, and a combination of reading comprehension techniques that include metacognitive strategies. The report concluded that "Teaching reading comprehension strategies to students at all grade levels is complex. Teachers not only must have a firm grasp of the content presented in the text, but also must have substantial knowledge of the strategies themselves, of which strategies are most effective for different students and types of content and of how best to teach and model strategy use . . . [Data from the studies reviewed on teacher training] indicated clearly that in order for teachers to use strategies effectively, extensive formal instruction in reading comprehension is necessary, preferably beginning as early as preservice" (National Reading Panel, 2000).

Studies of specific practices for teaching reading comprehension—for example, explicit strategy instruction (Duffy and others, 1987b; Duffy and Roehler, 1989) and reciprocal teaching (Palincsar and Brown, 1989)—have found that teachers can learn strategies that enable them to teach these complex comprehension skills and that specific teaching practices acquired through professional training enable teachers to improve student reading outcomes. These positive effects of

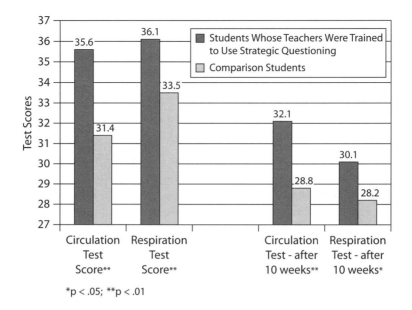

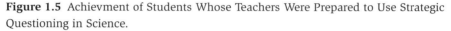

Figure 1.5 Achievment of Students Whose Teachers Were Prepared to Use Strategic Questioning in Science.

Source: Otto and Schuck, 1983.

strategy instruction have also been found in other fields, such as writing (see Chapter Seven) and science. (See "Linking Basic Research on Learning to Research on Teaching and Teacher Education" and Figure 1.5.) It is worth noting that many of these studies using experimental designs were conducted during the 1970s and 1980s when research funding favored this kind of inquiry. A recent resurgence of interest in such research designs has stimulated new research that is examining a wide range of teaching strategies and their effects on learning.

Linking Basic Research on Learning to Research on Teaching and Teacher Education

In science, learning theory suggests that certain kinds of questions can support strategic thinking on the part of students, particularly questions that ask students to develop hypotheses, make comparisons, analyze and synthesize data, evaluate possible solutions, and make judgments about what they have found. To translate these insights into teacher training and teaching practices, researchers randomly assigned ninety students from three rural junior high schools and six biology teachers to instructional groups of fifteen students each. Half of the teachers were taught questioning techniques through discussion, modeling, analysis of videotapes of teaching, and instructional planning supported by coaching. They were observed while teaching. Observers who did not know which teachers were assigned to which group found that the teachers who had received the training asked fewer managerial and rhetorical questions and more higher-order questions that dealt with strategic think-ing about data collection, analysis, and evaluation. Students taught by these teachers not only learned significantly more in tests after the units but also retained much more of what they learned when they were tested ten weeks later (Otto and Schuck, 1983).

Finally, *research on how teachers learn* to engage in successful practices is in many ways the newest area of research. Although there is foundational knowl-edge about teacher development and learning that parallels the basic learning research we talked about earlier, many of the applications of this knowledge are still being worked out (for a review, see Cochran-Smith and Zeichner, in press). So, for example, there is evidence that teachers' learning may also follow a developmental trajectory (Berliner, 1994; Feiman-Nemser, 1983; Richardson and Placier, 2001), that linking broad principles to concrete applications helps teachers understand more deeply and transfer what they are learning, and that reflecting on these attempts is as helpful to teachers in deepening their skills as it is to stu-dents (Cochran-Smith and Lytle, 1999; Feiman-Nemser, 2001a; Hammerness, Dar-ling-Hammond, and Shulman, 2002; Shulman and Shulman, 2004). Figuring out how specific learning opportunities and teacher education practices can capital-ize on these insights—and what the results are—is in some ways the most com-plex kind of research, because it requires tracking not only what and how teachers learn, but also how they use what they have learned and to what effect.

As one example of this kind of emerging research, a recent study examined the outcomes of preservice teacher education programs that have an intense focus on the teaching of reading and share critical curriculum features. The study found that their graduates were more able to construct rich, engaging literacy environ-ments, and they more frequently produced classroom gains in reading achieve-ment than a comparison group of beginning teachers (International Reading Association, 2003). (See "Strong Teacher Education Improves the Teaching of Reading.")

Strong Teacher Education Improves the Teaching of Reading

Researchers from the International Reading Association (2003) followed 101 recent program graduates from eight teacher education programs that were selected because they have a strong emphasis on teaching reading. Among the program features identified as important were:

- A cohesive curriculum treating how students learn to read as well as effective teaching strategies,
- A variety of course-related field experiences in which excellent models for the teaching of reading are available,
- A clear vision of literacy, quality teaching, and quality preparation informing the program design,
- Responsive teaching that is adaptive to the needs of diverse candidates,

- An active learning community among faculty, mentor teachers, and students that supports shared norms of practice and continual learning and improvement,
- Continual assessment of candidates and the program to guide decisions, and
- Adequate resources tied to the mission of the program.

The programs were public and private, large and small, in communities across the United States. These teachers were observed on multiple occasions over three years, as were beginning teachers from programs without an emphasis on literacy and teachers who were fully certified from a range of other programs. Data were collected about student achievement gains in reading comprehension in the classrooms of a subset of these teachers. The researchers discovered that the 101 teachers from the selected programs were more likely to construct high-quality text environments—using a greater variety, quality, and quantity of children's books and other texts in their classrooms. Furthermore, teachers from the eight selected programs had students who were more meaningfully engaged with texts and who showed greater growth in reading comprehension on a standardized test measure administered in the third year of the study. Beginning teachers from the eight teacher education programs performed like the experienced teachers: more of their classrooms experienced large gains and fewer experienced small gains than the comparison group of beginning teachers, whose classrooms generally gained little in achievement. (See Figure 1.6.)

Finally, some studies have begun to look at specific practices within teacher education programs and evaluate their influences on particular kinds of candidate learning and practice. A recent review of such studies considered teacher education pedagogies ranging from microteaching and various kinds of clinical experiences to the use of simulations, video cases, and other case methods

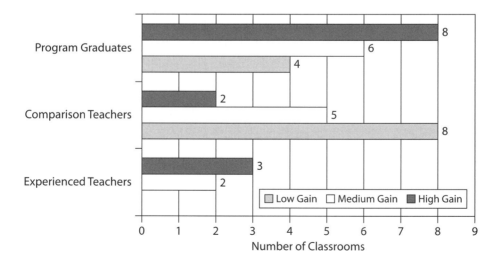

Figure 1.6 Student Achievement Gains in Reading Comprehension, by Classroom.

Source: Reprinted with permission from the International Reading Association.

(Grossman, in press). The review noted findings that suggest some promising directions for teacher education practice, as well as a need for greater consensus about measures and methods and greater reach of the research into practice.

This and other research suggests that *how* certain teacher education approaches are used may matter as much as the general approach itself. For example, a recent set of studies of the use of case methods in teacher education studied whether and how prospective teachers learned to analyze teaching and learning and how their success related to the pedagogy used by faculty. Some of these studies found evidence that, with careful scaffolding and feedback, as well as the skillful use of professional literature, teacher candidates could move from simplistic perspectives about the causes of classroom events to much more expert understandings of how aspects of teaching and students' development influence learning (Goodwin, 2002; Hammerness and others, 2002; Roeser, 2002). Others documented how, without specific teaching supports, the use of cases alone failed to move candidates decisively from novice ideas to more mature understandings of students and teaching (Whitcomb, 2002; Levin, 2002). As we gain greater knowledge about the effects of particular approaches to teacher education on teachers' knowledge, dispositions, and practices, and as we are able to follow these through to evidence about student learning, the consensus about what teachers should know and be able to do should be increasingly well connected to a consensus about how teachers can learn to do these things.

DOMAINS OF TEACHER LEARNING

Returning to our Figure 1.1, we describe here the ways in which knowledge of *learners,* conceptions of *curriculum,* and understanding of *teaching* might inform teacher education. These areas of teachers learning are developed further in Chapters Two through Nine.

Knowledge of Learners: Understanding Development and Learning in Social Contexts

The first area highlighted in Figure 1.1 involves teachers' knowledge and assumptions about learners' development in social contexts. Understanding how children develop and learn, as well as what they have learned during their early years and are continuing to learn outside of school, is critical for effective teaching. In particular, we focus on how people learn, how children develop over time, and how they acquire and use language.

Understanding Learners and Learning. People have speculated about how people learn for centuries. Based on research over the past thirty years, we organize our treatment of this vast literature using the *How People Learn* (HPL) framework

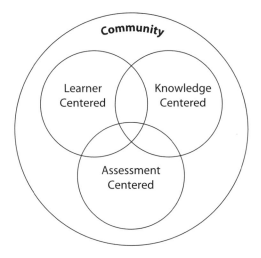

Figure 1.7 HPL Framework

introduced in several National Academy of Sciences reports, including *How People Learn: Brain, Mind, Experience and School* (National Research Council, 2000), and *How People Learn: Bridging Research and Practice* (Donovan, Bransford, and Pellegrino, 1999). As Figure 1.7 indicates, the framework provides a guideline for thinking about learning from the vantage point of

- The *learner* and his or her strengths, interests, and preconceptions;
- The *knowledge,* skills, and attitudes we want people to acquire and how they may be able to do so in order to transfer what they've learned;
- The *assessment* of learning that both makes students' thinking visible and, through feedback, guides further learning; and
- The *community* within which learning occurs, both within and outside the classroom.

Effective teachers know how to balance all four components of this framework. Teachers' knowledge of child development, language, cultural backgrounds, and special needs is important for being a *learner-centered* teacher. In the learning chapter we explore in more detail how connecting to students' knowledge and experiences helps them to learn. Furthermore, if they are to support learning that prepares students for life in a complex world, *knowledge-centered* teachers have to pay careful attention to what they teach and why. In addition to decisions about what is taught, which may be guided by national, state, and local standards, teachers must consider how specific topics and ideas may best be taught. The content to be learned shapes the learning process in important ways, as do preexisting beliefs and experiences of different learners. Among other things, teachers need to be able to anticipate student understandings and misunderstandings in specific areas like fractions, wave theory, planetary motion, and phonics.

Effective teachers connect *knowledge* with *learners* by being *assessment-centered.* Assessments, and the feedback they engender, are actually another source of learning, not just an evaluation of it. Research in cognitive science has shown that *formative assessment*, assessment carried out during the instructional process that makes students' thinking visible and provides them feedback for revising their efforts, can be a powerful tool for learning.

Finally, the process of learning is *community-centered,* as it is influenced by the norms and modes of operation of the community in which it occurs. In a sense, all learning is culturally mediated; that is, it arises from cultural activity. An important implication of this perspective is that providing supportive, enriched, and flexible settings where people can learn from one another is essential. Having strong social networks within a classroom, within a school, and between classrooms and outside resources produces a number of advantages for learning. Students learn more effectively in contexts where they can use the resources of their peers and where they believe their efforts matter to the welfare of the group. Students also learn more effectively when teachers build upon the "funds of knowledge" that exist in their communities and link their experiences outside of school to those within the classroom.

Understanding Development. In addition to a general appreciation of how people learn, teachers need to be able to support children's development across many domains that interact with one another, including physical, social-emotional, moral, and linguistic, as well as cognitive. Furthermore, children's development unfolds in social contexts that influence what they experience and how they respond to and make sense of the world around them. Consequently, a deep understanding of diversity is also extremely important for teachers. The classes of most teachers today include students with a wide range of cultural, language, and racial/ethnic backgrounds, as well as prior experiences and interests. The heterogeneity in prior knowledge in today's general classrooms has also widened greatly, and this presents challenges for teachers.

Teachers need to understand general developmental progressions as well as individual differences in development, so that they are able to figure out when children are prepared to learn particular things in particular ways, and how to support them as they take on new tasks. Teachers also need to understand how instruction can support development. In addition to understanding stages of development, an effective teacher needs to understand what is required by the tasks she assigns, and she must be able to observe students carefully to gauge their readiness and the resources they bring to the activity. Teachers who are able to evaluate a child's "zone of proximal development" can create tasks that address the things the child is ready to learn next, and they can provide the necessary supports for learning that will help children confront new challenges with confidence and growing competence. With that knowledge, teachers can help young children continue to feel successful and inspired to learn. Without it, they can stymie children's immediate learning and endanger their future success.

The Development and Use of Language. An especially important aspect of learners' development involves language. Virtually all school learning occurs through the medium of language. Not only do people need to acquire strong language skills to communicate with others, the very use of language enables people to acquire concepts and ideas and to sharpen their thinking. Teachers need to be aware of how language develops. They need to be concerned not only with developing students' general communication abilities in their first and second languages, they need to be able to help students engage in academic discourse, that is, to use the specialized language of the subject areas they are studying.

Furthermore, the language that children speak often affects teachers' and others' assumptions about students and their abilities. Teachers need to understand how "nonstandard" uses of English evolve and, while helping students learn to speak Standard English, avoid sending the message, either overtly or implicitly, that the language spoken by some groups of students is linguistically inferior to that spoken by others. The way students speak should be respected as something they learned effectively while growing up, with a recognition that children's linguistic differences are not a symptom of some inability to learn but a base of linguistic information to talk about, use, and build from.

Conceptions of Curriculum: Subject Matter, Skills, and Social Purposes of Schooling

In addition to understanding students as learners in social contexts, Figure 1.1 highlights a second area of professional knowledge that is important for teaching: the curricular understanding that enables teachers to organize the subject matter and skills they will teach in light of the goals they are aiming for. The focus here is on decisions about what to teach and why. Assumptions about the social purposes of schooling affect these decisions in important ways.

Guidelines about what to teach and why have been developed over the last decade by groups involved with setting national, state, and local standards. These new standards are a reflection of the changing purposes for education in our society and the implications these have for curriculum. It is beyond the scope of this volume to discuss all these content areas and standards; however, a companion volume to this one discusses issues of reading because of its pervasive importance. Our focus is on what effective teachers need to know to interpret these general guidelines and standards, think about how the teaching of specific kinds of knowledge and skills "adds up" over time, create purposeful learning plans, and adapt them to the particular students whom they teach.

Developing a Curricular Vision. Even when teachers are provided with texts and other materials for their classrooms, they must still construct a curriculum for their students in response to broad statements of goals and standards, the particular needs and prior learning experiences of their students, and the resources and demands of communities. They must make a wide variety of curriculum decisions, ranging from the evaluation and selection of materials to the design and sequencing of tasks, assignments, and activities for students, based on their learning needs. These demands on teachers have grown with the advent of standards-based reforms that presume that teachers will use data about student learning to help students acquire skills they have missed or struggled to learn. A curricular vision for teachers rests in an understanding of learning and learners as these intersect with educational goals and purposes, principles of instructional design, and an understanding of teaching options and possibilities.

Teachers need to think about the subject matters they teach in a broader context that includes an understanding of the social purposes of education, including the many functions of schools—academic, vocational, social and civic, and personal—that must be balanced in classrooms every day. In a democratic society, teachers must also evaluate their teaching decisions against the goals of preparing students to be equitable participants in a society that relies on interdependence. An important component of preparing students to participate in democracy is to allow them to experience democratic classrooms and schools. This includes a commitment to eliminate disparities in educational opportunities among students, especially those students who have been poorly served by our current system. It also includes ambitious learning opportunities and, in today's society, equitable access to the technological tools that citizens need to succeed.

Understanding Teaching: Designing Classrooms That Enable Diverse Students to Learn Challenging Content

The third area highlighted in Figure 1.1 involves the skillful teaching that enables learners to access the curriculum. The overall goal is to teach in ways that optimize learning for all students. This involves motivating and organizing students' work in settings that provide access to challenging content and frequent assessments of their progress, coupled with feedback and opportunities to revise and improve. At least four areas of knowledge and skill are essential for this process: the development of pedagogical content knowledge in the subject areas to be taught; knowledge of how to teach diverse learners; knowledge of assessment; and an understanding of how to manage classroom activities so that students can work purposefully and productively.

Teaching Subject Matter. To make content accessible to learners, teachers need flexible understanding of subject matter married to an appreciation for how students learn. Knowing how students understand (and sometimes misunderstand) their particular subjects and having a repertoire of strategies to help students engage ideas central to the discipline is at the core of pedagogical content knowledge. Teachers who understand the conceptual difficulties that students typically have with fractions, or metaphor, or acceleration—and who know how to diagnose these difficulties and provide strategies for overcoming them—have developed elements of the pedagogical content knowledge necessary to teach these aspects of their disciplines effectively. To build their understanding of students' subject matter reasoning and understanding, teachers need to observe students and study the processes of learning within a field. With this understanding, they can develop a storehouse of representations and other strategies for teaching specific topics to the range of students they will teach.

Teaching Diverse Learners. Students in today's classrooms pose a wide range of diverse learning needs that teachers must be prepared to address. Part of this process is learning how to understand and reach out to children who have a wide range of life experiences, behaviors, and beliefs about themselves and what school means to them. When teachers develop a "sociocultural consciousness," they understand that individuals' worldviews are not universal but are greatly influenced by their life experiences, gender, race, ethnicity, and social-class background (Banks, 1998; Villegas and Lucas, 2002a). This kind of awareness helps them better understand how their interactions with their students are influenced by their social and cultural location and helps them develop attitudes and expectations—as well as knowledge of how to incorporate the cultures and experiences of their students into their teaching—that support learning. In addition to constructing culturally responsive curriculum and teaching, teachers need to be prepared for learning differences and disabilities that are prevalent in the inclusive classroom. They need to understand how to evaluate students' strengths and difficulties, construct appropriate tasks and supports, and use strategies that enable students to learn how to guide their own learning.

Assessing Learning. If the central task of teaching is enabling learners with very different experiences, learning styles, and starting points to acquire common, high-level knowledge and skills, teachers must have many tools for tapping into what students think and adapting instruction to their needs. Assessment is a crucial element of the teaching and learning process. In addition to constructing thoughtful performance tasks and criteria for evaluating them that will guide students' learning and reveal what they have learned, teachers need a large repertoire of formative assessment strategies. These strategies need to be infused throughout the instructional process to help make students' thinking visible as they progress through a course of study, to give them feedback about their work that guides revisions in their thinking and performance, and to guide teaching so that it is responsive to what students need to know and how they learn. Helping students learn to self-assess is also important for learning. A number of studies show that achievement improves when students are encouraged to assess their own progress against internalized standards (National Reading Council, 2000; Lin and Lehman, 1999; White and Fredrickson, 1998). Finally, teachers need to learn how to use standards in constructing assessments and how to interpret standardized tests that their students will take, so as to make appropriate decisions about student learning and about their own teaching.

Managing Classrooms. Many beginning teachers, especially those who are underprepared, focus much of their concern on classroom management, especially as it pertains to what is generally thought of as student discipline. Organizing a classroom for learning is extremely important to safeguard valuable time and to create a positive environment for teaching and learning. However, effective classroom management extends far beyond rules for classroom conduct and procedures to deal with misbehavior. Research shows that effective classroom management starts with the creation of curriculum that is meaningful to students and with teaching that is engaging and motivating. Classroom management is further strengthened by the creation of learning communities that give students the opportunity to work together productively and to learn in a psychologically safe environment. It is critical for teachers to understand child development, motivation theory, and the management of groups as a starting point for constructing a successful classroom setting. In addition, teachers who know how to structure activities and interactions so that they are orderly, purposeful, and based on common understandings of what to do gain more learning time for their students and give students more opportunity to succeed because they understand what is expected of them. With these conditions in place, teachers will encounter less problematic behavior between and among students. However, teachers should be prepared with strategies to help students both attend to their learning and to repair and restore behavior respectfully. Psychological research on behavioral change and research on specific classroom management programs both provide insights for teachers about productive choices they can make. Finally, schools are expected to help students acquire basic moral values such as honesty, fairness, respect for others, and responsibility. We discuss how teachers can organize the classroom community to support students in learning these values that are essential for later life and for the society as a whole.

Collaborating to Create Strong Schools. Throughout these chapters we emphasize how important it is for teachers to adopt a whole school perspective, to learn to collaborate with their peers and with parents, and to be prepared to contribute to school reforms that will strengthen the learning environment for their students.

OVERALL ORGANIZATION

The chapters that follow are organized into two major sections. In the first section, we use the framework in Figure 1.1 to elaborate on the knowledge, skills, and commitments that beginning teachers need in order to help their students succeed. Eight chapters present "core concepts" to guide the development of curriculum. These include (1) learning, (2) development, (3) language, (4) curriculum goals, (5) teaching subject matter, (6) teaching diverse learners, (7) assessment, and (8) classroom management (see Chapters Two through Nine).

The "core concepts" we identify are related to the structure of the fields under study. Just as the concept of "mutual consent" is central to the study of contracts in the law, so the ideas of "transfer" and "prior knowledge" are central to the study of learning and teaching. Thus we organize our discussion around major linchpins in our understanding of learning and teaching rather than around lists of topics or sets of courses. As Bruner (1960/1977) argued: "The curriculum of a subject should be determined by the most fundamental understanding that can be achieved *of the underlying principles* that give structure to that subject" (p. 31, italics added). This makes a subject more understandable because it (1) allows students to generalize and make sense of later information by helping them develop a working sense of the entire field; (2) aids students' memory by helping them understand how information fits into a field; and (3) motivates students by focusing them on what is most worth knowing.

Furthermore, the domain areas used to define our chapters are not meant to represent courses. In fact, many of the core concepts in each of the domain areas might cut across many courses in a program. For example, at New York University, teacher educators use child development as a foundational base for the entire program. The content domain areas are integrated and the curriculum is conceptualized around a set of questions and "Inquiries" courses that are often tied to field experiences. In many of the programs highlighted in this report, faculty members have found innovative ways to integrate and deliver essential content.

In the chapters on these core concepts, we provide some examples of strategies used in teacher education programs that reflect widely used approaches and promising new methods to teaching these ideas, often in programs that have been found to be unusually effective. These examples are offered as illustrative, but not necessarily as superior to other potential strategies that are not discussed.

The second section of the book uses the same basic framework, but applies it to situations where *new teachers* are the learners. Many of the same assumptions about learning, development, assessment, and teaching are as relevant to teachers as learners as they are to students as learners. We discuss what is known about teacher development and learning, and we explore curriculum issues and promising pedagogies in teacher education that respond to what and how teachers need to learn. Finally, we treat questions of the policy context for teacher education and issues of institutional renewal and change. We focus especially on the need to improve the context within which teacher preparation programs operate, so that they, like their students, are optimally prepared to succeed.

CHAPTER TWO

Theories of Learning
and Their Roles in Teaching

John Bransford, Sharon Derry, David Berliner, and Karen Hammerness,
with Kelly Lyn Beckett

A Disturbing Discovery

It was one o'clock in the morning. Paul Nelson had spent the last eight hours grading final exams from the students in his high school astronomy classes. This was his first year as a teacher and he was exhausted and distressed because most of the essays showed clear evidence of misunderstandings on the part of the students.

The majority of the students wrote that summer temperatures were warmer than winter temperatures because the earth was closer to the sun in the summer. This was a false assumption that Paul had discussed several times in class. He had shown his students a model of the solar system and explained that summers were hotter than winters because of changes in the angle of the earth and the sun—not the distance of the earth from the sun. He knew he had mentioned this point at least three different times.

Paul wondered what had gone wrong. Were the students less capable than he had assumed? Were they not paying attention even though they seemed to be interested in the topic of astronomy? Was there something about having to put their thoughts into writing that caused them to do poorly? Given that he would be teaching the course the next year, was there something he should do differently? And if so, what and why?

Variations on the preceding scene occur again and again among K–12 teachers, college professors, people involved in business training, and others. They often feel that information was presented with great care and clarity and are stunned when students fail to perform as well as they had expected. Was it their fault, the students' fault, the curriculum's fault—some portion of all of these? And what is needed to help everyone be more successful the next time around?

The questions asked by Paul Nelson and other educators who experience similar difficulties involve questions about the nature of human learning. We all make assumptions about learning whether we realize it or not. We make assumptions about what is important for people to learn (understanding the earth's role in the solar system—including why it is warm in the summer— seems to qualify as worth knowing), about who can learn well and why, and about effective strategies for enhancing our own learning and that of helping others. Peoples' assumptions about learning can be considered to be tacit (unconscious) theories that affect their behavior, but tacit theories typically remain unexamined. By making tacit theories explicit, people can think more critically about them. This allows us to improve upon ideas and assumptions that may be partially true but far from complete. In cases like the one experienced by Paul Nelson, explicit theories of learning can help educators rethink their teaching processes. This is what people mean when they say: "There is nothing as practical as a good theory." The goal of this chapter is to provide a way of thinking about learning that can help educators improve their efforts to teach.

THE *HOW PEOPLE LEARN* FRAMEWORK AS A WAY TO ORGANIZE THINKING

We organize our discussion around the *How People Learn* (HPL) framework (see Figure 1.7 in Chapter One) that was used by a National Academy of Science Committee to organize what is known about learning and teaching (National Research Council, 2000). The framework's four components can be used to highlight areas where we all tend to have "mini theories" (often tacit) about learning and teaching. For example, we all make assumptions about

- What should be taught, why it is important, and how this knowledge should be organized (knowledge-centeredness)
- Who learns, how, and why (learner-centeredness)
- What kinds of classroom, school, and school-community environments enhance learning (community-centeredness), and
- What kinds of evidence for learning students, teachers, parents, and others can use to see if effective learning is really occurring (assessment-centeredness).

Teachers must learn to balance and integrate all four components of the HPL framework if they are to teach effectively. We begin by discussing each component separately and then explore the balancing act that effective teachers must continually orchestrate to help all students succeed.

Knowledge-Centeredness

The knowledge-centered aspect of the HPL framework seems obvious at first glance—so obvious that it hardly requires discussion. People often say, "Of course, learning involves knowledge (and skills, which we here assume are also a part of this knowledge). What else is new?" On second glance, however, issues about the nature of knowledge are extremely important and far from obvious. For example, it is easy to fall into the trap of assuming that schools should teach what we learned when we grew up. However, the world has changed and different kinds of skills and knowledge are required for successful and productive lives in the twenty-first century. People also have differing views of the purposes of education and hence the kinds of things that are worth knowing. The chapter on curriculum (Chapter Five) takes a special look at these issues. Among the points it discusses is how technology is changing our world and how people need to learn to use it to succeed.

Understanding the Nature of Expertise

Research in the learning sciences has explored the nature of the skills and knowledge that underlie expert performances, and this research is important for thinking about the design of effective curricula. For example, we know that experts notice features of problems and situations that may escape the attention of novices (see, for example, Chase and Simon, 1973; Chi, Feltovitch, and Glasser, 1981; de Groot, 1965). They therefore "start problem solving at a higher place" than novices (de Groot, 1965). This has a number of implications for teaching, including the need for teachers to frame what learners should pay attention to. For example, when teachers attempt to teach through video, field trips, internships, and other experiences in which students are expected to learn by observation and participation, teachers need to help students bring a mental organization to the learning experience. Consider videos: when teacher educators show them to teachers, or teachers show them to students, many features in the videos will be obvious to experts yet go unnoticed by novices unless the features are pointed out and discussed.

In addition to "noticing," problem solving and memory are strongly affected by the knowledge and skills available to the experts. For example, de Groot showed master chess players a five-second glimpse of a chess game in progress and then removed it from sight and asked them to reproduce what they had seen by using chess pieces that had been given them. The experts did extremely well at this task—much better than people less experienced in chess. One might conclude the experts did better because they are "more intelligent" or "have better memories." But it turns out that their abilities to remember are closely linked with their knowledge of chess.

One way that people tested this idea was to *randomly* place chess pieces on a chessboard (Chase and Simon, 1973). Under these conditions chess experts' knowledge is not nearly as useful because they are unable to detect meaningful patterns or "chunks" of information. And indeed, under random conditions, differences in memory between chess masters and less experienced players disappeared (see Chase and Simon, 1973).

An interesting variation on this experiment was conducted by Chi (1978). She compared the memory performances of college students and ten-year-old students who played a lot of chess. (The college students were not chess players.) When she asked participants in her experiment to remember strings of numbers, the college students did better than the ten-year-olds. However, when asked to remember parts of a chess game, the memory "abilities" reversed and the ten-year-olds did a much better job.

An Illustration of Expertise and Remembering. The studies about chess are among the many that show that peoples' expertise in an area affects their ability to remember and solve problems (National Research Council, 2000). One important component of these studies involves the amount of effort required to learn and remember new information. Sometimes we are able to learn almost "effortlessly"; we are able to rely on processes that are relatively automatic. At other times our learning depends on explicit strategies that are much more effortful (for example, see Hasher and Zacks, 1979). The degree to which a memory task fits our current levels of expertise can have strong effects on the amount of effort needed for processing. A demonstration that illustrates different effects of effortless processing on memory (depending on what we as learners already know) is provided in "Memory, Expertise, and Effortless Processing I."

Memory, Expertise, and Effortless Processing I

Differences between effortful and effortless processes are illustrated by the following demonstration experiment. In this exercise, please spend no more than four seconds reading each of the following sentences, and read each one only once. Most importantly, try not to use any fancy strategies such as generating elaborate images, rehearsing to yourself, and so forth. These are effortful strategies. Try to react to each sentence as effortlessly as you can.

John walked on the roof.
Bill picked up the egg.
Pete hid the axe.
Jim flew the kite.
Frank flipped the switch.
Alfred built a boat.
Sam hit his head on the ceiling.

Adam quit his job.
Jay fixed the sail.
Ted wrote the play.

Now try to answer the following questions without looking back at the preceding sentences.

Who built the boat?
Who picked up the egg?
Who walked on the roof?
Who quit his job?
Who flew the kite?
Who fixed the sail?
Who hit his head on the ceiling?
Who wrote the play?
Who flipped the switch?
Who hid the axe?

Most people have a very difficult time remembering who did what despite the fact that each statement was comprehensible. If you really approached these sentences in a relatively "effortless" manner, you probably could remember only two or three at most. To remember these sentences you would have had to use very effortful, sophisticated strategies such as thinking of someone you know with a particular name (for example, a friend of yours named John) and making an image of him walking on the roof.

Sentences similar to those presented earlier become much easier to remember if our knowledge base can do much of the work for us. As an illustration, spend approximately four seconds reading each of the following sentences. As in the earlier task, do not attempt to use any effortful, sophisticated strategies. Instead, react to each sentence as effortlessly as you can.

Santa Claus walked on the roof.
The Easter Bunny picked up the egg.
George Washington hid the axe.
Benjamin Franklin flew the kite.
Thomas Edison flipped the switch.
Noah built a boat.
Wilt Chamberlain hit his head on the ceiling.
Richard Nixon quit his job.
Christopher Columbus fixed the sail.
William Shakespeare wrote the play.

Now answer the following questions without looking back at the list.

Who built the boat?
Who picked up the egg?
Who walked on the roof?
Who quit his job?
Who flew the kite?

Who fixed the sail?
Who hit his head on the ceiling?
Who wrote the play?
Who flipped the switch?
Who hid the axe?

This demonstration experiment has been used many times (Bransford and Stein, 1993). Invariably, it is much easier to remember the second set of materials (about Nixon, Columbus, and so forth) than the first (about John, Robert, and so on). The second set of materials is designed to activate knowledge that, without much effort, permits a number of elaborations that make the problem of remembering quite easy to solve. For example, you have probably not heard the exact statement that "George Washington hid the axe," but your knowledge of George Washington is rich enough to easily generate elaborations such as, "it was the axe used to chop down the cherry tree—a tree he was not supposed to chop down." Similarly, for the sentence "Richard Nixon quit his job," you probably found yourself thinking that the job was the presidency, that he was forced to resign, and so forth. Because of the richness of your knowledge, a number of elaborations almost automatically come to mind.

There may have been a few people in the "named" list whom you didn't know. Younger generations often do not know Wilt Chamberlain, for example (a star basketball center). If you didn't know some of the names, you probably noticed that it made remembering more difficult.

Source: The IDEAL Problem Solver, 2nd edition by John D. Bransford and Barry Stein. © 1984, 1998 by W. H. Freeman and Company. Used with permission.

Expertise and Knowledge Organization. Research on expertise also provides important information on how knowledge should be organized. Experts' knowledge is much more than a list of disconnected facts about their disciplines. Instead, their knowledge is connected and organized around important ideas of their disciplines. This organization of knowledge helps experts know when, why, and how aspects of their vast repertoire of knowledge and skills are relevant in any particular situation (see Bransford, Brown, and Cocking, 1999; Chapter Two). Knowledge organization especially affects how information is retrieved.

Bruner (1960/1977), one of the pioneers in cognitive and developmental psychology, makes the following argument about knowledge organization:

The curriculum of a subject should be determined by the most fundamental understanding that can be achieved of the underlying principles that give structure to a subject. Teaching specific topics or skills without making clear their context in the broader fundamental structure of a field of knowledge is uneconomical . . . An understanding of fundamental principles and ideas appears to be the main road to adequate transfer of training. To understand something as a specific instance of a more general case—which is what understanding a more fundamental structure means—is to have learned not only a specific thing but also a model for understanding other things like it that one may encounter. (pp. 25 and 31)

Courses are often organized in ways that fail to develop the kinds of connected knowledge structures that support activities such as effective reasoning and problem solving. For example, texts often present lists of topics and facts in a manner that has been described as "a mile wide and an inch deep" (for example, see National Research Council, 2000). This is very different from focusing on the "enduring ideas of a discipline." In agreement with Bruner, Wiggins and McTighe (1998) argue that the knowledge to be taught should be prioritized into categories that range from "enduring ideas of the discipline" to "important things to know and be able to do" to "ideas worth mentioning." Thinking through these issues and coming up with a set of "enduring connected ideas" is an extremely important aspect of educational design.

The organization of peoples' knowledge affects process skills such as their abilities to think and solve problems. Links between knowledge organization and process skills (for example, evaluating and designing experiments) are illustrated in the experiment described in "Knowledge Organization and Problem Solving."

Knowledge Organization and Problem Solving

A group of college students received a challenge over the Internet before coming to class. The responses to the challenge help illustrate relationships between knowledge organization and problem solving. The challenge they received is described in the following section:

"As a group of biologists compare data from across the world, they note that frogs seem to be disappearing in an alarming number of places. This deeply concerns them, because the frogs may well be an indicator species for environmental changes that could hurt us all. The biologists consider a number of hypotheses about the frogs' disappearance. One is that too much ultraviolet light is getting through the ozone layer.

"One group of biologists decides to test the ultraviolet light hypotheses. They use five different species of frogs, with an equal number of male and female. Half of the frogs receive constant doses of ultraviolet light for a period of four months—this is the experimental group. The other half of the frogs—the control group—are protected so they receive no ultraviolet light.

"At the end of the four months, the biologists find that there is no difference in the death rates between the frogs in the experimental and control groups. This suggests that ultraviolet light is probably not the cause of the frog's demise.

"What do you think about the biologist's experiments and conclusions? Are there questions you would want to ask before accepting their conclusions? Are there new experiments that you would want to propose?"

Students responded to the challenge by posting written answers on the Internet before coming to class. They noted a number of good points about the experiment; for example, that it involved an experimental-control design that involved several different species of frogs, used stratified random sampling, and so forth. Students also raised a number of concerns such as, "Maybe the doses of ultraviolet light that were used were too weak"; "Maybe the light was provided for too short a time" (that is, only four months); "Maybe the experimenters didn't wait long enough to see the effects of the ultraviolet light, so maybe they should have looked at difference in illness between the two groups rather than compare the death rates." Not a single student questioned the fact that only adult frogs were used in the experiment (the multimedia materials that were part of the challenge that students viewed on the Internet showed clearly that the frogs were all adults). When the students arrived in class (remember that they had answered the challenge on the Internet before attending class), the instructor asked whether a flaw may have been to use only adult frogs rather than attempt to explore the effects of ultraviolet light on potentially vulnerable points in the frogs' life cycle. Every student immediately realized that the answer was "yes," and they stated they had all studied life cycles. However, they had learned about life cycles as isolated exercises (for example, they had been asked to memorize the stages of the life cycle of a fly or mosquito) and had never connected this information to larger questions like the survival of a species. As a consequence, the idea of life cycles had never occurred to them in the context of attempting to solve the preceding frog problem. To paraphrase Whitehead (1929), knowledge that was potentially important for exploring the frog problem had remained "inert."

The suggestion by Bruner (1960/1977) that was discussed earlier is highly relevant in this context; namely, that "Teaching specific topics or skills without making clear their context in the broader fundamental structure of a field of knowledge is uneconomical . . . An understanding of fundamental principles and ideas appears to be the main road to adequate transfer of training" (p. 25). The students in the class had all learned about life cycles, but their teachers and texts did not make clear the importance of this information in the broader structure of the field of knowledge.

The vignette presented at the beginning of this chapter (about the astronomy teacher who was dismayed that his students still believed that summer on earth was caused by its distance from the sun) is also relevant in this context. If explicitly reminded, students may have been able to remember seeing a demonstration of tilted orbits. Nevertheless, their thinking about the seasons was probably driven by other knowledge that they had available for them. For example, many experiences support the idea that distance from a heat source affects temperature. The closer we stand to radiators, stoves, fireplaces, and other heat sources, the greater the heat (National Research Council, in press).

Interestingly, there are also experiences in which we can manipulate the intensity of heat by changing the angle of a heat source—by pointing a hair dryer on one's head at different angles, for example. But without the ability to carefully control distance from the head or the tools to measure small changes in temperature (and without some guidance that helps people think to do this experiment in the first place), the relationship between heat and angle of the heat source can easily be missed.

Expertise and Teaching

Information about relationships between expert knowledge and teaching abilities is especially important for teachers to understand. At one level, teachers must have knowledge of their disciplines to teach effectively. Consider knowledge about elementary physics and simple machines (for example, levers, pulleys). Teachers who know a great deal about this topic can create classroom environments where students get to experiment with using simple machines and can ask the teacher questions about why certain things happened (for example, "Why did this way of using the lever work better than that way?"). Teachers need considerable knowledge in order to answer a wide range of questions that arise from the problems that students confront. Teachers who don't understand much physics will often have difficulty answering these questions. They may therefore be much more inclined to follow only the restricted set of activities in the textbook, where answers are provided in the teachers' edition of the text.

There is also a downside to having a great deal of knowledge about one's subject matter. Sometimes, the information becomes so intuitive that experts lose sight of what it was like to be a novice. In his studies with chess masters, de Groot (1965) notes how masters were often incredulous that lesser experienced players could not see "obvious" features of the game board that were "right before their eyes" and signaled clearly what the next move should be.

Nathan and colleagues (Nathan, Koedinger, and Alibali, 2001; Nathan and Petrosino, 2003) use the term *expert blind spots* to refer to downsides of content expertise. Experts are often blind to the fact that much of their knowledge of their subject matter has moved from explicit to tacit and hence can easily be skipped over in instruction. For example, experts in physics and engineering may not realize that they are failing to communicate all the information necessary to help novices learn to construct their own free body diagrams (Brophy, 2001). The reason is that many decisions are so intuitive that the professors don't even realize that they are part of their repertoire.

Shulman (1987) explains that effective teachers need to develop "pedagogical content knowledge" that goes well beyond the content knowledge of a discipline (see also Hestenes, 1987). It includes an understanding of how novices typically struggle as they attempt to master a domain and an understanding of strategies for helping them learn. Chapter Six in this volume explores the concept of pedagogical content knowledge in considerable depth.

Adaptive Expertise

An especially important analysis of expertise focuses on differences between "routine experts" and "adaptive experts" (for example, Hatano and Inagaki, 1986; Hatano and Osura, 2003). Both routine experts and adaptive experts continue to learn throughout their lifetimes. Routine experts develop a core set of competencies that they apply throughout their lives with greater and greater efficiency. In contrast, adaptive experts are much more likely to change their core competencies and continually expand the breadth and depth of their expertise. This restructuring of core ideas, beliefs, and competencies may reduce their efficiency in the short run but make them more flexible in the long run. These processes of restructuring often have emotional consequences that accompany realizations that cherished beliefs and practices need to be changed.

Figure 2.1 provides a characterization of adaptive expertise that is relevant for thinking about issues of learning and teaching (Schwartz, Bransford, and Sears, in press, in conjunction with the LIFE Center).

Schwartz and others note that the horizontal dimension in Figure 2.1 emphasizes efficiency; the vertical dimension emphasizes innovation. Sometimes these two dimensions are characterized as mutually exclusive ends of continuum (for example, high- and low-road transfer, Perkins and Salomon, 1989). However, because there are different processes involved, they are not necessarily exclusive of one another. Adaptive experts, for example, are presumably high on both dimensions (for example, Gentner and others, 1997; Hatano and Inagaki, 1986; Wineburg, 1998). Adaptive expertise is discussed as a "gold standard for learning" in *How People Learn* (National Research Council, 2000).

Schwartz and others (in press) note that "the horizontal dimension in Figure 2.1 is efficiency. People who are high on efficiency can rapidly retrieve and accurately apply appropriate knowledge and skills to solve a problem or understand an explanation. Examples include experts who have a great deal of

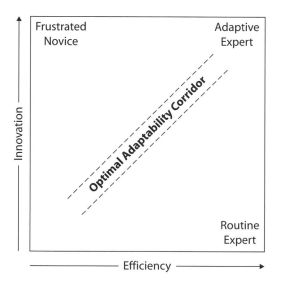

Figure 2.1 The Dimensions of Adaptive Expertise.

experience with certain types of problems; for example, doctors who have seen many instances of diseases in many different people or who have frequently performed a particular type of surgery. They can diagnose and treat a new patient quickly and effectively. Many instructional strategies are designed to develop the kinds of efficiency that enable people to act with fluency." Schwartz and colleagues (in press) also note the following:

> Researchers who study both people and organizations have learned a great deal about promoting efficiency. At a general level, probably the best way to be efficient is to practice at tasks and gain experiences with important classes and components of problems so that they become "routine" and easy to solve later. The best way to ensure transfer is to "teach for it" so that the problems people encounter on a test or in an everyday environment can be solved with high frequency because they are quite close to what has been learned previously. Transfer problems essentially disappear if we teach in contexts where people need to perform, and if we arrange experiences and environments so that the correct behaviors are driven by the environment.

There are ways to practice solving problems that are excellent from an efficiency perspective. Appropriate kinds of practice help people turn nonroutine, difficult-to-solve problems into routine problems that can be solved quickly and easily. Phrased another way, efficiency-oriented practice is often about "problem elimination" rather than about in-depth, sustained problem solving. A problem is typically defined as a gap or barrier between a goal state and one's present state (see, for example, Bransford and Stein, 1993; Hayes, 1990; Newell and Simon, 1972). By preparing people so that the problems they will face in life are essentially routine problems—or at worst very "near transfer" problems—the gap between goal states and present states is either eliminated or made to be very small. This allows people to perform quite effectively.

Schwartz and others (in press) proceed to note that all of this works well *provided* the environments for which we are preparing people are stable. However, people like Fullan (2001) and Valli (1996) argue that we live in a "whitewater world" where change is the norm and not the exception. Because efficiency is so emphasized in our time-limited society, it tends to take over as a prime way to assess progress. But, there are also potential downsides of an overemphasis on efficiency. For example, studies show that efficiency can often produce "functionally fixed" behaviors that are problematic in new situations (see, for example, Luchins, 1942). Similarly, Hatano and Inagaki (1986) discuss "routine experts" who become very good at solving particular sets of problems but do not continue to learn throughout their lifetimes (except in the sense of becoming even more efficient at their old routines). These potential downsides of an overemphasis on efficiency, especially in the face of change, make it especially important to attempt to reconceptualize learning and transfer as something more than the ability to apply previously acquired skills and schemas efficiently for routine problem solving. The argument is not to eliminate efficiency but to complement it so that people can adapt optimally.

Schwartz and others (in press) note that the vertical dimension illustrated in Figure 2.1 is innovation. It involves a movement away from efficiency, at least temporarily. It often requires the ability to "unlearn" previous routines (for example, unlearning how to type with two fingers in order to move to a new level of typing efficiency). It also includes the ability to "let go" of previously held beliefs and tolerate the ambiguity of having to rethink one's perspective. The study of history experts versus college students that was mentioned earlier (Wineburg, 1998) provides a good illustration of the need to resist efficient explanations and take the time to explore ideas more carefully. Instructional strategies designed to facilitate innovation are quite different from those that merely facilitate efficiency.

The importance of resisting one's initial ideas about a problem or challenge was discussed by Land, inventor of the Polaroid Land camera. With tongue in cheek, he described the processes of innovation (and the insights that precede them) as involving "the sudden cessation of stupidity." The "stupidity" comes from one's initial framing of problems—framings that contain assumptions that "put people in a box," or more technically, constrained the problem spaces within which they work (see, for example, Bransford and Stein, 1993; Hayes, 1990; Newell and Simon, 1972; Wineburg, 1998).

For educators, Figure 2.1 becomes especially useful when we ask how we can move people along both of its dimensions. Movement along one dimension alone is unlikely to support the development of adaptive expertise. Training dedicated to high efficiency can restrict transfer to highly similar situations. On the other hand, opportunities to engage in general, content-free skills of critical thinking or problem solving appear to provide a set of flexible "weak methods" (Newell and Simon, 1972) that are too inefficient for the large problem spaces found in many real-world tasks.

Researchers have conjectured that people will benefit most from learning opportunities that balance the two dimensions by remaining within the "optimal adaptability corridor" or OAC (Schwartz and others, in press). For example, children who receive nothing but efficiency-oriented computation training in mathematics may well become speedy at performing a specific routine, but this kind of experience will lead to limited capabilities in the face of new problems. Balanced instruction would include opportunities to learn with understanding and develop students' own mathematical conjectures *as well as* become efficient at computation. Instruction that balances efficiency and innovation should also include opportunities to experiment with ideas and, in the process, experience the need to change them. These kinds of experiences often require opportunities to interact actively with artifacts and people to discover inconsistencies and preconceptions that need further refinement. It is useful to consider when and how the instructional approaches discussed in this volume fit within the OAC.

Learner-Centeredness

The learner-centered lens of the HPL framework overlaps with knowledge-centeredness (for example, the idea of "pedagogical content knowledge" provides one such overlap), but the learner-centered lens specifically reminds us to think about learners rather than only about subject matter. When students enter our classrooms we can't help making assumptions about them. Some may sit straight in their desks and write down everything we say. Others may doodle, sprawl, or look out the window as we talk. Some may use language (for example, "I ain't got any") that can easily be misinterpreted as a sign of "poor upbringing" and perhaps "poor learning abilities." Assumptions about the capabilities of students often become "self-fulfilling prophesies" that affect how teachers interact with the students and hence how well they learn.

Chapters Three and Four in this section provide important insights into the complex task of understanding our learners. Chapter Three discusses theories of development and how they impact teaching and learning. Chapter Four discusses theories of language and how language usage (for example, saying "ain't") can act as a "marker" that inappropriately dooms some students to failure in their teachers' minds. Many of the other chapters in this volume also deal with issues of understanding learners and engaging culturally relevant teaching. This includes learning to build on students' strengths rather than simply seeing weaknesses. Several important aspects of being learner-centered are discussed in the following section.

Understanding the Constructive Nature of Knowing

One approach to thinking about learners is to imagine giving them pretests and then marveling at how much they *don't* know about the skills or topics we are teaching. If our focus is primarily on what learners don't know, we'll find lots of evidence that they indeed have lots to learn.

A different approach to understanding learners was emphasized by the famous Swiss psychologist Jean Piaget. He argued that children of all ages were active explorers of their worlds. The complexity of what they could understand was affected by what they already knew and their developmental levels (explained more in Chapter Three). Nevertheless, an important implication of his findings was that even young children were active learners who explored expectations about the world and how it worked. Piaget's theory emphasized the *constructive nature of knowing*. This refers to the idea that we all actively attempt to interpret our world based on our existing skills, knowledge, and developmental levels. Looking at the processes by which students actively attempt to learn is very different from simply testing them on facts or skills and seeing what they don't (for the moment) know.

The constructive nature of knowing is nicely illustrated in the children's story, *Fish is Fish*, by Leo Lionni (1970). *Fish is Fish* is the story of a fish who is interested in learning about what happens on land, but it cannot explore land because it can only breathe in water. It befriends a tadpole, who grows into a frog and eventually goes onto the land. The frog returns to the pond a few weeks later and describes the things it has seen like birds, cows, and people. As the fish listens to the frog's descriptions, he imagines each one to be fish-like. People are imagined to be fish who walk on their tailfins; birds are fish with wings; cows are fish with udders. This story illustrates both the creative opportunities and dangers inherent in the fact that people construct new knowledge based on their current knowledge. In Piaget's terms, the fish *assimilated* the information provided by the frog to its existing knowledge structures. In contrast to processes of assimilation are processes of *accommodation*. Here one changes a core belief or concept when confronted with evidence that prompts such as change.

Studies by Vosniado and Brewer illustrate *Fish is Fish*-style assimilation in the context of young children's thinking about the earth. They worked with children who believed that the earth is flat (because this fit their experiences) and attempted to help them understand that, in fact, it is spherical. When told it is round, children often pictured the earth as a pancake rather than as a sphere (Vosniadou and Brewer, 1989). If they were then told that it is round like a sphere, they interpreted the new information about a spherical earth within their flat-earth view by picturing a pancake-like flat surface inside or on top of a sphere, with humans standing on top of the pancake. The model of the earth that they had developed—and that helped them explain how they could stand or walk upon its surface—did not fit the model of a spherical earth. Like *Fish is Fish*, everything the children heard was incorporated into their preexisting views.

Fish is Fish is relevant not only for young children, but for learners of all ages. For example, college students often have developed beliefs about physical and biological phenomena that fit their experiences but do not fit scientific accounts of these phenomena. These preconceptions must be addressed in order for them to change their beliefs (see, for example, Confrey, 1990; Mestre, 1994; Minstrell, 1989; Redish, 1996). It is important to note that constructivism is a theory of knowing, not a theory of teaching. In particular, adopting a constructivist theory of knowing does not imply that all learning should be discovery oriented and that direct instruction should always be avoided (see, for example, National Research Council, 2000; Schwartz and Bransford, 1998). Instead, it implies that teachers must take account of students' prior conceptions in designing instruction, because these will influence what students learn—for good or for ill—whether or not the teacher is aware of them. The concept of "constructivism" is frequently misunderstood—analogous to the fish's understanding of birds, cows, and people.

Connecting to Students' Existing Knowledge. The *Fish is Fish* story illustrates how previously acquired knowledge can lead people to understand in ways that differ from what others intended. Another aspect of being learning-centered is to understand that previously acquired knowledge can also provide a powerful boost for new learning. Consider the statement: "The haystack was important because the cloth ripped." Most people actively attempt to make sense of the statement but have difficulty understanding it. Now consider the same sentence again but in the context of information about a "parachute." For most people, this provides a clue that allows them to construct a meaningful interpretation of the sentence. If you think about your interpretation, you probably made assumptions about a person using the parachute who jumped from a plane, about that person landing on the haystack, and so forth. None of this information was mentioned in the sentence but it didn't need to be. You supplied it based on your existing knowledge of the world (see, for example, Bransford and Johnson, 1972; Buhler, 1908).

Ideally, what is taught in school builds upon and connects with students' previous experiences, but this is not always the case. A story written in 1944 by Stephen Corey provides an informative look at one example of such disconnects. Entitled "Poor Scholar's Soliloquy," the article is written from the perspective of an imaginary student (we'll call him Bob—the "problem student") who is not very good in school and has had to repeat the seventh grade. Many would write Bob off as having a low aptitude for learning. But when you examine what Bob is capable of achieving outside of school, you develop a very different impression of his abilities.

Part of the soliloquy describes teachers' concerns that one of the reasons Bob is a problem student is that he is not a good reader. He can decode, but he doesn't read the kind of books teachers value. Bob's favorite books include *Popular Science,* the *Mechanical Encyclopedia,* and the Sears and Wards catalogues. Bob uses his books to pursue meaningful goals. He says, "I don't just sit down and read them through like they make us do in school. I use my books when I want to find something out, like whenever Mom buys anything second hand I look it up in Sears or Wards first and tell her if she's getting stung or not."

Later on, Bob explains the trouble he had memorizing the names of the presidents. He knew some of them, like Washington and Jefferson, but there were thirty altogether and he never did get them all straight. From this information, one might conclude that he has a poor memory. Yet Bob also talks about the three trucks his uncle owns and can describe the horsepower and number of forward and backward gears of twenty-six different American trucks, many of them diesels. Then he says, "It's funny how that Diesel works. I started to tell my teacher about it last Wednesday in science class when the pump we were using to make a vacuum in a bell jar got hot, but she said she didn't see what a Diesel engine had to do with our experiment on air pressure so I just kept still. The kids seemed interested, though."

Bob also discusses his inability to do the kinds of word problems found in his textbooks. Yet he helps his uncle make all kinds of complex plans when they travel together. He talks about the bills and letters he sends to the farmers whose livestock his uncle hauls and about how he made only three mistakes in his last seventeen letters—all of them commas. Then he says, "I wish I could write school themes that way. The last one I had to write was on 'What a Daffodil Thinks of Spring,' and I just couldn't get going."

Bob's soliloquy is as relevant today as it was to the 1940s. It highlights the fact that many students seem to learn effectively in the context of authentic, real-life activities yet have difficulty with the more artificial tasks required in school. A number of researchers have explored the benefits of increasing the learner-centeredness of teaching by actively searching for "funds of knowledge" in students' homes and communities that can act as bridges for helping them learn in school (for example, see Lee, 1995; Moll and Gonzalez, 2004; Moses and Cobb, 2001). Examples include helping students see how the carpentry skills of their parents relate to geometry; how activities like riding the subway can provide a context for understanding algebra; how everyday language patterns used outside of school often represent highly sophisticated forms of language use that may be taught in literature classes as an academic subject yet are not linked to students' out-of-school activities.

Bob's story illustrates the importance of learning more about people's histories as individuals. It is motivating for students to know that teachers care about them, but a teacher's knowledge of her students can affect aspects of learning even beyond motivation. The more we know about someone, the more we are able to connect to their specific interests and needs and explain things in ways that make sense to them. (See "How Personal Knowledge Affects Communication.")

How Personal Knowledge Affects Communication

Imagine playing a game where you hear target concepts and try to get someone you do not know to say them by providing clues but not giving direct answers. For example, in one study a participant received the target "red corvette" and said, "A sports car made by Chevrolet that's the color of fire." Given the target "videodisc" she said "An interactive medium for video that came out before CD-ROMs and was much bigger in size." For the target "brine shrimp" she said, "I'll pass on that one. It's too hard."

Consider the same contestant when told that she was communicating with a person with whom she had worked for over a decade and knew very well. For "red corvette" she said, "What Carolyn drives—be sure to name the color." For "videodisc" she said, "What our Jasper program was published on when it first came out" (Jasper was an interactive videodisc program). For "brine shrimp" she said, "The little orange things that are swimming around in the Ecosystem in my office." Knowing the person to whom she was talking provided a number of shortcuts to communication that otherwise could not have been taken.

Creating Bridges Between Prior Experience and New Knowledge. Even if teachers do not know a great deal about each student, they can encourage students to think about personal experiences that they have had that are relevant to a topic being explored. For example, Banks (2000) discusses a technique that he uses in his multicultural education class to help prospective teachers better understand how minorities often feel marginalized by society. He doesn't begin simply by giving a lecture on minorities and marginalization, as it can be difficult for nonminority students to develop a deep and empathetic understanding of the issues simply by hearing a lecture. Instead, Banks begins work on this topic by asking his students to write a short summary of a time when they felt marginalized by another group. He notes that almost everyone, whether from a minority culture or the majority culture, has had such an experience at some time in their lives. After writing their short essays, students are now in a better position to understand the significance of issues that Banks discusses in class.

Another example of being learner-centered is illustrated in "Connecting Content to Learners." This account of two teachers who approached teaching in very different ways provides an illustration of how "pedagogical content knowledge" (see Chapter Six)—that is, the ability to make subject matter knowledge accessible to students—is developed by combining an understanding of content with an understanding of learners' needs and perspectives. Taking learner's perspectives into account in this way integrates the knowledge-centered and learner-centered aspects of teaching.

Connecting Content to Learners

Two new English teachers, Jake and Steven, who graduate from elite private universities with similar subject matter backgrounds, set out to teach *Hamlet* in high school (Grossman, 1990). Jake went directly into teaching after graduating from college with a major in English. Steven spent an additional year after college in a master's degree program preparing to teach English.

In his teaching, Jake spent seven weeks leading his students through a word-by-word *explication du texte*, focusing on notions of "linguistic reflexivity," and issues of modernism. His assignments included in-depth analyses of soliloquies, memorization of long passages, and a final paper on the importance of language in *Hamlet*. Jake's model for this instruction was his own undergraduate coursework; there was little transformation of his knowledge, except to parcel it out in chunks that fit into the 50-minute containers of the school day. Jake's image for how students would respond was his own response as a student who loved Shakespeare and delighted in close textual analysis. Consequently, when students responded in less than enthusiastic ways, Jake was ill-equipped to understand their confusion: "The biggest problem I have with teaching by far is trying to get into the mind-set of a ninth grader . . . "

Thinking about how to connect the themes of *Hamlet* to his students' experiences, Steven began his unit without ever mentioning the name of the play. To help his students grasp the initial outline of the themes and issues of the play, he asked them to imagine that their parents had recently divorced and that their mother had taken up with a new man. This new man had replaced their father at work, and "there's some talk that he had something to do with the ousting of your dad" (Grossman, 1990, p. 24). Steven then asked students to think about the circumstances that might drive them so mad that they would contemplate murdering another human being. Only then, after students had contemplated these issues and done some writing on them did Steven introduce the play they would be reading. As described in Grossman (1990), the results of these different strategies were dramatically different in terms of students' engagement with and eventual learning of the text.

Learner-Centeredness, Metacognition, and Basic Cognitive Processes

Being learner-centered also involves an awareness of some basic cognitive processes that impact learning for all people. A branch of psychology called "information processing" (see, for example, Atkinson and Schiffrin, 1968) has explored a number of these processes. Work in this tradition becomes especially beneficial for education when it is used to help people learn about the cognitive processes that underlie their own abilities to learn and solve problems. This knowledge is often called "metacognition" (knowledge about one's own cognitive processes; see Brown, 1997b; Flavell, 1976). Some teachers have been known to introduce the idea of metacognition to students by saying, "You are the owners and operators of your own brain. But it came without an instruction book. It pays to learn how it works."

Attention and Fluency. Learning about attention is one important part of becoming a metacognitive learner. First, we can selectively attend to information. When reading the preceding sentence you probably did not attend to how often the letter "e" occurred, but you could do that if you wanted to. Second, our attention is limited; when we attend to one set of features (for example, whether the words in the earlier sentence contain the letter "e"), we miss other features (for example, the meaning of the sentences; see Craik and Lockhart, 1972; Hyde and Jenkins, 1969). There are important constraints on how much we can attend to at any particular point in time.

The amount of attention that we must devote to a task depends on how experienced and efficient we are at doing it. For example, unlike a novice driver, an expert can drive a car and carry on a conversation at the same time. Over time, driving has become "fluent" or "automatized" (highly efficient), which then frees up attention to do other things like converse with fellow passengers. But even for the experienced driver, intense weather or driving conditions can produce demands on attention that shut down the ability to also converse or, in some cases, even listen to the radio.

In contrast to experienced drivers, a novice has to pay a great deal of attention to each component of driving—turning the wheel the right amount, hitting the brake pedal rather than the accelerator, using the turn signals and shifting if the car has a stick shift. During early phases of learning, it is almost impossible for the novice to drive effectively and carry on a conversation. As driving becomes more automatic or fluent, the ability to multitask increases.

A number of studies have explored the concept of attentional demand and its relationship to fluency. When learning to read, for example, the effortful allocation of attention to pronouncing words can make it difficult to also attend to the meaning of what one is reading. When learning a new video game, students will often need to allocate all their attention to the game. Only when they become fluent at playing can they then begin to converse about everyday events or about what they are doing as they play.

The attentional demands that accompany attempts to learn anything new mean that all learners must go through a period of "klutziness" as they attempt to acquire new skills and knowledge. Whether people persist or bail out during these "klutz" phases depends in part on their assumptions about their own abilities. Some people may decide "I'm not good at this" and give up trying before they have a chance to learn effectively (see, for example, Dweck 1986). Wertime (1979) notes that an important part of being learner-centered is to help students learn to persist in the face of difficulty by increasing their "courage spans."

Short-Term Memory. Information processing theorists have also explored differences between short-term and long-term memory. If you look up a phone number and walk across the room to dial it (for example, 614-277-4883), you may rehearse it as you walk. This is one way to keep information active in short-term memory. However, after you dial the information you may not remember it later because it was not transferred to long-term memory. To achieve the latter you may need to rehearse for a longer period or use special strategies (for example, "the first part, 614, fits my brother's birthday (6/14) . . . " and so on).

Researchers have asked how knowledge about the need to use various strategies develops with experience. Consider the simple act of rehearsing information like a new phone number so that you won't forget it as you walk across the room to dial it. Are we born with knowledge of the need to rehearse or does it develop over time? (See "A Study of 'Metamemory.'")

A Study of "Metamemory"

Imagine that you and a number of first graders participate in an experiment where you are shown pictures of seven common objects such as car, table, book. An experimenter points to four of the pictures (for example, book, dog, tree, table). Your task is to wait fifteen seconds (you cannot see the pictures during this time) and then point to the pictures in the same order. After you report your answer, the experimenter points to another order of the set of pictures and you try to remember this order. This procedure is repeated for several trials. To be correct on each trial, what strategy would you use?

The answer to this question seems obvious. Most adults use the strategy of mentally rehearsing the names of the pictures to themselves during the fifteen-second segment between presentation and test. Thus they may say to themselves, "book, dog, tree, table; book, dog, tree, table," perhaps while also imagining these objects.

A classic study by Keeney, Cannizzo, and Flavell (1967) shows that younger children do not always rehearse even though they seem very motivated to remember. The researchers provided a task like the one described earlier to first graders. One of the experimenters was trained in lipreading. He watched for any subtle lip movements that might accompany the children's attempts to rehearse the information. Only some of the children showed signs of rehearsal, and rehearsal helped their performance. Those who rehearsed performed better than those who did not seem to rehearse.

Keeney and his colleagues also asked whether it was possible to teach strategies to the first graders who did not rehearse spontaneously. They found that it was possible to teach rehearsal and that, on trials when they were explicitly reminded to rehearse, the children's memory performance improved.

The experiment was extended to include additional trials, but without the explicit reminders to rehearse on each trial. A large number of the children stopped using rehearsal strategies on these extra trials despite the fact that they seemed motivated to remember the information. They apparently did not understand that rehearsal was necessary in order to do well in the memory task.

Storage Versus Retrieval. Another aspect of metacognition involves realizing the difference between storing information in long-term memory and being able to retrieve it. Having someone's name "on the tip of your tongue" is a good example of these differences—it's somewhere "in memory" but you can't quite get to it and hence are not able to generate the name (retrieve it). However, you can often recognize the name if someone gives you several choices and asks you to pick.

Different kinds of tests place different demands on retrieval. Multiple-choice exams place less emphasis on retrieval than essay exams. To perform on an essay test, people need to create retrieval schemes that can help them perform effectively. If you are writing about the history of different countries, for example, it can be helpful to think of a retrieval scheme such as "STEPS plus G," which can help you remember to write about science at the time, technology, economics, political systems, social and religious practices, and geography. Without some kind of retrieval scheme, people who have stored a great deal of relevant information may fail to retrieve all of it at the time of test.

Comprehension. Another important aspect of metacognition involves monitoring to see if we are comprehending something appropriately. Without active monitoring we often think we understand when we don't (recall the fish's interpretation of cows, birds, and so on). The ability to monitor our own understanding is not simply a general skill, it requires knowledge that helps people notice discrepancies between what they currently understand and what they need to know. If you are a detective, for example, you can understand a suspect's statement that "I visited my mother yesterday and she and her friends will testify that I was there." But you will also realize that you need more information—such as the exact time of day when the witness visited compared to the time of day of the crime.

Experts in various areas (for example, crime detectives, engineers, teachers, and so forth) develop specialized organizations of knowledge (often called scripts and schemas) that help them comprehend, remember, and monitor whether all the information necessary for particular schemas has been provided (see, for example, Black and Bower, 1979; Pichert and Anderson, 1977; Schank and Abelson, 1975). For example, the schemas available to crime detectives help them notice the significance of particular kinds of information and guide their search for additional information. Detectives know about phone records and other types of information that can be used to check on the accuracy of statements people make.

Often students who are new to a topic do not have enough experience in that area to have developed scripts and schemas that help provide internal standards for monitoring. It is therefore important to "make their thinking visible" so that teachers and peers can help this monitoring. We saw this earlier in the *Fish is Fish* example. Maybe the fish could have been a little more metacognitive and done more to check its interpretations. But without knowledge of the potential variation of creatures in the world, it can be difficult for the fish to know what else it needed to know or ask.

In other cases, people may have knowledge of standards that enable them to monitor their performances but do not do so spontaneously unless explicitly prompted. Studies show that "metacognitive training" can have powerful effects on helping students increase their abilities to comprehend by monitoring the current state of what they do and do not know (see, for example, Palincsar and Brown, 1984; White and Fredrickson, 1998).

Motivation. Helping students learn to identify what motivates them is also an important part of being learner-centered. Researchers have explored differences between extrinsic motivators (grades, money, candy, and so forth) and intrinsic motivators (wanting to learn something because it is relevant to what truly interests you). Both kinds of motivation can be combined; for example, we can be intrinsically interested in learning about some topics *and* interested in receiving extrinsic rewards as well (for example, praise for doing well, a consultant's fee). However, some research suggests that too much of an emphasis on extrinsic rewards can undermine intrinsic motivation because people get too used to the external rewards and stop working when they are removed (see, for example, Deci, 1978). (See also Chapter Nine.)

There appear to be important differences between factors that are initially motivating (the assumption that learning to skateboard seems interesting), and factors that *sustain* our motivation in the face of difficulty ("hmm, this skateboarding is harder to learn than it looked"). The social motivation support of peers, parents, and others is an especially important feature that helps people persist in the face of difficulties. It is also important to be provided with challenges that are just the right level of difficulty—not so easy that they are boring and not so difficult that they are frustrating. Creating the right kinds of "just manageable difficulties" for each student in a classroom constitutes one of the major challenges and requires expert juggling acts. (Explorations of the literature on motivation can be found in Deci and Ryan, 1985; Dweck, 1986; Stipek, 2002.)

Transfer. Learning about ourselves as learners also involves thinking about issues of transfer—of learning in ways that allow us to solve novel problems that we may encounter later. The mere memorization of information is usually not sufficient to support transfer; instead, it helps also to understand what we are learning. In Chapter One, we discussed differences between memorizing facts about veins and arteries versus understanding why each had particular properties (for example, why arteries needed to be more elastic than veins). Learning with understanding typically enhances the experience (see, for example, National Research Council, 2000). A classic study on learning, understanding, and transfer appears in "Learning for Transfer."

Learning for Transfer

In one of the earliest studies comparing the effects of learning a procedure versus learning with understanding, two groups of children practiced throwing darts at a target under water (described in Judd, 1908; see Hendrickson and Schroeder, 1941, for a replication). One group received an explanation of the refraction of light, which causes the apparent location of the target to be deceptive. The other group only practiced dart throwing, without the explanation. Both groups did equally well on the practice task, which involved a target twelve inches under water. But the group that had been instructed about the abstract principle did much better when they had to transfer to a situation in which the target was under only four inches of water. Because they understood what they were doing, the group that had received instruction about the refraction of light could adjust their behavior to the new task.

An important goal for transfer is cognitive flexibility (see, for example, Spiro and others, 1991). Experts possess cognitive flexibility when they can evaluate problems and other types of cases in their fields of expertise from many conceptual points of view, seeing multiple possible interpretations and perspectives. Wiggins and McTighe (1998) argue that understanding complex issues involves being able to explain them in more than one way. Spiro and others (1991) argue that the inability to construct multiple interpretations in analyzing real-world cases can result from instruction that oversimplifies complicated subject matter. Additional discussions of transfer occur later on.

Assumptions About "Intelligence." A major set of assumptions that can have important effects on learning and motivation are the assumptions that people make about intelligence—both their own and others'. Many Americans and Europeans have grown up with the belief that "intelligence" is something that is inherited and places limits on people's abilities to learn. In the first half of the twentieth century, many schools also accepted this belief and hence took it as a given that many students would fail.

More recent evidence suggests that is not productive to attempt to measure people's abilities on a single dimension like IQ (intelligence quotient). A number of researchers argue that people's capacity to be productive citizens and workers is multidimensional rather than unidimensional (see, for example, Gardner, 1983; Sternberg, 1985a). It has also been argued that human capacity is open-ended; hence people can "grow" their intellectual capacity (see, for example, Perkins, 1995; Resnick and Nelson-LeGall, 1998). As discussed in the following section, there is evidence from neuroscientists that learning not only depends on the structure of brain but also actually influences brain development (see, for example, National Research Council, 2000). An important implication of these positions is that no one really knows the upper limits of human intelligence.

Overall, there is growing agreement that even though there may be individual differences in biological aptitudes for learning certain kinds of things (music, social skills, and so on), most of functional intelligence is learnable and hence also teachable. People's *beliefs* about intelligence are a major factor in affecting what they can learn. A number of researchers have shown that many children in the United States (but not necessarily in many Asian countries) have come to believe that educational accomplishments are due to "aptitude" rather than "effort" (Resnick and Nelson-LeGall, 1998). Students who question their own academic aptitudes (often because of social stereotypes like "girls can't do math") are more likely give up when they experience difficulties (Mueller and Dweck, 1998). Similarly, even very able students who have come to think that achievement is a function of ability, rather than effort, often give up when they encounter a difficult task, believing that if they have trouble, it is because they are unable. As noted earlier, this is very serious because novices typically experience a "klutziness" phase when they are learning something new, and beliefs about intelligence affects people's interpretations of why this klutziness is happening to them.

Assumptions About Brain Development. Assumptions about intelligence are often linked to assumptions about "brain efficiency." It is a common misconception that individuals' intelligence and brain development are entirely predetermined by biology. In reality, education and experience actually help develop the brain. Physical and mental activities of various kinds help people develop their capacity to learn, and what teachers do can affect brain development by engaging students in activities that help them develop their capacities. This can range from the kind of neurological programming that occurs when musicians practice certain patterns of physical movement tied to symbol systems (reading music) and when readers practice letter-sound correspondences and learn comprehension strategies. Learning abilities can be developed by access to an environment that stimulates and uses the brain. (See "How Environments Affect Brain Development.")

How Environments Affect Brain Development
A pioneering study on the effect of the environment on brain development was conducted by William Greenough and his colleagues (1979). They studied rats placed in various environments and the resulting effects on synapse formation in the rats' brains. They compared the brains of rats raised in "complex environments," containing toys and obstacles, with those housed individually or in small cages without toys. They found that rats raised in complex environments performed better on learning tasks like learning to run mazes, and they had 20 to 25 percent more synapses per neuron in the visual cortex. This work suggests that brain development is "experience dependent," allowing animals to acquire knowledge that is specific to their own environments. These experiments suggest that "rich environments" include those that provide numerous opportunities for social interaction, direct physical contact with the environment, and a changing set of objects for play and exploration (Rosenzweig and Bennett, 1978b, cited in National Research Council, 2000, p. 119). Similarly, rich classroom environments provide interactions with others in the classroom and community, hands-on experiences with the physical world, and frequent, informative feedback on what students are doing and thinking.

New advances in technology are allowing scientists to go beyond the study of animals and explore how *humans* process information. In emerging brain research, imaging technologies are helping scientists localize areas of brain activity that underlie the cognitive components of a task; with imaging, areas of the brain are shown to "light up" under varying conditions. For example, the physical activity of the brain during reading differs for dyslexics and non-dyslexics. Some researchers have relied on these images to improve understanding of how to teach dyslexic students (Berninger and Richards, 2002).

Although research on the human brain is progressing rapidly, direct connections between brain science and specific teaching practices are not clear at this point. Bruer (1997) argues that, for now, educators should rely primarily on research on cognition, development, and teaching practices and keep an eye out for new developments in the neurosciences that have implications for these fields.

Community-Centeredness

The preceding discussion explored a number of issues relevant to being knowledge-centered and learner-centered. The community-centered aspect of the HPL framework is related to being knowledge- and learner-centered, but it focuses special attention on the social nature of learning, including the norms and modes of operation of any community we are joining. For example, some classrooms represent communities where it is safe to ask questions and say, "I don't understand this, can you explain it in a different way?" Others follow the norms of "Don't get caught not knowing something." A number of studies suggest that, to be successful, learning communities should provide people with a feeling that members matter to each other and to the group, and a shared belief that members' needs will be met through their commitment to work together (Alexopoulou and Driver, 1996; Bateman, Bransford, Goldman, and Newbrough, 2000). Many schools are very impersonal places, and this can affect the degree to which people feel part of, or alienated from, important communities of professionals and peers.

Community-Centeredness, Productivity, and Distributed Expertise

It is easy to do a quick *Fish is Fish* interpretation of the community-centered part of the HPL framework and assume that it is mainly an argument for creating classroom environments where students are helped to "feel good" about themselves but are not necessarily held to high standards. This is where the balance in the HPL framework plays a role—all four components affect the quality of the learning environments. Most importantly for present purposes, the idea of functioning as a community or team goes way beyond simply making everyone feel good because they are part of a group.

If you have ever been involved in a disaster such as a flood, hurricane, or tornado, you know what it is like for people to pull together in ways that are highly productive. Team activities often provide similar bonds of shared fate. Especially important is the fact that the ideal of being community-centered does not mean that everyone simply agrees with everyone else about everything. True learning communities learn from one another and know how to "argue with grace." As people share their understandings and reasoning with one another, they teach each other in a variety of ways. Not only are ideas shared, but modes of argumentation, reasoning, and problem solving are also modeled and shared. This helps others develop their thinking abilities as well as their store of knowledge. In addition, the various skills and interests provided by members of a learning community offer access to distributed expertise that can be skillfully used to support the learning of all participants in the community. A major part of classroom management involves the development of a respectful argument-based learning community in which students benefit from each other's knowledge and views (see Chapter Nine).

Concerns that many schools are impersonal and need to be smaller to be more learner- and community-centered can also be misinterpreted as simply being an argument for helping students feel good about themselves. This is very important, of course, but more is involved as well. The communication game discussed in How Personal Knowledge Affects Communication (for example, helping someone to guess "red corvette" or "brine shrimp") and the previous story about Bob (the "problem student" who nevertheless learned well outside of school) demonstrate the importance of searching for "funds of knowledge" in students' lives that can be built upon to enhance their motivation and learning. The more we know about people the better we can communicate with them and hence help them (and ourselves) learn. And the more they know about one another, the better they can communicate as a community.

Vygotsky and Community-Centeredness

The importance of creating and sustaining learning communities can be traced to Vygotsky's theory in which culture and human interaction play a central role in developmental processes. Earlier we discussed Piaget, who tended to focus on individual learners as they explored their environments. People do explore individually, of course. Nevertheless, Vygotsky (1978) emphasized that learning is highly social and mediated by one's culture. In his book *Mind in Society*, he argued that even the development of the human brain is influenced by activities of the cultures within which people participate. As noted earlier, these assumptions about the brain—made many years ago—are being confirmed by modern neuroscientists. The brain is not fixed at birth; instead, it develops as a function of the social activities in which people are engaged (see, for example, National Research Council, 2000).

Vygotsky also focused on the intersection between individuals and society through his concept of the zone of proximal development (ZPD). He defined the ZPD level as the distance between the actual developmental level as determined by independent problem solving and the level of potential development as determined through problem solving under adult guidance or in collaboration with more capable peers (Vygotsky, 1978, p. 86). What children can do with the assistance of others is even more indicative of their mental development than what they can do alone (Vygotsky, 1978, p. 85).

The zone of proximal development redefines everyday assumptions about people's "readiness to learn" by emphasizing upper levels of competence. These upper boundaries constantly change with the learner's increasing independent competence. What a child can perform today with assistance she will be able to perform tomorrow independently, thus preparing her for entry into a new and more demanding collaboration. These functions could be called the "buds" rather than the fruits of development. The actual developmental level characterizes mental development prospectively (Vygotsky, 1978, pp. 86–87). The ZPD is relevant to both learner- and community-centeredness. For the latter, teachers must balance the fact that, in most classrooms, multiple learning trajectories, or zones of proximal development, must be taken into account (see Brown and Campione, 1994). An example is provided in "Becoming Aware of Different Learning Trajectories."

Becoming Aware of Different Learning Trajectories

A research group wrote about an important lesson they learned that is relevant to one aspect of Vygotsky's theory of zone of proximal development (Cognition and Technology Group at Vanderbilt, 1997). The researchers were observing a teacher who had a reputation for being outstanding, but what they observed alarmed them. The teacher was working with middle school students on mathematical problems that were motivating but difficult to solve. Students typically worked in groups, but often they presented on their own. The problems could be solved in a variety of ways; a major goal of the presentations was to have the students explain why they had made particular choices in strategies. This is very different from simply repeating the computations that were used to get some answer at the end.

What shocked the research group was the fact that this allegedly outstanding teacher praised what was clearly a less than stellar performance by a student. The student's oral presentation of his mathematical solution to the complex problem was OK, but he provided no explanation of why he had chosen particular solution strategies. Despite this fact, the teacher praised the student and the class clapped. The research group became alarmed that the teacher's criteria for "good work" was much too low and that this would harm the students in the long run. They thought the teacher knew that the work in mathematics was supposed to focus on explanations, but evidently he did not.

The event occurred on a Friday and several members of the research group talked over the weekend about how to help the teacher. They didn't want to hurt his feelings, but the students' learning was at stake. Eventually the researchers decided to ask the teacher what he had thought about Friday's lesson, so they visited him on Monday and asked what he thought about Friday's class. His answer was: "It was one of the highlights of my teaching career." He explained that this was the first time in the entire year (it was early December) that the young man who had presented on Friday had gotten the courage to speak up in class. To be sure his performance wasn't perfect, and the teacher would have preferred that he offer explanations of his solution rather than simply recite his calculations. But overall the performance was a huge victory. The boy had told his parents about it and they had called the teacher to thank him. The class also realized that this was a big event, which is why they clapped.

The research group learned a valuable lesson. They didn't know enough about the young man to realize that his performance had represented true progress. They listened as the teacher explained how he carefully crafted expectations for different students depending on where they started—he didn't teach as if every student was on a conveyor belt where every student was expected to be able to the same thing at the same time. The teacher took seriously the idea that different students required different kinds of support (scaffolds) to make progress. At the same time, the teacher took seriously the need for all students to reach high standards. He was sure that, by the end of the year, the young man who had spoken for the first time on Friday would be able to explain his answers as well as simply describe them. He wanted high standards for all his students, and he realized that the kind of community culture that he developed in the classroom was an important part of helping him reach his goal.

A number of chapters in this book explore issues that are relevant to the community-centered aspects of learning environments. One is Chapter Nine, Classroom Management, which helps demonstrate how building such a community can be used in the service of stronger achievement.

At a broader level, being community-centered also means reaching beyond the walls of the schools to connect with students' out-of-school experiences, including experiences in their homes. In *How People Learn* (National Research Council, 2000), an analysis of time spent in school in a major school district during a calendar year indicated that even with perfect attendance, students spent only 14 percent of their time in school. A great deal of learning occurs outside of school, but often teachers do not know how to connect these kinds of experiences to school learning. Earlier we discussed the story of Bob (the so-called "problem" student) and related it to the idea of searching for "funds of knowledge" that exist in communities and can be built upon to help students succeed. Helping students build strong social networks within a classroom, within a school, and between classrooms and outside resources produces a number of advantages that are discussed in more detail in Chapters Three and Nine.

Assessment-Centeredness

We've discussed knowledge-, learner-, and community-centeredness; now we turn to assessment-centeredness. It is easy to assume that assessment simply involves giving tests to students and grading them. Theories of learning suggest roles for assessment that involve much more than simply making up tests and giving grades.

First, teachers need to ask what they are assessing. This requires aligning their assessment criteria with the goals for their students (part of being knowledge-centered) and the "readiness" of students in their classroom (learner- and community-centered). Assessing memorization (for example, of properties of veins and arteries) is different from assessing whether students understand why veins and arteries have various properties. (See Chapter One for the veins and arteries example.) Similarly, assessing whether students can answer questions about life cycles (of frogs, for example) is different from assessing whether they will spontaneously retrieve this information when attempting to solve problems. (Note the example in Knowledge Organization and Problem Solving about students' responses to the ultraviolet experiment that used adult frogs.) We also saw earlier that knowledge about students' zones of proximal development can help teachers decide to use different criteria for assessing students' progress. For example, in Becoming Aware of Different Learning Trajectories, we discussed the young man who presented his problem-solving solution in a way that did not fit ultimate standards for excellence, but the teacher applauded because he knew that this was the first time in the entire school year that the student had dared speak in front of the class.

At the most general level, issues of what to assess relate to issues of what students need to know and be able to do to have fulfilling lives once they graduate. Because of rapid changes in society, this is an issue that constantly needs to be reconsidered. Debates about standardized tests include concerns that they may "tip" teaching in a direction that is counterproductive for students because some teachers spend most of their time teaching to the tests, yet the tests do not assess the range of skills, knowledge, and attitudes needed for successful and productive lives in the twenty-first century. Chapter Eight, on assessment, explores this issue in more detail.

Different Kinds and Purposes of Assessment

An especially important aspect of the assessment-centered lens in the HPL framework is its emphasis on different kinds of assessments for different purposes. When most people think about assessments they think about *summative assessments.* These include standardized tests at the end of the year, final exams at the end of a course, and unit exams at the end of a unit. Summative assessments come in all forms: multiple-choice tests, essays, presentations by students, and so forth. These assessments are very important. Often they reveal important information that teachers wish they had seen earlier. The vignette at the beginning of this chapter about Paul Nelson, the astronomy teacher who discovered that his students still misunderstood important concepts about the earth and its seasons, provides an example of this point. Paul thought that everyone understood the lessons about the solar system and earth's systems, but the essay exams provided a different picture. If he had known earlier what the students were thinking, he could have returned to the topic and explored it from a different perspective. Now it was too late. The students had written their final essays and were finished with the class. Their *Fish is Fish* interpretations would follow them out the door. Paul's anguish could have been reduced if he had used what are called formative assessments. These are used for the purpose of improving teaching and learning. They involve making students' thinking visible *as they progress through the course*, giving them feedback about their thinking, and providing opportunities to revise.

The importance of frequent feedback was emphasized by one of the earliest research traditions in America to study learning—the Behaviorist tradition.

People such as J.B. Watson, Ivan Pavlov, and B.F. Skinner were major contributors to this line of thinking. They searched for universal laws of learning that could apply not only across individuals but across species (rats, pigeons, monkeys, humans). Their emphasis was on the role of positive and negative feedback in helping organisms learn to perform complex skills.

An early contributor to the Behaviorist movement was Thorndike, who became known as "The father of educational psychology." His famous "law of effect" stated that rewards strengthened connections between particular stimulus conditions and particular outcomes. When responses were rewarded, they tended to be repeated when those stimulus conditions appeared again.

Rewards and punishments carry information (feedback) about the "correctness" of one's actions (responses), and Thorndike emphasized the importance of feedback for learning. In a clever demonstration study (1931/1968), Thorndike decided to learn to draw lines that were exactly 4 inches long with his eyes blindfolded. He practiced for 3,000 trials but never received any feedback about how close each attempt was. Without feedback, he made no progress. On the first day of blindfolded practice, his lines varied from 4.5 to 6.2 inches. On the last day, they varied from 4.1 to 5.7 inches—still quite a ways from a perfect 4-inch mark.

Thorndike concluded that practice does not make perfect unless it provides the opportunity for feedback. Once he removed his blindfold, he improved very rapidly because he received feedback that allowed him to compare his behavior to a standard (a 4-inch line). Today, research in cognitive science has shown that formative assessment and the feedback it provides is extremely important for enhancing learning (see, for example, Black and William, 1998). The chapter on assessment (Chapter Eight) provides much more information about the importance of formative assessment for helping all students succeed.

Assessment and Theories of Transfer

It is also important for teachers to understand ways in which assessment practices relate to theories of transfer. Consider summative assessments, for example. We all want to make sure that these provide an indication of students' ability to do something other than simply "take tests." Ideally, our assessments are predictive of students' performance in everyday settings once they leave the classroom.

One way to look at this issue is to view tests as attempts to predict students' abilities to *transfer* from classroom settings to everyday settings. Different ways of thinking about transfer have important implications for thinking about assessment. Central to traditional approaches to transfer is a "direct application" theory and a dominant methodology that Bransford and Schwartz (1999) call "sequestered problem solving" (SPS). Just as juries are often sequestered to protect them from possible exposure to "contaminating" information, subjects in experiments are sequestered during tests of transfer. There are no opportunities for them to demonstrate their abilities to learn to solve new problems by seeking help from other resources such as texts or colleagues or by trying things out, receiving feedback, and getting opportunities to revise. Accompanying the SPS paradigm is a theory that characterizes transfer as the ability to directly apply one's previous learning to a new setting or problem. We call this the direct application (DA) theory of transfer. Some argue that the "sequestered problem-solving" methodology and the accompanying direct application theory of transfer are responsible for much of the pessimism about evidence for transfer (Bransford and Schwartz, 1999).

An alternative view that acknowledges the validity of these perspectives also broadens the conception of transfer by including an emphasis on people's "preparation for future learning" (PFL). Here, the focus shifts to assessments of people's abilities to learn in knowledge-rich environments. When organizations hire new employees they don't expect them to have learned everything they need for successful adaptation. They want people who can learn, and they expect them to make use of resources (for example, texts, computer programs, and colleagues) to facilitate this learning. The better prepared they are for future learning, the greater the transfer (in terms of speed and quality of new learning). Examples of ways to "prepare students for future learning" are explored in Schwartz and Bransford (1998), Bransford and Schwartz (1999), and Spiro, Vispoel, Schmitz, Samarapungavan, and Boeger (1987).

It is important to emphasize that the preparation for learning perspective on transfer does not assume the existence of a set of general learning skills that are content free. The expertise literature (see, for example, Bransford and others, 1999) shows clearly how strategies and knowledge are highly interdependent. Broudy (1977) provides an example: "The concept of bacterial infection as learned in biology can operate even if only a skeletal notion of the theory and the facts supporting it can be recalled. Yet, we are told of cultures in which such a concept would not be part of the interpretive schemata" (p. 12).

The absence of an idea of bacterial infection should have a strong effect on the nature of the hypotheses that people entertain to explain various illnesses, and hence would affect their abilities to learn more about causes of illness through further research and study, and the strategies one uses to solve new problems. The acquisition of well-differentiated knowledge is crucial for future learning (see, for example, Bransford and others, 1999; Schwartz and Bransford, 1998; Spiro and others, 1987). The more that this knowledge is acquired with understanding, the higher the probability that appropriate transfer will occur.

The sole use of static assessments may mask the learning gains of many students, as well as mask the learning advantages that various kinds of educational experiences provide (Bransford and Schwartz, 1999). Linking work on summative assessment to theories of transfer may help us overcome the limitations of many existing tests. An example of the difference between "sequestered problem solving" versus "preparation for learning" assessments of learning and transfer is provided in the following section.

"Sequestered Problem Solving" Versus "Preparation for Learning" Assessments of Transfer

Groups of fifth graders and college students were given the problem of developing a statewide recovery plan to protect bald eagles (Burgess, as discussed in Bransford and Schwartz, 1999). None of the students had studied eagle recovery plans before. The study was meant to see if the college students' general education experience would transfer to solving this problem. Both the college students and the fifth graders gave very inadequate solutions to this problem. Using a direct method of measuring transfer, it is apparent that the college students' general educational experiences did not transfer to solving this kind of problem. However, by measuring transfer as preparation for future learning, the college students' educational experiences did transfer. The researchers asked both groups to generate questions regarding important issues that they would need to research to develop an effective recovery plan. The differences between the college students and the fifth graders were convincing. The fifth graders' questions focused more on individual eagles (for example, What do they like to eat? What size are they? What kinds of trees do they live in?). College students' investigative questions focused more on the relationship between eagles and their habitat (for example, What kinds of ecosystems support eagles? What different types of experts are needed to carry out the recovery plans? Do other animals need to be recovered in order to recover eagles?). So, by this second measure of transfer, it seems college students used prior knowledge from other zoology or biology classes to help shape their future learning about a to-be-investigated topic. Several additional studies show that PFL measures of transfer can reveal the advantages of many kinds of educational experiences that remain relatively invisible when assessed from an SPS point of view (see, for example, Biswas and others, 2001; Schwartz and Moore, 1998; Schwartz, Lin, Brophy, and Bransford, 1999).

THE HPL FRAMEWORK IN ACTION

We have discussed all four components of the HPL framework, but we noted earlier that learning occurs most effectively when all four components are balanced. Underemphasizing one or more of the components can make it harder for all students to succeed. For example, teachers can be overly learner-centered and community-centered, yet fail to emphasize the acquisition of important concepts and skills (knowledge-centered) that students need for successful lives. And if teachers are not assessment-centered (especially in their use of formative assessments), they may fail to realize that students are not making adequate progress until the year is over and it is too late for them to help.

The HPL framework becomes a powerful conceptual tool for teachers when they use it to analyze the quality of various learning environments. With this goal in mind, imagine observing a middle school English teacher who is teaching a unit on stories and poetry that explore subjects of nature and ecology. She has instructed her students to read various nature writings and to select one of them to recite aloud to the class from memory. One of the students, Henry, chooses the following excerpt from Leopold's *Sand County Almanac*: "I now suspect that just as a deer herd lives in mortal fear of its wolves, so does a mountain live in mortal fear of its deer. And perhaps with better cause, for while a buck pulled down by wolves can be replaced in two or three years, a range pulled down by too many deer may fail of replacement in as many decades. So also with cows. The cowman who cleans his range of wolves does not realize that he is taking over the wolf's job of trimming the herd to fit the range. He is not thinking like a mountain. Hence we have dustbowls, and rivers washing the future into the sea" (Leopold, 1949/1990). Assume that Henry recites the piece flawlessly and the teacher and class applaud. How might the HPL framework help us think more deeply about this event?

Knowledge-Centeredness

Adopting this lens draws attention to questions about what should be taught and why. It is possible that this assignment was in a textbook and the teacher taught it simply because it was designed as "the next lesson." Ideally, more thought was involved in deciding that this unit was worth teaching. The teacher probably consulted national, state, and district standards for her discipline and aligned her teaching to these standards. And maybe the teacher even planned collaboratively with a science teacher so that both could focus on issues of ecology from different points of view (scientific evidence coupled with literature and art).

The knowledge-centered lens has implications for other HPL lenses such as assessment. For example, can we say that Henry learned effectively and that, for him at least, the lesson was a success? The answer depends on the teachers' goals for the lesson (which we will assume for this example are consistent with the district, state, and national standards).

The primary goal may have been to help students learn to perform by committing ideas to memory and delivering them in a powerful, emotional manner (rather than in a monotone, for example). This can be a valid and important goal for students, and from this perspective Henry has done very well. The goals might be different, however. For example, the teacher might have wanted all the students to develop a deep understanding of the pieces they are reciting. Based on Henry's performance as outlined so far, it is not clear if he understands what he has memorized.

Assessment-Centeredness

The assessment-centered lens of the HPL framework focuses on ways that different teaching and learning goals impact what teachers do to assess progress. If the goal is a dramatic recitation performance, the teachers will look at criteria for success that differ from those that signal learning with understanding. And if both of these are important, both need to be represented in the assessment criteria.

Assume that the teacher wants good oral performance *plus* a deep understanding of what the students have read. In Henry's case, the teacher might say: "Nice job Henry. Now tell the class what you think it means." Imagine Henry staring at the teacher for a few seconds and then saying, "Wolves are important. That's about all I can think of." Given the teacher's goal of having students understand as well as perform, Henry's answer is less than ideal. If the teacher treats this event as a summative assessment, she may simply assign Henry a grade (perhaps a "C" or "D") and go on to the next student. Ideally, this event is a formative assessment and the teacher's goal is to help Henry improve his abilities to comprehend the story. To do this the teacher must consider both the learner-centered and community-centered lenses of the HPL framework.

Learner-Centeredness

This lens from the HPL framework focuses attention on individual students and their special strengths, interests, and needs. The teacher's knowledge of Henry is very important for helping define his zone of proximal development, which will in turn help the teacher chose new learning goals and instructional procedures that will optimize Henry's learning.

It is possible that Henry is similar to the boy discussed in Becoming Aware of Different Learning Trajectories who had never before dared to speak in class. In that case, the teacher knew that the boy's attempt to say anything in front of the class was a huge leap forward. In Henry's case, however, we'll assume that he is used to talking in class and the teacher feels that he has the potential to more deeply understand what he read.

Here is an example of how the teacher might work with Henry:

TEACHER (T): So Henry, what do you think Leopold is saying here?

HENRY (H): I don't know. It doesn't make any sense to me, really.

T: Okay. Well, what do you know about overpopulation? (This represents an attempt to see if Henry already knows something that the teacher can use to help his comprehension.)

H: I know it's bad. (This suggests that Henry knows something about the concept of overpopulation.)

T: Is Leopold talking about overpopulation in this passage? (This represents an attempt to get Henry to use existing knowledge to interpret the present situation—similar to how "parachute" was used earlier to help you understand "The haystack was important because the cloth ripped.")

H: Yeah, he is! He's talking about how too many deer can hurt the side of a mountain and that's what overpopulation can do. (This represents one of those "lightbulb" moments when the application of previously acquired knowledge [overpopulation] provides an insight in a new context.)

T: Then, what do you think Leopold was saying when he said the cowmen were not "thinking like a mountain"? (This represents an attempt by the teacher to help Henry link his new insight to the most metaphorical part of the passage; for example, asking cowboys to think like a mountain.)

H: Well, I never thought of it this way but he's telling us that populations have to be kept in check or our world could end up like the side of that mountain. It's kind of a guideline for us and how we should live.

If teaching were always this easy everyone would rejoice. But even this situation illustrates the complexity of the teacher's juggling act. To be effective, teachers need to make moment-by-moment decisions based on their ongoing assessments of the learners' current levels of understanding and their zones of proximal development (ZPD). To use Piaget's terminology, the teacher's questioning enabled Henry to *assimilate* the meaning of the Leopold passage by incorporating the idea into an already existing schema: "overpopulation." This helped Henry take the next step, which was to expand his existing schema (what Piaget would view as an example of *accommodation* rather than pure assimilation) by viewing overpopulation from the perspective of a mountain rather than only from the perspective of humans. Overall, the more the teacher knows about Henry, the better she can guide instruction so that, eventually, Henry learns how to interpret stories and poems rather than merely recite them from memory.

For this particular lesson, the teacher may or may not adopt additional goals depending on her knowledge of Henry. The goal illustrated earlier was to ask questions that would help Henry understand *a particular story.* A more long-term goal might be to help Henry learn to ask questions that will help him develop the ability to understand a wide variety of stories, not just this one. A successful teaching strategy called "reciprocal teaching" has been shown to help students learn to ask their own questions about stories rather than have to rely on particular questions that their teachers have asked about a story they have read (Palincsar and Brown, 1984). To do so, teachers have to help students develop the abilities to self-assess their own understanding so that they don't always have to rely on someone else to ask the kinds of questions that enable them to decide if they have understood adequately (see, for example, Barron and others, 1998; Brown and Campione, 1994, 1996).

Community-Centeredness

The vignette involving Henry does not provide much explicit information about the community-centered aspects of the classroom and school in which the example took place. However, there are reasons to suspect that classroom norms have developed where the classmates respect one another's efforts to learn and realize that sometimes learning is a struggle for everyone. The teacher's use of questions to provide Henry with an opportunity for formative assessment and revision suggest that this may have become established as a norm in the classroom—and this is very important for creating a climate of shared learning and respect for learning. Not all classrooms are like this. The famous scene in the movie *Ferris Buehler's Day Off* in which actor Ben Stein lectures in a dead monotone while students struggle comically to stay awake is often appreciated by audiences because they remember many classrooms like it.

Another level of community-centeredness that is not visible in the preceding vignette involves the sense of community among fellow teachers and other adults in the school as a whole. When teachers get along and learn from one another, they provide models that help support student learning, and they are able to share their expertise with one another to improve the overall quality of instruction (see, for example, McLaughlin and Talbert, 2001). Finally, relationships among educators and parents and community members matter greatly. We noted earlier that, for a calendar year, a student with perfect school attendance spends only about 14 percent of his or her time in school. How students spend their time out of school is extremely important for their overall development, and it impacts their success in school. The more teachers can work with others to build upon the goodwill and intellectual resources of the community, the more successful they can be. In this case, it might include bringing in experts from the community who can talk about issues of overpopulation or other issues that are related to the topics being explored in class. Having community members be an audience for student presentation—an audience that asks questions—can be an especially powerful event for students *provided* that teachers have created a sufficient number of prior assessment and revision cycles to allow students to do a good job.

Issues of Motivation

Balancing all four aspects of the HPL framework helps motivation as well as learning. If students know they are learning content and skills that will be important in life, this is motivating. If courses connect with their interests and strengths, and provide interesting challenges to their preconceptions, this is motivating (Dweck, 1989). If students receive frequent feedback that allows them to see their progress in learning and gives them chances to do even better, this is motivating. And if students feel as if they are a valued part of vibrant, "high-standards" learning communities—at the classroom level, school level, and overall community level—this is motivating as well.

Learning Theories and Teacher Preparation

New information about learning, teaching, and transfer is as relevant for preparing new teachers as it is to the education of K–12 students. For example, simply having prospective teachers memorize facts about how to teach is as limiting as simply having students memorize facts about what scientists have discovered. Just as students studying science need to experience the inquiry processes involved in discovering and testing ideas relevant to science, prospective teachers need to experience what it is like to learn in environments that are consistent with learning principles (see, for example, National Research Council, in press). In fact, learning in the ways they are expected to teach may be the most powerful form of teacher education. Most people tend to teach in ways that mirror how they were taught. This means that teacher education programs can benefit from exploring the degree to which their courses and programs are consistent with what is known about how people learn. (See Chapter Ten, where we discuss teacher learning, for a more in-depth treatment of these issues.)

A Vision of Teaching Expertise

A major goal for any professional program is to help students begin to see themselves as developing professionals rather than simply as students whose primary goal is to get good grades (see, for example, the discussion of the six "commonplaces" shared by all professions in Chapter One). The argument here is not that good grades are unimportant. Instead, the argument is that prospective teachers need to be more than simply grade oriented. They need a clear vision of what it means to be a professional and intrinsic motivation to succeed so that they can monitor their progress and make corrections as needed. Without a clear vision of one's ultimate goals and responsibilities as a professional, the metacognitive reflection needed for assessing progress is difficult if not impossible to achieve.

Many education programs are adopting the idea of "adaptive expertise" as the gold standard for being a professional. We discussed the idea of adaptive expertise earlier in this chapter and differentiated it from routine expertise (see, for example, Hatano and Inagaki, 1986). Figure 2.1 (which appears earlier in this chapter) provides two dimensions of expertise (efficiency, innovation) that are very helpful for helping people develop a conception of what it means to be a professional. Adaptive experts are able to balance efficiency and innovation. Helping prospective teachers achieve this balance can be very beneficial: it can guide the "lifelong learning" needed to help all their students achieve.

The efficiency dimension in Figure 2.1 is a "magnet" for novices. Beginners in nearly every area often want step-by-step instruction on how to do things efficiently, and prospective teachers are no exception. Beginners learning to fish or sail want to learn what to do as quickly as possible. Similarly, beginning teachers want to be taught how to manage the classroom; how to organize curriculum and formative and summative assessments that align with local and national standards; how to teach fractions; how to manage group work; how to assign grades fairly; how to balance the hard work required of a teacher with a quality home life; and so forth. In many cases newcomers to an area request a heavy dose of "how to" techniques and are much less interested in theory and explanation about the "whys" and "whens" of the strategies they are taught.

Research on transfer provides important insights into "pure efficiency" training. In Learning for Transfer, for example, Judd's experiment on throwing darts at underwater targets is discussed. Beginners had to learn to throw darts effectively so that they would hit their intended targets. The initial learning rates for doing this were as fast for the "just do it" group as for the group that had been helped to understand the principles of light refraction that create visual displacements of the perceived underwater target. The advantage of learning about visual displacement appeared only when the depth of the underwater target was changed and people needed to adapt their previous learning. To the extent that the world is rapidly changing and that this change will continue to impact educational goals and teaching strategies, prospective teachers need to understand how the natural desire to say, "just tell me what to do" will not serve them optimally for the challenges they will face. As noted earlier, efficiency is extremely important; otherwise, we are overwhelmed by novelty. But efficiency is also insufficient if we want to adapt.

The innovation dimension in Figure 2.1 represents the need to go beyond one's existing efficiency-oriented skills and strategies to adapt to new situations. It is often said that innovation "favors the prepared mind," hence learning with understanding can support innovation and adaptation (for example, see the previous discussion of Judd). We noted earlier that innovation often involves "letting go" of cherished ideas and assumptions. Teacher educators must help prospective teachers prepare themselves for these kinds of tasks.

A major way to prepare teachers for innovation is to help them develop inquiry skills that support ways to look at student learning and adapt accordingly. Many of the chapters in this book emphasize inquiry. Inquiry represents a very different way of learning than simply memorizing facts about teaching and learning strategies without understanding why and when they are relevant.

Another way to prepare teachers to become adaptive experts is to help them explore where different theories of learning fall with respect to the efficiency and innovation dimensions. For example, many people contrast Thorndike (a behaviorist who emphasized trial-and-error learning and efficiency) and Dewey (a progressivist who liked projects and discovery) and argue about who is right. An alternative way to think about this issue is to assume that the choice is not one of "either/or." Thorndike's work falls primarily on the efficiency dimension in Figure 2.1 and Dewey's is closer to the innovation dimension. A conjecture currently being explored by learning scientists is that it is the balance among these that supports adaptive expertise (see, for example, Schwartz, Bransford, and Sears, in press).

Preparing Teachers to Understand and Support Learning

An important part of teacher preparation is to help people become familiar with technical concepts that support understanding—concepts such as summative versus formative assessment, normative versus criterion-based testing, pedagogical content knowledge, routine versus adaptive expertise, behavioral theory versus Piagetian theory, and so forth. But research on learning shows that people need much more than facts (for example, declarative knowledge) if the goal is to help them act and reflect responsibly. There are a number of strategies that teacher educators have developed to help preservice teachers understand and be able to thoughtfully apply the important ideas and concepts about learning discussed in this chapter, and these often emulate the strategies that research has found to be useful in developing *students'* learning—strategies that develop teachers' capacity to be adaptive experts who can take nonroutine aspects of the context into account in making sound teaching decisions.

Teachers can certainly profit from some direct instruction about broad principles of learning that may be highly generalizable, like many of those we have outlined in this chapter. At the same time, however, teachers also need to know that general theories of learning, although they provide guidelines for the design of effective learning environments, cannot produce a single recipe to use in all situations. One of the key features of modern learning theory is that optimal learning environments must be tailored to specific learning goals, to the students' backgrounds and prior knowledge, and to the contexts in which learning will occur. Thus teachers not only need to understand basic principles of learning but must also know how to use them judiciously to meet diverse learning goals in contexts where students differ in their needs.

Teachers' work is not unlike that of engineers building a bridge, who must not only understand principles of physics needed for safe structures and tricks of the trade (such as how to block off the water so that cement foundations can be poured); they must take into account the nature of the terrain, the overall length of the bridge, the uses to which it will be put and how much weight it must support, the nature of materials available for construction, the aesthetics of the design favored by the surrounding community, and whether there are earthquakes, floods, or other events common to the area. Like the engineers in this example, teachers need to learn how to evaluate the salience of many different conditions that influence learning and the potential effectiveness of different teaching strategies as they make decisions about what to do in particular instances.

To do this, teachers need to develop a conceptual map of the domain of influences on learning (including both contextual influences and the impacts of different teaching strategies), and they need to develop means for evaluating how these may be operating in specific instances. The *How People Learn* framework provides one way of organizing such a conceptual map. There are, of course, others as well. What is key is that teachers learn not just discrete facts about specific learning theories but a framework for the field as a whole. They also need analytic skills for interpolating between specific, highly contextualized teaching and learning events and general theories that can prove useful in interpreting them and providing guidance for how to proceed.

Among the specific pedagogies teacher educators have developed to help preservice teachers understand learning in relation to teaching are analyses of learning through careful observation of students and their work, analyses of novice teachers' own attempts to teach, and self-reflection on their own learning. Increasingly, these strategies ask teachers to examine teaching *in the light of learning* rather than simply asking teachers to implement discrete teaching behaviors culled either from theoretical principles or from studies about practices that were sometimes correlated with student achievement.

Quite often, research has found that strategies used successfully in one context have been less successful in others, or that overused, particular approaches prove much less effective, or that the mix of strategies is important, not just a single tactic by itself. For example, the degree of structuring or kind of scaffolding that is optimal for learning tasks depends in part on students' prior experiences and familiarity. How teachers *combine* inquiry-oriented learning and direct instruction is important for understanding, not just either alone. And the representations teachers choose will be most effective if they tap particular students' background knowledge. These contingencies are key for teachers to understand. Teacher education pedagogies that attend to how learning actually happens and how teaching actually affects learning for different students contrast with the older "technicist" era of teacher training, in which teaching was seen as the implementation of set routines and formulas for behavior, unresponsive to the distinctive attributes of either clients or curriculum goals (Darling-Hammond, 2001a). Examples of some of these emerging pedagogies are provided in the following discussion.

Developing a Conceptual Framework for Analyzing Learning and Teaching

An important way that teacher educators help new teachers understand and appreciate some of the complex factors at play in teaching and learning is to engage prospective teachers in the analysis of teaching and learning. Prospective teachers can examine videotapes of teachers, student work samples, teaching plans, assessments, and other materials from classrooms to help them attend more closely to the nature, focus, and character of the learning they demonstrate.

To make sense of learning, it is helpful for prospective teachers to develop a conceptual framework of influences on learning; to be able to identify and question their assumptions about learning, both in general and in specific instances; and to be able to organize their own inquiry process. One approach to developing these abilities was developed at Vanderbilt University by a group of instructors interested in applying both learning theory and technology to the preparation of teachers (PT3 Group at Vanderbilt, 2003). The AMIGO project uses the four lenses of the *How People Learn* framework as the basis for technology-based learning modules organized around challenges that trigger an inquiry process for the prospective teachers. The modules are designed to capitalize on what is known about how people learn through guided inquiry while also teaching the students about how people learn. A goal is to help the students learn to balance all four of these lenses simultaneously when they think about the learning process and the design of instruction by having them both study these ideas and experience them. (See "Developing a Conceptual Framework for Teaching and Learning.")

Developing a Conceptual Framework for Teaching and Learning

In the *How People Learn* course designed through the AMIGO project, the goal is for prospective teachers to look at learning situations and integrate knowledge through the four lenses of the framework—considerations of knowledge, learners, community, and assessment—in developing teaching responses. The challenges—questions like, "How could a test become a gift?" and "What shall we do about Bob?" (see earlier discussion in this chapter)—are the basis for students to first identify their initial thoughts, which are published to the Web, and then use resources that are available on-line (readings, audio and video clips of experts and teachers, simulations, suggestions for hands-on activities) to develop a deeper understanding of the issue, followed by a self-assessment of understanding (via tests that are provided or essays that receive feedback.) When they feel ready, students "go public" with a written essay or class presentation about what they have learned. Or they may construct challenges of their own for others to try. Students compare their thinking to their initial ideas. They may also respond to each other's answers to create a wider community of learning that provides access to multiple perspectives on the topic.

Research was conducted on the outcomes of one such class, taught on-line and in person using thirty-five modules developed to accompany the *How People Learn* text from the National Research Council. The goals of the course were to help students learn to analyze teaching and learning using the framework in order to evaluate the instruction of others as well as to design and assess their own instruction. The course strategies included inquiry using the on-line resources and others the students sought out, along with on-demand mini-lectures in class or on the Web that instructors designed to respond to students' questions and learning needs as these were revealed in their postings to the challenges and class conversations on the Web.

Pre- and post comparisons of students' initial and later responses to the challenges provided substantial evidence of learning throughout the course. Most interesting were students' own analyses of their learning. As one wrote of the "test as a gift" challenge,

Reviewing my initial response to this challenge was great because I think that this one really shows how much I have progressed in a semester regarding my understanding . . . I wrote, "How could a test be made positive? I do not know . . ." This is very exciting because I have since learned tons about formative assessment and have many ideas regarding "tests." Being in the class really caused me to question what a function of a test is. Partly, it is to hold teachers and students accountable, but additionally, and more importantly, it is to give students the opportunity to grow. Tests can be exciting; they can be "learner friendly" so to speak. The challenge asked the question, "How can a test be made like a gift?" My answers now is, "By giving students formative 'tests' or assessments. By providing students with opportunities to revise and improve their thinking, they are helped to identify problems and see their own progress, which is encouraging and worthwhile." (PT3 Group at Vanderbilt, 2003, p. 114)

The prospective teacher's perspective on what she would do to enhance her students' learning mirrored what she had just experienced in developing and refining her own ideas.

In another example of how analyses of learning situations can be used to reinforce the development of a conceptual framework, prospective teachers at Stanford University view videotapes of contrasting classrooms and are asked to write an analysis of them using the four lenses of the HPL framework. They examine how each classroom attends to knowledge, learners, community, and assessment in the process of teaching and how this influences learning. While watching the tapes, the student teachers need to take careful notes on the interactions they observe (in brief, field-note style) noting the setup of the classroom, jotting down direct quotes from the teacher and the children. These field notes comprise their perceptions and observations. The student teachers are then asked to consider what they observed in light of each element of the framework. How does the teacher organize the *knowledge* to be acquired so that it is accessible? In what ways does the teacher engage *learners'* interests and connect to their prior knowledge, experiences, and ideas? How does the teacher construct a *community* in the classroom? How does the teacher *assess* what the students know and are learning? Finally, the student teachers must evaluate the way in which the teacher scaffolds the learning process. What specific steps does the teacher take to ensure that learners are able to understand the material to be learned?

Completing this assignment helps prospective teachers look carefully at particular interactions between children and teacher. For instance, in an assignment using videotapes of a Japanese mathematics teacher from the Third International Mathematics and Science Study (TIMSS) tape, student teachers notice the careful selection of a challenging and authentic geometry problem for the class that opens up the mathematical questions effectively (knowledge-centered), as well as the way the teacher engages the students by using their names and personal interests in soliciting initial guesses to the problem (learner-centered). Prospective teachers often write about the way that the students are encouraged to work together to solve the problem and often remark upon how comfortable the students appear in coming to the board to present their particular approach to the problem in front of their peers (community-centered). Many student teachers write about the ways in which the students' presentations of different solutions make mathematical thinking visible to others (the teacher and other classmates), and some recognize the ways in which that approach actually reflects the academic mathematics community values of debate, discussion, and demonstration of methods (knowledge-centered). Finally, many notice the ways in which the teacher's emphasis upon public discussion and evaluation of a variety of students' solutions enables him to continually assess his students' current thinking and understanding (assessment-centered).

When asked to apply the HPL framework in this way on multiple occasions, it becomes a tool that enables prospective teachers to better understand what supports learning and how to design instruction. This kind of assignment helps new teachers begin to use the ideas and develop their own conceptual framework for organizing key ideas about learning—rather than simply memorize disconnected elements that remain abstractions.

Examining Learning in Relation to Teaching

Often, analyses of teaching have focused more on what teachers *do* than on what students *learn*. In recent years, there has been a great deal more emphasis on asking teachers to evaluate student work and learning together so that they can begin to understand the outcomes of instruction and to think about what would need to change to achieve stronger outcomes. Some teacher educators have begun to capitalize on such approaches by designing assignments that ask prospective teachers to collect evidence about student learning and to examine it in relation to the teaching that leads to it. One such strategy asks student teachers to collect three different kinds of evidence about student learning using different methods; for example, a test or formal essay, a free-write from the student about what she or he believes she has learned, an interview of the student about the material, or a performance in which the student is asked to apply the content to a new problem. The student teachers must then compare what can be inferred from these different methods about what the student did or did not appear to learn or understand, and to consider this in relation to the kind of teaching that the student experienced.

This kind of fine-grained evaluation of learning in relation to teaching raises questions about the learning process and the individual learner, the nature of different assessments and what they reveal or conceal, the kinds of knowledge sought and achieved, and the learning context. These questions can then be explored in more detail and connected to discussions of learning theory and instructional design. In addition, this kind of strategy sensitizes prospective teachers to the many aspects of learning, teaching, and assessment that can make a difference in the outcomes of their efforts.

Some teacher educators have found that asking teachers to write cases about teaching and learning can be particularly helpful. Case writing can focus teachers upon gathering evidence of learning, which pushes them to begin to articulate and understand what learning looks like (and does not) for their students and in their subject matter. Case writing can also be particularly helpful in aiding new teachers in analyzing how teaching contexts and approaches influence learning in the context of their own practice.

As an illustration, prospective teachers taking a course on Principles of Learning for Teaching at Stanford University write a "curriculum case" in which they detail the events of a learning segment (it can be a lesson that occurred over the course of a day or several days) and analyze it in light of learning theory (for details, see Hammerness, Darling-Hammond, and Shulman, 2002). Most critical to novices' ability to produce a powerful case is the use of evidence of learning combined with readings and discussions about learning theory. For the case, student teachers must not only describe what they did and said as teachers, but they are also asked to focus in particular upon how *their* students responded and what they learned, both individually and collectively. They must include substantive evidence of student learning, which can be in the form of samples of student work (essays, problem sheets, lab reports, and so on), transcriptions of classroom discussions, quotes from students, and even descriptions of the body language and other behaviors of their students. Student teachers then analyze this evidence after having described the learning context, the students whom they teach, their goals and intentions, and their instructional actions in order to consider the relationship between what they hoped for, what they did, and what their students learned (or didn't learn, as the case may be).

Quite often this exercise creates a common epiphany about the learning process, one in which student teachers see many of the learning principles they have been studying in action. For instance, one science teacher wrote her curriculum case about her unit on evolution and focused upon the difficulty of helping her high school students overcome Lamarckian conceptions of evolution. She noted that on the first day on this topic, their comments seemed to indicate that they immediately understood Darwin's theory. But a test on the concept (as well as comments she recorded from a later discussion) illustrated that misconceptions and misunderstandings about evolution still dominated in the class, even among some of her most accomplished students. The case author was disappointed and puzzled—if they understood Darwin's theory (even laughing at some of the Lamarckian interpretations of evolution), then why did they do so poorly on the exam?

By analyzing the evidence of learning she had collected for her case, she was able to identify the ways in which students' prior knowledge and commonsense explanations had interfered with the new disciplinary knowledge they had encountered in the class (a sophisticated rendering of the same *Fish is Fish* learning problem we discussed earlier in this chapter). Using key ideas from the course on learning, including ongoing assessment, metacognition, and prior knowledge, she was then able to identify some strategies she could use in the future to lead her students to more theoretically sound explanations and to more robust and deeper understandings of evolution. For instance, she discussed how she could have used a quick initial written assessment to determine how well the students understood after the first day and to test their growing understanding. That assessment would have probably revealed some of the misunderstandings and misconceptions that she did not encounter until later. She also suggested that a different summative assessment (an essay, instead of the test she had used) would also have pushed her students be more articulate about the differences between the two theories. She argued that if she had asked the students to compare and contrast the theories in writing, her students might have been able to attend to the more subtle but important distinctions (as well as some of the ways in which Lamarck's theory is intuitively appealing) and to be more thorough and careful in their presentation of the theories. (To read this case and examples of cases written by other prospective teachers, visit the Web site from the course: http://kml2.carnegiefoundation.org/gallery/khammerness/c_in_the_c/final/archive/archive.html.)

It is important to emphasize that these cases were the result of careful thinking and analysis over the course of several drafts, including feedback from peers and instructors and several "conferences" in which student teachers discussed emerging interpretations. Research analyzing the cases written for the course demonstrated that through the case-writing process, student teachers moved from naïve generalizations about their students' learning (students didn't "get it"; students hadn't tried hard enough; the teachers needed more time) to more expert, theory-based interpretations of the learning process (Hammerness and others, 2002). Through these case analyses, student teachers were able to begin to make distinctions about the nature of learning, what learning "looks like," and how to support and assess it—understandings that are critical to helping prospective teachers think about learning in much more complex terms than just a "lightbulb" in students' heads.

Developing Metacognition by Reflecting on Learning

Experiences like case writing and analyses of learning may be made even more effective if student teachers have also had an opportunity to think about and reflect upon their own learning experiences. New teachers who have had little experience with children or in teaching roles before coming to teacher education may benefit even more from such experiences. Reflecting on their own learning can also help new teachers take a first step in making their own assumptions about teaching and learning explicit—a key part of then critically examining them, as we have discussed in this chapter.

At San Jose State University in a course on learning, one teacher educator's first assignment asks prospective teachers to describe both a very powerful learning experience (either in or out of school) and a learning experience that was less successful, and then to compare and contrast the two. The students are not only required to describe these experiences, but also to analyze them to identify key characteristics of good learning experiences as well as poorer ones. In many programs, student teachers may be asked questions like the following as the basis for written reflections: "In general, what learning conditions and teaching strategies do you think most enable you to learn effectively? Think back to a specific time when you tried to learn something but felt you could not deeply understand it or become proficient. What was the nature of the learning situation? What impeded your learning? How did you feel? Can you imagine what would have allowed you to learn more effectively? Now think back to a time when you successfully learned something that was especially challenging. What was the nature of the content or skill that you were trying to learn? What made it difficult? What finally enabled you to succeed in mastering these difficult ideas or skills?"

Once students have had an opportunity to identify some of the key characteristics of good learning experiences in their own educational history, they are often more prepared to make sense of what they learn in their teacher preparation program about learning. Concepts of the zone of proximal development may have more depth when student teachers themselves have thought about how, for example, they learned to fix cars with their father over the course of several years. Concepts like metacognition have more power when teachers, for instance, have a chance to write about how opportunities to discuss the strengths and weaknesses of their writing with a supportive teacher helped them learn to write well. And in turn, student teachers are often able to appreciate better the nature of good learning experiences for their own students after having an opportunity to be metacognitive themselves about their own experiences.

In addition, courses for preservice teachers may be even more effective if they include opportunities to monitor their own learning in the course, to help them appreciate how thinking about one's own learning can facilitate greater understanding. For instance, in both the *How People Learn* course at Vanderbilt and the *Principles of Learning* course at Stanford, students were asked to write a reflection about their own learning after they completed a challenge or wrote a curriculum case. This allowed them both to gain more insights about their own learning and to give feedback to the instructors about what was useful, what could be more useful, and what more they wanted to learn.

Because prospective teachers' personal learning experiences are powerful predictors of their own teaching practices, the ways in which teacher educators model practices that are productive for learning is critically important. Student teachers will reflect on what they have encountered whether invited to or not, and they will draw implicit conclusions from their experience. Quite often teachers have in the past complained about preparation or professional development settings in which an instructor lectures them about the need to use cooperative learning techniques or tests them on formative and summative assessment principles without providing opportunities for constructive feedback and revision. Throughout the teacher education program, and especially in courses on learning, it is crucial that student teachers be asked to learn in ways that reflect what they are being taught about how people learn.

Connected Knowledge and Program Coherence

The discussion of expertise in the earlier part of this chapter emphasized the importance of well-connected knowledge that is organized around "big ideas" of the disciplines. For example, we noted that the concept of life cycles can be learned as a set of isolated facts (for example, students memorize the life cycle of some organism) or as an organizing principles that provides a basis for thinking about a variety of issues, including ways to prevent species from becoming endangered, ways to intervene to control pests, and so forth. Books like *Understanding by Design* (Wiggins and McTighe, 1998) provide important guidelines for "working backwards" by first identifying the enduring ideas of a discipline and then choosing particular strategies for instruction and assessment (see also Bruner, 1960/1977).

Teacher preparation programs need to consider issues of connected knowledge at the level of individual course design and at the level of the design of entire programs of study (including integration between college courses and classroom-based experiences). The second issue is often referred to as "program coherence," and it represents a challenge for all professional programs. Especially important is the degree to which *students* are able to understand how everything fits together, not simply the faculty. This set of issues is discussed in more detail in Chapter Eleven.

CONCLUSION

Concepts of learning (including ideas about transfer) are central to all attempts to improve education. Everyone has theories of learning, although they often remain tacit. We make assumptions about what is important to learn, who can learn, how to help people learn, and how to assess learning. By making tacit theories explicit, teachers can continually evaluate their assumptions and improve throughout their careers.

The concepts and theories in this chapter provide a way to begin to think about learning. By exploring these core ideas, prospective teachers can learn to identify many forms of evidence of learning, can appreciate how to evaluate and assess it, and finally, with support, can understand how to recognize and put into practice the features of classrooms that best support the kinds of learning they seek. Ideally, conceptualizations about learning can also provide a basis for connecting all of the important areas of expertise that teachers need to develop to help all students succeed.

CHAPTER THREE

Educating Teachers for Developmentally Appropriate Practice

Frances Degan Horowitz, Linda Darling-Hammond, and John Bransford, with James Comer, Kathy Rosebrock, Kim Austin, and Frances Rust

Good teachers understand what students everywhere can confirm: teaching is not just talking, and learning is not just listening. Effective teachers are able to figure out not only what they want to teach, but also how to do so in a way that students can understand and use the new information and skills. Furthermore, they know what students are ready for and need to learn, so they choose tasks that are productive, and they organize these tasks in a way that builds understanding. Finally, they monitor students' growth and progress so they can address specific needs and keep students engaged in school, learning productively, and growing as cooperative and thoughtful citizens who will be able to participate in society. To do all of these things, teachers need to understand children's development and how it influences, and is influenced by, their learning. A foundation of knowledge about child development is essential for planning curriculum; designing, sequencing, and pacing activities; diagnosing student learning needs; organizing the classroom; and teaching social and academic skills.

Anyone who has spent time in classrooms knows that a teacher cannot make headway without engaging students in the learning process, and this is not as straightforward as it might appear. As just one example, an observer in a successful primary classroom will see children intently and purposefully engaged in a variety of different learning tasks: measuring water at the water table, listening to a big book in the reading center, counting out manipulatives to solve an arithmetic problem, and writing or dictating a story about the recent classroom trip to the zoo. With all of this activity, the teacher knows what each child is doing, what the child understands in that domain, and what he needs to work on next to progress in his understanding. While the classroom activities may appear seamless, developing this kind of practice takes a great deal of knowledge and skill not immediately apparent to the casual observer or novice.

One first-year teacher, previously a successful lawyer, who was placed in a low-performing, urban middle school following a short summer preparation program, pinpointed the problem many new recruits encounter: when asked what he had found most challenging in that first year, the teacher said, "getting the children to sit still and pay attention." He did not return for a second year of teaching. Another midcareer teaching recruit who had not had the benefit of education training resigned on her second day. "The kids were nice enough," she said, "but they were running all over the place. There was no way I could teach them anything if I couldn't get them to sit down. I didn't know what to do" (Hegarty, 2001). Understanding where a child is developmentally is one of the most important keys to shaping appropriate learning tasks that are engaging for students—tasks that are both interesting and appropriately challenging. Tasks that are developmentally inappropriate not only breed academic failure for students, they also undermine motivation and encourage disruptive behavior.

A teacher who has a good understanding of child development and learning is more likely to be effective in the classroom; recent data show that new teachers who have had coursework in learning and development are also more than twice as likely to stay in teaching (National Commission on Teaching and America's Future, 2003, p. 84). This is probably because greater success follows from the ability to fashion developmentally appropriate instructional materials and lessons that meet students' needs. These abilities are critical factors in whether the teacher is able to manage a classroom. The challenge for the lawyer turned teacher was "how to keep the children still." When a teacher cannot create tasks that engage students at their developmental level, the result is a chaotic classroom environment where little learning can go on, and little success is achieved.

Teachers who understand development and how to support it encourage dramatically different results from those who do not. (See "Learning to Hate Mathematics and Developing a Classroom of Mathematicians.") This chapter describes how teachers' knowledge of development enables them to be effective in selecting and developing appropriate tasks, guiding the learning process, and maintaining children's motivation to learn.

Learning to Hate Mathematics

She was in first grade and already she was learning to hate mathematics. It was the one subject in which she was not successful. In fact, the class made her cry. Her parents, both successful professionals, heard for the first time the news about their daughter doing poorly in math at a meeting with her teacher at the end of the first two months of school. The teacher commented that the child had really earned a "D" but she had given her a "C" because the child had initially placed in the top math group. The teacher wondered if it might not be wise to move the child down to a lower-level math group.

The mother, a well-known and highly accomplished African American scientist, objected, realizing that failure in math and feeling incompetent in this subject was a recipe for severely curtailed options ten years hence. The parents said they would work with the child and see what they could do. This was a Thursday. By the following Monday afternoon when the mother visited the school for American Education week, the teacher reported that the child, who had not previously finished her math work, had not only completed it early but had done almost all of it correctly. This child had gone from failing work to "A" work in the space of four days.

The teacher wanted to know what the mother had done. The mother replied: "I figured it out. There were only a few things that could account for her poor showing in mathematics: she didn't know her facts; she didn't know how to express the facts in the way in which they were presented; or she didn't know how to express them in the time given." The mother discovered that her daughter was not connecting the amount of time she was allotted for the task to what she had to accomplish. So, the mother used a timer to help her daughter learn about the relationship between time allotted and completing the task at hand.

An eavesdropping teacher, upon hearing the mother's explanation, said, "Of course, many children at the age of first grade have not yet developed a sense of time and distance." The mother, reflecting on this incident years later, wondered if perhaps the teacher's failure to reach for this explanation and apply it correctively was due to an inadequate understanding of the developmental factors that could account for the child's failure, to expectations about learning abilities in African American children, to a lack of motivation or ability to do the diagnostic analysis that would reveal the learning problem the child was experiencing, or some combination of these things.

This true story provides a small window into what an effective teacher needs to know about child development, and how she should be able to apply that knowledge to help children learn and to grow. In addition to understanding stages of development, an effective teacher needs to understand the components of tasks she assigns and what they require, and she must be able to observe students carefully to evaluate not only what they know but how they learn and perform. With that knowledge, teachers can help young children continue to feel successful and inspired to learn. Without it, they can stymie children's immediate learning and endanger their future success. A teacher who does not understand development may conclude, as this teacher did at first, that a student who encounters difficulties is not learning or, perhaps, not even able to learn.

In contrast, here is a story of a new teacher who understands development, demonstrating how that understanding can make a difference for students' lives in school.

Developing a Classroom of Mathematicians

On a spring morning just before the last week of school, when many students are just biding time, Jean Jahr's classroom of twenty-eight second- and third-grade students is intently engaged in a mathematical investigation. A first-year teacher and graduate of Bank Street College, Jean teaches at P.S. 234, a New York City public elementary school. The multiracial, multilingual class of students is working in small groups on a single problem. Some children use calculators; others do not. Some have drawn clusters of numbers; others have developed a graphic display for their problem. As they finish, everyone takes their solutions with them as they sit on the carpeted meeting area facing the board. Jean begins by reading the problem with the group: In September, each person in classroom 113 brought one ream (one package) of Xerox paper. There are 500 sheets of paper in one ream. There are twenty-eight children in class 113. How many pieces of paper were there altogether?

She opens the discussion with an invitation, "Let's talk about how different people solved the problem, and why you decided to solve it that way." Over the next twenty minutes, students show, draw, and discuss seven different strategies they have used to solve the problem. Jane questions them to draw out details about their solution strategies and frequently recaps what students say. With patience and careful choice of words, she helps each member of the group understand the thought processes of the others. As the session nears its end, she asks if everyone understands the different solutions. Three children from one group seem in doubt and raise their hands. Jean asks one of the girls to come up and show "her way." Teacher and the other children observe patiently, obviously pondering the girls' thought process. Suddenly, Jean's face lights up as she sees what they have done. Her response clarifies their work: "That's how you did it! I was wondering if you had used tens groupings, but you had a totally different pattern. You started as if there were 30 children and then you subtracted the 1,000 sheets that would have been brought by the additional two children from the total number. You rounded to a higher number and then you subtracted. Wow. I get it. Let me see if I can show it to the others."

The young girl is pleased when the teacher shows the group "her" system. When everyone seems clear, Jean asks, "Does anyone remember where this problem came from?" A girl raises her hand and says: "That was my problem a long time ago."

"You're right," her teacher responds. "You asked that problem during the first week of school when all of you were asked to each bring a ream of paper for the year. You saw all those reams of paper stacked up in front of the room, and you wanted to know how many sheets of paper we had. I told you that we would find out some day but that at that point in the year it was hard to figure it out because you had to learn a lot about grouping, and adding large numbers. But now you all can do it and in many different ways."

Another child recaps by noting, "That means that we used 14,000 sheets of paper this year." Jean says, "You got it!" The problem stays on the board for the day, along with the students' multiple solutions.

This first-year teacher's practice demonstrates that she understands how to organize a developmentally supportive classroom so that young children are productively engaged in meaningful work. She creates a task that is grounded in the children's own experience, and she helps them use a variety of concrete tools—from manipulatives and drawings to graphic displays and calculators—to support their problem solving. Through careful observation and diagnosis, she has figured out what different tools and kinds of assistance will help different students make progress on the task. She has organized the task so that students can find a variety of entry points, and she creates a classroom dialogue showing a variety of solutions to make sure all students understand the answer and the process. She scaffolds the children's learning through structures for activities, access to peers, questions to guide students' thinking, and opportunities for children to learn social skills as well as cognitive ones. She listens and observes carefully to understand students' thinking, and she supports students in taking risks in sharing their ideas so that she will be able to move their understanding along. She also makes sure that students are affirmed in their efforts, thus stimulating self-confidence and ongoing motivation. Later we will see how her preparation in child development, as well as in pedagogical content knowledge, enabled her to do these things.

As we describe in this chapter, child development is tightly tied to learning in many ways. Novice teachers should understand that knowing about development is central to being an effective teacher, and being an effective teacher is central to whether children will make significant progress in the pathways necessary to healthy development and to becoming a fully educated person in a democratic society. Five major topics are discussed in this chapter:

1. **The importance of taking *a developmental perspective*:** When student development is the focus of teaching decisions, teachers plan in light of their students' needs and to support their progression along several developmental pathways—physical, social, emotional, cognitive, linguistic, and psychological. They understand that these dimensions interact with one another, and further, that students will have different developmental needs. Although there are many common aspects of the developmental process, milestones along each of these dimensions do not necessarily occur at the same age for all children nor does development in different arenas occur evenly within the same child. Although American schools are organized by grade, and to some extent by age, both age and grade are very imprecise indicators of development. At any grade level, there is usually a two- or three-year span of ages with an even wider span of skills, abilities, and developmental stages. Understanding developmental pathways and progressions is extremely important for teaching in ways that are optimal for each child.

2. **The inevitability of *individual differences* in development:** It is important for teachers to understand in considerable depth the diverse ways in which a child's development can evolve and even appear "splintered," departing from the norm in some areas but still within or close to the range of normal development. As noted in Chapter Two, effective teachers are learner-centered as well as knowledge-centered, and they use assessment to understand what their students need. The better they understand the ranges of variability in development and the areas where additional support is needed, the better prepared teachers are to help their students learn.

3. **The interactions among *development, knowledge, and learning*:** In contrast to earlier views of development as a set of biologically related stages clearly determining what students can do, current research shows that development, knowledge, and learning are related to one another. The older belief that development proceeds at a fixed pace that determines children's "readiness" for learning is no longer accepted by current developmental theorists. Instead, research demonstrates how learning can affect development, as well as the reverse. Newer studies show that, in addition to their age or apparent "stage," people's prior knowledge and experience with specific content affects the sophistication of their thinking. Hence the same person may think abstractly about one area of knowledge and much more concretely about another. Relationships between development and new learning are also important to understand. Vygotsky's concept of the zone of proximal development (ZPD) provides a framework for thinking about how to support learning and development for each child.

4. **The centrality of *cultural contexts* for development:** The fact that learning affects development (and vice versa), and that both learning and development are deeply embedded in cultural contexts, means that teachers must understand and appreciate the variety of ways children's experiences can differ, and be able to see and build upon cultural strengths if they are to help all students succeed.

5. **Strategies for helping prospective teachers acquire developmental expertise:** We noted in Chapter Two on Learning that "knowing" about an area, that is, being able to state facts about it, is not the same as being able to use this knowledge to solve important problems in the real world. This is as true for teachers as it is for students. Teacher educators have discovered a number of ways to help prospective teachers learn to go beyond simply "thinking about" development to being able to "think and act developmentally" as they teach.

THE IMPORTANCE OF TAKING A DEVELOPMENTAL PERSPECTIVE

To understand and support students' learning, a teacher must be able to take a "developmental perspective." This includes an understanding that development occurs along a number of different dimensions—physical, social, emotional, cognitive, and linguistic, among others—and that development along these dimensions, though following some common progressions, does not necessarily occur at the same age for each child or even at the same time within the same person. A useful metaphor for thinking about the course of development is in terms of "pathways" of development, which conveys the notion of movement along these several dimensions toward a set of important goals.

Progression Along the Developmental Pathways

At the core of effective practice is a teacher's ability to identify where a child is in his development and how to support his learning within the zone of proximal development (discussed in the next section). To do this, a teacher must understand general progressions in development as well as individual learning. Stage theories like Piaget's that posited large shifts in development at specific ages have been challenged by those who have found development to be more continuous and more individual, as well as more specific to particular contexts and content areas (Flavell, 1994; Siegler, 1998). It is increasingly clear that education can support development: Children can *become* ready to think and perform more complex tasks if they are given opportunities and guidance to develop these skills. Within some parameters, the teacher need not simply *wait* for children to "get ready." She can create a classroom that meets children where they are, takes advantage of what they want and need to learn, and moves them along the developmental pathways.

The idea of pathways encompasses the dynamic processes of physical, social-interactive, emotional, cognitive, linguistic, and moral-ethical development that interact to support the growth of the child. As James Comer and colleagues (1996) explain, "Balanced development, or maturity, is characterized by strong linkages among all of the developmental pathways. This metaphor of linkages among pathways enables us to explain simultaneously the complexity of development and the urgency of paying attention to all aspects of development" (p. 18).

As with all systems, any underdevelopment along one pathway has an impact on the whole system. This means that teachers need to attend to development along all of the pathways and look for opportunities to support growth in areas where attention is needed. In addition, it is important to understand that each one of these pathways develops within the child's particular social and cultural context, which can also contribute to individual differences among children.

Understanding development requires not only a sense of the "whole child" but also a consideration of the "whole child developing in particular social contexts."

A teacher who is developmentally aware will know, for example, how the child's prior knowledge and cultural experiences will inform what the child knows and how he may approach new ideas and tasks. Such a teacher will also understand the value of allowing children to explore the physical world with the use of their senses and to develop physical abilities, like balance, body, and space perception; rhythm and temporal awareness; and fine muscle activities, both for their own sake and because these abilities support other academic skills, including reading, writing, and the understanding of how physical principles work in the world, a foundation of mathematics and science. This teacher will know that a curriculum that encourages children to learn actively and concretely—by observing, collecting information, describing, counting, manipulating, and using what they have studied—will later support abstract thinking that relies on these concrete understandings.

A developmentally aware teacher will know that, for most students, teaching early reading skills in kindergarten (for example, helping students clarify the concept of words and letters and exploring sound-symbol relationships) will differ from teaching reading in later elementary grades (for example, using metacognitive strategies to enhance comprehension, integrating more extended reading and writing, extending knowledge of spelling and writing conventions). She will also understand that some students still need to learn skills others have mastered earlier, and will know how to diagnose these needs and target teaching and assistance accordingly. A developmentally aware teacher will know that as students progress in their understanding within a domain, they will be increasingly able to look for patterns, to think abstractly and contingently, and to manage multiple variables in more complicated ways. This teacher will be prepared to help students engage in this progression toward more systematic reasoning and symbolic thinking.

Pathways Interact. Different pathways of development *interact* with and influence one another; and these pathways and interactions have important implications for instruction. For example, understanding the general progression of *cognitive development* and the variations exhibited by individual children helps a teacher to structure, sequence, and pace instruction and choose instructional strategies that are likely to be effective. Understanding *language development*, including the ways in which language acquisition is related to cognitive development and cultural contexts, helps a teacher choose materials and teaching strategies that will support children's language proficiency and growing use of academic language. (Chapter Four explores language development in detail.) Understanding *social development,* including the development of social skills, is essential if a teacher is to develop a classroom in which students can work together and remain motivated. These skills need to be taught through modeling, coaching, and reinforcement. They do not always emerge spontaneously.

A teacher's understanding of the *psychological* and *emotional* pathways enables her to structure classroom experiences so as to maximize both the learning of subject matter and the development of positive self-concept, not with empty praise but by supporting and noting the development of competence, thus reinforcing the belief that putting forth effort will result in increased proficiency. This is critical because research indicates that if a student develops a poor academic self-concept (believing, for instance, that even with effort, he cannot succeed at schoolwork), he may de-emphasize effort in this domain to protect his overall self-esteem, developing a disengaged or oppositional stance to school (Harter, 1990; Tatum, 1999). A child who is socially insecure may be unwilling to risk engaging in classroom discussions for fear of being ridiculed, and may consequently fail to gain experience expressing his thoughts or securing feedback that would help him develop his ideas. The teacher may need to offer feedback in ways that reassure the student and help him learn strategies to support risk-taking (for example, writing down ideas before saying them aloud; preparing ideas ahead of time) so he can overcome his fears and benefit from other learning opportunities.

An important part of social development also includes the development of *moral* thought and action: the ability to respect the rights of others and to act in the interests of others as well as oneself. Teachers need to understand the developmental patterns that are associated with the development of concepts of justice and social welfare and the ways in which teaching can help support the development of character and the capacity to participate in a classroom community and, ultimately, a democratic society.

An understanding of different developmental pathways, and their interactions, is not only essential to the effective teaching of individual children but is critical to employing sound classroom management. In addition to the fact that children must be taught how to be members of a social community, children who are bored or who are presented with tasks at which they cannot succeed are the ingredients for out-of-control classrooms—the kinds of classrooms in which little learning takes place. The teaching that creates a constructive classroom environment in which children can work well with each other and in which tasks are appropriate and supportive of learning depends heavily on knowledge of development. An example of such an environment was illustrated in the earlier vignette about our new teacher, Jean Jahr.

Macro and Micro Elements of Pathways. The term *pathways* conveys the notion of movements toward a set of important goals. At a general (macro) level, children progress from point A to B to C. However, at a more micro level we know that development is not always characterized by linear progress and quantitative progressions. At various points in development there are spirals where the child's behavior appears to dip back before going forward. There are also qualitative transitions that involve a reorganization or new integration of functional abilities after which the individual operates at a qualitatively different level (Cole and Cole, 1993). Recognizing these micro processes while also understanding the general pathways and progressions of development is very important for effective teaching. For example, teachers who do not realize that a gain at one level can involve "backsliding" at another might think that their instruction has been ineffective, when in fact, it may be right on track. (See "Macro-Level Gains Can Produce Micro-Level Backslides.")

Macro-Level Gains Can Produce Micro-Level Backslides

At some point in their linguistic development, children learn how to speak in the past tense by adding a linguistic marker such as "ed' (for example, "We 'looked' at that book yesterday."). This is a definite advance over saying, "We look yesterday." However, progress at this level also often includes overgeneralizations that cause children to use a rule where it doesn't apply, thus appearing to make mistakes that they did not make previously. For example, they may begin to say, "We 'goed' yesterday," despite previously having used the word *went*. There are many examples of what appears to be "backsliding" that occur as children learn and develop. Teachers need to recognize when errors are simply momentary overgeneralizations that are actually healthy signs of new learning, and when they signal that children are truly misunderstanding and need help getting back on track.

Issues of Readiness. An understanding of developmental progression and of how different developmental pathways progress and interact is particularly important for helping teachers gauge children's "readiness" for new learning. For example, learning to read involves biological as well as cognitive development. Children's visual abilities (including binocularity and tracking) must mature before they can comfortably focus on and track relatively small print. This generally occurs sometime between the ages of four and eight, usually around the age of six or seven. At that point they typically also have a well-developed sense of one-to-one correspondence and can comprehend abstract symbols, which makes decoding of text easier (Cole and Cole, 1993, p. 476).

Developmentally prepared teachers further understand that children's development along various pathways can interact in many ways that affect readiness for specific tasks. For instance, a seven-year-old child with delayed small motor development will have difficulty writing. He may also have difficulty with certain visual and spatial concepts until the teacher engages him in small motor tasks that help him develop his physical skills. This will also enable him to engage in other kinds of academic learning. If the difficulties are severe, a developmentally aware teacher may encourage such a child to use a computer instead of a pencil when writing, so as not to slow the development of expressive written language skills while the child struggles with fine motor skills.

Neurodevelopmental differences, both within and beyond the ranges of what is considered "normal" development, are also important for gauging readiness. Individual children may process information most efficiently through different modalities (for example, visual, auditory, and kinesthetic), and some with more distinctive processing differences need teaching adaptations to learn content effectively. An effective teacher will ensure that a child with auditory processing difficulties has key information in written form so that the child can continue to learn content well while also developing her abilities to make sense of aural input. In the end, the goal of effective teaching is to move each child along each of the developmental pathways as far as possible at that point in time, with the ultimate goal of helping the individual achieve the levels of adult competence and functioning expected in our society.

Individual Differences

In traversing these developmental pathways, there is an enormous amount of normal variability among children of the same age. Teachers need to appreciate the range of normal differences that exists across children in classrooms even though they are all of the same age. In addition, teachers must be aware of within-child variability. For some children, development can be quite uneven—more advanced in one area, less so in another. Understanding these variations between and within children is critical to enabling a teacher to shape developmentally appropriate learning experiences for each child.

Unique Paths to Development

Studies of development show that people have much in common as they grow. Nevertheless, in a group of normally developing children who are of similar age, the teacher needs to realize that each child will have arrived at his or her age via a unique path of development influenced by biological factors, socioeconomic circumstances, and social and educational experiences. In a classroom where the backgrounds of the children vary considerably, it is obvious that one should expect great variability in the different domains of development. Even in classrooms where the backgrounds of the children are relatively homogenous, there will be considerable variability in development among the children, including individual differences in learning styles, attention spans, emotional reactions to success and failure, self-confidence, temperament, socialization, and prior experiences. For example, there is a two- to five-year range of ages during which just 50 percent of children can demonstrate Piaget's conservation tasks: six- to nine-year-olds demonstrate conservation of mass, four- to nine-year-olds can demonstrate conservation of length, seven- to nine-year-olds conservation of area, and eight- to ten-year-olds conservation of weight (Sroufe, Cooper, DeHart, and Bronfenbrenner, 1992).

Although variability in normal development is generally understood by teachers in the early grades, it is at least as great—but often less appreciated—in the adolescent years, offering special challenges to those teaching in middle and high schools. Wide variability in physical development and in the development of sexual characteristics is most obvious, but there are also major differences in cognitive and social development among twelve- to sixteen-year-olds. Differences in height and physical maturation, along with the cultural meanings attached to these characteristics, have consequences for self-concept, self-esteem, and self-confidence. Differences in the development of cognitive and social skills have consequences for academic progress when students confront more departmentalized, impersonal school environments with more rigid expectations for what is learned and how it is to be mastered and displayed (Eccles and others, 1993). These different developmental trajectories intersect with the developmental tasks of adolescents in American society—expectations with respect to independence, competence, and identity construction in relation to gender, sexuality, race, and culture, among other factors. The mix of these developmental trajectories in a class of adolescents means that the teachers in middle school and high school classrooms will necessarily be confronted with dealing with a large range of developmental needs.

The novice teacher needs to understand how individual differences manifest themselves and how individual differences can be employed to greatest effect in the service of learning. For example, children with short attention spans will need different pacing of tasks and activities than children with more enduring attention spans. Children with weak self-esteem may be more emotionally impacted by task failure and low evaluations than children with more robust self-esteem. The child who is less confident may learn more effectively in an instructional context designed to have a slower progression of small, supported steps so as to ensure successful performance, whereas the more confident child, even at the same skill level, may become bored by such an instructional strategy. The teacher may provide different kinds of feedback to children with different levels of self-confidence.

Overall, it is not unusual for development in one domain to be ahead of or behind development in other domains. For example, a child's language development may be somewhat advanced over the level of motor development at a particular age. A student may be able to solve a mathematical problem in the classroom with ease, but display less skill solving an interpersonal problem on the playground. Individuals display uneven growth across the developmental pathways. Just as gardeners understand that the plants in a healthy garden do not bloom simultaneously or even in the same season, teachers need to learn to see their children as multidimensional individuals—not "smart," or "slow," or "shy," but as complex individuals demonstrating varying levels of growth (Sprinthall, 1989, p. 136).

Splintered Development

The concept of *splintered development* refers to conditions where uneven development across domains is quite marked and exceeds normal variation. Splintered development is a special challenge for effective teaching because arrangements for learning experiences in one developmental area may need to be at a very different level than in another developmental level. For example, a child with advanced numeracy skills may lag significantly in language skills. A child who has advanced verbal language skills may have more difficulty with reading or written language production. Some of these sharp differences can signal learning disabilities that require diagnosis and special assistance. Whether or not this is the case, students will require attentive, focused instruction in the area where development is lagging. Teachers who have diagnostic skills and the capacity to individualize may be able to use changing groupings of students and individualized supports for different tasks to assure that students get the instruction they need without the negative effects of self-labeling.

Among the more challenging cases of splintered development are those in which a child has significantly advanced cognitive skills but whose emotional or social development is that which would be expected of a much younger child. In this case, the teacher needs to know how to foster the needed emotional or social development. The teacher needs to understand the possible strategies that can be employed to help the child learn to manage emotions, to behave in socially accepted ways, and to understand the perspectives and feelings of others.

Another very challenging case of splintered development is when a child with normal physical development is cognitively delayed. In many but not all cases, such children may be identified for special educational services. Whether identified or not, with the advent of mainstreaming, most such children will be educated in the regular classroom. In order for the student to continue to progress, the teacher needs to know how to adapt tasks so that the student can experience success and continue to learn along his own developmental trajectory. There is not nearly as much research or tested practice in dealing with sharply splintered development to guide a novice teacher as there is in developing effective teaching practices that reflect an understanding of normal individual differences. In these circumstances consultation with experts can be helpful. The well-prepared novice teacher should understand when consultation is needed and how to access that expertise.

An example of splintered development and its implications for making educational decisions about a student is discussed in "Splintered Development and

Educational Decisions." This example shows how assumptions about the productive instructional approaches for students should be examined in terms of the actual cognitive and other demands a setting makes as well as the supports that it offers for learning.

Splintered Development and Educational Decisions

A middle school student was having difficulty in school. Tests revealed that she had a language-processing problem that exceeded the ranges of typical variability. In particular, her ability to repeat sentences from short-term memory after hearing them was a problem: she could remember sentences that were only about one-half as long as those of typically developing children. However, her short-term memory for visual information was above normal.

Because of her learning problems, school officials decided to put her in basic courses rather than more enriched ones. For example, there was an enriched biology course that involved lots of hands-on experimentation and laboratory work in addition to the typical content of the basic course. The school officials were convinced that the basic course was all she could handle and enrolled her there.

A friend of the child's family was a leading learning scientist and immediately saw problems with this decision. The basic course was almost all verbal—students read texts and listened to lectures. This was precisely the area where the girl had processing problems. The "enriched" course provided an array of visual and tactile experiences and, because of that, played to the girl's strength.

The decision was finally made to put the girl in the enriched course and she did well, passing with a "C." There was no possibility of creating a control group and comparing the girl's performances in the two different environments. But the reasoning of the learning scientist is valuable to consider when trying to match students' strengths to particular ways in which courses are taught. Just because something is "enriched" doesn't necessarily mean that it makes learning harder. Opportunities for experiential, hands-on learning that are aimed at greater conceptual understanding often make learning more meaningful, and in that sense "easier," for students who have learning difficulties, as well as for those who are developing more typically.

Interactions Among Development, Knowledge, And Learning

Issues of students' "readiness" to learn certain kinds of information in certain ways highlights a topic that is especially important for teachers to understand; namely, what are the relationships among development, knowledge, and learning? Contrary to the earlier views of development—that is, that teachers just need to wait for it to "happen" at particular ages or stages—there is growing evidence that as children experience different contexts and learn about new content, their developmental capacities are enhanced. And as teaching supports children's development, their ability to learn in new ways is supported.

HOW PRIOR KNOWLEDGE AND EXPERIENCE SUPPORT DEVELOPMENT

A model of development that emerged from the early work of Piaget is that there are particular developmental stages that determine how people generally think about any kind of subject matter. Piaget's work (discussed briefly in Chapter Two) has had a profound and important influence on thinking about children's development. He developed well-structured clinical interviews that probed how students think about everyday events and how their reasoning changes. An illustration is shown in "An Example of Piaget's Work on Development and Thinking."

An Example of Piaget's Work on Development and Thinking

A child sees an adult take two identical pitchers, each filled with the same amount of water. One pitcher is used to fill one of the glasses (a tall, narrow glass); the other pitcher is used to fill the shorter, thicker glass. Do both glasses contain the same amount of water? Adults will say yes. Children around the age of five often say no and pick the glass where the water level is higher. But a few months later, that same child may begin to respond like an adult. What happened to cause this change?

Piaget's research findings led him to develop a "stage theory" that posited important qualitative shifts in development as children matured. The earliest stage involves sensorimotor development, followed by preoperational thinking, then concrete operational thinking when children are able to understand concepts like the conservation of matter, and finally, formal operational or abstract thought.

Piaget's stage theory has often been interpreted to assume that a person's current developmental level determines how he or she thinks about any subject matter. Newer studies show that people's knowledge of subject matter also affects the sophistication of their thinking; thus the same person may think abstractly about one area of knowledge and much more concretely about another. Overall, children's abilities to think and reason have been shown to *depend on the extent to which they are familiar with the content being reasoned about and have had a range of experiences upon which to draw* (Donaldson, 1978; Flavell, 1994; Siegler, 1998).

As an illustration, researchers have found that children as young as four can understand conservation if they can manipulate materials and discuss their reasoning with someone who already understands the concept (Field, 1987; Mayer, 1992). Older elementary-age students can learn to solve logical problems involving hypothetical ideas if they are taught the appropriate problem-solving strategies (S. Lee, 1985) and can separate and control variables if they are given instruction about how to do so (Metz, 1995). Conversely, adolescents and adults may think concretely about areas in which they are inexperienced (Byrnes, 1988; Kuhn, Garcia-Mila, Zohar, and Anderson, 1995; Pascarella and Terenzini,

1991) and yet be able to use higher-order thinking in areas where they have more knowledge (Girotto and Light, 1993; Schliemann and Carraher, 1993). De Lisi and Staudt (1980), for example, found that college students were more likely to show formal operational reasoning on tasks related to their majors but not on other tasks. Ormrod (2003) notes that, "Students may demonstrate formal operational thought in one content domain while thinking more concretely in another" (p. 33).

At a macro level, Piaget's general characterizations of development hold true. Generally, development follows a progression from egocentric thinking to thinking that takes account of multiple perspectives, from more reflexive behavior to more goal-directed activity, from reasoning based on rules to more contingent, multifaceted reasoning. Over time and with support, children develop abilities to generalize from and manipulate information, to act on their environment, and to learn from it in increasingly purposeful ways. However, as we have described, earlier beliefs about the details of what children could and could not do at various ages appear to have been overgeneralized. Given the chance to think about familiar content and experiences, preschool children can exhibit thinking that is not entirely egocentric, and they can reflect on their own thinking to at least some degree. Furthermore, formal operations do not appear to be solely the province of the adolescent years (Case, 1992; Feldman, 1980; Siegler and Richards, 1982). And the ability to use higher-order cognitive skills depends on the experiences children have had as well as their biological age or stage.

Studies of adolescents' abilities to engage in thinking that requires them to control variables in experiments provide an illustration of the interactions between knowledge and developmental "levels." In one study, thirteen-year-old students were shown a picture of four children fishing in four different ways (Pulos and Linn, 1981). Each child in the picture displays a different posture, a different manner of holding his fishing rod, and uses different types of bait, among other variables. Students were told, "These four children go fishing every week, and one child, Herb, always catches the most fish. The other children wonder why." Students who had experience fishing were better able to separate and control the multiple variables in this situation than those without fishing experience. Similarly, evidence of formal operations typically emerges in the physical sciences earlier than in such subjects as history and geography; students often have difficulty thinking about abstract and hypothetical ideas in history and geography until well into the high school years (Lovell, 1979; Tamburrini, 1982). These differences are likely related to the extent to which students have concrete experiences on which to build as well as to developmental maturation.

A major role of instruction is to build students' storehouse of experiences so that they can build their cognitive capacity. A skilled teacher understands that when she poses a task for students she should think about whether they have an experience base to draw upon in their thinking and reasoning. If some do not, she should be prepared to demonstrate, explain, or provide other opportunities for students to acquire the experiential knowledge they need in order to succeed. Many excellent teachers, like Jean Jahr in our earlier example, choose problems that come out of their children's experience, so that they can use what they know to picture the problem and think about solutions. Teaching strategies such as these have a great deal to do with whether and how higher-order thinking skills develop. Children need to have had many opportunities for exploration and practice that help them understand numerical concepts, physical phenomena, and the use of language, and they need to have been challenged with problems that encourage and support logical reasoning and contingent thinking (National Research Council, 2000; Kamii and Housman, 2000). When education that supports this kind of exploration is absent, many people do not develop these more sophisticated thinking abilities.

How Teaching Can Support Development

We have seen how students' abilities to think at different "developmental levels of sophistication" are affected by their prior knowledge of the topics being explored. It is also possible for teachers to organize knowledge so as to support developmental progress in thinking. The Russian teacher and psychologist Lev Vygotsky focused especially on ways that new instruction (rather than only previously existing knowledge) could actually encourage development. In one set of studies, Vygotsky and colleagues conducted experiments with students' storytelling. In general, students' ability to tell complex, well-structured stories improved with age. However, the studies found that story complexity also depended strongly on the nature of the knowledge that students were helped to *acquire* about the stories they were telling. For example, in one set of tasks, students were helped to organize a set of scientific concepts and then tell a story using these concepts. The stories they created were more coherent and complex than stories where they were asked to talk about a set of naturally occurring concepts that the children would have encountered outside of school but not necessarily been helped to organize in an optimal manner. Based on this study and others, Vygotsky conjectured that the adult structuring of a task could help people achieve at levels that were not possible without these supports. We noted in Chapter Two that the concept of the zone of proximal development (ZPD) provides important insights into the issue of "readiness" and its relationship to effective teaching. "The difference between what a child can do on her own and what she can do with some mentoring is the zone of proximal development" (Gage and Berliner, 1998, p. 112). Effective learning occurs when the distance between where the learner is developmentally (in terms of understanding and knowledge) and the understanding that is required for new learning is small enough to foster the new learning when assistance is provided, yet large enough to be challenging rather than boring. A teacher who teaches outside a student's

ZPD in a particular domain will provoke little new learning either because the lesson provides too little challenge or because it is so complex for the child that it is wholly out of reach.

Vygotsky argued that choosing tasks that meet children where they are—and appropriately stretching their performance—stimulates cognitive *development* as well as learning. "Tasks that children cannot do individually but that they can do with help from others invoke mental functions that are currently in the process of developing" (Berk and Winsler, 1995, p. 26). Vygotsky (1978) emphasized that cognitive development is supported through language, cultural symbols, and tools, as well as the nurturing of learning by teachers and caregivers. He encouraged teachers to assess where students are in a particular domain, what they understand, the experiences they have had, and to determine how, with assistance, students can be helped to advance to another level within their zone of proximal development. This assistance, when carefully offered to provide just enough support to allow steady progress in understanding, is often called "scaffolding." The analogy is to scaffolds that are erected around a building to allow workers, by working from these platforms, to reach heights and achieve goals that otherwise would be impossible or difficult to attain.

Working in the Zone of Proximal Development. A teacher who understands the zone of proximal development appreciates how to assess and support readiness for learning, how to use that readiness to challenge a child to learn, and, as a result, how to enable a child to make developmental progress. Recognizing a child's readiness to learn requires that the teacher understand the kinds of prior experiences a child has had with the ideas, concepts, or skills involved; these experiences and the child's current level of performance determine what kinds of learning opportunities the child will be most able to use and profit from next. Teachers need to be able to both watch a child for developmental signs of readiness and help the child become more ready for new accomplishments in each developmental pathway and domain. This is the full meaning of what it means to teach in a "developmentally appropriate" manner. It involves being cognizant of where students are in the process of their development and taking advantage of their readiness. It is also about teaching to enable developmental readiness, not just waiting for students to be ready.

The zone of proximal development has proved to be an intuitively attractive concept for helping teachers understand the proper sequencing of learning experiences and the appropriate distance to try to cover between where a child is and what it is reasonable to expect the child to learn next. The notion of ZPD helps teachers understand the size of the step a child can take in guided learning tasks to make developmental progress. For example, if a child knows how to add numbers, it is not too large a step to then teach subtraction, but it can be too large a step to go straight from knowledge of simple addition to trying to teach division. In addition to identifying the appropriate concept to teach next, teachers also need to provide just the right amount of assistance or scaffolding in the learning process, offering enough guidance to enable a student to see how he can reason through a problem without offering so much help that the student is not working on his own to try to solve the problem.

Accounting for Individual Differences in Readiness. Much of the knowledge incorporated in curriculum development and in the sequencing of tasks in the basic academic subjects, especially in the lower grades, has been developed to take into account the role of normal developmental progressions and of ZPD in effective instruction. The availability of standard and tried curricula materials that embody these principles can be very helpful to the novice teacher. However, not all curricula are as effectively organized for development as they should be. In addition, even well-developed teaching materials are no substitute for the individualized assessment a teacher must do in a classroom if she is to select appropriate curriculum materials and use them appropriately and effectively with individual children.

It is especially important to realize that the zone of proximal development can vary widely among a group of similarly aged and similarly skilled children. The size of a student's ZPD for a particular kind of learning—that is, the "bandwidth" of the strides a student can take from what he now knows about a domain to a new set of understandings—will vary depending on where the child is developmentally, as well as on what he has had the opportunity to learn previously and on the cognitive structures and schemas available to the child (Brown and Reeve, 1987). Individual differences, including emotional factors related to self-esteem and self-confidence, cognitive factors related to learning styles, and characteristics involving attention span, are only some of the individual differences that impact ZPD and need to be taken into account by the teacher determined to be effective with all the children in a class.

Adjusting Scaffolds to the Child. We noted that the term *scaffolding* is often used to describe support that can help people reach the upper bounds of their ZPDs. Scaffolding can be adjusted to the child in at least two ways: (1) by structuring tasks and learning environments so that demands are appropriately challenging, and (2) by adjusting the amount of adult intervention in response to the child's current needs and abilities (Berk and Winsler, 1995). Tasks may be structured in terms of the choices children are given, the guidelines provided, and the sequences into which problems may be segmented and defined. Adult intervention can be seen as a teacher circulates around the room, providing just-in-time assistance to individuals, or as she discovers a classwide misconception and leads a discussion to address the problem. An important goal of scaffolding is to foster self-regulation by gradually relinquishing control and assistance. This means giving children time to grapple with problems and intervening when the child cannot make progress. Learning and self-regulation are maximized when teachers ask open-ended questions that encourage children to participate in the problem-solving process in a meaningful way (Diaz, Neal, and Amaya-Williams, 1990; Roberts and Barnes, 1992; Gonzalez, 1994).

Examples of teachers' different sensitivities to children's zones of proximal development occurred at the beginning of this chapter where we began with two scenarios about teaching. The first scenario showed what happens when a teacher is not sensitive to the child's learning process and unaware of important scaffolds needed to support development—for example, assistance to understand how to evaluate time in conducting timed exercises. The second scenario provided an illustration of a teacher's sensitivity to multiple ZPDs among her students. When Jean Jahr encouraged her students to use help from one another and a variety of tools (drawing, manipulatives, calculators, graphic displays) to solve the mathematics problem they were working on, she used a strategy that allowed students at different zones of proximal development to gain access to the various kinds of assistance they needed to make sense of a new situation. When she asked students to share seven different solutions to the problem, explaining their reasoning, she further supported their cognitive development by allowing them to talk about their thinking, thus building conceptual understanding in both the presenters and the listeners. An additional example of a teacher's sensitivity to a student's ZPD was provided in Chapter Two (Becoming Aware of Different Learning Trajectories) when a teacher enthusiastically applauded the contributions of a student who had not before been confident enough to contribute in class, thus differentiating his feedback to support the student where he was in his development of this ability.

In Chapter Two we noted that teachers can also use children's experiences strategically in encouraging their further development. For example, if a student already knows a great deal about a particular topic because it is part of his home or community experience, this prior knowledge can be the basis of a writing assignment so that the development of writing skills can be fostered by the ready availability of "funds of knowledge" about the subject at hand (Moll and Greenberg, 1990). The teacher might help the student develop his thinking and ability to record details by asking questions about the topic that prompt the student to write an elaborated narrative. Thus experience and development in one area can be used strategically to foster development in another.

Teachers can also foster development by carefully watching students to see what they can do without assistance and then supplying strategic help to help them reach the next level of a skill—for example, seeing that a student has a grasp of basic linear measurement and then helping him learn to measure and calculate different object perimeters. For another student with a different zone of proximal development in this domain, the kind of assistance needed might be to learn basic measurement before moving on. Teachers can construct experiences for their students that fill in the necessary foundations for more abstract understanding. For example, when seventh graders express their confusion about why two-thirds, four-sixths, and eight-twelfths are all equivalent, a teacher might use concrete objects like sliced pizzas, pies, or linked beads to demonstrate how fractions with different denominators can be equal (Ormrod, 2003, p. 35).

Shaping Scaffolds to the Subject. By understanding the fundamental structures and key ideas of the disciplines *and* by understanding development, teachers can support learning more effectively. Bruner's (1960/1977) concept of a "spiral curriculum" is based on the idea that "any subject can be taught effectively in some intellectually honest form to any child at any stage of development" (p. 33). A fundamental concept can be taught at one age and then revisited in greater depth later. For example, even though most students are not generally ready to manipulate multiple variables until later childhood or early adolescence, a teacher can introduce some beginning concepts of algebra in the early grades using concrete objects rather than abstract representations of numbers like "x" and "y." Researchers have found that when teachers appropriately simplify the instructions and approach to a task, it can be completed by younger students (see, for example, Case, 1998; Siegler, 1998; Gelman, 1979) and that the success rate for students on a task can be related to the complexity of the instructions (Boden, 1980). Teachers can help students become ready to comprehend more complex ideas by providing a grounding that is appropriate to the students' level of developmental readiness.

There are many examples of how teachers can support the development of children's and adolescents' thinking. For example, analogies and models drawing on students' existing experience can be powerful vehicles for building bridges to complex concepts. Researcher and teacher Deborah Ball helps her students understand the concept of negative numbers by introducing a model of a building. Positive numbers are represented by the floors above ground; negative numbers are represented by the floors below ground. The model is used to introduce conventions of addition and subtraction involving integers and allows students to make observations such as "any number below zero plus that same number above zero equals zero" (Ball, 1993, p. 381 in National Research Council, 2000, p. 168). Ball asks her students to consider questions like, "How many ways are there for a person to get to the third floor?" Choosing effective ways of introducing and grappling with sophisticated concepts is part of what it means to teach in a developmentally appropriate manner.

Teachers can help students compose essays by providing writing prompts that work as scaffolds to support more sophisticated writing forms: "My main point is . . ." "An example of this would be . . ." "The reason I think so is because . . ." "I can tie this together by . . ." (Scardamalia and Bereiter, 1985; Ormrod, 2003).

By providing examples and guides for how to accomplish certain kinds of thinking and performance, teachers can support students in developing more sophisticated skills. Over time, these become internalized and students are able to regulate their own thinking about their work. Jean Jahr's classroom provided many such examples. (See "Using Scaffolds to Guide Student Work in Classrooms.")

Using Scaffolds to Guide Student Work in Classrooms

In Jean Jahr's room, children's work is displayed on walls, bulletin boards, and shelves, along with teacher-made charts listing information related to work that is underway. Near the book collections and writing materials, for example, three different charts pose guiding questions to help students meet the expected writing standards for content, mechanics, and personal goals as a writer.

The content standards ask:

- Does the beginning tell what my piece is about?
- Does the order in which I wrote it make sense?
- Did I use examples and details to create a picture in the reader's mind?
- Does my story make sense?

The chart on standards for mechanics asks:

- Have I checked for correct spelling?
- Have I used upper- and lowercase letters in the right places?

The chart on Being a Writer in a Community of Writers asks:

- Am I willing to share my writing?
- Do I listen to others, share, and give helpful feedback?
- Am I willing to revise my work?
- Can I say why I selected this piece for publication and what do I like best about it?

These reminders provide models of social interaction as well as guidance for learning and performance. It is clear in watching Jane at work that she cares equally about the quality of her students' work and about the quality of their experience as learners in a developmentally supportive classroom.

Capitalizing on Students' Developmental Interests. Teachers can also tap into students' developmental interests as a way of enhancing motivation in school tasks. For example, because children between the ages of about eight and twelve like to simulate things that adults do, such as playing at being firefighters, doctors, and so on, teachers can organize aspects of the curriculum around these interests and use them as a springboard for areas of skill development. In adolescence, students are particularly interested in both philosophical issues and issues of social justice. These interests and budding abilities can be tapped in the classroom. For example, in social studies, students can engage in structured debates that take advantage of their need to sort out and argue their opinions and can push them to learn systematic ways of assembling and organizing evidence and make a logical argument.

The following example ("Using Knowledge of Adolescent Development in Teaching History") shows how high school teacher Elizabeth Jensen prepares her students to understand the debates between the Federalists and the anti-Federalists. Because she understands adolescent development, she knows that she can build on their interests in trying on and debating ideas. She also knows that her students are unlikely to understand these debates unless she creates experiences that will allow them first to struggle with their philosophical underpinnings, so she plans her teaching to accomplish this.

Using Knowledge of Adolescent Development in Teaching History

[Elizabeth Jensen] knows that her 15- and 16-year-olds cannot begin to grasp the complexities of the federalist debates without first understanding that these disagreements were rooted in fundamentally different conceptions of human nature—a point glossed over in two paragraphs in the history textbook. Rather than beginning the year with a unit on European discovery and exploration, as her text dictates, she begins with a conference on the nature of man. Students in her eleventh-grade history class read excerpts from the writings of philosophers (Hume, Locke, Plato, and Aristotle), leaders of state and revolutionaries (Jefferson, Lenin, Gandhi), and tyrants (Hitler, Mussolini), presenting and advocating these views before their classmates. Six weeks later, when it is time to study the ratification of the Constitution, these now familiar figures—Plato, Aristotle, and others—are reconvened to be courted by impassioned groups of Federalists and anti-Federalists. It is Elizabeth Jensen's understanding of what she wants to teach and what adolescents already know that allows her to craft an activity that helps students get a feel for the domain that awaits them: decisions about rebellion, the Constitution, federalism, slavery, and the nature of government.

Source: Wineberg and Wilson (1991). Adapted from National Research Council, 2000. *How people learn: Brain, mind, experience, and school*, p. 163.

These developmental strategies require different approaches to teacher education. For example, researchers have found that teachers had to learn to think in a different way during text discussions in order to engage in responsive questioning techniques, using questions designed to help their students make connections and see relationships. Rather than simply deciding whether a response was right or wrong, teachers had to reflect on the meaning of what the child said and consider how to provide assistance when a child didn't understand or was having trouble making a connection (Gallimore, Dalton, and Tharp, 1986). This responsiveness to children's thinking is developed through close observation and a knowledge of teaching strategies for provoking more sophisticated thinking.

Understanding and Expanding "Readiness"

Research focused on issues raised by Piaget and Vygotsky has provided greater insight about the issues of readiness. Within some parameters, readiness can be encouraged, but stages of learning and growth necessary to consolidate understanding should not be skipped. For example, research has found that children who work with manipulatives and concrete objects to develop number sense and an understanding of scientific principles make stronger gains in advanced understanding than those who are asked to memorize information or learn algorithms without a solid grounding in concrete operations (Kamii and Housman, 2000).

Similarly, the value of play, which offers concrete learning opportunities in early childhood, has been confirmed in large-scale longitudinal studies as supporting academic achievement as well as social and emotional growth. One study compared fifty traditional-play kindergartens with fifty newly formed, academic kindergartens in the province of North Rhein-Westphalia in Germany. Teams of researchers from two different universities found that at the age of ten, children from the play kindergarten programs significantly outperformed those in the early-learning programs. Children who had attended play kindergartens were not only better adjusted socially and emotionally in school but were also more cognitively advanced in reading, mathematics, and other subjects tested, as well as excelling in creativity and intelligence, "industry," and "oral expression." In play or experience-based learning environments, students are busy with active, hands-on exploration, discovery, and social interaction—including the discussion and testing of ideas that build a foundation for later learning (Ewart and Brawn, 1978; Tietz, 1987; Winkelman, Hollaender, Schmerkotte, and Schmalohr, 1979).

Supporting Social and Emotional Development. An understanding of "readiness" and how it can be expanded is also important for social, emotional, and moral development. With appropriate social guidance, children can to begin to adopt another's perspective and consider intentions. With modeling, explicit teaching, and opportunities to explore the consequences of different behaviors and social systems, they become more able to cooperate with others and understand concepts like fairness and reciprocity. Teachers need to understand that *these abilities are learned* and must often be explicitly taught rather than assumed. For example, when children's behavior differs from classroom norms or expectations, it is important for teachers to explain and model the desired behavior rather than merely punishing students without explanation. This social teaching, far from deflecting from classroom goals, will translate into greater academic success as children are more able to work together and learn from each other (Comer, Haynes, Joyner, and Ben-Avie, 1996). Many children also need to be taught how to express their feelings and concerns, recognize others' views and feelings, and handle frustrations productively. These abilities support their ability to persevere in the face of difficulties and solve problems as they arise without losing control or giving up.

Supporting Identity Development. Children also develop a sense of self, including the kind of person they think they are and want to be, and a sense of identity, which determines not only how they feel about themselves but also what they see as salient to their lives and worthy of their effort. The self-concepts children develop in a number of domains (for example, academic, social and interpersonal, physical, and so on) guide their investments of time and effort (Harter, 1988). Students who have positive views of themselves and their capabilities are more likely to succeed academically, socially, and physically (Assor and Connell, 1992; Ma and Kishor, 1997; Pintrich and Garcia, 1994; Yu, Elder, and Urdan, 1995). Those who see themselves as "good students" and who see intelligence as something that can be developed (rather than something that is innate and unchangeable) are more likely to focus on the task at hand, try a range of learning strategies, and persevere when frustrated by challenging problems.

Teachers, parents, and other community members contribute to students' self-esteem and perceptions of their own abilities (Harter, 1988, 1996; Hartup, 1989; Ryan and Lynch, 1989). When adults communicate high expectations, encourage students as they pursue challenging activities, praise specific accomplishments, and create a climate of helpful feedback, students demonstrate more confidence in what they can achieve (Eccles and others, 1989; Eccles (Parsons), 1983; Marsh, 1990; Harris and Rosenthal, 1985). When teachers convey a genuine respect for their students and treat their problems, interests, opinions, and views as important, they are helping their students see themselves as valuable contributors to school and society (Katz, 1993). We saw how this looks in practice in our earlier example, when Jean Jahr vocally encouraged all of her students, asked them to share their solutions publicly, affirming that their ideas were important, sought to understand a puzzling solution so that she could explain it to the class, and gave a student credit for having posed the problem in the first place. She encouraged students to work together to give each other helpful feedback. As a consequence, her students clearly saw themselves as helpful contributors to the classroom and as confident learners of mathematics. Like Jean, teachers need to understand how social messages and their own behaviors can influence the development of a positive sense of identity and an academic self-concept that will support ongoing effort in school.

Teachers of adolescents should be aware of the ways in which self-concepts become more differentiated across domains (for example, scholastic competence versus romantic appeal) (Harter, 1998), and they should be aware of the critical changes in self-esteem that can occur at the onset of puberty, especially for girls (Simmons and Blyth, 1987). Teachers can help their students maintain positive self-images by identifying the strengths of individual students, demonstrating different pathways to success, and recognizing classwide progress (Rosenholtz and Simpson, 1984). Research on efforts designed to support adolescents' psychological development and connections with school have found positive outcomes when programs involve systematic reflection on experiences—for example, discussing biographies or keeping writing journals.

Students also have positive experiences when they have opportunities to take on responsible, real-life roles like peer teaching, peer counseling, or volunteering in the community (Sprinthall, 1989). Most critical is the development of earned self-esteem through the support of growing competence (Chapman, Tunmer, and Prochnow, 2000; Lerner, 1996).

Development of strong, positive, racial and cultural identities has been found to contribute to positive school outcomes for students from racial/ethnic minority groups (Spencer and Markstrom-Adams, 1990), enabling students to maintain a healthy sense of self, to focus on positive achievements, and to demonstrate resilience in hostile environments. Without this kind of strong identity, grounded in positive racial socialization as well as opportunities for trust, many children of color who experience racial stigmatization develop a "reactive racial identity"—an identity in opposition to school in order to protect themselves from rejection or negative messages about their identity or their group (Spencer, Dobbs, and Swanson, 1988).

Developmentally aware teachers encourage strong identity development by providing opportunities for all students equally. They are sensitive to the social messages and expectations students receive from the media and the society, and they affirm students' sense of themselves and help them find and develop areas of competence. They give students increasing opportunities to make decisions and to act responsibly within the school and the community.

When children receive appropriate support and guidance along each of the developmental pathways, they learn to use their growing cognitive capabilities to undertake increasingly complex tasks and to reason through things with growing independence. They become more socially aware and adept. They learn how to recognize and manage their emotions. They recognize their strengths and interests as pathways to learning and healthy identity development. And they develop a growing capacity to think and act ethically and in concert with others.

CULTURAL CONTEXTS AND DEVELOPMENT

Researchers have come to understand that human development is strongly social rather than something that occurs on a preset biological timetable and that development is a function of each person's cultural context. In fewer and fewer classrooms in the United States does the teacher encounter a racially, ethnically, and linguistically homogenous group of children. In many instances the teacher will come from a different cultural background than many or most of the children in the class. The novice teacher needs to be well prepared to work in a culturally heterogeneous environment and to understand the relevance of diverse cultural backgrounds to development issues. In addition, she needs to understand how her own culturally based perspectives influence her perceptions and expectations.

Learning in Diverse Cultural Contexts

Culture includes the many social contexts we inhabit simultaneously: family history, community, geographical location, designations of race and ethnicity, language, strong interest affiliations, religion, gender, and sexual orientation. Each of these individually and in combination can shape behaviors, expectations of social interaction, and social or individual views of what is possible for oneself and others to engage in or achieve. Culture is not just a backdrop to learning, but, as Rogoff (2003) argues, development *is* the process of learning the tools and tasks of a particular culture. In other words, the goals of development are culturally determined. Thus teachers must not only be aware of differences, but also be aware of what is important to learn and how that learning takes place in different cultures. Rogoff observes that "learning is a process of changing participation in community activities" (p. 284). These activities include those that occur both in the classroom and in the home and community. When the teacher's culturally based perspective is very different from those of the children in her classroom, she must do a great deal of learning about the cultural contexts the children bring with them into the classroom.

What is valued or emphasized developmentally in one cultural context may be different from what is valued or emphasized in another. The styles of collaboration of adults (experts) and children (novices) may also vary with respect to how linguistic, cognitive, emotional, physical, and social development are fostered. Different styles of social and emotional communication can lead to misunderstandings unless a teacher is sensitive to the range of approaches to communication. For example, in some groups children are taught to speak freely to adults; in others, children are taught to show respect by not talking. In some contexts, questioning is encouraged as a form of discourse; in others, it is not. Language differences and the complex nuances of the use of language in different cultural contexts can pose challenges for effective teaching. (See "Talking in Class: A Case of Cultural Difference.")

Talking in Class: A Case of Cultural Difference

A speech-language pathologist working in an Inuit school in northern Canada asked a principal—who was not an Inuit—to compile a list of children who had speech and language problems in the school. The list contained a third of the students in the school, and next to several names the principal wrote, "Does not talk in class." The speech-language pathologist consulted a local Inuit teacher for help determining how each child functioned in his or her native language. The teacher looked at the principal's notes and said, "Well-raised Inuit children should not talk in class. They should be learning by looking and listening."

When the speech-language pathologist asked that teacher about one toddler she was studying who was very talkative and seemed to the non-Inuit researcher to be very bright, the teacher said: "Do you think he might have a learning problem? Some of these children who don't have such high intelligence have trouble stopping themselves. They don't know when to stop talking." (Crago, 1988, p. 219. Adapted from National Research Council, 2000, p. 146.)

Examples of cultural misunderstandings abound. Nieto (2000) observes that many Puerto Rican children signify nonverbally when they do not understand something by wrinkling their noses. When her students do not respond verbally to her question, "Do you understand?" a new teacher may wrongly assume that they understand. Similarly, Shirley Brice Heath discovered that African American children in a Southern community she studied did not answer obvious, factual questions to which they assumed the teacher knew the answer. This kind of questioning—"What color is the dish?" "How many fingers do I have?"— common in many white, middle-class homes, was not part of their experience where questions were used only when the asker genuinely did not know the answer. The result was that they did not answer such obvious questions, and teachers assumed they were less able learners (Heath, 1983).

When students experience a dramatically different set of norms and expectations at home and at school, this can create boundaries that are difficult to cross unless the teacher facilitates connections within and beyond the classroom. The teacher's knowledge of how to make students feel confident in the classroom and how to help them understand and respect the norms that operate there will matter greatly to her ability to support student learning. Similarly, her ability to create culturally responsive learning experiences, including choices of content, representations, and forms of discourse that connect to student experiences, will help her create bridges for students into academic material. Research provides many examples of culturally specific practices that have been found to make a positive difference for student achievement. For example, Katherine Au found that when teachers incorporated communication patterns that resemble how Hawaiian families tell stories at home and incorporated students' home experiences as part of the discussion of reading materials, they were able to significantly raise the reading achievement levels of their native Hawaiian students (Au, 1980). Teacher and researcher Carol Lee demonstrated substantial learning gains when she drew on and incorporated the linguistic styles and strengths her African American students brought to the classroom (for example, irony, double entendre, satire, and metaphorical language) (C. Lee, 1995). By making students' tacit knowledge explicit, she helped them to make connections between their own language and the literature they were analyzing.

Researchers have noted that the teacher's own cultural background and experiences can influence the developmental and behavioral expectations the teacher has for children in a classroom, ranging from how she asks questions and expects them to be answered to how she structures learning tasks. Few Americans escape the pernicious effects of the pervasiveness of the subtle racism and sexism in our society that, in turn, influence the developmental goals teachers set for the children. Lower developmental expectations for children of color are too often the norm and become self-fulfilling prophecies, with negative consequences for the development of children. Teachers may treat students differently in the classroom unless they are aware of the assumptions they are making. For instance, researchers have found that teachers often have lower expectations, make less eye contact, and criticize children of color more frequently than white children (Brophy and Good, 1974; Wang and Lindvall, 1984). Similarly, lower expectations for female students and subtle, negative messages about their achievement can lead to fear of success (Hansen, 1977). Teacher education needs to enable teachers to examine these assumptions and develop countervailing practices that enable all students to develop in an environment of respect and encouragement.

SCHOOL AS A CULTURAL CONTEXT

It is important, too, for teachers to realize that schools have cultures, which can themselves be developmentally healthy or unhealthy, and that a teacher's work in the classroom can be much more effective if it represents shared values and norms throughout an entire school. As James Comer has demonstrated in his School Development Program, "a nurturing, challenging, and supportive school environment provides the nourishment that children need to be healthy, whole, and successful" (Comer, Haynes, Joyner, and Ben-Avie, 1996, p. xvii). This program, which helps educators learn how to embed principles of child development in every aspect of their work and to engage parents and communities as partners in education, has sharply improved student achievement in previously failing urban schools. Treating the school as an ecological system, Comer notes that the behaviors and attitudes of all of the adults in the school, ranging from the teachers and administrators to aides, counselors, cafeteria staff, and parents, create a powerful context shaping the behaviors, attitudes, and achievement of students. These behaviors include not only those directed toward the child in the classroom but between and among all the members of the community throughout the school:

> The child learns from the interactions that occur in the school setting, including interactions among the adults in the building and the connections between home and school. For example, the treatment of their parents by the school staff, of course, has an impact on how the students perceive the school and education in general. The children's learning process involves the environment in toto, including both the intentional, purposeful interactions and the offhand, seemingly inconsequential remark or gesture. Children learn by observing how their peers are disciplined, by overhearing how the adults in the building interact with one another, through contact with written and other cultural products, and especially, through significant adults who take an interest in them. (Haynes and others, 1996, pp. 44–45)

Changing interactions in this system is essential to changing the outcomes for students. If all of the adults work together to create norms of support and expectation, to model and teach students a consistent set of respectful, responsible behaviors, to support positive self-identities, and to support children's development along all of the developmental pathways, the climate in the school becomes a powerful support for children's development and learning. As Anson and colleagues (1991) note: "The greater the number and heterogeneity of adults endorsing mutual values, goals, and expectancies for a child, the more likely it is that the child will internalize these same goals as part of his or her own sense of identity" (p. 74).

Rather than looking only to the student to adapt to the environment, those who use an ecosystemic framework look also at the environment to see what needs to be modified to support healthy development. In research in middle schools, Eccles and colleagues (1993) have noted that many of the problems noted for early adolescents are actually the result of a "stage-environment" misfit—that is, the design of many junior high and high schools is out of sync with the developmental needs of students. When they most need intellectual challenge, opportunities to express opinions and participate in decisions, caring relationships, and affirmation in developing competence and identity, many adolescents are placed in large, impersonal, departmentalized structures where rules are more rigid, their participation is less sought, schoolwork is less engaging, they are less connected to adults, and their sense of identity is under attack. More personalized settings that allow more participation and responsibility-taking create greater achievement and greater affiliation with adults and with the academic enterprise.

In many cases, teachers will not find that the schools in which they teach are designed to be supportive of students and their healthy development. In these cases, they will need to understand what the features of a healthy environment are and how to work collaboratively with colleagues to develop changes that will allow their work with students to be successful.

In sum, effective teachers need to have a good grounding in normal development, an appreciation of the variations within normal development and the meaning of normal development within different cultural contexts, and the ability to employ the concept of the zone of proximal development for instructional purposes. Preparing an individual to be an effective teacher requires ensuring that the teacher develops her capacity to evaluate her own assumptions and behaviors, has tools to learn about the cultural backgrounds and experiences of the children in the classroom, and develops equitable and culturally responsive practices. We discuss some of these practices further in Chapter Seven, in the section on "Teaching Diverse Learners." Preparing the teacher to be a contributing member to a supportive school also means helping him or her understand how children's and adolescents' development is shaped by the overall environment, and how this environment must be consciously shaped by the efforts of all of the members of the school community.

Preparing Novice Teachers to Create Developmentally Appropriate Classrooms and Schools

A solid grounding in development is essential for good teaching. It helps a teacher create settings that allow students to learn how to behave and interact socially, manage their emotions productively, and engage purposefully in individual and group learning opportunities that foster cognitive progress. Developmental knowledge is also essential for helping a teacher select and construct tasks that take into account a student's attention span and developmental readiness, and to individualize instruction when necessary. Developmental knowledge is essential for enabling the teacher to assess and understand how children think and their readiness for particular kinds of learning activities. Developmentally responsive teachers provide strategic guidance and assistance within students' zones of proximal development, accommodating individual differences and moving all children toward greater competence. Finally, developmental knowledge and an appreciation of cultural contexts are essential to enable a teacher to work cooperatively with families and connect the child's home experiences to the curriculum.

In many respects, developmental knowledge is to a teacher what organic knowledge of anatomy and physiology is to a physician. It provides the underlying understanding of how children work—how they think, behave, grow, and learn—which allows the teacher to develop diagnostic abilities that guide what she looks for and how she interprets children's behavior as she plans for both the group and for individuals.

Research on a set of extraordinarily successful teacher education programs has noted that many of them have particularly strong coursework on child and adolescent development tightly linked to clinical work that fosters child observation and analysis of learning within school and out-of-school environments (Darling-Hammond, 2000b; Darling-Hammond and Macdonald, 2000; Miller and Silvernail, 2000; Snyder, 2000; Zeichner, 2000). Interestingly, these programs share very similar approaches—some of them growing out of the early child studies of pioneers like Maria Montessori, Jean Piaget, John Dewey, and Lucy Sprague Mitchell—that have become increasingly widespread in other programs. These approaches emphasize systematic observation of children and their development, child case studies, and analyses of student work and learning, using assessment tools and tasks to help gauge development and learning. Some also include family and community studies or family interviews that help novice teachers understand their students' developmental contexts.

These opportunities are generally embedded in courses about human development across the life span so as to enable a general understanding of issues related to the life course, developmental pathways and developmental trajectories. Beyond these general introductory courses, there is a strong focus on specific study of child and adolescent development, focused examination of cultural diversity and its relationship to effective teaching, and opportunities for classroom observations at several grade levels. Finally, in most of these programs, novice teachers have as background experience several opportunities for apprentice teaching or practicum experiences at multiple grade levels.

Curriculum Examples

One of these highly rated programs is Bank Street College in New York City, where Jean Jahr, the accomplished first-year teacher we visited at the start of this chapter, prepared to teach. Several studies have found that teachers rate their preparation at Bank Street extraordinarily highly, as do principals who employ these teachers (Darling-Hammond and Macdonald, 2000; Darling-Hammond, Chung, and Frelow, 2002), and the graduates are widely known to be successful urban teachers. Teachers and employers attribute these strengths to a deep understanding of and respect for children fostered in the teacher education program, an ability to diagnose students' strengths and readiness as well as their needs, and strong understanding of how to build curriculum that will foster learning from different starting points and take into account children's cultural contexts.

Jean attributed much of her skillful practice to a three-course sequence on child development at Bank Street College and to the developmental perspectives infused in most courses, including courses on content pedagogy in mathematics, literacy, science, social studies, and the arts. The three development courses include *Child Development* (one course for teachers of young children and another for teachers of older children and adolescents), *The Study of Children through Observation and Recording,* and *Family, Child, and Teacher Interaction.* In conjunction, these courses focus on children, how they grow and learn and the influences of societal factors in their development, as well as how teachers can use knowledge of students' strengths and needs to make decisions about curriculum, instruction, and assessment—and to communicate with families about their children's home and school lives. All of these courses explicitly address concerns for diversity in learning and cultures, including exceptionalities generally treated only in special education courses elsewhere. Jean noted in an interview: "Child Development was helpful (to my practice) because we read Piaget and started thinking about what is appropriate for a child and what isn't. What can you reasonably expect at different ages. And that is really the issue in teaching a combined second and third grade classroom . . . O and R [Observation and Recording] was very helpful in terms of a stance toward children. There was a huge amount of work, but it was worth it. One of the best things you can do is watch a child closely and try to understand why they're doing what they're doing" (Darling-Hammond and Macdonald, 2000, pp. 41, 44).

These understandings are reinforced with extensive clinical experiences in the Bank Street School for Children, an on-site PK–8 school where student teachers are found in virtually every classroom, and other partnering schools that model developmentally appropriate practice. Like other new Bank Street teachers, Jean attributes her ability to evaluate individual students' learning and support their progress to the consistency of her experience in courses, advisement, and field experiences at Bank Street. For example, the strategies Jean used with her students on a complex math problem were demonstrated in her preservice course on Math for Teachers, in which teachers would often begin a class by working in small groups solving the same problem and then demonstrating to one another the different ways they solved the problem. After groups present their solutions, the class discusses the different skills used in solving the problem and how they would teach students those skills.

The University of California at Berkeley's Developmental Teacher Education (DTE) program is another of the programs identified as exemplary in the same study (Snyder, 2000). DTE provides a four-seminar human development sequence that uses clinical methods for assessing levels of cognitive development and samples of children's spoken and written language for assessing their language development. Each seminar is connected to teaching methods courses and to one of the several student teaching placements through overlapping assignments and experiences. Issues of culture, context, and diversity are raised throughout these courses. As in a number of other programs with a strong developmental focus, two particularly powerful pedagogies shape student teachers' developmental learning: the use of systematic observation of children and the use of child cases.

Systematic Observation of Children

Child observation is widely used to help teacher candidates learn how to examine and assess child development and learning with enough care and detail to guide instruction. Students are guided in observing specific features of children's development and behavior that they will need to understand to guide their teaching through careful recording linked to specific developmental concepts and readings. Sometimes, these observations are linked to specific tasks (for example, Piagetian tasks assessing cognitive development) that the student teacher gives to students to observe their responses, with the goal of learning to observe where children are in their thinking in different domains. Sometimes the prospective teacher conducts interviews of students or collects work samples (written work or oral language samples) to gauge their learning about particular concepts or their reasoning about particular tasks. Observing and sampling across different domains of knowledge helps the prospective teacher to understand that one cannot find a "general stage of development" across domains or subject matter.

These experiences help prospective teachers begin to think about how to identify the zone of proximal development for students on different kinds of tasks as a guide to their later teaching. At Bank Street College, one of the early developers of the observational approach, the Observation and Recording course, popularly known as "O and R," is identified by students, graduates, and faculty as a critical means for prospective teachers to learn how to look closely at children. The course outline describes how the course is designed to sharpen the teacher's skills for seeking evidence while also allowing examination of the student teacher's own cultural and personal assumptions about children, so that the teacher can eventually observe and understand children more clearly and accurately:

> Almost everyone "observes" children informally, but what we "see" and remember is influenced by what we are looking for, what we expect to see and what we think about the nature and capabilities of children. Our observations of children are also influenced by our own values and feelings. In this course we will work toward sharpening awareness of our own cultural and personal assumptions when observing children. In this process we will work to develop greater sensitivity to ourselves as observers, to the language we use, and to the data we are choosing to attend to. The aim is to develop a personal style of observing and recording that is precise, vivid and non-judgmental, one that will serve us well in our work with children and families. Class time will be used to present, discuss and practice observational techniques. At times we will use films and videotapes in class in order to have common experiences for observation and discussion. (TE-502, Fall 1995; Darling-Hammond and Macdonald, 2000, p. 43)

Prospective teachers can study how students respond to particular learning tasks in order to figure out how to teach within the zone of proximal development. For example, an early assignment for candidates in the Developmental Teacher Education program at UC Berkeley asks:

> Select two learning tasks from the curriculum in your classroom which your students will understand at different levels. Administer interviews based on these two tasks to three children in order to investigate the different levels at which tasks might be understood using Piaget's method and his theory of development as a basis for interpretation. The focus in this assignment is on assessing the difficulty of the tasks in terms of the level of operational reasoning required for mastery. Write a report including a clear description of the tasks, a summary of the interview procedures and each child's responses, conclusions about each child's level of understanding, and about the level of reasoning required for mastery (Snyder, 2000, p. 113).

A similar approach is used at Wheelock College, yet another of the programs identified as extraordinarily successful in preparing urban elementary teachers (Miller and Silvernail, 2000). Keen observation is encouraged through guiding questions, and understanding in light of the literature on development is sought through specific readings that are provided as lenses for interpretation. In one observation assignment, for example, after reading about different theories of physical and cognitive growth in young children and examining findings about motor development, students are asked to observe and record at least two behavioral events of a child and analyze the events as follows:

> The goal of your analysis is to construct an understanding of your focus child's physical abilities. As you analyze your focus child's behavior, think about what you have learned about theory and research on physical development. In analyzing the behavioral event records, use the information about theory and research on physical development discussed by Cole and Cole (1993, Chapters Five and Six), and by Post, Williams, Witt, and Atwood (1990), as well as other course materials. Here are some questions to ask yourself as you begin your analysis:
>
> - What do the child's locomotion and large muscle coordination show you about her or his perceptual-motor development? What does the child's behavior and vocalizations reveal about her or his awareness of body, time, space, and direction, and visual and auditory cues? How does the child's level of large muscle control influence her or his interaction with objects and with other people? (See Cole and Cole, 1993, pp. 183–184, 213; Poest and others, 1990.)
> - What do the child's fine hand movements and small muscle coordination show you about her or his perceptual-motor development?
> - Does the child seem to be developing "normally" in the physical domain compared with other children of the same age and gender? If so, how do the child's physical abilities differ from what would be expected of a younger child, and of an older child? (Miller and Silvernail, 2000, pp. 80–81)

These kinds of courses and assignments help teachers develop the close observational skills and the ability to interpret developmental data they will need to construct tasks that meet children where they are and move them along the developmental pathways toward greater competence.

The Child Case Study

Another common approach is the development of child case studies in which the teacher candidate functions as a researcher. The case study is used to help teachers learn to apply knowledge of development, learning, motivation, and behavior to specific children as they function in their family, school, and community contexts. Many teacher education programs engage their students in conducting child and adolescent case studies to help them link theories of learning and development to observations of actual children. The goal of such case studies is to examine student learning and development with an eye toward identifying strengths, developmental progress, important influences, and needs. Collecting and analyzing data for the case study—from observations, interviews, records, and analyses of student work—helps teachers develop their skills of observation and documentation and their ability to analyze how children learn and how specific children can be supported in the process of development.

At Bank Street, the main assignment for the Observation and Recording course is an Individual Child Study for the purpose of "developing an increased awareness of the child's uniqueness, the relation of specific behavior to overall functioning, and the implications for learning" (Darling-Hammond and Macdonald, 2000, p. 43). This document is developed over several months from a number of different assignments, including short, weekly written observations of the child at school; a paper that examines the child in the context of his peers or group; an age-level study designed to see the child in light of developmental theory; and observations and interpretations of the child as a learner and member of a learning community.

Instructors review weekly observation and provide feedback designed to encourage the careful use of evidence and to suggest developmental theories and interpretations that will help the teacher make sense of what she is seeing. Specific data collection tools include a variety of techniques the teacher should be able to use in her own practice, such as a running record of a child's oral reading; observations of the child's use of language in different contexts; a collection of the student's work; recordings of children's responses to on-demand performance of specific tasks; and observations of children at play or in unstructured interaction with other children. The requirements ask that student teachers review all documentation, triangulate evidence to support their assumptions, make recommendations for teaching or further study, and use theoretical understandings to back up their recommendations.

In this kind of case, the narrative explicates with detailed examples a young person's thinking, learning, interactions, beliefs, concerns, and aspirations. In some instances, child case studies can be the basis for evaluating how better to work with a child who is having difficulty. Like some medical cases, written versions of such studies codify what is done by teachers when they evaluate a student using multiple tools of evidence, develop approaches to meet the child's needs, and examine the outcomes.

A vivid example of this kind of analytic child case study is provided in the account of Akeem, a third-grade student who entered Susan Gordon's classroom in a New York City elementary school after having been expelled for throwing a desk at a teacher in another school (Darling-Hammond, Ancess, and Falk, 1995, pp. 217–224). The case begins by describing Akeem's frequent outbursts, his efforts to disrupt classroom meetings, and his periodically surly and aggressive behavior. It continues by describing Gordon's efforts to document, using many tools of observation and assessment, exactly when these outbursts occurred, and her discovery that Akeem's misbehavior tended to occur when certain kinds of academic tasks arose, especially those requiring reading or writing. The case provides a detailed description of Susan's efforts, with her colleagues, to discover what Akeem could do well, to provide opportunities for him to build upon his strengths, and to develop strategies for addressing his specific literacy needs.

Like physicians who use a variety of tests to figure out the source of a problem and their knowledge of physiology and the etiology of disease to develop treatment strategies, Susan Gordon and her colleagues used their understanding of development and a range of assessment tools to evaluate Akeem's difficulties and strengths and to develop an approach that could address the former while building on the latter. From her knowledge of development, Susan suspected that Akeem's outbursts were an expression of a more fundamental discomfort. She closely observed what Akeem did when he had choices available to ascertain what his interests and abilities were, and she conducted a number of assessments of his reading abilities—miscue analyses, comprehension exercises, and analyses of his reading strategies—to figure out what he did and did not know how to do and how he approached the task of reading. As she understood what was impacting Akeem's performance, she allowed him to work in hands-on learning centers that tapped his artistic skills and his abilities to construct machines and models. She found him books and developed writing assignments that built on these interests, while systematically teaching him new strategies for reading. As the case unfolds, Akeem develops architectural drawings and creates sophisticated comics that he later annotates and turns into books; he is recognized by peers for his artistic and mechanical abilities and begins to gain status in the classroom; he joins classroom activities with increasing enthusiasm and less disruption; and, importantly, with specific coaching from an increasingly well-informed teacher, he learns to read and write. The case follows Akeem until he finishes middle school with a solid academic record, near perfect attendance, and admission into a specialized high school for the arts.

This kind of case, which illustrates expert practice that is developmentally informed, provides novices with an illustration of how to collect evidence about students' learning and behavior in light of broader professional knowledge; how to diagnose learning needs; and how to build a set of teaching strategies that addresses these needs. When novices construct their own case studies of children, they engage in similar kinds of diagnostic thinking and in an integration of information from many perspectives: cognitive, social, emotional, and physical. Such case analyses are most powerful when they are directly tied to formal study of development, so that students have a basis for understanding what they see. The case construction process enables novices to learn how to apply theoretical knowledge to concrete examples, and the completed case provides a basis for evaluating their ability to do so.

The School Development Process

All of the programs we have discussed here treat teaching as a collaborative activity and use a variety of strategies to help prospective teachers learn to plan and problem solve with their colleagues. This includes assignments that require novices to work together in planning and implementing curriculum and lessons and evaluating each others' practice. It also includes placing student teachers in schools where faculty work together and where they can see how professionals solve problems and pursue changes in schools that operate collaboratively. This preparation enables new teachers to see themselves as members of a broader school community and to develop skills for participating in creating a school culture that is supportive to children. In the best cases, novices are prepared in schools that have developed a strong developmental focus, and they are asked to examine aspects of the schoolwide approach, so that they can see how such a focus operates throughout the school and what good practice looks like beyond the individual classroom. Finally, in these and other programs, novice teachers are given opportunities to consider the processes of school change and reform, and to participate in both university-based and school-based deliberations about changes needed to create supportive environments for children. In this way, they develop a sense of the professional role as they become teachers who help to shape the environment of the school as well as their individual classroom.

CONCLUSION

The core purpose of formal education is to enable the development of *all* children to take their place in adult society with the competencies to be positively contributing members to the society. Nothing less is at stake when a teacher is given the responsibility for helping students make developmental progress. We emphasize preparing novice teachers with a well-grounded developmental perspective in service of this goal. Such teachers should be able to choose learning experiences, materials, and instructional strategies that are used strategically to meet students where they are within their zones of proximal development so as to move all children toward greater competence and help them develop strong identities as learners. To develop appropriate tasks and support students' progress along the developmental pathways, teachers must become keen observers of children, be able to analyze students' learning in the context of development, and be able to translate what they note into curriculum, instructional strategies, and classroom management approaches. In both elementary and secondary classrooms, the more developmentally prepared teachers are, the higher the probability that each child will learn and grow successfully.

CHAPTER FOUR

Enhancing the Development of Students' Language(s)

Guadalupe Valdés, George Bunch, Catherine Snow, and Carol Lee,
with Lucy Matos

There are different ways of looking at, and seeing, the children we teach. One prevalent perspective is to view schoolchildren as bundles of deficiencies, lacks, and problems. We are typically advised to begin each new school year by diagnosing problems in our students and then providing experiences designed to eradicate those problems. Diagnose, prescribe, and treat are medical terms which suggest that we view the child as an unhealthy, poorly functioning organism. But in the area of language, the child is an extraordinarily healthy organism who will continue to flourish in the rich environment we can provide. We are not trying to rid the child of language "problems," but rather to enhance her remarkable continuing language development.
—Lindfors, 1987, p. 25

THE MANY USES OF LANGUAGE

All teachers, regardless of the language backgrounds of their students, are directly and intimately involved with language. No matter what subjects they teach, and whether they work with kindergartners, middle school students, or high school students, teachers use language in many varied ways in all of their teaching activities. Although they may not be aware of it, most teachers use language skillfully to get students' attention, to present information, to emphasize particular points, to provoke discussion, to praise, to push for better answers, to explain, and sometimes to reprimand. Different teachers, of course, use language differently, but all skilled teachers are able to communicate both direct and very subtle messages to students about students' learning and their behavior.

For most experienced teachers, however, their own language use is completely unconscious. They seldom analyze the strategies they use to convey particular meanings and to achieve desired reactions and responses. Few notice the choices that they make in using particular strategies to convey tone or stance, and even fewer recall how they acquired these strategies. For many teachers, language only becomes a subject of discussion when it is suspected to be the underlying cause of students' problems. They are thus unable to analyze what is typical at different stages of language development and what is characteristic of all children or only a few. They may, in fact, "misdiagnose" children's conditions and provide treatment for nonexisting "illnesses."

In this chapter, we argue that an understanding of how language works in their own lives and in the lives of students who appear *not* to have language "problems" is essential for enabling teachers to effectively support all students' growth in academic language—the language used in schools to learn, speak, and write about academic subjects. Therefore we purposely avoid beginning this chapter with a discussion of what teachers need to know about "those students" for whom language appears to be a problem. Instead, we present the kind of information about language use and development that will help teachers first examine their own language use as well as their views about particular ways of speaking and writing. We then turn to the implications of what they have learned for their students from a variety of language backgrounds. We suggest that such an examination can provide teachers with important insights about how language varies inside and outside school and about the types of language differences that seem to matter in school.

It is our view that it is important for teachers to notice language and to attend to the taken-for-granted characteristics of everyday talk even before they take on the study of language structure or linguistics. Noticing language, even when it appears to be transparent, is essential for teachers committed to supporting the general intellectual and specific subject matter competencies of students at all levels. To illustrate the complexities of their own language use of which teachers may be unaware, we begin this chapter by introducing a fictional mathematics teacher named John. We give examples of the ways he speaks to different people for different purposes, and describe the various situations and interactions that cause him to select from a repertoire of possible choices (see Language in the Life of One Teacher). After the vignette and our discussion of John, we present the knowledge base that teachers must have about the language development of their students both before and into the school, focusing first on children from monolingual families and then on children whose families speak languages other than the dominant language of instruction. We then discuss the ways in which literacy development compares and contrasts with oral language development, and we demonstrate how a focus on learning the language valued by school is particularly crucial. Throughout this chapter, we highlight classroom implications of teachers' understanding (or not understanding) the nature of language use and development. We conclude with a summary of the "big ideas" essential for teachers to understand, classroom implications for each of those themes, and examples of how teacher education and professional development might help teachers develop those understandings.

Language in the Life of One Teacher

John is a young middle school teacher of Italian and Polish background, originally from Boston. He grew up speaking only English, but because his grandmother lived with them during most of his childhood, he also understands quite a bit of Italian. For the last five years, John has been teaching math in Tupelo, Mississippi, the hometown of his wife Alice. For the last two years, he has also been coaching the school's football team.

In this section, we follow John during a typical morning and eavesdrop on his conversations with family and friends. Our goal is to notice the many different kinds of English that John both hears and uses inside and outside of school.

At 6:00 A.M., John wakes up to the radio alarm. As usual, it is set to the local public radio station. Through a slight haze, John recognizes the unmistakable sounds of the talk show host and his Midwest accent: "Good morning and welcome to the program. The president has revealed a proposal that would make it easier to remove trees and brush from forests vulnerable to fires. A fire prevention strategy, the healthy forests initiative, would increase the amount of logging on public lands. Today's guests are all experts in forest management . . . "

John grins as Alice growls at him and chides him in her soft southern drawl, "Honey, it's bad enough waking up to one northern schoolteacher. Can't you wake up to anything a little less serious?" Absentmindedly he hits the other prerecorded stations. Alice growls again when she hears a series of space-age sounds blare and fade to the echoed special effects of an electronically enhanced voice: "Discover WHAT'S NOW! WHAT'S NEXT! WHAT'S NEW! right here on your only choice for the latest hit music." John then turns to the morning traffic report, read by an announcer who sounds as if he was born and bred right there in Mississippi.

"Now that sounds more like you and your kinfolk, don't it?" he jokes, in his best southern accent, exaggerating his impressions of Mississippi speech. Knowing it will make Alice want him to return to public radio, John turns to the shock jock station, aired in New York City. The host, in a high-pitched argument with a caller, berates the caller with slurs such as "Hey, genius, why aren't you at work?" and "You are the stupidest man I have talked to in a long time." The host's female assistant laughs as the caller is speechless for a moment, trying to compose himself to respond.

Alice mutters, "You win, but it's still your turn to get the baby ready," as a loud wail is heard from the next room.

John sighs and stretches a moment or two before he jumps out of bed. "I'm coming little fella," he calls out. "Mommy's being lazy, but here comes daddy. You just hold on there. Daddy's coming." Baby Matthew is standing in his crib, his face covered with tears and rubbing his eyes. He is tall for eighteen months, but has not yet begun to talk. "AAAAAh," he cries, as he holds out his arms to be picked up. "Well good morning to you too, Matt. Yes, Daddy had a very good sleep. Thank you for asking." Matt responds by wailing "Baaaaahhhh" impatiently and stretching out his arms once again. John continues his conversation with Matthew, as he skillfully removes pajamas, changes the wet diaper, and begins to get him ready for another day at his babysitter's. "Are you trying to say bear, Matt? He asks. Yes, wittle bear was right there all night. Wittle bear loves Matt. Give wittle Bear a wittle hug."

Forty-five minutes later John finally heads for Long Acres Middle School. It is a short drive to the school, but today he is in a hurry and is a bit annoyed when his cell phone rings. He hopes that he has not forgotten something at home.

"Hello?" (John's voice sounds impatient as he places his earphone in his ear.)

"Hey John, Sam here."

"Hey, man, what's up?" John yells into the faint connection.

"Well, it's about that racquetball game we had scheduled for this afternoon."

John pauses and says dramatically, "Don't EVEN tell me you're not going to make it!"

"Well, uh, I'm up to my ears in this project at work . . . If I don't finish it this week, the boss is gonna have my hide."

"Listen," John chides, "if you are afraid of losing to me AGAIN, just tell me—you don't have to make up some sorry excuse about your boss and some lame project at work."

Sam quickly retorts, "Man, with the way I am playing these days, you should be thanking your lucky stars that you don't have to face me today . . . it would NOT be pretty." They both laugh.

"Listen," John says, a little more seriously, "call me when your so-called project is done."

"Will do."

"Later, man." "Later."

John hangs up, smiling, and continues to drive.

On his way into the main office to check his mail, the first person John runs into is the school's assistant principal, Roberta Johnson, a forty-something African American woman. John greets her professionally, but with a playful (almost flirtatious) tone, as he checks his mailbox:

"Good MORNING, Mrs. Johnson."

"Good morning, Mr. Carlucci," she replies, smiling.

"Oh, Mrs. Johnson, by the way, what do you think the chances are of us getting that revised bell schedule today for next week's homecoming activities?"

"For you, Mr. Carlucci, anything. And if the photocopy machine is still broken, I'll just hand-copy them for all twenty-five teachers," she adds sarcastically but still smiling.

"I hear you," John replies, "thanks for lookin' into it."

"My pleasure. Have a great day Mr. Carlucci."

"You too," John smiles, as he begins the trek down the hallway to his classroom.

There are several students gathered around his door, obviously unaccustomed to being at school at this hour. John greets them all with a "Good morning, early birds, I'll be with you in one moment!" He unlocks his room, turns on the lights, throws his mail on an already large pile of papers on his desk, opens the blinds, and says cheerfully (but in a mock gruff tone) "OK you goofballs, get in here and WAKE UP!" The students, all on the football team, amble in, followed by others just arriving. As the students take seats and chat with each other quietly (some just sitting staring into space, others with their heads down on their desks), John prepares a video projector and screen, and then, in a much more serious voice, begins the meeting: "OK guys, we're gonna watch some film this morning, and we're gonna talk about what happened out there last week. But before we do, we're gonna start with the basics. There's rules to be followed. You gotta follow 'em in life; you're gonna have to follow 'em in football." (One boy leans over and whispers something to another.) "And I'll tell you one thing for darn sure. The next one that talks, I'm gonna bench for the next three games. In any phase of life, you have to listen and follow rules and follow orders. That's part of life. OK, now let's see what the heck happened last week."

After reviewing the film of last week's embarrassing loss and discussing specific plays and strategies, John decides to end on a positive note: "Now next week. I do see a lot of progress in you. By the time we get out on that field, you'll be very good football players, because I'm seeing a lot of progress. But we've got a lot of work to do before then. I'll see you after school. Jones and Anderson—I need to talk to you before you head off to your class."

As most team members file out of the room, four or five of the African American players cluster around Frank Jones and Jamal Anderson. Frank and Jamal have begun to engage in a display of verbal skill that is known as snapping or playing the dozens. Jamal begins by laying out the initial challenge in the game of ritual insults by saying: "Your mother is so fat that when she sits on a quarter she gets two dimes and a nickel." As the appreciative audience howls with laughter, Frank responds by saying, "Your mother is so old that when she read the Bible she reminisces." The cluster of onlookers laughs again.

John, overhearing the boys' talk, marvels at their quick wit. He knows, however, that he must interrupt a form of extended competitive play that can continue until one of the players is determined to be the winner by the audience. Breaking up the cluster with a stern face and motioning to the door, he says to Frank and Jamal, "I just wanted to let you both know how much leadership you showed during that game, even when we were losing so badly. Nice job."

A few minutes later, as John greets his students coming in for first period, he is back to being cheerful, fun-loving John. "Mornin', Anna, I read a great paper with your name on it last night!"

"Hey, Zack, welcome back. Hope you're feeling better."

"Hello, Sharon and Charisse . . . "

The final bell rings. "Good morning ladies and gentlemen. I hope everyone is ready for a great day of math! Take out your homework and let's get started." The students groan good-naturedly. It is 8:30 A.M., and John is ready to start his day as a teacher.

A careful analysis of John's use of language up to this point highlights many aspects of language that teachers may not have thought deeply about but which have profound implications for the learning of their students. First, we will notice that John hears, understands, and uses many different types of English. On the radio, it is not only accents that differ, but also styles and "rules" for what is acceptable to say, with the contrast between public radio and the shock jocks perhaps being the most extreme. With his son, John holds a one-sided conversation in which he speaks of himself in the third person ("Daddy's coming") and uses baby talk ("wittle bear") and repetition, practices he obviously would avoid with adults. John uses language differently to speak to his wife, the assistant principal, the football team, and his regular students. And he uses language differently for different purposes even when speaking to the same person. For example, his very direct and friendly greeting of the assistant principal is followed by a somewhat sarcastic and very indirect request for her to do something ("What do you think the chances are of us getting that revised bell schedule today?") and then an equally indirect, but much more polite, apology ("I hear you.").

Once teachers begin to think about the nature of language variation in their own speech and the speech of those with whom they interact regularly, it will not come as a surprise that their students also use variations of language depending on whom they are talking to or what the context of the interaction is. Some linguists refer to such differences as *registers.* Others prefer to think of them as specialized styles of speech used for carrying out particular types of tasks (for example, teaching class, motivating a football team, giving a public speech, presenting evidence before a court of law). What is clear is that styles or registers that are appropriate for speaking in one situation are not appropriate for speaking in another. John chooses very different types of language to convey friendliness and camaraderie with each person or group he is interacting with. For example, John and his wife use terms of intimacy ("honey"), but also mild sarcasm ("you win"). When speaking to the assistant principal, he uses formal greetings, but his intonation and body language demonstrated that this was not a formal exchange. With Sam, John uses language to demonstrate his friendship both by the way he addresses his friend ("Hey, man, what's up?") and by pretending to accuse his friend of making up a phony excuse to get out of the game. Different still are the ways John shows camaraderie with his football team (using the expectedly "tough" language of coaching) and his students (as with the assistant principal, a combination of formal features showing respect and more personal features indicating personal relationships). When speaking to his class, John first establishes cordiality by adopting a cheerleading style to greet students, and then authority by addressing the class as "ladies and gentlemen" and issuing a direct command: "Take out your homework." Table 4.1 summarizes John's use of language during a single morning.

What may not be very apparent from the transcribed examples of John's speech is that John's English is also different from the English spoken by his fellow teachers in Mississippi. English varies from region to region in pronunciation and in the use of particular words and expressions. Moreover, English varies depending on social status and ethnic background. A lawyer from Mississippi will speak very differently from a cowboy from Texas, and a white Appalachian grandmother will not sound like a polished New York society matron. Social dialects, as opposed to regional dialects, also vary in grammatical structure. Speakers from rural areas in all parts of the country, for example, might say, "He done come," and "I might could," expressions rarely heard in most suburban areas.

Like most other speakers of English, John is very probably not aware that judgments about features that are considered incorrect or nonstandard are social and not linguistic judgments. As Wolfram, Adger, and Christian (1999) point out: "The value placed on a certain way of saying something is very closely associated with the cultural identity and social status of the people who say it that way. The valuing is not an individual decision; it is society's evaluation of different groups, including their ways of speaking. As we are socialized, we learn these attitudes, sometimes unconsciously, sometimes through expressed regulations and rules, just as we learn eating behavior" (p. 11).

Examining such judgments can help teachers avoid sending the message, either overtly or implicitly, that the language spoken by certain groups of students is in some way inferior to that spoken by others. As we saw earlier, Alice jokes with John about having to wake up to "northerners'" speech, and John, in turn, ridicules Mississippi English by trying to imitate a southern drawl. Interestingly, he also uses a nonstandard feature in his imitation: "That sounds more like your kinfolk, *don't it*?" This suggests that for John, the speech of Mississippi sounds somehow less "correct" than his own. Although the construction, "he don't" is found in the nonstandard speech of most regions and is thus just as likely to be heard in Boston as it is in Mississippi, John pretends that this is not the case. Even though John would probably agree that the communicative effect of "don't it" and "doesn't it," are similar, he associates the former with what is socially unacceptable or incorrect.

Finally, from John's interactions with Mrs. Johnson and with his student Jamal, we saw examples of Standard African American English as well as of African American Vernacular English. As is the case with John's variety of English, the speech of both Mrs. Johnson and Jamal varies depending on a variety of factors including the cultural and ethnic background of the speakers engaged in the interaction. As Smitherman (2000) has pointed out, African American or black verbal style ranges from what she calls a southern sacred

Table 4.1 John's Use of Language

Situation	Features of Language
Makes fun of his wife Alice	• Imitates southern colloquial verb forms (for example, "don't it?") • Imitates southern (Mississippi) accent
Talks to baby Matthew	• Speaks about himself in the third person ("Daddy's coming") • Uses pronunciation typical of informal oral language (fellA instead of fellOW) • Uses "baby talk" ("wittle bear")

Converses with male friend on the phone	• Uses informal "male" style characterized by:
	  1. Elliptical language ("Will do." "Later man.")
	  2. Mock aggression and self-aggrandizement

Interacts with assistant principal	• Exaggerates standard polite greeting ("Good MORNING.") • Uses question form to make an indirect request ("What do you think the chances are of us getting the revised bell schedule?") • Uses grammatical structure typical of informal oral language ("the chances of **us** getting" versus "the changes of **our** getting") • Uses pronunciation typical of informal oral language for a single word ("lookin'") • Uses informal response drawn from the African American tradition of call and response ("I hear you.")
Conducts team meeting	• Uses pronunciation typical of informal oral language throughout ("gonna," "gotta," "wanna," "follow 'em") • Uses mildly profane language for emphasis ("For darn sure," "What the heck happened?")
Addresses Frank and Jamal	• Uses pronunciation typical of standard formal language ("I just wanted to let you know."). • Primarily uses grammatical structure typical of formal language. • Uses elliptical language in closing ("Nice job!" versus "You did a nice job.")

Greets students individually as they come into class	• Uses informal style characterized by:
	  1. Pronunciation typical of informal oral language ("Mornin' Anna.")
	  2. Elliptical language ("Hope you're feeling better.")

Addresses entire class	• Uses formal style that is characterized by
	  1. Careful pronunciation ("Good morning.")
	  2. Standard grammatical structure ("I hope everyone is ready . . .")
	  3. Direct command

style (associated with the black church tradition) to a secular style that is urban and northern and a product of both its southern roots and the unique experiences of inner-city African American people. Mrs. Johnson's speech when participating in a socially sensitive situation in which she interacts primarily with white colleagues is quite different from how she speaks when surrounded by close African American friends. Similarly, Jamal, who is an honors student, often exaggerates the hip hop nuances of his talk as he trades verbal insults with his homies. He knows quite clearly which features to use in dress, behavior, and language to maintain his standing among other African American students.[1]

From a single morning in John's life, we can learn a great deal about language. As some scholars have suggested (see, for example, Austin, 1975), speakers skillfully use language to carry out particular actions by means of words. For example, they approve, they disagree, they apologize, and they request; and they do so either directly or indirectly. In presenting themselves in public, people are engaged in what other scholars (Goffman, 1959) have called "impression management." They carefully select from a broad repertoire of speech styles (Gumperz, 1982) the best style for the purpose at hand. One scholar (Bell, 1984) has referred to the process of selecting the best language for particular situations and interactions as "audience design."

John's particular speech repertoire illustrates two very important facts that teachers need to know about language (whether it is English, Spanish, Chinese, or any other language): first, that language varies depending upon regional and social origins, and second, that there are no single-style speakers. As adults, the way we speak to a good friend, the way we speak in a courtroom, and the way we speak to a young child are not the same. More importantly, however, if young children's language is influenced by adults' language, which in turn varies according to geographic area and cultural factors, it is also influenced by how the various adults around them use language differently for different goals, purposes, and situations. As we saw in a single morning of John's life, there are different ways people convey meaning, even when they are talking about the same thing. In addition to varying language according to interpersonal purpose, to get things done effectively and efficiently with people

---

[1]According to Smitherman (2000), the oral style of young African American speakers is part of a complex and rich tradition that includes folk sayings, verbal interplay, and cultural rituals involving talk. Contemporary rappers, for example, build on traditional rhetorical qualities of African American discourse including exaggerated language, mimicry, proverbial statement, punning and plays on words, spontaneity and improvisation, metaphor, braggadocio, indirection, and tonal semantics. In Smitherman's words, "A black rap can [include] one, all, or any combination of these. Rappers must be skillful in reading the vibrations of their audience and situation, for the precise working depends on what is said to whom under what conditions" (p. 217). For additional information on African American language, see Baugh (1999, 2000); Morgan (1998); Mufwene, Rickford, Baily, & Baugh (1998); and Smitherman (2000).

who use a particular variety of language, people vary their language to present themselves in ways in which they want to be viewed (or, to be more precise, "heard") in particular situations. These choices in language variety may be overt (for example, consciously avoiding the use of obscene language around children or being extra polite around older people) or so subtle the speaker herself may not be aware of it (for example, the tendency to modify our speech slightly toward that of someone we are talking with whom we like and respect, both in word choice and pronunciation). Language is also an act of identity (Eckert, 1989; Gee, 1990; Norton, 2000). Choices in language use, as we saw in the case of Jamal, may signal broad categories to which people wish to demonstrate their allegiance, or they may represent momentary acts of "image control" (Goffman, 1959).

LANGUAGE BEFORE AND INTO SCHOOL

Teachers need to understand that language, unlike most school subjects, surrounds children from the time that they are born. Adults speak to each other as they hold young babies, feed them, care for them, and go about their everyday lives. As we saw in the case of baby Matthew, in some cultures and in some families, adults speak directly to even newborn babies. They carry on pretend conversations in which they act as if the baby had opinions and could respond to questions. In other families and in other cultures, adults may not treat children as conversational partners. These adults, however, will have clear expectations regarding when children begin to understand what is said to them, what kinds of language should be used with them, and what kind of language young children will first produce.

From anthropologists who have studied language all over the world and from psycholinguists who study first language acquisition, we know that all normal children, and even most children with disabilities, acquire the ability to use language. Parents engage in communicative acts that focus on meaning with their children, and children begin to "acquire" language from the input that surrounds them. Although initially they may be capable of producing sounds not used by the adults around them, during their first year of life infants start to constrain their babbling so that it sounds like their parents' language, and they lose the ability to hear sound distinctions that carry no meaning in their parents' language. By two or three years of age, children begin to develop the ability to communicate with the people around them, to use words learned from adults, to form new words that fit into the patterns licensed by their parents' language, and to create novel sentences, sentences that they have never heard before. Because language is extraordinarily complex, psycholinguists do not entirely agree about how the process of first language acquisition takes place.

Some linguists emphasize the remarkable ability that children have to extract the rules of the particular language or languages spoken around them from the varied and imperfect input that they hear. Even in homes of highly educated parents, children may hear utterances that are not always well-formed according to the rules of formal grammar. They will likely hear various versions of "baby talk," that is, speech that is modified to accommodate the supposed needs of the child. They will also hear the everyday elliptical talk that characterizes intimate conversations. Somehow, perhaps by extrapolating from the input, or perhaps from their own efforts to use language to communicate important messages, young children acquire vocabulary (some estimates suggest that first graders know 5,000–12,000 different words) and grammar (that is, how possible sentences in the language are formed and which words are possible words in the language) and make a good start on learning the sociolinguistic and pragmatic rules of communication within their communities that allow them to know what things to say and not say, how to be polite, and how to get others to fulfill their needs.

Although not everything that children hear is relevant to the acquisition of language, the ways in which language is used in particular families and in particular communities is of central importance in language acquisition. A child from Mississippi and a child from Boston will acquire the accents of the adults and children with whom they interact. The child from Mississippi will not sound like he comes from New York, and the child from Boston will not sound like she grew up in South Texas. Similarly, as Heath (1983) tells us, the child who grows up in the community or family where displaying information is emphasized will learn how to display information. In the same way, the youngster whose parents and siblings use careful school-like language and correct all stigmatized uses (for example, "Don't say 'gots,' say 'has.'") will grow up concerned about what her family considers to be correctness and incorrectness. By comparison, a child whose parents and community members care more about how effectively a child can think on her feet to defend herself when being teased by others may be much less concerned with norms of school correctness than with verbal expressiveness. It is important to emphasize, however, that speech communities and families within the *same* speech communities also differ in the ways in which they use language. Families of the same social class as well as the same racial and educational background will nevertheless socialize their children in the use of various speech genres (narrating, teasing) at different ages and in different ways. The structure of those genres, moreover, may differ as may the conditions under which the genre can be invoked.

Dramatic growth appears to take place in children's language during a very short period, although some scholars (for example, Aitchison, 1996, cited in Bialystok, 2001) argue that language acquisition takes as long as twenty years, with the first five years dedicated to acquiring basic structure, the next five to mastering complex grammar, and the last ten to acquiring a rich vocabulary.

When they start to speak, toddlers typically communicate their intents by using single words (for example, *up* with a gesture to request to be picked up, *gone* to request help finding something, *goggie* or *kiki* to direct the hearer's attention to a dog or a cat). They move gradually into early combinatory speech, in which these same intents are expressed with longer and more complex utterances (for example, "pick me up," "where cookie gone?" "dat a goggie"). Somewhat older children often produce forms ("goed," "runned") that are different from those produced by adults, or use words and expressions in ways that differ considerably from the standard adult use ("don't put me spinach!"). Such inventive uses occur in three- and four-year-olds, who typically have previously used correct forms ("went," "ran," "don't give me spinach," "don't put spinach on my plate") and are trying to integrate new forms they have encountered. Thus they suggest that children are active processors of the language they hear and try to generate regularities in it.[2]

In every case, children ultimately acquire the grammatical and sociolinguistic rules used by the adults and children around them. Thus a white child from the South whose parents speak a rural vernacular and use the form "done" to mark a completed action or event (for example, "I done told you not to mess up.") will acquire this rule as she internalizes the grammatical structure of English and will also use "done" to mark completed action. She may also acquire "fixin' to" to express what is about to be done or to happen ("It's fixin' to rain."). In Appalachia, a child whose parents use an "a"-prefix with –ing forms will produce sentences such as, "He was a-comin' home" or "He's a-laughin' at you." Similarly, a child whose family are speakers of African American Vernacular English (AAVE) and who use habitual "be" (for example, "Everyday he be tired.") to talk about an action or condition that occurs habitually will internalize this rule to produce sentences such as, "By the time I go get my momma, it be dark" to mean, "By the time I go get my momma, it is always dark." The child, rather than producing incorrect English, is using the grammatical resources of AAVE to express meanings that other varieties of English express differently.[3]

Teachers must know that when children arrive at school at the age of five, they have already acquired the ability to use language in important and effective ways within their families and their communities. However, teachers must also realize that only children whose families use language in ways that are very similar to the ways that it is used in school will have acquired the rules for using school-like language. Such children may already have been taught how to respond to questions that are requests for display of information (for example, "What is a baby cow called, Johnny?"). They may already know how to distinguish a true question ("Did you bring lunch money today?") from a polite request ("Don't

---

[2]Examples here are drawn from Lindfors (1987).

[3]Examples in this section have been adapted from Wolfram et al. (1999) and Smitherman (1986).

you want to put your toys away now and get ready for recess?"). Other children who have not had experience with the many different meanings that questions have in school settings will need to learn new mappings of forms to communicative intents, both to interpret school questions correctly and to decide whether to respond to such questions. Children also differ in how verbal they are. Children who are more verbal are often rewarded by schools if they conform their talk to school norms and punished if they use their verbal skills in other ways, while the contributions of less verbal children often go unnoticed.

In the United States, schools often value the particular varieties of English acquired by a particular subsection of the population, mostly that of families who have traditionally been largely white and middle- and upper-middle-class. Though schools rarely talk about these values overtly, it quickly becomes clear to students that different ways of speaking are valued differentially, and students often rapidly get the clear message that they have a "problem" with language or that they are not speaking "correctly." Children who are from working-class communities and who come to school speaking vernacular varieties of English can and will acquire the rules for speaking in school in very much the same way that they acquired the rules for speaking in their homes and communities, or in the same way that children who arrive at school speaking a language other than English acquire English. However, such acquisition will take time, and there may be many features of their home varieties of language that they will not abandon. Children from Boston will not sound like Mississippi children until they have been among Mississippi children for a period of time and until they want to sound like Mississippi children.

The important point for teachers is that the English that Boston children acquire is not a flawed Texas English, but rather Boston English, a very different and legitimate regional variety of the language. Similarly, children whose varieties of English have rules that are not identical to the rules of the standard language variety used in school are not speaking flawed school language. Rather, they are competently speaking a legitimate variety of English that also has strict rules for communicating meaning and that is used in everyday interactions by the adults in their homes and communities. Children, then, who arrive at school not speaking school language should not be faulted. It would tantamount to faulting a child who grew up speaking Japanese for not speaking German (Los Angeles Unified School District and LeMoine, 1999; LeMoine, 2002).

THE ACQUISITION OF MORE THAN ONE LANGUAGE

As outlined earlier, in monolingual English-speaking families, students acquire one or more varieties of English and, over time, a repertoire of registers and styles consistent with those with whom they interact. In such families, children need only one language to communicate with those around them. In other families and in many communities, children need more than one language to communicate with all the people who are important to them. They may have parents who have different language backgrounds and grandparents and other relatives who only speak the language of their home countries. In John's family, for example, an Italian-speaking grandmother always spoke to her grandchildren in Italian although, toward the end of her life, she understood quite a bit of English. As a result, John can still understand everyday household Italian, although he cannot read or write Italian. Teachers in the United States increasingly find themselves in classrooms with students from families in which languages other than English are spoken. In the following discussion, we outline the knowledge necessary for teachers to understand the language development of students from a variety of language backgrounds.

In some households, especially among middle-class professionals who come to this country in adulthood, much time and attention is given to the development of the children's two languages. For example, two highly educated, French-speaking parents who are fluent in English may carefully plan ways of exposing their children to both English and French. They may decide to use only French with their child but to hire a babysitter who speaks English, or they may decide that each of the parents will each use a different language with the child for all interactions. For such parents, bilingualism is seen as a valuable asset, and they assume that all educated persons are, by definition, bilingual. As is the case with other middle-class parents, such bilingual parents provide their children with books and recordings—but they provide them in two languages instead of only one. They might also travel to France or Canada on a yearly basis to provide the child with genuine models of the home language. For such middle-class children, the transition to a school in which only English is spoken is ordinarily painless. Because the children already speak English, they often pass undetected among monolingual, English-speaking middle-class children. Indeed, to avoid the stigma associated with bilingualism in many schools, the parents of such privileged bilinguals may not give information about the use of a non-English language at home to school personnel.

In the case of working class immigrant families, the situation is often quite different. Many individuals who come to this country, especially from very poor countries, have very little formal education. They do not speak English, and they move into neighborhoods where they are isolated among other immigrants, many of whom also speak little English. They work at jobs in which they have little contact with English-speaking people, and they have little opportunity to acquire English in ordinary interactions. Though they may enroll in English language classes within their communities, such classes are generally overcrowded and taught by inexperienced volunteers. Because of their geographical and economic isolation, they often make little progress in learning English. As compared to middle-class highly educated professionals, then, working class immigrants do not ordinarily design a language curriculum in the home for their children. They simply use their home language around their children, and it is the home language that their children acquire.

In those families where there are no speakers of English, such as relatives who have been here for many years or older siblings who have already begun to acquire English at school, children will remain monolingual in the home language until they arrive at school. In most schools, students who arrive with no English whatsoever, whether in early or late elementary school, middle school, or high school, present the greatest challenges. Such children must ideally be given access to the curriculum to prevent their falling hopelessly behind academically while they are in the process of acquiring English. Unfortunately, schools have few choices. When there are few children, they are often placed in ordinary classes with English-speaking peers and offered whatever support is feasible for the school. Teachers who work with such newly arrived children often wring their hands because they realize that their background and training has not prepared them to help children to develop English quickly at the same time that they are learning other subject matter.

When there are many immigrant children at the same school, the responsibility for working with them is primarily left in the hands of language specialists (that is, ESL teachers and subject matter teachers who teach special classes designed to simplify the language for such learners). Unfortunately, in many such schools, English language learners (ELLs) spend most of their school days isolated among other learners of English. They have few opportunities to interact with fluent speakers of English either at school, where most interactions are with the teacher and the ratio of learners to native speakers is 30 to 1, or in their communities, where they interact primarily with other immigrant families. Many children make very little progress in learning to speak fluent English under such circumstances even when they are taught exclusively in English. The situation is made even more complex when older immigrant students arrive at school in the later years without the same level of literacy background or exposure to school in their native language that their classmates have had, because of limited number of daily school hours in their countries of origin, interrupted schooling, and other social, political, and economic obstacles.

In families where both English and the home language are spoken, children will begin to acquire English at home. They may arrive at school speaking and understanding some English. As compared to children who have grown up in English-speaking homes, however, the English that immigrant children bring to school (even when they appear to communicate fairly well in interpersonal interactions) may still be limited. Their two or more languages will not develop in exactly parallel ways. Rather, their languages will be functionally specialized. They will use one of their languages to talk to certain people in certain contexts, and their other language to carry out other functions and to talk to other people about other topics. Because language development reflects language use, they will not be identical to monolingual children of either language who use one language exclusively for all purposes and in all contexts. Like monolinguals, bilinguals also have broad language repertoires and both styles and registers that they use for different types of interactions. In the case of bilinguals, however, this repertoire includes styles and registers in two languages.

Although addressing many of the challenges outlined earlier may be out of the control of individual teachers, an understanding of the nature of the development of more than one language *can* help teachers begin to understand and respond to the needs of their students. Unfortunately, the education profession has perpetuated a number of myths about bilingual students. Indeed the very term *bilingual* is often used as a euphemism for *disadvantaged.* Even though research for over forty years has clearly established the cognitive advantages of bilingualism (Peale and Lambert, 1962), beliefs about bilingual handicaps still persist, as do unrealistic notions about "perfect" bilinguals, often believed to be individuals who are two monolinguals in one. Few human beings attain such perfection, but most English language learners if given the necessary opportunities to acquire English and to learn *through* English can develop strong academic skills in their second language.

Like the process of first language acquisition, the process of second language acquisition is complex and in many ways poorly understood. Unlike for first language learners, who eventually become indistinguishable from native speakers of the same social and ethnic background, the end point for many second language learners is not necessarily native-like proficiency. Many speakers of English as a second language who sound non-native-like, however, are nonetheless dominant English speakers, capable of completing challenging communicative tasks in English and of learning and developing intellectually through English.[4]

LITERACY BEFORE AND INTO SCHOOL

Just as they learn that spoken language can be used differently for different ends in the same language, children in most communities also learn from an early age that communicating involves more than oral language. However, teachers

---

[4]Much confusion about the role of the first language in the education of English language learners has been generated by recent anti-immigrant and anti-bilingual education initiatives around the country. Educating students who do not speak the societal language is a complex endeavor that involves making difficult decisions about providing them access to the curriculum during the period that they are acquiring English. For information about controversies surrounding the prohibition of bilingual education, see the Web site of the Linguistic Minority Research Institute (http://lmri.ucsb.edu/index.htm) as well as the Center for Applied Linguistics (http://www.cal.org/pubs/bilinged_p.html). The following works provide information about the education of linguistic minority children in general: Arias and Casanova (1993); August and Hakuta (1997, 1988); Valdés (2001).

need to keep in mind that unlike oral language, written literacy is not a universal human characteristic. In fact, even though humans have been using language for tens of thousands, if not hundreds of thousands of years, it is only in the last several thousand or so that they have been using writing, and only much more recently that people have been called upon to use special forms of reading and writing for formal education (Gee, 1993; Halliday 1993).

The word *literacy* means different things to different people. Some people think of literacy as the most basic ability to read and write simple words and sentences. For others, literacy is synonymous with the particular kind of reading and writing commonly done in school. However, neither definition is sufficient. While literacy is more than simply reading words and writing letters, it also often takes forms very different from those practiced in schools.

Anthropologist Shirley Brice Heath (1986) uses the term *literacy events* to describe a wide range of children's interaction with text. According to Heath, literacy events can include practices as diverse as telling bedtime stories, looking at cereal boxes, noticing stop signs, watching TV ads, and following instructions for store-bought games and toys. James Gee (1990) defines literacy as not only the written but also the oral ways in which people control "secondary uses of language," which ultimately involve all the ways in which people communicate with social institutions beyond the family: schools, workplaces, stores, government offices, businesses, and churches. In an even broader view of literacy, some argue that in the current technological age, literacy is not limited to language at all. In this view, there is no such thing as "literacy," but instead "multiliteracies" (New London Group, 1996). In addition to language, these multiliteracies include visual meanings (images, page layouts, screen formats); audio meanings (music, sound effects); gestural meanings (body language, sensuality); spatial meanings (environmental spaces, architectural spaces); and multimodal meanings, which involve combinations of all of the above.

Regardless of the exact definition of literacy used, however, there is no question that (1) literacy, like language, is often experienced first at home and (2) also like language, there is no one "natural" way to be literate. As Heath (1986) puts it, "Ways of taking from books are as much a part of learned behavior as are ways of eating, sitting, playing games, and building houses" (p. 97). But these "learned behaviors" are learned in ways very different from the ways subjects are often taught in school. As Gee (1990) points out, "One does not learn to read texts of type X in way Y unless one has had experience in settings where texts of type X are read in way Y" (p. 43; see also Gee, 1998).

As with language acquisition, children growing up in different communities may be exposed to very different literacy practices. In her famous study comparing families' literacy practices in three nearby communities in the Carolinas, Heath (1983, 1986) demonstrated the potential differences in literacy practices, even in the same geographic area. As early as six months old, children of white, middle-class families from "Maintown" focused on books, acknowledged questions about books, and lived in rooms decorated with characters from books. From the time they could talk, these children were encouraged to engage in conversations about books and book characters, even when they were out in the "real world," and after the age of two they told imaginary stories and transformed real people and events into fictional stories. By age three, children also learned to listen and wait as an audience when adults read to them, and preschool children learned that books and book-related activities were entertainment and announced their own factual and fiction narratives.

Literacy practices were different for children in "Roadville," the white working-class community Heath (1986) studied. Parents in this community chose books emphasizing nursery rhymes, alphabet learning, Bible stories, and animals, and they directed their children both to repeat from and to answer factual questions about the content of the books. Children learned to see "stories" either as factual accounts of real life or as accounting from a book. In Roadville, according to Heath, "any fictionalized account of a real event is viewed as a *lie*; reality is better than fiction" (p. 111).

In the black working-class neighborhood Heath studied, literacy events were different from those in either of the two white communities. In contrast to the fiction-filled homes of Maintown nurseries or the story-as-account environment of Roadville, babies in Trackton "come home from the hospital to an environment that is almost entirely human . . . Infants are held during their waking hours, occasionally while they sleep, and they usually sleep in the bed with parents until they are about 2 years of age . . . They eat and sleep in the midst of human talk and noise from the television, stereo, and radio. Encapsulated in an almost totally human world, they are in the midst of constant human communication, verbal and nonverbal . . . " (p. 112).

Children in Trackton grew up in the midst of adults reading a variety of materials (newspapers, mail, the Bible and other church-related materials, political and community newsletters, parent notices from school, and advertisements), but there were no reading materials specifically for children, except those from Sunday school, and adults did not ritually read to children, either during the day or at bedtime. The types of questions adults asked children also were quite different from those in the white neighborhoods. Instead of questions eliciting information that adults already knew, children were asked analogical questions calling for comparisons, such as "What's that like?" as well as genuine requests for information not known by adults, such as "Where'd you get that from?" "What do you want?" and "How come you did that?" (p. 115). The ways in which children told stories were different too. Preschoolers in Trackton almost never heard "Once upon a time" stories, because the assumption was that the audience itself would be able to understand the context with proper cues in the story. Also in contrast to literacy in the white communities, one child did not hold the floor for an entire story, as storytelling was a competitive enterprise: "Everyone in a conversation may want to tell a story, so only the most aggressive wins out" (p. 116).

The differential ways of using language that Heath's work displays constitute one aspect of what has come to be called *emergent literacy*—the many practices and capabilities of preschool-aged children that can be seen as early points on the trajectory toward conventional reading and writing. In addition to using oral language in "literate" ways, some children arrive at school knowing a lot about letters, able for example to recite the alphabet, recognize most letters, and write many recognizably. Some children have had lots of practice in writing their own names, and perhaps also in doing "pretend writing" (making a shopping list with Mom, writing "thank-you notes," labeling artistic productions), and even invented spelling. Such children have experiences that map well onto the expectations of kindergarten and first-grade teachers, whereas others may have acquired emergent literacy practices that are puzzling to their teachers (for example, not handling books for fear of soiling them, writing only words they know how to spell correctly, copying in preference to writing stories, reading by memorizing rather than sounding out). Skilled literacy users, like skilled language users, have many different modes of interacting with text—recitation for some texts, expressive interpretation for others, reading for fun sometimes and for serious purposes sometimes, reading some texts to get information and others to assess writers' opinions, reading some for guidance about action and others for guidance about beliefs. All children arrive at school understanding and able to engage in only a subset of these literacy activities; school is meant to ensure that they all leave with a complete set.

Teachers also need to know that additional emergent literacy capabilities that some children develop before school and others only in kindergarten or first grade include an understanding of how letters represent sounds, which presupposes an understanding that words can be analyzed into smaller units of sound. The notion that the words *dog, log, fog, sog, bog, cog, hog,* and *jog* all share two sounds and differ in one represents a huge insight. This insight is key to profiting from phonics-based literacy instruction and to figuring out the nature of the alphabetic system. It is an insight that can be taught to children, or that some may discover on their own, particularly if they have many words in their vocabularies to work with. Successfully learning to read in the first and second grades requires putting together the insight that letters represent sounds with the capabilities to analyze sounds in words correctly, to recognize letters reliably, to remember how different sounds are spelled, to access the meaning of the words being read, and to do all this rapidly and effortlessly. Successfully reading in the later elementary and secondary grades means being able to do this with complex texts and novel words, and furthermore, to learn from the texts. It presupposes not just good primary-level reading, but wide vocabulary knowledge and considerable knowledge of how things work in the world. (For more about what teachers need to know about reading, see Snow, Griffin, and Burns, 2005.)

Heath's work, along with the work of others, shows that literacy practices in *all* communities have distinct potential advantages for engaging in learning in school and later on in life. For example, in Heath's study, the black working-class Trackton children, when they *started* school, already had the narrative skills rewarded in the *upper* primary grades, including sophisticated analogical reasoning and an understanding of the ways in which storytelling can be related to play (Heath, 1986, p. 121). However, schools in the United States have traditionally valued a relatively narrow set of literacy practices, matched closely with those of white, middle-class families. For example, according to Heath, Trackton children found themselves penalized in the early grades when they were unaccustomed to labeling shapes, colors, sizes, and numbers; answering questions adults clearly know the answer to; and participating in other literacy events that some students have been practicing almost since birth.

What teachers need to understand is that there is not one type of universal or "natural" literacy, that schools often value only a narrow set of all the literacy practices potentially powerful for learning, and that students can bring to school only the literacy practices they have been exposed to at home and in their communities. In the classroom, such an understanding is essential for teachers to realize that (1) students are not cognitively or linguistically deficient just because they have not mastered a particular set of literacy practices to which they have not been exposed, and that (2) if schools are going to continue to value certain literacy practices over others, it is the responsibility of teachers to help create the conditions necessary to foster the development of these practices.

LANGUAGE AND LITERACY PRACTICES OUTSIDE OF SCHOOL

Although literacy practices begin at home and are either challenged or supported at school (or both), teachers need to understand that a wide variety of literacy practices continue to develop throughout children's lives *outside* of school as well (Hull and Schultz, 2001). After John's son Matthew begins school, he will also, either at home or elsewhere, surf the Internet, communicate via e-mail, and participate in computer games requiring quite sophisticated and challenging literacy. He may decide to keep a journal, write poetry, or even experiment with graffiti. He will probably participate in clubs, activities, and religious organizations, each with its own literacy practices. Increasingly, he will participate in community service, either as a volunteer or to fulfill school or statewide graduation requirements. Some children, especially those from particular religious and immigrant communities, attend Saturday or evening school, sometimes in languages other than English. Many older children hold part-time jobs, either to earn extra income for themselves or to help their families make a living, and some accompany their parents to family-run businesses, late-night office cleaning jobs, and early morning paper routes. For students who are learning English, these activities are especially important language opportunities, either to help develop English or to help maintain students' heritage languages as they also learn English.

Clearly then, school is not the only place that students are "doing" literacy. In fact, many studies have documented how children struggling *inside* of school may be simultaneously quite successful using literacy *outside* of school in a wide variety of different contexts. For example, research has shown students who are struggling in school will often spend hours learning and succeeding in computer games that require interaction with complicated, text-rich information, and at least one case has been documented with a student diagnosed with attention deficit disorder who spent an entire night learning how to crack a computer code in order to cheat on a game (Gee, 2003a). Researchers have described how children ages nine through eleven at a community center in an inner-city African American neighborhood use a parking ticket as a literacy event, "problem solving, analyzing the ticket and sorting through strategies for dealing with it," and in so doing "draw on various literate and discursive strategies to find a way to obviate its influence—trying out scenarios, studying the artifact for information and directives, enumerating and questioning options" (Hull and Schultz, 2001, based on a study by Knobel, 1999, pp. 593–594). Heath, Soep, and Roach (1998) have described how students in a community-based arts program "engage . . . in learning, both for themselves and for others, through highly participatory projects that encompass listening, writing and reading, as well as mathematical, scientific and social skills and strategies" (quoted in Hull and Schultz, 2001, p. 595).

Being aware of the diverse literacy practices in which students participate outside of school can help teachers (1) envision alternative ways for students to access content and demonstrate content knowledge and (2) create the conditions under which students will be able build on the literacy skills they are developing elsewhere to learn and use the language of school power.

ADDING THE LANGUAGE VALUED AT SCHOOL

In school, students who have not grown up using language and literacy that is valued by schools are confronted with two challenges: (1) accessing content and demonstrating what they have learned in that content and (2) adding the language and literacy valued by school to their repertoire. To create a context in which the language that students bring to school can be enhanced, teachers must understand enough about language itself so that they can recognize the ways in which their students are already extraordinarily healthy. They must also gain a greater awareness of the types of language demands that are made on students by the teaching and learning process, so that they can help create the conditions under which students will have access to the essential content of instruction and opportunities to develop the language used in school to talk and write about that content.

In this section, we offer a brief overview of the types of language demands that schools make on students and conclude with some suggestions about ways that students can be helped to develop what we will refer to as academic English. In most classrooms, for example, students need to:

- Understand explanations and presentations of classroom and school rules, routines, and procedures
- Understand explanations and presentations of subject matter information
- Respond to questions about explanations and presentations
- Ask questions about explanations and presentations
- Understand and participate in class discussions
- Work in small groups
- Understand texts and materials
- Complete written assignments based on explanations and text materials
- Complete projects
- Demonstrate learning through oral presentations
- Demonstrate learning through written examinations

Although there are many grade-level and subject matter differences in the ways that students might be expected to participate in what we are calling here "class discussions," the kinds of language that students need to develop to participate in such discussions are outlined in Table 4.2.

Table 4.2 Language Demands Made by Class Discussions

Type of Interaction	Language Demands
Whole-group, teacher-led discussion:	Students must:
• Students take brief turns	• Follow points made in discussion
• Students take extended turns	• Self-select (bid for the floor)
	• Display information
	• Express opinions
	• Agree or disagree with others

Once a teacher identifies what students must do with language, she can then analyze the ways that students might best be helped in developing the appropriate language. The rules for self-selecting or bidding for the floor, for example, are very highly constrained in most classrooms. Some teachers allow students to speak out, whereas others require students to raise their hands and be recognized before they can take the floor. Once recognized, students must (1) get to the point and offer their contribution and (2) use a register and style considered appropriate or correct in the school context. In many classrooms, teachers spend a great deal of time teaching students how to self-select and reminding them to do so at different points. It is just as possible for teachers to model ways in which to express opinions or to disagree with others that are typical of academic or intellectual discussions (for example, "I am not sure that I agree with Charles. I would argue that there is another perspective.") Expecting that students learn and display the sociolinguistic rules for participating in such discussions enhances their development of school language in general. (See "In the Classroom: Modeling the Language of Academic Discussions.") It may not, however, result immediately in students eliminating all traces of their own vernacular or English learner varieties. A native speaker of English could very well say, "I would argue that he done did that on purpose," and a second language learner could still say, "I would argue that she explain me the lesson." Depending on the time available to the teacher to focus on form, she might wish to attend to such details. However, some scholars maintain that with enough sustained participation in such discussions in which there are other students present who use standard forms, both speakers of vernacular varieties and English language learners will slowly acquire and begin to use those forms as well. These scholars (Brown, 1997a; Brown and Campione, 1994, 1996; Brown, Palincsar, and Armbruster, 1994; Rutherford, 1995) also suggest that students can be taught that scientists, or mathematicians, or historians, speak in particular ways about their subjects. The inner-city African American students who worked with Brown and her colleagues, for example, eagerly presented results of their scientific investigations using good approximations of presentations that they themselves had heard.

In the Classroom: Modeling the Language of Academic Discussions

Ms. Jones teaches fifth grade in a diverse elementary school in New York City. Her classroom consists primarily of African American students who, as speakers of African American Vernacular English (AAVE), use features of language that differ from those used by many white students. Ms. Jones understands that children from different backgrounds use different kinds of language for different kinds of purposes. Her goal is not to get her students to stop speaking AAVE but to help them develop other language forms. One of Ms. Jones' goals is for her students to engage in scientific discussions in a variety of settings: with partners during labs, in small discussion groups, and in whole-class discussions. Ms. Jones realizes that for many fifth-grade students, regardless of the variety of English they speak, the language expected in scientific settings often uses different vocabulary and sentence organization that students may be unfamiliar with. To expand her students' academic language repertoire, and to promote the kinds of discussions that Ms. Jones believes "real" scientists engage in, she herself uses this language and encourages students to use it as well. To assist students in doing so, she places posters around the room, each featuring phrases that can be used for particular purposes. Ms. Jones discusses with students the ways in which specialized language is used in a variety of settings student may be familiar with, including politics, religion, advertising, and sports. Students are encouraged to use the language of the scientific phrases and to add new ones when they are encountered either in class discussions or in readings. The following are some examples of the posters around Ms. Jones's classroom.

Expressing an Opinion
I hypothesize that _____
In my opinion _____
It seems to me that _____
Reporting Results of an Experiment
We were surprised to find that _____
Predictably, we observed that _____
Our results indicate that _____
Asking for Elaboration and Clarification
Could you say more about that?
In other words, you think that _____
Could you give me an example of that?
Disagreeing
I don't really agree because _____
I see it in another way.
My understanding of the results is different.
Reporting What a Partner or Group Member Has Shared
_____ explained to me that _____
_____ pointed out that _____
_____ emphasized that _____

Adapted from Kinsella, K. and Feldman, K. (2003). Structures for active participation and learning during language arts instruction. *High School Teaching Guidebook for Universal Access.* Pearson Education, Inc.

Disciplinary Literacies

As students progress across their school careers, the demands of using language in oral and written communication, as well as comprehending language, particularly in written texts, become more specialized. In K–12 education, these issues crystallize in the secondary school curriculum. Although many assume that adequate preparation in reading and writing in the primary grades will lay the foundation for future success, assessment trends in reading on the National Assessment of Educational Progress (NAEP) suggest otherwise. On the most difficult reading tasks, those requiring the comprehension of complex texts, the vast majority of seventeen-year-olds do very poorly, as illustrated in Table 4.3.

Table 4.3 Percentage of 17-Year-Olds Meeting the Standard

	African American	Latino	White
Understands complicated information	17	24	46
Learns from specialized materials	1	2	8

Source: U.S. Department of Education, National Center for Education Statistics, 1999 NAEP Summary Tables. *Adapted from:* Education Trust, 2003.

The language registers of the academic disciplines and the kinds of speech events typical of the school-based work of these disciplines are often distinct and distant from the everyday experiences of students, regardless of social class or ethnicity. They pose distinct challenges for native speakers of English across language boundaries defined by ethnicity, social class, and region. These challenges may be even greater for English language learners. These challenges are certainly compounded by poor preparation in reading, composition, and a formal understanding of the grammar of the language.

By the grammar of the language, we do not mean understanding issues like subject-verb agreement in ways defined by the prescriptions of academic English. These prescriptions categorize the use of the habitual "be," for example, by speakers of African American English (as in, "he be there all the time") as incorrect English. Rather, we mean understanding that sentences in English, regardless of the variety of English, involve either single words or groups of words together that tell us who or what we are talking about (the subject); the action, which can be passive or active, carried out by the subject (the predicate); the word or words that answer the question "what?" after the predicate ["John throws what?"] (the direct object); and the word or words that answer the question "to whom?" or "to what?" [John throws *Mary* the ball]. Other individual words or groups of words can be placed around any of these core parts (subject, predicate, object, indirect object) to answer questions such as what kind, which one, or how many (adjectives); or to what extent, how (adverbs), or where (prepositions). And finally, relationships between subject-predicate clusters or subject-predicate-object clusters can be expressed through words that define the nature of the relationship (because, although, if, after, before), (conjunctions) [I arrived at the party late *because* the babysitter had not arrived].

Examples:

Lincoln (subject) signed (predicate) the Emancipation Proclamation (direct object).

John (subject) gave (predicate) Mary (indirect object) the ball (direct object).

This certainly sounds like a lead into a boring and irrelevant grammar lesson. However, the ability to read complex disciplinary texts often requires that the reader be able to draw on such knowledge to make sense of the reading. In history classes, students should be able to read documents such as the *Declaration of Independence*, or original documents that capture the political debates among the early U.S. colonies as to how power was to be distributed across the newly established states in the newly established nation (such as *The Federalist Papers*), or first-person narratives of enslaved Africans that were so important to the communication of the abolitionist movement (such as *The Autobiography of Frederick Douglass*). The entire opening paragraph of the *Declaration of Independence* is one sentence. There is little research to suggest that students in even the best high schools learn to read such texts or that students from more affluent white families learn to tackle such texts through either their dinnertime conversations, their joint storybook reading, or their visits to the museum.

If the reader is able to comprehend such texts on his or her own, based on a rich understanding of the content on which the text is based and a long personal history of reading such documents, the reader need not draw on the kinds of technical knowledge of grammar that we have described. Meanings will more or less flow. However, if one does not have extensive declarative or propositional knowledge regarding the topic, or one does not have much personal history in reading such texts, then the reader definitely needs such metalinguistic knowledge as one of the tools in his or her reading comprehension toolkit. Unfortunately, this is the case for many students entering high school, especially in urban and rural high schools in low-income communities. This problem becomes exacerbated when teachers presume, perhaps because of low reading comprehension scores on basic skills standardized assessments, that some students do not have the capacity to tackle such texts. These assumptions are often rooted in several misconceptions: (1) a belief that students who speak a national language or language variety other than academic English do not have the linguistic resources to even begin such intellectual endeavors; (2) a belief that students who enter high school as struggling readers will only be able to tackle texts with very simple language (in terms of vocabulary and sentence structure); (3) a belief that the kinds of metalinguistic knowledge we have described can only be understood intuitively; and (4) a belief that knowledge of English grammar is at best useful only to improve written composition.

We will illustrate how a reader might use a formal knowledge of English grammar to understand a complex text in science, one which represents the kind of primary source document that high school students should be able to understand and should have repeated opportunities to read and examine.

The following selection is taken from Charles Darwin's *The Origin of the Species.* One could argue this text, and others like it, provides a knowledge base on which participation in contemporary civic debate in this democratic society could be based. American Association for the Advancement of Science (AAAS) standards in science recommend that high school students be able to read and understand such primary source documents in science. This single sentence from the text is used to demonstrate how complex and specialized are the language demands of making sense of this sentence, let alone a significant chunk of the text or the text as a whole: "We have good reason to believe, as shown in the first chapter, *that* changes in the conditions of life give a tendency to increased variability; and *in the foregoing cases* the conditions have changed, and *this* would manifestly be favourable to natural selection, by affording a better chance of the occurrence of profitable variations" [italics added] (Darwin, 1999, p. 55).

In this single sentence, knowledge of sentence structure and semantics is required to understand that

- the word *that* signals that what follows is the same as what "we believe;"
- the single noun *conditions* points back to the earlier reference to the "conditions of life."

The subject is "we." The predicate is "have good reason to believe." The word *that* signals an object expressed as a clause, which tells the reader what it is that we have good reason to believe. The argument being made offers a proposition ("We have good reason to believe . . . that changes in the conditions of life give a tendency to increased variability"). The argument is complex because it is linguistically truncated. Its details are not explicitly stated in the sentence, but assume extensive prior knowledge. The argument applies the proposition to a set of cases ("in the foregoing cases the conditions have changed"). It then goes on to articulate a second proposition, which is a consequence of the first proposition, that is, the changes in conditions of life "would manifestly be favorable to natural selection." It then goes on to offer a warrant for both the first and the second proposition; namely, that changes in the conditions of life are favorable to natural selection by "affording a better chance of the occurrence of profitable variations." Additionally, being able to deduce the two propositions, the exemplar and the warranting of the claims are only meaningful if the reader also understands the specialized meanings of the terms *conditions of life*, *variability*, and *natural selection* in the topic of evolution in the domain of biology.

In addition to the problems of sentence structure required to understand complex disciplinary texts, students also face problems of vocabulary. In science, literature, history, and mathematics, words take on specialized meanings quite different from everyday informal language. Most students will have difficulty understanding what is entailed in these specialized vocabulary terms without extensive authentic and language-rich experiences, comparable in many ways to the kinds of experiences children require in situ to learn their native language. This includes an extended amount of time, opportunities to appropriate the meanings to experiences that are familiar, and opportunities to play with the language in ways that will likely demonstrate the same kinds of "errors" young children make as they deduce the rules of their first language (for example, applying the rule for regular plurals to irregular plural forms). In science and mathematics, it is possible that students who speak a language with Latin origins, such as Spanish, Portuguese, or French, will have greater access to terms in the sciences and mathematics with Latin roots. However, teachers would need to help students explicitly make such connections.

The problems we have identified so far tend to be localized within texts. However, to grasp the overarching claims or potential claims being made in a text, the reader also needs to understand the structure of argumentation within each of these subject matters. The student needs to understand how these structures of argumentation are taken up, how they are used, and to what ends in texts they read. Students must also learn to communicate, both orally and in written forms, what they understand and what positions they take on these arguments. Arguments that students create are expected to reflect the norms of the subject matters. These subject matter norms for argumentation may not be singular. For example, in the study of literature, various theories of literary criticism value different sources to warrant claims about what a reader thinks a work is trying to communicate. However, reasoning within the subject matters is not synonymous with the kind of everyday argumentation most of us engage in at the dinner table.

The problems of high school disciplinary literacy are real and pose huge hurdles for many students. However, there is the additional challenge to teachers to understand how to teach students to understand and overcome these problems. In many respects, the process of learning to understand the sometimes obtuse ways that language is used in disciplinary texts and the specialized ways of reasoning reflected in different subject matters is very much like learning a second language. Some have argued that learning academic discourses involves issues of identity and requires many supported opportunities to practice in authentic ways. This suggests the need for a relatively consistent pedagogical approach across the high school curriculum that allows students to try on these new roles and receive feedback, and to experience the kinds of failures and adaptations of the language that all second language learners experience. We are not arguing that high school students will become experts in the ways of using disciplinary language that, for instance, professionals in the discipline achieve. However, if high school students are to gain access to the texts such as *The Federalist Papers*, Lincoln's "A House Divided" speech, or *The Autobiography of Frederick Douglass* to engage in civic debate that is warranted in this country's history; if students are to read the works of Toni Morrison, William Faulkner, and Sandra Cisneros to grapple with the dilemmas of the human condition with which these authors wrestle; if students are to read Darwin and the evolutionists who followed him to take their own positions regarding Creationism or evolution and their own perspectives on how science has been and can be used for social ends—then schools must prepare students with the tools they will need to engage these texts and the kinds of argumentation that surrounds them.

Just as one cannot learn to use a second language in everyday speech in real settings simply by memorizing vocabulary words, learning correct pronunciations, and learning a descriptive grammar (for example, when to use "vouz" and when to use "tu" in French), so students cannot learn the second languages of the disciplines through rote memorization of rules.

Inservice and preservice teachers are expected to meet the academic standards of the subject matters by apprenticing students into modes of reasoning, ways of using language, and problem solving that are characteristic of each subject matter. At the secondary level, coursework is normally taught by subject matter specialists who have expertise in the subject matters, but little formal training in the reading and writing demands of their disciplines, and even less formal training in the systematic ways that acquiring such reading and writing skills are intimately linked to issues of language acquisition and language socialization. As illustrated in earlier sections of this chapter, the research literature makes a strong case for the language demands of emergent and novice readers and writers in the primary and elementary grades. However, there is less representation of these issues for older students in the research literature, and very little in the required coursework of those training to become secondary subject matter specialists (Moore, Bean, Birdyshaw, and Rycik, 1999; Alvermann and Moore, 1991).

In the second language teaching field, scholars often speak of "interlanguages" or "approximative varieties" to talk about the characteristics of learners' speech at different points in their acquisition of that language. What is useful about looking at students' language from this perspective is that there is an underlying expectation of change over time. The learner is seen as temporarily being at a particular stage of development. For many teachers, the shift from viewing children as bundles of deficiencies and problems to youngsters who are engaged in the remarkable process of language development will involve taking this very same perspective. This language development perspective will also lead teachers to realize that students need opportunities to hear and use as much language of the variety valued by schools as possible. Students need to be placed in situations where they have maximum exposure to the higher-level academic conversations happening in schools, rather than removed from them while their "problems" are "treated."

WORKING WITH ENGLISH LANGUAGE LEARNERS

In working with English language learners (who are also sometimes referred to as bilingual students, non-native English speakers, limited English proficient [LEP], English as a second language [ESL] students, and students of English for

Speakers of Other Languages [ESOL], it is essential for teachers to know that a single label often refers to students who are very different from each other in terms of their English language proficiencies. For example, English language learners may be newly arrived students who have very little knowledge of English. These students are described in Table 4.4 as Incipient Bilinguals. The

Table 4.4 Characteristics of Students Known as English Language Learners

Incipient Bilinguals	*Ascendant Bilinguals*	*Fully Functional Bilinguals*
Comprehend very little oral English	Generally comprehend oral English well. May have problems understanding teacher explanations on unknown topics.	Are native-like in their comprehension of oral English.
Comprehend very little written English	May have trouble comprehending written English in textbooks as well as other materials. Have limitations in academic and technical vocabulary.	Well-prepared students have no problems in comprehending most written English materials. At-risk students (like at-risk monolingual English speakers) who have trouble reading have reading problems and not language problems.
Produce very little oral English	Produce English influenced by their first language. May sometimes be difficult to understand. May have trouble expressing opinions, explaining statements, challenging others.	Produce oral English effortlessly. Can carry out presentations and work effectively in groups. Can challenge, contradict, explain, and so on. Traces of first language may be detected in their accent or word choice.
Produce very little written English	Written production may contain many "errors" that make it difficult for teachers to focus on students' ideas. Completion of written assignments and tests take longer.	Depending on students' previous experience with writing, written production may contain errors typical of monolingual basic writers. Dysfluencies reflecting first language influence may still be present.

term *English language learner* may also be used to refer to intermediate learners of English who can comprehend quite a bit of English but who are limited in their production of the language. The characteristics of these students are described in the table as Ascendant Bilinguals. Finally, the term *English language learner* is, unfortunately, also used to refer to fluent-functional bilinguals who are not identical to native speakers but who are, strictly speaking, beyond the "learner" stage. These individuals, described in the table as Fully Functional Bilinguals, like monolingual English-speaking students, will continue to grow in their development of English, but they have already acquired high levels of proficiency in the language.

Ordinarily, students who are incipient bilinguals should not be placed in mainstream subject matter classes (math, science, social studies) within which teachers must attend to their needs as well as to the needs of either monolinguals or more advanced bilinguals. Giving such students access to the curriculum requires special training. Specially designed instruction in which content is combined with language, sometimes referred to as "sheltered instruction" or "specially designed academic instruction in English" (SDAIE), is generally recommended only for students who are at the intermediate level of language learning. When faced with one or two incipient bilinguals in their classrooms, teachers should insist that the school provide additional support for these students in both subject matter and language. This support may include native language support, newcomer centers run by trained staff, two-way immersion programs, or other options (see Genesee, 1999, for a description of a variety of options). Stopgap practices in which teachers ask other students to translate materials or instructions to newly arrived students are seldom effective in giving students real access to the subject. Students asked to translate may not do an adequate job of communicating what is essential. Equally important, students asked to translate are often distracted from their own learning.

When working with intermediate students, those labeled in Table 4.4 as Ascendant Bilinguals, the most important task for teachers is to determine exactly how much classroom material students can understand. Rather than relying on standardized test scores, they should carry out informal assessments of their ELL students to see if they can follow a class explanation, understand the instructions on a worksheet, read assignments in the time allotted, and so forth. Once they have this information, teachers can reflect on strengths and weaknesses of lessons for ELLs of various language levels, and design ways to provide greater access to the lesson to ELLs without compromising access to academic content and language. Teachers' greatest struggles will involve designing ways of assessing student knowledge in ways that do not penalize ELLs for their limitations in oral and written English production. Teachers must understand that learner errors persist for quite some time. As students have an opportunity to interact with more English speakers, and to learn through

English, these errors will slowly disappear. It is not the case that more instruction in English grammar will significantly aid this process. Rather than focusing on errors, teachers will want to emphasize ways of speaking and writing in the classroom or in the discipline and offer many models of both written and spoken language that students can imitate.

In the case of fluent functional bilinguals, teachers need to be especially careful. They can make few assumptions about them without taking the time to find out about their previous schooling and preparation. If such students have academic problems, it is important that teachers not assume automatically that these problems are due to their incomplete acquisition of English. As is the case with other unprepared students who are native speakers of English, when fluent functional bilinguals have trouble reading, they need remediation in reading. If such students are basic writers and have received no instruction in organizing texts or in editing their own writing, they need instruction in these areas. Moreover, even well-prepared, fluent functional bilinguals will display non-native-like features in their written and spoken English. This does not mean that they should be sent back to ESL or sheltered classrooms. It is the responsibility of classroom teachers to help all students become better readers and writers, especially as it pertains to the subject matter being taught. (See "In the Classroom: Supporting Students' Writing Development.")

The most important advice that can be given to teachers who have English language learners placed in their classrooms is that, with some effort and attention, it is quite possible to incorporate ELLs at the intermediate level and beyond in mainstream classes. What needs to be remembered is that there are many differences in background and preparation among English language learners. Teachers must make a special effort of getting to know these students' strengths as well as their weaknesses. Teachers will often find that in contributing to ELLs' language development (for example, providing models of good narratives, explaining how to write a lab report, modeling a good classroom presentation, giving instruction in reading word problems) they will also foster the development of the academic language of monolingual students in their classrooms.

In the Classroom: Supporting Students' Writing Development

Mr. Martinez teaches social studies to seventh-grade students in a predominantly Latino community at a middle school in central California. Some of Mr. Martinez's Latino students, like Mr. Martinez himself, come from families who have lived in California for several generations and speak only English. Some students were born in the United States to parents who emigrated from Mexico and use predominantly Spanish at home. Other students were born in Mexico or El Salvador and have lived and attended school in the United States for several years. Because of their diverse backgrounds, Mr. Martinez's students are at different levels of English language proficiency, ranging from English monolingual speakers to students who are still in the process of acquiring the language. However, in these mainstream classes, all the students can use oral English to communicate with their peers and to participate in class discussions.

Using English for writing in social studies, however, is much more challenging for Mr. Martinez's students. Although he is not an English teacher, Mr. Martinez values students' ability to write a persuasive expository essay and takes responsibility for his students' development as social studies writers. Because he understands that writing is a skill that is not necessarily learned along with oral language, Mr. Martinez understands that not all of his students' writing errors are a feature of second language acquisition. Many problems encountered by both his monolingual students and second language learners are the same problems faced by all inexperienced writers of expository texts, such as difficulty maintaining consistent verb tenses throughout an essay or using vague pronoun references. He recognizes other errors as potential features of second language acquisition, such as students' difficulty using articles correctly or their consistent misuse of particular verb forms. Mr. Martinez also realizes that, although it is important to address both general writing errors and those specific to second language development, neither kind of error always detracts from his students' ability to write effective social studies essays.

What does detract from his students' ability to write effective social studies essays is a lack of exposure to the kinds of expository essays increasingly expected of middle school students, such as assignments that call for students to compare and contrast social phenomena, to construct persuasive arguments regarding political beliefs, or to explain historical events. Mr. Martinez realizes that unless they can read and analyze models of the kinds of texts they are expected to write, his students will not be able to write them. Therefore at the beginning of any assignment which calls for a new kind of social studies writing (compare and contrast, persuasive, explanatory, and so on), Mr. Martinez shows students a sample essay of the kind they will be writing. He elicits comments from students on what they notice about the organization of the text, and he highlights key features such as introductory paragraphs, topic sentences, and the organization of supporting evidence. Mr. Martinez then passes out a rubric students will use to guide their own writing, and students judge the model essay based on that rubric. Next, Mr. Martinez leads the class in writing a sample paragraph together. Suggestions are elicited from the students, and Mr. Martinez serves as scribe on the overhead projector as the class discusses the suggestions, edits them, and creates a sample paragraph together. With this exposure to a model, a rubric, and practice as a class, students are then free to begin to construct their own individual essays.

Language as an Act of Identity

Teachers must also remember that language is an act of identity, which means that even with their good faith efforts and supportive environment in which to develop additional varieties of language, students may not automatically incorporate new school varieties of language into their linguistic repertoires. A large number of factors influence how students choose to use or not use the varieties of language valued in schools at any given moment. Especially at early ages, most students desire to please their teachers and be seen as good students, but they also may resist school language norms at times or decide they would rather maintain solidarity with friends who do not use language in the ways schools demand. Students use language in sophisticated ways both to work within school language norms and to resist them, at times doing both simultaneously. In fact, students sometimes use school language to resist the very norms it represents, as when one member of a class mocks the disciplinary talk of the principal, or when speakers of AAVE use "Standard" English to make fun of certain teachers. And as we have seen earlier, students' language development continues to be influenced throughout their school years both by experiences at home and other places outside the school.

This section has argued that adding the language of school to the other forms of language students use involves much more than learning a particular set of vocabulary or mastering the grammatical structures of English. This does not mean, of course, that teachers are ill-served by understanding the more formal aspects of language. Particularly because academic language needs to be acquired by almost everyone largely through reading, helping students with strategies for analyzing the texts they are reading to help them understand those texts, infer meanings for words used in such texts, and reflect on the grammatical forms that one encounters in them, can be very helpful (Fillmore and Snow, 2002; Snow, Griffin, and Burns, 2005). Furthermore, understanding something about grammar and discourse can be a big help in assessing and improving students' writing.

Enhancing the Development of Students' Language: A Summary of Big Ideas

All teachers, no matter what subjects they teach, are engaged in the process of enhancing the continuing language development of their students. In this chapter, we have presented a number of big ideas that are basic to teachers' understanding of language differences.

- Speakers of English, like speakers of every other language in the world, use many different varieties or dialects depending on their regional and class origins. Even in classrooms consisting of all monolingual English speakers, teachers will encounter students who speak differently from each other and from the teacher. With a basic knowledge of regional and class language variation, teachers can understand that such differences are a natural result of human language development and not a "problem" to be rectified.

- Dialects of English known as "Standard" English also vary. Speakers of Standard English from different parts of the country (for example, Georgia, Kansas, Boston, New York City) and the world (for example, Ireland, Australia) will use a standard language that reflects their regional origin primarily in pronunciation and vocabulary but, in some cases, in grammatical structure as well. In the classroom, the fact that a particular student's language is different from the teacher's or other students' does not mean that that student is speaking "substandard" or "non-Standard" English. Teachers who understand that there is variation among forms of Standard English may be less likely to alienate their students by attempting to change their own standard dialects.

- Children come to school as competent speakers of the varieties spoken in their homes and communities. In the classroom, there is no such thing as a student who has not developed in his own native language (although there may be students who have not developed *literacy* in their native language). Teachers who understand the nature of language development may be less likely to view their students as deficient.

- Like speakers of all other languages, speakers of English use many different registers and styles of English in their everyday lives. These styles and registers make up their speech repertoire, and speakers draw from these repertoires to carry out different types of communicative activities. In the classroom, this means that all students will use language differently according to the context in which they are using it. Teachers who understand the nature of register variation can focus on expanding students' repertoire to include the styles of various academic conventions, such as a written paper or oral presentation, without expecting students to abandon styles appropriate for other contexts, such as collaborating with a colleague, seeking advice from a teacher, or socializing with a friend.

- For most children, enhancing children's language in school will involve helping them to expand their linguistic repertoires to acquire the ways that students are expected to speak and write in school in order to discuss ideas, to understand texts, and to demonstrate their learning. In the classroom, this means that students who come from language and literacy backgrounds different from those dominant in schools will need opportunities for modeling, practice, and feedback in using language for academic purposes in ways consistent with the expectations of schools.

Preparing Teachers

As we have argued throughout this chapter, without an understanding of the big ideas about language, future and current teachers may make decisions that, unwittingly, do much harm to children and their opportunities to learn. Teachers who do not understand dialectal differences send the message to the entire class that children from certain backgrounds do not speak as well as others, or, even worse, that they do not think as well. Teachers who do not understand the multiple variations of language that every speaker is capable of may criticize or even punish students for using languages or varieties of language that may be completely appropriate in the context in which they are being used. Teachers who do not understand that students expand their school repertoire by hearing and using the language of school may segregate some students from the very language needed for them to develop that repertoire. Teachers who do not understand the unique language demands of the disciplines they are teaching may not be able to support students in learning appropriate ways to talk or write about what they are learning in that discipline.

If teachers are to see language as a central concern of their teaching and not as an "add-on" requirement for dealing with "those students" outside the mainstream, then the language education of teachers must be integrated throughout their teacher education and professional development experiences. Language must become one of the basic strands of teacher preparation parallel to traditional foundation courses on human development and teaching and learning. Additionally, an understanding of language that will allow teachers to function as communicators, educators, evaluators, educated human beings, and agents of socialization (Fillmore and Snow, 2002) must be carefully woven into other areas of teacher preparation including domains of knowledge and skill that directly support the teaching of content. Ideally, a language strand would become an integral part of the required program for all teacher candidates. Such a strand would include a specially designed introductory course in linguistics that focuses on questions and concerns central to teaching and learning in schools and that is carefully planned to support students' understanding of oral language development and both reading and writing. The language strand would also be carefully woven into existing courses in the curriculum in a variety of ways.

In the sections that follow, we include suggestions for such a course, an example of a class project that has been successful in helping students reflect on language, a list of useful texts, and a brief discussion of ways in which language information can be woven into existing courses in the curriculum.

THE INTRODUCTORY LINGUISTICS COURSE

An introductory course for teachers will ideally be taught within schools of education or, if taught in a department of linguistics, by individuals who understand the practice of education well and who also understand the key issues facing educators in American schools. Such a course could begin with an introduction to noticing and talking about language, addressing questions such as what it means to know a language and how language is used in everyday life. The building blocks of language would then be introduced, including the sound system (phonology), the structure of words (morphology), and the structure of sentences (syntax). The second half of such a course would cover first and second language acquisition, language variation, and the relationship between language and literacy.

These topics are very similar to those covered in all introductions to linguistics. The difference is that, in covering each topic, applications to language issues that arise in connection with teaching and learning are directly made. In teaching the sound system, for example, teachers immediately apply what they have learned to the role of phonological awareness in reading, as well as to regional differences in pronunciation and "accents" among non-native English speakers. Similarly, in learning about syntax, they learn the difference between grammatical sentences (those sentences generated by internalized rules of grammar) and notions of good school grammar, and they consider how syntactic rules are similar and different across languages. When studying morphology, they consider how the structure of words matters in teaching.

These same basic concepts are underscored in the study of first language acquisition when prospective teachers examine the developing grammars of children at different stages of acquisition. They also examine first language development at home and at school. By focusing on language variation, they are encouraged to understand why people, themselves included, speak differently at different times with different people and to reflect on the styles of speaking and writing that characterize the discourse communities of which they are a part. They consider the implications of language variation for teaching. When studying second language acquisition—the process of becoming bilingual—prospective teachers consider the processes of learning language in everyday interactions as well as in classrooms, and they study the different processes of learning to speak, read, and write in a second language, examining the implications for teaching second language learners. Ideally, an introductory course for teachers would include course projects, such as the one included in Gathering Language Samples, that require students to examine language carefully.

Sample Course Project[5]

The following class project entitled "Gathering Language Samples" was used successfully with groups of beginning English teachers who enrolled in the course outlined earlier.

Gathering Language Samples

Your purpose in gathering language samples is to bring a greater awareness of how language works. For your class project you can choose to record (always with the

---

[5]These samples were taken from a course, 245B, taught at UC Berkeley by Guadalupe Valdés in 1991.

permission of the speakers you record) any type of language interaction that occurs naturally in a specific setting. Ideally, you will choose to focus on a type of language that particularly interests you. For example, in carrying out your teaching duties, you may wonder how you sound when you teach as opposed to how you sound when you talk with your friends. Therefore you would record yourself teaching and interacting with friends. Similarly, you might become intrigued with the variety of English spoken by some of your students, or your fellow teachers. You could ask permission to record them under a set of conditions that preserves the naturalness of their speech. What and who you record is wide open. What is important is that you get close to some aspect of language that interests you. Examples of types of interactions and language you can record are:

1. Child language

   Do you have a young child who is now acquiring language? Record your interaction or someone else's interaction with the child. Record different activities and different situations. Place a recorder near the bed when your child is falling asleep.

2. Adolescent speech

   Are you intrigued with the slang used by adolescents? How creative is it? How is it used to exclude or include? Record your students. Talk to me about how you might go about this.

3. Regional varieties

   Have you gotten interested in how people from different places speak? Record a speaker of a variety that appears to you to be different from your own.

4. The English spoken by non-native speakers of English

   Have you become aware of special characteristics of the English of speakers who are learning English? Record a speaker who is in the process of acquiring English.

5. Professional or occupational jargon

   Are you aware that special groups of people use jargon? Record jazz enthusiasts, baseball fans, and so on talking about their distinctive interests.

   The types of language and interaction you can record are almost limitless. For example, you can record:
   - Talk between intimate friends (telephone talk, gossip)
   - Talk in the classroom
     1. Teacher to student
     2. Teacher to whole group
     3. Student to student
   - Talk in school
     1. Principal talk
     2. Teacher to teacher

Transcription and Analysis

For your project, select a portion or segment of your sample. (Roughly fifteen minutes of taped interaction). Transcribe, that is, type out a segment of your taped recording word for word. You should use regular Standard English orthography for writing out what you hear on the tape. You may wish, however, to reflect the flavor of certain kinds of features (fast speech, casual speech, southern accents, and the like) by modifying the regular spelling of the items in question.

For example, you might reflect casual teenage speech as follows:

1. Tom: Whatcha' doin' Tom?
2. Pete: Nuttin' (nothing).
3. Tom: Ya gonna?
4. Pete: Wha?
5. Tom: Go to the game?

Notice that in this example, an interruption was indicated in Tom's utterance in line 3 by splitting this utterance with line 4. This is pretty fancy, though. The general rule you should follow is to decide whether a particular feature is central to your analysis. For example, if you are interested in interruptions, you would certainly want to show where and when they take place.

Examine your sample (especially the transcribed segment) and using the information discussed in class, describe what is going on, what you hear, why, what it means, and what implications it might have for teaching and learning.

Suggested Texts and Resources

In teaching an introductory linguistics course for teachers, the choice of texts is particularly important and would most likely include types of texts such as the following:

Texts Appropriate for an Introductory Linguistics Course for Teachers

An Introduction to Linguistics Accessible to Beginners:

Linguistics for non linguists: A primer with exercises (Parker and Riley, 1999)

Texts describing children's language:

Children's language and learning (Lindfors, 1987)
Language and learning: The home and school years (Piper, 2002)
The language of children and adolescents: The acquisition of communicative competence (Romaine, 1984)
Ways with words: Language, life and work in communities and classrooms (Heath, 1983)

Texts that focus on educational issues regarding English language differences and dialects:

English with an accent (Lippi-Green, 1997)
Out of the mouths of slaves (Baugh, 1999)
Talking and testifying (Smitherman, 1986)
Standard English: The widening debate (Bex and Watts, 1999)
Dialects in schools and communities (Wolfram, Adger, and Christian, 1999)
English for your success: A language development program for African American Children, Grades Pre-K–8: A handbook of successful strategies for educators (Los Angeles Unified School District and LeMoine, 1999).

Texts that focus on educational issues regarding second language acquisition and speakers of languages other than English:

How languages are learned (Lightbown and Spada, 1999)
Second language acquisition (Ellis, 1997)
Educating language-minority children (August and Hakuta, 1998)
The power of culture: Teaching across language difference (Beykont, 2002)
Learning and not learning English: Latino students in American schools
     (Valdés, 2001)
Teaching by principles: An interactive approach to language pedagogy
     (Brown, 2001)

Texts that focus on other aspects of language important to teachers:

Language myths (Bauer and Trudgill, 1998)
Using language (Clark, 1996)
Introducing language awareness (van Lier, 1995)
Linguistics for teachers (Cleary and Linn, 1993)

Other resources:

American tongues [Videorecording] (Kolker, Alvarez and Holliday, 1986)
Language policy in schools: A resource for teachers and administrators
     (Corson, 1999).

Weaving Language Awareness into Other Curricular Strands

A course such as that previously outlined will provide teachers with a solid foundation that they can use to support the general intellectual and subject matter competencies of all their students. This core knowledge, however, must be further strengthened by a continuing exploration of language in other foundational courses as well as in courses focusing on particular subject matter areas. For example, in a course on child development, a unit or module or even a set of readings on the role of language in cognitive growth or on the role of language in the development of academic skills might be included. In a course on the sociological foundations of education, materials could be included that examine the symbolic significance of language (see, for example, Bourdieu, 1991). A course on learning theory might explicitly note that most existing theories of learning are based on the investigation of monolingual individuals and invite students to consider the implications of this fact given that the majority of the world's population speaks more than one language. Finally, a course on assessment could include among other topics the problems raised by the use of standardized tests with non-English-speaking populations (Valdés and Figueroa, 1994), the difficulties surrounding the measurement of language (August and Hakuta, 1997), and the importance of taking language difference into account when developing classroom assessments.

In the case of classes focusing on curriculum and instruction in particular subject matter areas, language must clearly be given attention. It is important for students to make connections between what they learned in the introductory course about discourse communities and the particular discourse community of which they, as professionals and as teachers of particular subjects, are a part. They must examine how their particular disciplines (math, science, social studies) use language, and they must become aware that ways of speaking and writing in these disciplines—in addition to the specialized vocabulary used in the discipline—make particular demands on students. For example, as Gee (2003b) points out, there are obvious linguistic differences that make it easy to pick out from the following two statements the one more appropriate for a science class: "Hornworms sure vary a lot in how well they grow" or "Hornworm growth displays a significant amount of variation." It is not enough, however, for teachers to learn the linguistic differences between the two statements. Teachers must also understand that the more scientific sounding of the two statements is recognizable as scientific because it applies not only to the speakers' actions (for example, observing hornworms), but rather because it also appeals to the activities, norms, and values of a particular discourse community, in this case the discourse community of biologists. For students to succeed at sounding like biologists, they must (1) understand how the communicative functions of biology match up with the social practices of biology and (2) view themselves as part of a biology "community of practice" (Lave and Wenger, 1991). For teachers, discussions about the implications for language use in their particular disciplines make most sense not as part of an "additional course" in an already overcrowded schedule, but rather as integrated throughout their core course in curriculum and instructional practices in their subject area of expertise.

Teachers must be taught how to become aware of these particular uses of language, and they must be taught how to bring them to the level of awareness of their students. In preparing to teach math, for example, teachers must engage in the examination of the demands made by reform-oriented mathematics on children's language proficiencies. As Moschkovich (1999a) points out, in such classrooms, it is no longer enough for students to acquire technical vocabulary, to read and comprehend their textbooks, and to develop strategies for understanding word problems. Students "are now expected to participate in both verbal and written mathematical discourse practices, such as explaining solution processes, describing conjectures, proving conclusions, and presenting arguments" (p. 6). As will be evident, to succeed in such classrooms, *all* children must be supported in their efforts to participate in the discourse of mathematics, and all teachers must be prepared to scaffold both the development of mathematical language *and* conceptual development.

Elementary and secondary-level teachers, whether they teach English, social studies, mathematics, science, or all primary-school subjects, must be prepared to create communities of learning of the type described by Ann Brown and her colleagues (Brown, 1997; Brown and Campione, 1994, 1996; Brown and others,

1994). Such communities include activity structures that support research, children teaching children, and sharing information. They carefully take into account the centrality of discourse in communities of practice and the importance of distributed expertise in acquiring deep content knowledge. To create such communities, teachers must understand how language and discourse practices mediate learning in their classrooms and the ways that such practices can include and exclude particular children. Ideally, prospective teachers will have the opportunity to observe and assist in classrooms that model these strategies, as well as to analyze classrooms with a range of practices and outcomes.

Beyond student teaching, another way of developing this kind of applied understanding is modeled at the University of Massachusetts at Amherst where an emphasis on praxis in the learning process for teachers involves preservice teachers in a number of collaborations with practicing teachers. In a variety of courses, teachers undertake projects to improve the learning of language-minority students. For example, in a course on *Assessment, Testing, and Evaluation*, one group of pre- and inservice teachers worked to develop culturally responsive ways of preparing linguistically diverse students for the mandated statewide standardized test. Another group worked with teachers and students in a local school to address the academic and social needs of Cambodian students who were not successfully engaging in academic work. In a course on *Teaching Heterogenous Classes*, teachers worked in teams with practitioners in local schools to design curriculum for linguistically diverse classrooms, including schools serving Hmong-, Russian-, and Spanish-speaking students that experienced different language and literacy concerns and posed different problems for teaching (Gebhard, Austin, Nieto, and Willett, 2002).

Within teacher education programs, attention to language cannot be limited to content and pedagogy courses intended for teachers of language arts or even to required courses in reading in the content areas developed for secondary teachers. For new teachers to attend to language consistently over the course of their careers, they must have modeled for them a consistent awareness of language by their instructors. New teachers will only become aware of the language demands made by their particular curriculum if they are guided by members of their own discipline in analyzing the kinds of receptive and productive language that is normally taken for granted in ordinary teaching. They must, therefore, be invited by their instructors to constantly problematize language and to examine the kinds of oral and written proficiencies that are required for their students (1) to access textbooks and other written material; (2) to comprehend teacher explanations; (3) to participate effectively in group discussions; and (4) to demonstrate what they (the students) have learned in class, on classroom evaluations, and on formal assessments. Because language demands are unique to each discipline and curriculum, this can only be done in the context of students' work on their area of specialization. Preparing to teach math or English or science must also involve understanding what counts as "good" language in particular classes for particular purposes. Student teachers can only be prepared to enhance what Lindfors (1987) called "the remarkable continuing language development of children" (p. 25) if a strong and well-planned language strand is meaningfully woven into every aspect of their teacher education experience.

CHAPTER FIVE

Educational Goals and Purposes: Developing a Curricular Vision for Teaching

Linda Darling-Hammond, James Banks, Karen Zumwalt, Louis Gomez, Miriam Gamoran Sherin, Jacqueline Griesdorn, and Lou-Ellen Finn

Having grown up within schools, most adults share the common experience of seeing teaching through the eyes of a child. Like the audience member's view of an orchestra conductor (see Chapter One), the child's view of teaching can produce a highly simplified image of what it means to teach, focusing on the superficial trappings of lectures, discussions, and assignments without an appreciation for the knowledge, planning, and analysis that undergird expert practice. For laypersons, it is easy to believe that we know most of what is important about K–12 schooling: we know how to teach because we watched teachers for many years. We understand children because we were once children ourselves, and we may have our own children. We know K–12 content because we took the required courses in school.

However, when students enter the field of teaching they quickly find out that the real mysteries of teaching were hidden to them as children. They were never involved in the intensive planning that is required for even one day of teaching, much less several weeks and months. They never had to develop relationships with children and parents who did not speak their language. They never had to work with colleagues who had very different perspectives, opinions, and personalities. Prospective teachers soon discover that the fact that they were able to learn math quickly or learned to read without realizing it does not mean that all other children will do the same. For a variety of reasons, what they learned about the content of schooling is not enough to guide curriculum decisions in their new roles as teachers. For one thing, curriculum changes. When many of us were in grade school, the Soviet Union was still a unified power, and space-craft had not yet reached other planets. In addition, the deeper structure of the curriculum—how key concepts and ideas connect and add up to a solid under-standing of a discipline—is not generally obvious to students as they learn. Finally, the "hidden curriculum" of the classroom (Anyon, 1980)—how teachers create conditions that enable or disable certain kinds of learning and identity construction for students—is often invisible to students and novice teachers.

In this chapter we focus on what teachers need to know to understand the "big picture" that guides their efforts: to be clear and purposeful about what and how they teach, to organize the formal curriculum, and to influence the informal curriculum of the classroom taking into account the social purposes of schooling in the United States as well as the children and the content they teach. We define curriculum as the learning experiences and goals the teacher develops for particular classes—both in her planning and while teaching—in light of the characteristics of students and the teaching context (Beauchamp, 1982; Macdonald and Leeper, 1965). This conception of curriculum includes the *formal curriculum*, which outlines topics or concepts to be taught; the *enacted curriculum* as it occurs in the activities, materials, and assignments teachers select and develop and in the interactions that occur between and among teach-ers and students; and the *hidden curriculum* that tacitly implements the under-lying goals and perceptions schools and teachers hold for students individually and as a group.

We assume that in the United States these curriculum goals are, or should be, shaped by the requirements of preparation for citizenship in a democracy. Given the substantial evidence that schools often reinforce unequal social statuses and differential expectations through the allocation of resources and learning opportunities (Darling-Hammond, 2001b; Gamoran and Berends, 1987; Oakes, 1990), this goal implicates teachers as change agents (Fullan, 1993b). If all students are to be prepared for democratic engagement on an equal foot-ing, teachers in many schools will need to create new conditions for learning that provide more equal access to challenging curriculum and more engagement in decision making. Furthermore, many of the "regularities of schooling" (Sarason, 1990), including the fragmentation of students' learning experiences and the paucity of opportunities for teacher collaboration, undermine the con-ditions needed for powerful teaching. This poses additional challenges for change that teachers should be prepared to face. These conditions suggest atten-tion to curriculum issues both within and beyond individual classrooms, includ-ing decisions about what learning experiences students have access to in the school as a whole.

Finally, we assume that in contemporary society, expectations and uses of new technologies play an important role as both a goal and a support for curriculum. By technologies, we mean both the standard suite of desktop productivity tools—including things like word processors, presentation managers, and spreadsheets—and common networking tools: e-mail, Web browsers, and audio, video, and text-based conferencing.

We focus on what beginning teachers need to know about the nature of curriculum decision making and the curricular planning process as these are embedded in and informed by social contexts and purposes for education. We believe a social perspective on curricular questions is important for at least three reasons. First, the broad social purposes of public education, the preparation of a citizenry for life in a democracy, must be considered as a foundation for decision making about what is taught and how it is taught. Second, successful learning is closely tied to the social contexts of learning environments, including the school, the classroom, and the community. Teachers need to be able to skillfully negotiate those contexts, both for the sake of the children and to discharge the professional responsibilities that are required of them. Third, although the teacher education content potentially included under the umbrella of social context and purposes (history, sociology, philosophy, culture, and policy) is vast and could be studied throughout a teacher's career, there is some specific information that is necessary for teachers to know during their first year in a classroom. For example, a teacher needs to know that under the law all children have a right to free and appropriate public education, and that children, regardless of their challenges, have a right to be educated in the least restrictive environment in which they can receive proper services. Teachers need to be aware of these and other policies so they can advocate for parents, children, and conditions that allow their work to be successful.

In what follows, we provide illustrations of teaching that is mindful of curricular and social purposes in both elementary and secondary schools. We discuss how teachers can develop a curricular vision and the skills needed for curriculum planning and curriculum inquiry. (The ways in which teachers apply some of this knowledge in teaching specific subject matters are further examined in Chapter Six.) We discuss the role of technology in contemporary and future classrooms as both a goal for curriculum and a resource for curriculum planning and teaching. Finally, we describe teacher education approaches that are productive for developing the knowledge, skills, and dispositions we have described.

WHY SHOULD TEACHERS BE CONCERNED ABOUT THE SOCIAL PURPOSES OF EDUCATION?

Lewis Carroll observed in *Alice in Wonderland,* "If you don't know where you are going, any road will get you there." The teacher who lacks clear goals and a sense of purpose is likely to have difficulty making sensible, consistent decisions about what to teach, when, and how. Yet teachers' goals must be developed based on more than their own individual interests.

Knowledge of our country's educational history is important if teachers are to understand the broader social purposes of education, beyond their own personal experiences and views. This includes debates about the aims of education and current perspectives and policies that shape contemporary aims. Over more than two centuries, these debates have included questions such as: Which children will get access to education and which will not? Which students should get preparation for college and which will be prepared for non-college occupations? To what extent should curriculum aim for transmission of specific facts and to what extent should it emphasize acquisition of critical-thinking and inquiry skills that allow students to seek out knowledge for themselves? Should classrooms seek to build skills for social interaction and collaboration as well as individual achievement? Should students be encouraged or allowed to learn in a native language other than English?

These questions are both educational and political in nature, and they are decided in a variety of ways, through federal, state, and local policy decisions that govern school offerings, curriculum content, and student assignments to various schools and programs, among other things. Issues of who decides what students will be asked to learn are fundamental to curriculum development, and teachers should understand the contexts in which these decisions are made, as well as their implications. Teachers should understand that curriculum is not static, but is continuously negotiated, and they should understand that their role as professionals is to bring an understanding of how different decisions are likely to affect student learning, identity, and future educational opportunities.

There are also a number of different functions of education that deserve consideration. In his book *A Place Called School*, John Goodlad (1984) identified four purposes of schools: academic, vocational, social and civic, and personal. The academic function involves the development of intellectual skills and knowledge; the vocational function prepares people for work; the social function prepares people to be citizens; and the personal emphasizes the development of the individual. All of these purposes have been strongly endorsed by members of our society—to greater and lesser extents in different communities and at different times—and are embedded in the policies and practices that continue to govern schools. Decisions about curriculum, instruction, and schooling should be made with all of these ends in mind.

Teachers are expected to pursue broadly held purposes for education, including, in today's context, new state-adopted learning standards and curriculum frameworks as well as instruction that responds to students' cultures and prior experiences, supports for language learners, and adaptations for students with exceptional needs. Additionally, such knowledge can help teachers understand the varied perspectives of parents and community members. Some emphasize preparing their children to have knowledge that enables them to compete in a competitive workforce. Others especially want their children to be taught to be good citizens who will grow up to make a difference in the world. Still others focus on their desire for their children to develop themselves as individuals. Even a first-year teacher should understand these perspectives and recognize how her personal philosophy and vision about the purposes of education, as well as her professional obligations, fit within broader societal expectations. Teachers also need a moral compass that enables them to follow through on their commitments for all children. This requires some explicit consideration of ethical issues that arise in teaching.

In addition to the importance of equal access to education in a democracy, contemporary theorists maintain that democratic education in a diverse society such as ours should seek to foster civic equality, toleration, and recognition, and it should help students develop the capacity to deliberate in public discourse (Gutmann, 1999). Just as philosophers and educators such as Julius Drachsler (1920) and Horace Kallen (1924) argued at the beginning of the twentieth century, so contemporary scholars like Will Kymlicka (1995) and Renato Rosaldo (1997) contend that diverse societies need to develop *cultural democracy* that enables immigrants and social minorities to maintain important aspects of their community cultures and languages, while integrating these contributions within the nation's overarching democratic ideals. This enables diverse groups to have allegiance and commitment to the nation's ideals and ownership in the political process. It also gradually enlarges the common intellectual and cultural space that citizens share, as this space comes to reflect aspects of more and more of the society's members.

As Parker (2003) points out, democrats are created, not born. A major task of the public schools in the United States is to educate citizens for effective participation in our diverse, democratic nation-state and society. Democratic nation-states become imperiled when their citizens do not have the knowledge, attitudes, and skills to participate in the civic and public culture of the nation-state, or when they are alienated because they do not feel that the nation-state reflects their interests, experiences, hopes, and dreams (Banks, 1997, 2004). Preparing democratic citizens requires a curriculum that connects students to the society by inviting them into the school culture, respecting their home and community traditions while also forging a common culture among the diverse members of the school community.

If these broad social goals are to be achieved, teachers need to learn to select and construct curriculum that (1) represents and connects to their students' lives and experiences; (2) allows students to develop habits of participation in a diverse community, beginning with the classroom itself; (3) supports academic, vocational, civic, and personal goals; and (4) supports equitable achievement. To accomplish these goals, teacher educators can draw on deeper bodies of knowledge than they have used in the past. This knowledge includes information about the social contexts and purposes of education, the influences of culture on learning and schooling, and the development of curriculum, including responsive curriculum, pedagogy, and assessment. We deal with these bodies of knowledge in this and subsequent chapters.

PROFESSIONAL RESPONSIBILITIES AND THE POLICY CONTEXT

In addition to knowledge of social contexts and purposes, teachers need to be aware of a range of policies that define their rights and obligations to children and should be reflected in their curricular thinking. These include policies that aim to protect the general welfare and educational rights of children—for example, policies regarding child abuse and neglect or special education responsibilities— as well as those that aim to define aspects of curriculum, teaching, assessment, and professional responsibilities teachers are meant to implement.

Although it might be tempting to suggest that these many and varied expectations should not be the concern of beginners, it is not legally or ethically acceptable to say to a special needs child whose new teacher fails to implement necessary accommodations that the teacher will learn how to attend to these needs some day, long after the child has failed or moved on to another classroom. Neither is it acceptable to say to a parent who expects her third-grade child to learn the district standards that the new teacher did not understand she had to attend to these standards and did not know how to develop a curriculum that would enable her third graders to learn them.

Discharging professional responsibilities and those defined by policies is much more complex than simply learning the law or reading a list of professional expectations. It requires knowledge about the nature of the responsibilities and what is required; skills to deal with children, parents, and other professionals in identifying and solving problems; and dispositions to accept responsibility, listen carefully, take into account many perspectives, and exercise judgment carefully. The importance of all these abilities can be illustrated with the example of a teacher who is faced with protecting a child who is being abused. In this situation, the teacher first must know the signs of abuse in order to diagnose a problem. She must be able to sort out the cultural considerations that sometimes complicate determinations about why a child is behaving in a certain way or what a parent's behaviors may have been. She must know the laws regarding child abuse in this country and the school policies and procedures surrounding the reporting of abuse. She must have the moral courage to stand up against an injustice and follow through with reporting the abuse. She must know how to work with other professionals and community agencies, including counselors, child protective services, and the courts. And, most important, she needs to know how to interact with children who may be abused and parents who may be abusive. She must refrain from biased inter- actions that could leave a child (or parent) afraid or unwilling to seek help in the future.

To discharge many kinds of responsibilities, teachers need to understand the social context of schools as organizations: how they reflect and relate to the communities in which they are located, and how they operate as organi- zations with norms, expectations, people, and structures that must be interde- pendent if the members of the school are to accomplish their jobs effectively. Although teachers' knowledge about these matters is clearly important for chil- dren, it is also important for the survival and success of novice teachers. By the time teachers enter the classroom, if they do not understand how to work with a diverse group of children, if they are thwarted by the difficulties of nego- tiating a bureaucracy, or if they have trouble handling a complex community of parents, colleagues, and administrators, they will most likely leave the field. Most teachers enter the profession with good intentions, moral commitments, and a caring attitude toward children. Many of these same people find them- selves looking for other careers when they are not able to negotiate the chal- lenging social and political contexts of schools.

A first step toward understanding these complex relationships is the consid- eration of educational goals and purposes from a *social* perspective, that of the local community as well as the broader society, not just an unconsidered per- sonal perspective. A second step is understanding the professional role in terms of the expectations of the teacher as a purposeful actor in the social process of education. This carries with it responsibilities for planful teaching and work with colleagues that extends beyond the implementation of daily classroom lessons.

WHY SHOULD TEACHERS LEARN ABOUT CURRICULUM?

People use the term *curriculum* in many ways and often encounter difficulties in talking with one another about the extent to which curriculum should be developed within or outside a given classroom because they have different def- initions in mind. A common conception of curriculum is that it refers to the topics taught and the books or materials used. However, two teachers who use the same text or "cover" the same topics may teach very different things in quite different ways. Our conception of curriculum extends beyond a textbook series, a specific curriculum package, or a state or local curriculum guide. Beyond these formal content guides, we include the decisions and adaptations teachers make to ensure that the ideas and skills they hope to teach are made accessible to students. Although teachers may or may not be working with a formal curriculum approach, framework, or set of materials outlined by a state or district, these resources, no matter how useful, cannot determine all that the teacher does. Curriculum materials alone do not determine how the teacher can create equitable classrooms that support all students, draw connections to students' prior knowledge and experiences, choose appropriate starting places and sequences of activities, develop assignments and assessments to inform learning and guide future teaching, and construct scaffolding for different students depending on their needs.

Nor can these broader curriculum resources by themselves resolve the many competing goals teachers must balance in the classroom. For example, teachers must rely on their own curricular vision and understanding of educational purposes as they address the differing needs of various individual children at any moment in time; as they decide among the competing uses of instructional time that they are always faced with; and as they pursue a variety of goals, such as encouraging independence versus the importance of adequate support when a student is struggling, the continual tension between investigating ideas deeply and covering a wide terrain, and the development of social and academic skills. These goals and decisions are informed both by broader social goals for education and by social policies such as those governing coeducation, education of children with special needs, and student and educator rights and responsibilities.

Although the study of curriculum and its development have not always been part of the teacher education curriculum, for all of the reasons we have discussed, we believe such knowledge is essential for all teachers. Curriculum guides, texts, and tests help the teacher respond to a subset of local and state expectations; however, by their very nature they cannot dictate a curriculum for a particular class. Because what is taught must connect to student readiness and interests as well as to community contexts, even topics that are routinely taught or presented in texts require curricular deliberation and development. Subject matter teaching needs always to be infused with a developmental perspective and sensitivity to social contexts. As an experienced teacher observed: No textbook writer, curriculum developer, or department head can know exactly what it is that a particular teacher must do within that classroom. The teacher can, and the good teacher does. Guidelines imposed by the subject, the mandated curriculum, and superiors must be shaped and molded to fit the teacher's vision of what needs to be done and the needs of the students in that classroom. The good teacher does so consciously, making priorities and following through on them (John Dore, 1988, in Zumwalt, 1989, p. 174).

The capacity to plan instruction so that it meets the needs of students and the demands of content, so that it is purposeful and "adds up" to important, well-developed abilities for students, is not something that most people know how to do intuitively or that they learn from unguided classroom experience. For example, a study of experienced teachers who had not had previous formal preparation found that among the things they felt they learned from the graduate-level pre-service program that they entered after several years of teaching were the abilities to engage in curriculum planning; to set long-term goals and organize instruction and assessment in support of these goals; to assess, reflect on, and improve their teaching; and to make decisions grounded in useful theoretical frameworks about teaching and learning (Kunzman, 2002, 2003). Many of these experienced teachers spoke of their previous lack of long-term vision in curricular planning, such as one who admitted, "I didn't have a big vision for where my class needed to go: What was my end result? Where did I want to be at the end of the semester, both in content and in skills? So I couldn't work cogently toward those goals." Another teacher described her former planning process:

> I would sit down and I would plan things, but I never . . . really thought, "Okay, what is it that I want them to know? How are they going to know it? And how am I going to know that they know it?" I never did that kind of stuff. Time would go by and I'd say, "Well, I'd better do an assessment here, or a test, or I'd better have some sort of project here." You know what I mean? It's kind of just a natural feeling (Kunzman, 2003, p. 246).

As another teacher noted about what she had learned, "You really need a tighter purpose. You really need to know where you're going . . . you know, look at the work as a whole: 'What do I want out of this year?'" (Kunzman, 2003, p. 246). According to these experienced teachers, the teacher education program taught them the rudiments of lesson planning and the elements of instruction a lesson should encompass as well as the more complex skills of thematic planning around a central question with extensive scaffolding involved in getting students to a performance goal (Kunzman, 2002).

Well-prepared teachers have developed a sense of "where they are going" and how they and their students are going to get there. They are able to create a coherent curriculum that is also responsive to the needs of students and to construct a classroom community in which the "hidden curriculum" fosters respectful relationships and equitable learning. They have thought about social purposes for education as well as their own vision and have integrated these so that their students can be successful in the world outside of school as well as within the supportive environment of the classroom. The following vignettes demonstrate how two young teachers, a high school English teacher prepared at the University of Virginia in Charlottesburg, Virginia, and an elementary teacher prepared at Alverno College in Milwaukee, Wisconsin, create a purposeful curriculum—both formal and "hidden"—and enact it with attention to the responses of learners.

Selena Cozart: Focusing on Competence and Community

On a sunny Wednesday morning in April, Selena Cozart, a graduate of the University of Virginia's teacher education program, is listening intently as groups of her ninth-grade students are making presentations on the different novels each group has read. Their assignment is to share the central ideas with their classmates, who, in turn, are asked to write a paragraph summarizing the plot of the unfamiliar novels. The students have Selena's full, undivided attention. After the third group has made its presentation in a talk-show format, Cozart steps forward. Immediately, one can feel that Selena has a clear sense of purpose for her work with these youngsters as well as a deep respect for each of them. Encouraging her charges to write their paragraphs, she manages several other tasks at once, including collecting books, checking make-up work, and coaching students in their writing by quickly reading drafts and making direct, focused comments. She undertakes these tasks with equanimity and good humor, matched with a firm expectation about getting the job done. This is a class in which students clearly are expected to learn about novels, their structure, and content. Students seem comfortable speaking up in class, and Selena insists that there be no interruptions when students are talking.

Cozart explains that she has worked hard to create a "sense of community" in her classroom. She appears certain of her role and of the classroom structure that will help her achieve her purpose. Permeating this culture and structure is a sense that this classroom is a warm, safe, and caring place. Cozart is in tune with her students and thinks carefully about the needs of each individual. She stresses the importance of classes with clear goals, but also champions the importance of structured choices, so that students can control their learning. For example, though all must meet a common objective, she allows students to choose groups and partners, and she gives them options on paper topics, stressing that there are multiple ways to reach a stated goal.

Cozart's personal passion for literature is palpable and infectious. "I love language," she declares, and indicates that she hopes to help her students share her passion. She works hard to communicate her knowledge and love of literature so that her students will learn to appreciate literature and revisit it later in their lives. However, she is also quick to acknowledge that students need more than passion for a particular subject or genre. They need skills. Selena is unwavering in her commitment to help her students gain sufficient skills to write well and communicate clearly. Cozart is clear with her students about the need for these skills in the "real world." Invoking a belief in the importance of basic skills and the responsibility of teachers to teach them, Selena states, "I do teach grammar [but] we talk about what the purpose is." She expects her students to spell correctly—spelling matters in the real world, she tells them—but she also teaches the students how to correct and check their work using dictionaries, spell-checkers, and peer and adult tutors. Her teaching exhibits the influence of a clear and strong philosophical perspective combined with an array of instructional strategies to achieve her purpose.

In addition to her own efforts to act on behalf of the learners, Cozart also pushes others in her school to make decisions that will improve conditions for students. She participates actively in policy decisions about resource allocation in her department and tries to engage other teachers in learning opportunities that she has identified outside of the school. During a discussion with her colleagues about the use of a $2,000 technology grant to her department, she "spearheaded a discussion of what we were going to do [with the money] and how we were going to get there." In this discussion, she wanted her colleagues to be aware of their decision-making process and to acknowledge its implications for students. Cozart is not shy about the power of inquiry and the obligation that teachers have to question what decisions mean for students.

Source: Adapted from Merseth and Koppich, 2000.

Berthina Johnson: Reinforcing Learning with Home and Classroom Connections

At 8:30 A.M., after a half-hour informal period in which students read from the many trade books that are scattered throughout the room and engage in a spirited recitation of the school creed emphasizing pride in self, school, and academic success, Berthina Johnson gathers her twenty-six first graders on the floor in front of the calendar. Adams School is located in one of Milwaukee's poorest neighborhoods. About 93 percent of the 746 pupils in the school qualify for the free breakfast and lunch program and the school has a mobility rate of 34 percent. Like their teacher, all twenty-six of Ms. Johnson's pupils are African American.

After a brief career in the insurance industry, Berthina graduated from Alverno College with a degree in elementary education. Almost every inch of space on the walls of her bright, cheery classroom is used to review and reinforce concepts and words found in the students' everyday world with colorful materials related to the alphabet, numbers, colors, shapes, days of the week, and basic vocabulary words. Several learning centers throughout the classroom provide opportunities for children to work on math and reading skills with computers, to write and draw, and to listen to a tape while following along in a book.

One of Berthina's major goals for her first graders this year is to encourage them to become more independent and responsible for their actions over the course of the year. Throughout the morning, Berthina continually reminds her pupils that they are first graders and not kindergartners so they must do things like speak in complete sentences, and take responsibility for their own behavior. Throughout the morning, she repeatedly poses questions to the class as reminders of things discussed beforehand and invites a choral response from the class to such questions as, "How can we become good readers?" The response each time is, "By reading good books." Pupils are focused intently upon the activity at hand for the whole morning, and the class is lively and buzzing with talk about the things students are working on.

Today, Berthina reviews and reinforces with her pupils ideas such as the date, the meaning of the words *yesterday*, *today*, *tomorrow*, and *weekend* and basic math concepts such as place value and counting forwards and backwards. The pace is quick and the expectations are high for student success. Berthina poses one question after another and asks for a response from either an individual child or the whole group. If a child or the group does not answer a question correctly, she keeps encouraging the children until they are able to figure out the answer. If students respond to Berthina's questions with phrases instead of complete sentences, Berthina is very persistent in pushing them in a friendly and supportive way to respond in complete sentences, and she sticks with them until they do.

The class moves immediately upon finishing the calendar lesson to a reading activity. The pupils cut out and color a cap with the letters "ap" marked on it and slip in sheets of paper with consonants and consonant blends and read the words together as a class, and in pairs. Berthina encourages the children to take their materials home that night and read the words to someone else. The rest of the morning is spent working on math problems involving place value. For an addition problem, the pupils are asked to draw a picture to show how they have solved the problem. Two pupils who have solved the problem using different strategies are then asked to draw their pictures on the board and to explain to the rest of the class what they have done. During the half hour when students are free to choose to work at any one of the various learning centers in the room, students read, work at computers on games that provide practice in math and reading, draw, or listen to tapes and follow along in a trade book.

Throughout all of the academic tasks, Berthina is very attentive to individual children and their needs, creating a warm, caring environment along with clearly articulated expectations. Two boys complain of feeling ill and require individual consultations about whether they want to go home (both decide to stay), and a girl complains about her eye hurting. Another young boy, who is crying because he cannot find his pencil, also requires a few minutes of hugging and support. Several parents come into the room and speak with Berthina about various matters. Each time she warmly welcomes them into the room and spends a few minutes talking with them. In her responses to her pupils throughout the morning, she reveals knowledge of all of the special circumstances involved with contacting the children's homes. In one case, an older brother is to be contacted to pick up an ill child. In other cases, Berthina refers to a child's grandmother, uncle, mother, or father. She seems to know in each case who needs to be contacted.

Berthina has made a conscious decision to blend "process" and "skill-oriented" instruction in her classroom, combining learning centers and trade books with specific instruction in phonics and other skills. Consistent with the focus of her preparation at Alverno, she has focused first and foremost on what she perceives to be in the best interests of her pupils. Also, consistent with the focus of the Alverno program, Berthina is a member of the school district's assessment team and is involved in piloting the use of portfolios to assess the work of her pupils. Finally, like many of the other graduates from the program, Berthina has remained involved with the program after her graduation by mentoring Alverno College field students who work in her classroom and by talking about her teaching to Alverno College students on campus.

Source: Adapted from Zeichner, 2000.

Both of these young teachers have clear goals about what they intend to accomplish in their year with their students, in terms of content, habits of mind and communication, and interpersonal relations. They enact these goals with well-chosen, engaging activities and consistently reinforce them in a variety of direct and indirect ways, creating purposeful synergy among the many things students do, as well as a sense of academic press. They have made conscious decisions about what they do in their choice of content and teaching strategies, considering the needs of their students and their sense of the demands of their disciplines and of society. Their classrooms prepare students for the world beyond, from consciousness about the use of language to competence in the use of computers. The "hidden" curriculum emphasizes respect, high expectations and strong supports for all students, social responsibility, and community, including the involvement of parents as welcome members of the classroom. Both take broader roles in the school to improve the quality of instruction for all students. These young teachers have developed a curricular vision with a deep appreciation of the social contexts within which they work and the broader purposes of education.

DEVELOPING A CURRICULAR VISION FOR TEACHING

Zumwalt (1989) suggests that beginning teachers' initial knowledge of curriculum should include an understanding of (1) different views of curriculum and what they suggest for educational goals and the teacher's role; (2) how to develop and carry out curricular plans that are coherent and have a high probability of success; and (3) how to make sound curricular decisions and address curricular issues that arise. Without these understandings and skills, beginning teachers are likely to lurch along from day to day, not able to develop plans that "add up" for their students and move them purposefully from point A to point B. They are also less likely to be able to make much sense of what is working or not working in the classroom or to figure out how to address problems in ways that are more than ad hoc guesswork.

Understanding Curriculum in Terms of Learning Experiences

Curriculum has many meanings. To many laypeople, the curriculum is the subjects that students must study, such as math, English, and biology, or the list of topics included in a course or syllabus. Sometimes people think of curriculum as the textbook or curriculum guide or set of skills measured on a test. These are all legitimate uses of the term *curriculum*; however, from the student's perspective, what actually happens in the classroom—the enacted curriculum and how it plays out—is what constitutes the real set of learning experiences she encounters. For example, a group of students may be enrolled in a course called algebra for which the list of topics in a curriculum guide includes nonlinear functions. There is a chapter on this in the required text. However, if their teacher spends only thirty minutes explaining nonlinear functions, without opportunities for practice and review, the enacted curriculum is not comparable to what some other students might experience in a different course by the same name, even using the same textbook, where the teacher spends weeks on the same topic. What counts as the curriculum for the students are the learning experiences that actually occur. Although it may seem odd to those who do not work in or study schools, there is evidence that what occurs in different classes and schools in courses with similar names is substantially different in content, emphasis, and method (see, for example, McKnight et al., 1987).

Similarly, *how* teachers approach the teaching of a given topic or body of content influences the curriculum that students experience. For students and teachers, curriculum and teaching are intertwined. Furthermore, assessment is also an integral part of how content is conceived, how teaching is structured, and how learning unfolds. So, for example, contrast the experiences of two real groups of students in different English classes studying Sophocles' *Oedipus the King.* In one group, the teacher assigns the reading of the book as homework, holds two days of discussion about the book in class, and has students take a test on the book emphasizing new vocabulary and facts about characters and plot details. In the other group, the teacher provides a choice of essay questions, such as "Was Oedipus the victim of fate or did he create his destiny?" a month in advance. She begins the unit with a contemporary essay about the *Oedipus complex,* relating this common term to what students are about to read. They read the book over two weeks, combining daily read-alouds and dramatic presentations of the play with nightly reading for homework and guided journal questions. The journal questions ask students to reflect on aspects of the unfolding characters and plot related to the essay topics that are ahead. The teacher reviews these journals throughout the weeks to give feedback and gauge students' understanding, which she uses to adjust her teaching and to ensure that she finds a way to get every student participating in the conversation. Class discussions in large and small groups take up these questions and probe them further. The class also stages a debate on the question of Oedipus' responsibility for his fate; students then write a series of drafts regarding the essay question chosen, with peer review and teacher review before completing a major essay on the book.

In terms of what the teacher does to support student learning systematically, in terms of what students experience, and in terms of the understanding and skills students have as a result, these classrooms offer very different curricula. These curricular differences not only have implications for the content students encounter but for the extent to which the classroom produces equitable outcomes. The more extensive scaffolding and multiple modes of learning offered in the second classroom are more likely to produce strong outcomes for a wider range of students, thus supporting social justice goals as well as content learning goals.

New teachers are often shocked to learn that what they had hoped students would be able to do as a consequence of instruction does not magically happen when they present a topic. Prospective teachers need to understand the interrelationships between how they *organize* what they teach (in addition to specific teaching techniques or strategies) and what they hope to accomplish if they are to help students achieve what they hope for them. The second teacher's strategy reflects a kind of purposeful teaching pointed at significant outcomes embedded in a performance assessment they work toward. This kind of instruction has been found to produce stronger outcomes in a number of studies. For example, a study of more than 2,000 students in twenty-three restructured schools found higher achievement for students who experienced instruction organized around clear performance assessments calling for higher-order thinking, extended writing, and an audience for student work and who were engaged in active learning toward that end (Newman, Marks, and Gamoran, 1995). A study of 820 high schools in the National Education Longitudinal Study (NELS) also found that students in schools with high levels of this kind of instruction experienced greater achievement gains on standardized tests (Lee, Smith, and Croninger, 1995).

Decisions made explicitly and implicitly during the planning and interactive phases of teaching influence what students learn and are influenced by the teacher's intentions for and vision of student learning. Many competing visions of learning and of curriculum exist in and around schools. Bloom's taxonomy (Bloom, 1956), for example, articulates many kinds of learning, ranging from recognition and recall of information to analysis, synthesis, and production of ideas and performances. Though all of these kinds of learning are important, educators, parents, policymakers, texts, and tests vary in the emphasis they place on each kind. To evaluate curriculum materials and to converse with other professionals and parents, teachers need to be conversant about the assumptions people are making about educational goals, purposes, and methods when they discuss curriculum ideas.

Teachers need to be able to ascertain what kind of learning is implied by different materials and recommendations for curriculum and determine whether the goals they and others hold are likely to be achieved if particular approaches or materials are adopted. Teachers also need to evaluate their own strategies: is a teacher satisfied only to have students learn to recall the ideas they have read or heard about, or does she want students to be able to evaluate ideas, weigh and use evidence, synthesize a variety of kinds of evidence, and produce arguments, ideas, and products such as research reports, critiques, and science experiments? Teachers need to understand how their goals for instruction should be related to the assignments and assessments they devise, the activities they plan, the materials they select, the feedback they give, and the ways in which they interact with students. As Zumwalt (1989) observes:

> Decisions, made explicitly and implicitly during the planning and interactive
> phases of teaching, influence and are influenced by one's vision of what one
> hopes students learn. When one makes instructional decisions (e.g., use whole

group instruction in math; use reading workbooks for practicing separate component skills; use the tests which accompany the social studies texts), the nature of the curriculum for students . . . is affected. Choices of "how" are more than instrumental; they influence the curriculum, often in profound ways. Prospective teachers need to understand this interrelationship if they are to be thoughtful and reflective about their practice. (p. 175)

Planning Curriculum

Given that teachers are responsible for enabling students to achieve some overarching instructional goals and not just for "getting through the book," beginning teachers should have knowledge of a planning process that enables them to plan curriculum beyond the individual lesson. This expectation has become even more pronounced since the advent of learning standards in most states; these standards articulate what children are expected to know and be able to do but do not typically set out how these goals might be achieved. Teachers need to be able to figure out how to organize their curriculum around the most important learning elements implied by the standards and configure a sensible sequence and set of activities for the particular students they teach. There are a number of curricular planning processes that can serve as touchstones, ranging from Tyler's (1950) objectives-based model, which has dominated much of the work of curriculum designers and textbook publishers for a half century, to Wiggins and McTighe's (1998) *Understanding by Design,* which outlines an instructional design process that enables teachers to "map backward" from their goals to desired performances to activities and elements of scaffolding needed to support student progress.

These and other strategies (see, for example, Barnes, 1982; Doll, 1982; Eisner, 1985; Posner and Rudnitsky, 1982; Walker and Soltis, 1997) are organized around the generally accepted commonplaces of curriculum development, which treat the nature of the subject matter, the learners, the context, and the teacher's role (Schwab, 1973) in the planning and evaluation of teaching. These four commonplaces are placeholders for areas of knowledge that inform instructional decisions. For each of the commonplaces there is a diverse knowledge base drawn from research and theory across many disciplines and fields of study, for example, developmental and cognitive psychology, linguistics, sociology, philosophy, and others. Understanding curricular decision-making in terms of commonplaces that continuously influence each other helps teachers think about the interactive quality of curricular decisions: for example, how best to choose and organize content for particular learners, given the school and classroom context and the nature of the teacher's role.

Elements of Curriculum Planning. In addition to the knowledge of content, learners, contexts, and teaching reflected by these commonplaces, there are at least three interrelated elements in any curricular planning process that prospective teachers need to know about: educational purposes, learning experiences, and evaluation.

In terms of *educational purposes,* beginning teachers should have a conception about what is important to study in the content areas they teach based on social needs and expectations, learning standards, and research about the kinds of understandings that are necessary for transfer and for further learning. They should be able to define and defend the goals they select to their students, parents, colleagues, administrators, and themselves. And they should be able to translate their broad goals into more discrete objectives that can guide particular lessons and units of study. At the same time, teachers must be able to find the right "grain size" for objectives around which they plan—one that does not become so microscopic as to trivialize the skills sought, resulting in the "triumph of technique over purpose." There is evidence that when objectives and associated tasks are overly narrow and decontextualized (for example, "students will be able to identify the 'schwa' sound with 80% accuracy" or "students will recount the first 5 elements of the periodic table"), children's learning fails to add up to transferable knowledge (Bransford and others, 1999, pp. 41–46). Similarly, teachers need to know how to develop an appropriate level of detail for planning—one that provides strong guidance for a coherent progression of activities but does not prevent the teacher from remaining flexible in the face of student responses that suggest the need for adjusting pacing or strategies to ensure that students are understanding. Some research, for example, suggests that students learn less when teachers' planning is too detailed and rigid, such that the teacher focuses more on getting through the plan than on ensuring that students learn (Peterson and Clark, 1978; Duchastel and Merrill, 1973; Yelon and Schmidt, 1973).

In our earlier examples, Selena Cozart and Berthina Johnson were clear about their educational purposes, were able to explain their choices of goals and activities to their students, and were able to weave their most fundamental purposes into the informal as well as the formal curriculum, by, for example, helping students develop habits of communication, such as speaking in complete sentences or reviewing and revising their writing. These were not just discrete tasks on a given day but were infused in ongoing everyday expectations. In addition, these teachers worked with others in their buildings to develop expectations and practices that would extend across classrooms, thus creating a more powerful and coherent educational experience for students throughout their schooling years. A focus on educational purposes in teacher education should help prospective teachers learn to create coherent, connected learning experiences both within and beyond the classroom and evaluate curriculum options in light of what they and their colleagues are trying to accomplish.

Planning *learning experiences* to achieve educational purposes requires attention to selection and organization of content and activities—what is often called "scope and sequence." Teachers must decide what is important to include, given their goals, and know how to make it accessible to a particular group of students. This requires thinking about how to give students a schema or conceptual map of the domain to be studied (National Research Council, 2000) as well as planning specific activities in light of students' levels of readiness for various kinds of learning experiences. It also requires consideration of the kinds of information, demonstrations, models, inquiry opportunities, discussion, and practice students need over time to understand particular concepts and develop particular skills. Although research has found that all of these features of instruction can support learning, the process of instructional design requires that teachers figure out which things students should do when, in what order, and how.

Attention to organizing elements, principles, and structure is important to avoid a curriculum that is just a sequence of interesting activities (Tyler, 1950). In addition, task analysis is important to figure out the prerequisite knowledge and skills that must first be taught if students have not already acquired them. This analysis should guide careful scaffolding of the learning process to ensure that students have explicit opportunities to acquire the requisite knowledge and skills systematically (Collins, Brown, and Newman, 1989). Also important is knowledge of different ways of organizing students' work (for example, small group or whole group discussion, lecture, practice opportunities, individualized instruction) and how to manage them, along with an understanding of what kinds of tasks are best suited to which kinds of organizational structures.

Cognitive psychologists have developed a base of research on learning that brings new insights that can help teachers with many aspects of instructional design. For example, in the choice and sequencing of activities, studies suggest that opportunities for hands-on inquiry coupled with conceptual explanations are more effective than either discovery learning or direct instruction alone (Schwartz and others, 1999).

There is a recent awareness that assessments are also a part of learning experiences, as they both guide the teaching and learning process—operationalizing learning goals and making clear the criteria for good performance—and provide opportunities for feedback about how students can improve their learning. There is evidence that attention to formative assessment with concrete, specific feedback throughout the learning process increases student achievement (Black and William, 1998). Planning strategic opportunities for such feedback throughout a sequence of learning activities in the form of carefully planned assignments and assessments is critically important.

Finally, teachers need to know how to *evaluate* their curriculum decisions— to collect diagnostic, formative, and summative information about what is working and how students are learning against the variety of different goals they may have for their classroom. They need to be aware of trade-offs that can occur as well: for example, an exclusive emphasis on students learning to recall arithmetic facts might reduce the time students are spending exploring the underlying number concepts, leading to an inability to evaluate whether a hastily recalled answer or algorithmic solution is sensible or meaningful. Overemphasis on group work without sufficient individual work might leave the teacher with inadequate diagnostic information about individual students' learning and, thus, unexplained outcomes on other assessments. Focus on too many topics might undermine adequate attention to some critical areas of learning that are foundational for many others. And so on. To figure out how curriculum decisions contribute to the outcomes teachers observed, they must be able to collect and analyze information from their students through formal and informal assessments of what they are understanding and what they are having difficulty with on classroom measures as well as standardized tests.

The Role of Technology. Increasingly, teachers need to be able to consider the role of technology as they plan curriculum. Although early expectations that technology would transform the practice of teaching and learning have not yet been realized, evidence is beginning to suggest that recent investments by schools and school districts are starting to pay off (Becker, 2001; Ronnkvist, Dexter, and Anderson, 2000). Most teachers have ready access to a desktop computer and e-mail while in school (Ronnkvist and others, 2000), and 43 percent of teachers who teach in self-contained elementary school classrooms report frequent use of computers by students in their classrooms (Becker, 2001). (In contrast, however, teachers of high school subjects like English and social studies report much lower percentages: 24 percent and 12 percent, respectively.)

Technology influences curriculum thinking and planning in many ways. First, fluent use of new technologies is now a societal goal for curriculum. Today's students will need to use a variety of technologies in their future lives as workers and citizens, thus schools must play a role in closing the gaps in access to this knowledge represented by the current "digital divide" in home and community access. Second, technology provides a resource for curriculum development, as it enables teachers to find and assemble materials and to guide their students in doing so as they take on independent inquiries. Today's networks give schools access to much more information and many more people than was ever before possible. This poses additional needs for students to learn how to locate and critically analyze information. Internet browsers and the World Wide Web give students and teachers access to information that is situated in domains of practice (Shulman, 1986). Today's networks also make it possible for teachers and children to join communities of people well beyond their schoolhouse doors. With synchronous and asynchronous conferencing, teachers and students can join with varied communities in the discourses of those domains (New London Group, 1996).

Third, technology can provide tools that are analytically useful in various domains of practice, for example, simulation, modeling, and visualization tools in science, and text analysis tools in literature. Technologies that permit scientific visualization and dynamic modeling, for example, make it possible for people in schools to use tools that are the same or very similar to the tools that people who engage in professional practice use in their own work (Edelson, Gordin, and Pea, 1997). These tools also make abstract concepts like feedback tangible and dynamic for learners (Jackson, Krajcik, and Soloway, 2000).

Finally, technology provides tools that aid in reflection and improvement, including video tools that allow teachers and others to consider and analyze their personal practice and the practice of others. Computing applications that are readily available to learners, like multimedia authoring tools, allow learners to display what they know in a variety of ways that extend well beyond text or stand-and-deliver presentations (Mott and Klomes, 2001). These tools are also a way for public and concrete reflection on what learners know and what teachers do. These tools can allow teachers to show students models of good performances and support formative assessments of learning in the classroom. Video tools can also help teachers evaluate and improve their curriculum, by assembling and aggregating student work so that teachers can look at it collectively and can explore what curriculum revisions may be needed to improve student performances.

Making Curriculum Decisions

Research indicates that curriculum choices at both the classroom level and the school level can matter a great deal to student learning. Not only do the courses students take influence their overall achievement (Jones, 1984; Pelavin and Kane, 1990), so does the nature of the content they experience within courses, in terms of the topics that are taught and the depth with which key concepts are studied (Gamoran and Berends, 1987; Gamoran and Weinstein, 1995; McKnight et al., 1987; Lee and others, 1995). Curricular approaches that take advantage of what has been learned from research on learning and cognition have been found to promote greater conceptual understanding. For example, students better acquire complex skills when their teachers help them recognize patterns and develop self-monitoring strategies, model thinking, scaffold the learning process, and provide coaching while students use their knowledge in a variety of applications. In addition, students are better able to generalize and transfer knowledge when their teachers help them develop the ability to evaluate and regulate their own learning, see patterns for transferring their knowledge, and gradually take on more independence in their learning (Anderson, 1989; Good and Brophy, 1995). Curricular approaches built on these principles have been found to develop higher-order skills and greater conceptual understanding in the areas of reading (Duffy and others, 1987b; Palincsar and Brown, 1984,

1989), writing (Englert and Raphael, 1989; Englert, Raphael, and Anderson, 1992), mathematics problem solving (Carpenter, Fennema, Peterson, Chiang, and Loef, 1989; Fennema, Carpenter, and Peterson, 1989; Wood and Sellers, 1996), and science (Otto and Schuck, 1983; Rubin and Norman, 1992). Teachers need to understand the principles that underlie such successful approaches and be able to gauge how their curricular decisions are likely to influence their students' achievement.

Research on many decades of curriculum reforms also demonstrates that curriculum materials do not teach themselves. Even very well-developed curricula that are successful when taught by teachers who understand the way they approach content and the methods they require have been much less successful when used by teachers who do not understand them (Good and Brophy, 1995). Thus teachers need to be able both to make good choices among curriculum options and to study and deeply understand the teaching implications of the choices they or others in their schools or districts have made.

Knowledge of the types of curriculum material and resources available at particular grade levels and for particular subject areas—and the ability to evaluate the utility of these for various purposes—is particularly useful to beginning teachers. Prospective teachers should be aware of major resources in their field and those that are in use locally, and know how to find additional resources and critically assess what is available. For example, if the Success for All reading program, the writing process approach, and the Integrated Mathematics program are common in the schools local graduates are likely to teach in, initial preparation might focus on these programs, plus some other major programs in the field, allowing students to examine their methods, strengths, and weaknesses for various purposes and the ways they might be adapted and augmented.

Teachers should be able to examine these kinds of materials in light of a state's or district's standards, curriculum frameworks, and assessments to evaluate to what extent and in what ways they can be aligned, or to determine if there is a substantial mismatch between the content and skills included in the curriculum materials and those students are expected to learn. Teachers also need to understand the professional and contextual constraints on their curriculum decisions—constraints that are inherent in the role of the teacher (Buchmann, 1986). These include such things as the expectations of the school board and professional colleagues, as well as parents and students; available resources; class size and composition; state or local curricular mandates; tests that students will be held accountable for; diversity of learners and the professional obligation to support the success of all learners.

It is helpful for teachers to understand that there are a number of endemic curricular issues (Kliebard, 1988; Walker and Soltis, 1997) that derive from the unavoidable ethical and political dimensions of curricular decision making. Addressing the fundamental curricular issue—What knowledge is worth knowing?—is a recurrent question that shifts over time and across locales and for different learners with different goals. There are always questions about whose knowledge becomes part of the curriculum, what topics and human experiences will be represented, and who will have access to different kinds and forms of knowledge (Anyon, 1981; Banks, 1996). Among the many enduring curricular problems are those associated with such dilemmas as the rights of the individual versus the rights of the class, the desirability of homogeneous versus heterogeneous grouping, the trade-offs between wide coverage of topics versus deep mastery of central ideas and skills, the tensions between socialization of children to common norms versus the desire for individualism, the relative importance of cognitive goals versus affective goals, the utility of a common curriculum versus differentiated curriculum for different students, the tug of war between local versus state control of educational decisions, and many more (Zumwalt, 1989).

Other ongoing curricular concerns involve how to avoid fragmentation, offer relevance and rigor, achieve balance among various topics and approaches to teaching and learning, deal with censorship concerns, manage accountability, address the influence of textbooks and tests, and negotiate the role of the teacher among all of these issues. Knowledge that these dilemmas are enduring tensions that must be continually reengaged rather than problems that can be easily resolved by simple either/or solutions will help novices place their decisions and their experiences in context, and perhaps ease the frustrations they may otherwise experience and help them think productively about how to engage these issues from a broad perspective.

It is also important for teachers to know how to evaluate, in light of research about teaching and learning, the many competing recommendations for curriculum and the innumerable fads that come and go in education, so that they can be professionally informed decision makers about what to adopt and what to reject among the many ideas they will be asked to consider in their local schools and districts.

The study of curriculum proposed here is more than a body of knowledge; rather, it is a way of thinking and dealing with the many knowledge bases described in this volume and with the "personal practical knowledge" (Clandinin, 1985) teachers construct for themselves as they interact with students, subject matter, and their local communities. It is a combination of knowledge, skills, and dispositions about how to create curriculum and make curriculum decisions that enables teachers to be responsible practitioners and to learn from their own teaching.

Implications for Teacher Education

How can prospective teachers develop a curricular vision for their work, and learn to ground it in students' needs, curricular demands, and social purposes for education? As Deborah Ball once framed a central aspect of this question: "How do I create experiences for my students that connect with what they now know and care about but that also transcend their present? How do I value their interests and also connect them to ideas and traditions growing out of centuries of mathematical exploration and invention?" (Ball, 1993, p. 375).

Whereas most schools of education once reserved courses in curriculum design for advanced master's or doctoral students who planned to become specialists at textbook companies or in central offices, most strong programs today see the development of curriculum as intrinsic to the process of learning to teach. They help prospective teachers learn to evaluate, select, and organize important subject matter concepts and bring these concepts to students in ways that will provoke deep learning. Some offer courses in curriculum development; others embed curricular planning in courses on instructional methods or in integrated seminars. A common tool in these courses is the development of a curriculum unit, which we discuss further in the following section. Another emerging tool is the curriculum or teaching case. As we have discussed, to be useful, these kinds of exercises must be informed by knowledge of development, learning, and language, as well as by knowledge of the content to be taught and teaching methods that are likely to be effective.

Strong teacher education programs generally include at least three major kinds of learning experiences that prepare teachers to develop a curricular vision. These include:

- Consideration of educational goals and purposes in general and within content areas, including review of national or state learning and teaching standards and practice with how to embody them in curriculum;

- Learning about instructional design, including guided practice in developing, implementing, and reflecting on and revising curriculum plans; and

- Review and evaluation of curriculum plans and materials from the perspectives of instructional design, evaluation of the implementation of others' curriculum efforts, and study of research on curriculum and its implementation.

Considering Educational Goals and Purposes

Constructing an Inclusive Curriculum. Prospective teachers need opportunities to consider how they will support the social purposes of education to develop an equitable society in which all citizens can develop their potential and make a contribution. In addition to learning strategies for teaching diverse learners successfully (see Chapter Seven), and incorporating content that allows students to see themselves represented in the curriculum (Banks, 1996), this requires a sense of the historical trends that frame contemporary schooling and that influence students' lives. Foundations courses are often the place where prospective teachers deal for the first time with the history of education and contemporary social, political, and legal contexts for schooling. These are also often the places where equity issues are explicitly addressed, including concerns of racism, classism, and sexism, as well as the implications of multiculturalism, extending beyond race and ethnicity to include cultural factors such as geographic locale, family norms and roles, and parents' aspirations for their children.

When such study is connected to student teachers' classroom experiences, it can support a much deeper understanding of educational purposes. At Bank Street College, for example, students study these issues in Foundations courses while they also visit a variety of schools to consider their educational philosophies, how these are manifested in curriculum and teaching, and what they are able to accomplish as a result. Students assess educational purposes and outcomes as they contrast the nature of teaching and learning in a Montessori school, a Waldorf school, a school oriented to a "back-to-basics" curriculum, and one organized around child-centered pedagogy, and they reflect on the explicit and hidden curriculum of each and their accessibility to and outcomes for different students. This allows them to develop a vision of how a whole school develops practices to pursue its goals. Contrary to the assumption that Foundations courses are "too theoretical," many Bank Street graduates cite such courses as having helped them to develop a broad understanding of schooling, shape a personal philosophy, and use analytic skills. In a study of the program, one current student explained:

> I took a Foundations course that really taught me about being a critical thinker. That had not been part of my educational experience before. Even college was about, "let me figure out what this or that teacher wants and what I will need to give back to them at exam time and get a good grade." I was good at that. So this whole thing about reflecting in a deeper way about the philosophical questions, about what I want to teach and why and how will it be meaningful, is new for me, and I learned it through Social Foundations. (Darling-Hammond and Macdonald, 2000, p. 49)

A beginning teacher in New York City public schools found this kind of study crucial to her survival, noting: "The Foundations class was very helpful to me for the kind of children that I'm encountering in my school. There are a lot of children in this school from homeless shelters who have a lot of emotional and behavioral needs. In this class, we studied a lot about children from these types of environments and the effect that it has on them, the types of education they respond best to, what they need, and what helps them. And the class made me come to a whole new understanding of how to deal with them" (Darling-Hammond and Macdonald, 2000, p. 50).

In this teacher's elementary classroom, researchers saw twenty-six children from some of the most economically disadvantaged parts of New York involved in mathematical problem solving using multistep word problems often considered suitable for much older children, reading of children's literature, and studies about the authors of their favorite books. The teacher's ability to construct this environment was, she believed, a function of her clarity about her educational purposes, her commitment to an equitable, high-quality education, and the knowledge of children and curriculum she had acquired in her preservice preparation (Darling-Hammond and Macdonald, 2000).

Why Teach the Disciplines? In addition to clarifying their thinking about broad educational purposes, teachers need to be clear about what they are trying to accomplish in specific subject matter domains. When students ask, "Why should we learn this?" teachers need to be clear about the answer they will provide and must be prepared to organize their actions to accomplish their goals. In many teacher education programs, one of the first questions student teachers confront in their content methods courses is *why* students should learn science, or mathematics, or English, or history, or art and why a teacher should care about teaching it. (We discuss these issues further in Chapter Six.)

At the University of Virginia, for example, from the first day in the Mathematics Methods course, students reflect on the nature of mathematics, why mathematics is taught, and what it means to teach mathematics. A second activity often asks students to think about "What's worth knowing?" as a teacher of a given discipline. In Selena Cozart's English Education class, she was asked, as part of this assignment, to list "what you think you need and/or want to know at this point in your preparation in order to create a classroom in which both you and your students experience success." Student teachers' responses to this assignment raise questions that guide their thinking over many months and years to come. For example, "How can I be a questioning, inquiry-focused teacher and still cover the required curriculum?" Or, "What is the best way of determining what is relevant to my students, especially if their backgrounds are different than mine or unfamiliar to me?" (Merseth and Koppich, 2000).

These kinds of iterative questions and reflections teach a habit of mind that focuses teachers on their goals for their own and their students' learning, leading to the kind of clear and purposeful teaching we saw in Selena's and Berthina's classrooms at the start of this chapter. This focus on "Why am I teaching what I'm teaching?" also encourages teachers continually to evaluate the extent to which they are accomplishing their larger purposes as they engage in the daily work in which it is otherwise so easy to lose track of the big ideas. Finally, it sets the stage for the understanding that the usefulness of any given lesson, method, or technique can be assessed only in relation to the purposes that a teacher hopes to accomplish.

Incorporating Learning Standards. A major aspect of the process of considering educational goals is studying national and state learning standards within the disciplines and learning how to incorporate these goals productively into curriculum planning and assessments.

In content methods courses, student teachers increasingly study curriculum and content standards promulgated by various national organizations (for example, National Council of Teachers of Mathematics, National Council of Teachers of English) as well as analogous state standards, develop lessons and units reflecting those standards, and assess work produced by children in relation to content and performance standards. This process helps prospective teachers think about the specific objectives embedded in standards in relation to the big ideas of their disciplines and figure out how to address them meaningfully in the classroom, rather than just marching through topics in ways that become superficial and fail to add up to deep understanding and proficient performance.

Teacher education programs especially need to help prospective teachers consider how to locate the most important and generative ideas among the standards—concepts and skills that link together many of the core ideas of the discipline and allow students to have a map of the field that will help them make sense of many other facts and ideas. This is essential so that teachers can figure out what to emphasize, what may be the sine qua non for other areas of learning or the key to opening up concepts that will otherwise remain mysterious. By some estimates, if one looked across the many statements of learning standards that have been promulgated in the last decade, the numbers of individual facts and skills posited for students to learn could take them a lifetime if they marched through them one by one (Darling-Hammond, 1997, p. 228). Programs should help teachers analyze standards documents to understand the key concepts and modes of inquiry that sit at the core of understanding within a discipline, so that teachers can use the standards productively and strategically, while continuing to conduct in-depth inquiry in the classroom.

Designing Curriculum and Instruction

Enacting educational goals requires strong knowledge of instructional design and curriculum planning. Many programs use the development of a multiweek curriculum unit as the centerpiece of this study, which can be a particularly powerful experience when it is critiqued, revised, taught, and revised again. The experience is an epiphany for many students. One mature teacher education student, who was in the midst of a transition from a management career, noted of the curriculum course at Bank Street, for example: "Curriculum was very worthwhile, because I'd never seen this holistic way where you . . . can teach everything in a connected way. I'd never known that. This was an eye-opening experience for me. Having to devise a curriculum really helped me think out every little process. I liked this course a lot, and then I did a new curriculum for my directed essay. Now I can think in terms of the big picture" (Darling-Hammond and Macdonald, 2000, p. 53).

Berthina's training for curriculum planning at Alverno College, like that offered at Bank Street and other schools of education with a strong emphasis on curricular thinking, was grounded not only in planning curriculum units around content standards but also finding ways to connect the interests of children to the goals of the curriculum and articulating clear performance standards for their learning (Zeichner, 2000). Alverno graduates repeatedly described how they felt they really knew how to get to know their pupils as whole people and to then construct learning activities for their classrooms based on what they learned. One graduate described to a researcher how she manages the interface between the child's interests and the required curriculum: "This unit on the solar system came about because we were studying dinosaurs. With our study of dinosaurs the kids got interested in comets and asteroids because they learned that is maybe how the dinosaurs became extinct. They became so interested that I decided to plan the unit on the solar system. So first I listen to what is going to pique their interest and from there I try to set my goals. I try to find ways to get to all of the skills that I'm required to cover" (Zeichner, 2000, p. 45).

The Alverno faculty's explicit efforts to model in the program the kinds of teaching practices that they hope to have their students consider is another factor that has seemed to strengthen graduates' curriculum planning abilities. For example, the explicitness of the criteria that are used to evaluate students' performances on the various abilities that the Alverno curriculum aims to develop—and the emphasis on continual revision to meet performance standards—leads graduates to use these practices as they plan curriculum for their own classrooms. Just as we saw in Berthina's classroom, other graduates note that they were prepared to "plan backward" from their goals to coherent learning activities, and to incorporate the expectation for review and revision in their units:

> Our teachers give us criteria before we do something. When we have a project or a visit to do or something, they give us criteria: what we have to do to successfully complete the task. I'm doing that in the classroom, letting my students know what is expected before they start on something. Then there is no fuzzy area. They know right away what is expected.
>
> They're always asking you how you could have done it differently, how you could have done it better, what are some changes you would have made? They always throw the ball in your court at Alverno. They are asking me to be just better and better, to constantly revise and reassess. (Zeichner, 2000, pp. 48–49)

A key point is that the kinds of curriculum and teaching that are modeled in teacher education programs have a great deal to do with what graduates do when they launch their own classrooms. Another important influence on prospective teachers' learning about curriculum development is the extent to which they understand school goals and contexts beyond the classroom, child development and learning processes, and the structure and purposes of the disciplines. The importance of building these understandings deliberately, brick by brick, is suggested by the sequence of courses at the University of Virginia, where the development of curricular vision occurs over several years that enable students to gain a broad perspective on what students are learning in school over time.

Beginning in the sophomore year, students in the teacher education program participate in an extensive array of field placements designed to expose them to many elements of teaching. During this year, all prospective teachers, regardless of their intended level of teaching, observe in both elementary and middle schools in a variety of settings within a school (including regular and special education classrooms, the library, media center, and the principal's office) to get a sense of schoolwide goals and purposes. During the junior year, the focus of courses and practica is on individual learners, and the field experience requires students to serve as tutors, often to students with special educational needs, while also completing an extensive child or adolescent study, thus focusing on goals for the individual child. In the senior year, field experiences require that students observe, describe, and analyze teaching and learning behaviors in the classroom; develop and teach model lessons in peer sessions and in the classroom; identify an organizing theme for a unit of instruction; and develop the unit and teach it in a classroom. This work in the classroom is undertaken concurrently with a two-course sequence on teaching methods.

Later, students read each other's units and identify areas for improvement: "If the unit were yours to revise, identify three to five things that you would do differently." Based on this feedback and feedback from the instructor, students then draft a plan for revising the material, answering the following kinds of questions:

- What do I like most about this unit and want to retain?
- What are the key conceptual changes I would like to make?
- Based on my reading and class experiences to date, what are some new contents and instructional strategies I would like to include, and where might I include them?
- What are three goals I would set for myself in creating a stronger unit, that is, what planning skills do I want to improve upon?

In this reflective process, students have their work assessed in ways that establish the habit of further critique, insight, and revision (Merseth and Koppich, 2000).

Evaluating Curriculum Plans and Materials

Evaluating one's own efforts to develop curriculum, like those described earlier, brings home many of the features of good instructional design that prospective teachers are taught as they learn to develop curriculum. These include:

- Planning with the end in mind,
- Constructing thoughtful performance assessments with clear criteria,
- Carefully scaffolding children's learning process based on their experiences, their readiness, and their starting points,
- Providing engaging questions and experiences that stimulate interest and effort, using a variety of teaching strategies—including models, representations, and entry points—that can make strong connections for different students,
- Incorporating lots of guided practice and application so that abstract ideas are made real and knowledge is used, and
- Strategically using formative assessment and feedback to guide the teaching and learning process (Wiggins and McTighe, 1998).

Although these may be understood in the abstract, it is when a novice teacher seeks to incorporate them into a unit of instruction, teaches it, and evaluates the resulting learning that they become deeply understood. One strategy used in a growing number of teacher education programs is the guided analysis of teaching and student learning from a unit of instruction the student teacher has designed and taught.

Sometimes, this is done through the development of a "curriculum case"—a deep analysis of a segment of teaching and learning focused on a central educational goal. At Stanford University, for example, prospective teachers write a case about the teaching of a curriculum unit in which they were trying to teach a key concept, problem, topic, or issue that is central to the discipline, such as the concept of irony in English, evolution in science, or pi in mathematics. The process of writing the case requires repeated analysis of the curricular and student context, the teaching goals and activities, and the students' learning—all examined in light of a set of readings about learning theory and with ongoing peer and instructor review of the emerging interpretations. The use of case writing combined with case consultations is intended to help students move away from naïve generalizations about their experiences toward more sophisticated understandings of the connections between what they choose to teach, how they teach the material, and what their students learn; in short, to learn how to "think like a teacher," asking productive questions about how learning is shaped by students, content, context, and teaching decisions (Hammerness and others, 2002).

Data from a study of the outcomes of this process suggest that it enables most prospective teachers to move from simplistic hypotheses about their teaching to much more systematic understandings of what influences student learning, showing evidence of what Berliner (1986) has described as the movement from novice to expert thinking. As one student noted:

> The experience of writing a case turned out to be a profound experience. When I finished teaching the unit in November I knew the lessons needed a little tuning . . . I talked to my CT about what happened and left it at that . . . Writing the case I was able to get a lot more out of what happened. I had my eyes opened to seeing the implications of time allotment, lesson sequencing, prior knowledge and pre-assessment, and making choices on the fly to ensure the success of a lesson. If I had not written and re-written the case as I did, I would not have the deeper insights I have . . . Before the development [of] my case study, I thought I would simply add a day or two and try it again . . . [but] I now know that I have to put more effort into my assessment of prior knowledge and concepts and that I have to not move on to new material until I am certain that I have achieved the goals I set out at the beginning. (Hammerness and others, 2000, p. 227)

A similar evaluation of curriculum and teaching outcomes can also be encouraged through the kinds of portfolio assessment of beginning teachers now in use in states like Connecticut that require beginning teachers to plan and teach a unit of instruction and then to assess it based on evaluations of student learning and on daily reflections about what is happening in the classroom. (See also the discussion of the PACT portfolio in Chapter Eight.)

Finally, it is important for new teachers to have opportunities to learn how to evaluate and integrate particular curriculum materials into instruction in ways that are appropriate for the teacher's goals, for the content under study, and for the particular students. These efforts seem to be most useful when they allow for the application of materials in practice rather than through abstract discussions only. There is some evidence, for example, that substantial changes in practice can occur when teachers are involved in integrating particular curriculum materials and units into their instruction and reflecting on the results of these efforts with one another as a part of fine-tuning their instruction (Cohen and Hill, 2000).

Infusing Technology

As we have noted, the importance of technology for today's students and tomorrow's citizens means that infusing technology into learning and teaching is an increasingly important instructional goal as well as a tool. Although some analysts have suggested that observers would find teachers' work at the beginning of the twentieth and twenty-first centuries fundamentally the same (Cuban, 1992, 1993), most classrooms now have technology tools available, and many teachers are using them. For widespread change to occur, teachers need to incorporate the opportunities of the emerging technological infrastructure into their overall curricular thinking.

If teachers are to develop a curricular vision with respect to the use of technology for learning, teacher education programs need to think of their responsibilities as including the production of technically literate teaching professionals who have a set of ideas about how their students should be able to use technology within particular disciplines. Like traditional literacies in text, technical literacy requires general fluency and specific fluencies. In the world of teaching, general fluency is probably best thought of as a deep, workable understanding of the use of standard productivity tools for the work of teaching. Teachers also need a number of specific fluencies in the use of technological tools that are coupled to their specific domains of expertise.

Teachers, and the school districts that employ them, should have the expectation that when teachers arrive on the job they already know how to use general desktop productivity tools, including word processing, spreadsheets, and other applications like general search tools, in ways that are linked to the practice of teaching. Many teacher education programs have found that the best way to accomplish this fluency is to infuse the use of such tools into all of the courses in the teacher education program, requiring the frequent use of e-mail, information searches, multimedia presentations, and data analyses.

In addition, today's technologies offer teachers and students the opportunity to participate in specialized communities of practice. Enabling students to participate in these communities is an important goal of instruction. For example, readily available technologies like those for multimedia composing, visualization, and database searches are important tools of the content disciplines. A key component of teachers' specific fluency is understanding how to use the technical tools of the discipline in ways that are consistent with the broader community of practice. As several scholars have noted, the tools people use carry important information about the communities in which they work (Hutchins and Klausen, 1996).

Chemistry teachers, for example, should understand and be able to explain how chemists use visualization, which may be different than the use of visualization in biology. In a similar vein, social studies teachers require technical fluency with database tools that allow them to explore original documentation for argument in the social sciences. The use of probeware in biology and graphing calculators in mathematics, as well as computer-based language tools in English and world languages, are part of this discipline-based technical fluency that will allow teachers to build curriculum around tools that are part of the communities of practice their students are joining. As a consequence, students should become fluent in the use of tools that will be part of their long-term repertoire for ongoing learning.

For teacher preparation institutions to ensure that teachers know how to use the technologies that are part of the professional communities of practice, these, too, need to be infused into the content pedagogical courses that teachers take, so that they are using the tools within the disciplines themselves, not just learning about them in the abstract. In the course of these efforts, schools of education can provide opportunities for teachers to think reflectively about the roles these technologies play as gateways into deeper engagement with the disciplines.

Finally, many school districts, large and small, use information technology for the data-intensive clerical functions of school district operations including attendance, grading, and collection of performance information from tests, performance tasks, portfolios, and other sources. Schools of education should prepare teachers to use data from systems like these to analyze teaching and student achievement as a basis for curriculum planning. In a world in which teachers are generally technically fluent, they would be able to use data from district systems to analyze their own practice and student achievement and perhaps, for deeper analysis, compare their practices and student classroom achievement to that of other teachers in their buildings and across the school district. The information infrastructures that are making their way into schools bring this information to teachers' desktops quickly. But to be useful, teachers must be fluent in techniques that help them use the data pedagogically.

Teachers should be able to look at data about student progress in terms of different areas and qualities of learning and then be able to consider the relationship of this learning to the curriculum and teaching they have designed. This kind of evaluation is encouraged by teacher education strategies like those associated with the Oregon work sampling system, which asks student teachers to design, collect, and analyze pre- and postassessment data for students in relation to a unit the student teachers design and teach (Schalock, 1998).

This kind of analysis is a good start toward the ability to thoughtfully steer a classroom and to discuss curriculum improvements needed within a school. Even more important, especially in today's standards-based education systems, teachers must have knowledge of what changes they might make in how they organize and deliver instruction to strengthen student learning for individual students, groups of students who are underperforming, or the entire class or school. This understanding is the subject of the remainder of this volume. When their teachers have these tools, students can benefit from the kind of curricular vision that underlies the seemingly effortless classroom orchestration good teachers are able to conduct.

CHAPTER SIX

Teaching Subject Matter

Pamela Grossman and Alan Schoenfeld, with Carol Lee

What do teachers need to know about the subjects they teach? Various versions of this question have long interested practitioners, policymakers, and researchers alike. In this chapter we begin with the assumption, grounded in research, that teachers should possess deep knowledge of the subjects they teach (for examples, see Shulman, 1987; Wilson, Floden, and Ferrini-Mundy, 2001). We focus specifically on the pedagogical understandings of subject matter—or pedagogical content knowledge—which include, among other things, the ability to anticipate and respond to typical student patterns of understanding and misunderstanding within a content area, and the ability to create multiple examples and representations of challenging topics that make the content accessible to a wide range of learners.

We have framed this chapter around a set of questions that provide a framework for pedagogical content knowledge. We then respond to these questions within the subject areas of mathematics and English/language arts as two illustrative content areas. A discussion of the pedagogical content knowledge for teaching reading is considered in a separate volume (see Snow, Griffin, and Burns, 2005). We believe that any teacher preparation program should provide opportunities for student teachers to explore these questions in their own subject matter domains. Such an argument poses particular challenges for elementary teacher preparation, in which teachers are being prepared to teach multiple subjects, a challenge we address in the conclusion of this chapter.

THE CENTRALITY OF CONTENT IN TEACHING

In his essay "I, Thou, and It," David Hawkins (1974) outlines the critical importance of content in the relationship between teacher and student. What distinguishes teaching from other helping professions or from parenting, he argues, is the centrality of a common involvement in subject matter and the need for the teacher to develop an attitude of respect toward the student as a learner of that content. Like John Dewey before him, Hawkins argues for the need for teachers to become diagnosticians of children's interests and ideas and to engage students in explorations of subject matter that extend the reach of their understanding. To respond in such a manner, teachers need to understand deeply not only the content they are responsible for teaching but how to represent that content for learners of all kinds (for examples, see Shulman, 1987; Wilson, Shulman, and Richert, 1987). This chapter argues for the centrality of pedagogical content knowledge in the teacher education curriculum and the need to engage teachers in explicitly pedagogical considerations of the subject matter. We begin with examples of tasks that illustrate one aspect of pedagogical content knowledge: the ability to anticipate student thinking within the domains of mathematics and language arts.

An Illustrative Example of Pedagogical Content Knowledge

What kinds of knowledge are important for teaching? Imagine that you have been teaching elementary school students to work with fractions. It is time to assess what they know.

Assessing Student Understanding of Fractions

Which of the following tasks would best assess whether a student can correctly compare fractions? (These examples are drawn from Swan and Ridgway, 2002.)

1. Write these fractions in order of size, from smallest to largest: 5/8; 1/4; 11/16
2. Write these fractions in order of size, from smallest to largest: 5/8; 3/4; 1/16
3. Write these fractions in order of size, from smallest to largest: 5/8; 3/4; 11/16

Can you explain why the two tasks you did not select are not good assessments of students' understanding of fractions?

Let us examine what it would take for teachers, or prospective teachers, to answer this question. It goes without saying that they would need to know the relevant mathematics, in as deep and connected a way as possible (Ma, 1999). Note that there are at least two ways to solve each of these problems, which we will illustrate with task 1. It is possible to solve the task by converting the given fractions to decimals and comparing them. Doing so is not pretty—11/16 is not a "nice" fraction to convert—but the task is straightforward, even without a calculator. Awareness that this represents one way to work the problem is important, because some students may approach it this way. Equally important, converting fractions to decimals can be a very useful technique at times. Alternatively, it is possible to reason through the task by comparing the fractions themselves. Of the three fractions, only one, 1/4 is less than 1/2 (its numerator is less than half its denominator). So, 1/4 is the smallest. And then? Because 5/8 = 10/16, and 10/16 is less than 11/16, 5/8 is less than 11/16. Thus the order is 1/4, 5/8, 11/16.

So far, so good: there are at least two ways to solve the problem, both of which might be used by students. But the real issue for teachers concerns how their own students will tackle the problem. Research shows that many students who have yet to master fractions will focus only on the number of pieces, not their relative size. Given task 1, such students will think, "1/4 has only one piece, so it's the smallest; 5/8 has five pieces, so it's in the middle; and 11/16 has eleven pieces, so it's the largest." Note that this very common form of incorrect reasoning produces the right answer to task 1! Putting task 1 on the test will fail to reveal students' possible misconceptions.

Another misconception developed by many students as they learn fractions is that "the smaller the pieces, the smaller the fraction." If students hold this conception, they attend only to the denominator of the fraction. Because sixteenths are smaller than eighths, which are smaller than fourths, students with this misconception will reason incorrectly and yet arrive at the correct answer to task 2. In contrast, students who use either form of incorrect reasoning will get the wrong answer to task 3—and their incorrect answer will suggest why they got it wrong. Their answers to task 3 will provide diagnostic information to the teacher, who can then work to clear up students' misconceptions.

Assessing Student Understanding in Early Reading

Imagine you are a second-grade teacher working with a small group of children around a short fairy tale. Concerned about Juan's reading, you take him aside and ask him to read a short section of the fairy tale aloud to you. The original text reads: "Once upon a time, an old man and his wife lived in a little house in the woods. They were very poor. The man was going to cut wood for the fire. His wife gave him a little rice cake take with him. It was the last bit of food they had."

Juan reads: "Once upon a time, an ol man and his wif lived in a little hus in the wuds. They were very poor. The man was going to cut wud for the fir. His wif gave him a little ras cak to tak with him. It was the last bit of f-f-f-food they had."

As Juan's teacher, which two of the following would be most important for you to focus on during instruction?

- Work on high-frequency sight words
- Practice with reading for meaning
- Instruction on CVCe patterns
- Work on consonant sounds
- Use of background knowledge

Source: This example is drawn from Sheila Valencia, University of Washington, who developed it as one of a number of items designed to assess teachers' knowledge about teaching reading.

Most teachers could read the fairy tale assigned to the students without difficulty. But only those prepared to teach elementary reading can probably assess Juan's reading ability from listening to him read. Such understanding requires knowledge of reading development, of the demands of text, of specific children's repertoires of strategies and skills, and so forth. (see Snow, Griffin, and Burns, 2005). Without such knowledge, teachers may misdiagnose children's errors, or provide inappropriate instruction or scaffolding, such as encouraging them to sound out words, like "two," that are phonetically irregular—words that are best taught as high-frequency sight words. Based on this sample of Juan's reading, an experienced teacher would observe that this brief segment of text is at Juan's frustration level for reading, and is therefore inappropriate for independent reading. The number and type of errors Juan makes support the need to provide him with easier text. Although it is difficult to get a firm understanding of Juan's strengths and needs from a text at his frustration level, skilled teachers could get some initial insights. Juan's performance indicates that he is not reading for meaning. In the very first sentence, he misreads several words (*wife, woods, house*) and substitutes nonsense words for them (*wif, hus*). This suggests that he not only has difficulty decoding these words (which are all decodable) but that he does not recognize that they do not make sense in the sentence. It does not appear that Juan self-monitors his reading, or uses the context to reread for meaning. Although it seems as if Juan has not yet learned that reading should make sense, this conclusion is complicated by the fact that Juan is an English language learner. From the information provided, we do not know his level of English proficiency and we have no way of knowing if the words he misreads (*wife, house, fire*, and so on) are a part of his English listening or speaking vocabulary. It is also complicated by the fact that the passage is at his frustration level, where he misreads many words, making it more difficult to for him to use context to aid in self-monitoring, an issue the teacher would want to explore further.

An experienced teacher would also notice that many of the words that Juan misreads are CVCe words. CVCe words are words that follow the pattern of *con*sonant, *v*owel, *c*onsonant, followed by a silent "e." The CVCe generalization, familiar to most experienced readers of English, is that words of this pattern (wife, kite, bite, mate, and so on) generally have a long vowel sound; without the "e" at the end, the vowel becomes short (bit, kit, mat, and so on).

Juan pronounces the consonant sounds correctly, but mispronounces the medial vowels in these words as short vowel sounds. He has not yet learned the orthographic pattern that signals a long vowel sound, something that could be targeted for instruction.

The General Case Illustrated by the Example

We now return to the issue of pedagogical understanding of subject matter. Knowing the subject matter terrain, in a variety of ways, is the foundation for pedagogical content knowledge. Effective teachers need subject matter competence; they need to know how to solve the problems they pose to students and to know that there are multiple approaches to solving many problems. But such competence is not enough. Making the right choices as a teacher depends on knowing what kinds of errors or mistakes students are likely to make, being able to identify such mistakes when they occur, and being prepared to address the sources of the students' errors in ways that will result in student learning. We stress that such errors will occur no matter how good the instruction may be. Errors are a part of learning, which is why "learning from your mistakes" is folk wisdom. But learning from mistakes often takes an experienced other—be it teacher, parent, or friend—to provide the necessary feedback and perspective.

Effective teachers know much more than their subjects, and more than "good pedagogy." They know how students tend to understand (and *mis*-understand) their subjects; they know how to anticipate and diagnose such misunderstandings; and they know how to deal with them when they arise. This kind of knowledge has been termed *pedagogical content knowledge* (Shulman, 1987). Such knowledge differs from knowledge of generic teaching skills, because it is content specific. Knowing that it is important to "check for understanding" in teaching does not guarantee that teachers will be able to anticipate specific student understandings and misunderstandings of fractions or of CVCe words. Nor does it guarantee that teachers know what sophisticated understandings or polished performances might look like within a subject matter.

Teachers can begin to develop this knowledge, along with the tools and the predilection to continue developing it, in professional education, both before and after obtaining the credential. When they know what to look for, teachers develop more of this knowledge on the job as they gain experience with patterns of student responses. In this way, teachers begin to build their understanding of students' subject matter reasoning and understanding. They learn about predictable patterns in student understanding (that irony is hard for students to comprehend, for example, or that students are likely to misunderstand exactly how to explain seasonal differences) as well as how to support the movement to more disciplinary understandings. Learning about students' content-related understandings goes beyond mastery of the content, and beyond common sense pedagogy, and deserves serious and sustained attention in the teacher education curriculum.

Subject Matter Knowledge

To argue that teachers need to know the subject matter they teach seems almost tautological, for how can we teach what we do not understand ourselves? Yet the links between content knowledge and teaching performance are not all that easy to document. In their review of research on teacher education, Wilson and colleagues (2001) examined the empirical evidence related to teachers' subject matter knowledge. They found that although several studies found a relationship between teachers' subject matter preparation and student achievement (see, for example, Darling-Hammond, 2000a; Goldhaber and Brewer, 2000; Monk, 1994), the findings of some studies are equivocal. For example, Goldhaber and Brewer (2000) found that a major in the subject area was a significant predictor of student achievement in mathematics, but not in science. Monk (1994) found generally positive relationships between the number of undergraduate mathematics courses teachers had taken and their students' achievement. However, this relationship did not continue to grow stronger after a certain number of courses (about five in this study), and holding a major in mathematics was not significantly correlated with student achievement. Wilson and colleagues concluded that although subject matter knowledge of some form is important, the field needs to learn more about the specific kinds of subject matter knowledge that matter in teaching.

The kind of content knowledge that supports good teaching may, in some cases, be different in kind than that generally acquired by individuals who pursue a college major in a content field. For example, Liping Ma's (1999) work on expert teachers of elementary mathematics indicates that such teachers often have a deeper, richer organization of elementary subject matter knowledge (called "profound understanding of fundamental mathematics") than do mathematics professionals, because their knowledge is organized for teaching. From this perspective, "more mathematics" is not a sufficient prescription for content preparation; it is mathematics knowledge related to teaching that matters.

We argue that, at a minimum, prospective teachers need a solid foundation in the subject matters they plan to teach and the requisite disciplinary tools to continue learning within the subject matter throughout their careers, an argument that is consistent with the finding that having undergraduate coursework in a subject area is important. Such tools include understandings of deep connections in the subject matter that inform curricular and pedagogical choices, an understanding of big ideas and productive patterns of thought within the discipline, and an understanding of how knowledge is generated within a field (see, for example, Ball and Bass, 2000; Ma, 1999).

Typically, potential teachers develop their subject matter knowledge within the arts and sciences component of teacher preparation rather than within the professional curriculum. Because this volume is centrally concerned with the professional component of the teacher education curriculum, we will not address subject matter preparation within the arts and sciences. However, we also argue that some aspects of subject matter understanding are critical to pedagogical content knowledge, and so deserve to be addressed within courses related to the teaching of subject matter. We also believe that teachers continue to learn about content through the practice of teaching, and that teachers deserve ongoing opportunities to continue to learn within the subjects they teach.

Pedagogical Content Knowledge

Pedagogical content knowledge has been defined as

> The most regularly taught topics in one's subject area, the most useful forms of representations of those ideas, the most powerful analogies, illustrations, examples, explanations, and demonstrations—in a word, ways of representing and formulating the subject that make it comprehensible to others. Pedagogical content knowledge also includes an understanding of what makes the learning of specific topics easy or difficult; the conceptions and preconceptions that students of different ages and backgrounds bring with them to the learning of those most frequently taught topics and lessons (Shulman, 1986, pp. 9–10).

Although the term itself was first introduced by Shulman, the ideas behind pedagogical content knowledge are not new. Dewey (1902), for example, talked about the need to "psychologize the subject matter," to connect disciplinary knowledge to students' experience. In an otherwise scathing critique of teacher education, Conant (1963) noted the importance of helping prospective teachers understand subject matter from a more pedagogical perspective. He argued that although a physicist might understand the important physics content to teach, or which concepts are most central to the study of motion, for example, she might not be able to address whether ten-year-olds are able to grasp these concepts.

In the review of research on teacher education mentioned earlier, Wilson and others (2001) noted that some studies found that courses in education were as important as content courses. For example, Monk (1994) found that "courses in undergraduate math education contribute more to student gains than do courses in undergraduate math" (as cited in Wilson and others, 2001, p. 8). Wilson and her colleagues note that this finding probably relates to the need for teachers to develop pedagogical content knowledge in a subject, something that is most likely to be addressed in subject matter methods classes rather than subject matter courses (see, for example, Grossman, 1990).

A Framework for Pedagogical Content Knowledge

In this chapter, we address the knowledge of content for teaching through a series of questions that lie at the heart of pedagogical content knowledge—what it means to understand one's subject matter for the purpose of teaching it to others. One purpose of teacher education is to initiate inquiry into these questions and to provide frameworks to help prospective teachers construct answers to these questions. But teachers, assisted by ongoing professional development, will continue to generate ever more refined and elaborate responses to these questions throughout their careers. The role of teacher education is not to provide definitive answers to these questions, especially considering the time frame typically allowed for teacher preparation. Its role is to help prospective teachers begin to generate productive answers to these questions and to provide them with the intellectual tools to continue to inquire into these questions over their careers. Figure 6.1 provides an overview of these questions.

This set of questions engages both subject matter knowledge as well as pedagogical content knowledge, although the questions focus more on the latter. To answer most of these questions, teachers would need to have a solid grasp of the subject matter itself. Moreover, teachers would also need to understand the broader political and educational contexts that help shape our notions of what it means to know and teach a subject, as well as draw on an understanding of

---

Q1. How do we define the subject matter? What are the central concepts and processes involved in knowing the subject matter? According to whom? Are there competing definitions of the subject matter? What are the consequences of multiple definitions of subject matter? How do national and state standards or frameworks define both the content and what it means to know the content?

Q2. What are the different purposes for teaching the subject matter in public schools? Why is the subject important for students to study? What aspects of the subject are most important? Are there different purposes for teaching the subject matter depending upon the age of students?

Q3. What do understanding or performance look like with regard to this subject matter? What are the different aspects of understanding and performance? What are students likely to understand about the subject matter at different developmental stages? How do student understanding and proficiency develop? How can instruction support the development of student understanding and proficiency?

Q4. What are the primary curricula available to teach the subject matter? What definitions of the subject are embedded within the curriculum materials? How are curricula aligned with national and state standards? How are they articulated across grade levels? How can teachers use curriculum materials effectively to support student learning?

Q5. How do teachers assess student understanding and performance within a subject matter domain? What tools are most useful for assessing student competence? How do teachers use the results of these assessments to inform instruction?

Q6. What are the practices that characterize the teaching of particular content? What practices and approaches have been shown to be effective in promoting student learning? Are there practices that are particularly effective with specific groups of learners? What representations, examples, analogies are particularly useful in helping students grasp particular concepts or ideas?

Figure 6.1 Questions That Underlie Courses in Content-Specific Pedagogy.

Source: Adapted from Grossman, 2002. Reprinted with permission from author.

their students. Most importantly, from the perspective of this volume, these six questions provide the underpinnings for courses in content-specific pedagogy during teacher education.

Although the questions themselves are general, responses to these questions will play out differently in every subject. Let us address for a moment the first question, which concerns the definition of the subject matter and its relationship to education standards. In no content area is there an absolute consensus. For example, in mathematics, at the national level, there is clarity and a fair amount of consensus regarding standards, as represented by the National Council of Teachers of Mathematics' (2000) *Principles and Standards. Principles and Standards* defines and focuses on five content standards and five process standards, demonstrating how they serve as the core of the K–12 curriculum. Yet the story is not that simple. Most states also define their own frameworks and standards, which may or may not be aligned with those at the national level. In English, there are competing definitions of the subject matter. Debates over the definition of the subject matter spill over into the effort to create national standards in almost all subject areas. Even the sciences, which one might think are straightforward, are not uncontroversial: the path to the development of the National Research Council's (1995) *National Science Education Standards* was by no means easy, featuring arguments about the teaching of science between traditionalists concerned primarily with the acquisition of information on one side and reformers concerned with the understanding and use of scientific inquiry on the other. Various state frameworks line up on one side or another of this controversy. There are also controversies about the content of science, for example, attempts to discredit the teaching of evolution or elevate the status of creationism so it can be taught as "creation science." Social studies may represent the most extreme case of the difficulty of defining the subject matter. Social studies, as a school subject, is a marriage of many distinctive disciplines, including history, geography, political science, economics, sociology, and even psychology. There are many competing definitions of social studies, some of which feature the importance of history, whereas others stress the centrality of civics. These competing definitions of the subject matter have made it difficult for the field to develop a commonly embraced set of standards.

As these examples suggest, pedagogical content knowledge is inherently subject specific. For this reason, we will explore potential responses to these questions across two domains to illustrate the subject-specific dimensions of inquiry into these questions and the subsequent need for prospective teachers to investigate these questions in the context of specific subject matters.

Responses to the Questions in Illustrative Domains

We argue that well-prepared teachers should be able to respond to the questions in Figure 6.1 within their own domain, and that high-quality teacher education programs can help prospective teachers begin to generate responses to these questions that will continue to be refined through classroom experience. We also recognize that responses to these questions are often a reflection of professional judgment rather than empirical conclusion. No program of research can answer the question of why science might be important for all students to learn, although it might be helpful in developing a better understanding of students' everyday beliefs about scientific phenomena.

As noted earlier, we could not hope to address these issues for the entire school curriculum in a brief chapter. Hence we illustrate the kinds of responses that might be given in two important subject areas: mathematics and English/language arts, while attempting to suggest the range of responses in other disciplines through prefatory or concluding comments. Teachers in each field need opportunities to continue to learn about and address the questions in their own areas.

Q1. How do we define the subject matter? What are the central concepts and processes involved in knowing the subject matter? According to whom? Are there competing definitions of the subject matter? What are the consequences of multiple definitions of subject matter? How do national and state standards or frameworks define both the content and what it means to know the content?

This set of questions sits at the intersection of subject matter knowledge and pedagogical content knowledge. As the research on teachers' knowledge of subject matter suggests, knowing a number of facts within a subject is less powerful preparation for teaching than knowing the big ideas and deep structures of the disciplines (see, for example, Schwab, 1964). Emerging standards in the disciplines (including mathematics, English, social studies and its constituent disciplines, science, and the arts) all focus on content *and* process. A learner needs to know things and how to do things—how to engage in the practices of the discipline, including learning to explore new arenas. In most problem-solving domains, competence includes knowledge of facts, procedures, and concepts; fluency with strategies; skill at monitoring and self-regulation; and dispositions and beliefs consistent with productive engagement with the discipline (see, for example, de Corte, Verschaffel, and Greer, 1996; Greeno, Pearson, and Schoenfeld, 1997; Schoenfeld, 1985.)

The questions regarding the definition of the subject matter and the central concepts and processes involved in knowing the subject matter point to the epistemological issues that underlie the various disciplines and the subject matter we teach. As work on teachers' subject matter knowledge suggests, how teachers define the subject will influence how they organize both curriculum and instruction. In their article on teaching social studies, for example, Wineburg and Wilson (1988) described the different ways that beginning teachers organize the curriculum and traced their organizations back to the teacher's undergraduate major. The anthropology major, for example, organized the course around the concept of culture, whereas the political science major organized the course around an exploration of political history. Grossman and Stodolsky (2000) found that math teachers could hold quite different definitions of the subject, and that these differences had consequences for how they thought about teaching their subject.

Sample Response: Mathematics. At the national level, the *Principles and Standards* of the National Council of Teachers of Mathematics (NCTM) (2000) provide great clarity and a fair amount of consensus about the central concepts and processes of mathematics. This document, the process of whose development was endorsed by all of the major professional mathematical societies, defines five content standards (number and operations; patterns and algebra; geometry; measurement; probability and statistics) and five process standards (problem solving; reasoning; communication; connections; representation). It shows how these play out from pre-K through grade 12. Specific attention is given to central, difficult concepts and their development over time. All concepts are not created equal: at times (depending on student readiness), some ideas are more heavily weighted in the curriculum than others.

The situation is, however, more complex than simply saying, "There is a general consensus around *Principles and Standards.*" The 1990s saw the math wars, in which advocates for "basics"—usually characterized as emphasizing computational and procedural skills—argued strongly against "reform"—usually characterized as focused on understanding mathematical concepts and reasoning as well as facts and procedures. Most states have their own standards, frameworks, and assessment systems. Depending on how those frameworks were developed, they may be more or less aligned with the national ones. Issues of alignment are critical, for teachers will have to balance the desire to teach for understanding with the knowledge that their students (and they) are likely to be judged by the state assessments, which may sometimes differ substantially in emphasis. Negotiating these tensions takes a significant degree of curricular knowledge and instructional skill.

Sample Response: English/Language Arts. English teachers in the United States cannot seem to agree on a definition of the subject matter. As Peter Elbow (1990) asks plaintively in his book on a conference of English teachers, *What is English?* One of the challenges for beginning teachers is to understand the radically different approaches their colleagues might take toward the subject, differences that often reside in conflicting definitions of the subject matter of language arts. Some would argue that the field of English is most concerned with the reading of canonical texts, whereas others would argue that the proper definition has more to do with the consumption and production of a much broader array of texts. Still others might argue that the field of English should be defined by the skills involved in reading, writing, listening, and speaking. Within these various components of the subject are competing theories of what it means to read a text represented by different literary theories, and different theories of what it means to write.

The existence of multiple and competing conceptions of the subject matter has had consequences for the development of common standards at the national and state levels. Because there are such competing views, consensus is possible perhaps only at a fairly high level of generality. The National Council of Teachers of English standards, for example, represent a very broad definition of the subject matter organized around the processes of reading, writing, and communication, all in the context of social community. These standards represent as much a theory of language learning as a theory of the multidisciplinary subject of English/language arts.

Within elementary language arts, definitions of the subject matter are less contentious, although there are fierce debates about how to teach the subject matter. Most elementary teachers and researchers would agree on the centrality of reading and writing to the subject matter in the broader contexts of uses of language and communication. There is an emerging consensus on standards for teaching a "balanced literacy" program, although there is still variation in how people might define the balance. (See Snow, Griffin, and Burns, 2005.)

Q2. What are the different purposes for teaching the subject matter in public schools? Why is the subject important for students to study? What aspects of the subject are most important? Are there different purposes for teaching the subject matter depending upon the age of students?

If the first set of questions focuses rather squarely on the discipline, the second set focuses on the school subject. Prospective teachers may assume that what they do as math majors in a university is the same as what they might do in a high school classroom. But the purposes for teaching math to all students in public schools may be quite different than the purposes of math professors, who are trying to prepare the mathematicians of the future. This set of questions also engages the kinds of subject matter standards produced by a wide range of professional organizations.

Teachers need to have some grasp of the history of their subject matter, how it has been defined and is currently being defined, in order to understand the curricular choices they will need to make. Choosing a textbook, for example, may involve privileging a particular definition of the subject matter; teachers should make such decisions mindfully. To understand some of the debates that take place in schools over the curriculum, prospective teachers may need to explore the histories of those debates and how those histories reverberate in the school curriculum.

As part of these historical excursions, prospective teachers need to investigate how different purposes for teaching a subject may be constructed for different groups of students. For example, the historical purposes for teaching math have varied radically across tracks in high school, also reflecting systematic differences in curricular access by race and class. Students in higher-track math classes may engage in disciplinary problem solving, for example, whereas students in "business math" may learn to balance their checkbooks instead. In history classes, students in the higher tracks may be asked to engage in rigorous interpretation of historical evidence whereas students in lower tracks may encounter a very different version of history. Research on tracking has typically found that students' achievement is more a function of the curriculum they receive than their previous ability level (for reviews, see Gamoran and Berends, 1987; Slavin, 1990b). Professional education should help students interrogate how differing purposes for teaching the subject matter to different groups of students can reinforce existing inequities and affect access to higher education.

Sample Response: Mathematics. Understandings of the purposes of mathematics teaching and learning are evolving. Mathematics, once the province of the "elite" or "college-intending," is now seen as necessary for a number of purposes, including (1) preparation for the increasingly quantitative demands of the workplace; (2) preparation for literate citizenship, given that the issues voters confront often depend on mathematical or scientific understanding; (3) the ability to make life decisions (about mortgage payments, and so on) that depend on quantitative understandings; and (4) preparation for higher education. Citizens are handicapped if they do not have these understandings.

Principles and Standards argues that it is possible to prepare all students for all of the above-mentioned purposes, while giving students a solid grounding in the five content and five process standards defined as central to the curriculum.

It may be fair to say that the purposes do not change with students' age, if one thinks along a developmental spectrum. The goal is for students to develop understandings in all these ideas. At different ages, various aspects of these understandings are most appropriate. For example, students can start to examine patterns at an early age, codifying them with symbols (algebra) later on. Similarly, they can start to make reasoned arguments ("This is why I think this is true") at an early age, but should only be expected to produce mathematically correct formal proofs in high school.

Sample Response: English/Language Arts. As Douglas Barnes and colleagues (1984) illustrate, there are essentially competing "versions of English" operating in classrooms. Some of these versions include (1) a basic skills approach, in which the major purpose is to teach the skills of reading, writing, speaking, and listening; (2) a personal growth approach, in which the major purpose is to help students develop as human beings through engagement in reading and writing; (3) a disciplinary approach, in which the purpose is to prepare students to engage in the disciplinary practices of literature and writing; and (4) a critical literacy approach, in which the purpose is to help students use literacy to critique the world around them. Each of these versions of the subject highlights particular aspects of the subject matter and obscures others. The basic skills approach, for example, features grammar, whereas the personal growth approach emphasizes personal meanings and may downplay the importance of grammar and conventions. These different purposes are reflected in both curriculum materials and standards and have varied in importance throughout the history of the subject (Applebee, 1974).

One of the consequences of competing purposes for teaching English is a certain amount of cacophony within departments. Prospective teachers need opportunities to inquire into these different approaches and their consequences for curriculum and instruction, as well as opportunities to understand how departmental debates may be rooted in differing beliefs about the purposes for teaching English. Another consequence, as suggested earlier, is that students in different tracks, who often differ by race and class, may encounter quite different versions of English (for examples, see Applebee, 1974; Barnes, Barnes, and Clark, 1984).

There is a general consensus about the need to teach reading as a subject in and of itself and also as a set of skills that are critical to learning within other subject matters (learning to read and reading to learn). There is an emerging consensus that teaching reading involves both teaching students to decode written texts and to make meaning from those texts, and recognition that part of teaching reading involves teaching students comprehension and interpretive strategies, as well as metacognitive strategies for monitoring their comprehension. Writing, too, is seen as a fundamental skill both within the subject and to support achievement in other arenas. There is general agreement that students need to learn to write in multiple genres and for multiple audiences. The purposes of teaching grammar and the strategies that are most productive to use toward these ends are more contested at both elementary and secondary levels. Elementary and secondary teachers alike need opportunities to explore how, and in what ways, grammar instruction supports students in learning to read and write, and how the strategies for instruction might differ depending upon a student's English language proficiency.

Q3. What do understanding or performance look like with regard to this subject matter? What are the different aspects of understanding and performance? What are students likely to understand about the subject matter at different developmental stages? How do student understanding and proficiency develop? How can instruction support the development of student understanding and proficiency?

This set of questions focuses squarely on students and their understanding. In order to teach for understanding, teachers need to have a sense of what understanding looks like in a particular subject matter domain. What does it mean to understand literature, for example? How would you know if students had developed a deep understanding or a superficial understanding of a literary work? What should students be able to say about characters, plot, and the way the work is constructed? How would students approach the fractions problem we posed at the introduction of this chapter? What misconceptions might they hold about the relative size of fractions? What indicates substantial understanding in science? Can a student state a law or principle, for example? Can he or she use it to explain a "real-world" event, or solve a problem? Can the student reason as to likely causes or consequences of events (for example, what are the advantages and disadvantages of genetically modified foods?)? What does skilled performance look like in a foreign language? Do students need to develop fluency across multiple registers in another language to be considered proficient?

Responses to these questions depend both on subject matter and on students' ages. Students are full of ideas and have relevant experiences for the study of relevant subject matter at almost any age, and their knowledge and experience base (as well as their cognitive development) change substantially with time. For example, younger children are more likely to face challenges in identifying a theme in a literary work, or in revising an initial interpretation. Whatever their age, students do not enter our classrooms as *tabulae rasa*, or empty vessels. Thus it is essential for teachers to determine what kinds of understanding of the subject their students already possess, and to craft instruction that is appropriate for the students' level of knowledge and development.

Although it is important for teachers to know the range of possible responses students might theoretically generate to a subject matter problem, some research suggests that it is even more important for teachers to understand their own students' approaches to the subject matter. In their study of elementary teachers' pedagogical content knowledge in math, Peterson, Fennema, and Carpenter (1991) created opportunities for teachers to learn about children's various strategies for arithmetic. They found that it was not enough for teachers to know theoretically that primary students use different strategies for addition; rather, teachers' ability to anticipate their *own* students' strategies for addition correlated to student achievement. This suggests that teacher education will need to provide tools for the continued investigation of student understanding within the subject matter, so teachers continue to develop their knowledge of their own students.

Sample Response: Mathematics. Documents such as NCTM's (2000) *Principles and Standards* illustrate intended levels of understanding, and a massive literature (including handbooks such as the soon-to-be-revised *Handbook of Research on Mathematics Teaching and Learning* [Grouws, 1992]), fleshes it out. One key idea is that knowledge and understanding are *generative.*

Understanding mathematics means being able to recognize when a particular kind of mathematics is useful to help one understand or analyze a situation, and to use it appropriately. This goes far beyond being able to do calculations or symbolic manipulations. For example, an instructional program called "cognitively guided instruction," or CGI, helps teachers work with the many valid approaches to representing and solving simple word problems generated by students rather than presenting just one canonical approach. Other approaches, such as "conceptually based instruction" (CBI), "supporting ten-structured-thinking" (STST), and the problem-centered mathematics project (PCMP) focus, likewise, on rich views of mathematics that intermingle conceptual and procedural competencies. (For a discussion of these programs and others, see Fennema and Romberg, 1999.) Teachers should be aware of instructional programs and teaching methods focused on developing robust understandings.

A second key idea is that robust understandings come from seeing the same concepts from multiple perspectives and representing and using them in multiple ways, thereby developing connected webs of understandings rather than rote memorization of facts and procedures. Doing mathematics is a form of sense-making. As a consequence, students must learn it as such—actively engaging in problem solving, grappling with problematic situations rather than simply memorizing formulas and rules. Some instructional programs, such as the Algebra Project (Moses and Cobb, 2001), focus on providing students concrete experiential referents as a base from which to build more abstract mathematical understandings. Understanding connections within mathematics (via multiple representations) and outside mathematics (to real-world phenomena) are both essential parts of coming to grips with mathematical ideas (National Council of Teachers of Mathematics, 2000).

A similar idea that is relatively recent and important is the idea that one can develop and sharpen one's understandings by solving problems. Some years ago it was assumed that one had to "master" a huge amount of mathematics, and then "apply" it to problems. It is now understood that one can give students problems that they can grapple with, and that if the problems are carefully chosen, students develop mathematical ideas as they work through the problems.

Developmental readiness, and growth in sophistication, are very important ideas. Some hints regarding this were given in the response to question 2, regarding the purposes of teaching subject matter. *Principles and Standards* lays out content and process sequences that are consistent with developmental growth—the idea, for example, that proof is the codification of a coherent line of reasoning, that one can begin with informal arguments about why something makes sense, and proceed to the point where such arguments are formalized. Similarly, there are progressions in terms of the complexity of content. Third graders can make and explore conjectures about whole numbers, producing reasoned and reasonable arguments for their claims. They might, based on experience, conjecture that the sum of two odd numbers is always even. If they have defined odd numbers as "numbers that have one left over when you try to group them by pairs," they can discover an argument that two "representative" odd numbers, say 5 and 7, must add up to an even number, because the unit "left over" in 5 and the unit "left over" in 5 can be combined to make a pair. Years later, as an elementary exercise in algebra, they can codify this understanding with a proof, the central argument being

$$(2N + 1) + (2M + 1) = (2N + 2M + 2) = 2(N + M + 1).$$

Later on, this kind of argument will be one of many in their mathematical toolkit that can be used for approaching a wide range of problems in many subject areas.

Questions of "developmental readiness" raise thorny issues with regard to mathematics curricula. If one assumes that the mathematics curriculum is, in essence, immutable and hierarchical, then a desire to place students in courses they are "ready for" would result in tracking. There are alternatives to this kind of approach. One option is to devise curricula that contains many rich problems or problem situations, which can be worked on at varied levels. Given sufficiently rich situations, some students could explore straightforward patterns, coming upon a solution inductively; some could symbolize the situation and derive analytic representations and solutions of problems within it; some could generalize the problems and their solutions. This might be considered the curricular equivalent of giving students complex texts that can be read and discussed at multiple levels. (For examples of such approaches in mathematics and the consequences of them, see Boaler and Greeno, 2000; Horn, 2003.)

In addition, teachers and curricula both must provide mathematics learning opportunities for English language learners. This issue becomes especially critical as curricula increasingly include the modeling and discussion of complex situations. Care must be taken not to disenfranchise English language learners, but instead to capitalize on the linguistic resources they bring to the classroom. Providing multiple representations that create multiple handholds into the content becomes especially important for such students (see, for example, Brenner, 1994; Khisty, 1995; Moschkovich, 1999a, 1999b, 2002).

Sample Response: English/Language Arts. People who choose to become English teachers are often avid readers and writers themselves. Part of the challenge for professional education is to help prospective teachers move beyond their own experiences as readers and writers and understand how a diverse group of students learn to read and write. A second challenge in the area of reading and writing is to help prospective teachers see that understanding in these domains involves procedural, conceptual, and strategic knowledge. Learning to write, for example, can be conceptualized as a form of problem solving, in which students need to understand the kinds of problems posed by a specific writing task and how to address those problems. Understanding the role of audience in composition requires both a concept of audience, and a set of skills and strategies for the consideration of audience. In the area of reading, teachers might need to investigate students' abilities to decode text: the kinds of strategies students use to comprehend both expository and narrative texts, as well as their approaches to interpreting literary text. Understanding literature means much more than the ability to decode and comprehend the specific words, as any reader of Toni Morrison will know.

Research in the area of English that has investigated student understanding has documented some of the ways in which students develop their ability to read and write over time. For example, some research illustrates how students move from relatively global assessments of literature to more refined and analytic understandings over time; other research documents younger students' tendency to develop a fixed interpretation of a text early on that is then difficult for them to revise, something more experienced readers do as a matter of course; this distinction may also characterize differences between weaker and stronger readers. Another line of research illustrates the difficulty that struggling readers have in visualizing the details of a literary text; such readers need more assistance getting "into" a text and using details to build an image of the world created by the author (see Grossman, 2001, for a review of this literature). In investigating questions of students' understanding of literature, prospective teachers should have opportunities to get inside of students' thinking about text and to compare the kinds of interpretive strategies used by skilled readers to those of less experienced readers.

Reading also varies by the nature of text; we do not read the newspaper or a textbook in the same way we read *House on Mango Street* or a Billy Collins poem. For this reason, teachers need opportunities to explore the reading demands of different kinds of texts (expository, narrative, poetic, and so forth) and the kinds of reading strategies children need to read such texts successfully.

Teachers also need opportunities to explore how students' cultural backgrounds may affect their interactions with texts. We know, for example, that children come to school with different experiences in interacting with text (Heath, 1983). We also know that readers' prior knowledge will affect their ability to comprehend text. For example, a reader who is unfamiliar with the history of India and its revolution would find it difficult to comprehend *Midnight's Children* by Salman Rushdie, just as a reader who lacked knowledge of slavery would find *Beloved*, by Toni Morrison, even more challenging. Students may also respond to text based on their cultural or racial identities; teaching *The Adventures of Huckleberry Finn*, for example, poses particular pedagogical challenges in its portrayal of Jim (see, for example, Booth, 1988). Teachers need to be alert to the cultural knowledge and identities students bring to reading and writing, and how to anticipate the ways students can draw on such knowledge in learning to read and write complex texts. One line of research has begun to explore how to use students' cultural knowledge as a resource in comprehending difficult literary texts (see, for example, Lee, 1995).

Lee's work in Cultural Modeling (1995) demonstrates the complexity of prior knowledge in the interpretation of literary texts. Lee designed a curricular intervention that scaffolded the rhetorical knowledge of African American adolescent speakers of African American English to support literary reasoning of canonical texts. She assessed students' prior knowledge of African American cultural knowledge as related to two target texts, *The Color Purple* by Alice Walker and *Their Eyes Were Watching God* by Zora Neale Hurston. She also assessed their knowledge of signifying, a genre of talk in African American English that involves ritual insult characterized by high use of innuendo and figurative language, using material close to the students' out-of-school experience. (See Building on Students' Knowledge Through Cultural Modeling, which illustrates how one teacher in the Cultural Modeling Project used her knowledge of students' out-of-school knowledge to evoke literary explanations.)

Building on Students' Knowledge Through Cultural Modeling
Students had been given the lyrics to the rap song "The Mask," by The Fugees. In each stanza of the song, characters are said to wear the mask.

Teacher: Okay, "My posse up town wear the mask, my crew in Queens wear the mask, stick up kids with Tommy Hill wear the mask." Who is he talking about here?

Student 1: So they trying to say that little kids are stickin' up people too with masks on? Is that what they trying to say?

Teacher: They actually have masks on?

Student 2: No. Well, basically, they tryin to hide their true identity. Even if they don't actually have a mask, it's like an illusion in a sense, because obviously, they don't walk around with a mask on, but they walk around with this cover like, you know how some people try and act like they're hard, but they really not. And they, you know, but that don't mean that they have. They got like a cover, you know, a shield over 'em; but it's not, it's an invisible shield.

Students here have distinguished between the literal and the figurative. They have imputed an archetypal literary theme to explain the internal states of the characters in the lyrics. By sequencing instruction in ways that first elicit students' relevant cultural knowledge and by making explicit how the structure of their everyday reasoning maps onto the problems of literary interpretation they will meet in canonical texts, over time students are able to construct complex interpretations of canonical texts without explicit continued scaffolding by the teacher.

Source: Adapted from Lee, in preparation. Reprinted with permission from the author.

Lee's research suggests that understanding the significance of students' cultural knowledge for instruction is not a simple matter. Examining relationships between students' prior knowledge of social codes, their knowledge of signifying, and scores on pre and post tests of literary comprehension, Lee notes that ". . . prior social knowledge, in and of itself, does not assure the kind of interpretation of texts sought in this instructional unit. I argue that the missing link here is knowledge of signifying as a code or framework on which to map a literary stance toward the interpretation of figurative language" (p. 90).

Such pedagogical understanding requires not only a deep understanding of the subject matter, akin to Li Ping Ma's conception of the "profound understanding of fundamental mathematics" that superior teachers of mathematics hold; it also requires an equally profound understanding of the knowledge, world experiences, dispositions, and habits of mind that students construct through their history with schooling as well as through their out-of-school experiences in families, communities, and peer social networks. To draw on students' cultural knowledge to support learning, teachers must think critically about how that knowledge maps onto the demands of the academic domain. They must plan text selection and sequencing with this understanding in mind. They must be sufficiently flexible in their understanding of relationships between cultural knowledge and domain knowledge to recognize what students' moves reveal about their understanding of the problems presented in texts.

In the area of writing, prospective teachers need to explore the different demands of a variety of writing tasks, and how students develop the resources to meet those demands. How do students develop a sense of written academic discourse distinct from spoken language? How do those who are still mastering spoken English engage in a variety of writing tasks? Research on writing provides numerous starting points for investigating students' developing understanding of writing (see Sperling and Freedman, 2001). In the area of elementary language arts, prospective teachers need to understand how students develop as readers over time. The use of informal reading inventories can help teachers identify students' proficiency in decoding and comprehending text. Teachers can also investigate the kinds of metacognitive strategies used by skilled readers and the ways in which students might employ such strategies in their reading of different kinds of texts. As is true across levels, teachers also need opportunities to assess the relative difficulty of texts and how best to match text difficulty with reading ability. This knowledge of how young readers read—the kinds of strategies they use, their development over time—is fundamental for elementary teachers (see Snow, Griffin, and Burns, 2005). Elementary teachers also need to know how students develop as writers, the relationship between learning to read and learning to write, the demands of different genres and how students might understand those demands, and how students are likely to understand different components of the writing process.

Q4. What are the primary curricula available to teach the subject matter? What definitions of the subject are embedded within the curriculum materials? How are curricula aligned with national and state standards? How are they articulated across grade levels? How can teachers use curriculum materials effectively to support student learning?

Curriculum materials are powerful professional tools, but teachers need to learn how to use them (Ball and Cohen, 1996; Ball and Feiman-Nemser, 1988). Part of pedagogical content knowledge involves knowing the kinds of curricular tools that are available for teaching a particular subject. In addition to knowing what is available, teachers must also know how to critique curriculum materials; what visions and purposes for teaching subject matter are embedded within curriculum materials? For example, what different perspectives on biology are represented by the different versions of the Biological Sciences Curriculum Study (BSCS) curriculum in science? What assumptions do curriculum materials make about what students already know? Teachers must also be able to critique curriculum materials with an eye toward the accuracy of the subject matter being represented.

Sample Response: Mathematics. There has been a sea change since the early 1990s. Traditional curricula, which predominated before then, were oriented toward basic skills. They consisted of K–8 packages focusing on arithmetic, followed by a year (grade 9) of algebra, a year (grade 10) of geometry, a year (grade 11) of advanced algebra/trigonometry, and a year (grade 12) of precalculus. Following the 1989 issuance of the first NCTM *Standards,* various "reform" or "standards-based" curricula were developed. These curricula focus much more on applications, mathematical contexts, statistics, and sense-making. They tend to be much more "hands-on" at the early grades, with manipulative materials. They tend not to fractionate into separate content areas (algebra, geometry, trigonometry, and so forth) at the high school level, as did the traditional curricula.

These reform curricula were controversial, because many feared that students would be deprived of the core knowledge and skills found in the traditional curricula. (For a discussion of these debates, see Schoenfeld, 2004.) However, evidence is now accumulating that shows that the new standards-based curricula are working. A growing body of both small-scale and large-scale studies indicates that students in the reform curricula do as well on traditional tests of basic skills as students who study the traditional curricula, and they are much more successful on tests of concepts and problem solving (see, for example, Riordan and Noyce, 2001; Schoenfeld, 2002; ARC Center, 2002; Senk and Thompson, 2003). Teachers need to know about these reforms and their implications: what the new curricula look like, how they differ from the traditional ones, that they work when they are taught right, and what it means to teach them right. The new curricula often call for different pedagogical practices than have typically been featured in many mathematics classrooms, for example, the use of group work, the use of extended problems or projects. Teachers need to develop the facility for implementing and assessing such curricula, including how to assess a broader set of desired student outcomes. Standardized assessments that focus largely on procedures and the solution of routine exercises may fail to capture aspects of problem representation and problem solving that are central to new standards and curricula (Ridgeway and others, 2000).

Sample Response: English/Language Arts. Within elementary language arts, basal readers have been a traditional part of the curriculum, in addition to sets of trade books aimed at different grade levels. More recently, there have been a number of packaged reading programs (Open Court, CIRC) used as the curriculum for elementary reading. Prospective teachers need opportunities to explore what these different curriculum materials offer for teaching the range of language arts, as well as their potential limitations. Prospective teachers will also need a sense of how to use these curriculum materials to support student learning. Elementary teachers generally have a number of additional resources for teaching other components in the language arts, including grammar and vocabulary, among others. Teachers should have the opportunity to study some range of the available materials, the theoretical orientations toward teaching reading instantiated in these materials, and how to use them in putting together a balanced literacy program. As curriculum materials used by some districts become more prescriptive, teachers need the opportunity to analyze what they are being asked to implement and how the curriculum supports, or does not support, the range of learners in their class.

In secondary English, although there are textbooks for teaching various components of the language arts, teachers generally rely heavily on literary texts as the basis of the curriculum. For this reason, prospective teachers need opportunities to examine the recommended and required literature for students of different ages and consider the curricular possibilities of the literary texts for teaching about reading, literature, writing, and language. The literature in the secondary curriculum has remained relatively static over time (Applebee, 1991), so prospective teachers also need opportunities to think about the ways in which the literature curriculum does and does not reflect contemporary literature and the diversity of their students. In addition, they should have opportunities to survey the kind of textbooks and curriculum materials available for teaching writing, language, and grammar and assess how they might use such materials to support students' learning.

Part of the challenge in the domain of English/language arts involves learning to coordinate a variety of curriculum materials that cut across a range of areas to create a coherent curriculum for students. Curriculum materials that integrate more aspects of the language arts (what Grossman, Thompson, and

Valencia [2003] have termed the "scope of the materials") are likely to help beginning teachers think about how to integrate these different content areas in the classroom. For example, some curriculum materials may focus only on the teaching of writing, detached from the teaching of literature, whereas others integrate the teaching of writing and literature in both reading and writing activities. The latter could help students and teachers see that "reading and writing are complementary acts that remain unfinished until completed by their reciprocals" (Scholes, 1985, p. 20).

Q5. How do teachers assess student understanding and performance within a subject matter domain? What tools are most useful for assessing student competence? How do teachers use the results of these assessments to inform instruction?

To design and improve instruction, teachers need a sense of what students already know within a given subject matter, and what they learned through instruction. Although there is knowledge of assessment that cuts across subject matters, such as how to design a multiple-choice test or how to create a scoring rubric (see Chapter Eight), much of the assessment teachers actually do requires subject-specific tools. In early reading, for example, teachers need to have tools to assess their students' developing literacy skills. They might know about informal reading assessments, which help them assess students' decoding skills and their fluency and comprehension in reading. In writing, teachers would need to know how to use different kinds of writing assessments, from holistic assessments of a piece of writing to the use of analytic scales. Just as important, they need to know how to use such information to inform instruction. In addition to knowing how to assess student learning within a subject matter, teachers also need to know how to use the assessments to develop instruction that helps students develop skills and understanding.

Sample Response: Mathematics. The example that began this chapter shows how a great deal of thought must go into assessing student understandings of even as simple a topic as putting fractions in order. As that example indicates, good assessment should not only provide accurate indications of what students can do, it should also reveal student difficulties, and point to the sources of those difficulties. Chapter Eight discusses issues of assessment in general. Above and beyond this general knowledge of assessment, however, teachers of mathematics will need to know the specifics for mathematics, as discussed in volumes produced by the National Research Council, for example (1993a, 1993b), and in professional development materials such as the *Balanced Assessment* (1999) packages at the elementary, middle, high school, and advanced high school levels.

Sample Response: English/Language Arts. The field of reading actually has much more developed ways of assessing students' reading than exist for secondary English. Prospective teachers should have opportunities to explore the kinds of assessment instruments, both formal and informal, that are used to assess students' reading and writing. For example, prospective elementary teachers might have the opportunity to conduct informal reading inventories with students and use the inventory to develop a sense of that student's proficiency in decoding and comprehension, as well as assessing fluency. This kind of opportunity can build prospective teachers' understanding of how students read, the predictable problems they might have with texts, and information about how best to design instruction to meet student needs. Such opportunities to look closely at students' reading performances are much rarer for secondary teachers. With the current concern over adolescent reading, however, prospective secondary teachers may also need structured opportunities to conduct such reading assessments with students for the purposes of informing instruction.

Similarly, in writing there are a range of ways to assess students' writing ability across both elementary and secondary school, from holistic evaluations of writing to primary trait scoring approaches, to assessment of intellectual strategies used in writing (Cooper and Odell, 1977). Prospective teachers need opportunities to experiment with a range of ways to assess student writing and to explore what they can learn from different kinds of assessments.

Learning to use these different tools for assessment can help sharpen teachers' ability to listen and look carefully for student learning, enabling them to see students' classroom performances as opportunities for informal, formative assessment (see Chapters Two and Eight, on Learning and Assessment, for discussions of formative assessment). Teachers also need to learn to use and develop assessments that track the learning of their students over time, particularly in areas that are not well captured on standardized tests.

Q6. What are the practices that characterize the teaching of particular content? What practices and approaches have been shown to be effective in promoting student learning? Are there practices that are particularly effective with specific groups of learners? What representations, examples, analogies are particularly useful in helping students grasp particular concepts or ideas?

This final set of questions has to do with knowledge about teaching specific content. As was true of assessment, there is knowledge about teaching that is relatively general—such as how to organize effective small groups in a classroom, how to design direct instruction, how to manage a classroom so that students stay on task (see Chapter Nine, Classroom Management). But within each subject area, there are differences in how such instruction might unfold. For example, designing small-group work around a laboratory experiment is not the same as designing small-group work around a peer-editing task in writing. The roles of group members are likely to be different, as is the nature of the task. Each subject area may also have distinctive approaches for teaching the subject matter, and teachers in these subjects will want to explore how to design and orchestrate such classroom practices. For example, in the teaching of literature, there are a range of instructional practices that may be part of teachers' pedagogical repertoires, such as having students direct and perform dramatic works, engaging in small or large group discussion around a literary text, or conducting readers' theater. Similarly, in elementary reading, teachers may be familiar with guided reading instruction, reciprocal reading, or literature circles. The laboratory experiment is part of the distinctive pedagogy of science classrooms. Social studies classes often incorporate debate, mock elections, simulations of historical events, the careful reading of primary source materials, or structured academic controversies. To teach the subject matter effectively, teachers need a pedagogical repertoire for the particular content they teach.

In addition to subject-specific repertoires of instructional practices, teachers may also need to consider the issue of the most effective practices for different groups of students. One set of practices might include culturally responsive pedagogy, and what this might look like in different subject matters (see, for example, Delpit, 1995; Ladson-Billings, 1994; Moll, Amanti, Neff, and González, 1992; Secada, Fennema, and Adajian, 1995). (For a further discussion, see Chapter Seven, Teaching Diverse Learners.) What does culturally responsive pedagogy look like in science, in math, in history, or in English? Another group of students that might benefit from a specific set of practices is English language learners. There is, for example, a growing literature on effective mechanisms for enfranchising language learners in mathematics and science (see, for example, Khisty, 1995; Moschkovich, 1999a, 1999b; Warren and Rosebery, 1995). For example, the *Cheche Konnen* project seeks explicitly "to define a new perspective on scientific practice in the classroom that admits diverse sense-making practices, carries with it more egalitarian values, and ensures that linguistic minority students acquire the mainstream literacies they need to succeed in school and beyond . . . [This calls for] a new kind of relationship between students and science, one that is distinctly different from that enacted in traditional school science" (Warren and Rosebery, 1995, p. 324). Prospective teachers should have opportunities to learn the kinds of instructional practices recommended for English language learners, and how these practices might play out within a particular subject matter arena. There is also a body of work on ways of teaching and assessing writing for English language learners (see, for example, Reyes de la Luz, 1991) that can inform the work of teachers.

In addition to more general kinds of instructional practices, there are also the examples, analogies, and representations that are particular to subject matter. Teachers will develop many of these as they engage in the practice of teaching. But examining different analogies or examples for teaching particular subject matter, and considering how different representations may be useful for students based on their prior knowledge and experiences, can help prospective teachers understand how to build bridges between their own understanding of the content and students' understanding.

Sample Response: Mathematics. As is the case with almost all subject matter, students are not likely to develop certain kinds of understandings unless they have the opportunity to practice them. Students will not develop skill at communicating mathematical ideas in written or oral form unless they have ample opportunity to do so in class; they will not get good at making connections unless they are given problems that call for making connections. Thus teachers must develop a repertoire of classroom practices that support their students' development of important mathematical understandings. Fortunately, many of the new curricula provide such opportunities and suggest forms of interaction in the classroom. (Examples of some such programs were given earlier; see Fennema and Romberg, 1999, for additional examples.)

Some recommended practices for teaching mathematics may be enacted in ways that render them ineffective in the classroom. One example is "cooperative learning," which became a bandwagon approach to instruction in the 1990s. For many teachers this simply meant having students work together in small groups. Classroom studies soon revealed that many small-group conversations were not focused on the mathematics, and when conversations were not focused, mathematics learning did not take place. In short, it takes work to make sure that this technique—having groups of students engage meaningfully with mathematical content—is implemented successfully. Teachers need to learn how to structure successful groupwork (see, for example, Slavin, 1990a; Cohen and Lotan, 1995). The same goes for all other techniques.

Sample Response: English/Language Arts. In the area of elementary language arts, there are a number of common practices for teaching reading, such as guided reading, literature circles, and reciprocal teaching. Although some of these, such as reciprocal teaching, are quite well defined and are supported by a strong research base, others, such as literature circles, are much more open to interpretation and variability in enactment. Similarly, in the area of writing, there are practices such as writers workshop, authors chair, peer editing groups, and mini-lessons that are commonly used for teaching writing, although what such practices look like in classrooms can differ widely. In the teaching of literature, classroom discussion is probably the most prevalent practice. Forms of discussion that build on and extend student thinking have been shown to have a positive relationship to student achievement in the area of literature (Nystrand, Gamoran, Kachur, and Prendergast, 1997). However, as is also true for mathematics, how discussions are organized and facilitated influences what students learn. For example, Nystrand and his colleagues found that teachers' uptake of student ideas in whole group discussions of literature was positively related to student achievement. Small-group discussions of literature had widely varying results. For all of these practices, the diversity among practices bearing the same name is enormous. Prospective teachers need opportunities to see common, concrete examples of forms of instruction, ideally through videotape, in order to develop their understanding of how such practices can be used effectively to promote student learning. Prospective teachers could also benefit from understanding some of the critical features of effective instructional practices, such as uptake in group discourse, that are essential for student learning. Finally, teachers need to understand how such instructional practices represent theories of learning as well as disciplinary understanding.

Implications for the Teacher Education Curriculum

Much of teaching effectively depends on understanding student thinking—or better yet, anticipating and preparing for student understanding ahead of time. In fact, the design of many exemplary Japanese lessons includes as a matter of course not only the questions that should be posed to students, but a list of the typical correct and incorrect responses students provide, and information about how the teacher can capitalize on such responses. This kind of *subject matter knowledge for teaching,* or pedagogical content knowledge, is an important and unique aspect of the kind of knowledge that teacher preparation programs can provide opportunities to develop, and that appropriately structured professional development programs can continue to foster. Such a perspective, however, raises questions about both the preparation of subject matter specialists, who are typically secondary school teachers, and the preparation of elementary teachers who must teach across multiple fields. We address these issues in the following discussion.

PROFESSIONAL EDUCATION IN SUBJECT MATTER AS AN OPPORTUNITY TO INVESTIGATE CORE QUESTIONS

If the questions posed about the teaching of subject matter in Figure 6.1 are taken as generative, then it should be possible to design rich learning experiences for teachers around these questions. We will now return to these questions and explore the kinds of activities teacher educators and those in charge of professional development might design.[1]

In preservice teacher education, teachers confront the definition of the subject matter as they engage in curriculum design, analyze curriculum materials, and design classroom activities. For example, in some methods classes, students

---

[1]The examples in this section were taken from EMST 224A, "The Nature of Mathematical Thinking and Problem Solving" taught at UC Berkeley, and ED 262A-C, "Curriculum and Instruction in English" taught at Stanford University.

use the work of Grant Wiggins on backward design to create curriculum units (Wiggins and McTighe, 1998). Wiggins recommends designing curriculum units around a question that is essential to both the subject matter and the students. For example, the question, "How can fiction be true?" addresses core issues within literary study. Generating essential questions thus forces teachers to think about their own definitions of the subject matter, what is central and what is peripheral to the study of a subject. Similarly, teachers can analyze textbooks to see how textbooks define and represent the subject matter, and how these definitions, in turn, match teachers' understandings. Such activities are rooted in practices of teaching, and therefore prepare prospective teachers for the work they will be doing as professionals, while also calling upon their developing content and pedagogical content knowledge.

In grappling with the question "Why teach the subject matter?" preservice teachers can analyze standards documents and curriculum materials for explicit and implicit rationales for the school subject. They can study some curricular controversies with an eye toward understanding the underlying motivations behind the stances taken. For example, in a methods class on the teaching of English, students can be given several articles that argue for quite different purposes for teaching English and then be asked to develop their own rationale for teaching English in the public schools. Likewise, preservice teachers can explore controversies such as those embodied in the "math wars" in a variety of ways, including touring the Web sites of groups that are for and against reform. They can think about different perspectives on content by imagining social studies topics as seen through the lens of an anthropologist, a political scientist, and a historian. In observing in schools, preservice teachers might also talk with experienced teachers about their own beliefs about the purposes for teaching their subject. Understanding that different purposes can and do exist might also help prospective teachers navigate departmental politics, in which such differences often surface. Practicing teachers can continue to grapple with this set of questions by serving on curriculum committees and contributing to standards documents or to department or school philosophy statements. Preparing for the National Board for Professional Teaching Standards' certification assessment also requires teachers to return to this set of questions regarding the purposes of teaching subject matter.

Perhaps one of the most fruitful venues for professional education lies in the set of questions regarding students' understanding and performance in a subject matter. Many of the activities both in methods classes and in field experiences could be designed to help preservice teachers explore the question of student understanding. For example, in one preservice English methods class, the teacher has a series of assignments that focus on developing teachers' understandings of their students. Students first interview a high school student about his or her experiences as a reader and writer, both in and out of school, to move student teachers beyond their own experiences in the subject and inquire about what others might have experienced. Because prospective English teachers are generally people who love to read and write, they are often surprised by the negative reactions many of their students have toward these activities. Later, students examine a set of student papers from their own classroom and draw some conclusions about what students already know about writing, and what they are struggling with. Later in the class, they assess one student's understanding of literature using three different approaches. In their analysis they need to draw some conclusions about what this student understands about literature and the usefulness and limitations of each assessment strategy. Analogously, in one preservice mathematics class, prospective teachers take a standard assessment (perhaps a test given in one of the classes they are observing, or something similar) and ask individual students if they would be willing to be videotaped as they work the problems out loud. Quite often what the students say as they work the problems bears only passing resemblance to what finally makes its way onto the page; the prospective teachers see aspects of student thinking that were heretofore invisible.

All of these assignments draw on and extend teachers' developing pedagogical content knowledge. In engaging in a close assessment of one student, prospective teachers are both beginning to develop case-based knowledge of students' understanding by looking at a single student in depth and developing the tools with which they can continue to construct their understanding of student understanding. One of the primary functions of preservice teacher education is to provide prospective teachers with the tools to learn from experience. Teacher educators cannot possibly teach them everything they will need to know as professionals; but by focusing their attention on key issues related to the teaching and learning within a subject matter, and by equipping them with the tools to continue their inquiries, we can help them keep on learning.

These kinds of activities are based in the core practices of teaching (Ball and Cohen, 1999). Teaching involves helping students to develop understanding. That means finding out, via both formal and informal assessments, what knowledge the students bring to the task. All teachers must design preassessments in order to learn more about what students already do and do not understand about a subject. Teachers must also analyze student work, with an eye toward what it reveals about students' understanding. Although practicing teachers seldom have the opportunity to engage in the kind of in-depth analysis of a single student that this assignment requires students to do, they do engage in a variety of forms of action research that might use such tools and that select a few students for in-depth analysis.

For each of the sets of questions in Figure 6.1, there are sets of activities and practices that help teachers investigate these questions. The activities designed for preservice teachers have their analogue in the kinds of activities that classroom teachers might engage in, fulfilling Dewey's admonition that "only by extracting the full meaning of each present experience are we prepared for doing the same thing in the future" (Dewey, 1938, p. 49). Such activities also provide prospective teachers with the tools they will need to continue learning throughout their careers. As Sharon Feiman-Nemser (2001a) suggests:

> The study of teaching requires skills of observation, interpretation, and analysis. Preservice teachers can begin developing these tools by analyzing student work, comparing different curriculum materials, interviewing students to uncover their thinking, studying how different teachers work toward the same goals, and observing what impact their instruction has on students. Carried out in the company of others, these activities can foster norms for professional discourse such as respect for evidence, openness to questions, valuing of alternative perspectives, a search for common understandings, and shared standards. (p. 1019)

CULTIVATING PEDAGOGICAL CONTENT KNOWLEDGE IN ELEMENTARY TEACHER EDUCATION

The question of subject-specific preparation for teaching becomes more complex when we consider the preparation of elementary school teachers, both in the area of content knowledge and in pedagogical content knowledge. First, we argue that elementary teachers need a strong grounding in disciplinary ways of knowing, preferably within a discipline that is closely connected to the elementary school curriculum. Though not everyone would agree with this stance, and little research would help us resolve this issue, we believe that the ability to answer the kinds of questions we have posed relies, in part, on the opportunity to delve deeply into a field of study and to understand how questions are generated and pursued within a field. Although a smattering of survey courses across the liberal arts might convey some of the necessary content for elementary teaching, such an approach is unlikely to help prospective teachers develop the ways of thinking within any particular discipline; such a survey would provide a "rhetoric of conclusions rather than a rhetoric of inquiry," as Schwab (1964) suggests. We believe that a grounding in inquiry in a particular discipline will help prospective teachers create inquiry-oriented classrooms for their students. We also believe that elementary teachers, no less than secondary teachers, need a strong liberal arts education, one that introduces students to different ways of thinking and to knowledge and understandings that provide the foundations for the elementary school curriculum. We argue, then, for both depth and breadth of subject matter preparation—depth in a particular content area that is related to the elementary curriculum and breadth across the liberal arts.

These recommendations focus on subject matter knowledge rather than content pedagogy. Although the questions we have posed for pedagogical content knowledge are just as important for elementary teachers to explore as they are for secondary teachers, teacher educators need to wrestle with how to design the subject-specific component of the professional curriculum to reflect the fact that elementary teachers teach multiple subjects.

One approach would be to prepare elementary teachers as subject-specialists, especially at the intermediate level. To develop this kind of "profound understanding of fundamental" content (Ma, 1999), upper elementary teachers may need the opportunity to focus deeply on teaching and learning within fewer subject areas.

An alternative position would be to maintain that certain content areas have high priority, specifically, the content areas that are seen as core to academic success across the curriculum: literacy and mathematics. Teacher education could then provide greater attention to these two areas, helping prospective elementary teachers develop pedagogical content knowledge, including deep understanding of content standards and grade band curricula, and familiarity with students' common understanding and misunderstandings in these two content areas. Teacher education could continue to provide opportunities to learn to teach science, social studies, and the arts; following an introduction to these content areas, prospective teachers then might choose to specialize within one of these areas. Such a position would pose consequences for how we staff elementary schools, as principals would need to make sure that the faculty includes teachers with specialties in all of the content areas. Such distributed expertise would also affect the organization of teachers' work. All teachers would be expected to teach literacy and mathematics to students in their own classroom, but teachers might then teach their specialty area (for example, science or art) to a broader range of students in the school or they might help the colleagues in their grade level team to plan instruction in their specialty area.

Another possibility would be to create more opportunities within the liberal arts component of teacher education for prospective teachers to begin to think about both the ways of thinking within different disciplines and the pedagogical entailments of different subject matters. Within a liberal arts curriculum, prospective teachers might learn physics in classes that model an inquiry-oriented approach to the teaching of physics, and history in courses that emphasize the use of primary source materials (Wilson and McDiarmid, 1996). Such courses already exist; the challenge would be to harness their power for the education of prospective teachers. Whether there are subject matter specialists who consult and help with instruction, whether teachers team up and share distributed expertise, or some other arrangement is established, the bottom line is clear: we owe it to our students to guarantee that their teachers develop the rich kinds of pedagogical content knowledge that will enable them to teach most effectively.

CHAPTER SEVEN

Teaching Diverse Learners

James Banks, Marilyn Cochran-Smith, Luis Moll, Anna Richert,
Kenneth Zeichner, Pamela LePage, Linda Darling-Hammond,
Helen Duffy, with Morva McDonald

In today's schools, teachers must be prepared to teach a diverse population of students. Of course, diversity is the nature of the human species, and students are and always have been different from each other in a variety of ways. However, schools have not always had the mission to support achievement for all students, and children's assignments to schools and classrooms have, during many periods in history, fostered segregation rather than encouraging inclusion and acceptance of heterogeneous groups.

In recent years, classrooms in the United States have changed rapidly. Just over thirty years ago, in 1972, students of color constituted 22 percent of the school population; by 2000 this proportion had increased to 39 percent (National Center for Education Statistics, 2002a). Thirty years from now (by 2035) demographers project that students of color will constitute a majority of the student population in the United States (Hodgkinson, 2001; U.S. Bureau of the Census, 2000). The number of children in schools who are English language learners has also increased dramatically in recent years, more than doubling from about 1.5 million in 1985 to about 3.2 million in 1995 and continuing to grow since then (Villegas and Lucas, 2002a). Diversity in the range of academic abilities within classrooms has also grown as schools have included more students with exceptional needs in mainstream classrooms. In 1998–1999, 13 percent of students participated in special education, and nearly half of them (47 percent) spent 80 percent or more of their time in general education settings, a sharp increase from only a decade earlier (National Center for Education Statistics, 2002b).

Thus all teachers must be prepared to take into account the different experiences and academic needs of a wide range of students as they plan and teach. The recommendations in this section are based on research that indicates that when teachers use knowledge about the social, cultural, and language backgrounds of their students when planning and implementing instruction, the academic achievement of students can increase (see, for example, Au, 1980; Philips, 1972; Lee, 1995; Gandara, 2002; Garcia, 1993). And, when teachers know how to address learning needs associated with cognitive differences and disabilities, children's academic achievement also increases (Palincsar and Brown, 1987; Reynolds, Walberg, and Weissberg, 1999). These kinds of knowledge can augment a teacher's knowledge of content in powerful ways. For example, a study of mathematics and science teaching found that student achievement was greater for those whose teachers had a degree in the field they were teaching *and* had had preparation regarding multicultural education, special education, and English language development (Wenglinsky, 2002). This chapter extends the recommendations offered in other chapters in the volume to consider the realities of diverse classrooms where knowledge of development, learning, language, and pedagogy must be integrated by the teacher.

This chapter's recommendations are based on the assumption that to support democracy, educators must seek to eliminate disparities in educational opportunities among all students, especially those students who have been poorly served by our current system. Furthermore, in order for all citizens to be prepared to participate in a democracy, children must experience democracy in schools. Therefore teachers need to have the knowledge, skills, and attitudes to create democratic classrooms and to implement a culturally responsive and inclusive curriculum (Gay, 2000).

In addition, teachers need to be aware of—and be prepared to influence—the structural conditions that determine the allocation of educational opportunity within a school: the kinds of courses, curriculum, and teaching that are offered to different students, the kinds of student groupings that are created, the ways in which students are assigned to teachers, and the kind of norms and expectations that govern their treatment and the treatment of their families. Teachers also need to be aware of family and community values, norms, and experiences, so that they can help to mediate the "boundary crossing" (Davidson and Phelan, 1999) that many students must manage between home and school. All of these things influence student achievement and access to educational opportunity as much as the efforts of the individual teacher in the classroom.

In this chapter we focus on what new teachers must understand and be able to do to enhance the academic achievement of all students. We consider aspects of diversity including culture and racial/ethnic origins, language, economic status, and learning challenges associated with exceptionalities. As Banks (1993) notes, all of these factors—and their interactions—are important for teachers who want to construct an "equity pedagogy" (p. 5). We incorporate aspects of the knowledge base regarding development, learning, and learning differences (see Chapters Two and Three of this volume) as well as content pedagogy, assessment, and classroom management (see Chapters Six, Eight, and Nine) with knowledge about culture and its influences on learning (Cazden and Mehan, 1990; Heath, 1983). We also discuss what teachers need to know to construct culturally responsive and learner adaptive pedagogy, curriculum, and assessment (Gay, 2000; Villegas and Lucas, 2002a; Palincsar, Magnusson, Collins, and Cutter, 2002) and to work with communities and parents (Moll and Gonzáles, 2004). Finally, this chapter discusses the kinds of teacher preparation experiences that may enable prospective teachers to more effectively teach diverse students (Nieto, 1999; Villegas and Lucas, 2002a; Zeichner, 1993a; Wolfberg, 1999).

CHALLENGES OF TEACHING DIVERSE LEARNERS

The following three vignettes portray teachers and students in U.S. public schools. Although necessarily incomplete, they provide a sense of the complexity of teaching in today's diverse schools. In particular, these vignettes point to some of the decision making required of teachers and the multiple, sometimes competing, contexts that influence those decisions. They also reveal how the demands of today's schools require that we rethink traditional teacher education as well as K–12 curriculum and instruction.

Ms. Cowen and a Special Education Placement

Ella Cowen has been teaching kindergarten for five years in Boston, Massachusetts, where the majority of children in her class are African American and Asian. Today she is attending an IEP (Individualized Education Plan) meeting for Julie Lee, who is part of her class only three times a week for two hours. Julie spends most of her time in a special education class down the hall. She was diagnosed with developmental delays when she was three years old and was given early intervention opportunities. Today, a team of professionals is trying to decide a correct placement for Julie for next year. Should she repeat kindergarten? Should she continue in special education? Should she be promoted and placed in an inclusive first-grade classroom? Julie's adoptive parents believe that she has serious language delays and would like to keep her in special education. Ms. Cowen, however, suspects that Julie was diagnosed at a time when she simply needed to adjust to a new country, new parents, and a new language. In the last few months, Julie has made noticeable progress, and Ms. Cowen believes Julie has the potential for more challenging work. Ms. Cowen is not sure whether a special education placement is appropriate, and she knows about the research showing that grade retention rarely raises achievement and can have other unfortunate side-effects. But what if Julie needs special education services that will not occur in a mainstream classroom? How can Ms. Cowen tell the difference between behaviors associated with cultural differences, language learning, and context and challenges associated with specific disabilities? What type of classwork should she take to the meeting as evidence for her recommendations? What kind of instructional plan will best serve Julie's needs next year? What are the parents' expectations, Ella wonders, and how can she be both respectful and professional?

Mr. Levy and a Student Paper on Immigration

Mr. Levy is a teacher who has been teaching social studies at Fairfax High School for fifteen years. Living close to Washington D.C., he loves teaching government and is considered a very good teacher. He recently asked his students to write a paper about the causes of unemployment in the United States. Roger Davenport's first draft concerned him. Mr. Levy was surprised to find that Roger blamed the unemployment rate on immigration and on what he described as more and more of "those people" coming into "our country." In the paper, Roger argued that too many people were being allowed into the country and were taking jobs away from Americans. He explained that not only was the government letting in too many unskilled laborers, but they were also letting in highly qualified computer people from other countries like Russia. He blamed employment problems on illegal immigration and talked about the difficulties of dealing with "boat people." He also explained that many immigrants were taking college scholarships away from Americans because people felt sorry for them.

Mr. Levy pondered about how to respond to the paper, especially given the fact that his own Jewish grandfather had emigrated from Europe in the 1940s to avoid religious persecution. Should he simply tell Roger he needed to develop a better argument based on historical evidence and more accurate knowledge of immigration policy and immigrant populations? Should he make a personal and moral plea? Should he confront the racism implicit in the paper head on? Was this a private issue to discuss with Roger only or did his ideas represent broad misconceptions that needed to be addressed in class? If yes, how should he approach the topic? Should he provide a well-researched lecture on the economics of immigration to ensure that students hear accurate information? Or should he develop an activity where the students inquire into the topic and come to their own conclusions?

Ms. Carrington: Teaching Shakespeare to English Language Learners

Ms. Carrington is a student teacher at John Burroughs Middle School in San Leandro, California. Her English class has twenty-eight students who speak five different languages other than English, including Spanish, Tagalog, Mandarin, and Cantonese. The children are African American, Samoan, European American, Chinese, Filipino, Cambodian, and Latino. Some students walk to school whereas others take public transit, and although many choose not to eat the free lunch, most qualify for free or reduced lunch.

Ms. Carrington's choices about what and how to teach are tightly constrained by districtwide curriculum frameworks and the state-mandated proficiency tests in every major subject area now given every spring to all children in third through eighth grades. Ms. Carrington is required to teach a unit on Shakespearean sonnets, although her students have shown little interest in any kind of poetry, let alone Elizabethan sonnets.

In previous lessons, Ms. Carrington has used modern music to spark the children's interest in poetry, which worked well to capture their attention. At this point, she doesn't want the children to lose interest. She wonders whether she should stray from the required curriculum and teach modern poetry in order to maintain their interest or continue with the required curriculum and try to connect to their experiences to keep them engaged in the required texts. If yes, what strategies should she use to bridge the gap between her children and Shakespeare? Some of her colleagues have suggested using technology, which seems a good idea because many of her students excel at the computer and have already responded well to audio. But, what type of activity would be most effective, a Web quest, some educational software, a Shakespeare Web site with interactive sound and video? What strategies would effectively engage the children and support academic content?

As these vignettes indicate, teachers in today's public schools, whether they are beginning teachers or highly experienced veterans, face new challenges. The classes of most teachers in the twenty-first century—unlike like those taught 50 years ago—are highly diverse in terms of the cultural, language, racial, and economic backgrounds of the students. Thus teachers must have the tools for inquiring into the cultures, groups, and individuals represented in their classrooms. In addition, because the span of ability and experience levels in today's classrooms has widened greatly, with many students who traditionally would have been segregated from other students into special education classes now included in general classrooms, teachers need to have more knowledge about the nature of learning differences and disabilities as well.

The Demographic Imperative

The phrase "the demographic imperative" has been used to make the case that teacher educators and others must take action to alter the disparities in opportunities and outcomes deeply embedded in the American educational system. The argument for the demographic imperative usually includes statistics about the increasingly diverse student population, the still relatively homogeneous teaching force, and "the demographic divide" (Gay and Howard, 2000, p. 1), especially the marked disparities in educational opportunities, resources, and achievement among student groups who differ from one another racially, culturally, and socioeconomically.

A Homogeneous Teaching Force. Although statistics point to the growing diversity of our nation's schools, the composition of the teaching force is much less diverse. The most recent federal data from the Schools and Staffing Surveys

(1999–2000) indicate that teachers of color make up about 16 percent of the nation's teaching force—an increase from only 10 percent in 1986 (National Center for Education Statistics, 2003)—but still much less than the 40 percent of public school students who are students of color. Although beginning teachers include a somewhat larger proportion of teachers of color (21 percent of those with fewer than three years of experience), it seems clear that it will be some time before the population of individuals entering and remaining in teaching closely resembles the population of students in most schools.

More important than simple differences in racial or language backgrounds, there are also marked differences in the biographies and experiences of most teachers and their students. Most U.S. teachers are European Americans from middle-class backgrounds who speak only English. Many of their students are racial and ethnic minorities, live in poverty, and speak a first language other than English. Thus most teachers do not have the same cultural frames of reference and points of view as their students (Au, 1980; Heath, 1983; Lee, 1993). The importance of connecting new learning to prior experiences and the intrinsically cultural nature of learning and knowing (see Chapters Two and Three of this volume) suggest that teachers will need knowledge to understand students' backgrounds and experiences in order to structure meaningful learning experiences for all of them. Even if a teacher has a similar racial or ethnic background as her students, this does not guarantee all students access to educational opportunities (Foster, 2001; Montecinos, 1994). Indeed, all teachers need to develop cultural competence in order to effectively teach students with backgrounds different from their own.

The Demographic Divide: Differences in Educational Outcomes and Resources. There are marked discrepancies in the educational outcomes and learning conditions for students who vary by race, culture, language, socioeconomic status, and learning differences. With one in four children living in poverty, the United States has the highest rate of childhood poverty among Western democratic nations, with the percentage of African American and Hispanic children living in poverty much higher than the average, at 42 percent and 40 percent, respectively. The achievement levels of African American and Hispanic students on the National Assessment of Educational Progress (NAEP) mathematics and reading assessments are consistently and markedly lower than levels for white students, as are high school graduation rates. Villegas and Lucas (2002a) conclude that "the consistent gap between racial/ethnic minority and poor students and their White, middle-class peers . . . is indicative of the inability of the educational system to effectively teach students of color as schools have traditionally been structured" (p. 9).

While there is a long history of research demonstrating the many ways in which poverty contributes to low achievement by reducing access to prenatal and childhood health care, safe housing, and a variety of out-of-school learning opportunities, unequal and inadequate education also contributes to these outcomes. Many studies have documented large disparities in the allocation of resources (for example, equipment, supplies, physical facilities, books, access to computer technology, access to qualified teachers, and class size) to schools serving white and affluent students in comparison with those serving low-income students and students of color. Recent analyses of data prepared for school finance cases in Alabama, California, New Jersey, New York, Louisiana, and Texas have found that on every tangible measure—from qualified teachers to access to technology and curriculum offerings—schools serving greater numbers of students of color tended to have significantly fewer resources than schools serving mostly whites (Darling-Hammond, 2004; see also, National Center for Education Statistics, 1998, 2001a, 2001b, 2001c). In 2001, for example, students in California's predominantly minority schools were five times more likely to have uncertified teachers than those in largely white schools (Shields and others, 2001) and had less access to every category of instructional resource, including textbooks, supplies, and computers, than did schools serving predominantly white and middle-class students (Oakes and Saunders, 2002).

These differences in outcomes have increasingly severe consequences for students and for society. Those who do not succeed in school are becoming part of a growing underclass, cut off from productive engagement in society. In addition to the increasingly strong correlations between educational attainment and income (National Center for Education Statistics, 2000a, p. 432), success in school is increasingly related to the ability to engage in any kind of productive employment. Whereas a high school dropout in 1970 had two chances out of three of getting a job, by 1998, only 44 percent of recent high school dropouts were in the labor force and employed (National Center for Education Statistics, 2000a, p. 430). These proportions are generally even lower for students of color. Furthermore, 30 percent of Hispanic sixteen- to twenty-four-year-olds and 14 percent of African American youth of the same age had dropped out of school (National Center for Education Statistics, 2000a, p. 127). For students diagnosed with learning disabilities, as many as 60 percent drop out of school before graduating from high school (Levin, Zigmond, and Birch, 1985; National Center for Education Statistics, 2000a, p. 129). At a time when the economy demands that more citizens attain higher levels of education, these trends, which have not improved for more than a decade, are deeply troubling.

Differential Treatment of Students in Schools. The differential allocation of skillful teachers appears to play a particularly important role in these disparate outcomes. For example, a number of studies have found teacher expertise (as measured by certification status and test scores, education, and experience levels) to be a significant determinant of student outcomes (Betts, Rueben, and Danenberg, 2000; Ferguson, 1991a; Ferguson and Ladd, 1996; Fetler, 1999; Goldhaber and Brewer, 2000; Strauss and Sawyer, 1986). These and other studies have suggested that much of the difference in school achievement found between more and less advantaged students is due to the effects of substantially different school opportunities, in particular greatly disparate access to high-quality teachers and teaching (Barr and Dreeben, 1983; Dreeben and Gamoran, 1986; Dreeben and Barr, 1987; Oakes, 1990).

However, teachers alone do not account for all of the educational opportunities that make a difference to students' learning. The ways schools are organized for instruction, what curriculum they offer to whom, what teachers are assigned to which students, how families are involved, and whether and how teachers are encouraged to collaborate all matter for the quality of opportunity different students receive. There is substantial evidence, for example, that curriculum differentiation or tracking matters greatly for student achievement, and that at any given achievement level, students who are "tracked up" or who are exposed to a more rigorous curriculum learn more than same-ability students who are "tracked down" or offered a less challenging course of study (Gamoran, 1990; Hallinan, 2003: Hoffer, 1992; Slavin, 1990b). Differences in access to high-quality course content are associated with race and class and contribute to differences in achievement (Dreeben and Gamoran, 1986; Jones, 1984; Jones, Burton, and Davenport, 1984; Moore and Smith, 1985; Pelavin and Kane, 1990).

Researchers have found that students placed in lower tracks are typically exposed to a more limited, rote-oriented curriculum and ultimately achieve less than students of similar aptitude who are placed in academic programs or untracked classes (Gamoran, 1990; Gamoran and Mare, 1989; Oakes, 1992). Teacher interaction with students in lower-track classes has been found to be less motivating and less supportive, as well as less demanding of higher-order reasoning and responses (Good and Brophy, 1994). Presentations are often less clear and less focused on higher-order cognitive goals (Oakes, 1985). These interactions are also less academically oriented and more likely to focus on behavioral criticisms, especially for minority students (Eckstrom and Villegas, 1991).

Some evidence suggests that teachers themselves are tracked, with those judged to be the most competent and experienced, and those with the highest status, assigned to the top tracks (Oakes, 1986; Talbert, 1990). Students in the lowest tracks are most likely to be assigned teachers who are underprepared, unlicensed, inexperienced, and out-of-field (National Commission on Teaching and America's Future, 1996). Disparate outcomes can also result from differences in class sizes, as well as texts, materials, and equipment, available to students in different courses and tracks.

Furthermore, some research suggests that race and socioeconomic status can determine assignments to tracks even after grades and test scores are controlled

(Gamoran, 1992; Oakes, 1992; Oakes, 1993). There is evidence that decisions about grouping influence not only achievement, but also how students relate to each other interpersonally: when students are grouped in racially or linguistically separated classes or programs, especially when these have different statuses within the school, they form fewer positive intergroup relationships (Khmelkov and Hallinan, 1999). And when student groupings are more segregated, racial climate is less positive within classrooms and schools (Braddock and Slavin, 1993). Conversely, when students of different backgrounds are placed together in classrooms and work together in well-managed cooperative groups, interracial relationships can improve (Slavin, 1995) as can achievement (Johnson and Johnson, 1989; Slavin, 1990a).

School personnel make many organizational decisions that have broad consequences for student outcomes, and teachers should be aware of the consequences of these decisions, so that they can help shape productive school environments. School personnel also need to be aware of how the norms and values they may take for granted in school accord with those that students experience in their homes, and how school decisions may either bridge or exacerbate differences that may exist between home and school. Many researchers have identified how students' cultural or subgroup norms may differ from those of the school. These school norms are expected to govern students' academic and social behavior (as well as their social status), and the extent to which students' behavior abides by these norms has a great deal to do with their academic and social success, as well as their treatment by school personnel (Comer, Haynes, Joyner, and Ben-Avie, 1996; Cusick, 1973; Heath, 1982, 1983). If the norms and values that pertain in a student's home or community diverge significantly from those that pertain in the school, the student experiences conflict, and the way this conflict is resolved by both the student and the school has much to do with whether the student experiences success.

For example, as we described in Chapters Three and Four, different cultural norms may cause educators and families to communicate in ways that inadvertently cause misunderstandings. In addition to linguistic norms, there are norms of engagement with schools and staff that differ across communities, with some parents feeling that they should be active partners in their child's education (and having the time to do so) and others feeling that efforts to do so might convey mistrust to the school personnel, whom they see as in charge of the process. Still others who have had poor experiences themselves in schools may have deep fear or mistrust of schools as institutions and feel inadequate or unsure about how to advocate for their children (Epstein, 2001).

Furthermore, in some communities, where few, if any, families have completed high school or gone to college, there may be little information about the college preparatory process and little experiential reason to expect that students will pursue such goals. Schools may expect that students have reference books and computers at home; quiet, secluded places and time to study; health care for themselves and their families; encouragement for time spent on academic pursuits; and other supports for school achievement that are not always present when families struggle economically. Teachers, both individually and collectively, need to be aware of the contexts within which students are learning at home as well as at school in order to ensure necessary supports. Individual teacher and schoolwide awareness of cultural contexts, family experiences, and norms can be built through home visits, community study, and family involvement initiatives, which can help shape school policies that bridge normative differences (Delgado-Gaitan, 1991; Villegas and Lucas, 2002a).

Students face different kinds of borders as they negotiate a variety of sociocultural, economic, linguistic, and structural differences between home and school, which can be bridged by school efforts or made into chasms into which students fall (Davidson and Phelan, 1999; Phelan, Davidson, and Yu, 1998). If efforts to include parents in the educational process are infrequent, not informative about substantive issues affecting the students' learning, linguistically inaccessible, or held at times when working parents cannot attend, opportunities to reduce key barriers to student achievement will be missed. In addition to school policies governing parental involvement, students' challenges in negotiating these boundaries are exacerbated or ameliorated by policies regarding discipline, curricular and extracurricular inclusiveness, and outreach regarding information about college and other opportunities (Davidson and Phelan, 1999).

Some of these are among the informal systems that operate in schools alongside the formal ones—systems that recognize and reward some kinds of students and activities rather than others; systems that provide students access to information about extracurricular or outside of school opportunities; systems that make it more or less possible or welcoming for parents to participate in the life of the school; and systems that directly and indirectly convey norms about how students are treated, the so-called "hidden curriculum" of the school (Anyon, 1980). These signals about what and who matters in the school have strong consequences for whether students feel they belong in the school, whether they become attached to school and academic work, whether they believe they can achieve, and whether they feel it is worth investing effort and trust in the school and its members.

Part of the informal system are practices and signals that determine the treatment students receive in school. In addition to differences in resources, some studies have found, for example, that teachers often hold more negative attitudes about black children's ability, language, behavior, and potential than they do about white children, and that most black students have fewer favorable interactions with their teachers than white students (Irvine, 1990). Other studies have found that children of color are more likely to be punished for offenses that white students commit without consequence, and that black students, particularly males, are more likely to be suspended from school than whites (Fine, 1991; Nieto, 1992; Carter and Goodwin, 1994).

Research also suggests that males and females tend to have different experiences in school, and these experiences can affect their potential for academic achievement and success. Females are less likely to be called upon by name, are asked fewer complex and abstract questions, receive less praise or constructive feedback, and are given less direction on how to do things for themselves (Jones and Wheatley, 1990; Sadker and Sadker, 1995). Although girls are identified for gifted programs more often than boys in elementary school, by high school fewer girls remain in gifted programs; this is particularly true for African American and Hispanic females (U.S, Department of Education—Office of Civil Rights, 1999; American Association of University Women, 1998).

On the other hand, boys receive more teacher attention than females, including more negative attention, and may be disciplined more harshly than girls for violating the same rules (Mid-Atlantic Equity Center, 1999; National Center for Education Statistics, 2000b), and males, especially African American males, are disproportionately placed in special education, often inappropriately (U.S. Department of Education—Office of Civil Rights, 1999). If we are to create schools where all students have opportunities to learn, teachers must know how to be alert for these kinds of disparities and aware of how to provide classroom environments that are both physically and psychologically safe for all students.

Responses to the Demographic Imperative. During the last fifteen years, professional organizations and institutions charged with the preparation of teachers have responded in a variety of ways to this demographic imperative. Currently, among the various professional organizations concerned with the preparation, licensing, and certification of teachers, there is general consensus both about the need for teacher preparation content that is related to sociocultural contexts and about important areas of teacher knowledge and skill. In 1972, the American Association of Colleges for Teacher Education formed the first of several commissions on multicultural education to help revise the preparation of teachers for a diverse society. In 1976, the National Council for the Accreditation of Teacher Education (NCATE) added multicultural education and teaching for diversity to its standards, requiring that institutions seeking accreditation show evidence that they incorporate such content in their programs. By 1993, sixteen of the seventeen national subject area curriculum guidelines approved by NCATE had incorporated multicultural guidelines, and forty states required schools or teacher education programs to include the study of ethnic groups, cultural diversity, human relations, or multicultural/bilingual education in their programs.

Over the last decade, teacher preparation programs throughout the United States have revised courses, curriculum, fieldwork experiences, and policies to include attention to social contexts, diversity, and multicultural education. In addition, the Multicultural Education Consensus Panel (Banks and others, 2001), sponsored by the Center for Multicultural Education at the University of Washington and the Common Destiny Alliance at the University of Maryland, identified twelve essential principles for teaching and learning in a multicultural society that are derived from research and practice. Consistent with previous syntheses and related bodies of research (Ladson-Billings, 1995; Villegas, 1991; Zeichner, 1993a), the first principle describes what teachers need to know and learn to teach effectively, including identifying their own attitudes toward different cultural groups, acquiring knowledge about the histories and cultures of diverse groups, becoming acquainted with diverse perspectives within different ethnic and cultural communities, understanding the ways that institutions and popular culture can perpetuate stereotypes, and translating that knowledge into classroom practices that provide all students access to academic rigor.

What Teachers Need to Know: Building a Culturally Responsive Practice

Clearly, teachers' technical competence in teaching and classroom management, as well as their knowledge of subject matter, are factors that strongly influence whether they will be successful in helping students learn. However, technical competence in teaching skills (such as leading discussions and managing groups), solid knowledge of subject matter, and knowledge of how to teach are essential but not sufficient for effective teaching. Teachers' attitudes and expectations, as well as their knowledge of how to incorporate the cultures, experiences, and needs of their students into their teaching, significantly influence what students learn and the quality of their learning opportunities. In this report, it is not possible to describe all the strategies that can help teachers work with diverse children. Instead, we provide examples of the approaches found over the last three decades to enhance instruction for children who have traditionally been poorly served by our system.

Research on Culturally Responsive Teaching. To build a culturally responsive practice, teachers need to have a broad set of teaching strategies for working with diverse children. Teachers need to know how to examine their own cultural assumptions to understand how these shape their starting points for practice. They also need to know how to inquire into the backgrounds of their students so that they can connect what they learn to their instructional decision making, in a sense becoming anthropologists who explicitly seek to understand their students' cultural practices (Gutiérrez and Rogoff, 2003). As Geneva Gay (1993) argues, a teacher needs to be prepared to be a "cultural broker" who "thoroughly understands different cultural systems, is able to interpret cultural symbols from one frame of reference to another, can mediate cultural incompatibilities, and knows how to build bridges or establish linkages across cultures that facilitate the instructional process" (p. 293).

Efforts to reduce the gap between the cultures of students and the often unexamined norms of teachers are one major aspect of culturally responsive teaching. There are many ways in which different conceptions about the nature of meaningful communication exacerbate such gaps. (See also Chapters Three and Four.) For example, Philips (1972) found that the participation structures used on the Warm Springs Indian reservation differed in substantial ways from those used in the school. At home, parents rarely engaged in questioning of their children as a mode of teaching, and verbalization between adults and children was relatively infrequent. Consequently, Indian students were reluctant to participate in class discussions because they were required to speak in front of the class and because the teacher dictated the speech. Similarly, Heath (1982) found that the patterns of interactions between adults and children were quite different at home and at school for African American children in Trackton. These children's parents did not generally ask them stylized "known answer" questions of the sort common in school (for example, "What color is this leaf?" "Who sat on a tuffet?"). Consequently, the children often did not respond to such seemingly obvious questions asked by their teachers, or they responded to them in ways that the teachers found unsatisfactory. When teachers modified their interaction styles with the students to ask more authentic questions, they talked more and became more deeply involved in the lessons.

Efforts to create cultural connections between the school and children's communities have often led to increased achievement. For example, Au (1980) found that when teachers incorporated participation structures into their lessons that were similar to "talk story" in Hawaiian culture, the reading achievement of Hawaiian second-grade children significantly increased. Tharp (1982) studied reading comprehension in the Kamehameha Early Childhood Program in Hawaii. He found that a culturally relevant, comprehension-oriented reading program using active instructional methods can be more effective than a program focused more on discrete subskills using instructional methods that do not incorporate the students' cultures.

Lee (1995) investigated the effects of using the African American tradition of signifying as a scaffold for teaching skills in literacy interpretation to African American students. She found that when teachers incorporated this cultural knowledge into instruction, the students provided longer and more sophisticated comments on the texts. In a four-year evaluation of the High School Puente Project in California, Gandara (2002) found that Mexican American and Latino students who participated in a rigorous academic preparation program that incorporated community-based research and writing, academic counseling, and opportunities to interact with community leaders applied to and attended universities at nearly twice the rate of those who did not participate in the program. In a longitudinal study on the use of students' "funds of knowledge" in classroom instruction, Luis Moll and colleagues (2004) found that Latino students' academic performance is strengthened when students' community knowledge is tapped.

Other research has examined the practices of successful teachers of students of color and English language learners to discover what such teachers do. This research suggests that effective teachers of students of color form and maintain connections with their students within their social contexts. They are familiar with community speech patterns and often incorporate elements of such communication patterns, such as "call and response," even while they instruct in standard English. For students of varying language backgrounds, they allow the use of multiple languages while teaching the target language; and they celebrate their students as individuals and as members of specific cultures, asking students to share who they are and what they know with the class in a variety of ways (Cochran-Smith, 1995; Garcia, 1993; Irvine, 2003; Murrell, 2002; Nieto and Rolon, 1997; Strickland, 1995).

Jacqueline Irvine (1992), Gloria Ladson-Billings (1994), and Eugene Garcia (1993) have all summarized research finding that effective teachers of students of color—who include white teachers as well as members of minority groups—link classroom content to students' experiences, focus on the whole child, and believe that all of their students can succeed. They use an active, direct approach to teaching: demonstrating, modeling, explaining, writing, giving feedback, reviewing, and emphasizing higher-order skills while avoiding excessive reliance on rote learning or punishment. They see the teacher-student relationship as humane and equitable, and characterized by a sense of community and team. Their classrooms typically emphasize cooperation rather than competition and feature cooperative learning strategies and student-initiated discourse and participation.

Knowledge for Building a Culturally Responsive Practice. Teachers who "think pedagogically" about diversity are able to build a practice that is both academically challenging and responsive to students. Building a culturally responsive practice requires teachers to build a broad base of knowledge that grows and changes as students, contexts, and subject matters shift. Knowledge of self and of others (students, parents, community) is an essential foundation for constructing, evaluating, and altering curriculum and pedagogy so that it is responsive to students. In the classrooms of culturally responsive teachers, the methods of instruction and assessment, the curriculum, and the classroom climate work together to support the academic achievement of all students.

The teachers in our opening vignettes demonstrate the challenges of developing a practice that meets the needs of diverse populations of students, especially when that diversity is constantly in flux and the consequences of the differences between and among students are crucial to determining student outcomes. In addition to drawing upon her knowledge of child development,

Ms. Cowen's (see Ms. Cowen and a Special Education Placement) awareness that she is working within multiple contexts in evaluating Julie's needs and placement is critical. Expectations of the school and home, state legal mandates, as well as a moral sense of what might serve this particular student all inform her recommendation about Julie's placement, as does her careful observation of Julie's classroom performance. Teachers are often the first professionals to become aware of learning challenges experienced by children in their classrooms. These insights can be as straightforward as noticing that a child cannot see the blackboard to recognizing that a child is having significant problems with auditory processing and retrieval of information.

This type of "problem spotting" must be accompanied by care and sensitivity. A teacher must have some knowledge of children and typical patterns of development, as well as normal differences. She must know her students well because even young children can find ways to hide what they see as weaknesses. At the same time, children develop differently, and a delay in one area may gradually disappear over time. If a teacher suggests to a child that the child may have a learning disability, it can discourage or embarrass a child who believes that disability or special education carries with it a stigma and it can initially upset parents if they are not aware of ongoing learning challenges.

In addition, as Ms. Cowen's vignette illustrates, teachers should be aware of the research that shows children of color and those who are new English language learners are often overidentified with certain disabilities. At the same time, because of inappropriate attributions of some difficulties to language barriers or "cultural deprivation," such students may fail to be identified for special education services in other cases. A range of in-classroom and standardized evaluations are necessary to gain a more complete picture of student strengths and needs that should inform instructional decisions. Knowledge about Julie's individual history, her knowledge of child and language development, her knowledge regarding the overrepresentation of English language learners in special education, and her ability to assess student work all combine to inform this important professional recommendation. Also important is how Ms. Cowen worked with Julie to find and build upon her strengths and to keep work samples to guide assessment, which informs both her teaching and this placement recommendation.

Mr. Levy (see Mr. Levy and a Student Paper on Immigration) found himself confronting a student's attitudes toward and misinformation about new immigrants when he read Roger's paper, which connected unemployment to immigration and "those people" who were taking jobs away from people who "belonged" in the United States. In thinking about how to respond to Roger, Mr. Levy had to consider many factors, including Roger's lack of knowledge about immigration (a subject matter issue), and his attitudes and beliefs about "others." Mr. Levy also had to decide the pedagogy he would use to approach Roger given the many other students in the class who were themselves immigrants and who had varying kinds of knowledge and experiences with unemployment.

Ms. Carrington (see Ms. Carrington: Teaching Shakespeare to English Language Learners) had to know a great deal about her students as she embarked on the challenging path of teaching them Shakespearean sonnets—a requirement of the state curriculum. Her challenge concerned how to provide access to the Shakespeare text given both the language and cultural differences among her twenty-eight students. For both Mr. Levy and Ms. Carrington, the work has to begin by learning about their students: who they are, what they know, and what meanings and strengths they bring with them to school. As previous chapters in this volume make clear, all students need scaffolds to connect what they know from their lives outside school to their life and work in school. Ms. Carrington needed not only a deep understanding of her students, but also an understanding of the content in relation to the students; for example, language or themes that could make Shakespeare difficult for that particular group of students and themes that could make it engaging and increasingly well understood.

Teachers need to be able to understand student cultures and differences without falling victim to the cultural stereotypes that might result from a superficial understanding of students and their experiences. It is this kind of superficial knowledge, and the potentially damaging stereotypes that can result from it, that Cazden and Mehan (1989) warn against when they observe that it can be dangerous to attempt to transmit shorthand knowledge about a list of different cultures to prospective teachers. Instead, prospective teachers must learn how to learn from their students and members of the communities where they teach, borrowing strategies from anthropology and sociology. Although some knowledge of the histories of cultures is certainly necessary, teachers need access to the particular experiences of the students they work with to inform their decisions.

The importance of connecting with students and their communities for the purposes of mutual information and support suggests a "reciprocal and interactive" orientation toward practice. In such a practice, students and teachers work together to construct meaning out of content, rather than teaching a decontextualized set of skills that are passed from teacher to student. The collaborative interactive model suggests instead that curriculum and pedagogy be connected in direct and intentional ways with the lives of children (Cummins, 1986; Delpit, 1995; Delgado-Gaitan, 1991; Nieto, 2000; Olsen and Mullen, 1990; Moll, 1988). To accomplish this, teachers need to know how to generate and sustain a genuine dialogue with students so that they will be able to draw on what the students know and care about and monitor their engagement and success. The following vignette featuring a successful sixth-grade teacher illustrates the sort of interactions that enable students' experiences to become an official part of the classroom curriculum. The vignette demonstrates not only a range of pedagogical strategies, but also how her knowledge of assessment, learning, and development informs her choices.

A Case of Culturally Responsive Teaching

In Ann Lewis's 6th grade class, the students were listening as one of them read aloud. The class was studying *Charlie Pippin* by Candi Dawson Boyd. The novel is about an eleven-year-old African American girl who attempts to win the approval of her father, a decorated Vietnam War veteran who has buried all of his feelings about the war within him. The girl feels alienated from her father and wants to find a way to reach him. There were 29 students in the class (20 African Americans). When the student who was reading finished, an African American boy, Jerry, asked, "Is she [the story's protagonist] going to stay eleven years old in this book?"

Lewis responded with a question, "What about in *Driving Miss Daisy*? Did the main character stay the same age?"

Students (in unison): "No."

Ann: "How do you know?"

Jerry: "Because she was using one of those walkin' things when she got old."

Ann: "A walker?"

Jerry: "Yeah, and then she was in the old folks home."

Ann: "Can you see without a video?"

Calvin (another African American boy): "Yes, you can see when you're reading. So we'll see how old Charlie is in the book! . . . [Referring to the protagonist], she got feelings her dad doesn't understand and he got feelings she don't understand."

Ann: "Do you know anybody who ever feels like this?"

Calvin: "Me!"

Ann drew a Venn diagram to represent similarities and differences between Calvin and the character in the story. "You have your own video of your entire life in your head. Every time you read, you can get an image of how the story connects with your life. Do you want to get back to the story?"

"Yeah!" the class says in unison.

A third boy began to read. When he finished, Lewis said, "Close your eyes. Let's put on your video." She then re-read a section of the book describing the mother in the story. "How can you relate this to your life?" One of the African American girls commented, "That's just like when I kiss my mom."

Students then took turns reading passages from the book. For some, this was the first "chapter book" they'd read in school. Some of these slower readers had trouble with some of the words. Lewis encouraged them and urged other class members to help. "Remember, we're all a team here. We've got to help each other." When Charlene (an African American girl) asked a question about a dispute the main character had with her father, Lewis suggested the students role play to understand better. Two students struggled a bit with the role play. Two others gave it a try and got a round of applause from the rest of the class.

After the role-play, Ann asked, "What do we know about Charlie's dad?" The class erupted with excitement—many wanted to contribute. Lewis began to develop a "character attribute web" on the board . . . Ann filled the board with the student responses and shouted, "That was perfect! You're a perfect class! If you're perfect raise your hand!" Twenty-nine hands were in the air.

Over the course of the next several months, *Charlie Pippin* became the centerpiece for a wide range of activities. One group of students began a Vietnam War research group. One group member who assumed a leadership position was a very quiet Vietnamese girl whose relatives had fought in the war. She brought in pictures, maps, letters, even a family member to talk to the class about Vietnam. In the book, the main character made origami to sell to her classmates. Lewis taught her students how to make origami. She introduced them to Elanor Coerr's *Sadako and the Thousand Paper Cranes*. A second group of students researched nuclear proliferation. . . .

Although [many of Lewis's students] had had previous problems, including poor academic performance, truancy, suspension, recommendation for special-education placement, and at least one threatened expulsion, Lewis's class represented an opportunity for a new academic beginning.

One of Lewis's star students, a boy named Larry, had had a particularly troubling history. Although he was short and slightly built, he was the oldest child in the class. He had been left back several times and was 13 in a class made up of 11 year olds. He had been traumatized by the drive-by shooting of a favorite aunt. Other teachers in the school referred to him as "an accident just waiting to happen." None wanted him in their classrooms. Lewis referred to Larry as a "piece of crystal."

"He's strong and beautiful but fragile. I have to build a safe and secure place for him and let him know that we—the class and I—will be here for him. The school has been placing him in the kitchen junk drawer. I want him to be up there in the china closet where everyone can see him."

By the end of the school year, Larry had been elected president of the school's sixth grade. He was involved in peer conflict mediation and was earning A's and B's in every subject. . . . While Larry represented a special example of accomplishment, the classroom was a special place for all of the children, including the nine non-African Americans. (They were Latino, Pacific Islander, and Vietnamese.) The work was challenging and exciting. The students were presumed to have some level of literacy, which formed the foundation for increased competency. Reading, writing, and speaking were community activities that Lewis believed all students could participate in—and they did.

Source: Excerpted from Gloria Ladson-Billings. © 1994. *The DreamKeepers*, pp. 107–112. This material is used by permission of John Wiley and Sons, Inc.

Ann Lewis's classroom demonstrates a variety of pedagogical strategies that culturally responsive teachers use to engage students' interests and support their learning and development. It also illustrates important aspects of curriculum and assessment that support these strategies.

Pedagogy. A first glance at Ann Lewis's classroom shows how interaction and collaboration, which are central to a reciprocal approach, produce a great deal of talk about what students read and research about related issues, both within and beyond the current text. Lewis clearly knows how to create multiple opportunities for students to engage in collaborative dialogue that supports the relationships within which teaching and learning occur while also supporting students' cognitive growth. There are many ways to create opportunities for students to engage in meaningful oral and written exchanges in the classroom through such practices as journal and essay writing, reciprocal teaching, cooperative groupwork, and peer tutoring, among other strategies (For examples, see Garcia, 1993; Irvine and Armento, 2001; Nieto, 2000; Weiner, 1999; Villegas and Lucas, 2002b).

However, as the vignettes in this chapter indicate, knowing a set of practices is not sufficient. Teachers also need to know when and how to use specific approaches to achieve their goals under a range of different circumstances (Moll, 1988; Nieto, 2000; Neito and Rolon, 1997; Reyes, 1992; Valdes, 1996; Weiner, 1999). For example, in Mr. Levy's vignette, we saw him weighing his next instructional move: an individual lesson? A whole class lecture on the economics of immigration? An activity to encourage student inquiry and discovery? Deciding between these instructional options requires not only knowledge of his students' interests, but a careful assessment of their abilities and knowledge of which instructional strategy can most effectively lead them to the next level of understanding.

In this short segment from Ann Lewis's classroom we see her use several different strategies to engage her students in the material. At first glance, the classroom looks like one that would be recognizable to many: students listened while one student read the text aloud. When the reading finished, another student raised a question about the reading that created an opportunity for Lewis to activate and build upon students' prior knowledge. Rather than answering Jerry's question directly, Lewis responded with a question of her own, asking students to make connections to their prior knowledge by thinking about another character they knew, this one from a film. With the contribution from another student, she is able to demonstrate that students can use clues that help them visualize what they read and connect themselves and their experiences with the text.

She extends and makes explicit this reading strategy using one of the characters in the book and a Venn diagram as a visual tool for students to see similarities and differences between one of the characters and a student in the class. Doing this demonstrates to students one way experienced readers connect with literature and gives them a visual means of representing that knowledge. When a student asks another question about a dispute the main character has with her father, Ms. Lewis once again does not simply answer the question. Instead, students do a role-play to understand the conflict more clearly. After the role-play, the students build their knowledge of the main character rather than having the answer handed to them. This shifts the responsibility for generating knowledge from teacher to students and teacher collectively. Ms. Lewis has not disappeared from the process, but she has skillfully supported the students in taking increased control over their learning and has modeled strategies they can use to help answer their own questions in the future.

Ms. Lewis' pedagogical moves in this brief selection illustrate the use of a wide range of strategies, which provide multiple opportunities for students to engage with the material and expand the probabilities that students who learn in different ways can gain an understanding: students read aloud, they listened, they talked, they produced visual representations, and they acted things out. Ms. Lewis needed to know not only the range of pedagogical choices she had and how to use them successfully, she also needed to know which approaches were likely to achieve particular goals with this group of students.

Ms. Lewis also displays knowledge of literacy development. We are told in the vignette that this is the first chapter book that some of the students have read. Ms. Lewis understands that for some inexperienced readers it is difficult to visualize what they read in the text. When Jerry asks a question about the protagonist in the book, Ms. Lewis suspects that he needs to remember to use clues from the text to help visualize and connect what he knows to his reading. The instructional moves she makes pick up on this cue from Jerry's question and explicitly provide some strategies that students can draw upon to read complex texts: visualizing text, making comparisons, and making predictions. Ms. Lewis also knows that if students use those strategies with the support of their peers, they are more likely to use the strategies independently in the future, so she practices the strategies together as a large group.

Curriculum. Culturally responsive teachers need to know how to develop a curriculum that takes into account the understandings and perspectives of different groups while also attending to the development of higher-level cognitive skills (Banks, 1991, 2003). This involves selecting material that is inclusive of the contributions and perspectives of different groups (Delpit, 1995; Ladson-Billings, 2002) and that is responsive to the particular cultural context within which one teaches (Irvine and Armento, 2001; Knapp and Shields, 1991; Sleeter and Grant, 1999; Villegas, 1991). To create a curriculum that creates connections for their students, teachers need to have wide-ranging knowledge of subject matter content, so that they can construct a curriculum that includes multiple representations addressing the prior experiences of different groups of students (Lee, 1993; McDiarmid, 1994).

Ann Lewis's knowledge of curricular material also allows her to build upon student interests while pushing students to more sophisticated academic work. She needed an awareness of a range of multicultural resources in order to select the novel they read together. In selecting the novel, Ms. Lewis needed to consider not only its potential for student interest, but the difficulty of the book—where some students would be challenged and where some would find the reading easy—and needed to consider her goals for them as readers as well as the district's grade level standards. The book she selected is not one that many of the students could read on their own, but with her help and the help of their peers, they can read the book together. Anne selected the book in light of her knowledge of students' zones of proximal development in this area. With her careful scaffolding, the book stretches the students to read at a higher level than they might have been able to on their own. Another aspect of her pedagogy is represented in her explicit attention to reading. She knows what experienced readers do when they encounter texts that are challenging and she shares those strategies explicitly with students.

In addition, the vignette shows that she uses students' excitement and engagement in the novel and moves them into research projects, allowing the students to shape their own inquiries. In the process, she not only teaches students about doing research, but creates a place for students to share and learn from traditional resources and each other's histories (and, in fact, creates opportunities for students to learn their own histories more deeply). In encouraging one student whose parents had fought in the Vietnam war to share some artifacts of the period—maps, pictures, and the like—and inviting a family member to talk with the class, Ms. Lewis connected her school work with the home environment while enriching the cultural and historical knowledge of all her students.

Assessment. Developing and modifying assessment strategies so that they are sensitive to children's differences can also enhance student learning (Darling-Hammond, 1996; Goodwin, 1997a). This requires knowledge of a range of assessments and what each reveals about student learning. (See Chapter Eight in this volume.) Ms. Cowen's vignette, for example, demonstrates her awareness of a variety of tools that provide her with a fuller view of Julie's strengths and areas that need development. In addition, Ms. Cowen's knowledge of development helps her articulate precisely where she sees Julie's progress. Ms. Cowen also reveals that she has a complex view of student achievement that goes beyond a single measure.

Ms. Lewis clearly had specific goals for reading the novel her class was working on together, and she challenged all students to reach those goals. Before she selected the novel, she needed to assess her students' strengths, abilities, and interests as readers and the areas where they needed to work. Thus she used the knowledge gained from her assessments of them as readers to inform not only her text selection, but also her goals for teaching the text.

Another important feature in Ms. Lewis's practice was her explicit articulation of strategies available to readers. Explicitly teaching those strategies makes it more likely that students will use them in their future reading. Had she not been able to articulate them, she might have just waited for students to discover those strategies accidentally. Some students might have done so, whereas others would never have figured them out. Delpit (1995) makes this point quite powerfully, noting that, especially for students whose home culture is different from that of the school, demystifying school expectations and learning strategies is critical.

Teachers' Attitudes and Expectations: The Importance of Dispositions

Another aspect of culturally responsive teaching is the ability to build upon the strengths that students bring to school. To capitalize on students' strengths, teachers need to be able to assess what knowledge and beliefs students bring to the classroom, evaluate how they learn in different domains, and structure conditions that will facilitate their academic achievement (Au, 1980; Mehan, Villanueva, Hubbard, and Lintz, 1996; Tharp, 1982). We saw how, in preparation for an IEP meeting regarding her student, Ms. Cowan reflects on the abilities she has seen Julie demonstrate in her classroom. Her careful observation has allowed her to see beyond the initial special education diagnosis to a nuanced understanding of several aspects of Julie's learning. Similarly, Ms. Lewis is able to see the leadership potential in her student Larry, and she creates experiences for him that generate increased effort, motivation, and success. Students' learning is facilitated when teachers view them as learners who have experiences, ideas, and home and community resources that can be built upon to help them master new knowledge and skills (Moll and others, 1992; Moll and Gonzalez, 2004).

Developing a Sociocultural Consciousness. The vignettes featured in this chapter point to research indicating that there are some beliefs and attitudes that are critical for teachers to be effective with all students, including respect for all learners and their experiences, confidence in their abilities to learn, a willingness to question and change one's own practices if they are not successful in a given case, and a commitment to continue seeking new solutions to learning problems (see, for example, Delpit, 1995; Ladson-Billings, 1994, 1995; Gay, 2000; Irvine and Armento, 2001; Murrell, 2002; Tharp, Estrada, Dalton, and Yamaguchi, 1999; Villegas, 1991; Villegas and Lucas, 2002b). In addition to building on students' strengths, developing a "sociocultural consciousness" enables teachers to realize that the worldview they may have grown up with is not universal but is greatly influenced by their life experiences and aspects of their cultural, gender, race, ethnicity, and social-class background (Banks, 1998; Harding, 1991; Villegas and Lucas, 2002a). Mr. Levy's awareness that his own family's immigration history is one factor shaping his response to Roger's paper demonstrates an aspect of this sociocultural consciousness (Willis and Lewis, 1998; Tatum, 1997). Teachers are more aware of how they interact with their students—and what their choices are—when they develop self-knowledge, in particular, an awareness of themselves as cultural beings as well as an awareness of the ways their culture shapes their views. Those teachers who develop this consciousness are not only aware that multiple perspectives exist, but they can also create opportunities for students to articulate their views and discover ways in which their experiences and popular culture shape these views.

When prospective teachers develop greater sociocultural consciousness, it becomes a vehicle for the development of a more affirming and positive attitude toward students. Teachers begin to better understand how their interactions with their students and the world in general are influenced by their social and cultural location and that of the students. Bernstein (1972) summed it up nicely when he said, "If the culture of the teacher is to become part of the consciousness of the child, then the culture of the child must first be in the consciousness of the teacher" (p. 149).

By building on the experiences and knowledge of their students, teachers can create more personalized and motivating social contexts for teaching. Veteran teachers such as Ms. Cowen and Mr. Levy realize the importance of continuing to learn about their students throughout their careers. Ms. Lewis masterfully channels the excitement generated by a novel they read together, allows students to pursue a variety of interests generated by the novel, and draws from a variety of resources to do so. In the process, she creates opportunities for students to share their knowledge across cultures, developing a cross-cultural or sociocultural awareness in students as well. When prospective teachers develop greater sociocultural consciousness, it can become a vehicle for developing a more affirming and positive attitude toward students and a foundation for building curriculum.

It is most important that teachers not make quick assumptions about children. It is easy to label a child unmotivated when he is lost and unable to connect to instruction or is underchallenged and bored. It is tempting to label a child slow who is simply confused by directions on how to complete an assignment. Teachers must believe that it is possible to develop and adapt instruction to engage all children, to help them learn, and to help them become responsible members of a classroom community. They must also know how to provide clear, organized directions—using multiple modes of communication so that students who process information differently will be able to understand them—and well-scaffolded tasks that provide many entry points into the material so that students *can* learn. To teach all children well, teachers must tailor their curriculum and instruction so that their students will be engaged in meaningful work.

These concerns for affirming environments and meaningful learning opportunities operate at the school level as well. There is evidence that when schools have adopted a philosophy and set of pervasive practices that are based on an understanding of children's development and experiences—that affirm students, offer a strong curriculum to all, and promote individual development as well as positive intergroup relationships—attachments to school, positive interactions among adults and children, and achievement can be strengthened (Comer, Haynes, and Joyner, 1996; Khmelkov and Hallinan, 1999; Newmann and Wehlange, 1995; Nieto, 2003; Slavin, 1995).

Without an explicit agenda to develop such norms and to look for ways to recognize and support all students, to offer all individuals and groups a rich and meaningful curriculum, and to build positive relationships across students, many schools inadvertently (and sometimes knowingly) distribute opportunities for learning and success inequitably. Individual teachers who seek to change these norms within their classrooms will be much less effective than if they work within a context that reinforces their efforts. Consequently, teachers need to be aware of how the formal and informal systems of the school operate to construct opportunity and how to participate in school-level change processes that call attention to organizational needs and help develop a supportive culture schoolwide.

Teaching Children with Exceptional Needs: Building an Inclusive practice

The ideas of *culturally responsive classrooms* and *inclusive classrooms* are not entirely the same, but they are similar. Specifically, both terms suggest that schools and teachers need to develop classrooms that are supportive of children and accepting of difference. Within both of these conceptions, children's strengths are emphasized and differences are considered a positive part of a learning environment because they allow children to share and experience diverse perspectives. In the past, children with exceptional needs were largely taught in isolated special education classrooms, and special education was associated primarily with a deficit orientation. Today, although special education is still connected closely to a medical model because children are "diagnosed" with certain disabilities, most educators understand that learning differences exist along a vast continuum, that human beings typically develop compensatory strengths—often formidable ones—to allow them to expand their learning even though they may have some areas of difficulty, and that strategic instruction can make a large difference in what students achieve. Moreover, many believe that viewing disability as a type of insurmountable deficit is a socially constructed notion that is detrimental to children and should be challenged (McDermott, 1996).

Other lingering misconceptions include the equating of special education with behavioral models of teaching featuring a focus only on rote acquisition of skills or with a legalistic model that focuses on labels and procedures that must be followed. In this chapter, we present an inclusive model that reflects a broad view of diversity, one which recognizes that students have multiple and complex experiences, strengths, and identities that include interests and talents as well as ethnicity, gender, social status, family experiences, and learning differences, among others. These complex sets of experiences require that students be taught as individuals by teachers who are observant and diagnostic in their approach and who are also aware of the more general patterns in learning to be considered as they assess and plan instruction. Quite often, teachers who are prepared to teach students with exceptional needs become more skillful teachers of all students because they develop deeper diagnostic skills and a wider repertoire of strategies that are useful for many students who learn in different ways.

To instruct special needs students effectively, teachers need to understand the nature of various disabilities, ranging from mild to moderate learning disabilities—for example, dyslexia, dyscalculia, developmental aphasia, or perceptual problems—to other concerns such as developmental delays, mental retardation, hearing impairments, visual impairments, autism, emotional and behavioral disorders, speech and language impairments, physical impairments (mobility), emotional disturbance, and attention deficit, hyperactivity disorder (ADHD). Teachers should be aware that certain conditions such as cerebral palsy and autism are associated with a spectrum and can be very mild (hardly recognizable) to very severe. For common disabilities (for example, auditory or visual processing problems), teachers should at minimum have a basic repertoire of strategies and adaptations that can help students gain access to the material they are teaching in an appropriate way.

In addition, a teacher should have some understanding of the eligibility and placement process and how to work with other professionals and parents within these processes. Although it is not necessary for novice teachers to know the details of all the various highly specialized tests used for assessment purposes for all the different types of disabilities, they should be able to talk with parents about how their child will be assessed, given the learning difficulties the teacher has reported. They should be able to communicate with professional colleagues about the findings of assessments and the services to be offered. They need to know where to find additional information—from research or from professional colleagues—about specific diagnoses, disabilities, and services when it is necessary to work with an individual child and his family. They should be prepared to work with parents who have varied reactions to news concerning their children. For example, one parent might be upset and argue that her child has no learning challenges, whereas another parent will use legal means to obtain resources for his child that are not readily available.

Teachers will need to know how to contribute to and implement Individualized Education Plans (IEPs) for students in their classrooms, and they should be aware that the IEP process was developed as way to ensure that children have access to best possible educational opportunities within the least restrictive environments, and that parents are assured due process. Teachers should understand students' rights and have a working knowledge of the laws and policies associated with access to education, such as the Individuals with Disabilities Education Act (IDEA), so that they can meet the spirit of these policies.

What Teachers Need to Know About Teaching Children with Exceptional Needs

To teach children with learning differences, it is important for teachers to have a deep understanding of child development, learning, language development, and sophisticated strategies for teaching content, managing the classroom, and assessing both *how* children learn and *what* they are learning—aspects of teaching we have treated elsewhere in this volume. In this section, we address how teachers can use that knowledge and specific knowledge about distinctive learning needs to move children forward in their progress. For example, children identified with learning disabilities often need adaptive instruction and supports in various areas of development (see Chapter Three), including speech and language, gross and fine motor, cognition, and social and emotional development. In this chapter, it would be impossible to talk about all the instructional adaptations to assist children with special learning challenges, so we provide a few examples of particularly powerful strategies that illustrate key principles of instruction used with students of different ages who have learning disabilities. General education teachers will not generally know all the adaptive techniques available to children with disabilities, but they should have some understanding about important principles of instruction as well as information about where to find these special adaptations and strategies when they need them.

Example #1: Young Children with Speech, Language, and Social Delays. Young children with speech and language delays have difficulty connecting with peers and developing meaningful relationships. This can interfere with social and emotional development. Many children with social problems, particularly children with autistic spectrum disorders, face serious challenges learning how to play and socialize with peers. They experience problems conveying and interpreting social-communication cues that make it difficult to coordinate social activities with other children or to join peers in play. Attempts to socialize are often subtle, obscure, or poorly timed and mistaken as signs of deviance or limited social interest. Many children spend inordinate amounts of time alone pursuing repetitive and unimaginative activities. Without appropriate intervention, they are at high risk for being excluded from their peer culture and failing to learn the communication skills they will need throughout life (Wolfberg, 1999). Knowledge of these learning and development issues—and of strategies that can counteract these problems—is critical for teachers to appropriately support students' social learning, interpersonal skills, and their symbolic capacities. One such strategy includes engaging children in an Integrated Play Group. This strategy creates play groups with special needs children and nondisabled children and uses principles of cognitive apprenticeship to engage children in guided play with scaffolding that enables "expert" assistance from more skilled peers to teach communication and play strategies (Wolfberg, 2003) (see The Integrated Play Groups Model).

Many knowledgeable preschool teachers use augmentative communication symbols (picture symbols that enable children who cannot read or talk to communicate by pointing to a sequence of pictures) to develop materials to help all children with and without disabilities learn language skills. These teachers use the playgroup models to help all children learn to interact, to develop social and communication abilities, and to become caring citizens in their learning communities.

The Integrated Play Groups Model

Integrated Play Groups are designed to support children of diverse ages and abilities with autism spectrum disorders (novice players) in mutually enjoyed play experiences with typical peers and siblings (expert players) within school, home, and community settings. The intervention seeks to maximize each child's developmental potential as well as intrinsic desire to play, socialize, and form meaningful relationships with peers through a carefully tailored system of support described as "guided participation" (Rogoff, 1999). This system monitors play initiations by children;

Outcomes for Novice Players	Outcomes for Expert Players
• More frequent and sustained social interaction and play with peers—decreased isolate play • Advances in representational play, developmentally/age-appropriate play—decreased stereotyped play • Advances in related symbolic activity (writing and drawing) • Improved social-communication skills • Improved language skills in verbal children • More diverse range of play interests • Higher degree of spontaneous social engagement (initiation and responsiveness) with peers • Increased affect—emotional expression • Sheer enjoyment—"fun factor" • Formation of reciprocal relationships—friendships with peers	• Greater awareness, tolerance, acceptance of individual differences • Greater empathy, compassion and patience for others • Increased self-esteem, confidence, sense of pride in accomplishments • Increased sense of responsibility to cooperate and include others • Ability to adapt to children's different play interests and ways of relating and communicating • Sheer enjoyment—"fun factor" • Formation of reciprocal relationships—friendships with atypical peers

Source: Based on the findings of Gonsier-Gerdin, 1993; O'Connor, 1999; Wolfberg, 1988, 1994; Wolfberg and others, 1999; Wolfberg and Schuler, 1992, 1993; Zercher and others, 2001.

builds on these by providing assistance through directed and modeled play as well as verbal and visual cueing; and immerses novice players at their level of development in more advanced play experiences with expert players through partial participation. An equally important focus is on teaching the peer group to be more accepting, responsive, and inclusive of children who relate and play in different ways (Wolfberg, 2003). Research shows that children learn and develop in a multitude of ways through shared experiences in play (Vygotsky, 1966, 1978). Moreover, peers perform a distinct role in fostering children's socialization and development that cannot be duplicated by adults (Hartup, 1979, 1983; Wolfberg and others, 1999). To test the effectiveness of the playgroups model, scholars have conducted a number of empirical studies on children with and without disabilities (see the following summary). In many of these studies, there was evidence that children made gains in both social and symbolic play while participating in playgroups, and acquired improved communication and symbolic skills in the areas of spoken language, writing, and drawing.

Example #2: Older Children with Learning Disabilities. In contrast to earlier beliefs that students with learning disabilities need highly repetitive, rote activities in order to learn, researchers have discovered that strategic instruction—helping students learn approaches to solving problems or producing work—is highly beneficial to students with special needs. This includes helping students develop some of their own strategies for learning and retention, including memory aids (for example, mnemonic devices) and organization strategies (task analysis, webbing, and outlining). It also includes highly effective strategies for enhancing metacognition. Like the strategy instruction used in the Integrated Play Groups, discussed earlier, researchers have found that learning disabled and nondisabled students benefit from strategy instruction in many academic subjects, including writing. (See "Teaching Metacognitive Strategies for Writing to Students with Learning Disabilities.")

Teaching Metacognitive Strategies for Writing to Students with Learning Disabilities

Studies of learning have found that students are more able to learn complex skills when they are able to think "metacognitively," that is, to think about their own thinking and performance so as to monitor and change it. Vygotsky (1978) suggested that talking things through, internally or aloud, actually helps people learn by helping them organize and manage their thought process. In fact, studies of writers have found that they engage in an internal dialogue in which they talk to themselves—sometimes even muttering aloud—about audience, purpose, form, and content. They ask and answer for themselves questions about who they are writing for, why, what they know, and how ideas are organized as they plan, draft, edit, and revise. They guide their thinking with metacognitive strategies that help them write purposefully.

This basic research has led to strategies for teaching writing that help novice writers learn how to engage in this kind of self-talk and self-monitoring as they go through similar processes. In one study, teachers of fourth- and fifth-grade learning disabled and non-learning disabled students were taught how to implement these strategies in their classrooms by analyzing texts, modeling the writing process, guiding students as they wrote, and providing students with opportunities for independent writing over the course of a year. Analyses were conducted for an intervention group of 32 students and a matched comparison group of 31 similar students selected from a pool of 500 students in seven urban schools participating in a broader research study. In each group, half of the students were learning disabled and half were non-learning disabled. The study found that the groups whose teachers had received the special training engaged in more self-regulating metacognitive strategies and were more able to explain their writing process. This ability was positively and significantly related to measures of their academic performance in reading and writing. Although there were significant differences in the writing knowledge of learning disabled and non-learning disabled students within the comparison group, the learning disabled students whose teachers had had the special training were just as able to describe and use the writing strategies—such as the ability to organize, evaluate, and revise their papers in appropriate ways—as were the regular education students in the comparison group. Sometimes, the learning disabled students who had received this strategy instruction even outscored the regular education students.

Source: Englert, Raphael, and Anderson (1992).

Example #3: Elementary-aged Children with Reading Disabilities. There are also specific kinds of instruction that can help students with particular learning disabilities, such as dyslexia. In a review of research on teaching reading to students with reading disabilities, the National Research Council's report *Preventing Reading Difficulties in Young Children* (1998) found that a useful instructional strategy for working with many elementary-aged children with reading difficulties is phonemic awareness training (see, for example, Williams, 1980). Word recognition skills of severely disabled readers can often be substantially improved through intensive supplementary training including either explicit instruction in phoneme awareness and letter-sound patterns or training in using common orthographic patterns and analogies to identify unfamiliar words (Lovett and others, 1994). Recent analyses on an expanded sample indicate that the two training conditions are about equally effective for older (grades 5 and 6) and younger (grades 2 and 3) children with reading disabilities (Lovett and Steinbach, 1997).

These studies indicate, first, that intensive training, even over relatively short periods, can substantially improve the word-reading skills of children with serious reading disabilities and that these positive outcomes are maintained over months or years after the cessation of training. Second, it is clear that phonologically oriented training programs are not the only type of intervention that can facilitate word recognition, although this approach produces the strongest gain in phonemic awareness and phonological decoding when combined with training in other reading skills. Teachers who work with students who have difficulty with reading need to be able to assess students' reading difficulty and be aware of the range of possible interventions and what research says about which interventions would profit students the most.

Example #4: General Accommodations. There are a number of different types of adaptations that teachers have at their disposal. Teachers need to know how to teach specific strategies to children, how to use adaptive materials to help children with speech and language difficulties socialize with other children, and how they can focus on particular instructional strategies (such as phonemic awareness training) to help children with reading disabilities. More generally, teachers also need to know how to create adaptations of the work they plan for learners with particular needs. These can include adaptations of:

Size: The length or portion of an assignment, demonstration, or performance learners are expected to complete. For example reduce the length of report to be written or spoken, the references needed, or the number of problems.

Time: The flexible time needed for student learning. For example individualize a timeline for project completion, allow more time for test taking.

Level of Support: The amount of assistance to the learner. For example students work in groups, with peer buddies, or mentors.

Input: The instructional strategies used to facilitate learning. For example use of videos, computer programs, field trips, and visual aids to support active learning.

Difficulty: The skill levels, conceptual levels, and processes involved in learning. For example provide calculators, tier the assignment so the outcome is the same but with varying degrees of concreteness and complexity.

Output: The ways learners can demonstrate understanding and knowledge. For example to demonstrate understanding, students write a song, tell a story, design a poster, or perform an experiment.

Degree of Participation: The extent to which the learner is actively involved in the tasks. For example in a student play, a student may play a part that has more physical action rather than numerous lines to memorize.

Modified Goals: The adapted outcome expectations within the context of a general education curriculum. For example in a written language activity, a student may focus more on writing some letters and copying words rather than composing whole sentences or paragraphs.

Substitute Curriculum: The significantly differentiated instruction and materials to meet a learner's identified goals: For example in a foreign language class, a student may develop a script that uses both authentic language and cultural knowledge of a designated time period, rather than reading paragraphs or directions (reprinted with permission: Cole, S., Horvath, B., Chapman, C., Deschenes, C., Ebeling, D., and Sprague, J., 2000).

Some of the strategies for working with special needs learners can and should be used with all children. For example, all teachers should use visual aids, plan concrete examples, and provide hands-on activities for students who have had little prior experience in a domain. Teachers need to know the range of common adaptations that exist, know how to implement them, and know under what circumstances they are most effective.

What Teachers Need to Know About Developing an Inclusive Practice

Developing an inclusive practice goes beyond understanding special education policy and identifying specific instructional strategies that will help students with disabilities. Teachers must also know how to develop a supportive classroom community in which all students feel safe with the teacher and with each other. This involves sophisticated skills in classroom management. For example, it is important for teachers to be able to design groupwork in which children with varying abilities can work together productively. This requires identifying the strengths of special needs learners in ways that allow them to contribute and helping other students learn how to work within a heterogeneous group that supports contributions from all members (Johnson, 1985; Johnson and Johnson, 1989; Cohen and Lotan, 1995).

To develop inclusive classrooms teachers need to be able to observe, monitor, and assess children to gain accurate feedback about their students' learning and development. Thus they need to have skills in systematic inquiry, including the ability to observe not only an individual child in interaction with different tasks, but also the interactions among students. (See for example, the story of Akeem in Chapter Eight on Assessment.) Given the context of the classroom, the interactions between children, the individual nature of the learning challenges, and the child's life outside school, they need to determine why children may be responding or behaving in particular ways. Then they need to be able to develop interventions, track changes, and revise their strategies as necessary.

As mentioned earlier, teachers also need to attend to cultural and language differences as well as differences in how students learn and interact with one another. Most often this requires that teachers actively work to develop classroom communities where students are not only accepted, but are valued for their diverse experiences inside and outside the classroom. Teachers need to find ways to bring those experiences into the classroom. To develop an inclusive community students need to feel safe, not only with the teacher, but also around their peers. Developing this type of community can be difficult and takes some skill. For example, the teacher should be able to develop activities that are not overly competitive. If a teacher encourages children to talk about their disabilities and their backgrounds, the teacher needs to know how to direct conversations and to support people who are disclosing information. Teachers may also need to provide direct instruction on how children should interact with their peers. In fact, some children need to be taught how to be empathetic.

Developing an inclusive practice also requires that teachers work closely with other professionals. The necessary collaboration skills are complex, sometimes requiring that a teacher move beyond "being polite" with other teachers and professionals in order for them to communicate about serious educational issues that require debate and may create conflict. These may range from issues concerning individual students and whether they are being appropriately placed or treated in school to issues concerning broader school practices, such as tracking or curriculum differentiation, student placement policies, curriculum or teaching policies, or issues related to the quality of services provided in special education or in other parts of the school program. Teachers need to know how to raise questions and issues in a professional manner, seek appropriate information about student performance and school practices and bring that information to the table for discussion, and suggest strategies for clarifying goals and taking action. They need to know how to listen carefully so as to understand different positions and points of view, look for consensus and identify differences in ways that move the conversation forward, and take steps to resolve conflict. In the next section, we talk more about how teacher education programs can help teachers develop both the skills and the dispositions they need if they are to work successfully with diverse children and help create school environments that support equity and progress for all students.

IMPLICATIONS FOR TEACHER EDUCATION

Acquiring the kinds of knowledge we have described in this chapter—self-knowledge, cultural and linguistic knowledge, culturally informed pedagogical knowledge, knowledge about the nature of learning differences, knowledge of teaching methods and materials suitable for different kinds of learning needs, and knowledge of home-school relationships—is a complex undertaking. The teacher education community has responded to the challenge of helping prospective teachers acquire this knowledge base in a number of different ways that include instructional and curricular offerings that put teacher candidates in closer contact with the students and communities they serve. New program structures and recruitment processes for students and faculty also strengthen opportunities for teachers to expand their cultural knowledge and experiences.

The challenge of teaching diverse learners starts the moment teachers begin planning ways to connect their students with the subject matters they intend to teach. For this connection to occur, teachers must know their students—who they are, what they care about, what languages they speak, what customs and traditions are valued in their homes. This suggests that teacher education needs to include a variety of opportunities for teachers to learn about their students and the communities from which they come. At the same time they must know how to continue to learn about their students because their students will continue to change for every class and every year. Not unrelated is what teachers need to know about themselves—who they are, how their past school experiences frame their ways of knowing and being in school, and how that, in turn, tends to influence what they believe and what goals they set for doing the work. Teacher education pedagogies that stress all three of these knowledge domains—knowledge of learners, knowledge of self, and knowledge of how to continue to learn in teaching—suggest how we might begin to consider the implications of considering the "diverse learners" when thinking about learning to teach.

Learning About Students and Communities

We have suggested in this chapter that knowing one's students is important for teaching them well, as is believing that all students can learn and achieve high levels of academic success. The challenge of knowing one's students well and continuing to believe in their potential is fortified as teachers develop the knowledge and skills that enable them to succeed in teaching children from diverse backgrounds. There are several promising teacher education pedagogies that have emerged to prepare teachers to accomplish this goal. What kinds of activities might teacher educators design to prepare teachers for meeting the coupled challenge and opportunity of teaching our nation's diverse student population?

In *Educating Culturally Responsive Teachers,* Villegas and Lucas (2002a, p. 138) describe four types of field experiences that can help prospective teachers understand the school and community contexts in which they practice, and gain skills for becoming agents of change. These include guided school and community visits; service learning opportunities in both schools and other community organizations; studies of students, classrooms, schools, and communities; and practica in diverse contexts with teachers who are engaged in an equity pedagogy. All of these require care in structuring and guiding the learning experience, and each offers the possibilities for personal insights, professional learning, and deeper understanding of the social and structural features of schools and communities that shape opportunity.

One way to get to know one's students is to spend time with them and time in their communities paying careful attention to who they are, what they know, and what is the context for their experiences. In some teacher education programs, teacher candidates engage in various assignments and activities that take them into the communities where their students live and where their students' parents work. The "funds of knowledge approach" developed by Moll and González (2004) provides an example. This approach, which builds on ethnographic methods, centers on visiting students' households for the purpose of developing social relations with family members to document their knowledge and social capital so that it can be integrated into the work of the school (Moll and González, 2004). Through their inquiries teachers can document the funds of knowledge found in their students' households, including knowledge about vocations and avocations as well as community resources. In becoming theoretically and methodologically adept with this form of inquiry, they can rediscover those cultural resources in their students and incorporate them into the curriculum (González and others, 1995; Moll, Amanti, Neff, and González, 1992). Through their engagement with the inquiry process the teachers learn to employ this methodology as they continue to learn about their students in future years.

Rather than isolated in one experience or even one course, opportunities for novice teachers to spend time in the communities where their students live need to occur in a variety of ways and throughout the teacher's professional preparation (Bennett, Okinaka, and Xio-Yang, 1988; Grant and Koskella, 1986; McDiarmid and Price, 1990; Sleeter and Grant, 1988). These kinds of learning opportunities can also be offered through Child or Adolescent Case Study assignments that require teachers to come to know the life circumstances of a particular child very well (Roeser, 2002), for example, or extended fieldwork assignments that have teachers working in neighborhood or community settings (Ladson-Billings, 2001).

Community experiences in and of themselves are not necessarily educative, however. What makes them so are opportunities for students to reflect on and challenge the initial assumptions they carry with them into the field. Undoing prior assumptions is an important part of this process of learning to teach children who are not one's own. Ladson-Billings (2001) emphasizes this point when she notes that because of some teachers' prior experiences, they sometimes view their work through the lens of "helping the less fortunate" which provides little room for "the need to really help children become educated enough to develop intellectual, political, cultural, and economic independence" (pp. 82–83). Thus in the program Ladson-Billings describes, students complete a six-week assignment in a community-based agency or neighborhood center while they are enrolled in two courses: *Teaching and Diversity*, and *Culture, Curriculum, and Learning*, in addition to a seminar designed to help students debrief their community experiences. Furthermore, the work of this experience goes on throughout the remainder of the program year, which is tightly integrated around the ideas that teachers need to know the communities where schools are located, teachers need to develop a "humanizing pedagogy," and teaching is "an unfinished profession" (p. 109). Thus the program seeks to prepare teachers as learners and includes regular reflection as part of that process.

The occasion for guided reflection helps teachers make sense of what they have seen and heard and helps them to learn how to use their emerging knowledge to design curriculum and assessment materials appropriate to the students they teach. This time for guided reflection also allows teacher educators to be explicit about the processes involved in learning from one's experience as foundational for the continued work of learning in teaching.

Learning About Self

The importance of learning about one's students is paralleled by the importance of learning about oneself. Activities or experiences that place students face to face with their entering beliefs and assumptions both about themselves and others, and about learning, schooling, and intelligence, are essential as novice teachers prepare to teach students who are often different from themselves, in schools that are also different from the ones they attended, in a society that is changing with rapid intensity every day. A number of pedagogical approaches have been developed that provide this opportunity for students. For instance, autobiography, narrative, and life history are all methodologies teacher educators have developed to help prospective teachers question their existing beliefs about themselves and others (see, for example, Gomez and Tabachnick, 1992).

A study of one such methodology showed how ethnic literature and autobiography can become a means for prospective teachers to conduct studies of their own lives, which allows them to see themselves as cultural beings, and can lead to changes in their beliefs about literacy, schooling, and cultural identity (Florio-Ruane, 2001). In another teacher education program, novice teachers were asked to write a number of short narratives about instances of learning in the classrooms where they teach. They were startled by their own unquestioned assumptions and beliefs, which became evident when they were asked to analyze the collection of narratives they had produced (Richert, 2002). In addition, some narratives that portray instances of culturally responsive pedagogy or that provide portraits of students inside and outside academic settings provide ways to challenge assumptions prospective teachers might hold. The skillful use of autobiography, family histories, and contemporary and historical narratives can help prospective teachers learn about their own views, their students' experiences, and about the role of culture in learning, teaching, and schooling. We describe how this can be done in the account of Professor Holt's teacher education course, which is a composite account illustrating practices in several teacher education programs. (See "Professor Anderson Holt's Teacher Education Course.")

Professor Anderson Holt's Teacher Education Course

Anderson Holt is a professor in the teacher education program at a large state university in the Midwest. The demographics of the teacher education population at his university mirror the national population of teacher education students and teachers. Approximately 80 percent of Holt's students are white and about 75 percent are female. Many of Holt's students attended predominantly white elementary and secondary schools and grew up in rural areas or in small towns. Their experience at the large state university is the first opportunity they have had in their lives to interact with African Americans, Latinos, and American Indians in equal-status situations.

Among the major goals that Holt has for his course are to help the students understand the ways in which race is constructed in American society, how some racial groups are privileged and others are disadvantaged by established racial categories, and the pernicious effects of the "color-blind" approach to dealing with racial issues and problems in school (Schofield, 2003). Another aim of Holt's course is to help students understand the ways in which they are ethnic and cultural beings and the significant ways in which culture influences teaching and learning (Irvine, 2003; Ladson-Billings, 1994). Holt often hears student comments like these at the start of his multicultural teacher education class:

"I am just American. I don't have a cultural or ethnic group."

"Why do we have to talk about ethnic and racial differences? Why can't we all be just Americans?"

"Kids don't really see colors and these kinds of differences. I am afraid that if we bring them up we will just be teaching kids about them."

Helping Teacher Education Students Rethink Race, Culture, and Ethnicity

Although many students in teacher education programs view themselves as monocultural beings who are color-blind and raceless, evidence suggests that "color-blind" perspectives often mask unacknowledged biases about racial/ethnic minority groups. For example, in an important ethnographic study of a school, Schofield (2003) found that teachers who said they were color-blind suspended African American males at highly disproportionate rates and failed to integrate multicultural content into the curriculum. Color-blindness was used to justify the perpetuation of institutionalized discrimination within the school.

Teacher education students need to understand, for example, the ways in which the statement "I am not ethnic; I am just American" positions other cultures as non-American. A well-meaning statement such as "I don't see color" fails to legitimize racial identifications that often define the experiences of people of color and are used to justify perpetuation of discrimination. If educators do not "see" color and the ways in which institutionalized racism privileges some groups and disadvantages others, they will be unable to take action to eliminate racial inequality in schools.

In his introductory teacher education course, Holt incorporates readings, activities, lectures, and discussions designed to help students "unlearn racism" and to read the "racial text" of U.S. society (Cochran-Smith, 2000). Assignments include a personal reflection paper on the book *We Can't Teach What We Don't Know: White Teachers, Multicultural Schools* (Howard, 1999), as well as a family history project. In his book, Howard (1999) describes his personal journey as a white person to come to grips with racial issues and to become an effective educator. In their reflection papers, Holt's students describe their powerful reactions to Howard's book and how it helps them to rethink their personal journey related to race and their ideas about race. Howard makes racism explicit for most of Holt's students for the first time in their lives.

In their family history project, the students are asked to provide a brief account of their family's historical journey and to give explicit attention to the ways in which race, class, and gender have influenced their family and personal histories. Although the family history project is a popular assignment, many students struggle to describe ways in which race has influenced their family and personal histories because race is largely invisible to them (McIntosh, 1997). Gender is much more visible to the women students in Holt's class. More of the female than male students are able to relate gender to their family and personal stories in meaningful ways.

Challenging the Metanarrative

A series of activities in Holt's course is designed to help students examine the U.S. metanarrative, to construct understandings and narratives that describe the development of U.S. history and culture in ways that incorporate the histories and cultures of the nation's diverse racial, cultural, ethnic, and language groups. These activities include historical readings, discussions, and role-playing events. The perspectives in these historical accounts are primarily those of the groups being studied rather than those of outsiders, because the students have already had much more experience with outsider perspectives than the voices of the people themselves (see, for example, Takaki, 1993; Banks, 2003). To function effectively in culturally, racially, and language diverse classrooms, teacher education students need to understand the experiences and perspectives of various communities and to understand how race, culture, and ethnicity are related to the social, economic, and political structures in U.S. society (Nieto, 1999; Omi and Winant, 1994).

Videotapes that powerfully depict the perspectives of ethnic groups of color on historical and contemporary events supplement the historical readings in Holt's course. These videotapes include *The Shadow of Hate: A History of Intolerance in America* (Guggenheim, 1995), which chronicles how various groups within the United States, including the Irish, Jews, and African Americans, have been victimized by discrimination. One of the most trenchant examples of discrimination in the videotape is the description of the way Leo Frank, a Jewish northerner living in

Atlanta, became a victim of anti-Semitism and racial hostility when he was accused of murdering a white girl who worked in a pencil factory he co-owned.

The Leo Frank case provides the students an opportunity to understand the ways in which race is a social construction, is contextual, and how the meaning of race has changed historically and continues to change today (Jacobson, 1998). Leo Frank was considered Jewish and not white in 1915 Atlanta. Holt presents a lecture that gives the students an overview of Brodkin's (1998) book that describes the process by which Jews (and other white ethnics, such as the Irish and Italians) became white in America by assimilating mainstream American behaviors, ideologies, and perspectives, including institutionalized attitudes toward groups of color (see also Ignatiev, 1995; Morrison, 1992). The students in Holt's class are surprised to learn how the meaning of race has changed through time and that the idea that whites are one racial group is a rather recent historical development.

A videotape that deals with a contemporary Native American issue is used to help students understand the ways in which the United States' past and present are connected. *In Whose Honor?* (Rosenstein, 1997) chronicles the struggle of Charlene Teters, a Native American graduate student, to end the use of a Native American chief as a football team mascot at the University of Illinois in Champaign-Urbana. The team is called The Fighting Illini, after Chief Illiniwek. During halftime, a student dresses up as Chief Illiniwek and dances. Teters considers the chief and the dance sacrilegious and demeaning to Native Americans. The videotape describes the social action taken by Teters to end the tradition, as well as the strong opposition by the board of trustees and alumni who want to maintain a tradition that is deeply beloved by vocal and influential alumni and board members. This leads to a consideration of how the construction of the Indian in U.S. society is controlled by mainstream institutions, including the mainstream media. Through questioning and discussion, Holt helps the students relate Columbus' construction of the Native people of the Caribbean as Indians, Cortes' construction of the Aztecs as savages, Turner's construction of the West as a wilderness, and the selection of Chief Illiniwek as a mascot. They consider which groups have the power to define and institutionalize their conceptions within the schools, what is the relationship between knowledge and power, and who benefits (and who loses) from the ways in which Native Americans, and other people of color, have been and are often defined in U.S. society.

An Unfinished Journey

Holt's course is designed to help his teacher education students better understand race, culture, and ethnicity, and how these factors influence the teaching and learning process. Holt seeks to communicate the respect he has for his students while at the same time encouraging them to seriously challenge their deeply held beliefs, attitudes, values, and knowledge claims. The course is a beginning of what Holt hopes will be a lifelong journey for his students. One course with a transformative goal can have only a limited influence on the knowledge, beliefs, and values of students who have been exposed to mainstream knowledge and perspectives for most of their prior education. Students are required to take a second multicultural education course at the state university where Holt teaches. Also, other members of the teacher education faculty are trying to integrate ethnic, cultural, and racial content into the foundations and methods courses. The goal is to enable teachers to learn to understand and successfully engage the students they will meet, and to work on their behalf for effective education and social justice.

Source: Banks, James A. (2001c). Citizenship education and diversity: Implications for Teacher Education. *Journal of Teacher Education, 52*(1), 5–16, copyright © by Sage Publications. Reprinted by permission of Sage Publications, Inc.

Learning About How to Learn from Teaching

Although dispositions and commitments are clearly important, teachers do not continue to believe that "all children can learn" unless they have developed knowledge and skills that enable them to succeed in teaching diverse children. As described further in Chapter Eleven, reading and writing cases is one strategy to develop prospective teachers' capacities to spot issues, frame problems in complex teaching settings, develop teaching strategies, and learn from their own experiences (Kleinfeld, 1990, 1991; Merseth, 1996; Shulman, 1987). A number of educators have developed written and video cases that raise issues of culture and learning for teachers, allowing them not only to become more conscious of their own beliefs and perspectives, but also to become more aware of strategies for reaching their students (Banks, 1991; Kleinfeld, 1998). For example, the Teachers for Alaska program at the University of Alaska Fairbanks has used cases skillfully to explore concerns of multicultural teaching in local contexts. Cases in this program offer students a preview of situations they may encounter in their teaching careers; provide descriptions of strategies successful teachers use in handling these gnarly situations; and help novices develop tools for handling the "messy dilemmas that require all the imagination, intellectual resources, and tact at a teacher's command" (Kleinfeld, 1998, p. 145). (See "Using Cases to Support Learning from Practice in Multicultural Contexts.") Although such cases can be extremely valuable, they need to be constructed with great care, so that they avoid the risk of inadvertently stereotyping students or situations, or attributing to cultural or other characteristics of students behaviors that may have other origins (Darling-Hammond and Snyder, 2000).

Using Cases to Support Learning from Practice in Multicultural Contexts
The Teachers for Alaska program at the University of Alaska Fairbanks replaced the traditional sequence of foundation courses and methods courses followed by student teaching with a program organized around curriculum blocks, each of which emphasizes the study of a case that is thematically related to the subject matter being taught. The cases consist of actual stories of situations confronted by teachers in the culturally diverse classrooms and communities of Alaskan villages. They are modeled on the "dilemmas" approach to case method teaching used by the Harvard Business School to prepare practitioners for action in complex and uncertain con-

texts (Christensen and Hansen, 1987). These cases introduce students to the "tangled issues of teaching in remote villages—the simmering animosities between local people and high-paid outsiders, unfamiliar cultural rules that new teachers could unwittingly violate, the organization of power in village communities, the injustices the educational system has visited on villagers, and also the injustices visited on outside teachers" (Kleinfeld, 1998, p. 142).

The teaching cases consist of two parts. Part one poses the dramatic problem nested within a web of related issues. For instance, one case begins with a classroom fight between an Eskimo student and an Anglo student. As the case develops, the teacher realizes the fight is related to the Anglo student's cutting remark about the Eskimo students' work ("D minus, huh?"). Later the teacher discovers that the Eskimo student's interpretation of this remark cuts to the core of his identity, "He thinks I am dumb because I am native." The case also develops such contextual issues as the stress of culture fatigue, the hostility of the local community, and lack of support from school administration. In the case, the teacher considers such pedagogical and ethical issues as: What is a fair grading system in an English class where some students are children of "outside professionals" and native speakers of English whereas others are Yup'ik-speaking children of subsistence hunters? What alternative grading options might be considered? How can competence be supported and recognized? The case presents teaching problems not as prepackaged neatly solved exercises but as difficult issues to be explored. The critical task for students in their discussion of the cases is first to understand the range of considerations and from that understanding to determine what else to explore.

Part two of the case shows how experienced teachers go about addressing the issues raised in the first part. The advantage of part two is that it features specific strategies that candidates can consider using themselves. In the previous example, for instance, the teacher revises his grading system with goals for each student and grades students on their success in meeting their individualized goals. He creates a bulletin board entitled "The Theme is Excellence" to post students' work, pictures of them doing homework, and articles about their parents from the local newspaper. With other teacher colleagues, he organizes a community relations campaign with a successful poster showing an Eskimo mother with a baby superimposed over a classroom of students. The caption reads, "WE TEACH . . . the children you love." During the program, students write a case from their own student teaching experience. Many of these cases become part of the curriculum for the program the following year. They provide a base for assessing students' success at understanding their work in a multicultural context and for developing productive strategies for reaching their students.

The case-based approach, coupled with carefully structured coursework and clinical experiences, appears to make a difference for candidates' learning. Evaluations of the Teachers for Alaska program show measurable improvement in students' cross-cultural teaching skills from the point of entry until graduation. In a recent evaluation, at the end of their first semester on campus and again after their student teaching experiences in the villages, trained observers documented sample lessons graduates taught with culturally diverse students. At their entry into the program, 28 percent of the candidates took into account students' cultural frames of reference. At the program midpoint, 62 percent did so. At the end of the program, 83 percent did so. Other measures, such as the use of active teaching strategies, showed similar changes (Kleinfeld, 1998). Examining and practicing teaching in cultural and community context appears to strengthen teachers' ability to take account of their students.

Ideally, in their clinical placements, student teachers will have the opportunity to observe firsthand schooling that seeks to confront the long-standing barriers created by tracking, poor teaching, narrow curriculum, and unresponsive systems. If prospective teachers have long-term placements in schools where they can work collaboratively with other teachers on classroom and schoolwide issues, as is the case in many professional development school partnerships, they can learn to become part of a team that works to transform the contexts for teaching and learning. (For examples of such partnerships, see Darling-Hammond, 1994; Guadarrama, Ramsey, and Nath, 2002.) One set of such partnership schools, for example, working with California State University at Fullerton, has created a collaborative approach to preparing special education teachers and regular education teachers involved in inclusion. Creating several sites that seek to demonstrate exemplary practices to special education and that restructure the ways in which students are educated, these teacher education partnerships have demonstrated steady increases in student achievement while educating new and veteran teachers as both skilled inclusion teachers and as agents of school change (Glaeser, Karge, Smith, and Weatherill, 2002).

Clearly, however, inequities are not solved overnight. Some programs focus on arming prospective teachers with skills to evaluate what is working and not working for groups of students in their schools as the basis for planning and implementing changes. By exploring inequities in their teaching contexts through action research, student teachers can also be taught to critically examine current school structures, practices, and outcomes as they visit and study schools and evaluate school policies and reforms (see, for example, Darling-Hammond, French, and Garcia Lopez, 2002; Gebhard, Austin, Nieto, and Willett, 2002).

Studies of schools often involve prospective teachers in investigating particular issues or questions—sometimes generated by the course and other times by the candidates themselves—by systematically collecting information, observing interactions in classrooms and other parts of the school, looking at statistical data, examining artifacts or records, and interviewing students, parents, and staff. School studies can examine policy issues that are under discussion (for example, curriculum adoption or development, looping, family involvement policies, language learning policies); grouping practices and how they affect different students, teachers, and practices; inter- and intraschool resource allocations; discipline policies and practices; or other topics. These studies can expand understanding of different perspectives, provide skills for collecting and interpreting data, and develop candidates' knowledge of how school organizations operate—and how they can be influenced to change. As Villegas and Lucas (2002a) note, however, about the process of such studies, guided reflection is essential. "Without it, preservice teachers might interpret problems they observe as deficiencies within the students, their families, and their communities while overlooking how inequitable conditions in schools and society contribute to those problems" (p. 143).

Considerations of Program Design

It warrants mentioning under the umbrella of the pedagogical approaches that structural changes in programs of teacher education are needed to make space for the kinds of learning experiences we are highlighting here. More time and opportunity for teachers to spend in the communities where they teach makes learning about those communities possible. Student teaching placements that are carefully chosen to enable teachers to work with expert veterans who are knowledgeable, skillful, and committed to all of their students are also important to this work. It is difficult to learn to teach well by imagining what good teaching might look like or by positing the opposite of what one has seen. Rather, placing students carefully with cooperating teachers who are teaching in culturally responsive ways and then structuring those field placements to connect with courses that help teachers understand those experiences are both essential to providing learning opportunities for students doing this work. Many professional development school relationships have been developed so that prospective teachers not only learn to teach from strong practitioners but also so that they work in a school context that has developed formal and informal structures to promote equity (see, for example, Darling-Hammond, 1994; Guadarrama and others, 2002). In these settings, candidates generally are able to experience many aspects of school functioning and learn from many practitioners beyond the individual classroom, including the aspects of the school like special education or language support services, the school governance process, extracurricular activities, and the like. In this way, they have the opportunity to see what schools do when they are committed to serving all of their students well and when they engage in continual self-reflection and improvement.

Another structural factor that impacts a program's ability to provide the kinds of learning opportunities we have highlighted concerns the admissions and hiring procedures that shape the learning community itself. A key building block for the curriculum of any school, from pre-K through graduate school, is the knowledge and set of experiences of those who are members of the learning community. When a diverse group of people gather to teach and learn from one another they become resources for each other. The opportunities for in-depth conversations, teaching examples, inquiry, and other opportunities to learn and grow are enhanced as people with diverse prior experiences come together. It is for this reason that scholars and practitioners have emphasized the recruitment of more faculty of color in teacher education programs as well as the recruitment of individuals who have taught successfully in settings serving diverse learners. Similarly, having a diverse population of teacher candidates contributes to the learning climate for developing a culturally responsive pedagogy. The more diverse the array of prior experience and perspective among participants, the more generative can be the work of learning to teach.

However, just providing more diversity and experience among the professoriate and student population is not a magical solution to the needs teacher education programs face in preparing teachers to teach in culturally responsive ways. As we have already discussed, programs must develop a curriculum and pedagogy that helps people learn how to learn from those opportunities when people from diverse backgrounds come together to study teaching practice. Learning to learn together is part of this challenging work. An example comes in learning to actively confront stereotypes about the traits of students as well as teachers from various groups in order to correct the tendency to "exceptionalize" successful people of color while maintaining lower expectations of most. With this comes learning how to actively examine how classroom and school-level practices work to enhance or undermine achievement for different groups of students (Ladson-Billings, 1999). Teachers need to be supported in developing the commitment to teach all children to high standards. Holding onto the belief that all pupils can learn and that intelligence is not something immutable or fixed, teachers are then ready to develop the cultural sensitivity and intercultural competence that will create the foundation on which they can base their learning about their students over the duration of their professional careers.

Although considerable work has been done to develop pedagogies that prepare teachers to meet the needs of the widely diverse population of learners they face, at the same time there is much work to be done. New pedagogical approaches are needed, as is a broader inclusion of such efforts in programs nationwide. Similarly, continued effort needs to be made to create programs where these efforts are not standalone courses, but rather integrated experiences throughout the professional preparation program. Research has shown the limited impact of single, standalone courses on prospective teachers' knowledge, attitudes, and practices (Bennett, Okinaka, and Xio-Yang, 1988; Grant and Koskella, 1986; McDiarmid and Price, 1990; Sleeter, 1988). Similarly, single standalone community experiences are not enough to overcome years of prior conditioning. Ultimately, the goal must be to design programs that make attention to diversity, equity, and social justice centrally important so that all courses and field experiences for prospective teachers are conducted with these important goals in mind.

CHAPTER EIGHT

Assessment[1]

Lorrie Shepard, Karen Hammerness, Linda Darling-Hammond,
Frances Rust, with Joan Baratz Snowden, Edmund Gordon,
Cris Gutierrez, Arturo Pacheco

Assessment of student learning is an integral part of the learning process. A generation ago, it was considered sufficient if teachers knew how to give tests that matched learning objectives. Today, research in cognitive science has shown that formative assessment, used to discover what a student understands or does not understand, can be a powerful tool in targeting instruction so as to move learning forward. *Formative assessment* is defined as assessment carried out during the instructional process for the purpose of improving teaching or learning. To be effective, teachers must be skillful in using various assessment strategies and tools such as observation, student conferences, portfolios, performance tasks, prior knowledge assessments, rubrics, feedback, and student self-assessment. More importantly, they must have a deep understanding of the formative assessment process and understand its close relationship to instructional scaffolding. They must be able to use insights from assessment to plan and revise instruction and to provide feedback that explicitly helps students see how to improve.

Teachers also continue to have their traditional responsibilities for giving grades and reporting to parents about student progress. *Summative assessment* refers to those assessments that are generally carried out at the end of an instructional unit

---

[1]Portions of this chapter were adapted with permission from Shepard, L. A. (in press), Classroom assessment. In R. L. Brennan (Ed.), *Educational Measurement* (4th ed.). Westport, CT: Greenwood Publishing Group.

or course of study for the purpose of giving grades or otherwise certifying student proficiency. In contrast to earlier times, principles for effective grading practices derived from research findings in the areas of motivation, cognition, and measurement suggest that students should be afforded multiple ways to demonstrate their proficiency and should be judged in relation to performance expectations rather than in comparison to other students.

Today's classrooms are greatly affected by external accountability assessments that often have high-stakes consequences for schools, teachers, and students. Teachers should be informed about research results on both the positive and negative effects of high-stakes testing. They should know how these findings relate to the particular testing programs in their state and district and should be able to evaluate how well tests align with content standards and meaningful curriculum goals. Although teachers have a responsibility to ensure that students are prepared for the specific demands of important external tests, they should not narrow the curriculum in ways that harm the breadth and depth of student understandings.

This chapter is organized in four main sections. The first three elaborate on the uses of assessment described earlier. Each of these sections presents research documenting the effect of various assessment practices on student learning with corresponding recommendations for the knowledge and skills needed by beginning teachers. The fourth section focuses on the models of assessment that are currently in use in some strong teacher education programs.

Before proceeding, however, a caveat is needed. The ideal assessment practices described in this chapter are based on research and they are consistent with the practices of particularly adept, expert teachers. However, these ideals do not necessarily reflect typical assessment practices. In particular, the majority of practicing teachers may have limited knowledge of formative assessment strategies and may think about assessment as being primarily for the purpose of grading. In some sense then, novice teachers may have an easier time developing conceptually coherent curricular, instructional, and assessment repertoires than experienced teachers for whom such practices would require substantial change. Where relevant we identify misconceptions associated with current practice that would have to be overcome in order for research-based assessment practices to flourish.

FORMATIVE ASSESSMENT

For teachers to be effective in supporting student learning they must constantly be checking for student understanding. Moreover, they must convey to students the importance of students themselves taking responsibility for reflecting on and monitoring their own learning progress. A landmark review by Black and

Wiliam (1998) found that focused efforts to improve formative assessment produced learning gains greater than one-half standard deviation, which would be equivalent to raising the score of an average student from the 50th percentile to the 85th percentile. In other words, formative assessment, effectively implemented, can do as much or more to improve student achievement than any of the most powerful instructional interventions, intensive reading instruction, one-on-one tutoring, and the like.

In this section, we present a model of formative assessment followed by several of the specific strategies and tools that teachers use as part of everyday instructional routines. These recursive assessment processes are essential for ongoing revision and improvement of teaching as well as for improving student learning. Formative assessment may involve informal methods such as observation and oral questioning or the formative use of more formal measures such as traditional quizzes, portfolios, or performance assessments.

An Example of Formative Assessment in the Classroom

A vivid example of the value of this kind of formative assessment is provided in the account of Akeem, a third-grade student who entered Susan Gordon's classroom in a New York City elementary school after having been expelled for throwing a desk at a teacher in another school (Darling-Hammond, Ancess, and Falk, 1995, pp. 217–224). In the early weeks of school, Akeem had outbursts of temper, made frequent efforts to disrupt classroom meetings, and was either periodically surly or aggressive. Gordon immediately began a focused effort to assess Akeem's strengths as well as to locate where he found difficulty. Along with completing a set of observational records that helped her determine his progress in literacy and numeracy, she documented exactly when and under what circumstances his outbursts occurred. She also carefully documented those moments when Akeem seemed most at ease, focused, and productive. She discovered that Akeem's misbehavior tended to occur when certain kinds of academic tasks arose: Akeem's actions seemed designed to deflect attention from the fact that he could not read well or write with any ease. At the same time, she discovered that he was very interested and skilled at complex and creative drawings, and he displayed a passion for and strength in building and designing architectural models.

Susan encouraged Akeem to work in hands-on learning centers that tapped his artistic skills and his abilities to construct machines and models. Because her close assessments of his reading and writing had identified particular areas where he struggled, she was able to develop a plan that would help provide him some focused instruction with those needs in mind. She found him books and developed writing assignments that built on his interests, while systematically teaching him new strategies for reading. Gradually in concert with these activities and assessments, Akeem began to experience greater success academically.

Akeem developed architectural drawings and sophisticated comic books which he later annotated and turned into books; he was recognized by peers for his artistic and mechanical abilities and began to gain status in the classroom; he joined classroom activities with increasing enthusiasm; and, not incidentally, he learned to read and write. Akeem was able to finish middle school with a solid academic record, near perfect attendance, and gained admission into a specialized high school for the arts.

This kind of account provides an illustration of how to collect and diagnose evidence about students' learning and behavior in light of broader knowledge about both. It shows us how to diagnose learning needs and how to build a set of teaching strategies that addresses these needs. As the case of Akeem demonstrates, formative assessment insights are an essential part of effective curriculum and pedagogy.

A Model of Formative Assessment

Sadler (1989) provided the most widely accepted model of formative assessment. He pointed out that it is insufficient for teachers merely to give feedback about whether answers are right or wrong. Instead, to facilitate learning, it is equally important that feedback be linked explicitly to clear performance standards and that students be provided with strategies for improvement. This model of formative assessment is further explicated in a recent report on classroom assessment in science by Atkin, Black, and Coffey (2001). They frame the learning-assessment process with these key questions:

- Where are you trying to go?
- Where are you now?
- How can you get there?

By answering the assessment question (#2, Where are you now?) in relation to the instructional goal (question #1) and specifically addressing what is needed to reach the goal (question #3), the formative assessment process directly supports improvement.

Setting clear targets for student learning involves more than posting an instructional goal for students to see. It also requires elaboration of the criteria by which student work will be judged. How will the teacher and student know that a concept is understood? How will the student's ability to defend an argument be evaluated? Then, the assessment step must occur during the learning process, while the student is working on tasks that directly embody the intended learning goal. This assessment, in the midst of learning, could happen by means of student questioning during group work, at the overhead projector when students explain to the class how they solved a problem, or by examining written work. In the third and final step, feedback must be given that provides insight to both teacher and student about how to close the gap. For example, when a student is still confused about a fundamental concept, the teacher might try taking a different approach to the problem or revisit prerequisite knowledge. If the reasoning in a paper is poorly developed, the teacher might ask the student to revise after first considering what is lacking in relation to assessment criteria.

This formative assessment model is more than a data-gathering step. It is a model for supporting learning that is designed to advance a student within his or her zone of proximal development (ZPD). (See Chapters Two and Three.) As envisioned by Vygotsky (1978), the zone of proximal development is the region, on an imaginary learning continuum, between what a child can do independently and what the same child can do with assistance. Wood, Bruner, and Ross (1976) further developed the idea of *scaffolding* to characterize the support, in the form of guidance, coaching, hints, and encouragement, that adults provide in the ZPD to enable (and, indeed, challenge) the learner to perform at a level of accomplishment that she would otherwise not have been able to reach. The assessment step in the formative assessment model (Where are you now?) provides the insight needed to enable effective support. The complete formative model, which includes clarification of the goal and identification of the means to get there, is essentially synonymous with instructional scaffolding. Indeed, Sadler's fully elaborated version of formative assessment requires that teachers and students have a shared understanding and ownership of the learning goal and, ultimately, that students be able to self-monitor their own improvement. This corresponds to the goal of scaffolding, which is to foster internalization and the assumption of responsibility by the learner (Tharp and Gallimore, 1988).

In the real world, teachers rarely have time for one-on-one tutoring sessions or dynamic assessments that would allow them to pursue scaffolded instruction with one student through an entire learning cycle. And, to be sure, planning instruction for an entire classroom filled with students whose ZPDs are highly varied is challenging. Nevertheless, classroom routines can be established to ensure that the basic elements of formative assessment and scaffolding are in place and functioning in the guise of ordinary instructional interactions. One of the reasons that classroom discourse has received such attention in research on instructional reform is that patterns of group interaction, especially students questioning and explaining their reasoning, can scaffold student learning without requiring one-on-one teacher time. In addition, if students have learned to work independently and in groups, then teacher time can be used efficiently to assist individual students at just those points where a student is stuck. Cobb, Wood, and Yakel (1993) describe scaffolded whole class discussions in which students are able not only to clarify their understandings of mathematical concepts but also to practice the social norms and ways of speaking in that discipline. Hogan and Pressley (1997) similarly describe interactions in science inquiry classrooms where students learn to provide evidence to support a position and also to critique their classmates' unsupported conclusions—a valuable form of feedback. Such public displays of developing thinking also afford the perfect opportunity for formative assessment.

Ideally, then, formative assessment should be seamlessly integrated with instruction. In the pages that follow, we elaborate on the specific elements of the formative assessment process that have an extensive research base. We begin with a focus on content, because assessment is meaningless if it does not engage those things that we most want students to learn. Then we consider learning progressions because, within subject matter domains, teachers must also have a working idea of typical learning progressions so that they know what they are helping students toward, and also how to back up when comprehension fails. Then we consider specific aspects of assessment-instruction interactions, accessing prior knowledge, making criteria explicit, providing feedback, and so forth. None of these processes, however, needs to interrupt instruction; instead, assessment should continuously feed back into ongoing learning. Even if time is taken for a formal quiz, the results can be used for instructional diagnosis to decide what concepts still need further discussion and work. And students can come to understand that such assessments have a learning purpose.

The Importance of Content: Selecting Instructional and Assessment Tasks That Embody Learning Goals

Assessment cannot promote learning if it is based on tasks or questions that divert attention from the real goals of instruction. Historically, traditional tests have often misdirected instruction, if they focused on what was easiest to measure instead of what was important to learn. Classroom instruction should engage students in learning activities that are, to the greatest extent possible, instantiations of the real goals for learning. For example, if we want students to be able to read books, newspapers, and poems, they should, in fact, do these things and not be given shortened, simulated materials except to make them age appropriate. Similarly, in science, if we want students to be able to reason with and use scientific knowledge, then students should have the opportunity to figure out how things work by conducting investigations and developing explanations in their own words that connect their experiences with textbook theories. Assessment, then, must be conducted as part of such meaningful learning activities. Often this means that instructional and assessment tasks are merged.

A defining feature of standards-based reform has been the development of curriculum standards that served to reinvigorate and elevate what it means to know and demonstrate proficiency in each of the disciplines. For example, the National Council of Teachers of Mathematics (NCTM) *Curriculum and Evaluation Standards for School Mathematics* (1989) set out expectations, emphasizing problem solving, communication, mathematical reasoning, and drawing connections that went well beyond the mastery of basic skills and concepts. Not surprisingly, assessment reform was an equally important part of the standards movement because of the need to address these more ambitious goals.

The term *alignment* has been used to specify the desired correspondence between assessments and curriculum standards. Unfortunately, the meaning of alignment has been cheapened somewhat when test publishers show that all of their multiple-choice items can be matched to the categories of a state's content standards, even if, altogether, they tap only a narrow subset of the intended standards. Shepard (2003) has suggested that the term *embodiment* might better be used to characterize the more complete and substantive alignment that occurs when the tasks, problems, and projects in which students are engaged represent the range and depth of what we say we want students to understand and be able to do.

As illustrated by Wiggins and McTighe (1998), devising assessments that *embody* the standards and goals of instruction is central to good teaching, not just a matter of measuring outcomes. Instead of instructional planning that focuses on interesting activities, Wiggins and McTighe use a process of "backward design" that begins with the goals, then asks what would be compelling evidence or demonstrations of learning, and last plans activities that would enable students to perform. With understanding as the goal of instruction, Wiggins and McTighe emphasize the need to spell out what evidence of understanding would look like. These descriptions of performance in turn propel them to provide students with opportunities to develop and practice these skills that might otherwise have been missed if "understanding" had been left only as the globally stated goal of the unit. For example, evidence of understanding would be found if students could explain, interpret, apply knowledge, evaluate perspectives, demonstrate empathy, and reveal self-knowledge. And each of these facets can be further elaborated to make clear what it is that students would be able to do as evidence of understanding. A student who understands can explain, which means "providing complex, insightful, and credible reasons—theories and principles, based on good evidence and argument—to explain or illuminate an event, fact, text, or idea; providing a systematic account, using helpful and vivid mental models" (p. 66).

In sum, teachers must be knowledgeable about the content standards in each of the disciplines and know how to select instructional activities and both formal and informal assessment tasks that embody content standards. For many experienced teachers, focusing on standards has meant moving away from rote knowledge and skills used in isolation toward a greater focus on conceptual understanding of core ideas and on students' abilities to solve problems and formulate an argument. Beginning teachers should be able to design or select assessment tasks that probe for students' conceptual understanding and reflect important learning goals.

Learning Progressions

An understanding of learning progressions or learning continua is important for monitoring and supporting learning and development over time. Although most teachers have some intuitive sense of what comes next (or they would not be able to help students do better) even master teachers could benefit from more formally developed models of how learning typically unfolds within a curricular domain as well as knowing the natural variations and departures from the typical pattern. Empirically validated progressions can enable more insightful instructional scaffolding; however, progressions should never be interpreted as lockstep or an absolute sequence of prerequisites.

The *progress map* in "Progress Map for Counting and Ordering" is an example of a learning progression from Australia's Developmental Assessment program. A student's progress in understanding number concepts can be mapped or charted on this continuum, which provides a picture of individual growth against a backdrop of normatively established expectations. In contrast to assessment reports that look more like a checklist of grade-level objectives, progress maps have more direct implications for instruction because they provide simultaneously a picture of strengths and weaknesses and a way to look ahead at what comes next for each facet of the domain. For example, a fourth-grade student may be adept in the use of decimal fractions, and may even be ready to use percentages to make comparisons—a fifth-grade expectation that builds on and extends understanding of decimals and place value. At the same time, however, that same student may still be struggling with the relative size of common fractions, thereby functioning closer to the third-grade level. Knowing these strengths and weaknesses, targeted instruction would not only focus on developing a better understanding of fractions but would draw on the student's understanding of decimal fractions to do so.

Progress Map for Counting and Ordering

The following is the lower portion of a counting and ordering progress map. The map shows examples of knowledge, skills, and understandings in the sequence in which they are generally expected to develop from grades 1 through 5. This type of map is useful for tracking the progress of an individual child over time. An evaluation using tasks designed to tap specific performances on the map can provide a "snapshot" showing where a student is located on the map, and a series of such evaluations is useful for assessing a student's progress over the course of several years.

1. Counts collections of objects to answer the question "How many are there?"
   Makes or draws collections of a given size
   (Responds correctly to Give me 6 bears)
   Makes sensible estimates of the size of small collections up to 10
   (For 7 buttons, 2 or 15 would not be a sensible estimate, but 5 would be)

Skip counts in 2s or 3s using a number line, hundred chart, or mental counting (2, 4, 6, . . .)

Uses numbers to decide which is bigger, smaller, same size

(If he has 7 mice at home and I have 5, then he has more)

Uses the terms first, second, third (I finished my lunch second)

2 Counts forward and backward from any whole number, including skip counting in 2s, 3s, and 10s

Uses place value to distinguish and order whole numbers

(Writes four ten dollar notes and three one dollar coins as $43)

Estimates the size of a collection (up to about 20)

Uses fractional language (one-half, third, quarter, fifth, tenth) appropriately in describing and comparing things

Shows and compares unit fractions (finds a third of a cup of sugar)

Describes and records simple fractional equivalents

(The left over half pizza was as much as two quarters put together)

3 Counts in common fractional amounts

(Two and one-third, two and two-thirds, three, three and one-third)

Uses decimal notation to two places

(Uses 1.25 m for 1 m 25 cm; $3.05 for three $1 coins and one 5 cent coin; 1.75 kg for 1750 kg)

Regroups money to fewest possible notes and coins

(11 × $5 + 17 × $2 + 8 x $1 regrouped as 1 × $50 + 2 × $20 + $5 + $2)

Uses materials and diagrams to represent fractional amounts

(Folds tape into five equal parts, shades 3 parts to show 3/5)

Expresses generalizations about fractional numbers symbolically

(1 quarter = 2 eighths and 1/4 = 2/8)

4 Counts in decimal fraction amounts (0.3, 0.6, 0.9, 1.2, . . .)

Compares and orders decimal fractions

(Orders given weight data for babies to two decimal places)

Uses place value to explain the order of decimal fractions

(Which library book comes first—65.6 or 65.126? why?)

Reads scales calibrated in multiples of ten

(Reads 3.97 on a tape measure marked in hundredths, labeled in tenths)

Uses the symbols =, <, and > to order numbers and make comparisons

(6.75 < 6.9; 5 × $6 > 5 × $5.95)

Compares and orders fractions (one-quarter is less than three-eighths)

5 Uses unitary ratios of the form 1 part to X parts

(The ratio of cordial to water was 1 to 4)

Understands that common fractions are used to describe ratios of parts to whole

(2 in 5 students ride to school. In school of 550, 220 ride bikes)

Uses percentages to make straightforward comparisons

(26 balls from 50 tries is 52%; 24 from 40 tries is 60%, so that is better)

Uses common equivalences between decimals, fractions, and percentages

(One-third off is better than 30% discount)
Uses whole number powers and square roots in describing things
(Finds length of side of square of area 225 sq cm as a square root of 225)

Source: Extract from *Mathematics Profile for Australian Schools,* reproduced courtesy of Curriculum Corporation, first published in 1994 by Curriculum Corporation, Carlton pp. 26, 40, 56, 70, and 86. http://www.curriculum.edu.au

One of the obstacles to the development of instructionally useful learning progressions has been the patchwork fashion in which large-scale assessment systems have been developed over time. State and national assessments, originally intended to monitor large-scale trends, have often focused on grade-level expectations for milestone grades (for example, 4, 8, 12). More recently, with increased requirements for individual testing, states have filled in the intervening grades and interpolated curricular expectations. However, these expectations, especially when "world-class standards" are set on never-before-implemented curricula, do not necessarily reflect the developmental trajectory of real students. At the same time, there is the danger that relying on normative means for establishing progressions will reify outmoded curricular expectations. For example, when the National Assessment of Educational Progress first attempted to establish vertical scales in science, it appeared that scientific concepts would have to be mastered in the order of biology-chemistry-physics. Yet this apparent progression was merely an artifact of the traditional sequencing of high school courses—originally alphabetical, not based on what scientists believe about productive ways to sequence concepts and skills development.

Although world-class, subjectively determined progressions may be overly ambitious, empirically determined progressions may set expectations that are too low, because they "average in" the results of failed instruction. For example, based on empirical data, the Keymath Diagnostic Arithmetic Tests uses items in the form of $4\ 1/4 \times 5$ as an example of the arithmetic that students would be expected to master during the ninth-grade year. What is needed is a development process based on both research and expert judgment that includes validation of proposed continua in the context of well-implemented curricula. To date, the most grounded and instructionally relevant work has been done in the area of emergent literacy, with documentation of typical development in reading, writing, and spelling. For example, the sequence in Table 8.1 illustrates the typical progression of children's increasing mastery of the phonemic principle underlying spelling.

Beginning elementary teachers should be familiar with the learning progressions in early literacy and mathematics development and be able to plan instructional and intervention strategies that help students take the next steps. Teachers at all grade levels should understand how "skills," such as hypothesis testing, reasoning from evidence, and explaining one's thinking, are developed over time, and they should be able to use rubrics to evaluate and guide that development. To aid their own learning about learning trajectories as well as for use in communicating with parents and students, teachers should collect work at

Table 8.1 Strategies in Children's Spelling

Prominent Strategy	Description	Example
Prephonemic	Letters are used to write words but the sound-symbol relationships are unrelated to target word.	"c" for "hat"
Early phonemic	Some phonemes are represented by letters, typically most salient phoneme(s) in a word.	"dr" for "dear"
Phonetic	Attempts are made to represent most sounds in words, often letter name that most closely resembles sound.	"wns" for "once"
Simple associations	Simple vowels and consonants are represented correctly but complex patterns are not.	"bid" for "bird"
Strategic extensions	With complex vowels and consonants, attempts reflect complex English patterns, although not the conventions of English.	"bote" for "boat"
Conventional		

Source: These strategies are summarized by Hiebert and Raphael (1998) and represent an elaboration of stages originally proposed in J. R. Gentry's (1982) "An Analysis of Developmental Spelling in GNYS AT WRK" (pp. 192–199). From *Early Literacy Instruction* (1st ed.) by Hiebert and Raphael. © 1998. Reprinted with permission of Delmar Learning, a division of Thomson Learning: http://www.thomsonrights.com.

key intervals throughout the school year as a means to translate static content standards into models of expected growth.

Prior Knowledge Assessment

Prior knowledge is essential to learning. In fact, the process of learning can be thought of as what one does to connect and reintegrate new understandings with existing knowledge. Prior knowledge includes formal learning, such as a preschooler learning the rule about not crossing the street without looking both ways, but it also includes a multitude of implicit, self-taught explanations about how the world works. These intuitions or self-taught theories can sometimes facilitate new learning, as when scientific explanations are easily mastered because they "make sense" and jibe with our previous experience. Intuitive theories can also be the source of serious misconceptions that hinder new learning and are relatively impervious to instructional change unless students are given a structured way to work through the inconsistencies between their intuitions and contradictory evidence.

Effective instructional strategies draw on students' prior knowledge as a resource. Moreover, by using knowledge-activation routines at the beginning of new lessons and units of study, teachers help students develop the habit of asking, when faced with a new learning or problem-solving task, "What do I already know to help me figure this out?" Many prior-knowledge activities, such as instructional conversations (Tharp and Gallimore, 1988) and K-W-L techniques[2] (Ogle, 1986), are not seen as assessments per se by either students or teachers. Nevertheless, they do yield valuable data for revising instruction, as when teachers find gaps in assumed knowledge or discover that students know far more about a topic than anticipated. Given the research evidence on the need to engage misconceptions when they occur, explicitly acknowledging assessed misconceptions as the reason for subsequent instructional activities could be a way to heighten students' awareness that assessment serves learning purposes.

Prior knowledge is more than a set of facts that a student has amassed at home and in previous grades. Prior knowledge also includes language patterns and ways of thinking that students develop through their social roles and cultural experiences. Differences in cultural practices can sometimes be misinterpreted by teachers as evidence of "deficits." For example, white middle-class children are more accustomed to being asked decontextualized questions like "What color is this?" than children from other social groups (Heath, 1983). Implicit rules of interaction can make it difficult for teachers to see the strengths of students outside their own social group unless they have a means for drawing out those strengths in a way that is culturally responsive. For example, Moll and others (1992) use "funds of knowledge" as a way to describe the household knowledge that children bring with them to school. This knowledge may be based, for example, on farming, carpentry, medicine, religion, childcare, and budget management activities, which can be used to support school knowledge.

As we have noted, novice teachers need to understand the role of prior knowledge in enabling, and sometimes impeding, new learning. And they need

---

[2]K-W-L refers to a technique in which teachers help students think about what they know, what they want to understand, and later, what they have learned.

to know strategies for eliciting prior knowledge in a way that allows students from different ethnic and cultural groups to bring relevant resources to bear. This is an important form of assessment.

Explicit Criteria and the Use of Rubrics

The formative assessment model requires that teacher and student have a shared understanding of the goals for learning. Furthermore, to really be helpful in learning, the goals cannot be vague and amorphous but must be reasonably specific. Frederiksen and Collins (1989) use the term *transparency* to express the idea that students must have a clear understanding of the criteria by which their work will be assessed. Understanding and internalizing the standards of excellence in a discipline—that is, what makes a good history paper or a good mathematical explanation—helps students develop the metacognitive aware-ness of what they need to attend to as they are writing or problem solving. In fact, learning the rules and forms of a discipline is part of learning the disci-pline, not just a means to justify grading.

Novice teachers should be able to develop rubrics that communicate the essential features of good work to students in age-appropriate language. Rubrics must capture what is most important to the *quality* of work and not just what is easiest to count or quantify. Wiggins (1993) pointed out, for example, that it was difficult to get English teachers to use how "interesting" a paper was (as well as how organized it was) as a basis for scoring, because it was harder to score "interesting" reliably. Yet writing papers that are interesting and com-pelling should ultimately be the goal of writing instruction. Novice teachers should be able to use student work to identify learning continua and to develop descriptors of performance at each level that clearly communicate each level's distinguishing characteristics.

Feedback

One of the oldest findings in psychological research (Thorndike, 1931/1968) is that feedback facilitates learning. Without feedback about conceptual errors or an inefficient backstroke, the learner is likely to persist in making the same mis-takes. In an extensive meta-analysis of 131 controlled studies, Kluger and DeNisi (1996) reported an average effect size or gain due to feedback of .40. They also acknowledged significant study variation with roughly one-third of studies showing negative effects. In attempting to identify characteristics of feedback most associated with positive effects, Kluger and DeNisi found that learning is more likely to be fostered when feedback focuses on features of the task and emphasizes learning goals. This important finding from the feedback literature is consistent with our previous argument for rubrics that allow performance to be judged in relation to well-defined criteria (rather than in comparison to other students), and it jibes with findings from the motivational literature discussed later in the context of grading practices.

According to research evidence, it is a mistake to give false praise in an effort to motivate students and boost self-esteem. At the same time, straightforward, let-the-chips-fall-where-they-may, negative feedback can undermine learning and students' willingness to make subsequent effort. Therefore an understanding of the motivational consequences of feedback is as important as knowing its cognitive purposes. The formative assessment model, consistent with the cognitive literature, shows that feedback is most effective when it focuses on particular qualities of a student's work in relation to established criteria, identifies strengths as well as weaknesses, and provides guidance about what to do to improve. In addition, teachers must establish a climate of trust and develop classroom norms that enable constructive criticism. This means that feedback must occur strategically throughout the learning process (not at the end when teaching on that topic is finished); teacher and students must have a shared understanding that the purpose of feedback is to facilitate learning; and it may mean that grading should be suspended during the formative stage. Given that teachers cannot frequently meet one-on-one with each student, classroom practices must allow for students to display their thinking so the teacher will be aware of it, and for students to learn to become increasingly effective critics of their own and each other's work.

Novice teachers should be able to analyze student work and identify patterns of errors and gaps that most need to be addressed (not every possible error). In an intervention study, Elawar and Corno (1985) found that teachers dramatically improved the effectiveness of feedback by focusing on these questions: "What is the key error? What is the probable reason the student made this error? How can I guide the student to avoid the error in the future?" (p. 166). Teachers must also understand the theory of how feedback enhances learning so that they can develop classroom routines that check for student understanding and ensure that students are not left alone to persist in bad habits or misconceptions.

Teaching and Assessing for Transfer

Transfer refers to the ability to use one's knowledge in new contexts. Transfer is obviously a goal of learning. What good is knowledge if it can't be accessed or applied? Yet, studies of students' abilities to use relevant information even from a recently successful lesson are notoriously disappointing. Transfer is inhibited when students learn by rote and go through mechanical routines to solve problems without thinking. Examples are numerous ranging from regrouping (or borrowing) by rote in second-grade arithmetic to "plug and chug" problem solutions in college physics. In contrast, expert-novice research and transfer studies show us that transfer is more likely to be supported when initial learning focuses on understanding of underlying principles, when cause-and-effect relationships and reasons why are explicitly considered, and when principles of application are directly engaged.

Teaching for transfer requires that initial instruction focus on understanding. It also means visibly working to extend students' understandings. For example, it should be commonplace—as soon as students appear to have mastered a new problem type or one way of solving a problem—for teachers to ask a new question that connects with but extends that knowledge. The two tasks in "Assessment Tasks Illustrating 'Find a Rule' and Near Transfer" are from *Measuring Up: Prototypes for Mathematics Assessment* by the Mathematical Sciences Education Board (1993). These are exemplary tasks in a number of respects. First, they illustrate that good assessment tasks can be interchangeable with good instructional tasks. Second, the sequencing of questions within each part clearly supports development of understanding of an underlying principle. Third, Part 2 can be thought of as a near-transfer task that can be used to make sure students can generalize what they learned in Part 1. However, they will have to think a little bit about the unique features of the new task. They cannot just apply the rule from Part 1 by rote to Part 2. One reason that experts have better transfer skills than novices is that they are able to recognize the features of problems that are the same and different from problems previously solved. Therefore it is important for students to learn to think specifically about how they can use what they already know. In this sense, strategies involved with teaching for transfer, especially far transfer, also dovetail with strategies used to assess prior knowledge.

Assessment Tasks Illustrating "Find a Rule" and Near Transfer

Part 1

All of the bridges in Part 1 are built with yellow rods for spans and red rods for supports, like the one shown here. This is a 2-span bridge like the one you just built. Note that the yellow rods are 5 cm long.

1. Now, build a 3-span bridge.
   a. How many yellow rods did you use? _____
   b. How long is your bridge? _____
   c. How many red rods did you use? _____
   d. How many rods did you use altogether? _____
2. Try to answer these questions without building a 5-span bridge. If you want, build a

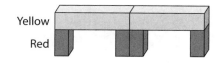

Figure 8.1

5-span bridge to check your answers.

    a. How many yellow rods would you need for a 5-span bridge? _____

    b. How long would your bridge be? _____

    c. How many red rods would you need? _____

    d. How many rods would you need altogether? _____

3. Without building a 12-span bridge, answer the following questions.

    a. How many yellow rods would you need for a 12-span bridge? _____

    b. How long would your bridge be? _____

    c. How many red rods would you need? _____

    d. How many rods would you need altogether? _____

4. How many yellow rods and red rods would you need to build a 28-span bridge? _____ yellow rods and _____red rods. Explain your answer.

5. Write a rule for figuring out the total number of rods you would need to build a bridge if you knew how many spans the bridge had.

6. How many yellow rods and red rods would you need to build a bridge that is 185 cm long? _____ yellow rods and _____red rods. Explain your answer.

Part 2

The bridges for this part are built like this 2-span bridge:

The black rods are 7 cm long, and the light green rods are 3 cm long. Notice that the supports are *shared* between spans, except at the ends.

1. Build a 3-span bridge of this same kind, with black and light green rods.

    a. How many black rods did you use? _____

    b. How long is your bridge? _____

    c. How many light green rods did you use? _____

    d. How many rods did you use altogether? _____

2. Try to answer these questions without building a 5-span bridge. If you want to, build a 5-span bridge to check your answers.

    a. How many black rods would you need for a 5-span bridge? _____

    b. How long would your bridge be? _____

    c. How many light green rods would you need? _____

    d. How many rods would you need altogether? _____

3. Without building a 13-span bridge, answer the following questions.

    a. How many black rods would you need for a 13-span bridge? _____

    b. How long would your bridge be? _____

    c. How many light green rods would you need? _____

    d. How many rods would you need altogether? _____

4. How many black rods and light green rods would you need to build a 56-span bridge? _____ black rods and _____ light green rods. Explain your answer.

5. Write a rule for figuring out how many rods you would need to build a bridge if you knew how many spans the bridge had.

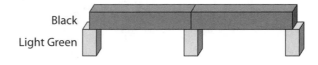

Black

Light Green

Figure 8.2

6. How many black rods and light green rods would you need to build a bridge that is at least 429 cm long? _____ black rods and _____ light green rods. Explain your answer.

Source: Reprinted with permission from *Measuring up: Prototypes for mathematics assessment* by the National Academy of Sciences, ©1993, courtesy of the National Academies Press, Washington, DC.

Novice teachers must understand the concept of transfer and know how to avoid narrow instruction-assessment matches that encourage rote learning. The ability to devise transfer tasks is an important component of the more general requirement that teachers be able to select and develop tasks that embody important learning goals. They also need to be able to assess initial understanding before working on extensions, because transfer cannot happen if the student is still struggling with initial concepts. Teachers' understanding of transfer and knowledge generalization will also be germane when we later consider appropriate preparation for high-stakes, external tests and the problems of too much teaching to the test.

Student Self-Assessment

Engaging students in critiquing their own work serves both cognitive and motivational purposes. Ultimately the habit of self-assessment leads to the self-monitoring of performance that is the goal of instructional scaffolding as well as the goal of Sadler's (1989) formative assessment model. The process of self-assessment builds on the benefits of explicit criteria by requiring students to think about and apply criteria in the context of their own work. In so doing, students make sense of and come to understand what the criteria mean in a deeper way than if they merely read a list. More broadly, this kind of supported practice—that is, where students learn strategies to monitor their own learning—helps develop students' metacognitive abilities. At the same time, self-critique can increase students' responsibility for their own learning and make the relationship between teacher and student more collaborative. This does not mean that teachers relinquish responsibility, but by sharing it, they gain greater student ownership, less distrust, and more appreciation that expectations are not capricious or out of reach. Furthermore, students begin to internalize the expectations, so they no longer belong only to the teacher.

In case studies of two Australian and English sites, Klenowski (1995) found that students who participated in self-evaluation became more interested in the criteria and substantive feedback than in their grade per se. Students also reported that they had to be more honest about their own work as well as being fair with other students, and they had to be prepared to defend their opinions in terms of the evidence. Klenowski's (1995) data support Wiggins' (1992) assertion that involving students in analyzing their own work builds ownership of the evaluation process and "makes it possible to hold students to higher standards because the criteria are clear and reasonable" (p. 30). In an experimental study by White and Frederickson (2000), students learned to use science inquiry criteria to evaluate their own work. As part of the protocol, students in the experimental group had to write a rationale each time they self-evaluated, pointing to the features of their work that supported their ratings. In addition, students used the criteria to give feedback to classmates when projects were presented orally in class. Compared to controls, students who had participated in self-assessment produced projects that were much more highly rated by their teachers (on the shared criteria). In addition, initially low-achieving students showed dramatic gains on a measure of conceptual understanding.

Novice teachers should understand the basic principles of cognitive and motivational theory that explain why self-assessment works to improve learning. (Research findings about the effects of evaluation on students' motivation are taken up in the next section.) Teachers should also know some simple strategies for including self-assessment and peer-assessment as a normal part of classroom instruction. For example, "author's chair" is a literacy practice where students learn explicitly the norms for listening and giving feedback to classmates about a piece of writing (Routman, 2000). Conferencing with students can also be a means to see if they are developing the ability to self-evaluate. Both the Klenowski and White and Frederiksen studies noted earlier involved a self-assessment step that became a part of normal instruction. Importantly, the purpose of engaging students in self-assessment is not to give a grade but to gain insight that can be used to further learning.

Evaluation of Teaching

The formative assessment model focuses on student learning. An equally important use of classroom assessment is the evaluation and improvement of teaching. At the same time that teachers are gathering evidence about student understanding, they should also be considering what teaching practices are and are not working, and what new strategies are needed. The NCTM (1995) *Assessment Standards for School Mathematics* identified three types of instructional decisions that are informed by assessment data: moment-to-moment decisions, short-term planning, and long-term planning. When assessment and instruction are effectively intertwined, then assessment insights can be used in real time to adjust instruction. For example, if several students are making the same type of error, it may be useful to stop and spend some time on the underlying misconception. Whereas formative assessment focuses on what the student can do to improve, the parallel evaluation of teaching asks whether students have had adequate opportunity to learn. This leads to consideration of how instruction can be modified or extended so that adequate opportunities are provided for each student to master the concepts or skills.

Teachers who are reflective about their practice use data systematically to make judgments about the specific aspects of instructional strategies that may be hindering learning. They look for explanations of learning success or failure, and especially for teaching decisions that may be the cause. For example, they may ask questions such as: "Are there certain tasks that seem to elicit a great deal of student thinking because they are high-interest and allow multiple solutions? Are there some activities that engage most of the boys but leave the girls slumped in their seats? Do second-language learners struggle with assignments when there is not adequate time to talk about relevant background knowledge or to clarify expectations?" In a now classic reexamination of his own teaching, Mazur (1997) discovered that students could do problems like number 2 in "Assessing Conceptual Understanding," but not problems like number 1. His extended analysis of why students could do algorithmic problems but not conceptual ones and what he was doing to foster their search for recipes (including the form of his exams), led Mazur to completely revise his teaching to focus on more active learning strategies.

Assessing Conceptual Understanding

1. A series circuit consists of three identical light bulbs connected to a battery as shown here. When the switch S is closed, do the following increase, decrease, or stay the same?
   (a) The intensities of bulbs A and B
   (b) The intensity of bulb C
   (c) The current drawn from the battery
   (d) The voltage drop across each bulb
   (e) The power dissipated in the circuit

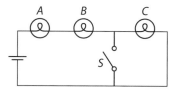

Figure 8.3

2. For the circuit shown, calculate (a) the current in the 2-Ω resistor and (b) the potential difference between points P and Q.

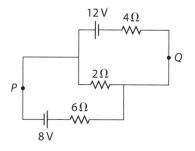

Figure 8.4

Conceptual (top) and conventional question (bottom) on the subject of DC circuits.

Source: From Mazur, Eric. *Peer instruction: A user's manual,* 1st ed., © 1997. Reprinted by permission of Pearson Education, Inc., Upper Saddle River, NJ.

When teachers use assessment data to modify their instruction they are also setting an important example for students. Shepard (2000) argued that "if we want to develop a community of learners—where students naturally seek feedback and critique their own work—then it is reasonable that teachers would model this same commitment to using data systematically as it applies to their own role in the teaching and learning process" (p. 12). Novice teachers should understand the joint purposes of assessment for the improvement of both teaching and learning. They should know how to use assessment data in instructional planning and be able to communicate with students about changes they are making based on feedback received from student work, student questions, or comments.

A Repertoire of Assessment Tools

Although experienced teachers are more adept at using a wide variety of assessment strategies, even beginning teachers should be familiar with a range of assessment tools and know how they fit into instructional routines. Assessment tools include oral questioning of students, observation, written work products, oral presentations, interviews, projects, portfolios, tests, and quizzes. These strategies may be either formal, where students know that they are being assessed, or informal, where the gathering of assessment data is done entirely within the context of ongoing instruction. As suggested earlier, there does not need to be an exact equating of informal-formative assessment, nor of formal-summative assessment. Although these pairings are the most common in traditional practice, they are not necessary. Indeed, efforts to change the culture of the classroom to focus more on learning and less on grading might suggest that fewer assignments be graded and that more formal assessment occasions be used clearly as a means to improve subsequent performance, with opportunities for revision built in.

Flexible use of multiple forms of assessment is important for several reasons. First, the goal of capturing important learning is best served by using a wide variety of formats. Second, the availability of multiple formats makes it more feasible to integrate assessment with instruction. Third, multiple sources of evidence protect against the biases inherent in any one form of measurement. Because it is not possible to see inside a student's head to directly measure understanding, we rely on various indirect means, such as how he explains or how he approaches a problem. Each indirect way of assessing has its own biases or artifacts—things that are features of the assessment strategy and not the thing we are really trying to assess. For example, a student may have oral or written language problems that inhibit demonstration of his mathematical understanding, but when asked to demonstrate what he knows with symbols or manipulatives, he is able to do so.

Ideally, the assessor looks for convergence across sources of evidence to be able to evaluate the level of a student's understanding. However, teachers can also learn from the pattern of differences, especially if a student consistently shows the same pattern of strengths and weaknesses over time. Then it becomes important for the teacher to draw on the student's strength in developing conceptual understanding, while at the same time, not ignoring areas of weakness. In fact, having insights in math could enable a student first to agree with another student's explanation, then begin to verbalize her own explanations, and finally to draw pictures or graphic representations and develop proficiency in writing explanations. Note that multiple forms of assessment also help in teaching for transfer. Although subject matter experts may think that they have developed tasks that measure the same underlying construct, empirical evidence suggests that format makes a big difference in how readily students can solve problems. As we saw in the transfer literature, students who have learned and applied concepts in a variety of contexts are better able to generalize their knowledge to new settings.

Novice teachers should know how to use a variety of assessment strategies so as to capture important learning goals and support the learning process. They should understand the ideal of one-on-one tutoring-assessment interviews and know, realistically, how to create opportunities for this same type of insight from ongoing classroom interactions and written products.

Equity Concerns

Assessment, like instruction, will be ineffective if it is unresponsive to differences in children's experiences and cultural knowledge. Several of the assessment strategies discussed earlier clearly require that children's home, community, and prior schooling experiences be taken into account. For example, while learning progressions help envision the next steps in learning, developmental trajectories in some fields may be different for English language learners than they are for monolingual English speakers. Similarly, third-grade students who are still struggling readers should not be taught using only first-grade early reading materials, even if they are reading first-grade-level texts. The materials they use need to be designed to build their content knowledge on grade level and to tap their interests and experiences.

Prior knowledge assessment is one of the most important assessment strategies to ensure that students have equal opportunity to learn. Ironically, the validity of efforts to assess prior knowledge are themselves affected by a student's knowledge base and by cultural practices. Using skills checklists or a pretest that mirrors the end-of-unit test is likely to underestimate the relevant knowledge of less sophisticated members of the class because they will be unable to make the translation between pretest vocabulary and their own intuitive knowledge gained in other contexts. Open discussions or conversations are more likely to elicit a more coherent version of students' initial conceptual understandings and the reasoning behind their explanations (Yackel, Cobb, and Wood, 1991).

Multiple modes of assessment are also important as an ongoing part of instruction to ensure equal opportunity to learn. Teachers must become familiar with relevant experiences and discourse patterns in diverse communities so that children who come to school with very different experiences will be able to demonstrate their competence rather than appear deficient because they are unfamiliar with the teacher's mode of questioning (Heath, 1983).

Putting it All Together

In the past, assessment training for teacher education candidates focused on learning to write and score different kinds of tests, especially essay and multiple-choice tests. Today, teacher candidates are being asked to do something much more complex. As documented in Chapter Nine, effective classroom management depends centrally on meaningful curriculum and engaging pedagogy. In addition, the formative assessment processes described here must be an integral part of curriculum and teaching. Formal tests and instructional tasks in which assessment is embedded must capture important learning goals because they become the enacted curriculum, and the processes of interaction (written feedback, conferencing, oral questioning, students commenting on each others' work, and self assessment) must all be understood as being for the purpose of learning. Thus formative assessment practices contribute to, but also require support from, a larger shift toward the development of a community of learners.

Idealized assessment systems are often viewed by novice and veteran teachers alike as too daunting to undertake. Ironically, once they are built into classroom routines, these strategies are not onerous and do not take away from instructional time, but research on reform has found the change process itself to be extremely time consuming (Putnam and Borko 1997; Putnam and Borko, 2000; Shepard, 1995). These findings suggest that it is important for teacher candidates to have access to clinical experiences where mentor teachers are using strategies such as writing portfolios and writing conferences or reform-based mathematics curricula typically structured around extended problems for students to solve and discuss. They need to gain experience with formative assessment that is already integrated with instruction. Some formative assessment strategies are so seamless a part of instruction that there is no need to limit their intrusion on instruction. This is true, for example, when students are explaining their thinking to the class or in a small group. Other strategies, such as the formal aspects of scoring portfolios or conducting one-on-one assessments, tap the scarce resource of teacher time and must be used strategically—although as the account of Akeem illustrated, if used effectively, they can produce important gains for individual children. Thus the time an assessment strategy may take away from other types of teacher-student interaction should be considered "worth it" if the insights gained help the teacher work with students more effectively. For example, one-on-one assessments with only two or three students can often help the teacher gain an understanding of how students are thinking that will be relevant to many more students in the class.

SUMMATIVE ASSESSMENT AND GRADING

Formative and summative assessments have different purposes. One enables learning and the other documents achievement. To be mutually supportive, formative and summative assessments must be conceptually aligned. They must do a good job of representing important learning goals and should use the same broad range of tasks and problem types to tap students' understandings. However, summative assessments should not be mere repeats of earlier formative tasks. Rather, they should be culminating performances that invite students to exhibit mastery and to use their knowledge in ways that generalize and extend what has come before. Summative assessments can be thought of as important milestones on the same learning continua that undergird formative assessment.

In this section, we consider first the purposes for summative assessments and what can be learned from them. We follow this with a summary of research on current grading practices and then reprise concerns about the substantive quality of classroom assessments. After reviewing relevant empirical findings from the measurement, cognitive psychology, and motivational psychology literatures, we outline the grading practices that are expected to be both valid in reporting achievement and conducive to student learning. Most importantly, we address the relationship between summative and formative assessment practices. A list of best practices for grading does not automatically produce a system that is compatible with a learning community and with the formative assessment model. However, if one understands that the underlying theory or model of assessment should be one that supports the developing competence of students, then formative and summative assessment practices can be coherent and mutually supportive.

Context for Summative Assessment

Most teachers dislike evaluating their students and giving grades (Brookhart, 1993; Nava and Loyd, 1992). However, there is some evidence of positive cognitive benefits from summative assessments that should be considered along with more troubling findings from the motivational literature. Significantly, students appear to study more and learn more if they expect to be tested. As summarized by Crooks (1988), the benefits from testing can be explained by three factors. First, follow-up testing engages students in review and relearning, which works like a limited form of distributed practice. Second, the testing experience itself engages students in mental processing of the content, although this depends very much on the quality of the test questions. Third, for good or ill, the test directs attention to the topics and skills tested, which has implications for subsequent study.

Cognitive theory also suggests that students benefit from the opportunity to demonstrate competence and to work toward increasing proficiency as defined by criteria that are mutually understood by teacher, student, and the community (Pellegrino, Baxter, and Glaser, 1999). As described earlier, providing students with a clear understanding of goals makes goals more attainable, and helping students learn the meaning of criteria in the context of their own work helps them develop the metacognitive awareness of what they need to do to improve. Internalizing what criteria mean in a particular discipline is not just about learning the rules for grading—it literally means learning the discipline itself.

Although there have not been systematic studies of circumstances where students received only feedback from formative assessment with no summative assessment, cognitive theory would not predict that withholding summative evaluations would improve learning. In fact, from a cognitive perspective, the best system would be one where formative and summative assessments were mutually aligned with conceptually oriented learning goals, and where summative assessments were used as milestones of accomplishment (perhaps acknowledged by family and friends) following successful learning periods supported by formative assessment.

Audiences for Grading

There are three important audiences for grades: parents, external users such as employers and college admissions officers, and students themselves. Evidence is limited about what kind of information parents find useful. Shepard and Bliem (1995) found that 77 percent of the parents of third graders whom they sampled placed the highest value on talking with the teacher about their child's progress. Sixty percent of these parents said that seeing graded samples of their children's work was useful. Forty-three percent found report cards useful, and only 14 percent were interested in standardized test scores. In interviews, parents explained that talking with the teacher was valued most because of the firsthand knowledge such conversations gave them of their children's specific strengths and weaknesses in the context of the classroom curriculum. One additional generalization from this research has significant implications for grading practices: parents want normative comparisons. However, rather than requiring information from a norm-referenced test, they appear to be willing to have teachers tell them how their child is doing in relation to grade-level expectations. This substitution of grade-level standards for norm-referenced comparisons is important in the context of standards-based reporting and, as we will see, because of the demotivating consequences of normative grading practices.

Students become the primary audience for grades because what others are told about their achievement comes to play a powerful role in learning interactions. By the time students reach high school, there is an expectation that grades should have meaning for external audiences. For example, a grade of A or B in English should mean that the student can write a well-organized essay; and a G.P.A. of 3.0 should mean that a senior is well prepared for college work.

In contrast, it is much more difficult to conduct formal assessments of young children and much less necessary. Therefore the salience of grades in classroom life should be very different for young children than for high school students. In "Guidelines for Appropriate Assessment for Children Ages 3 through 8" we have reproduced assessment principles from the position statement on appropriate curriculum and assessment practices for children ages three through eight issued by the National Association for the Education of Young Children (NAEYC) (1990). These principles emphasize that assessments of young children should be based on observations conducted during the ordinary activities of classroom life and should be used for formative purposes and to report to parents. The NAEYC concluded that for children in the early grades, "The method of reporting to parents [should] not rely on letter or numerical grades but rather [should] provide more meaningful, descriptive information in narrative form" (p. 15).

Guidelines for Appropriate Assessment for Children Ages 3 through 8

1. Curriculum and assessment are integrated throughout the program; assessment is congruent with and relevant to the goals, objectives, and content of the program.
2. Assessment results in benefits to the child, such as needed adjustments in the curriculum or more individualized instruction and improvements in the program.
3. Children's development and learning in all the domains—physical, social, emotional, and cognitive—and their dispositions and feelings are informally and routinely assessed by teachers' observing children's activities and interactions, listening to them as they talk, and using children's constructive errors to understand their learning.
4. Assessment provides teachers with useful information to successfully fulfill their responsibilities: to support children's learning and development, to plan for individuals and groups, and to communicate with parents.
5. Assessment involves regular and periodic observation of the child in a wide variety of circumstances that are representative of the child's behavior in the program over time.
6. Assessment relies primarily on procedures that reflect the ongoing life of the classroom and typical activities of the children. Assessment avoids approaches that place children in artificial situations, impede the usual learning and developmental experiences in the classroom, or divert children from their natural learning processes.
7. Assessment relies on demonstrated performance during real, not contrived, activities, for example, real reading and writing activities rather than only skills testing (Engel, 1990; Teale, 1988).
8. Assessment utilizes an array of tools and a variety of processes including, but not limited to, collections of representative work by children (artwork, stories they write, tape recordings of their reading), records of systematic observations by teachers, records of conversations and interviews with children, teachers' summaries of children's progress as individuals and as groups (Chittenden and Courtney, 1989; Goodman, Goodman, and Hood, 1989).

9. Assessment recognizes individual diversity of learners and allows for differences in styles and rates of learning. Assessment takes into consideration children's ability in English, their stage of language acquisition, and whether they have been given the time and opportunity to develop proficiency in their native language as well as in English.

10. Assessment supports children's development and learning; it does not threaten children's psychological safety or feelings of self-esteem.

11. Assessment supports parents' relationships with their children and does not undermine parents' confidence in their children's or their own ability, nor does it devalue the language and culture of the family.

12. Assessment demonstrates children's overall strengths and progress, what children can do, not just their wrong answers or what they cannot do or do not know.

13. Assessment is an essential component of the teacher's role. Because teachers can make maximal use of assessment results, the teacher is the primary assessor.

14. Assessment is a collaborative process involving children and teachers, teachers and parents, school and community. Information from parents about each child's experiences at home is used in planning instruction and evaluating children's learning. Information obtained from assessment is shared with parents in language they can understand.

15. Assessment encourages children to participate in self-evaluation.

16. Assessment addresses what children can do independently and what they can demonstrate with assistance, because the latter shows the direction of their growth.

17. Information about each child's growth, development, and learning is systematically collected and recorded at regular intervals. Information such as samples of children's work, descriptions of their performance, and anecdotal records is used for planning instruction and communicating with parents.

18. A regular process exists for periodic information sharing between teachers and parents about children's growth and development and performance. The method of reporting to parents does not rely on letter or numerical grades but rather provides more meaningful, descriptive information in narrative form.

Source: Reprinted with permission from the National Association for the Education of Young Children (NAEYC)(1990), *Guidelines for appropriate curriculum content and assessment in programs serving children ages 3 through 8.* Washington, DC: NAEYC, pp. 14–15.

Research on Current Practice

Brookhart (1994) identified nineteen studies published within ten years of her review that examined teachers' grading practices. Study methods varied from teacher surveys to case studies. Supported by highly consistent results across studies, Brookhart identified the following generalizations:

1. Teachers try hard to be fair to students, including informing them up front what the components of a grade will be (Briscoe, 1991; Brookhart, 1993; Stiggins, Frisbie, and Griswold, 1989).

2. Achievement measures, especially tests, are the major components in grades, but effort and ability are also commonly considered (Agnew, 1985; Frary, Cross, and Weber, 1993; Friedman and Manley, 1991;

Griswold and Griswold, 1992; Gullickson, 1985; Manke and Loyd, 1990, 1991; Nava and Loyd, 1992; Pilcher-Carlton and Oosterhof, 1993; Stiggins and others, 1989; Terwilliger, 1987; Wood, Bennett, Wood, and Bennett, 1990).

3. There is a grade-level effect on grading practices. Elementary teachers use more informal evidence and observation. At the secondary level, paper-and-pencil achievement measures and other written activities compose a much larger portion of the grade (Bateson, 1990; Griswold and Griswold, 1992; Gullickson, 1985; Nava and Loyd, 1992; Wilson, 1990).

4. There is individual variation among teachers' grading practices. Different teachers perceive the meaning and purpose of grades differently, and consider achievement and nonachievement factors differently (Brookhart, 1993; Frary and others, 1993; Nava and Loyd, 1992; Pilcher-Carlton and Oosterhof, 1993).

The practices identified in findings 1 and 3—that teachers try to be fair and communicate grading standards and that they use more informal evidence at younger grade levels—are consistent with research-based professional standards. However, findings 2 and 4 regarding the use of effort and ability factors to adjust achievement grades create dilemmas for grading because these factors are difficult to measure accurately, they may create inequities or invite students to dissemble, and they may confuse audiences about the meaning of grades. Cizek, Fitzgerald, and Rachor (1995/1996) argued that teachers use a diverse array of nonachievement factors in ways that create a "success bias" helping them to raise student grades.

In trying to explain the large gap between practice and theory, Brookhart (1994) advances several arguments for this practice. Teachers tend to see effort as part of "earning" a grade; work habits are closely related to the feedback that students need about how to do better; and participation is essential to the student's relationship with the teacher as coach. Although it is critical to understand teachers' viewpoints and the practical realities of classrooms, teachers' intuitive beliefs about what is fair and motivating to students may not always be supported by research evidence. We must also consider whether teachers are using effort grades to *manage* student behavior, which is not the same thing as creating a learning environment that is *motivating* to students. In a case study of teachers' assessment methods (Lorsbach, Tobin, Briscoe, and LaMaster, 1992) a major finding was that "Tasks and systems of aggregating scores often reward completion of tasks and motivation to learn rather than what is known" (p. 310). Teachers sometimes appeared to be operating within a "school is work" metaphor (Marshall, 1988), creating an elaborate system to keep track of student work, but without always emphasizing the quality or content of that work.

Content and Format

We addressed the issue of assessment content previously in the context of formative assessment and will visit it again when considering the effect of external tests on teaching and learning in the classroom. The content of tests—what gets tested and how it is tested—and the content of assignments that are evaluated for a grade communicate the goals of instruction to students and focus their attention and effort. Note that merely giving points for assignments does not ensure attention, if the quality of work is never examined (see Lorsbach and others, 1992, noted earlier).

In 1983, Fleming and Chambers analyzed 8,800 test questions from elementary through high school tests and found that nearly 80 percent were at the lowest level in Bloom's taxonomy—the *knowledge* level. Similar results were found a decade later in a nationally representative survey by Madaus, West, Harmon, Lomax, and Viator (1992). The researchers found that 53 percent of high school and 73 percent of elementary math teachers reported using textbook tests at least once a month. Based on a content analysis, Madaus and others (1992) found that only 3 percent of items on text-embedded final tests sampled high-level conceptual knowledge and about 5 percent sampled higher-level thinking skills of any type. The remaining 95 percent of items sampled recall of information, computation, and use of algorithms and formulas in routine problems similar to those students had worked in the text. A higher percentage of teachers reported making their own tests, but when these were examined in field studies, Madaus and others (1992) found them to be close adaptations of textbook tests. More recently, Cizek and others (1995/1996) reported a surprising finding that novice teachers were more likely to develop their own assessments than were experienced teachers who tended to rely on commercially prepared tests. This finding could be the result of more attention to assessment in teacher education with changes in preparation standards in the early 1990s, as well as to beginning teachers having more access to reform-based materials and problem types with the advent of standards-based reforms.

As we have stressed previously, assessment reform has been an integral part of educational reform because of the need to engage students in authentic tasks so as to develop, use, and extend their knowledge. More meaningful work aimed at conceptual understanding not only provides better evaluation data about how well students are doing; it also has both cognitive and motivational benefits. In an early study, Marton and Saljo (1976) found that students' approaches to learning tasks could be categorized as either *deep* or *surface* approaches. Deep approaches involved an active search for meaning, underlying principles, and structures that linked different concepts. Surface approaches focused primarily on memorization of isolated facts without looking for connections among those facts. Although other factors affected students' tendency to use deep or surface approaches, especially interest and motivation, their perceptions of the demands of anticipated evaluations were clearly influential in their choice of strategy. These research findings have been cor-roborated in subsequent studies examining the link between evaluation format and the study strategies of college students (Crooks, 1988).

For these reasons, many researchers and educators have worked to develop more thoughtful performance assessments that require and promote deeper analysis and learning than do close-ended items primarily measuring recall and recognition. Subject matter experts value conceptually rich instructional tasks because they capture what is most important for students to learn. Cognitivists prefer challenging tasks because they engage students in reasoning and they support generalization, if transfer tasks are used as a normal part of instruction. In a practice-oriented synthesis of research on motivation, Stipek (2002) explained that authentic tasks also increase student motivation to learn. Tasks that require higher-order thinking and active problem solving are intrinsically more interesting than memorizing or applying simple procedures. For example, Mitchell (1993) found that students' beliefs about the real-world significance of what they are learning were a strong predictor of their interest and enjoyment in math class. Challenging tasks increase intrinsic motivation by enhancing students' feeling of competence. Newmann (1992), for example, found that students give the highest interest ratings to classes that make them think hard and require them to participate actively in thinking and learning.

Grades and Motivation

The most devastating evidence showing the negative effects of many grading and schooling practices comes from the motivational literature. Strikingly, in a comprehensive review of research on children's motivation, Wigfield, Eccles, and Rodriguez (1998) report that many aspects of classroom organization have such pervasive negative effects that children's competence beliefs, achievement goals, interest in school subjects, and intrinsic motivation to learn all decline as students move through the elementary and middle school years.

With respect to grading practices, the most important issues have to do with the role of grades as rewards (or punishments), students' orientations toward performance or learning goals, and the use of normative versus mastery evaluation standards. These factors, along with other factors such as students' loci of causality and feelings of competence, all interact in complex ways. Here we summarize only the most significant and consistent patterns.

The use of grades as rewards contributes to what Lave and Wenger (1991) termed the "commoditization of learning" (p. 112). When there is no cultural value for increasing one's skill and participation in an endeavor, the only reason to participate is to obtain surface knowledge that can be displayed for evaluation. In reviews of experimental studies, researchers found that the use of external rewards can actually undermine students' intrinsic interest in a task (Deci and Ryan, 1985; Lepper, 1983), and, as summarized by Stipek (1996), rewards work to decrease intrinsic motivation when they are perceived as controlling and are not directly related to successful performance. Consistent with the positive findings from research on feedback, rewards or praise that convey positive information about competence are more likely to increase intrinsic motivation.

Perhaps the most serious negative consequences of traditional grading practices have come from the use of normative comparisons. As Ames (1984) suggested, competitive class structures make social comparisons and judgments about ability more salient. In a series of studies, Butler (1987, 1988) and Butler and Nisan (1986) found that normatively distributed grades resulted in lower interest, less willingness to persist, and lower performance compared to students who received substantive feedback. In a classic study, Harackiewicz, Abrahams, and Wageman (1987) found that evaluation based on social norms reduced interest in a task whereas evaluation based on achieving a predetermined standard increased interest. Stipek's (1996) general conclusion from this literature was that evaluation, especially of difficult tasks, tends to undermine intrinsic interest. However, the exception she identified is noteworthy and foreshadows our own recommendations for grading practices: "Substantive evaluation that provides information about competencies and guidance for future efforts, and evaluation that is based on mastery rather than social norms, however, appear not to have these negative effects and can even enhance intrinsic interest in academic tasks" (p. 99).

Findings about the effects of rewards are closely related to research on students' goal orientations. Dweck (1986) distinguished between children with mastery goals and those with performance goals. These dispositions are independent of students' academic abilities. Students with mastery goals are intrinsically motivated. They seek challenging tasks and enjoy opportunities to develop new competencies. They are less likely to be fearful of evaluation because they see the teacher as a resource. When students with a mastery orientation are faced with a difficult task, they are likely to persist, maintain a positive attitude, and look for solution strategies. A mastery orientation has also been termed a *task orientation* by related theories. In contrast, students with a performance orientation are extrinsically motivated. They are more concerned about looking competent rather than being competent and will tend to avoid situations where they might appear to be incompetent. Related theories refer to structures that induce a performance orientation as ego-involving environments. When faced with a difficult task, performance-oriented students will often comment on their lack of ability, act bored or anxious, and exhibit a marked deterioration in performance. Dweck came to call these behaviors "learned helplessness." Because of their fear of evaluation, students in this category may try to hide their lack of understanding from the teacher.

Importantly, mastery versus goal orientations are not fixed student attributes; they can be created or elicited to different degrees by the learning environment and have been experimentally induced (Elliot and Dweck, 1988). In a study of college students, Benware and Deci (1984) found very different levels of conceptual understanding in the group that was told they would be tested at the end of the study versus the group that was told that they would need to teach the material to others. Ames (1992) and Stipek (1996) identified the following classroom practices as those likely to foster a learning orientation among students:

- Provide diverse opportunities to demonstrate mastery.

- Adapt instruction to students' knowledge, understanding, and personal experience.

- Provide opportunities for students to participate in decision making and take responsibility for their own learning.

- Emphasize effort, learning, and working hard rather than performing or getting the right answer.

- Treat errors and mistakes as a normal part of learning.

- Evaluate students' progress and mastery, rather than only outcomes, and provide students opportunity to improve.

- Allow sufficient time for different students to complete their work.

When and How to Grade

Given the known negative effects of grading, a critical question becomes "How often to engage in summative assessment?" Measurement specialists argue for frequent grading of assignments to gather sufficient data to ensure reliability. Cognitivists want students to have practice with the criteria that will be used to evaluate culminating performances. However, the formative assessment model and motivation research argue that grading could undermine students' learning orientation. Therefore to make formative assessment truly for learning, teachers may need to postpone giving grades or use only student self- and peer assessment and, when needed, provide "as if" grades to help students stay focused on substantive feedback. Most certainly, teachers should avoid interrupting and judging for a grade the quality of learning that is still in progress. Of course the issue of reliability is important. And students should not be graded on the basis of only one or two isolated formal tests. However, if summative assessments are embedded in learning progressions, then the reliability of graded events is supported by other evidence of each student's developing competence along that underlying continuum.

Summative assessments and the grades based on them should represent achievement. However, consistent with Stipek's (1996) review of motivation research noted earlier, evaluation of achievement should be based on mastery standards rather than social norms. Achievement-based grades will be more transparently aligned with feedback on the same standards used for formative assessment and will communicate better to external audiences. In heterogeneous classrooms, grading in terms of mastery standards will require other support systems for students of different abilities. These should include strategies such as differential pacing for learning and timing of benchmark assessments; identification and assessment of intermediate, attainable goals; and differential scaffolding. If taken seriously, the commitment that grades represent achievement could mean reducing or doing away with various elements of compliance grading such as extra credit points on unrelated tasks, points for turning in note cards and preliminary drafts, points for turning in homework that is never graded, and so forth. The effects of assignments that help students learn should be evaluated ultimately in culminating assessments where that learning should be manifest. At the same time, other ways of helping students focus on learning rather than merely worrying about grades would be allowed, when they provide opportunities for students to develop and demonstrate mastery. These would include routine revisions and regrading of work to meet standards, replacement assignments and replacement tests, and throwing out test scores when learning is verified by subsequent assessments. The key is the focus on ultimate learning.

EXTERNAL, LARGE-SCALE ASSESSMENTS

National, state, and district-level assessments are used to collect data to answer the questions of policymakers at some distance from the classroom. Ideally, collecting information to monitor trends in student achievement would be no more disruptive than reporting attendance data. Yet, because of the public attention and consequences attached to achievement scores, external tests can have profound effects on what goes on inside of classrooms. Although teachers seldom have the power to determine the content and design of external assessments, they do normally have control over instructional decisions that can increase positive effects and mitigate the negative effects of external tests.

In this section, we first summarize what teachers need to know about the purposes of external tests and about the relationship of testing purpose to both test design and test validity. Then we review the research on the positive and negative effects of high-stakes testing. *High-stakes* is the term used to refer to accountability tests that have serious consequences for schools, teachers, or students. Given what is known about the effects of testing, it is possible to recommend instructional practices that protect against curriculum distortion while at the same time ensuring that students receive adequate test preparation. Related strategies, based on a domain analysis of the high-stakes test, can also be used to ensure valid interpretation of test results. Finally, we consider important uses of large-scale assessment results to evaluate curriculum and improve one's teaching.

Purposes, Design, and Validity of Large-Scale Assessments

Large-scale assessments serve distinctly different purposes from classroom assessments. They are used to monitor achievement trends over time, to evaluate educational programs, or to hold districts, schools, and teachers accountable. In some states, they are used to report on the performance of individual students or to determine high school graduation or grade-to-grade promotion. Teachers can be the most effective in dealing with large-scale assessments if they know what they are good for as well as what their limitations might be. For example, it has been beneficial to have data from the National Assessment of Educational Progress (NAEP) to document the achievement gap between majority and minority groups in the United States, as well as the progress made over the last thirty years toward closing that gap. Data from state assessments can be used to identify schools that have had the most sustained success in raising the achievement of low-socioeconomic students and to identify the schools with the greatest needs for improvement. Most importantly for teachers, state tests that do a good job of representing curriculum frameworks and conceptual learning goals can be used to evaluate one's own curriculum and instruction to identify those aspects that are more or less effective.

Technical testing standards of the American Educational Research Association, American Psychological Association, and National Council on Measurement in Education (1999) require that tests be developed and evaluated for the specific use for which they are intended. A test designed and validated for one purpose may not be valid for other purposes. Because large-scale assessments are used to answer broad policy questions, assessment design must be tailored to serve this purpose. For example, testing procedures must be standardized to ensure comparability of achievement results across schools or for different groups of students over time. Comparisons would be invalid if one school took the test in March and another in May or if one group of students received help from their teachers but another group worked independently. Comparative data purposes also require that test content be relatively broad even if this means that the level of the test is too easy for some students or too difficult for others. In contrast, classroom assessments are only useful if they are closely focused on students' specific strengths and weaknesses. Pellegrino, Chudowsky, and Glaser (2001) referred to these tensions as the inevitable trade-offs in assessment design.

Because of the consequences associated with test results, large-scale assessments must meet more stringent standards for technical accuracy than any one classroom assessment. In classrooms, teachers assess on an ongoing basis and have the luxury of revising decisions as new insights are gained about students' developing understandings. For practical reasons, external assessments must also be efficient and cost-effective. Because they are not tied closely to ongoing instruction, they should take as little time as possible away from regular instruction. The desire for efficiency, however, often exacerbates the lack of authenticity in problem types and writing tasks used in large-scale assessments. Some features of present-day large-scale assessments, such as reliability of school scores, are essential to ensure that the assessments serve their intended purpose of allowing comparisons across sites. Other features, such as overreliance on multiple-choice question formats, are an artifact of cost constraints and desires for efficiency in an era when government has substantially increased the amount of testing required. Teachers should have an appreciation of what features of large-scale assessment are essential to its purpose and which features are rightly criticized. They cannot ask that state assessments share all the characteristics of good classroom assessments, but they could ask that state assessments become more like the best existing examples of large-scale assessment.

Knowing What Students Know (Pellegrino and others, 2001) was a landmark report by a National Academy of Sciences committee. The authors brought together the findings from cognitive science and measurement research to make recommendations for improved assessment systems. They identified several alternatives, such as curriculum-embedded assessments, that would make it possible to do a better job of representing the complexity of student learning and still ensure comparability of data. For the future, they envisioned a more balanced assessment system in which classroom and large-scale assessment would work together in a more coherent and supportive fashion. Coherence between the two levels of assessment would require that both share the same underlying model of learning. This means that in addition to being tied to the same curriculum frameworks, the two levels of assessment should also hold in common the full range of cognitive demands, similar tasks and means for eliciting student proficiency, common standards for judging the quality of student work, and the same underlying continua or benchmarks representing how student proficiencies are expected to develop over time.

As we discuss later, teachers need to be able to analyze their own state or district accountability test in relation to this ideal. The best state assessments include tasks that align with professional curriculum standards and represent ambitious learning goals. Reflecting upon one's teaching and revising instruction to improve student performance on exemplary tasks should enhance not constrain student learning. In contrast, some state tests ask only closed-form questions about a limited range of content. As we discuss in the following section, teachers should be wary about allowing such assessments to drive most instruction in the classroom.

Research on Testing Effects

When standards-based educational reform began in the late 1980s, one of its defining principles was that accountability assessments must be improved to lead instructional change in a positive rather than negative direction. Summarizing research on effects from basic-skills accountability testing, Resnick and Resnick (1992) concluded that assessors get what they assess, do not get what they do not assess, and therefore should build assessments toward which they want educators to teach (p. 59). Similarly, in their conception of systemic school reform, Smith and O'Day (1990) argued that the pressure on teachers to tailor their instruction to the form and content of standardized tests "might be productive if tests were constructed to measure complex thinking and problem-solving and thus served to move curriculum and instruction in the direction of developing these skills" (p. 243). In response to these ideas, many state testing programs were revised in the early 1990s to include more open-ended problem types and to reflect more challenging learning goals.

In keeping with the original intention of standards-based reform, a number of studies have shown that these kinds of large-scale assessments can influence instruction in demonstrably positive ways. For example, in an early study of testing that included more open-ended tasks, teachers reported that they were having their students write more essays because of the state's new writing test and that their students' writing had improved (Shepard and Dougherty, 1991). In a study of Kentucky's Instructional Results Information System (KIRIS), which included a writing and mathematics portfolio and performance tasks, Koretz, Barron, Mitchell, and Stecher (1996) found that, consistent with the goals of the program, four-fifths of teachers reported increasing the emphasis or instructional time devoted to problem solving, communicating mathematically, and writing. More recently, Stecher and Chun (2001) surveyed Washington state teachers who reported substantial increases in the amount of time spent teaching probability and statistics and the mathematical processes represented in state learning goals and on the state's performance-oriented assessments, such as analyzing information, drawing conclusions and verifying results, constructing solutions, relating concepts to real life, organizing and interpreting information, and so forth.

Some of the innovative assessment programs begun by states in the early 1990s have been replaced by more traditional-looking tests because demands for individual student scores and testing in every grade have come into tension with the costs of reliably scoring performance assessments. Although some states and districts have continued to develop assessments that measure student writing, thinking, and performance, in others, the idea expressed in *Knowing What Students Know* (Pellegrino and others, 2001)—that "large-scale assessments can serve the purposes of learning by signaling worthwhile goals for educators and students to pursue" (p. 248)—continues to be more of a hope than reality.

There is some limited evidence that standards-based reforms, along with other reforms of school funding, teacher education, and professional development, have contributed to improvements in student achievement. In a book-length analysis of changes in state scores on NAEP, Grissmer, Flanagan, Kawata, and Williamson (2000) concluded that reform efforts most likely accounted for mathematics score gains in Texas and North Carolina over the decade of the 1990s because these gains were greater than could be expected based on changes in population or resource variables. It is interesting to note that survey studies conflict as to whether curriculum standards or tests have the greater influence. In Washington, Stecher and Chun (2001) found that teachers "pay more attention to the WASL [the state tests] than to the EALRs [learning goals] that the tests are supposed to reflect" (p. 22); whereas in Colorado, teachers more often attributed positive changes in their classrooms (such as increased emphasis on higher-order thinking skills) to state standards, not CSAP testing (Taylor, Shepard, Kinner, and Rosenthal, 2003).

Positive effects of high-stakes testing on instruction, however, are also accompanied by negative effects, which may often be of greater magnitude. The most pervasive research finding from both the United States and abroad has been that high-stakes testing narrows the curriculum (Heubert and Hauser, 1999; Pellegrino and others, 2001; United States Office of Technology Assessment, 1992). Narrowing occurs both by reducing the amount of time devoted to nontested subjects and by reshaping instruction in tested subjects to more closely resemble the test formats. In elementary schools, for example, teachers consistently report either eliminating or cutting back on the amount of science and social studies they teach (Stecher and Chun, 2001; Taylor and others, 2003). In a national survey of 12,000 teachers, Pedulla and others (2003) found that the extent of curriculum narrowing was directly associated with the degree of stakes attached to assessment outcomes. The higher the stakes, the greater the exclusive focus on tested content.

Depending on stakes and the format of the test, teaching-the-test efforts have also had distorting effects on instruction, particularly on the ways in which reading, writing, and mathematics are taught. Instead of spending one or two hours to make sure that students were comfortable with item formats, the majority of elementary teachers in Pedulla and colleagues' (2003) national survey reported spending more than twenty hours in specific test preparation activities. They practiced with items similar to those on the test, used commercial test preparation materials tailored to their state test, and gave their students released items provided by the state. Seventy percent of teachers in states classified as high-stakes by the researchers, as compared to 43 percent of teachers in states with moderate stakes, reported using these strategies throughout the school year, not just the month or weeks before the test.

Teacher interview studies reveal further why learning may be harmed if testing formats become the template for regular instruction. For example, being able to identify the main idea of a reading passage is an important aspect of comprehension but it is fostered better by having students discuss what they have read and formulate a summary themselves rather than practice choosing the best story title from a multiple-choice list. In writing, practicing on decontextualized prompts and drilling on adherence to the state rubric can produce lifeless student essays, in contrast to classroom practices where writing grows out of student interest and is used to help students gain new knowledge and develop their ideas (Hillocks, 2002; Strickland and others, 2001). Teachers also acknowledge that adhering to a test-driven curriculum necessitates superficial coverage. It requires giving up content-based, in-depth units and moving quickly even if some students are lost in the process (Clarke and others, 2003).

Empirical evidence shows a strong connection between teaching-the-test instructional practices and test-score inflation. Students who have been drilled for a specific test, particularly one that is based on knowledge of specific facts and problem types, do not develop deep understandings and are not able to generalize their knowledge or use it in even closely related contexts. A study by Koretz, Linn, Dunbar, and Shepard (1991) found a substantial decline in performance by students in high-stakes states when they were retested on independent tests that covered the same content as the taught-to test. More generally, steep gains in state assessment scores like those in Texas have not been confirmed by gains on the National Assessment (Klein, Hamilton, McCaffrey, and Stecher, 2000). The negative effects of test-driven curricula for student learning are especially worrisome because they fall more heavily on poor and minority students, the very groups that standards-based reform policies are intended to help. When Madaus and others (1992) compared high- and low-minority classrooms, they found that teachers with high percentages of minority students more often reported pressure from their districts to increase test scores, and more often reported test-oriented teaching practices such as teaching topics known to be on the test and providing test practice throughout the school year.

What becomes apparent from the research on testing effects is that teachers are the mediators who determine how much external tests will reshape the curriculum. Thus teachers have a responsibility to understand that raising test scores is not always the same thing as improving learning, and they should recognize how instructional choices make the difference in fostering real or spurious gains. In the next section, we consider strategies for test preparation that protect against curriculum distortion and maintain a commitment to real learning and accomplishment for students.

BALANCED CURRICULUM AND APPROPRIATE TEST PREPARATION

Good teachers naturally want their students to do well on accountability tests, not only because of the importance of test results, but because of how the students themselves feel while they are taking the test. How can teachers prepare their students to make sure they will be able to do their best without succumbing to teaching-the-test practices known to limit learning? Ethical standards in the field of testing and measurement assume that some limited amount of practice with test formats is legitimate and even desirable to ensure that students are not impeded from demonstrating their knowledge because of unfamiliarity with the types of questions asked or the modes of response. Most commercial test publishers include practice tests with test batteries for children in the early grades who may not have had prior experience choosing from among multiple-choice options or bubbling in separate answer sheets.

Research studies show that practice with test formats does improve performance, but the effect is slight unless the exact same test is repeated (Hopkins, 1998). Moreover, the benefit of practice comes from taking *one* practice test; performance does not keep increasing to the same degree with each subsequent retesting. Because of this evidence, major testing companies, such as ETS, maker of the SAT, provide released test forms to be used as practice materials. The intention is to level the playing field so that all test takers will have adequate familiarity with test format, time constraints, and so forth.

Practice with test formats such as open-ended math tasks or writing to a prompt should be provided in the context of the instructional goals to which they connect. And given what we know about the lack of transfer when only one problem type is used, teachers should ensure the development of more robust understandings by focusing on underlying principles and continuing to probe—by asking questions again in a new way and looking for extensions and applications (Shepard, 1997). At the same time, teachers should approach test practice with care, keeping in mind the implicit messages conveyed to students about the nature of subject matter and the purposes for learning. In an analysis of reading readiness tests, for example, Stallman and Pearson (1990) concluded that the demand characteristics of the tests were in many cases antithetical to what children would be expected to do as readers.

Teachers may not realize that improving student achievement in the long run is more likely to occur by teaching concepts and skills deeply than by rushing through a list of topics that might be on the test or by drilling students on specific items or item-types. For example, analyses have found that the frequency of teachers' use of written assignments to assess student progress in reading correlates positively with student achievement on the NAEP tests, whereas the frequency of using multiple-choice or short-answer tests to evaluate reading correlates negatively with student performance (National Center for Education Statistics, 1994).[3] In addition, recent studies show that students who engage in a curriculum focused on mathematical reasoning and problem solving do as

---

[3]NAEP 1992, 1994, National Reading Assessments, Data Almanac Grade 4: Teacher Questionnaire (http://nces.ed.gov/pubsearch/getpubcats.asp?sid=031#017).

well on traditional tests of basic skills as students who engage in a basic skills curriculum more closely aligned to the test, and they are also much more successful on assessments of concepts and problem solving (see, for example, Riordan and Noyce, 2001; Schoenfeld, 2002; Senk and Thompson, 2003).

The amount of time spent on specific test practice should be limited to a few hours and should try to convey to students an approach of strategic good sense. Measurement textbooks (Airasian, 1996; McMillan, 2001) suggest guidelines such as the following:

- Pay careful attention and follow directions.

- Be sure you understand the question before answering.

- Don't worry if some questions are too difficult, you can skip hard questions and come back to them if you have time.

- Learn how to eliminate wrong answers on multiple-choice, and guess if you need to from the remaining choices.

- Organize essay answers before writing them.

Parents are a significant source of pressure that teachers say forces them to focus on raising test scores. The same domain mapping strategy that can be used to keep instruction focused on student learning can also be used as a tool for communicating with parents. A Venn diagram that shows test results as a subset of a teacher's reading or mathematics curriculum can be used as the backdrop for reporting test results along with other (perhaps more important) evidence of student progress. The more a teacher's own assessment system is able to document student understandings and student work as they relate to expectations, the less emphasis there will need to be on external tests to set standards or to measure progress.

Using Results to Improve Instruction

Teachers should know how to use results from large-scale assessments to make appropriate improvements in curriculum and instruction. As we discussed earlier, formative assessment tools will be more helpful in improving instruction than large-scale assessments because they are available more frequently and are directly tied to instructional decisions. Nonetheless, external assessments can provide important insights especially if they are aligned with challenging curriculum frameworks. As Wiggins (1998) pointed out, good teachers have the ability to self-assess, but still there are blind spots and a lack of external referents.

State assessments and other large-scale assessments are most often used to declare that a problem exists, but teachers are typically left on their own to decide what to do about poor test results. Ironically, test and measurement textbooks tell preservice teachers how tests are made and the meaning of stanine and percentile scores but not how to improve instruction in responses to test results. The *Assessment Standards for School Mathematics* (1995) developed by the National Council of Teachers of Mathematics (NCTM) provides perhaps the best framework for considering how a school team or individual teacher might use assessment data to evaluate their instructional program. In particular, NCTM's vision calls for the use of multiple data sources—combining evidence from external and classroom assessments—and for disaggregation of data to track the performance of important subgroups.

No Child Left Behind legislation now requires that progress be charted for subgroups identified by race and ethnicity, free and reduced lunch, special education, and English language learners, but it is also important that teachers consider whether there are apparent gender differences or differences in progress for the lowest-achieving and highest-achieving students. Merely charting progress will not be helpful, however, unless professional judgment is brought to bear to explain the causes of differences in performance and constructive follow-up to ensure that stronger instruction occurs.

Most large-scale assessment programs provide content breakdowns to allow for analysis of major topics and cognitive skills within each content area. Relative strengths and weaknesses are the first place to look for needed program improvements. For example, in an analysis of ITBS scores for one Chicago school, Chen, Salahuddin, Horsch, and Wagner (2000) found that seventh and eighth graders were doing relatively better on factual meaning test items than on inferential and evaluative meaning items. Thus they suspected that instructional practices were not providing opportunity for higher-order thinking. In another example, North Carolina state assessment staff used NAEP Mathematics Assessment data to identify test item topics, such as the Pythagorean theorem and estimation, where state students were doing poorly in comparison to the national sample (Stancavage, Roeber, and Bohrnstedt, 1993).

Additional insight can also be gained by examining student work. Student work may occur directly on state assessments, and teachers may have access to this work in scoring sessions or professional development workshops, or work may be gathered from subsequent classroom assessments intended to help understand reasons for difficulties on the external assessment. Murnane and Levy (1996) document how teachers in Vermont became more knowledgeable about curriculum, teaching, and students' thinking as they collaboratively evaluated student portfolios from the state assessment system in summer scoring sessions. Wood and Schmidt (cited in Shepard, 2003), provide two relevant case studies of how state assessment data were used to improve science teaching in Delaware. In the first case, teachers reviewing student answers on an eighth-grade weather assessment found that the majority of students believed that weather fronts always move from west to east and therefore were unable to answer questions about ocean breezes on the east coast. In the second case, lead teachers in a planning session recognized but could not explain why the state-level score on a simple graphing problem was alarmingly low. When they tried this item type with their own students, the performance level was as low as that of the state as a whole, thus prompting a reexamination of what students were understanding and a subsequent change in teaching strategy.

Of course, the most difficult challenge is to know what to do when score profiles are low or high across the board. A common pattern in low-performing schools is for teachers to cite the home background of students and poor resources as explanations for poor performance. Just as "funds of knowledge" (Moll and others, 1992) is an important formative assessment tool that can help teachers overcome a deficit approach to children's learning, there are external assessment strategies that help to focus on effective instructional strategies that do not blame results on children's circumstances. In the field of large-scale assessment there has always been controversy between two extreme reporting practices: one simply ranks schools, which always makes rich schools look as if they have the best teachers; the other adjusts results for differences in socioeconomic status, but this method implicitly sets lower standards for poor children. A compromise strategy creates comparison schools that have similar demographic characteristics but then sets as the comparison standard the performance of the top 10 percent of schools in each category (Just for the Kids).[4] This method of comparison can serve to ratchet up performance expectations, and at the same time studies of the top schools in each category can provide credible evidence of instructional approaches that are effective with specific groups of students. Comparisons to similarly situated schools also create a greater challenge for high-performing schools and could stimulate important reexamination of curriculum if the state assessment is reflective of challenging learning goals.

TEACHING PRESERVICE TEACHERS ABOUT ASSESSMENT

Teacher educators have developed some pedagogical approaches that seem particularly promising in helping new teachers develop an understanding of the core ideas addressed in this chapter. In this section, we focus upon four of those pedagogical approaches: analysis of student work and learning; engagement in assessment design; examining motivation and learning and how they relate to assessment; and working with standards to design and evaluate assessments for accountability. We conclude with an example of how student teachers' clinical experiences can be designed to both mirror and reinforce important ideas about assessment developed in program coursework.

---

[4]Just for the Kids uses the top ten schools in each category, but we have modified our recommendation to be the top 10 percent of schools for greater statistical stability.

To illustrate some of the tasks that novice teachers can engage in to develop and display their understanding of assessment, we draw upon the work of the Performance Assessment for California Teachers (PACT) project, which is a consortium of fifteen colleges of teacher education.[5] The PACT has developed a performance assessment called the "Teaching Event," which is substantially modeled on the portfolio of the National Board for Professional Teaching Standards and which is currently being piloted in all the colleges. This assessment, completed near the end of the preservice period, asks teachers to plan and teach a unit of instruction, including development of an assessment plan, and to analyze their students' learning in relation to their teaching. We describe the PACT tasks that probe teachers' assessment knowledge, and we discuss examples of course components and assignments used in one of the PACT teacher education programs to help student teachers develop these assessment skills.

Analysis of Student Work and Learning

A strategy increasingly used in teacher education and professional development to help teachers examine student learning—and reflect on the teaching associated with this learning—is *analysis of student work.* Teacher educators may engage student teachers in examining samples of students' work (for example, writing, projects, lab reports, mathematical equations and explanations) and of student learning (video of student discussions, for instance) in order to evaluate and assess the learning of the student or of a group of students. The purpose of these kinds of analyses is to help new teachers develop an understanding of how such evaluations of learning can inform their instructional choices. As we noted earlier, there is evidence that teachers feel they can improve their practice when they collectively review student work to analyze what has been learned by different students, uncover misconceptions or difficulties, and reflect on curriculum or teaching adaptations that may be needed to produce stronger understanding on the part of students. Such review processes also allow teachers to apply standards in evaluating this work, to compare their evaluations, and to develop their ability to assess aspects of student thinking and expression fairly and with clarity about what counts as proficient performance.

The PACT assessment provides two examples of such assignment, one focused explicitly on formative assessment and the other more focused on a summative assessment, which participating institutions can use as anchors for their instruction about assessment, as it relates to planning and instructional decision making. The first of these, adapted from a task used in some of the

---

[5]The colleges and schools of education participating in PACT as of this writing include California State University campuses at Sacramento, San Diego, San Francisco, and San Jose; Mills College; Stanford University; the University of Southern California; and all of the University of California campuses (Berkeley, Davis, Irvine, Los Angeles, Riverside, Santa Barbara, San Diego, and Santa Cruz).

National Board for Professional Teaching Standards portfolios, examines the work of two students over time, focusing on how their learning is unfolding in relation to the teaching they experience. Teachers need to demonstrate that they can appraise each student's strengths, weaknesses, learning process, and instructional needs and reflect on how their teaching contributed to the progress shown across multiple work samples. To do this they need to draw on their knowledge of learning and development, as well as principles of assessment, including how to give useful and appropriate feedback and follow up to ensure that the feedback is used. (See "Analyzing Individual Student Work Over Time.")

Analyzing Individual Student Work Over Time

As part of the PACT assessment, student teachers are asked to select two students in their class who represent different instructional challenges. At least one must be an English language learner. Students must provide three samples of each student's work that represent learning progress. For each student, they must then write a commentary that addresses these issues and questions:

1. Describe the student as a person and learner. What are the student's strengths and approach to learning, levels of knowledge and skills, academic needs, individual learning goals, and other relevant characteristics?
2. Discuss what each work sample illustrates about the student's developing skills and understandings. What was the student able to do? In what areas did the student have difficulty?
3. Describe what learning progress you can see across the samples. Are there aspects of the student's learning you have observed that are not well represented in these particular assessments?
4. Describe how you assess each response. What feedback did you give to the student?
5. Discuss what you believe supported or impeded the student's progress. Were there particular modifications you made to support the student's success?
6. Finally, discuss what you have done or you will do as a teacher to build on what the student has already accomplished and to support the student's ongoing learning.

Source: Reprinted with permission of the PACT Consortium.

Assessing student work in this way helps student teachers develop an appreciation of how learning unfolds over time, how different students learn, and how these students respond to their instruction. It can also strengthen the teachers' commitment and capacity to see it as their responsibility to develop student understanding and proficiency over the course of the school year, rather than merely grading students. And it can develop teachers' abilities to plan instruction that responds to students' evolving learning needs.

The PACT portfolio also includes a more summative assignment in which candidates evaluate the results of a whole class assessment associated with the learning segment they have taught and documented in print and video. (See "A

Sample Analysis of Whole Class Learning.") Engaging in this kind of analysis of student work linked to a specific unit of instruction can help new teachers appreciate the range of understandings students may exhibit in their classroom and to identify some of the typical challenges students may encounter in understanding key ideas in their subject matter. Candidates have the opportunity to consider to what extent their goals were reached and, by analyzing the teaching associated with this learning evidence, what may have contributed to these outcomes. Building upon this understanding, student teachers can be helped to then think about how to respond pedagogically to such learning challenges and consider how they will revise or focus instruction in response to what they have learned from analyzing student work and learning.

A Sample Analysis of Whole Class Learning

As another part of the PACT assessments, teacher candidates are asked to assemble data from an entire class for one formal assessment that was part of the learning segment they taught (for example, homework or other papers, tests, projects, logs, journals, presentations, and so on). They must summarize the performance of the entire group and provide samples of three students' responses to the assessment that together illustrate (1) what students generally understood and (2) what a number of students were still struggling with.

Candidates then write a commentary that uses data—evidence from their analysis—to discuss the achievement of the whole class. They identify one or more learning objectives measured by the assessment on which they focus their analysis, and create a summary of whole class student achievement relative to the learning objective(s). For the summary, they discuss what they learned about the achievement of the class as a whole from looking at their collected work. (For example, what did most students appear to understand well? What misunderstandings, confusions, or needs were apparent for some or most students?) The last part of the assignment requires student teachers to consider the impact of their analysis upon their upcoming instructional choices. They conclude with a discussion of what this analysis suggests are important next teaching goals for the class as a whole, and for individuals in the class.

Assessment Design

Another pedagogical approach teacher educators are finding useful in helping students understand some of the central ideas in this chapter is engaging students in assessment design as part of their learning about instructional design. Rather than planning activities for lessons or units in isolation from thinking about assessment, candidates design an assessment plan as part of a unit or curriculum plan. They learn to "map backward" (Wiggins and McTighe, 1998) from what they hope to accomplish to the design of culminating assessments that will measure these goals and the development or identification of ongoing formal and informal assessments to examine students' initial knowledge and ongoing progress. Enacting the idea of "backwards mapping" reinforces the idea that all activities should connect to and build understanding, and assessments should deliberately measure and reflect progress toward those goals. Candidates also are asked to consider a grading plan that will appropriately evaluate students' progress toward these objectives and will maintain motivation and effort for the range of students in their class. (See "An 'Assessment Plan' Assignment.")

An "Assessment Plan" Assignment

In this assignment, student teachers are asked to develop an assessment plan for a unit of instruction. The plan should include a description of the informal and formal assessments they will use to gauge student learning and adjust their teaching, including the type, format, and purpose of each assessment; a description of what they expect the assessments will reveal about students' learning of content, skills, and academic language; what kind of feedback they will provide; and how the assessment will inform their teaching. Student teachers are also asked to describe any accommodations planned for students who have special educational needs and how the accommodations address their needs. Finally, they must include a discussion of their grading plan, accompanied with a justification of what they are valuing and why, how this relates to their goals and activities in the unit, and how they will handle grading in a fashion that sustains motivation and effort for the range of students in their class.

Involving candidates in designing an assessment-infused unit can help student teachers think about the importance of including an appropriate variety of summative and formative assessments throughout the unit; it can also help them gain experience in developing and selecting from a repertoire of possible assessments, each of which has possibilities, advantages, and disadvantages for developing and illuminating different aspects of student understanding.

In particular, teacher educators can ask student teachers to articulate the reasons for their choices—that is, why certain assessments are appropriate, and for what purpose—so that students begin to think about what they want to assess and why, and how they will use what they learn to inform their practice.

Some teacher educators have found that it is important to spend time focusing on the design and critique of instruments candidates are likely to use frequently in assessing student learning in their content area. For instance, in one course on assessment, students learn about the design and purposes of a number of different assessment strategies, such as designing rubrics, performance assessments, and paper and pencil tests. The faculty begins by introducing some core ideas such as the links between assessment and instruction and the relationship between assessment and individual student growth and development (as well as individual differences). They also introduce the concepts of *reliability, standardization, validity,* and *practicality* (or, *RSVP* as they termed it), ideas that the class continues to focus upon throughout the various activities and experiences. Faculty then design a series of activities to help student teachers learn about different forms of assessments. Students learn, in particular, how to devise a rubric that reflects appropriate skill and understanding of development, what qualifies as appropriate language in rubrics, and how to ensure that the rubric actually relates to and measures the goals of the assignment. Students examine different rubrics and compare effective and less effective aspects of the design, language, and purpose of each one—answering questions like, "Does the rubric capture the essential features of a good performance in your subject?"

The faculty also ask student teachers themselves to complete a performance assessment in their own subject matter, one which typically might be given to their own students (that is, complete a difficult lab assignment, engage in a debate, or write an essay) and then student teachers are asked to critique the assignment. Student teachers are asked to consider whether (or not) the assessment actually measured what it was designed to measure, what kinds of knowledge it assessed, and how effective it was in doing so. They are then asked to modify the assessment to address any concerns or weaknesses they have identified while doing the assessment, so it would be more appropriate, effective, and accurate as an assessment for students. Finally, students also spend some time learning about paper and pencil test design, and how to write effective and clear essay prompts—again, paying close attention to the language of assessment, the purposes of the assessment, and the design of powerful learning experiences.

Teaching Key Concepts of Motivation and Learning as They Relate to Assessment

In addition to analyzing samples of student work and creating assessment design, teacher educators have found that it is extremely important to help prospective teachers understand core principles of learning that relate to assessment, such as motivation and metacognition. For instance, in a course on learning, faculty at one university have found it useful to help student teachers understand the concepts of intrinsic and extrinsic motivation in light of the design of feedback and rubrics. They focus upon the concept of "clear criteria" and how that aids in developing understanding. During the course, faculty share key principles of feedback. For instance, they discuss the ways in which the principle of "providing specific positive feedback first before constructive critique" is important not only because it helps fuel students' motivation (by helping them feel a sense of accomplishment in their current work) but also because it contributes to students' metacognitive awareness of the progress of their current learning (students become more able to identify their strengths, current levels of understanding, and then the gaps and areas needing development).

They also discuss how the principle of "providing specific, grounded suggestions" is more helpful than broader comments to students because this enables students to engage in a thought process focused upon particular learning goals and specific features of good work, and it enables students to understand in concrete terms how they can improve. Faculty follow these principles of feedback themselves when responding to work by student teachers (see Chapter Five for a description of the curriculum case assignment) so that student teachers can themselves appreciate and experience how appropriate feedback can motivate learners and lead to greater learning.

Faculty also engage students in thinking about the design of rubrics for evaluating their own work during the course. For instance, during an assignment to write a curriculum case, students read a series of cases written by previous students and by experienced teachers. Students then generate a list of the features of "good cases," which then leads to the creation of a rubric by the whole class to be used with their own written case. Faculty feel that the experience of creating a rubric (during which students spend time discussing appropriate language for the rubric, the features of good work, and the relationship between rubric and actual case) enables students to think about their own work in relation to a rubric and to the features of good work, and helps them more explicitly attend to the criteria of the assignment. It also helps them internalize the underlying rationales and features of such assessment tools they will need to understand to create rubrics for their own students.

Standards, Assessment, and Accountability

Finally, teacher educators have developed some pedagogical approaches that seem particularly effective in helping new teachers understand the relationship between their own curriculum and standards and standardized testing, as well as big ideas like norm-and-criterion-referenced testing. Some teacher education programs engage student teachers in a technique we call "domain mapping." Starting with the state's curriculum frameworks or national content standards, they draw a Venn diagram or construct a table to illustrate what subpart of the desired curriculum is covered by the test and what is not. This activity helps them recognize what parts of each content strand are represented by state- or commercially developed tests and what parts are not. Candidates can then see, for example, that if a test may cover the easiest-to-measure part of each content strand in a domain, this does not mean that the domain has been adequately represented. Saying what has been left out helps to make clear the limitations of the test as a curriculum guide. Based on this explicit analysis, preservice teachers can then consciously plan units of study and allocation of instructional time in ways that keep attention to tested content in its proportional place.

In addition, some teacher educators have found it effective to engage prospective teachers in completing a subset of real test items on typical standardized tests in their subject area in order to better understand the tests, the cognitive functions they draw upon, and the kinds of learning they assess. They then ask the preservice teachers to evaluate the clarity of the items, to identify any typical misunderstandings associated with some of the items, and to recognize some of the skills involved in test-taking that might be helpful for students to acquire. They also ask preservice teachers to evaluate the nature and type of knowledge being assessed by the tests, as well as to consider the kinds of knowledge and understanding that are *not* represented and evaluated by the test. Overall these kinds of activities can help preservice teachers understand the utility and limitations of specific tests and consider the choices inherent in test design and their consequences for what kind of learning is measured and encouraged. This understanding may inform candidates' own classroom test design and may help to assure that they continue to focus upon the design and conduct of assessments that are conceptually based.

BRINGING IT ALL TOGETHER: INFUSING ASSESSMENT INTO THE PROCESS OF LEARNING TO TEACH[6]

All the assignments and experiences described earlier are likely to be most effective when they are part of a program that seamlessly integrates and strategically develops student teachers' understandings of core ideas about learning, assessment, and development both in theory and in practice. In this final section, we describe a program that has effectively been able to help its teachers develop a theory- and practice-based understanding of assessment through the integration of coursework and clinical work. At the University of Southern Maine, interns in the Extended Teacher Education Program (ETEP) encounter these ideas not solely in their coursework, but also find these ideas deeply embedded in the classrooms in which they do their practice teaching. For instance, Tom Taylor, an ETEP intern in the Gorham school district, finds himself learning to teach in a classroom of a recent ETEP graduate where many of the conceptions he is learning about in ETEP are at play. The University of Southern Maine has a long-standing professional development school relationship with the district and school where Tom is learning to teach and has worked collaboratively with this district to develop a system of performance assessments that are part of the

---

[6]Much of this section is drawn from Whitford, B.L., Ruscoe, G., and Fickel, L. (2000) "Knitting it all together: Collaborative teacher education at the University of Southern Maine"

district and school policy environment and professional culture. Thus Tom's learning about assessment is predictable and coherent in both his university coursework and his school placement.

Tom's First Placement: The Classroom of an ETEP Graduate

At first glance around the room, the scene seems commonplace—a fairly typical elementary classroom: students are seated at individual table-type desks with detached chairs; the room is lined with instructional materials; and a teacher, Mrs. Kopp, is standing by her desk holding an open book. Beth, one of the students, is at the front of the room, quietly talking about a book and occasionally referring to a diorama she has made to illustrate it. The other twenty-five or so students are generally attentive and quiet.

When she concludes her report, one's first impression of "typical" begins to change. Without prompting, several students immediately raise their hands. Beth calls on Jeff, seated at the back of the room, and, smiling, he asks, "On a scale of one to ten, how would you rate this book?" Beth quickly replies, "Ten." Jeff immediately comes back, "Why?" A few students groan. (Observers later learn that the "one-to-ten-and-why" is Jeff's stock question during their monthly "book talks.") Another student asks Beth to give more detail about the plot, and she does. Referring to a half-size sheet of paper (upon which criteria for presentations is listed), another suggests that more eye contact with the audience would help. Still another comments that she was not loud enough to be heard at the back of the room. As she listens to these comments from her classmates, Beth seems at ease and unembarrassed.

A second adult gently asks her what she specifically liked about the book. This is Mr. Blackstone, a special needs teacher whose five students are part of this class. Later, observers are surprised to learn that Beth is one of them. Mr. Blackstone praises her for her diorama. Several students quickly point out that the visual is really a "triorama," not a diorama. At this point, Mrs. Kopp cautions the students about talking out of turn. Beth's presentation ends with the students applauding.

Mrs. Kopp asks another student, Austin, if he is ready to give his report. Nodding "yes," Austin positions himself confidently on a stool at the front of the room, which makes him more visible to those at the back. He speaks in a clear, steady voice with enthusiasm about his book, maintaining eye contact with the audience throughout. At the conclusion of his report, hands from perhaps one-third of the students fly up. Smiling, Austin calls on Jeff, who asks his "one-to-ten-and-why" question. Then Austin calls on another student, who asks, "What genre would you place this book in?" Austin replies, "Well, it's sort of an adventure book and a thriller, too." The questioner, nodding, seems satisfied. That is when observers notice that, in addition to asking questions, the children are also scoring the presentations using criteria printed on the half sheet of paper. A third adult stands and reminds the students to be sure to turn in their "rubrics"—the half sheet of paper. This is Tom Taylor, an ETEP intern, who will work with these teachers and students all day, every day, until the December holiday break. Tom collects the scoring guides as students hold them in raised hands.

Later in the year, small groups of students work on projects related to a unit on regions of the United States. Their culminating activity for this unit is an oral presentation to the class designed to persuade Mr. Taylor, now role-playing an immigrant Italian businessman, to settle and start his business in their group's region. Gorham educators call this type of culminating assessment activity an "exhibition" because it is a way for students to demonstrate, or exhibit, what they have learned during their study of the unit.

These glimpses of Tom's first placement demonstrate several ways in which some of the core ideas expressed in this chapter are central to the workings of this classroom—and hence are part of his experience in learning about assessment as an ETEP intern. The first feature one might note is the emphasis on student performance assessment and public critique of that performance using shared criteria—something that is common practice in this school district. Two districtwide scoring guides are routinely used, one for oral presentation and one for writing. These are used in classrooms by teachers and students as well as by parents and other non-school community members serving as judges during district-level exhibitions. Student exhibitions occur each spring as all third, sixth, eighth, and eleventh graders publicly demonstrate their knowledge on a predetermined districtwide topic. A goal is to have each student's exhibition judged by at least two adults from outside the school.

Second, the work of students (and teachers themselves) is organized around explicit goals and standards to which all students work, and against which all students are assessed. Gorham educators call these standards the "Gorham Outcomes," and these outcomes reflect a philosophy about teaching and learning that emphasizes particular approaches to learning that students are expected to develop. These outcomes, or "habits of mind," state that students are expected to be self-directed learners, collaborative workers, complex thinkers, quality producers, and community contributors. On each student's desk is taped a set of goals toward which the student has agreed to work during the school year. These goals, set during parent-teacher-student conferences held at the beginning of the year and often led by students, are structured around the five Gorham outcomes. Throughout the year in individual portfolios, students accumulate evidence bearing on the goals along with other examples of their work. Student teachers in Gorham learn how to teach in this assessment-oriented environment, using these tools and strategies.

Mirroring Ideas About Assessment in the ETEP-Gorham Program

Tom and his fellow ETEP student teachers experience many of these core ideas about assessment, development, and learning reflected in their coursework and assignments. For instance, just as students in Gorham classrooms become accustomed to performance assessment, so too, do interns in the ETEP-Gorham program. They participate in at least three formal, public exhibitions of their knowledge: first, when they share their "short project" from orientation called "All About Gorham" with teachers new to the district in August; second, when they display their interdisciplinary units for teachers and administrators in April; and finally, when they formally present their portfolios to a five-member committee composed of administrators, district teachers, and ETEP instructors in May. And just as students and teachers in Gorham classrooms create scoring guides or rubrics for particular classroom projects, which they use to assess their work and the work of others, so too, do ETEP interns create scoring guides and rubrics for their own work. Although performance assessment is routine with Gorham students it is also a central part of the ETEP interns' experiences as they learn to assess and improve their own knowledge and practice.

And just as students complete goals developed around district outcomes, ETEP interns complete similar "goal-and-evidence" portfolio assessment. As part of completing the Master of Teaching and Learning degree from USM, the final phase of ETEP involves preparing a portfolio organized around the five "Gorham Outcomes." For instance, Mrs. Kopp's portfolio presented evidence from her teaching—curriculum materials, student work, reflections from journal entries—to show how each of the Gorham themes was addressed in her teaching. Among other things, she showed how she monitors and evaluates her current practice by using student work to assess her teaching. In these ways and others, there is a parallel between what is emphasized in the Gorham school district and what is emphasized in ETEP: the conception of assessment and understanding as a performance, the role of self-assessment, the importance of content in assessment, the close relationship between goals and evaluation and evidence, and the role of the learner in making explicit one's own learning. What makes the experience for ETEP interns particularly powerful are the connections between the ideas they encounter in their coursework and in their clinical work. Together, the clinical and coursework reinforces understanding about assessment and its role in learning and development, substantiates what that looks like in practice, and ultimately, makes it possible for ETEP graduates to integrate those understandings of assessment in their future classrooms.

Research on the effects of formative assessment (Black and Wiliam, 1998) shows its potential to dramatically improve student learning. Yet, surveys of current classroom practice continue to suggest that grading is the main focus of assessment rather than assessing for the sake of improvement. Most teacher candidates cannot rely on their own experiences growing up for models of effective assessment practices; and in contrast to the Gorham example described earlier, many cannot necessarily rely on the models they observe in their field experiences. Therefore teacher education programs must provide both new theory and research evidence and specifically structured assignments that provide candidates with well-grounded practical opportunities for gaining this experience. Most particularly, teacher candidates need experience identifying, constructing, and evaluating assessment tasks that tap conceptual understanding. They need opportunities to focus on assessment as a step in instruction so that they can see how assessment insights lead to next steps for students and for themselves. They also need practice with grading procedures and philosophies that accurately reflect important learning goals but avoid the demotivating aspects of traditional grading practices. Finally, in an era of high-stakes accountability testing, teacher candidates need to be able to analyze tests well enough that they can help students gain sufficient familiarity with test formats and thereby do their best, while still preserving the integrity of classroom instructional decisions, keeping the focus of time and effort on learning, not on test-taking.

CHAPTER NINE

Classroom Management

Pamela LePage, Linda Darling-Hammond, Hanife Akar,
with Cris Gutierrez, Evelyn Jenkins-Gunn, Kathy Rosebrock

Teacher candidates have long rated knowledge about classroom management as one of the most crucial topics to be learned in preservice teacher education, yet often one of the most ignored (Burnard, 1998; Stallion and Zimpher, 1991; Martin, Linfoot, and Stephenson, 1999; Silvestri, 2001). Contrary to common misperceptions, classroom management is not simply the process of arranging desks, rewarding good behavior and choosing consequences for misconduct. Classroom management encompasses many practices integral to teaching, such as developing relationships; structuring respectful classroom communities where students can work productively; organizing productive work around a meaningful curriculum; teaching moral development and citizenship; making decisions about timing and other aspects of instructional planning; successfully motivating children to learn; and encouraging parent involvement. The goals of classroom management include academic achievement, social and emotional development, collaboration, and character development. Classroom management involves the practical application and integration of much of the foundational knowledge outlined in this book. Skillful classroom management makes good intellectual work possible.

The ways in which these many aspects of teaching and planning come together in a well-managed classroom are seen in the following observation of a first-year teacher who graduated from the University of California at Berkeley's Developmental Teacher Education Program. (See "A Classroom That Supports Productive Learning.")

A Classroom That Supports Productive Learning

Mary Gregg teaches in a portable classroom at Wilson Elementary School in an urban district in the San Francisco Bay Area. Wilson's 850 students, most of them language minority, constitute the largest population of Title I–eligible students in the district. Mary's room, a small portable with a low ceiling and very loud air fans, has one teacher table and six rectangular student tables with six chairs at each. Mary has thirty-two first graders (fourteen girls and eighteen boys). Twenty-five of the children are children of color; a majority are recent immigrants from Southeast Asia, with some African Americans and Latinos, and seven European Americans.

Despite the small size of the room, Mary fosters an active learning environment with her students. She has plastered the walls from floor to ceiling with student work—math graphs, group experience stories, and student collages. Hanging down from the ceiling so that adults have to duck or wend their way through the room are student-constructed science mobiles and a variety of What We Know and What We Want To Know charts. In one corner, a reading area is set up with books and a carpet.

At noon, half of her class leaves the room to participate with a bilingual class for the science lesson while half of the bilingual class comes to her. She groups the students in mixed language and gender cohorts and introduces the science activity she has designed. The room is full of materials needed for the lesson. There are cups in large tote trays, two trays filled with saltwater; two with regular tap water; small totes full of small plastic bears, different kinds of tiles, quarters, rocks, and paper clips. The goal is to see how many objects it takes to sink the cup in the different types of water.

The thirty students conduct experiments, record on yellow post-its how many objects it takes to sink the cup, and then place the post-its on a large piece of chart paper she has labeled in two columns, saltwater and tap water. Before starting the activity she reads the labels and asks students to read the labels. She has the students point out interesting language and spelling features. Two children excitedly point out, "That's the same weird spelling we saw this morning." While organizing the groups she gives directions for students to go to their assigned tables and sit on their hands. She points out that they will be unable to put their hands in the water if they are sitting on them. This is one of many "management techniques" she combines to assure students the opportunity to engage in the work. Among the others are a "Peace Treaty" hanging from the ceiling that lists a set of student-generated rules that the students signed. It includes a promise to be peaceful in room 31, and, "to help make our room a place of learning and friendship," the following pledges: "We won't pick on anyone. We won't fight at school. We won't mess up the room. We will be peaceful and good. We will listen. We won't say any bad words. We will be quiet. We won't fight with guns. We won't touch anyone's plant. We won't karate kick. We won't push."

Once into the science activity, management appears invisible. There is, of course, some splashing and throwing things into the water, but as the lesson progresses, the teacher engages in on-the-spot logistical management decisions. For instance, everyone is supposed to get a chance to go to the table to choose objects to be placed in cups. After choosing the first person to go, Mary sets them to the task. Very quickly, it is the second person's turn and the students do not know how to choose who should get the next turn. At first she says "you choose," then foresees an "It's my turn. No it's my turn" problem and redirects them with a counterclockwise motion to go around the table.

At the end of the experiment, she brings the class together to discuss the recorded information. Students generate their own hypotheses and then, with teacher encouragement, match their hypotheses with the data. When the language becomes more abstract, she asks students to come to the front of the room and demonstrate their science concepts with the materials all had used. This is one aspect of what in California is called Specially Designed Academic Instruction in English (SDAIE), a pedagogical approach focused on increasing the learning opportunities of English language learners.

Mary skillfully uses a range of other strategies throughout the day to keep her students working peacefully and purposefully. These include frequently praising those who are behaving; stopping and waiting until she has everyone's attention; questioning if all can hear; recording stars on the board when the group is attentive and erasing the stars to call their attention to the need to settle down; ending or extending an activity based on students' willingness and ability to focus ("I have time for one more. Is the class ready for one more?"); and positively refocusing disruptive behavior. To call the group together, she asks them to "sit on their stars." (Stars are marked on the group rug to help students locate a place to settle during group meeting times.) Other aspects of Mary's teaching include cooperative groups that enable communication, peer teaching, and development of group interaction skills; performance tests, portfolios, and journals; hands-on and minds-on activities such as the development of products, simulations, and research projects; extensive use of visuals such as slides, posters, tapes, and realia (for example, classroom aquariums, terrariums, field trips); inclusion of community members as conduits of language and culture; integration of first language and culture into class activities; and well-developed scaffolding techniques to accommodate multiple levels of language proficiency within a single classroom.

Source: Adapted from Snyder (2000).

Mary's ability to organize her classroom is clear, but there are other important aspects of classroom management being demonstrated in this observation. For example, Mary designs tasks that allow students to explore important curriculum ideas in developmentally appropriate ways, using hands-on materials that give them a concrete experience of the concepts they are studying. She organizes the materials and activities so that all of the children can be successful and all can understand. She scaffolds their ability to categorize their findings by developing a comparison chart and giving them tools to collect and fill in the data. In her manner and her strategies, she demonstrates an obvious respect for children's experiences, their work, their families, and their communities. She has created a caring community, where children hold themselves responsible for their actions. Through the construction of the class "peace treaty," she is teaching them to be good citizens and to collaborate. Through thoughtful curriculum planning and pedagogy focused on meeting children's needs, she emphasizes the prevention of disruptions rather than intervention (Snyder, 2000).

Like Mary's classroom, this chapter presents a comprehensive view of classroom management and reviews research that suggests (1) why knowledge of classroom management is important, (2) what prospective teachers need to know about classroom management, and (3) how teacher education can help teacher candidates acquire the essential skills to become effective classroom managers.

THEORETICAL BASES OF CLASSROOM MANAGEMENT

Classroom management has been broadly defined as actions taken to create and maintain a learning environment that supports instructional goals (Brophy, 1988). For teachers to be prepared to create and maintain an effective learning environment, they must have a variety of knowledge and skills that allow them to effectively structure the physical classroom environment, establish rules and procedures, develop relationships with children, and maintain attention and engagement in academic activities.

In the last twenty years, classroom management has undergone a paradigm shift from a focus on intervention—the recognition and punishment of misbehavior—to a focus on prevention through the development of classroom communities in which norms are established and academic routines promote constructive work (Brophy, 1988; Weinstein, 1999).

Evidence of this paradigm shift can be seen in the metaphors used to describe classroom management. Earlier metaphors describe classroom management from an authoritarian or industrial perspective that viewed teachers as managers or technicians and schools as factories (Glasser, 1990; Bullough, 1994; Lasley, 1994; McLaughlin, 1994). Teachers reinforced students with tangible compensation in exchange for good behavior, like rewarding workers for producing good products. Later metaphors described teachers in terms of leadership qualities and effective teaching and motivational skills (McLaughlin, 1994; Weinstein, Woolfolk, Dittmeier, and Shanker, 1994). The "manager" metaphor was replaced by an "orchestration" metaphor meant to reflect a learner-centered environment that emphasizes the social context for academic tasks (Randolph and Evertson, 1994).

The early foundations for classroom management recommendations included Pavlov's behavioral theories of conditioning and reinforcement suggesting the importance of providing specific stimuli to produce desirable behaviors.

Research on behavioral approaches today emphasizes approaches that highlight good behavior and use punishments sparingly, given findings about the perverse effects of punitive measures for managing behavior (Mayer, 1995; Mayer and Leone, 1999).

For example, in a situation where a teacher asks a group of children a question and they randomly shout out the answer, a teacher might be advised to praise a student who is raising her hand, by saying, "Thank you Jane, I liked that you raised your hand when you wanted to talk. I cannot hear the right answer when everybody shouts at the same time." In this example, the teacher is praising Jane, not only to reward her for her good behavior, but also to encourage her classmates to model this behavior. This kind of positive reinforcement is still used in classrooms today and can be helpful. New teachers should understand the role that behavior management plays in classroom management. But, in contemporary classrooms, there are a number of reasons why teachers must also look beyond behaviorism. First, an emphasis on controlling behavior often leads to resistance rather than buy-in (Lewis, 2001), thus failing to develop self-maintenance of positive behavior in the long run. Second, analysts have found evidence that the overuse of extrinsic rewards and sanctions can undermine intrinsic motivation and eventually affect moral development because it fails to help children develop self-responsibility and an internal moral compass (see, for example, Kohn, 1996a; Ryan and Deci, 2000). Third, teachers need more than behavioral controls to manage a classroom effectively: misbehavior can be the result of poorly planned activities, inadequate scaffolding and modeling (leaving children unaware of what to do), or insufficient attention to developing norms and participation routines in the classroom.

There appears to be a relationship between teachers' abilities to manage a set of complex activities in the classroom and their ability to teach intellectually challenging material. Because the novel tasks required for problem solving are more difficult to manage than the routine tasks associated with rote learning, lack of knowledge about how to manage an inquiry-oriented classroom can lead teachers to turn to passive tactics that dumb down the curriculum (Carter and Doyle, 1987). In a recent study of four high schools, McNeil (2000) confirms that intellectual expectations can be lowered when teachers "teach defensively," choosing methods of presentation and evaluation that simplify content and reduce demands on students in return for classroom order and minimal student compliance on assignments.

It is important for teachers to understand the theoretical foundations that underlie their classroom management and instructional strategies because an effective teacher needs a management system that is consistent with her instructional system. For example, if a teacher's goal is to instill an intrinsic love of learning and develop autonomous learners, it would be self-defeating to construct heavy-handed monitoring systems and emphasize extrinsic rewards for motivation. If a teacher asks students to collaborate, then creating a system of competitive incentives and norm-referenced grading (see Chapter Eight) could cause behavior problems as children struggled to work through contradictory messages.

This chapter is based on contemporary research about practices that support participation, effort, and learning. This research illustrates that classroom management relies as much on developing relationships and orchestrating a productive learning community as it does on determining consequences for inappropriate behavior. The chapter is built on the assumption that teachers must understand various approaches to behavior management and be prepared to choose appropriate strategies for the individual child, given the context. It describes what teachers should know to manage classrooms well, including:

1. Creating meaningful curriculum and engaging pedagogy to support motivation,

2. Developing supportive learning communities,

3. Organizing and structuring the classroom,

4. Repairing and restoring behavior respectfully, and

5. Encouraging moral development.

The chapter concludes with sections that describe research on some classroom management programs and provide insights into how this material might be taught in teacher education programs.

CREATING MEANINGFUL CURRICULUM AND MOTIVATING INSTRUCTION

Engaging Pedagogy

To develop and maintain an effective learning environment, children must be interested and engaged in the learning activities presented in the classroom. Teachers must choose tasks that are developmentally appropriate and intellectually meaningful and make sure that children can understand their instruction. The teacher must provide appropriate scaffolding so that children are not frustrated by material that is too hard, or bored by material that is too basic. We saw many examples of this in Mary Gregg's instruction when she engaged students in an intrinsically interesting hands-on inquiry with concrete materials and then allowed them to collect, display, and interpret data. She used groupwork to enable students to learn from their peers and demonstrations to make the concepts understandable to second language learners.

Her approach illustrates the findings of research summarized by Brophy (1987) and Lepper (1988), which concludes that a student's interest in academic activities is enhanced when teachers (1) emphasize intrinsic reasons for learning rather than stressing grades or other rewards; (2) relate material to students' lives and experiences or to current events; (3) offer choices about what, where, how, or with whom work is done; (4) assign tasks that are varied and that include novel elements; (5) assign problems for students to solve that are realistic and challenging; and (6) assign work that involves creating a product or provides some concrete form of accomplishment.

Supporting these recommendations, in a recent study of ten fifth- and sixth-grade science classes in four different schools, Blumenfeld, Puro, and Mergendoller (1992) found that in science classrooms where students reported higher levels of motivation to learn, teachers stressed conceptual understanding and made material more concrete and interesting by providing examples and relating them to their students' experiences or to current events. They also assigned varied tasks and encouraged students to work cooperatively in groups. They concluded that four factors characterized teacher practices in classrooms where students reported high levels of cognitive engagement: (1) teachers created a variety of opportunities to learn, (2) teachers pressed students for thinking through feedback and participation, (3) teachers used scaffolding to support students' attempts to understand, and (4) teachers' evaluation emphasized understanding and learning rather than work completion, performance comparison, or right answers.

Support for Intrinsic Motivation

Many people think that motivation is something that inheres to the individual, rather than something that teachers can influence. Teachers should know that students are likely to be motivated to learn when they have interesting tasks, expectations that they can be successful, and appropriate support for learning (Blumenfeld and others, 1992), and they should know how to construct these conditions. Research demonstrates that children are motivated to learn when they have confidence in their abilities (Bandura, 1997; Eccles, Wigfield, and Schiefele, 1998; Pintrich and de Groot, 1990; Schunk, 1991; Stipek, 1996), and when they have a good relationship with the teacher (Goodenow, 1993; Roeser, Midgley, and Urdan, 1996; Ryan and Powelson, 1991). Intrinsic motivation for learning also derives from the fact that humans typically want to understand the world, have control over their lives, and be self-directed.

Learners are intrinsically motivated when they perceive themselves as the cause of their own behavior, whereas learners who are extrinsically motivated are motivated by external sources (Stipek, 2002). Motivation theorists offer evidence that human beings are naturally disposed to develop skills and engage in learning-related activities. Individuals appear to learn best when they see themselves as engaging in learning behavior for their own internally generated reasons, because they want to learn, rather than to avoid punishment or gain rewards (Stipek, 2002).

There is strong evidence that when children are given external rewards extensively, especially for the purpose of control, they will often attribute their behaviors to external factors and lose their sense of self-determination, along with interest in engaging the task again. In addition, task quality can decline under conditions of extrinsic motivation (Ryan and Deci, 2000; Pintrich and Shunk, 1996; Brewer, Dunn, and Olszewski, 1988; Lepper, Keavney, and Drake, 1996). However, the relationships are not entirely straightforward. A large body of research in the 1970s investigating the impact of positive and negative verbal feedback on intrinsic motivation revealed complex patterns of heightened or diminished motivation associated with reward structures (Deci, 1971, 1972, 1978; Lepper and Greene, 1978). There is evidence that when changes in behavior are sought, positive extrinsic rewards can help children exert effort toward desired ends. When skillfully used, and then reduced or eliminated, these rewards can ultimately be used to develop self-efficacy and self-determination—factors that enhance intrinsic motivation (Cameron, 2001).

Stipek (1988) argues that "The challenge to the teacher is to create tasks and learning contexts that shift students from extrinsic to intrinsic motivation" (p. 81). To promote intrinsic motivation, Spaulding (1992) suggests that "perceived control" and "perceived competence" are important. Teachers need to learn how to create academic environments in which students perceive themselves as being competent and having a measure of self-control, and they need to use scaffolding strategies to help their students overcome the difficulties or obstacles they face (Spaulding, 1992; Brophy, 1981; Burden, 2000).

Deci argues that the effects of rewards are dependent not only on the recipient's perception and interpretation of them, but also on the intention and manner of the person presenting the awards. From his research, Deci concluded that students who believe that tangible rewards or praise are controlling them lose interest in the task. However, those who perceive that feedback gives them information about their progress and performance have enhanced interest in the task, and their locus of causality remains internal. This indicates the importance of teachers learning how to use concrete, specific feedback about task performance rather than generalized praise or disconnected rewards such as stickers or candy for completing assignments. If a teacher is trying to create tasks and learning contexts that shift students from extrinsic to intrinsic motivation, then extrinsic rewards should be verbal, based in social interaction, and also unexpected (Ryan and Deci, 2000). In other words, rewards become informative and useful when they are linked to actual performance or progress (Harackiewicz and Sansone, 2000).

Culturally Responsive Pedagogy

Finally, if students are to feel competent and in control, and if teachers are to develop strategies that are appropriate for their needs, teachers must know and respect their students. There is evidence that many teachers attribute inaccurate characterizations of both behavior and academic ability to students based on race and ethnicity (Kaplan, Gheen, and Midgley, 2002; Irvine, 1990). This type of bias can lead to negative expectations—which can trigger the behaviors that teachers want to avoid (Kaplan and others, 2002). Students may come to expect bias (Sheets and Gay, 1996), which influences their behaviors. Teachers need to understand how their attitudes toward their students can significantly shape the expectations they hold for student learning, their treatment of students, and what students ultimately learn (Irvine, 1990; Valdes, 1996). Affirming attitudes, for example, have been shown to support students' achievement (Ladson-Billings, 1994; Lucas, Henze, and Donato, 1990; Nieto, 1996).

Teachers who respect cultural differences are more apt to believe that students from nondominant groups are capable learners, even when these children enter school with ways of thinking, talking, and behaving that differ from the dominant cultural norms. Teachers convey these attitudes by exposing students to an intellectually rigorous curriculum and supporting them in mastering it; by teaching students strategies they can use to monitor and manage their own learning; by encouraging children to excel; and by building on the individual and cultural resources they bring to the school. Strategies such as these, which convey respect for students to affirm their differences, become the basis for meaningful relationships and favorable academic results (Gay, 2000; Irvine, 1990; Ladson-Billings, 1994; Lucas and others, 1990).

Beyond the development of nondiscriminatory and antiracist behaviors, engaging in culturally responsive pedagogy also requires that teachers understand the views and learning preferences children may bring to school (Gay, 2000; Martin and Van Gunten, 2002), including, for example, how students communicate in their communities and whether some students feel more comfortable with communal rather than individualistic approaches. Based on a review of literature on culturally responsive teaching, Villegas and Lucas (2002) observed that culturally responsive teachers recognize that there are multiple ways of perceiving reality; hold affirming views of students from diverse backgrounds; believe they should and can bring about change to make schools more equitable; know about the lives of their students and incorporate sociocultural experience in the classroom; and know how children construct knowledge, and provide situations for promoting knowledge construction. By knowing children well and being attuned to diversity, teachers can develop instruction that is engaging and that is developmentally appropriate for children with different temperaments, backgrounds and cultures.

DEVELOPING LEARNING COMMUNITIES

School and Classroom Community

Many contemporary scholars argue that establishing relationships and developing community are as critical for classroom management as having classroom environments free from disruptions (see, for example, Brophy and Alleman, 1998). In collaborative communities, "members feel valued, personally connected to one another, and committed to everyone's growth and learning," (Brophy and Alleman, 1998, p. 56). Research suggests that teachers and students who work together in supportive communities have higher levels of self-understanding, commitment, performance, and belongingness (Sergiovanni, 1994), and that children who feel a sense of belonging in school are less likely to have discipline problems. In a recent review, Parke and colleagues (Parke and others, 1998) highlighted a recent cross-sectional study of 12,000 adolescents showing that school connectedness has very broad and significant benefits, including lower levels of alcohol use, marijuana use, early sexual behavior, emotional distress, suicide, and violent behavior (Resnick and others, 1997).

Research also suggests that a strong link exists between social and academic performance and that being in a strong classroom community affects academic achievement. A study of six elementary schools that measured classrooms' "sense of community" found that students who experienced a high sense of community showed significantly greater academic motivation and performance; stronger liking for school; greater empathy and motivation to help others; and more ability to resolve conflicts (Battistich, Watson, Solomon, Schaps, and Solomon, 1991). The researchers' approach to helping teachers develop such classrooms has shown significant benefits. In a more recent study, Battistich, Solomon, Kim, Watson, and Schaps (1995) found that, although schools serving low-income students typically show lower levels of community than schools serving affluent children, low-income schools that have developed high levels of community also reduce the gaps in performance and attitudes toward school typically found between more- and less-affluent students. These scholars conclude that a high sense of community helps to "level the playing field" for poor children.

An effective classroom learning community develops respectful relationships not only between teachers and students, but also among the students themselves. In such a community children are taught how to develop social competence. Research indicates that social competence typically leads to happier and more academically successful children. In a recent study, Welsh, Parke, Widaman, and O'Neil (2001) examined the direction of effects between social competence and academic competence over time. Findings indicated that lower levels of social acceptance in kindergarten were predictive of lower academic performance as revealed in standardized test scores in the first and second grades (Parke and others, 1998), and that a bidirectional pattern of influence emerged between social and academic competence from second to third grade.

The development of a learning community helps teachers manage the classroom, not only because children feel more connected, but because it provides an environment for stimulating learning opportunities and greater assistance in learning. In such classrooms, teachers help students construct knowledge through social interaction in active learning processes where they engage in guided collaborative inquiry with their peers. Classrooms that promote and take advantage of these kinds of social interactions can produce more effective learning. Thus creating such classrooms is a major goal of classroom management (Brophy and Alleman, 1998).

Contemporary researchers have built on Lev Vygotsky's ideas about learning as a social process and have developed principles of effective pedagogy based on research in a wide range of classrooms (see, for example, Tharp, Estrada, Dalton, and Yamauchi, 2000). This body of research suggests that learning is enhanced when teachers and students work together in "joint productive activity," which occurs when experts and novices engage in activities together (as they do in families and communities) and have an opportunity to talk about their work. In this context, teachers share decisions about the selection of topics and responsibilities for how to proceed, helping students learn to engage in dialogue, negotiation, and compromise. Tharp and colleagues (2000) have found that learning is accelerated when teachers make instruction meaningful by connecting it to students' own experiences and interests, creating engaging tasks and applications, and showing how ideas are related, and when activities are cognitively challenging, requiring thinking and analysis rather than merely memorization and recall. They suggest that the foundation of this kind of instruction is dialogic, implemented through exchange and discussion around a specific academic goal in purposeful "instructional conversations." These conversations not only guide the work and thinking process, they also help students develop competence in the language of instruction, including an understanding of how members of academic disciplines use specific language to describe, categorize, and study things.

Much research has demonstrated that students in cooperative learning environments typically perform better than those in competitive or individualistic situations in terms of their reasoning, the generation of new ideas and solutions, and how well they transfer what they learn from one situation to another, as well as on traditional test measures (Jensen, Johnson, and Johnson, 2002; Cohen, 1994; Slavin, 1990a). David and Roger Johnson reviewed more than 500 experimental and 100 correlational research studies conducted on cooperative, competitive, and individualistic educational efforts, finding consistently large effects on student achievement of cooperative learning strategies (see Johnson and Johnson, 1989, for a review of these studies).

For groupwork to have an impact, however, teachers must be taught to design collaborative instruction effectively. Effective groupwork requires teachers to create truly interdependent tasks, establish clear goals, effectively organize discussions, monitor activities to reinforce how students can help one another, and facilitate frequent evaluations of how the work is progressing. Teachers can also informally recognize a particular student's strength or ability so that others may rely on that student for assistance. Cohen and Lotan (1995) call this "assigning competence"; in their classroom research, they have found that identifying students' strengths publicly can increase the participation rates of low-status students. A classroom climate of trust, where students have opportunities to share their views without fear of being wrong, is essential to promote healthy student-to-student interactions.

Community Beyond the Classroom

To be most effective, a community orientation should move beyond the classroom. Children benefit from a cohesive community, especially when all of the members of the school staff work with the community to create a shared vision of child development and learning (Comer, Haynes, Joyner, and Ben-Avie, 1996). It is important for the principal and other administrators to provide leadership in developing a school community, but teachers can also take leadership in developing a caring school community in which staff collaborate and share ideas. Teachers in cohesive communities work past balkanization and superficial interactions so they can develop strong relationships, both with each other and with the families they serve.

Parental involvement is especially important to a strong school community. There is a growing body of empirical evidence that shows that well-structured family participation in education enhances students' academic success, improves school behavior, and reinforces stronger self-regulatory skills and work orientation (Chavkin, 2000; Moles, 1987; Baker, 1997; Morris and Taylor, 1998). A bond between parents and teachers and schools contributes to student learning (Epstein, 2001), as well as positive attitudes and behavior (Lee, Burkam, Zimiles, and Ladewski, 1994; Carpenter-Aeby and Aeby, 2001; Simon, 2001). In a longitudinal study that involved 11,000 parents of children from more than 1,000 high schools with diverse student populations, Simon (2001) found that parent involvement had a positive influence on student grades, course credits completed, attendance, behavior, and school preparedness regardless of the child's background. The study found that when students communicated with their parents about school and college planning, they were more likely to attend classes and be prepared.

However, parents are largely uninvolved in many schools. Moles (1993) found that there are three main obstacles to parent involvement in schooling: (1) teachers' insufficient knowledge, skills, and strategies to collaborate effectively with parents; (2) restricted opportunities for interaction due to school policies; and (3) psychological and cultural barriers that may exist between teachers and families in the community. Developing a relationship with parents can be complicated: research reveals that parent-teacher communications often center on children's academic problems, misbehavior, or negative attitudes, which makes it difficult for parents and teachers to develop positive relationships (Epstein, 2001). When their interactions are not problem based, a study by Hanafin and Lynch (2002) found that parental involvement was typically limited to giving and receiving of information about their children, restricted consultation, and engagement in providing supplemental help.

Some schools have found effective ways to encourage parent-teacher communication and connection, using practices ranging from home visits, frequent positive calls home, on-line connections for homework and information sharing, parent-teacher-student conferences, exhibitions of student work, and parent participation in school activities among many other strategies (see Mattingly, Prislin, McKenzie, Rodriguez, and Kayzar, 2002, for an extensive review of parent participation programs).

It is not difficult to convince new teachers that parent involvement is important; the difficulty lies in preparing teachers to work with diverse adult personalities in the context of schooling. Some parents must be encouraged to participate, whereas others are not reticent and may have strong ideas about how their children should be educated. Some have gentle, easygoing styles whereas others will be assertive and even litigious when solving problems for their children. Some parents have access to the schools and have time to be involved; others find schools intimidating and have schedules not conducive to frequent school visits. Some speak English and are well versed in educational jargon; others have more difficulty communicating about their children's educational needs. Teachers also differ in their temperaments and assumptions about the roles of parents. Many may believe their job is to work only with children and not with their families. If they are to be maximally effective, it is important for teachers to understand the importance of learning to work with parents, administrators, and other community members to address the needs of children.

Ultimately, teachers need to know how to find ways to work with parents to enhance children's learning. Teachers should be aware of recent literature that provides strategies on how to work with parents and how to set up successful parent participation programs (see, for example, Epstein and others, 2002; Lieber, 2002), including situations where parents do not agree with the teachers (see, for example, Collins and Dowell, 1998). It is also important for new teachers to understand the children's experiences outside of school. For example, according to Elkind (1994), the way parents raise children has changed significantly in the last thirty years. In the past, many believed children should obey parents without question. Now, however, many children have more voice, and parents spend a lot of time negotiating with their children. Children's experiences carry over to school, where they expect adults to behave in ways that are similar to their parents. It is important for teachers to get to know children's parents or guardians to find out whether and how the teacher's management, discipline, and instructional strategies are aligned with the beliefs of the child's at-home teachers, as well as to figure out how to negotiate different beliefs and interaction styles.

Organizing the Classroom

Classroom management is often erroneously equated only with organizing classroom routines and dealing with misbehavior. Relevant concerns about curriculum, pedagogy, motivation, and community development are often missing. For that reason, we purposefully did not present this limited view at the beginning of the chapter. However, that does not mean that the knowledge and skills for organizing and structuring classrooms are unimportant or unnecessary. An efficient classroom organization and structure is crucial to maintaining an orderly and effective learning environment. An orderly classroom arrangement optimizes learning time, whereas inadequate planning causes disruptions and delays (Emmer, Evertson, Sanford, Clements, and Worsham, 1984). Arranging the classroom thoughtfully supports orderly movement, few distractions, and efficient use of available space (Emmer and others, 1984).

Early research by Kounin (1977) uncovered a number of ways in which teacher behavior affects student behavior and learning. Kounin videotaped eighty different classrooms that were defined as either orderly or disorderly. His observations and analyses led him to conclude that effective classroom managers frequently monitored classroom behaviors and interactions in ways that allowed teachers to address problems before they arose. Good teachers, he claimed, had "eyes in the back of their head"—an alertness to what is occurring that he called "withitness." Kounin's years of research led him to create a set of principles for preventive discipline. He observed that certain actions by the teacher could hinder the momentum and smoothness of a lesson. For example, he found that when a teacher terminates one activity, starts another, and then returns to the first activity it disrupts the flow. Teachers also disrupt the flow when they are pulled away from the activity by unimportant matters, or when they slow down the instruction (for example) by explaining instructions in detail when children already understand. He introduced teaching concepts, techniques, and strategies that would increase the level of on-task activity and allow for a well-run, problem-free classroom.

Effective classroom organization not only has an impact on student behavior, it also impacts academic achievement (see, for example, Evertson, 1989,

1997; Moles, 1990). For example, the relationship between instructional time and learning is in substantial part mediated by classroom management practices. The well-known Beginning Teacher Evaluation Study was one of the first, but not the last, to note that there is a wide variability across schools and classrooms in the amount of time students spend learning the curriculum and the amount of instructional time spent is often associated with student achievement (Fisher and others, 1980).

Learning time is optimized by using strategies that maintain the flow of the activities, minimize the disruptions that occur during transitions, and help students develop responsibility for their actions. Research reveals that teachers who start the school year by developing a set of rules and procedures are more effective classroom managers (Sanford, Emmer, and Clements, 1983; Weinstein, 1996). For example, Evertson, Emmer, and Anderson conducted in-depth observations in twenty-seven elementary classrooms in eight schools and found that teachers who were clear about rules and routines in the first few weeks of the school year had fewer misbehavior problems than teachers who did not make these clear at the beginning (Evertson, 1997). Data from this study were used to identify effective and ineffective classroom managers. Better managers routinely analyzed the procedures and expectations required of students, included instruction on rules and procedures, analyzed their students' needs for information about how to participate in class activities, kept their students in view, and dealt with problems quickly. Subsequent studies showed that good managers were also more consistent, developed a system for student accountability, communicated effectively, and preserved their instructional time.

From these kinds of observational studies, Evertson (1989) identified six major kinds of routines or procedures that are important for teachers to consider in setting up a well-functioning classroom. These include (1) the physical setting of the room; (2) transitions in and out of the room; (3) procedures during groupwork; (4) general procedures such as distributing materials or being on the playground; (5) procedures specific to particular classroom routines, such as attendance or putting homework on the board; and (6) procedures or routines associated with student-initiated and teacher-led instruction. Being clear about productive arrangements in each of these areas enables teachers to run their classrooms smoothly by minimizing disruptions and, in return, maximizing students' learning time (Jones and Jones, 1990; Emmer and others, 1984; Burden, 1999).

New teachers also need to consider that different classroom arrangements facilitate different kinds of teaching. For example, the physical environment of the classroom determines the role of the teacher and the students and whether the work is more competitive or collaborative. It influences power relations among the students and between the teacher and the students (Rosenholtz and Simson, 1984). In the last few decades, many teachers have started using more cooperative learning strategies in their classrooms and have arranged seating to accommodate this type of learning, with tables or small clusters of desks organized for groupwork rather than desks in rows. A particular seating arrangement may facilitate certain kinds of learning, but it does not predict that that learning will occur in an effective manner. What is key is that physical space arrangements fit the teaching plans and allow work to go smoothly. These arrangements may change from day to day or week to week depending on what kinds of activities students are engaged in and what the teacher is trying to accomplish.

When teachers choose particular kinds of learning activities, they need to consider how to organize other classroom plans to support the strategies they have chosen to use. For example, novice teachers sometimes hold the misconception that active classrooms in which students are engaged in activities and group inquiry are "less structured" and require less planning and organization than classrooms featuring teacher-led whole group instruction. In truth, activity-based classrooms are highly structured and take a great deal of time to plan and organize. The quality of the learning depends on substantial prearrangement and preparation of materials, planning of activity structures, and skillful management of workflow.

In sum, to organize and structure classroom environments effectively, teachers must be able to design an appropriate physical layout for the classroom, develop rules and procedures, optimize learning time by developing smooth transitions between activities, set an appropriate pace for learning, and involve children in creating a democratic space where they have a sense of ownership and autonomy.

Repairing and Restoring Student Behavior

When teacher candidates are asked about the anxieties they hold regarding their future classroom, most express concern about dealing with potential student misbehavior or disruptions (Martin and others, 1999). New teachers often search for the "right way" to handle various disruptive behaviors. With the other features of instruction we have described earlier in place, misbehavior should be occasional. When students behave in ways that are counterproductive to the classroom goals and norms, teachers need to know, first, that there are many strategies to choose from and second, that their decisions should be based on several factors, including the student's particular learning situation and needs, the history of the student's behavior, the context of the class, the severity of the problem, and school policy.

It is helpful for teachers to think about how to respond to various disruptions based on the underlying cause and the severity (and perhaps frequency and duration) of the behavior. Charles (2001) describes five types of misbehavior that should occasion different kinds of responses: *aggression*, which includes physical and verbal violence; *immorality*, such as cheating; *class disruptions*, which entail acts that are against the set rules or routines; *defiance* of authority or opposing to the teacher's expectations; and *goofing off* or being indifferent to tasks. For example, if a teacher must confront one or more students who are "goofing off," interventions should be as unobtrusive as possible and preserve the students' attachment to the teacher and classroom (Weinstein and Mignano, 1993). Some unobtrusive methods include using body language, approaching the child, keeping eye contact, or calling the child's name out loud (Weinstein, 1996). Similarly, teachers might choose a minor intervention, such as the use of "I-messages," for example, "I feel concerned when I see that everyone is not yet working on their task." Such messages might also be called "responsibility messages," because they leave the responsibility of the behavior with the student and avoid labeling the student or triggering a negative impact of the intervention (Gordon, 1974).

If the problem is more serious, such as one that involves aggression against other students, the teacher may want to develop a more substantial intervention plan such as designing and implementing a program for conflict resolution. Johnson and Johnson (1994) found that, even in elementary school, students who learn and practice skills of conflict resolution become more inclined to work out problems among themselves before the problems escalate. In addition, Tyrrell, Scully, and Halligan (1998) found that a peaceful environment can be established when the community works together to create a conflict resolution program. The purposes of such programs often aim at fostering the values of compassion, respect, and appreciation of others' differences, building character and strengthening the practice of nonviolent resolution of conflict. Students who are frequently aggressive benefit especially from learning specific skills for managing conflicts peacefully that differ from what they have previously learned at home or from peers.

In another study of the effects of training in conflict resolution and cooperative learning in an alternative high school in New York City, Deutsch (1992) found positive effects on children's academic performance and social development. The student training in cooperative learning involved five principles: (1) positive interdependence; (2) face-to-face interactions; (3) individual accountability; (4) interpersonal and small-group skills; and (5) processing (that is, analysis of group functioning with the goal of improvement). The conflict resolution training taught active listening, I-messages, reframing the issues in conflict, criticizing ideas and not people, differentiating between underlying needs versus positions, distinguishing between negotiable and non-negotiable conflict situations, developing "win-win" solutions, and destructive and constructive negotiation styles. The results showed that students improved in managing conflicts, and they experienced increased social support, improved relations, higher self-esteem, increases in personal control, and higher academic performance.

Although there are many options for teachers in managing student behavior, teachers also need to know about ineffective choices. Research suggests that misuse of authority tends to reinforce a sense of weakness, passivity, subordination, and victimization among children (Lewis, 2001). For example, in a study involving twenty-one elementary schools and twenty-one secondary schools, Lewis (2001) found that coercive discipline inhibited the students' development of responsibility and distracted them from their schoolwork. As we describe in the following section, the success of different discipline plans has been found to vary, and these differences are associated with the extent to which various approaches are consonant with research on children's moral and cognitive development, motivation, and learning.

Based on an analysis of the research literature, Brophy (1998) argues that teachers who approach classroom management as a process of developing and maintaining effective learning environments are more likely to become successful than teachers who emphasize their role as authority figures or disciplinarians. A recent study that supported this conclusion compared a sample of eighty-eight "teachers of the year" to a group of ninety-two other teachers matched by gender, years of service, grade levels taught, and highest degree earned (Agne, Greenwood, and Miller, 1994). The authors found teachers of the year to be significantly more humanistic than others in their dealings with children. These teachers emphasized "trust, acceptance, friendship, respect, self-discipline, democratic climate, flexibility, student self-determination, and nonpunitive, nonmoralistic attitudes" (p. 149).

Classroom Management Programs

There are various programs that have been designed to provide teachers with guidance about how they can set up conflict resolution programs (see, for example, Bodine and Crawford, 1998; Gordon, 1974; Teglasi and Rothman, 2001), create learning communities (Freiberg, 1999; Sergiovanni, 1994; Kohn, 1996b), and develop systematic strategies for discipline (Curwin and Mendler, 2000; Fay and Funk, 1998). Teachers need a professional base of knowledge both for evaluating programs that may be suggested to them and for developing their own programs.

Approaches to classroom management have varied in the extent to which they are based on what Burden (2003) describes as low-, medium-, or high-control strategies. Methods that are founded primarily on behaviorism are generally considered high control as they emphasize external rewards and punishments to shape behavior. For example, *Assertive Discipline* (Canter and Canter, 2002) has been identified as a high-control program. In that program the authors emphasize the teacher's rights to reinforce desired behaviors and establish consequences. Low-control methods are based more on cognitive psychology and on the philosophical belief that students have primary responsibility for controlling their own behavior and that, with guidance, they have the capability to make sound decisions. The child's thoughts, feelings, and preferences are taken into account when dealing with instruction, classroom management, and discipline. *Teaching with Love and Logic* (Fay and Funk, 1998) has been identified as a low-control approach. In this approach, the authors emphasize shared control with students, maintaining student self-concepts, and balancing consequences with empathy.

Medium-control approaches are based on the philosophical belief that development comes from a combination of innate and outer forces. Thus the control of the student behavior is a joint responsibility of the student and the teacher. *Discipline with Dignity* (Curwin and Mendler, 2000), has been identified as a medium-control approach. In that approach, the authors suggest that teachers establish social contracts and teach students to make responsible choices. There are many other programs developed by various educators that teachers can evaluate and draw upon. (See Burden, 1999, and Charles, 2001, for a short description of many of these programs and their theoretical foundations. See Moles, 1990, for research on outcomes of various programs.)

There has been much controversy over which methods are most effective, not only for purposes of achievement and management, but also for promoting citizenship and longer-term responsibility. Current research suggests that low- to medium-control methods of management are more effective than high-control methods not only for regulating behavior, but also for improving achievement (Lewis, 2001; Brophy, 1998; Kohn, 1996b).

For example, an evaluation of a community-oriented classroom model called Judicious Discipline found that, based on repeated measures of student outcomes, participating students developed a better self-concept, achieved higher levels of moral development, demonstrated a greater sense of ethical decision making, established better student-educator and student-student relationships, and spent more quality time in school and classrooms (McEwan, Nimmo, and Gathercoal, 1999). This comprehensive approach to democratic classroom management is a medium-control approach that provides educators with a foundation for teaching citizenship each day through student-teacher interactions. Judicious Discipline seeks to create a common language based on the principle of human rights and responsibilities, emphasizing that it is the educator's professional responsibility to create an equitable environment that affords every student the opportunity to be successful.

Similarly, a program called Consistency Management and Cooperative Discipline expands the leadership roles in the classroom from the teacher to the students. According to third-party evaluations of this program, researchers found there was an increase in student and teacher attendance; a reduction in discipline referrals; and improvements in classroom climate, time to learn, and long-term student achievement (Freiberg, 1999).

By contrast, studies of high-control approaches have found that, over time, student misbehavior can actually increase, as students increasingly abandon their own self-responsibility for their learning and behavior (Mayer, 1995; Mayer and Leone, 1999), and teachers' use of increasingly punitive approaches creates resistance and student opposition to learning and school, while exacerbating discriminatory treatment of students (Leone, Mayer, Malmbren, and Meisel, 2000; Townsend, 2000). These findings are consistent with the decidedly mixed empirical findings about the effects of programs like Assertive Discipline on student behavior (Emmer and Aussiker, 1990; Render, Padilla, and Krank, 1989). Such programs that rely heavily on reward tokens and escalating punishments while de-emphasizing discussion about behavior or efforts to create classroom communities tend to externalize responsibility rather than help students take initiative in creating a constructive classroom environment.

Low- and medium-control approaches may be more desirable because they are associated with high-quality teaching and greater intrinsic motivation for students, but most agree they require more teacher skill to implement (Epstein and Sheldon, 2002). Thus teacher education programs must incorporate effective strategies of general pedagogical development alongside efforts to teach specific classroom management techniques.

Moral Development

In addition to enabling students to engage in purposeful academic learning and to behave in prosocial ways, teachers are also called upon to support children in their moral development. Nel Noddings (1997) argued that a morally defensible mission for the schools in the twenty-first century "should be to produce competent, caring, loving, and lovable people" (p. 28). When teachers are focused on controlling children and classrooms, it can be difficult for them to see that children can be taught to be good citizens, and that a moral perspective can positively impact their classrooms. Psychosocial and moral development are seldom part of the formal curriculum, and given what is expected of teachers today, they have very little time to use teachable moments and other opportunities to present moral lessons. This is unfortunate, because behavior management is closely connected to social, moral, ethical, and emotional development. As Butcharts (1998) notes, discipline is a moral endeavor and moral qualities are learned through moral actions and reflection.

As we discussed earlier in the section on learning communities, when children are taught to get along with others, to make moral choices, to care for others, and to be good citizens, it is not only easier for teachers to manage the classroom and to produce confident children, they will also help children develop academically (Schaps, 1998; McEwan, 1996; Parke and others, 1998; Battistich and others, 1995).

Moral development is often misunderstood in part because people have different opinions on what it means to be moral. LePage and Sockett (2002) describe these confusions as arising from four main sources. First, many believe that morality must derive from religious beliefs. Second, many believe that to express a moral viewpoint is merely to express an opinion, and an opinion is by definition subjective. Third, some believe that morals are relative, differing from society to society or from age to age so that any form of moral condemnation of another society cannot be warranted. Finally, many equate morality with very limited categories of human experience, for example, sexual behavior.

This is not the place to counter all these confusions in detail but simply to say that, as with many serious misconceptions, there is a kernel of truth lurking in each of them. First, although those with religious beliefs do draw implications for their (moral) acts and actions from their religious beliefs, people do not have to be religious to be moral. Second, although it is essential that a moral person act from his or her own will (rather than under orders), that does not mean that the moral beliefs the person has or the opinions she or he expresses are entirely idiosyncratic. Third, although it is true that there are dissimilarities between many societies on certain things, there are many areas in which there is moral congruence (for example, caring for family members or telling the truth). If we focus on our individual moral views, we risk ignoring the moral character of a community and the similarities between such communities (Etzioni, 1996). Finally, to think of moral behavior as referring to just private or interpersonal sexual matters is to ignore the communal moral issues of honesty, fairness, courage, justice, trust, loyalty, and so on.

Educational thought is influenced by these confusions as, for example, where teachers feel they dare not "impose their values" on children. Although teachers frequently worry about this important issue, polls show that the public strongly favors the teaching of core civic values in school (Farkas, Johnson, Duffett, and McHugh (1998). Most would agree that teaching is a caring profession focused not only on educating children, but also on improving our society. And it is certainly true that teachers' work presents difficult moral choices that need constant consideration, experimentation, and reflection (Jackson, Boostrom, and Hansen, 1998; Sockett, 1993).

In classrooms today, the confusion about what it means to be moral is often played out in various perspectives on character education. Some believe that character education should focus on teaching children to obey the rules, get along with others, and be good citizens in a classroom. Others believe that character education should focus on teaching children to be autonomous thinkers who question injustice and adopt a critical stance toward citizenship. In fact, some of these advocates believe that teaching children to simply "follow rules" can be damaging (see Kohn, 1997). Still others believe that character education should focus on teaching children virtues—to be responsible, caring, honest, trustworthy, and so on. New teachers must understand the different perspectives on morality and character education so they can make informed decisions about their own strategies based on well-examined philosophies and perspectives about children's moral development.

New teachers also need to understand the different domains of emotional, moral, ethical, and psychosocial development and how development in each of these areas affects development in the other areas. For example, as students are enabled to develop emotional empathy with others by considering their experience or point of view, they are also better prepared to engage in moral and ethical thinking about individuals' responsibilities to one another and to the community or group. Furthermore, teachers can use this developing empathy and moral thinking to teach about productive social interactions and encourage growth in the psychosocial realm.

One misconception often held by new teachers is that psychosocial, moral, and emotional development has no impact on intellectual development—that teachers must choose between teaching academic topics and teaching about character. Not only can these two topics be instructionally integrated, but according to Kohlberg (1981), moral development and cognitive development are closely intertwined. As students learn how others think and feel, they increase their ability to see multiple perspectives, an ability that transfers across other academic as well as interpersonal domains.

It is useful for teachers to know that there are many scholars who have conducted research about the processes of moral development and related aspects of intellectual development, which leads to strategies for fostering students' growth in these domains (see, for example, Belenky, Clinchy, Goldberger, and Tarule, 1996; Damon, 1990; Gilligan, 1982; Jackson, Boostrom, and Hansen, 1998; Kohlberg, 1981; Noddings, 1992; Piaget, 1999; Sockett, 1993). Teachers should have familiarity with stages of moral development and have some knowledge of this research that can provide a foundation on which to build as they continue their professional development.

Can Morality Be Taught?

Two common misconceptions among novice teachers are that morality cannot be taught and that it should be the sole responsibility of the parents. There are at least two ways to encourage, or teach, moral development in schools. One is through a moral communities approach, which involves setting up environments where children make moral choices and engage in moral action—something they would do in any event—with teacher guidance for thinking about the implications of their decisions for others. The second approach involves directly teaching character education.

Kohlberg (1981) held early on that moral education required more than individual reflection. It needed to include experiences for students to operate as moral agents. Therefore Kohlberg and his colleagues developed the Just Community Approach. The Just Community Approach (JCA) draws on two different traditions in moral education theory. The first is the psychological tradition expounded by Dewey and Piaget, who proposed that schools should become democracies nurturing moral development by providing children with opportunities for cooperative decision making. The second is the sociological tradition articulated by Durkheim, who advocated that schools should become communities fostering moral socialization by building strong group norms and group attachment. In a research study that evaluated the Just Community Approach, Jennings and Kohlberg (1983) found that a JCA program for youthful offenders led to significantly higher levels of moral reasoning (using a moral stage development inventory) than did a behavior modification or transactional analysis program. The extent of change in moral development measured in these youth was equivalent to the extent of change measured when developmental moral education programs for nondelinquent high school students had been evaluated in the past.

Similarly, in a longitudinal study, Schaps (1998) evaluated the results of an intervention designed to improve relationships and "sense of community" in classrooms. He found that as the children's "sense of community" increased, so did their concern for others. Specifically, the study showed an increase in empathic awareness, democratic values, prosocial conflict resolution skills, altruistic behavior, intrinsic motivation, enjoyment of helping others learn, positive attitudes toward out-groups, and positive interpersonal behaviors in class. In another study of five schools, researchers found that schools that developed a community orientation in support of learning demonstrated gains in prosocial behavior and in academic achievement (Schaps, 1998).

Teachers may benefit from being aware of character education programs, such as Character Counts and Kids for Character. Most use similar strategies, providing literature, video, computer programs, and other forms of narrative to present moral tales that can be analyzed in class. Many of these programs offer case studies, for example, of children acting morally or immorally in certain situations. Children are expected to write about the cases or act them out and discuss them. One example of a high school program that focuses on moral development is called Facing History and Ourselves (Web site: http://www.facinghistory.org). For more than twenty-five years, Facing History has engaged teachers and students of diverse backgrounds in an examination of prejudice and discrimination in order to promote the development of a more humane and informed citizenry. By studying the historical development of the Holocaust and other examples of collective violence, students make the essential connection between history and the moral choices they confront in their own lives. Examining history in all of its complexities, including its legacies of prejudice and discrimination, resilience and courage, encourages young people to engage in critical discussions and debates regarding their community and nation. An outcome study found that participating students showed increased relationship maturity and decreased fighting behavior, racist attitudes, and insular ethnic identity relative to comparison students (Schultz, Barr, and Selman, 2001), indicating that moral development and associated prosocial behaviors can, in fact, be taught.

IMPLICATIONS FOR TEACHER EDUCATION

In the past, when teachers were asked how they learned to manage their classrooms, many claimed they learned on the job. For example, in a study involving 126 teachers from twenty-one randomly chosen secondary schools in the Midwest, Merrett and Whendall (1993) found that only 18 percent of teachers claimed they learned management skills during initial training, whereas 82 percent learned them on the job. These teachers believed that a course focusing on behavior management in their preservice education would have helped them reduce the level of pupil misbehavior and their own stress. Most of the participants in this study thought that their colleagues spent too much time on order and control, and 38 percent thought they themselves did also.

This is beginning to change as preparation programs incorporate more explicit attention to all of the elements of pedagogical planning and classroom management we have described here. For example, a survey of Kentucky teachers found that more than 80 percent of beginning teachers who graduated from Kentucky colleges of education—where statewide reforms of teacher education had been undertaken in the early 1990s—felt well prepared for virtually all aspects of their jobs, including classroom management (Kentucky Institute for Educational Research, 1997). A 1998 survey of 3,000 beginning teachers in New York City found that the great majority of teachers who were prepared in teacher education programs felt adequately prepared for the many tasks of teaching related to classroom management, whereas those who lacked preparation or entered teaching through alternative programs rated this as an area in which they felt the most inadequately trained (Darling-Hammond, Chung, and Frelow, 2002). Similarly, well over 70 percent of the graduates of the California State University felt well prepared for virtually all aspects of their jobs, including classroom management. Those who had had student teaching (just over half of the total) felt significantly better prepared—and were viewed as better prepared by principals—than those who had completed certification through an internship program or who had taught on an emergency credential without student teaching (California State University, 2002a, 2002b). Another study found that these emergency hires clamored for information about classroom management in the teacher education courses they were taking while they were teaching, but they often failed to understand the strong connections between effective curriculum planning and student behavior (Shields and others, 2001).

When it comes to management, first-year teachers need to be as well informed as fifth-year teachers. If teachers deal with misbehaviors inappropriately and ineffectively, they can cause serious damage to children's psychological well-being as well as to their own sense of competence, which often leads to quitting the profession. In a research study that included 243 secondary teachers from fifteen randomly selected schools, Brouwers and Tomic (2000) found that teachers who did not have confidence in their classroom management skills were confronted by their incompetence every day and quickly "burned out." They found a significant relationship between emotional exhaustion and low levels of perceived self-efficacy in classroom management. Luczak's (2004) study of beginning teachers surveyed in the federal Schools and Staffing Surveys confirmed that beginning teacher attrition is strongly related to teacher preparation in general and to classroom management training in particular. Martin and others (1999) found that teachers who lacked confidence in their classroom management skills were more likely to refer children to other school personnel, less likely to work with non-school professionals, and less likely to use positively focused strategies in response to behavior.

Brophy (1988) suggests that, in addition to knowledge about subject matter, pedagogy, and students, teachers initially need three types of knowledge to become effective classroom managers: propositional knowledge that concerns principles of classroom management, procedural knowledge that addresses the implementation of these principles, and conditional knowledge that pertains to when they should be implemented and for what reason. Others argue that successful classroom management also depends on the development of dispositions toward children and teaching, including dispositions of respect and care; dispositions to inquire into children's lives and thinking so as to better understand their experience; and dispositions toward education that value children's broad development in social as well as academic domains (Tobin and Johnson, 1994; Martin and Van Gunten, 2002; Kaplan and others, 2002; McAllister and Irvine, 2002; Winitzky, 1992).

As teacher educators help teachers learn to successfully manage classrooms, three important elements of preparation should be considered. First, teachers need practical experience working with children under the guidance of expert practitioners as they learn about classroom management. Second, practical experience needs to be supplemented by useful classroom pedagogies that link theory with practice. Third, teacher educators must themselves model good classroom management.

Strategies for Preparing Teachers for Classroom Management

At the beginning of this chapter, we described an observation of Mary Gregg's classroom during her first year of teaching (Snyder, 2000). It is important to ask what type of program can prepare such a skillful teacher so early in her career. Mary was taught in the Developmental Teacher Education Program (DTE) at the University of California, Berkeley. This program is a two-year postbaccalaureate program that includes a year focused substantially on coursework and observation followed by a second year of intensive clinical experience with ongoing connected coursework.

DTE includes a number of design features that contribute to candidates' high levels of skill (Snyder, 2000). Among other things, the program emphasizes the relationship of developmental theory to teaching practice throughout a set of four connected courses that extend over the full two years. Candidates develop a sophisticated practice as courses are sequenced in a spiral curriculum to provide the opportunity for repeated consideration of teaching-related issues at higher levels of understanding over the two years. Candidates engage in five carefully selected student-teaching placements so they experience diverse settings where teaching issues can be addressed with a variety of teaching role models as guides. These placements are selected to model the practices taught by the program, with expert practitioners in each. A weekly student-teaching seminar with a complex and flexible organization promotes integration of theory and practice, small-group problem solving, and interaction between first- and second-year students. Individual clinical supervision is provided by highly experienced staff. Although the introduction to teaching is gradual, the amount of supervision remains relatively constant over the five placements.

These features are important in the following ways: Because classroom management is a practical art that is theoretically grounded, extensive student teaching in well-run, developmentally appropriate classrooms provides a solid foundation for understanding how teachers can engage students in meaningful learning and manage classrooms toward that end. That the classrooms serve very diverse student populations gives student teachers practice in learning to work successfully with children and families whose backgrounds may be different from their own. That the program integrates learning about children, learning, curriculum, and teaching and revisits key concerns allows candidates' practice to "take root," growing more thoughtful and reflective as well as more competent on the ground in the classroom. That the faculty is well rooted in research on instruction grounds the practical work the candidates engage in. The DTE program suggests that to effectively teach propositional, procedural, and conditional knowledge, as well as dispositions, teachers benefit from hands-on experience working with children, classroom activities that tie theory to practice, and personal experience of good classroom management in their placements and their own preparation programs.

Practical Experience—Working with Children. Preparation for classroom management typically should involve clinical experiences involving observing and modeling with guided reflection. Although experience is important, learning alone from trial and error is not at all the same as learning through supervised practice from a cooperating teacher who can demonstrate how to organize productive learning activities and respond to both predictable and unexpected problems that arise in classrooms. It is important for student teachers to get guided hands-on experience with children before taking responsibility for a classroom. (See Chapter Ten on teacher learning in this volume.) The quality of the modeling and the opportunities to practice skills are key. As Burnard and Yaxley (1997) point out, learning classroom management skills by observing mentor teachers during apprenticeships has had two main flaws. First, mentor teachers do not always have effective classroom management skills. Some are still engaging in the trial-and-error method; others have adapted strategies that are not highly effective for managing behavior *and* supportive learning. Second, many student teachers do not have the opportunity in their internships to use various strategies under difficult circumstances so they lack confidence when they are alone in a class.

Choosing strong mentors and structuring the internship to allow for graduate responsibility are both important elements for successfully learning to manage the classroom. Having a student teaching placement begin at the start of a school year allows student teachers to see how classroom routines are established; how teachers learn about students, their families, and their communities; and how curriculum planning concords with classroom management procedures. Staying long enough to be able to take over elements of teaching allows student teachers to practice implementing management techniques first-hand and problem solve classroom events with the mentor teacher before having to take on a classroom independently.

Prospective teachers can also benefit from strong modeling, both in clinical sites and in coursework, about how to work with parents. They can be asked, as some programs do, to make positive calls home to parents and to conduct parent conferences or home visits using models and protocols that demonstrate how to make these conversations productive. Understanding that these kinds of connections outside of class can make an important contribution to students' effort and cooperation inside of class is an important realization for new teachers, who may otherwise think of their teaching skills as applying largely within the confines of classroom time.

Reflection on Management Through Class Activities. Brophy (1988) argues that it is important to develop classroom management skills through the apprenticeship approach involving modeling, coaching, and scaffolding. However, he also argues that this approach needs to be supplemented with didactic instruction in basic concepts and skills, structured classroom observations, and the use of case materials and simulation exercises. Today, these kinds of materials include interactive video and computer-based simulations, such as the interactive multimedia program *Classroom Management,* developed by the Vanderbilt Cognition and Technology Group (Smithey, 1996). The program provides research on classroom management key issues tied to video examples of teachers practicing what the hypertext narrative is describing, and assignments to design plans for addressing that particular issue in students' own future classrooms, based on research findings, what they viewed in a real classroom, and what they believe is effective management. Through the use of the program, students are able to visit a wide variety of teachers and observe the ways in which they arrange their classrooms for instruction, the different ways in which they conduct instruction, and the methods they use to manage student behavior. In reflections and analyses, students are challenged to move past their "derivative" knowledge and to develop their own knowledge about teaching to create learning environments that are positive and well managed.

Through these and other cases and classroom exercises, teachers can learn to reflect critically on their teaching. A teacher's ability to reflect on his or her experiences is an important dispositional skill for successful classroom management (Winitzky, 1992; McAllister and Irvine, 2002; Jadallah, 1996). Winitzky (1992) studied how teachers reflect on their practice to understand their teaching, finding that the way teacher candidates organize their knowledge of classroom management has a bearing on their ability to reflect about classroom management. Teachers with more organized and complex structures for framing their knowledge were better able to reflect on classroom events at all levels, from the technical through the moral. Coursework specifically treating classroom management, particularly if it embodies the comprehensive frame we have described here, can give teachers a conceptual map or schema to understand what they are experiencing and trying to accomplish in the classroom. There may be particular benefit in having this coursework occur while prospective teachers are in student teaching placements, so the theory can be immediately connected to practice.

Through reflective practice, teachers can move beyond the trial-and-error stage quickly. Engaging in action research about specific problems can help them learn to use systematic research techniques that go beyond intuitive reflection. Teachers who have reflective dispositions are less likely to blame children or parents for lack of progress. They are more likely to engage in critical self-assessment in order to change their strategies. When one strategy does not work with a child, they learn to move on to the next strategy (Zeichner and Liston, 1996; Valli, 1989). A reflective teacher does not communicate to a child, a parent, or other colleagues that a child is unreachable. Lack of success means that for this particular child, given these strategies, in this context, the plans were unsuccessful. Therefore the teacher needs to develop new plans.

Following is an example of how teacher educators have tied teacher research to a simulation using readers' theater to analyze a case involving classroom management issues. In this study, high school teachers reflected on their experiences as instructors in an in-school suspension (ISS) program where the children were sent when they were expelled from classrooms (Sevcik, Robbins, and Leonard, 1997). These teachers realized that a large number of the children being sent to ISS were referred because of obscene language, and the same children were sent over and over again. Obviously, punishing children by having them sent to ISS was having no effect on decreasing the behavior. So, as part of their research study, the teachers worked to understand why the children chose to use obscene language despite the consequences and how they might more effectively eliminate this behavior. In this short excerpt of the actual dialogue from one group discussion, one of the teachers is asking one of the students (John) why he was sent to ISS on this one particular occasion:

TEACHER: I can remember reading your response, the one where you got tapped in the head or smacked in the head or something. What happened?

JOHN: Yea, I was . . . I had my head laying down like this . . . and Eugene—I guess it was Eugene, smacked me in the back real hard.

CHRIS: Smacked him in the back of the head real, real, hard.

JOHN: And I jumped up and said, "Who in the f . . . did that?" Mrs. Turner goes, "Go out in the hallway!" I said, "Well, who hit me in the back of the head?" She started going off . . . "It doesn't matter who hit you in the back of the head . . ."

KRYSTAL: And, John, he was like, "F . . . ing b . . . ," and walked out.

TEACHER: And, who were you talking to?

JOHN: Mrs. Turner when she did that because . . .

TEACHER: Because she told you your language was inappropriate?

JOHN: No, because . . .

CHRIS: When there was a problem, she didn't address the problem. She refused to address problems in the classroom. Like when something happens . . .

MARK: She sends us out in the hallway . . .

JOHN: Yeah, she sends the guys out in the hallway, but she won't like say anything to a girl.

The researchers used this kind of excerpt to help teachers raise questions about the various elements of the situation. For example, this dialogue can be read simplistically. Some might argue that John called the teacher a name, he should be suspended—end of story. Others might question whether the teacher was unfair in her response, or biased against this particular child. Was there a way the teacher could have addressed the initial disturbance without escalating the problem? Could this entire incident have been prevented in the first place? What does the dialogue say about the children's relationship with this particular teacher, not only her relationship with John, but with the other children in the group who were helping John describe the incident? What do we know about how this school addresses misconduct? We know that when children act out in certain ways, they are "sent away." How does this assist in the development of the children's moral decision making or citizenship? What are the students learning from ISS and the school's methods of discipline management?

To prepare teachers to think about classroom management (broadly conceived), this particular research project has been used in a master's program at George Mason University (Sockett, Demulder, LePage, and Wood, 2002) as an exercise to stimulate discussions about issues of classroom management. Teachers have been asked to read the transcript dialogue aloud in class, taking various "roles." After the transcripts are read aloud, the class is asked to analyze the data together. Many themes are discussed, not only about the strategies used, but also about the children's views of obscene language, how they respond to the teachers, and how they view the classroom and school community. The teachers are also asked to discuss what it means to be moral, not only for the children, but also for the teachers involved in the study, and for themselves. The student teachers also read the published report (Sevcik and others, 1997) and discuss the researchers' conclusions. Among these is the recognition that the children's use of obscene language is complex. Particular words are used at various times for specific purposes depending on the context: there are rules and norms that govern the use of obscene language.

This activity also encourages the development of dispositions by allowing the teachers to confront their biases. Often when the dialogue is read, many of the teacher candidates immediately label the children as ethnic minorities from poor urban areas or children with learning disabilities (because one of the ISS teachers is a special education teacher). In fact, the majority of the children in the study were white children from a middle-class suburban area—not diagnosed with disabilities.

Student teachers are also asked to discuss the ISS teachers' strategy for dealing with misbehavior. This strategy is called "the inquiry method" of behavior intervention. In this strategy, children are asked to think through the reasons for their behavior, articulate those reasons, and justify their behavior with little or no adult interference. Part of the goal is to have the children struggle with the logic of their actions. The researchers found that by the end of their focus group interviews, the children, who were not proscribed from cursing during the focus group interviews, significantly decreased their use of obscene language by the end of the study.

Modeling by Teacher Educators. Finally, in teaching about classroom management, it is also important that teacher educators model good practice. Teachers are often asked to model the behaviors and rules they impose on children, from "come to class on time" to even more significant goals like "respecting each other's rights." Much of the literature on this issue explores the complexity of "practicing what we preach" (Wiest, 1999).

Teacher educators, too, have worked hard to "practice what they preach" (see, for example, Lehman, 1991; Kroll and LaBoskey, 1996; Phillips and Hatch, 2000). In addition to using active teaching methods when asking student teachers to use such methods, teacher educators should plan carefully to optimize learning time, structure appropriate transitions, develop community, be organized, and provide engaging and meaningful, well-scaffolded activities. Debriefing with student teachers on the choices they have made and strategies they use in managing their own classrooms is one way to teach thorough modeling and reflection. In addition, teacher educators need to model moral practices and a caring approach. This may seem obvious, but providing a moral model in academia can be complex. For example, it is not unusual for professors to turn a blind eye to other faculty members or administrators who are not treating students, staff, or colleagues appropriately. If teachers are expected to enforce professional norms with their colleagues for the sake of children, then teacher educators should be willing to do the same. Modeling is important because teachers are more likely to adopt certain pedagogical strategies if they have experienced the benefits of those strategies themselves in their own learning environments (Ertmer, 2003; Phillips and Hatch, 2000).

For years classroom management has perplexed new and experienced teachers alike. Poor skills in classroom management have caused many teachers to quit their jobs and move on to other careers. This is not an inevitable consequence of new teaching. It is clear that teachers like Mary Gregg, the first-year teacher featured at the beginning of the chapter, can learn strategies that will help them organize and manage a classroom effectively to prevent most, if not all, difficult behaviors, and when they do, they can engender meaningful learning from their earliest days as teachers.

CHAPTER TEN

How Teachers Learn and Develop

Karen Hammerness, Linda Darling-Hammond, John Bransford,
with David Berliner, Marilyn Cochran-Smith, Morva McDonald,
Kenneth Zeichner

How teachers learn and develop as professionals is a question that has compelled teacher educators and researchers for many years. How do teachers learn to draw upon and use their understanding of subject matter, learning, development, culture, language, pedagogy, and assessment in addressing concrete problems of practice? How do they learn to balance the individual needs of diverse learners with the demands of the curriculum and the goals of the larger group? How do they learn to become members of a professional community that works together to improve student learning? How can teacher educators help prospective teachers learn to address the multiple challenges of classroom and school life?

This chapter reviews classic and contemporary theory and research on teacher learning and development. Our discussion is divided into four major sections. In the first, we return to a theme mentioned in Chapter One and discussed in more detail in Chapter Two: namely, the theme of adaptive expertise that supports lifelong learning (Hatano and Inagaki, 1986). Clearly, the knowledge, skills, and attitudes needed for optimal teaching are not something that can be fully developed in preservice education programs. Instead, teacher education candidates need to be equipped for lifelong learning. This is especially true in societies like ours where expectations regarding academic standards and equitable education are constantly being refined as our world changes. Rethinking what is most important to teach is one example: Do we need to teach a wider range of foreign languages and more about international relations as the world gets smaller? Do we need to teach the calculation of square roots in an age of calculators? Rethinking how to teach and assess is another example. Can spreadsheets become a powerful tool for helping students understand the power of algebra? Can distance-learning technologies enhance global understanding? What strategies are most effective for teaching new English language learners in mathematics, in reading, and in other subject areas?

To successfully prepare effective teachers, teacher education should lay a foundation for lifelong learning. However, the concept of lifelong learning must become something more than a cliché. Given the relatively short period available for preparing teachers and the fact that not everything can be taught, decisions must be made about what content and strategies are most likely to prepare new entrants to be able to learn from their own practice, as well as the insights of other teachers and researchers.

In this chapter we explore theory and research relevant to the goal of helping teachers become professionals who are adaptive experts. We pay particular attention to three widely documented problems in learning to teach. First, learning to teach requires that new teachers come to think about (and understand) teaching in ways quite different from what they have learned from their own experience as students. Lortie (1975) called this the problem of "the apprenticeship of observation" to refer to the learning that takes place by virtue of being a student for twelve or more years in traditional classroom settings. These experiences have a major effect on preconceptions about teaching and learning that new teachers bring to the task of becoming professionals.

Second, helping teachers learn to teach more effectively requires them not only to develop the ability to "think like a teacher" but also to put what they know into action—what Mary Kennedy (1999) has termed "the problem of enactment." They need not only to understand but also to *do* a wide variety of things, many of them simultaneously. Meeting this challenge requires much more than simply having students memorize facts and procedures or even discuss ideas. As Simon (1980) notes, there is a major difference between "knowing that" and "knowing why and how."

A third issue in teacher preparation involves "the problem of complexity." Teachers typically work with many students at once and have to juggle multiple academic and social goals requiring trade-offs from moment to moment and day to day (Jackson, 1974). Although some aspects of teaching can be made somewhat routine, what teachers do will still be influenced by changing student needs and unexpected classroom events. And many other decisions in teaching cannot be routinized because they are contingent upon student responses and the particular objectives sought at a given moment. Helping prospective teachers learn to think systematically about this complexity is extremely important. They need to develop metacognitive habits of mind that can guide decisions and reflection on practice in support of continual improvement.

Some approaches to learning to teach do not adequately respond to these problems. For example, telling teachers in general ways about strategies that might be used in the classroom, without examples and models, does not typically lead to deep understanding or enactment. Developing routines can be helpful and can free up teachers' attention for other aspects of their work; however, offering only routines does not help teachers develop the diagnostic and instructional skills for dealing with students who require different approaches or additional supports if they are to learn successfully.

The third section of this chapter examines research on the development of teaching expertise and its implications for instruction. We discuss evidence that suggests that teachers' development is influenced by the nature of the preparation they received initially, and we show how changes in some teacher education programs seem to influence what teachers are able to do early in their careers. The final section provides a framework for considering the knowledge, skills, and dispositions needed for effective teaching, and for helping teachers learn throughout their lives.

TEACHERS AS ADAPTIVE EXPERTS

Carter (1990) notes that "how one frames the learning-to-teach question depends a great deal on how one conceives of what needs to be learned and how that learning might take place" (p. 307). This is consistent with Wiggins and McTighe's arguments (1998) that the design of effective learning opportunities needs to begin with a clear idea of what we want people to know and be able to do. It is also consistent with the problem-solving literature that suggests that the ways people initially frame problems has major effects on their solution strategies because different framings open up different "problem spaces" for people to explore (see, for example, Bransford and Stein, 1993; Newell and Simon, 1972).

As discussed in Chapter Two, the development of "adaptive expertise" provides an appropriate gold standard for becoming a professional. Figure 2.1 illustrates the hypothesis that there are two dimensions of expertise: efficiency and innovation (Schwartz and others, in press). In teaching, these dimensions might reflect a teacher's ability to efficiently and effectively use a specific classroom technique—such as reciprocal teaching conducted in small groups for reading—on the one hand, and her ability to develop a set of new strategies for a recently enrolled new English language learner for whom the existing routines are not enabling success. An important feature of adaptive experts lies in their abilities to balance these two dimensions.

Expertise along the *efficiency* dimension involves greater abilities to perform particular tasks without having to devote too many attentional resources to achieve them (see, for example, LaBerge and Samuels, 1974; Atkinson and

Schiffrin, 1968). Expert teachers are able to perform a variety of activities without having to stop and think about how to do them. Examples include how to manage a classroom while students are working in groups, how to give directions and hand out materials while keeping everyone's attention, how to predict the range of answers that students may give to a particular question about a concept in math, history, science, and so forth. Expert teachers are also able to notice patterns of classroom activity that, to the novice, often seem like disorganized chaos. (See "A Study of Teacher Expertise.")

A Study of Teacher Expertise

Expert and novice teachers notice very different things when viewing videotapes of classroom lessons. For example, when examining the same segment of videotape, experts are able to see patterns of activity and quickly draw inferences about what is happening in the classroom, whereas novices see activity that is confusing and not patterned. Here is one example:

EXPERT 6: On the left monitor, the students' note taking indicates that they have seen sheets like this and have had presentations like this before. It's fairly efficient at this point because they're used to the format they are using.

EXPERT 7: I don't understand why the students can't be finding out this information on their own rather than listening to someone tell them because if you watch the faces of most of them, they start out for about the first 2 or 3 minutes sort of paying attention to what's going on and then just drift off.

EXPERT 2: I haven't heard a bell, but the students are already at their desks and seem to be doing purposeful activity, and this is about the time that I decide they must be an accelerated group because they came into the room and started something rather than just sitting down and socializing.

NOVICE 1: I can't tell what they are doing. They're getting ready for class, but I can't tell what they're doing.

NOVICE 3: She's trying to communicate with them here about something, but I sure couldn't tell what it was.

ANOTHER NOVICE: It's a lot to watch.

Adapted from Sabers, D., Cushing, K. S., Berliner, D. C. (1991). Differences among teachers in a task characterized by simultaneity, multidimensionality, and immediacy. *American Educational Journal, 28*(1), 63–88.

Lifelong learning along the *innovation* dimension typically involves moving beyond existing routines and often requires people to rethink key ideas, practices, and even values in order to change what they are doing. These kinds of activities can be highly emotionally charged, and the capacity to consider change without feeling threatened is an important ability. Land's (see Nierenberg, 1982) tongue-in-cheek definition of innovation as "the sudden cessation of stupidity" can be helpful for maintaining a sense of humor in the midst of the need for fundamental change.

The processes of efficiency and innovation are assumed to be complementary at a global level, although they can sometimes appear to be antagonistic at a local level. They are complementary when appropriate levels of efficiency make room for innovation. For example, assume that a student in a classroom generates an answer to a math word problem that is novel for a particular teacher. If the teacher is able efficiently to predict and understand the range of other answers given by students in the class, it becomes possible to think creatively about the novel answer and figure how and why the student might have generated it. With experience and instruction, problem situations change from being novel, nonroutine problems to routine problems (that is, problems that have been solved before or are very similar to ones solved before). However, if the entire range of answers generated by students seems novel to the teacher, he or she will be overwhelmed and unable to cope. Hence learning about common conceptions and misconceptions about specific topics in one's field supports teacher problem solving by allowing teachers to be more efficient in their planning and more effective in their responses to students. (See Chapters Two and Six, for example.)

An example of a teacher's attempt to deal with what to her was a student's novel response to a mathematics problem is illustrated in "The Capacity to Innovate: Dealing with a Puzzling Answer."

The Capacity to Innovate: Dealing with a Puzzling Answer

A second-grade teacher asked students to solve 3 + 3. One boy, whom we'll call Jimmy, excitedly answered that the answer was 8. After asking him to rethink and still hearing the same answer, the teacher held up three fingers on each hand and asked Jimmy to count them. This time he got the answer "6." "Great," said the teacher, "so what is 3 + 3?" Jimmy again said "8," leaving the teacher perplexed.

Eventually it was discovered that Jimmy was highly visual and considered "8" to be the answer because a 3 and a reversed 3 made 8 visually. Initially it took considerable time for the teacher to understand the reasons for Jimmy's answer (which was far preferable than simply saying "you are wrong" and not helping him understand why).

Once the teacher understands Jimmy's reasoning, it should become much easier (more efficient) for her to diagnose similar answers from others who might also have a proclivity to think visually about these kinds of problems. Adding this information to the teachers' repertoire of familiar (routine) problems helps her become more likely to handle new sets of novel (nonroutine) teaching problems that may occur subsequently.

Efficiencies and innovation are antagonistic when one blocks the other. For example, a well-learned routine for teaching fractions, genetics, or other subject matters may turn out to limit a teacher's ability to help students develop a deep understanding of the subject matter if the teacher does not have a flexible command of alternative explanations (for example, see National Research Council [in press]). Under these conditions, attempts to "unlearn" the efficient set of routines and learn new approaches can be difficult and emotionally painful. Indeed, during the process of learning new strategies, teachers may initially become less efficient than previously, as they let go of techniques that have been comfortable and well practiced for them. In these instances, it is important to help people understand that "letting go" of previously learned ideas and routines or incorporating new information into their practice—choosing what to abandon and what to keep or modify—is a big part of what it means to be a lifelong learner and an adaptive expert. For an adaptive expert, discovering the need to change is perceived not as a failure but, instead, as a success and an inevitable, continuous aspect of effective teaching (see, for example, Cognition and Technology Group at Vanderbilt, 1997; Wineburg, 1998).

TEACHING STRATEGIES AND EFFICIENCY VERSUS INNOVATION

Teaching strategies vary according to the degree to which they emphasize the innovation versus efficiency dimensions. For example, some educators advocate teaching strategies that are highly scripted (see Sawyer, 2004). The goal is to reduce variability in implementation and produce outcomes that are better than what could be expected from a significant subset of teachers if they were left to their own devices. The effort to develop more routinized approaches to teaching is a response to at least two factors: (1) the perception of low levels of teaching skill on the part of practitioners, and (2) an attempt to create more standardization in students' experiences across classrooms and schools.

Other educators argue that effective teaching needs to be highly interactive and should vary depending on the needs of each learner. For example, Gay (personal communication, March 12, 2004) suggests that effective teaching is sensitive to students' needs and backgrounds and should be viewed as a creative act. Ball and Cohen (1999) also emphasize the role of innovation in teaching, "[Our] perspective views teachers' capacity not as a fixed storehouse of facts and ideas but as a source and creator of knowledge and skills needed for instruction" (p. 6). For these educators, effective teaching ranks particularly high on the innovation dimension, but always with a base of efficiency for reasons noted earlier. For this reason, for example, Sawyer (2004) sees the alternative to "scripted teaching" as "disciplined improvisation," with as much emphasis on the disciplined or structured elements of instruction as on the improvisation.

In each of these accounts of teaching there is implicit acknowledgment that being appropriately innovative requires the development of automatized schemas and routines that provide enough background efficiency to keep teachers from becoming overwhelmed and losing sight of important goals. Although highly scripted approaches have been criticized as not allowing enough room to meet the needs of individual students who learn in different ways, thoughtfully considered curriculum materials, assessment tools, and classroom routines that are based on solid learning theory and well-grounded teaching strategies help teachers develop useful efficiencies in some areas of their teaching that then set the stage for additional innovation and adaptation.

However, if teachers have simply learned automatized routines "by rote" (for example, in a strictly scripted manner) they will not be prepared to be the kinds of adaptive experts who will solve problems that arise while continuing to meet the needs of students and improving over time (see, for example, Cognition and Technology Group at Vanderbilt, 2000; Judd, 1908). Although some have argued that teachers should begin with scripts for teaching with the goal of having them become more innovative over time, this could result in teachers learning a nonresponsive practice in which they do not know how to, nor expect to, individualize to meet students' needs. They may also lack a theoretical foundation and tools for reflection that would allow them to change course when what they are doing is not working well.

It is important to note that even the most scripted approach to teaching requires some room for innovation—for example, pausing one's teaching routines to accommodate an unexpected issue in the classroom. And as noted earlier, "disciplined improvisation" is far from simply being freewheeling—it involves innovation within a set of general constraints (for example, to ensure that relevant standards are met) and structured analysis of the innovation process to continue to evaluate and adapt the strategies that are used. Adaptive experts attempt to be particularly aware of the larger social contexts within which they operate. This helps them adapt in ways that are novel *and* appropriate: it helps them innovate within constraints. (See "Innovation Within Constraints.")

Innovation Within Constraints

The importance of "innovation within constraints" surfaced at a meeting at University of Washington in Seattle where teacher educators met with school professionals to identify potential gaps in the teacher education program. The school professionals identified one potential gap that was particularly important; namely, that University students are often taught "ideal" curriculum and teaching practices for teaching specific subject areas, including reading, mathematics, science, history, and so forth. To help students understand differences between strong and weaker approaches, students are often introduced to contrasting cases of curricula—some of which are very good and some that are far from ideal.

The school professionals were quite supportive of the goal of helping students develop deep understandings of stronger versus weaker approaches to teaching particular concepts and strategies, and they agreed that the use of contrasting cases was quite valuable. However, the school professionals added that new teachers often enter schools where particular curriculum content and practices are mandated by the district. What if the curricula that are mandated fall in the "less than ideal" range according to the students' training? Should the new students quit their job, fight to change the system, simply comply and forget their previous training? These are dilemmas that many new teachers will face.

Once this issue was identified, teacher educators at the Seattle meeting realized the need to reframe their instruction and focus on the goal of helping students think about the challenges of "teaching effectively in an imperfect world." There are always constraints on people's activities. For teachers, there are usually ways to learn to teach creatively within these constraints. Indeed, being creative means being novel and appropriate (see, for example, Bransford and Stein, 1993). So constraints must always be acknowledged and taken into account.

In schools, "appropriate" is defined by both professional and community standards and by the needs of particular students. Prospective teachers must learn to understand the reasons for various constraints in their particular school and its community, and they must learn to find ways to teach effectively within them. Over time, teachers also need to understand how to work with others in the school and community and to become leaders who can collaborate to change system constraints when they seem clearly less than ideal. Helping prospective teachers see themselves as potential innovators and change agents who operate within systems that are much larger than their classrooms means that issues of organizations and leadership are important issues for prospective teachers to explore (see, for example, Fullan, 1993b; Hargreaves and others, 1994; Knapp and Turnbull, 1990).

An especially important aspect of adaptive expertise involves the ability to learn from others. This is not overly difficult when what is learned simply makes a teacher's existing teaching routines more efficient and elaborated. As noted earlier, however, lifelong learning often involves the kinds of changes (innovation) that require giving up old routines and transforming prior beliefs and practices. This is much easier said than done. A major part of the vision for future teachers must involve efforts to help them see that being a professional involves not simply "knowing the answers" but also having the skills and will to work with others in evaluating their own performances and searching for new answers when needed, both at the classroom level and the school level. Helping teachers learn to work in teams where they learn from one another is therefore extremely important. For example, watching a videotape of one's teaching with peers or inviting a colleague into the classroom to gain feedback is very helpful but can also be intimidating. When teachers have learned to develop their teaching in these collaborative contexts, they welcome rather than avoid such feedback. The propensity to seek rather than avoid feedback is important along a number of dimensions. For example, it is important when a school team asks how well students are doing in different classrooms and areas of the curriculum and considers how school curriculum, professional development, or organizational structures might need to change. While seeking feedback can be challenging, teachers who have experienced working in teams to consider such questions will see this as part of the professional role and an important, ongoing activity rather than as a threat to what they have previously been doing. True adaptive expertise for a teaching professional involves a deep appreciation of the value of actively seeking feedback from many sources in order to make the best decisions for children and to continue to learn throughout one's life.

SOME LEARNING PRINCIPLES FOR FACILITATING TEACHER DEVELOPMENT

Helping prospective teachers become adaptive experts who are able to engage in effective lifelong learning is not something that can be accomplished by simply telling them the information we have discussed in this volume. In this section we discuss research and theory relevant to key learning principles involved in helping people learn to teach and to improve their practices throughout their lives.

We organize our discussion around three major principles of learning that have been summarized in several reports from the National Academy of Sciences (National Research Council, in press; National Research Council, 2000). These three principles complement the *How People Learn* framework that we discussed in Chapters One and Two (see Figure 1.5). We use these principles to organize this discussion because they help readers align issues of teacher learning with other organizing principles for learning that are based on a strong body of research about how children and adults learn and acquire competence. The three principles are:

1. Prospective teachers come to the classroom with preconceptions about how the world, and teaching, works. These preconceptions, developed in their "apprenticeship of observation," condition what they learn. If their initial understanding is not engaged, they may fail to grasp the new concepts and information, or they may learn them for purposes of a test but revert to their preconceptions outside the classroom.

2. To develop competence in an area of inquiry that allows them to "enact" what they know, teachers must (i) have a deep foundation of factual and theoretical knowledge, (ii) understand facts and ideas in the context of a conceptual framework, and (iii) organize knowledge in ways that facilitate retrieval and action.

3. A "metacognitive" approach to instruction can help teachers learn to take control of their own learning by providing tools for analysis of events and situations that enable them to understand and handle the complexities of life in classrooms.

The Importance of Addressing Student Preconceptions

In Chapter Two we discussed Lionni's (1970) *Fish is Fish* story as an illustration of the constructive nature of knowing. Just as the Fish had preconceptions that affected what it learned from the Frog, prospective teachers have preconceptions that affect what they learn from teacher educators and in-classroom experiences. These preconceptions come from years and years of observing people who taught them and using this information to draw inferences about what good teaching looks like and what makes it work.

The sociologist Dan Lortie (1975) used the term *apprenticeship of observation* to refer to the processes by which prospective teachers develop conceptions of teaching based on their own experiences as students. The good news of these apprenticeships is that students have had a great deal of experience in classrooms, and many draw inspiration from outstanding teachers who taught them. The bad news is that these apprenticeships can result in serious misconceptions about teaching. As Lortie (1975) notes: "Students do not receive invitations to watch the teacher's performance through the wings; they are not privy to the teacher's private intentions and personal reflections on classroom events. Students rarely participate in selecting goals, making preparations or postmortem analysis. Thus they are not pressed to place the teacher's actions in a pedagogically oriented framework" (p. 62).

The difficulty of inducing a deep understanding of actions through observation alone is illustrated in "Learning Through Observation and Induction."

Learning Through Observation and Induction

Amy had learned to cook delicious ham dinners by watching her grandmother. For the grandmother's 85th birthday, Amy cooked a ham "just like grandmother used to make" and the grandmother stood by proudly to watch.

One of the secrets that Amy had observed was that her Grandmother always cut off a rather large piece of the end of the ham before cooking it. Amy had explained to her children that this allowed the juices to simmer in a very special way. As the Grandmother watched her granddaughter slice off the end of the ham, she asked, "Why did you cut off the end of the ham, Amy?" Amy replied, "Because you always did it, Grandmother, and your hams were always the best." The Grandmother smiled and explained, "I did it to fit the ham into my oven—it was much smaller than yours!"

(Author unknown)

Lortie (1975) concludes that students' long apprenticeship of observing teaching often leads to a number of misconceptions. One is the widespread idea that teaching is easy. Rather like the audience members watching the orchestra conductor we referred to at the beginning of Chapter One, students observe the superficial trappings of teaching, but not the underlying knowledge, skills, planning, and decision making. Part of the problem is that the limited vantage point of the student does not result in the acquisition of professional knowledge; that is, knowledge that allows the selection and implementation of different strategies that will support learning for different purposes and different students. Instead it produces a tendency to imitate the most easily observed aspects of teaching. Munby, Russell, and Martin (2001) add that even when observing good teaching or experiencing it for oneself, one cannot easily glean a deep understanding of the complexity of the work: "Good teaching tends to reinforce the view that teaching is effortless because the knowledge and experience supporting it are invisible to those taught. Good teaching looks like the ordering and deployment of skills, so learning to teach looks like acquiring the skills" (p. 887).

Kennedy points out additional preconceptions that can make learning difficult for novice teachers. For example, many of the concepts and ideas discussed in preparation courses are ideas that already seem familiar to the students—concepts such as group learning, assessment, and diversity. Preservice teachers often already have clear beliefs associated with these concepts and therefore tend to assimilate what is being taught to their preexisting schemas. This can make it very difficult to develop deeper, more nuanced understandings of these concepts. For example, effective collaboration requires the use of tasks or problems that actually require diverse perspectives, the allocation of time for making sufficient progress, scaffolding of critical skills, and so forth (see, for example, Brown and Campione, 1996). Prospective teachers may have experienced groupwork yet have been totally unaware of the degree to which the tasks they were assigned or the procedures they followed actually supported collaboration. They may therefore think they understand collaborative learning when in fact they do not. Whether they had poor experiences in unguided, poorly planned groupwork or good experiences with well-designed collaborative tasks, they may not know what elements caused the experience to be more or less productive.

As noted earlier, novice teachers often use the same language as teacher educators but signify different things with their language than do teacher educators. One method for overcoming this overassimilation problem is to use carefully calibrated sets of contrasting cases, grounded in practice as well as theory, that help people progressively differentiate their understanding rather than simply assimilate new information to preexisting ideas (see, for example, Schwartz and Bransford, 1998). In Chapter Eleven we discuss the use of written and videotaped cases to illustrate teaching and learning concepts in ways that make more vivid the consequences associated with different kinds of practices.

In an extensive review of research on teacher change, Richardson and Placier (2001) have documented the beliefs about teaching that preservice teachers tend to bring to their classrooms. Many beliefs consist of unexamined assumptions that need to be made explicit and explored. These views tend to focus on affective qualities of teachers (for example, caring), teaching styles, and individual children, with little appreciation of the role of social contexts, subject matter, or pedagogical knowledge (Paine, 1990; Sugrue, 1996). As Paine (1990) notes from a study of five teacher education programs, novices typically bring "an enthusiastic appreciation of personality factors and an underdeveloped sense of the role of content and context" (p. 20). Richardson and Placier (2001) note that many preconceptions in teacher education are hard to change and require interventions that are time-consuming and difficult. But if these preconceptions are not addressed, prospective teachers may retain problematic beliefs throughout their programs.

One important preconception that many candidates hold about *learning* is that it is the simple and rather mechanistic "transfer of information" from texts and teachers to students who acquire it through listening, reading, and memorization (Feiman-Nemser and Buchmann, 1989; Richardson, 1996). We noted in Chapter Two that constructivist theories play a major role in modern theories of learning and teaching, and that they are theories of knowing—not theories of pedagogy (teaching). A great deal of research establishes that individuals process and understand new information (correctly or incorrectly) in light of their experiences and prior knowledge and beliefs, and that they will often fail to remember, understand, or apply ideas that have no connections to their experience and no context for acquiring meaning. Although constructivist theorists acknowledge that there are indeed "times for telling" (Schwartz and Bransford, 1998), these theories help explain why attempts to "directly transmit" new information often fail and offer alternatives that have been found to foster learning much more successfully (see, for example, Schwartz and others, in press). Preconceptions that teaching is only about "transmission" can make it difficult for teacher educators who seek to prepare teachers to teach in ways that are more compatible with what we now know about how people learn. These more successful methods are often fundamentally different from how the student teachers were taught, and, sometimes, from how the teacher educators themselves learned as students (Borko and Mayfield, 1995).

Studies suggest that there is a wide distribution of preconceptions about teaching that are held by novices. In a review of the literature, Wideen, Mayer-Smith, and Moon (1998) concluded that prospective teachers are not an undifferentiated group and instead, hold a variety of images of and understandings about teaching and learning. These entering beliefs are more nuanced—and extend across a wider range of possibilities—than many people had imagined. These findings suggest that teacher educators will have different work to do with different candidates and warn against a "one size fits all" approach.

Many short-term interventions have shown little capacity to change preconceptions (Wideen and others, 1998). In contrast, longer-term approaches that explicitly seek to elicit and work with novice teachers' initial beliefs and concerns have shown some success. For example, in a three-year longitudinal study, Gunstone and colleagues (1993) found that teachers' beliefs and understanding about the teaching and learning of science changed significantly as they completed a one-year preservice program that explicitly drew upon and addressed their experiences, concerns, and needs. The program consciously provided new information and experiences relevant to those evolving concerns. Similar findings in other teaching fields have also been reported (see, for example, Fosnot, 1996; Graber, 1996). All of these studies involved cases where teacher educators used their students' "apprenticeship of observation" as a springboard from which to begin the process of conceptual and behavioral change.

The Importance of Learning for Understanding and Enactment

The preceding discussion focused on the importance of taking account of prospective teachers' preconceptions about the nature of teaching. A second challenge of learning to teach is what Mary Kennedy (1999) has termed the *problem of enactment*. If it is difficult to help preservice teachers learn to "think like a teacher," it is even more complicated to help them learn to put their intentions into action. Teachers must learn to weigh difficult dilemmas and to make and implement decisions on the fly; to put their plans into action effectively as well as to alter plans for unforeseen circumstances while they are in the midst of teaching; to respond to children and to represent well the material they are teaching. This challenge relates to the second *How People Learn* principle discussed by the National Research Council (in press), one that focuses on ways to help novices develop the kinds of organized understanding and skills that support effective action. This principle can be described as follows: "To develop competence in an area of inquiry, students must: (a) have a deep foundation of factual knowledge, (b) understand facts and ideas in the context of a conceptual framework, and (c) organize knowledge in ways that facilitate retrieval and action" (National Research Council, in press).

A strong body of research indicates that learning experiences that support understanding and effective action are different from those that simply support the ability to remember facts or perform rote sets of skills (see, for example, Donovan and others, in press; Good and Brophy, 1995, pp. 293–318; Resnick, 1987). Furthermore, actions that are supported by understanding are often more effective than those that occur without understanding. An example is provided in Experience and Understanding, which continues the story of *Fish is Fish*.

Experience and Understanding

In the first part of Lionni's (1970) *Fish is Fish* story (discussed earlier), we saw the Fish imagining fish-like birds, cows, and people, and we noted that this illustrated the role of preconceptions in constructing new understandings. Lionni's story continues with the Fish beginning to act on the knowledge that it thinks it has learned from the Frog. In particular, the Fish is so excited by the Frog's descriptions that it leaps from the water to experience life on land for itself. Because it can neither breathe nor maneuver on land, the Fish must be saved by the amphibious Frog. This part of Lionni's story illustrates how knowledge of events affects subsequent actions and decisions. The Fish did not have a real understanding of the differences between life in water and on the land.

Experience played a critical role in helping the Fish understand some key aspects of life on the land. Thankfully, the experience was "supervised" by the Frog, who could avert potentially disastrous consequences. However, experience alone is not enough either. The Fish's misunderstanding would presumably have persisted even if it had seen real birds, cows, and humans, or accurate pictures of them. The National Research Council (in press) argues the following:

> Some additional, critical concepts are needed: for example, the concept of adaptation. Species that move through a medium of air rather than through water have a different mobility challenge. And species that are warm blooded, unlike those that are cold blooded, must maintain their body temperature. It will take more explaining of course, but if the fish is to see a bird as something other than a fish with feathers and wings, and a human as something other than an upright fish with clothing, then feathers and clothing must be seen as adaptations that help solve the problem of maintaining body temperature, and the upright posture and wings must be seen as different solutions to the problem of mobility outside water. Conceptual information such as a theory of adaptation represents a kind of knowledge that is unlikely to be induced from everyday experiences. It typically takes generations of inquiry to develop this kind of knowledge, and people usually need some kind of help (e.g. interactions with "knowledgeable others") in order to grasp organizing concepts such as this (e.g. Hanson, 1970).

Source: Reprinted with permission from *How Students Learn: History, Mathematics, and Science in the Classroom,* © 2005 by the National Academy of Sciences, courtesy of the National Academies Press, Washington, D.C.

Our earlier discussion of Lortie's (1975) work on the "apprenticeship of observation" touched on the difficulty of inducing important levels of understanding simply by watching. In the *Fish is Fish* example in Experience and Understanding, it is quite plausible that the Fish would not have deeply understood adaptation and mobility even if the Frog had tried to explain these concepts. But after it experienced its own inabilities to breathe and move when on land, a "time for telling" emerged where new opportunities for learning should now be possible. As we discuss in the following section, the time and the manner of telling, however, have to be carefully considered.

Because Wisdom Can't Be Told. In his 1940 article, "Because Wisdom Can't be Told," Charles L. Gragg of the Harvard Business School begins with this quotation from Balzac: "So he had grown rich at last, and thought to transmit to his only son all the cut-and-dried experience which he himself had purchased at the price of his lost illusions: a noble last illusion of age" (see Gragg, 1940).

Except for the part about growing rich, many educators find that Balzac's ideas fit their experiences quite well. Educators frequently attempt to prepare people for the future by imparting the wisdom gleaned from their own experiences. Sometimes these efforts are rewarded, but often they are less successful than people would like them to be and we need to understand why. Examples of this problem are discussed in "Using Knowledge in Action."

Using Knowledge in Action

College students were taught about problem solving from the perspective of the IDEAL model—a model that emphasizes the importance of *I*dentifying problems, *D*efining them from at least two perspectives, *E*xploring strategies for solution, *A*cting on the basis of strategies, and *L*ooking at the effects (Bransford and Stein, 1993). Students were able to learn the material; for example, they could explain the purposes and steps of the IDEAL model and provide examples of how to use it to solve problems assigned in class. Nevertheless, students often failed to use the model spontaneously, when not asked to do so. For example, unless explicitly prompted to do so, students often failed to apply the model to their attempts to formulate their own topic for a paper related to discussions of problem identification and definition. They could think about the model, but they tended not to "think in terms of the model" (Bransford, Nitsch, and Franks, 1977) or "think with" the model (Broudy, 1977). The model had not become what some call a *conceptual tool* (Bransford and Stein, 1993).

Bereiter and Scardamalia (1989) provide an additional illustration of failure to spontaneously use important information. They note that a teacher of educational psychology gave her students a long, difficult article and told the students they had ten minutes to learn as much as they could about it. Almost without exception, the students began with the first sentence of the article and read as far as they could until the time was up. Later, when discussing the strategies, the students acknowledged that they knew better than simply to begin reading. They had all had classes that taught them to skim for main ideas, consult section headings, and so forth. But they did not spontaneously use these strategies when it would have helped.

The problem of knowing something but failing to have it guide one's actions is ubiquitous. Many years ago, Alfred Whitehead (1929) warned about the dangers of inert knowledge. This involves knowledge that that is available to people in the sense that they can talk about it when explicitly asked to do so (for example, when asked to explain the IDEAL model, or explain strategies for reading research articles). However, the knowledge is inert in the sense that it does not guide one's thinking and actions in new settings. Whitehead made the provocative claim, demonstrated by research several decades later, that traditional educational practices tend to produce knowledge that remains inert (see also Bereiter and Scardamalia, 1989; Brown, Campione, and Day, 1981; Gick and Holyoak, 1980).

Gragg's (1940) "Wisdom Can't be Told" article discusses problems with Harvard Business School graduates in the 1930s. Employers said that the Harvard graduates had acquired an impressive array of knowledge and skills, but they were not "prepared for action" (for example, they could not make useful decisions in business settings). Barrows (1985) noted similar problems with respect to medical education. Michael, a language therapist, provides a particularly interesting story about this problem. She served for several years as a clinical supervisor of college students who were beginning a practicum in language therapy for language-delayed children. The students had all passed the required college course on theories of language and their implications for therapy, but there was almost no evidence that the students ever attempted to use this knowledge in the clinical therapy sessions. Michael concluded that the college course must have been very poorly taught.

Michael was later asked to teach that college course herself. She did what she thought was a highly competent job and was pleased with the general performance of the students on her tests. A year later, she encountered a number of students again in the clinical practicum on language therapy. Much to her surprise and dismay, these students also showed little evidence of applying what they had learned in their language course. Many could remember facts when explicitly asked about them, but they did not automatically draw on that knowledge to help them solve problems in the clinic.

Because she had taught the practicum, Michael was reluctant to conclude that her college students performed poorly because of poor instruction. Instead she was motivated to explore problems with traditional approaches to instruction and to study ways to overcome them. Her Ph.D. thesis successfully explored new teaching methods that were designed to improve the degree to which her students were prepared for action when they moved from the classroom to the clinical lab (Michael, Klee, Bransford, and Warren, 1993).

To better prepare people for action, a number of professional schools (law schools, medical schools, and business schools, for example) use a variety of approaches called "case-based" and "problem-based" instruction. (See Williams [1992] for an excellent review and analysis of this general approach.) The essence of the approach is to organize instruction around actual situations that students are likely to encounter later in their careers or perhaps have already encountered. In business, for example, a case might focus on a company that is in trouble and needs to be restructured. In medicine, a case might involve a patient with certain symptoms that need to be diagnosed. In Michael's work on language therapy (discussed earlier), faculty anchored their instruction around videos of language experts who were working with children, and students analyzed these examples from different theoretical perspectives (for example, behavioral, linguistic, social/linguistic).

In all these examples, students work on cases over some fixed period, set learning goals for acquiring new information that is needed to solve the problem, and eventually discuss their ideas with classmates and with the professor. Ideally, students move from simple cases to more complex ones. In the process, they acquire relevant knowledge while learning to analyze problems, set learning goals, and present and discuss their ideas. Overall, these kinds of experiences appear to help students think and act more professionally when dealing with everyday problems relevant to their disciplines (see, for example, Hmelo-Silver, 2004; Michael and others, 1993). These approaches to instruction represent attempts to avoid Whitehead's lament that many traditional forms of instruction tend to produce knowledge and skills that tend to remain inert once students leave the classroom and enter the world. Research like this underlies a number of the pedagogies for teacher education that we describe in Chapter Eleven.

Challenges of Enactment in Teacher Education. The issues teachers face regarding enactment are similar to those encountered in other professional fields, but there are differences as well. The preconceptions about educational ideas carried into teacher education by prospective teachers may be stronger than those of other novice professionals because of the long apprenticeship of observation in elementary and secondary schools. In addition, even when novice teachers have developed solid ideas about teaching, putting them into action is extremely challenging, as teachers do many more things at once, with many more clients assembled at one time, than do most other professionals. Developing an authoritative classroom presence, good radar for watching and interpreting what many different students are doing and feeling at each moment, and skills for explaining, questioning, discussing, giving feedback, constructing tasks, facilitating work, and managing the classroom—all at once—is not simple.

A number of scholars have specifically explored the challenges involved in preparing *teachers* for effective action. Schön (1983), for example, suggests that there are some kinds of professions—he includes teaching as a prime example—in which much of the information needed to make effective teaching decisions *emerges in the context of the practice.* For example, information about what ideas students have developed about a topic, how they are understanding or misunderstanding the material being taught, and how different students learn best emerges in the actual work of teaching—and guides future planning and instruction. How different strategies work with this or that *group* of students, as well as individuals, also emerges in the course of enacting plans, and cannot be fully known ahead of time in the abstract.

Some describe learning for understanding and enactment as learning to "apply" knowledge to practice. However, our earlier discussions of adaptive expertise suggest that effective actions involve *more* than the ability to simply apply previously acquired routines and schemas. The efficiency dimension (see Figure 2.1) highlights the importance of acquiring and using well-learned schemas and routines that set the stage for effective action without commanding too much attention. However, the innovation dimension involves "disciplined improvisation" (Sawyer, 2003) where new ideas and actions often emerge in the context of ongoing interactions. As discussed earlier, the upshot of this analysis is that "application" and "innovation" are tightly intertwined and need to be learned together, in the context of a schema that provides a means for reflection and further learning.

If the information needed to teach well emerges during the practice itself, then learning how to think and act professionally is unusually difficult at the start of a teaching career, and many ways of preparing prospective teachers will not be sufficient to guide their actions. For example, if a teacher preparation program emphasizes "book learning" rather than opportunities to practice and reflect in supervised classrooms, students' actual postgraduation teaching experiences would be expected to have more effect on their subsequent teaching than their book-based classroom experiences. And indeed, data show that, for good or for ill, teachers' initial classroom experiences, especially in the first one or two years, are consistently a predictor of teacher effectiveness (Rowan, Correntti, and Miller, 2002). Evidence also shows that these initial classroom experiences are much different for candidates who have had strong preservice preparation and those who have not (see, for example, Darling-Hammond, Chung, and Frelow, 2002).

One inference from these studies of learning is that teacher educators need to make sure that candidates have opportunities to practice and reflect on teaching *while enrolled in their preparation programs.* During both the preservice period and initial years in the field, new teachers need support in interpreting their experiences and expanding their repertoire, so that they can continue to learn how to become effective rather than infer the wrong lessons from their early attempts at teaching. Findings from several studies suggest that how teacher education is conducted can make a difference in teachers' abilities to enact what they are learning. These studies have found that, when a well-supervised student teaching experience precedes or is conducted jointly with coursework, students appear more able to connect theoretical learning to practice, become more comfortable with the process of learning to teach, and are more able to enact what they are learning in practice (Chin and Russell, 1995; Darling-Hammond and Macdonald, 2000; Koppich, 2000; Snyder, 2000; Sumara and Luce-Kapler, 1996; Whitford, Ruscoe, and Fickel, 2000). Other studies suggest that when teachers learn content-specific strategies and tools that they are able to try immediately and continue to refine with a group of colleagues in a learning community, they are more able to enact new practices effectively (Cohen and Hill, 2000; Lieberman and Wood, 2003).

Metacognition and the Problem of Complexity

A third challenge in learning to teach is that teaching is an incredibly complex and demanding task (Lampert, 2001; McDonald, 1992). Effective teachers become increasingly aware of the complexities involved in teaching and learn how to think systematically about them so that they can better assess their own performances. As McDonald explains, "Real teaching happens within a wild triangle of relations—among teacher, students, subject—and the points of this triangle shift continuously. What shall I teach amid all that I should teach? How can I grasp it myself so that my grasping might enable theirs? What are they thinking and feeling—toward me, toward each other, toward the thing I am trying to teach? How near should I come, how far off should I stay? How much clutch, how much gas?" (1992, p. 1).

A principle of learning that is extremely important for helping teachers become adaptive experts who can manage complexity involves the concept of metacognition—or the ability to think about one's own thinking. John Flavell (1979) described two aspects of metacognition: *metacognitive knowledge*—that is, understanding one's own thinking and developing strategies for planning, analyzing, and gaining more knowledge—and *metacognitive regulation*—that is, being able to define learning goals and monitoring one's progress in achieving them (see also National Research Council, 2000). A continuation of the *Fish is Fish* story provides more information about the nature and role of metacognition in learning (see Developing Metacognition in the Cause of Learning).

Developing Metacognition in the Cause of Learning

Hero though he is for saving the Fish's life, the Frog in our story gets poor marks as a teacher. But the burden of learning does not fall on the teacher alone. Even the best instructional efforts can be successful only if the student can make use of the opportunity to learn. Helping students become effective learners is relevant to the third key principle: a metacognitive, or self-monitoring, approach can help students develop the ability to take control of their own learning by defining learning goals and monitoring their progress in achieving them.

Our Fish accepted the information about life on land rather passively. Had it been analyzing and monitoring its understanding, it might have noted that putting on a hat and jacket would be rather uncomfortable for a fish, and would slow its swimming in the worst way. Had the Fish been more engaged in figuring out what the Frog meant, it might have asked why humans would make themselves uncomfortable and compromise their mobility. A good answer to the Fish's questions might have set the stage for learning about differences between humans and fish, and ultimately the notion of adaptation.

Source: Reprinted with permission from *How Students Learn: History, Mathematics, and Science in the Classroom,* © 2005 by the National Academy of Sciences, courtesy of the National Academies Press, Washington, D.C.

There is a strong research literature demonstrating that efforts to help students become more active monitors of their own learning facilitate their performances (see, for example, Brown, Bransford, Ferrera, and Campione, 1983; National Research Council, in press). Data showing the benefits of metacognitive reflection range from work with children to adults. Metacognition is an especially important component of adaptive expertise (National Research Council, 2000). People with high levels of metacognitive awareness have developed habits of mind that prompt them to continually self-assess their performances and modify their assumptions and actions as needed. People who are less metacognitive rely on external feedback from others to tell them what to do and how to change.

Effective teachers particularly need to be metacognitive about their work. The more they learn about teaching and learning the more accurately they can reflect on what they are doing well and on what needs to be improved. For example, beginning teachers frequently focus on their teaching practices rather than on what their students are learning. They need to be able to figure out what they do and do not yet understand about how their students are performing and what to do about it. They also need to be able to ask themselves and others questions to guide their learning and decision making. These include questions about the spheres of decision making that matter in interpreting what is going on in the classroom—for example, the aspects of learners' experiences, content representations, and social contexts that are in play in a given situation. And they need to be able to analyze acts of teaching as well as reactions and interactions that occur, so that they can reflect on these outcomes and adapt what they do.

In describing the complexity of teaching, Lampert outlines some of the many factors a teacher must consider and some of the areas in which metacognitive deliberations are critical to her ability to make sound decisions:

> One reason teaching is a complex practice is that many of the problems a teacher must address to get students to learn occur simultaneously, not one after another. Because of this simultaneity, several different problems must be addressed in a single action. And a teacher's actions are not taken independently; there are interactions with students, individually and as a group. A teacher acts in different social arrangements in the same time frame. A teacher also acts in different time frames and at different levels of ideas with individuals, groups and the class to make each lesson coherent, to link one lesson to another, and to cover a curriculum over the course of a year. Problems exist across social, temporal, and intellectual domains, and often the actions that need to be taken to solve problems are different in different domains.
>
> When I am teaching fifth-grade mathematics, for example, I teach a mathematical idea or procedure to a student while also teaching that student to be civil to classmates and to me, to complete the tasks assigned, and to think of himself and herself and everyone else in the class as capable of learning, no matter what their gender, race or parents' income. As I work to get students to learn something like "improper fractions," I know I will also need to be teaching them the meaning of division, how division relates to other operations, and the nature of our number system. While I take action to get some particular content to be studied by a particular student in a particular moment, I simultaneously have to do the work of engaging all of the students in my class in the lesson as a whole, even as I am paying different kinds of attention to groups of students with diverse characteristics. And I need to act in a way that preserves my potential to keep acting productively day after day, throughout the year. [Lampert, M. (2001). *Teaching problems and the problems of teaching.* New Haven: Yale University Press.]

Lampert's account of the multiple considerations that shape her teaching of mathematics to fifth graders suggests at least four elements for reflecting on the complexity of teaching. First, *teaching is never routine*. Students do not learn at the same pace or in the same ways. Their needs are both diverse and ever-changing. The "wild triangle" to which McDonald refers is constantly shifting—teachers must constantly cope with changing situations, learning needs, challenges, questions, and dilemmas. Second, *teaching has multiple goals* that often must be addressed simultaneously. As Lampert explains, for instance, at the same time a teacher is teaching content, she is simultaneously teaching social and intellectual development, helping students work in groups, and paying attention to the way she interacts with the child who needs some extra support and the child who needs to be the center of attention. Third, *teaching is done in relationship to very diverse groups of students.* In contrast to the individual problems confronted one at a time by doctors, lawyers, or architects, teachers must find a way to meet the needs of a group of students who are diverse in terms of their learning needs, strengths, backgrounds, areas of challenge, and range of abilities. Finally, *teaching requires multiple kinds of knowledge to be brought together in an integrated way.* For instance, teachers must constantly integrate their knowledge of child development, of subject matter, of group interactions, of students' different cultures and backgrounds, and of their particular students' interests, needs, and strengths together in a way that advances the learning of all their students. In sum, helping new teachers learn about and reflect upon the multidimensionality and simultaneity of teaching (Jackson, 1974) is clearly important. And it is also no easy task.

Not only is there great complexity in the classroom, but there is also a complicated set of factors from outside the classroom that influence teachers and students. The way the school is organized shapes the prior experiences—norms, access to knowledge, and supports—students will have had before entering a given teachers' classroom, as well as their current experiences. Furthermore, the conditions and relationships existing in the community served by the school will influence how children are raised, what resources have been available to them, how alike or different groups served by the school are and what kinds of expectations and values they bring. To be effective over the course of a career, teachers need to understand and manage these factors, and, eventually, to influence them on behalf of the students they serve.

THE PROCESS OF TEACHER DEVELOPMENT

It would be helpful if there were predictable phases of teacher development that could guide teacher educators. As is the case with child development (see Chapter Three), it is important to understand different theories of development and the contributions of each.

Developmental Progressions

A number of stage theories have been advanced to describe teachers' development (Berliner, 1994; Feiman-Nemser, 1983; Fuller, 1969; Richardson and Placier, 2001; Sprinthall, Reiman, and Theis-Sprinthall, 1996) as well as the course of their careers (Huberman, 1989). For example, drawing upon a review of ten studies of teacher's concerns, Fuller (1969) proposed that new teachers develop through phases in which they focus initially on themselves and their teaching—for instance, their ability to control the classroom, what their supervisors think about them as teachers—and then eventually on concerns that are related to student learning, such as designing curriculum, finding effective teaching strategies, and assessing student learning. This developmental progression—from early concerns with "self" to a gradual focus upon issues related to students and student learning, and, eventually, conditions of schools and schooling—has been observed in a number of studies.

Descriptions of classroom practice suggest that some teachers eventually develop a strong focus on student welfare and learning that drives their teaching decisions and self-improvement efforts, whereas others stop short of this state, developing techniques of teaching that "work," in that they get teachers through the day, but that do not result in high levels of learning for students or high levels of teacher concern when learning does not occur. Both the speed and endpoint of this progression appear to be related to teachers' preparation, as we discuss in the next section.

Other research has focused on the development of teaching knowledge by examining the differences in thinking between expert and novice teachers (Berliner, 1994, 1986; Carter, Cushing, Sabers, Stein, and Berliner, 1988; Lin, 1999). This line of research, described at the beginning of this chapter, has found, for example, that when beginning and experienced teachers are asked to evaluate classroom scenes, novices tend to offer superficial, general observations that do not attend to the intellectual work of the classroom. (See "A Study of Teacher Expertise," p. 361.) On the other hand, more expert teachers attend to specific aspects of the classroom that are linked directly to the intellectual work of students, to generate more detailed observations and hypotheses about what they see, to qualify their observations and interpretations, to weigh the relative importance of certain kinds of information, and to "take into account the complexity of problems which exist in classrooms" (Carter and others, 1988).

Like experts in other domains, teaching experts quickly recognize patterns in what they observe; see more complexities and bring to bear many sources of knowledge about how to respond to them; are more opportunistic and flexible in their practice than novices, responding to demands of the situation and the task; and have a broad repertoire of skills they can easily access and implement to achieve their goals (Berliner, 2001). Studies of expertise in fields such as physics (Chi, Feltovitch, and Glasser, 1981; Chi, Glaser, and Rees, 1982), chess (de Groot, 1965; Newell and Simon, 1972; Chase and Simon, 1973), and history (Wineburg, 1991, 1998) suggest similar features in other fields.

Berliner (1994) has proposed that teachers develop expertise through a set of stages—from novice to advanced beginner, competent, proficient, and ultimately to expert. Over time, they progress from learning the basic elements of the task to be performed and accumulating knowledge about learning, teaching, and students to making conscious decisions about what they are going to do, reflecting on what is working based on their experience, and, ultimately, at the expert level (Stage 5), sensing the appropriate responses to be made in any given situation. Teachers appear to develop competence over a period of about five to seven years, and only a small percentage of teachers continue to develop into experts (Berliner, 2001). Some research, described later, suggests that the metacognitive elements that are involved in the development of expertise can be developed in teacher education, enabling more teachers to reach this level of strong competence and to do so earlier than might otherwise be the case (see, for example, Hammerness and others, 2002).

Finally, some researchers have examined the process of development of specific teaching skills. For example, Joyce and Showers (2002) have described how teachers go through an iterative process of learning, experimenting, and reflecting as they develop new skills for use in their classrooms. They have also studied how the developmental process of learning to enact new skills can be supported by skilled coaching in peer support groups that allow teachers to explore, develop, strengthen, and refine teaching skills together. Both the feedback and the collegial nature of the process appear to stimulate reflection and greater skill development. Approaching this kind of process from a developmental perspective strengthens both implementation and student achievement gains.

Stage theories have been useful in describing the trajectory of teachers' development and the nature of teachers' expertise. However, they do not tell us as much about the characteristics of the learning experiences that may help teachers progress in their concerns and acquire expert skills (Berliner, 2001). Furthermore, many stage theories that have guided teacher education decisions have been interpreted as suggesting that teachers' development progressed in a linear fashion, in fairly fixed stages, suggesting teacher development is "invariant, sequential and hierarchical" (Richardson and Placier, 2001). Yet, other frameworks for describing teacher development suggest more complex paths in learning to teach, as well as differences in teachers' concerns and capacities when they have had different kinds of preparation (see, for example, Grossman, 1992, in response to Kagan, 1992).

Furthermore, many studies describing teacher development in terms of what beginning teachers "can" and "cannot" do were conducted at a time when most teacher education programs were fairly weak interventions. Thus they may underestimate the potential of new teachers to practice in more sophisticated ways, particularly if those new teachers are prepared in programs that can leverage their development productively. Some recent studies designed to examine the kinds of teacher education that support teacher learning suggest that, under the right circumstances, with particular kinds of learning experiences, new teachers can develop a more expert practice even as beginning practitioners (Darling-Hammond, 2000b; Darling-Hammond and Macdonald, 2000; Hammerness and others, 2002; Koppich, 2000; Merseth and Koppich, 2000; Miller and Silvernail, 2000; Snyder, 2000; Whitford and others, 2000; Zeichner, 2000).

These findings parallel recent findings in cognitive development demonstrating that, given well-chosen tasks with appropriate scaffolding and supportive learning environments, children can learn much more than may have been anticipated by earlier biologically based theories of development (Boaler, 1997; Brown and Campione, 1994; Lee, 1995; Palinscar and Brown, 1984; Rogoff, 1990; Vygotsky, 1978). This recent evidence of powerful novice teaching is also particularly important because the studies examined teacher education features that appear to make a substantial difference for preservice teachers' learning and development. These features are discussed more fully in Chapter Eleven.

This research does not suggest that new teachers can immediately develop the kind of expertise that a master teacher develops over years of experience. Such learning about teaching, students, culture, development, and subject matter develops over time. Grossman, Smagorinsky, and Valencia (1999) have distinguished between "appropriating tools" and "mastery," suggesting that "If mastery means the skill to use a tool effectively, then this more fully realized grasp of a concept most likely would take years of practice to achieve" (p. 18). However, this recent research does suggest that new teachers can demonstrate more accomplished practice than previously thought when they experience stronger, more purposeful preparation.

Studies of teacher development have provided evidence for a potential trajectory of teacher development. And although the sequence and timing of particular stages may not be invariant, particularly when new teachers can benefit from especially well-designed teacher education, the descriptions of expertise have helped undergird much of our understanding of what accomplished practice might look like. They provide a basis for characterizing some of the practices we might hope teachers begin to learn and demonstrate as skilled and thoughtful practitioners.

THEORIES OF TEACHER DEVELOPMENT
IN COMMUNITIES OF PRACTICE

Current conceptions of learning to teach have also been informed by theories of learning in a community (Au, 2002; Cochran-Smith and Lytle, 1999a; Grossman and others, 1999; Oakes, Franke, Quartz, and Rogers, 2002). A focus upon learning in communities of practice has evolved out of multiple research traditions in the United States and other countries. It can be traced back to scholars such as Kurt Lewin, a social psychologist; to the educational philosophy of John Dewey; and to movements that called for teachers to collaborate and participate in research in their classrooms alongside university researchers, which were in evidence as early as the 1950s (see Zeichner and Noffke, 2001, for a review of these traditions). In addition, this work has been informed by the work of cognitive psychologists who have focused in particular upon the situated and contextualized nature of learning within such communities (see, for example, Bruner, 1996; Cole, 1977; D'Andrade, 1981; Lave and Wenger, 1991; Vygotsky, 1978).

Research on teacher development within learning communities also emphasizes the importance of a particular kind of knowledge development: knowledge that is developed within both teaching contexts and professional contexts. Cochran-Smith and Lytle (1999) outline several approaches to knowledge development, including the development of knowledge *for* practice, knowledge *in* practice, and knowledge *of* practice. The first of these refers to the kinds of knowledge teachers may need to rely upon in developing their practice: knowledge of subject matter content, content pedagogy, theories of learning and development, and research about the effects of various teaching strategies. This kind of knowledge has been the traditional emphasis of teacher education and it has often been thought of as knowledge to be transmitted from scholars to teachers or from experts to novices.

The second perspective emphasizes knowledge in action: what accomplished teachers know as it is expressed in their practice, their reflections, and their narratives. To be sure, some of this knowledge is reflected in the first category, when it has been the subject of formal research on teaching. However, the notion of knowledge *in* practice emphasizes that much of the knowledge of accomplished teachers is practical, highly situated, and acquired through reflection upon experience. Although one teacher's knowledge in practice, when studied by other teachers, can become knowledge for practice, learning from the actions of expert teachers as they make choices and decisions depends upon learning how to "think like a teacher"—how to observe students, reflect upon their needs, evaluate curriculum options, and put plans into action.

Finally, knowledge *of* practice emphasizes the relationship between knowledge and practice and the theoretical aspects of both, assuming that "the knowledge teachers need to teach well emanates from systematic inquiries about teaching, learners and learning, curriculum, schools and schooling. This knowledge is constructed collectively within local and broader communities" (Cochran-Smith and Lytle, 1999a, p. 274). It emphasizes the role of the teacher in constructing knowledge and learning, and growing through that process. And, it suggests the importance of ongoing inquiry by teachers in their own classrooms and into other systematic and practical sources of knowledge for addressing critical problems of practice. In this conception, communities of practice play a central role in developing and transmitting knowledge from practice to research and back again. These notions of knowledge for practice, developed within a professional community of inquiring teachers, inform many of the emerging pedagogies in teacher education that have been found to be associated with implementation of new teaching strategies and improvements in student learning (see, for example, Joyce and Showers, 2002; Cohen and Hill, 2000).

These conceptions of teacher development within professional communities highlight the ways in which the learning of beginning and experienced teachers is similar. As Cochran-Smith and Lytle (1999) explain, "Working together in communities, both new and more experienced teachers pose problems, identify discrepancies between theories and practices, challenge common routines, draw on the work of others for generative frameworks, and attempt to make visible much of that which is taken for granted about teaching and learning" (p. 293). This conception poses an image of the teacher as a member of a professional community and as a lifelong learner, focusing upon collegial, career-long development.

CRITICAL ASPECTS OF IDENTITY DEVELOPMENT IN TEACHERS

In addition to developing knowledge and skills, teachers are developing along many other dimensions. Teachers are developing as professionals (Feiman-Nemser, 2001a); as scholars and practitioners within a subject matter context (Shulman, 1986; Grossman and Stodolsky, 1995); as change agents (Ayers 1995; Darling-Hammond, French, and Garcia-Lopez, 2002); as nurturers and child advocates (Cummins, 1986); and as moral agents (Fullan, 1993b). As teachers develop a vision for what teachers do, what good teaching is, and what they hope to accomplish as a teacher, they begin to forge an identity that will guide them in their work (Hammerness, in press). Developing an identity as a teacher is an important part of securing teachers' commitment to their work and adherence to professional norms of practice.

Preparation programs deliberately and inadvertently reinforce the development of different kinds of teaching identities as they emphasize various aspects of what it means to be a teacher and as they place student teachers in different environments where they will see certain kinds of norms modeled. Though not always explicitly considered, this aspect of preparation is critically important, as the identities teachers develop shape their dispositions, where they place their effort, whether and how they seek out professional development opportunities, and what obligations they see as intrinsic to their role.

Teachers are also developing in their identities as members of racial/ethnic groups and in their views about members of other groups. Research on the development of racial identity suggests that through childhood (as early as three or four years of age) and into adulthood, people move through a variety of stages in making sense of their own racial/ethnic identity and culture and those of others (Katz, 1982; McAllister and Irvine, 2000; Phinney and Rotheram, 1987; Tatum, 1997). This process of racial identity development influences how teachers treat the students they teach as well as how they see their role in confronting social and institutional barriers to equity. This process can be facilitated by teacher education if teacher educators understand how it unfolds and can be supported (Carter and Goodwin, 1994).

Of course, children in the classrooms of teachers also go through these stages. Thus it is equally important to note that teachers play a particularly influential role in the development of children's racial/ethnic identity and their academic self-concepts. As Banks (1988) argues, "Teachers are even more important than the material they use because the ways in which they present material highly influence how they are viewed by students" (p. 88). As teachers bring their own assumptions and beliefs (and even prejudices and biases) to bear upon the materials they use in the classroom, the way they interact with materials or describe them to children can create a lens with which the children themselves view the materials. In this process, teachers can reinforce or counteract racial biases and stereotypes that children bring into school with them, and can display negative or positive attitudes to children of color. Because of teachers' critical role in the identity development of children, teacher educators argue that teachers need to develop consciousness about their own racial identity and consider how they can support positive racial identity development among their students (Carter and Goodwin, 1994).

Furthermore, as Hernández (1989) asserts, teaching is always a cross-cultural encounter no matter what the ethnicity or race of teachers and students, because culture so deeply informs the entire teaching and learning process. Teachers naturally bring their own cultural values, beliefs, and understandings to their work with children, and children always bring their own cultural understandings and ways of knowing to their experiences with teachers, with knowledge and ideas, and with each other.

Of particular challenge is helping preservice teachers from the majority culture develop an understanding of cross-cultural issues and experiences such as discrimination. Surveys suggest that many white teachers have limited awareness of these issues (Sleeter, 2001). Qualitative studies suggest that many have had few cross-cultural experiences, and this lack of experience may lead them to unintentionally or unconsciously accept forms of racial, ethnic, language, or cultural discrimination (McIntyre, 1997; Smith, Moallem, and Sherrill, 1997; Valli, 1995). This limited experience also affects many teachers' understanding of culturally appropriate classroom practices. Many preservice teachers have trouble imagining what multicultural teaching can look like (Goodwin, 1994), in part because of the lack of models of multicultural practices in their own experiences as students and in their placements. Indeed, for these same reasons, preservice teachers of color do not necessarily know more about culturally relevant pedagogical practices than white preservice teachers (Goodwin, 1997b). As we describe in Chapter Seven, preservice programs can provide much-needed opportunities for teacher education students of all backgrounds to develop culturally relevant practices and pedagogical approaches that can serve a diverse range of students (Ladson-Billings, 2001; Sleeter, 2001).

A FRAMEWORK FOR TEACHER LEARNING

In recent years, a number of scholars have offered theoretical frameworks for teacher learning that incorporate much of the research described earlier (Cochran-Smith and Lytle, 1999; Feiman-Nemser, 2001a; Grossman and others, 1999; Shulman and Shulman, 2004). In addition, professional standards for teaching, especially those offered by the Interstate New Teacher Assessment and Support Consortium (INTASC) and the National Board for Professional Teaching Standards (NBPTS), also build upon this research in describing what competent beginners and accomplished teachers need to know and be able to do in order to teach challenging content to diverse students.

We draw from these efforts in offering a framework for teacher learning. As depicted in Figure 10.1, this framework suggests that new teachers learn to teach in a community that enables them to develop a *vision* for their practice; a set of *understandings* about teaching, learning, and children; *dispositions* about how to use this knowledge; *practices* that allow them to act on their intentions and beliefs; and *tools* that support their efforts.

As we argue in Chapter Five, teachers need to have a sense of where they are going and how they are going to get students there. Zumwalt (1989) has called this a sense of "curricular vision." This vision, along with powerful images of good practice (Feiman-Nemser, 2001a; Shulman and Shulman, in press; Zumwalt, 1989) can help new teachers reflect on their work, guide their practice, and direct their future learning (Hammerness, in press). Feiman-Nemser argues that these images are critical for teacher learning: "Teacher candidates must . . . form visions of what is possible and desirable in teaching to inspire and guide their professional learning and practice. Such visions connect important values and goals to concrete classroom practices. They help teachers construct a normative basis for developing and assessing their teaching and their students' learning" (2001a, p. 1017). Developing a vision for teaching is the first step toward addressing the apprenticeship of observation and the process of enactment.

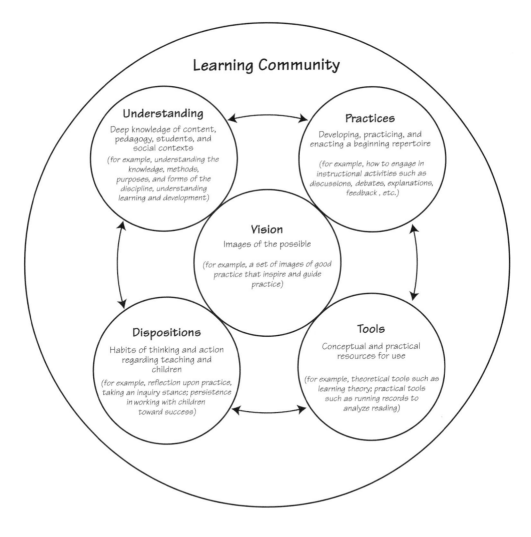

Figure 10.1 Learning to Teach in Community

As we discussed in Chapter Six, scholars agree that teachers need to have a deep knowledge, or *understanding*, of their subject and how to make it accessible to others (Shulman and Shulman, 2004). Making content accessible relies, in turn, on an understanding of students and their prior knowledge and experiences, and an understanding of the learning process. In their definition of disciplinary understanding, Boix-Mansilla and Gardner (1997) argue that deep disciplinary understanding includes understanding the knowledge, the purposes, the methods, and the forms of a subject. This model suggests that teachers need to possess a coherent and rich conceptual map of the discipline (knowledge); an understanding of how knowledge is developed and validated within different social contexts (methods); an understanding of why the subject is important (purposes); and finally, an understanding of how one can communicate knowledge of that subject to others (form). Communicating that knowledge effectively rests upon an understanding of students' thinking, experiences, development, and learning processes and of how curriculum can be constructed and classrooms managed to allow the learning process to unfold productively.

To put these understandings into practice, teachers also need to develop *tools* (Grossman and others, 1999)—conceptual and practical resources for use in the classroom. Grossman and colleagues make the distinction between conceptual and practical tools, noting that *conceptual tools* can include learning theories, frameworks, and ideas about teaching and learning (concepts such as the zone of proximal development or culturally relevant teaching). They suggest that *practical* tools include particular instructional approaches and strategies, and resources, such as textbooks, assessment tools, and other materials. Such tools help teachers to work smarter and to enact their intentions in practice.

These understandings and tools need to be integrated into a set of *practices,* or what Feiman-Nemser (2001a, p. 1018) has termed a *beginning repertoire* of classroom enactment. These practices can include a variety of instructional activities to promote student learning, such as explaining concepts, holding discussions, designing experiments, developing simulations, planning debates, and organizing writing workshops (Feiman-Nemser, 2001a). Practices also include activities like learning to design and carry out unit plans and daily lessons that build understanding; developing and implementing formative and summative assessments; and offering feedback that is constructive and specific. Feiman-Nemser points out that student teachers should be learning not only the content of these strategies, but "when, where, how and why to use particular approaches."

In addition to understanding that is connected to tools and practices, teachers need to develop a set of *dispositions*—or habits of thinking and action—about teaching, children, and the role of the teacher. Teaching dispositions include the disposition to reflect and to learn from practice, which Cochran-Smith and Lytle have termed *inquiry as stance* (1999, p. 250). Dispositions toward children include determination and persistence that support the ability to work with children until they succeed (Haberman, 1996), including the inclination to take responsibility for children's learning and the will to continue to seek new approaches to teaching that will allow greater success with students. Ladson-Billings, for example, has found that the belief that all children can succeed is a particularly important attribute of successful teachers of African American children (1994). Dispositions can also include a personal orientation (Haberman, 1996) characterized by appreciation of the need for good rapport and strong relationships with children, and of valuing, respecting, and caring for children.

This framework also takes into account the understanding that learning to teach occurs within communities (Cochran-Smith and Lytle, 1999). Professional communities include those found in classroom and clinical settings, such as the peers and faculty candidates work with in their coursework and in student teaching. Purposefully constructed professional communities that share norms and practices can be especially powerful influences on learning. In addition, teachers learn to teach in different kinds of local and regional communities that offer different kinds of opportunities for learning and practice. These settings—which can differ by culture, socioeconomic status, language diversity, political and social norms, and many other factors, pose distinctive challenges for teacher preparation. If their candidates are to be successful, teacher preparation programs must take into account the role of community contexts in children's learning and development and must respond to the particular diversity of children, schools, and communities served by their programs (Haberman, 1996).

This model of teacher learning also invites teacher educators to examine whether and how teachers' learning in school settings complements what is learned in university settings and vice versa (Grossman and others, 1999). Visions of good practice may differ in different settings, and different settings may emphasize or demonstrate different tools, practices, and even dispositions. This model helps demonstrate the importance of coherence—or at the very least, helps teacher educators consider the potential conflicts and differences their students may encounter as they learn to teach in different settings.

Finally, this framework helps us to think about how teacher educators can equip teachers in ways that address the three persistent problems of learning to teach that we identified earlier in this chapter. For example, Feiman-Nemser has pointed out that developing vision, or a set of images of the possible, is a critical step in addressing the problem of the apprenticeship of observation: "Unless teacher educators engage prospective students in a critical examination of their entering beliefs in light of compelling alternatives and help them develop powerful images of good teaching and strong professional commitments, these entering beliefs will continue to shape their ideas and practices" (2001a, p. 1017). Similarly, Cochran-Smith and Lytle point out that the disposition to take an inquiry stance can help teachers deal with the complexity of teaching;

they offer illustrations of "colleagues working together, bringing their perspectives to bear on inquiries into the complexities and messiness of teaching and learning" (1999, p. 279).

From this model, we can see that rather than conceptualizing the process of teacher development as moving in lockstep through a series of universal stages (regardless of setting or experiences), teacher educators are now emphasizing the interrelationships between teachers' *learning and development* and the *context* of teachers' learning. In turn, they are beginning to focus upon the particular features of those contexts and experiences that might help teachers develop these capabilities. This perspective parallels the development of learning theory over the past twenty years, as psychologists have moved from behaviorists' quest for a direct relationship between stimulus and response, to cognitive psychologists' exploration of how individual learning unfolds, to the broader focus offered by sociocultural theory on the contexts and conditions that promote learning.

Although some researchers have previously interpreted research on stage theories to imply that beginning teachers cannot profitably focus on student learning or curriculum issues until they have mastered classroom routines (Kagan, 1992), recent research supports Grossman's (1992) argument that new teachers have the potential to make fruitful strides on these matters even as novices, if they have the right kinds of support. In Chapter Eleven, we focus on some of the characteristics of teachers' learning experiences that appear to contribute to the development of teachers' visions, understandings, tools, practices, and dispositions.

The Design of Teacher Education Programs

Linda Darling-Hammond, Karen Hammerness,
with Pamela Grossman, Frances Rust, Lee Shulman

Given what we know about how teachers learn and develop, how can we create teacher education programs that are effective in enabling teachers to acquire the knowledge, skills, and dispositions that will allow them to succeed? In Chapter Ten, we examined the nature of teachers' learning and identified three particular problems in learning to teach: the problems associated with the "apprenticeship of observation," the difficulty of enacting teaching intentions, and the enormous complexity of teaching, which requires integrating many kinds of knowledge and skills in making judgments about how to pursue multiple goals with learners who have diverse needs.

In this chapter, we examine some central issues in curriculum and program design, including issues of content and coherence, as well as concerns about scope and sequence. We then explore some of the features of programs that appear to support teacher learning and development. Finally, we move to an exploration of long-standing and emerging pedagogies that are used in teacher education and their implications for teacher learning. These include the construction of clinical experiences, including student teaching and strategies like microteaching; the use of performance assessments and portfolios; analyses of teaching and learning; case methods; teacher inquiry; and autobiography.

Some of these approaches have been developed explicitly to address one or more of the "problems of teaching" we described earlier. Some have been designed to help new teachers develop and practice particular skills they will use in the classroom (the "efficiency" dimension of our adaptive expertise schema, described in Chapter Ten). Others are designed to enable teachers to make judgments in the face of uncertainty, to innovate, and to be able to continue to learn from their practice; that is, to become adaptive experts. We explore the uses of these pedagogies for various purposes and goals of teacher education. We present them not as a "top ten list" of best strategies, but as examples of approaches that have gained currency because they are viewed as meeting particular needs or solving particular dilemmas in the learning-to-teach process.

Several lines of research have been helpful in outlining features of teachers' experiences that influence their learning. Many decades ago the Teacher Education and Learning to Teach (TELT) research program at Michigan State University explored the features of different teacher education programs that appear to change teaching practices and affect student learning outcomes. A series of case studies of exemplary teacher education programs by the National Commission on Teaching and America's Future provided empirical data about the nature of preservice teachers' learning experiences in programs viewed by graduates and employers as highly successful. Recent studies by researchers at the University of Michigan offer important large-scale data about the nature and features of professional learning experiences in the context of mathematics and science teaching reforms, whereas researchers at Ohio State University have examined the features of urban teacher education programs. In addition, a line of research from the University of Pennsylvania and the University of Wisconsin–Madison has documented how teachers can learn to generate knowledge about practice and to critically analyze the social contexts of schooling by working in teacher research, action research, or inquiry communities.

These studies and others suggest that, although there is no single best way to organize teachers' learning experiences in a preparation program, there are some common considerations in developing programs and a growing repertoire of strategies to draw upon in doing so.

ISSUES OF PROGRAM DESIGN

Connection and Coherence

In the recent past, many teacher education programs have been criticized for being overly theoretical, having little connection to practice, offering fragmented and incoherent courses, and lacking in a clear, shared conception of teaching among faculty. Indeed, conceptual and structural fragmentation is a consistent theme in studies of teacher education, especially those conducted throughout the 1980s (Feiman-Nemser, 1990; Floden, McDiarmid, and Werners, 1989; Goodlad, Soder, and Sirotnik, 1990; Howey and Zimpher, 1989; Zeichner and Gore, 1990). Programs that are largely a collection of unrelated courses without a common conception of teaching and learning have been found to be relatively feeble change agents for affecting practice among new teachers (Zeichner and Gore, 1990). In a large-scale study of a wide range of programs, Goodlad (1990) found only a small number of programs that provided prospective teachers with opportunities to learn to teach consistent with a particular vision of teaching and learning.

Beginning in the late 1980s, teacher education reforms began to produce program designs representing more integrated, coherent programs that emphasize a consistent vision of good teaching. These programs seek to create stronger links among courses and between clinical experiences and formal coursework, in part by using pedagogies that are connected to classroom practices (Cabello, Eckmier, and Baghieri, 1995; Graber, 1996; Grossman, 1994; Grossman and McDaniel, 1990; Hammerness and Darling-Hammond, 2002; Oakes, 1996; Ross, 1989). These pedagogies emerged as programs were restructured around theories of professional learning that suggest that teachers need to do more than simply implement particular techniques; they need to be able to think pedagogically, reason through dilemmas, investigate problems, and analyze student learning to develop appropriate curriculum for a diverse group of learners.

Since then, a number of studies have offered empirical evidence that teacher education programs that have coherent visions of teaching and learning, and that integrate related strategies across courses and field placements, have a greater impact on the initial conceptions and practices of prospective teachers than those that remain a collection of relatively disconnected courses. In a set of studies of seven exemplary teacher education programs—programs in which graduates and their employers find they are significantly better prepared than most other beginning teachers—one of the most striking characteristics is that the programs are particularly well integrated and coherent: they have integrated clinical work with coursework so that it reinforces and reflects key ideas and both aspects of the program build toward a deeper understanding of teaching and learning. These programs are founded on a set of big ideas that are continuously revisited and hence more deeply understood. In addition, researchers found that the programs are built around a strong, shared vision of good teaching practice; they use common standards of practice that guide and assess coursework and clinical work; and they demonstrate shared knowledge and common beliefs about teaching and learning among university and school-based faculty (Darling-Hammond, 1999; for cases, see Darling-Hammond and MacDonald, 2000; Koppich, 2000; Merseth and Koppich, 2000; Miller and Silvernail, 2000; Snyder, 2000; Whitford and others, 2000; Zeichner, 2000).

These findings echo those of Howey and Zimpher (1989), who found in their study of teacher education that strong programs

> . . . Have one or more frameworks grounded in theory and research as well as practice: frameworks that explicate, justify, and build consensus around such fundamental conceptions as the *role* of the teacher, the *nature* of teaching and

learning, and the *mission* of the school in this democracy . . . Programs embedded in such frameworks clearly establish priorities in terms of key dispositional attitudes and behaviors that are enabled and monitored in repeated structured experiences . . . Conceptually coherent programs enable needed and *shared* faculty leadership by underscoring collective roles as well as individual course responsibilities. Programs also contribute to more mutual endeavors in research and evaluation beyond the individual course level. (p. 242)

Similarly, a study of nine teacher education programs conducted as part of the Institute of Research on Teaching's Teacher Education and Learning to Teach (TELT) study found that more coherent programs, those with a strong vision of the type of teaching they were aiming to develop and consistent goals across courses, were more influential and effective in supporting student teacher learning and, for programs that emphasized constructivist learning theories, in helping new teachers understand the nature of teaching diverse populations (Tatto, 1996).

The importance of program coherence was further emphasized in the conclusions of a review of ninety-three empirical studies on learning to teach that examined efforts to change entering student teachers' beliefs, understanding, and behaviors with respect to teaching, learning, and students. The authors concluded that

> In the short-term interventions, which in all but one or two cases involved a single course, we saw little reported impact. In the studies of year-long programs, however, it was much more common for the researchers to report positive effects. Duration of intervention, as such, was not the main variable. More significant was what a given time period enabled those in the program to do. In the short-term interventions there seemed a tendency for the other elements of the program to interfere with or even nullify the effects of the intervention . . . the hidden curriculum in this case emanates from the type of structured fragmentation Gore and Zeichner (1991) refer to. *Longer-term programs on the other hand were effective when the teacher educators maintained a consistent focus and message.* (Wideen and others, 1998, p. 151, emphasis added)

That coherence should be important is not surprising. Studies of learning suggest that learning is enhanced when learners encounter mutually reinforcing ideas and skills across learning experiences, particularly when these are grounded in strategically chosen content and conveyed through effective pedagogies (National Research Council, 2000; Bruner, 1960/1977, 1990). Repeated experiences with a set of conceptual ideas, along with repeated opportunities to practice skills and modes of analysis, support deeper learning and the development of expertise (Ericsson, Krampe, and Tesch-Romer, 1993; Gick and Holyoak, 1983). It is particularly important for learners to be able to use theories and practices that can help them make sense of the phenomena they experience and observe rather than encountering mixed messages, contradictory theories, and ideas that are superficially conveyed. Tatto (1996) argues, however, that having a coherent program does not necessarily require that all faculty think alike, as diversity of thought contributes to rich learning experiences. She emphasizes, rather, that coherence should abide in the common ground among faculty around professional norms and expectations, as well as in the way that learning experiences are organized and conceptualized.

An effort to develop coherence in professional visions, norms, and expectations has implications for the policies used to staff and manage teacher education programs. In none of the highly coherent and impactful programs that were the subjects of the research noted earlier was it the practice to staff the program with large numbers of adjunct instructors who changed frequently. All of these programs had dedicated, long-term faculty members who worked out the program plan together and revisited it frequently. Although there were adjunct instructors employed in most of the programs, these were generally school-based faculty who taught or cotaught courses on a regular basis as members of the faculty team, rather than temporary employees who came and went without engagement in the intellectual life of the program. It is extraordinarily difficult to create a coherent program if much of the teaching is conducted by part-timers with different notions about what good teaching is and how to get there, and who have little opportunity to connect with what else is happening in the program.

In addition, the faculty in many of the programs cited earlier included many who themselves had been K–12 teachers before becoming university professors; some continued a teaching presence in schools as well as conducting research about teaching. Engagement in scholarship on curriculum, teaching, and learning was widespread among the university-based faculty and often extended to school-based faculty as well. This engagement supported a continuous dialogue about how to improve the program in light of the outcomes participants sought and observed.

Organizing Content: Considerations of Scope and Sequence

Research suggests that several elements make a difference in the design of a teacher education program, including:

1. The *content* of teacher education—what is taught and how it is connected, including the extent to which candidates are helped to acquire a *cognitive map* of teaching that allows them to see relationships among the domains of teaching knowledge and connect useful theory to practices that support student learning;

2. The learning *process*—the extent to which the curriculum builds on and enables candidates' *readiness* and is grounded in the materials and

tools of practice in ways that allow teachers' understandings to be enacted in the classroom; and

3. The learning *context*—the extent to which teacher learning is situated in contexts that allow the development of expert practice; such contexts include both subject matter domains and a community of practitioners who share practices, dispositions, and a growing base of knowledge.

Content: The Subject Matters

Although much research has focused on the processes of teacher learning, evidence suggests that *what* teachers learn matters at least as much as how they learn. It is worth noting, first of all, that teachers learn different things from diverse preparation programs (Kennedy, 1998, 1999); that they feel differentially well prepared for specific aspects of teaching, depending on the kind of pathway into teaching they have pursued and program they have completed (Darling-Hammond, Chung, and Frelow, 2002; Imbimbo and Silvernail, 1999); and they vary in their sense of efficaciousness and effectiveness as a consequence of their learning experiences (Andrew, 1990; Andrew and Schwab, 1995; Cohen and Hill, 2000; Denton and Lacina, 1984; Desimone, Porter, Garet, Yoon, and Birman, 2002).

Considering What is Taught. This entire volume has sought to provide a rationale for critical content to be considered in initial teacher education. But do decisions about the content of the curriculum matter to what teachers know and can do? Though it may seem hardly worth stating, decisions about what gets taught in teacher education matter.

A number of large-scale studies have found relationships between teacher effectiveness and the quantity of training teachers have received in subject matter and content-specific teaching methods (Begle, 1979; Druva and Anderson, 1983; Ferguson and Womack, 1993; Goldhaber and Brewer, 2000; Monk, 1994; Monk and King, 1994). Although these studies were unable to examine the nature of this training, more recent studies have examined the substance of training as well as the amount. For example, Wenglinsky (2002) found that, in addition to subject matter background, more effective middle school math and science teachers had more professional preparation in how to work with diverse student populations (a combined measure of training in cultural diversity, teaching limited English proficient students, and teaching students with special needs), how to develop higher-order thinking skills, and how to use hands-on methods.

Although some studies have found effects from the amount or length of training, other research suggests that the duration of professional learning experiences is less influential in its effects on teacher practices than the content of the learning experience and the pedagogy used to teach that content. (For a review, see Kennedy, 1998.) Another set of studies that followed students from eight different teacher education programs over time found, among other things, that the substantive content of programs made a difference for what teachers learned, and teachers prepared in programs with different content emphases learned to practice in different ways. For example, Kennedy (1999) reported that teachers who participated in "traditional" programs that emphasized management and the technical aspects of teaching tended to become more concerned about grammar, conventions, and prescriptive aspects of writing than about students' abilities to communicate their ideas. Similarly, Desimone and colleagues (2002) found that teachers who participated in what they called "reform-oriented" professional development programs tended to focus more upon students' own strategies and purposes. In a study examining the effects of professional development on teachers' instructional practices for 207 teachers in thirty schools, these researchers found that the content of the learning experience—opportunities to review student work, to obtain feedback on teaching, and its connection to other current activities—had strong effects on teachers' using those practices in their classrooms.

Other research suggests that when teachers have opportunities to interact with their subject matter in ways that they aim for their own students to do (such as engaging in writing workshops, getting feedback on their own writing, giving critiques), they are more likely to engage in those practices in their classrooms (Lieberman and Wood, 2003). Earlier studies suggest these differences in teaching practice matter for what students learn, and that certain kinds of teacher education and associated teaching practices appear to be more effective in bringing about basic skills learning, whereas other approaches to teaching and teacher development appear to be more effective in supporting more transferable learning of more complex higher-order skills (Brophy and Good, 1986; Crawford and Stallings, 1978).

Recognition that various practices are differentially useful for different learning goals has caused conceptions of the teacher education curriculum to change dramatically over the years. In the past, ideas about what teachers needed to know in order to teach were quite limited, often to a bit about classroom management and some "tricks of the trade" that might include how to present a lesson or how to introduce a lecture to one's students. Little emphasis was placed upon the importance of understanding how people learn or the design of curriculum and assessment. However, the growing emphasis on student learning—and teachers' responsibility for it—has stimulated the development of a curriculum for teachers that includes knowledge about influences on learning, including child development, social contexts of education, language acquisition, educational purposes, and aspects of pedagogy, along with specific building blocks for teaching, including content knowledge and how to teach it to diverse students at different stages, and the design of curriculum, classroom environments, and assessments.

Creating a Cognitive Map of Teaching. This volume has organized its discussion around a number of domains of knowledge for teaching. However, there is a danger in considering domains of the curriculum in a piecemeal fashion. Research suggests that when learners begin with a sense of the whole and are helped to see how ideas are connected and related, it deepens their understanding and allows them to integrate and use more of what they learn. Studies of memory and learning have found that students learn best when they have a *conceptual framework,* a *cognitive map,* or a *schema,* which enables them to organize categories of information and to recognize the relationship among concepts (Singley and Anderson, 1989), something that is much more difficult when they encounter an unrelated set of facts or a decontextualized introduction to discrete skills. Learners benefit from encountering a curriculum that is organized around the structure of a subject—the fundamental ideas, concepts, and issues of a field—noting that, as Bruner has argued, "to learn structure, in short, is to learn how things are related" (1960/1977, p. 7). Learning ideas within the context of an overarching conceptual framework not only helps students understand the "big picture" but also enables them to begin to recognize how all the individual ideas and theories fit together and relate to one another.

Having this structure explicitly described and explained is helpful for candidates' later learning. Clearly, for this to take place, teacher educators themselves must have worked out such a framework, both within and across courses, so that they can structure the content they are teaching and explain this structure to prospective teachers. Whereas at one time, teacher educators had not generally considered this kind of conceptual framework, recent standards from NCATE and other accrediting agencies require that programs develop and defend such a framework, thus increasing the likelihood that a shared understanding of how it all "fits together" will be held across the faculty. Going a step further formally to articulate this conceptual map to the teacher candidates themselves could help candidates better use the ideas they encounter.

One way to give novices a sense of the big picture is by explanation and illustration. As illustrated in Chapter Two, helping students develop and use a cognitive map (for example, the frameworks offered by the book *How People Learn* [Donovan and others, 1999]) can help in creating a basis for understanding and analyzing teaching and learning. Standards for teaching, such as those developed by the National Board for Professional Teaching Standards and by state certification agencies, also provide a schema that can help people understand what dimensions of teaching are important and how they are supposed to fit together. An experientially powerful way to help build a schema is to develop a sense from guided observations and engagement in practice of what the act of teaching is and what kinds of knowledge it may require before or while encountering an intellectual framework for interpreting practice.

For this reason, many programs now emphasize the importance of providing clinical experience early and throughout a teacher education program—so that prospective teachers develop an image of what teaching involves and requires. This allows them to begin to understand some of the challenges and thinking involved so that they can better make sense of how the ideas and theories they encounter in their coursework fit in the process of developing practice. Some teacher educators contend that providing novices with these early practicum experiences actually provides a conceptual structure for them to organize and better understand the theories that are addressed in their academic work. Some empirical work lends support to this claim, suggesting greater effectiveness on several measures of teaching for those with more and earlier clinical experiences (Denton, 1982; Denton, Morris, and Tooke, 1982; Henry, 1983; Ross, Hughes, and Hill, 1981; Sunal, 1980).

Helping candidates understand the bigger picture allows them to locate what they are learning. In addition, deep understanding involves *returning to central ideas and concepts* again and again, so that over time students are able to understand them more thoroughly and to appreciate their relationship to other concepts, ideas, and theories. Bruner's (1960/1977) notion of a "spiral curriculum" suggests that "a continual deepening of one's understanding of [key ideas] comes from learning to use them in progressively more complex forms." Bruner argues, "A curriculum as it develops should revisit these basic ideas repeatedly, building upon them until the student has grasped the full formal apparatus that goes with them" (p.13).

Research on learning and transfer supports this conception. Studies of transfer indicate that when ideas are taught in multiple contexts and include both attention to key principles and examples of how the ideas are applied (Biederman and Shiffrar, 1987), learners are more likely to be able to abstract the relevant and important features of key concepts and to develop more flexible knowledge about the topic at hand (Gick and Holyoak, 1983). This kind of learning is facilitated both by a curriculum that is coherent and reinforcing across settings and by an iterative design, like that described earlier in the Developmental Teacher Education Program at the University of California at Berkeley, where developmental concepts are reencountered over the four semesters of a sequence of developmental courses. (See "The Power of a Coherent, Purposeful Teacher Education Program.")

The Power of a Coherent, Purposeful Teacher Education Program

Recent research on powerful teacher education programs not only suggests that new teachers may be able to move farther along in the journey of developing as a teacher more quickly than was previously thought, but also that it is possible for new teachers to learn much more about teaching and to attend to more aspects of the classroom than previously expected. For instance, in a case study of the University of California–Berkeley's Developmental Teacher Education Program (DTE), Snyder (2000) describes the classroom of a graduate who is a first-year teacher, revising curriculum based upon her perception of her first-grade students' needs and interests. (See Chapter Nine.) She was able to revamp a "packaged curriculum" so that it engaged students in authentic science inquiry in which they recorded data, generated and evaluated hypotheses, and drew data-based conclusions. She was also able to create and use cooperative groups that balanced the racial, language, and ethnic diversity of her students and that encouraged students' leadership and interpersonal skills; scaffold work for students' different levels of language proficiency; and manage a classroom expertly so that students got their work done and could focus on the intellectual work at hand.

Snyder details a connection between this beginning teacher's skills, abilities, and approaches and the experiences DTE offers candidates in their teacher preparation programs. For instance, the DTE program involves students in four "core" seminars on human development in which students observe children's behavior in classrooms, evaluate their developmental levels, and offer explanations of children's learning and activity based upon theories of child development. Student teachers also take courses in subject matter teaching methods, which focus upon actively engaging students in "hands-on" science and mathematics. As Snyder explains, the purposeful links between the "core" and "methods" courses create a consistent, cumulative experience for the student teachers:

> The content of the teaching methods is only half the story. The concurrent experiences provided in the core seminars link the study of development with the developmental demands of schools and school subjects. Introducing an activity that holds the interests of the students is only one half of the task. The other half is to identify the knowledge that is the target of the activity, and how this knowledge relates to previous and future understandings. To do this well requires an understanding of developing cognitive abilities within a particular content area, the kind of activities that promote their development, and how the same abilities are manifested in other areas of the curriculum. (2000, p. 108)

While DTE students are taking their courses, they are "always in classrooms simultaneously." In fact, students have five placements in different classroom settings (to vary by age groups as well as context) over the period of two years in their master's degree program, designed so that student teachers can begin to consciously integrate what they are learning across a variety of contexts—as well as to develop a rich understanding of what teaching practice can look like.

The Learning Process

Considering how to introduce, work with, and revisit key concepts so that they are truly understood in ways that can be enacted and integrated into a sophisticated practice is no small problem. To do this well, teacher educators need to consider how to develop candidates' readiness for learning about particular aspects of teaching and how to bring to life theory in practice and practice in theory.

Developing Readiness. The concept of *readiness* undergirds approaches to scope and sequence, which involves identifying key foundational ideas and experiences that can lay the foundation for later learning. The starting point for learning is always one's own prior knowledge, which must be connected in some way to new learning opportunities. As we have noted, in teacher education, candidates' prior knowledge poses both problems and possibilities that derive from the apprenticeship of observation they have all experienced. To both confront and use this prior knowledge, and to help candidates begin to realize that students will learn in different ways and have different experiences and perspectives, many preparation programs begin with candidates' personal experience as a productive way to trigger discussion of beliefs and their bases as well as to build more systematic knowledge. Some programs begin courses of study in teaching by engaging students in writing and sharing educational autobiographies and narratives, which can assist students in critically examining their own educational experiences and becoming ready to engage in professional pedagogical thinking.

As is true in children' development, considerations of readiness should not be used to restrict learning experiences but instead to guide decisions about where to start and how to scaffold learning so that students are *enabled* to develop critical skills and abilities. So, for example, although research on new teachers indicates that they do not often begin with a focus upon student learning and are instead concerned with their own actions in the classroom, novices can be helped to focus upon their students and the learning process through purposefully constructed experiences and coursework. Many successful teacher education programs begin their course of study in teaching with work on learning and development—hoping to start new teachers with a focus upon students and student learning from the beginning. Such courses require students very early on in their programs to observe children and to collect detailed information about their development and learning, as well as their learning contexts, thus bringing the child's experience and learning into focus.

Often assessments of student learning and related analyses of curriculum and teaching are a trigger for this process of focusing on learning and its relation to teaching decisions. Tying close observations and discussions of children's behavior and learning to analyses of teaching also allows novices to understand the relationship between curriculum plans and what children do. This helps them realize that their early concerns about control and classroom management will be as much addressed by their learning about effective planning and teaching as by their development of classroom rules or routines.

Finally, if teacher educators want novices to develop expert thinking and skills of enactment, they need to think about what the components of that skill set are, which understandings and skills are the foundation for others, and what experiences will be needed to help ensure that candidates can make progress toward the broader goals of the program. Just as in other kinds of cognitive apprenticeship, the processes of clarifying goals, articulating what the desired performance consists of and what it looks like, modeling and demonstration, scaffolding, making thinking visible, and practice with coaching are essential. These processes need to be thought out across courses and clinical learning experiences, so that the overall curriculum for teacher education makes sense and adds up to readiness for teaching.

Learning About Practice *in* Practice. A key element for successful learning is the opportunity to apply what is being learned and refine it (National Research Council, 2000). Indeed, cognitive psychologists have found that "deliberate practice"—purposefully and critically rehearsing certain kinds of performances—is particularly important to the development of expertise (Ericsson and others, 1993). Whereas in the traditional undergraduate program, student teaching was often placed at the end of a program, as a kind of culminating experience, many programs are now entwining carefully designed clinical experiences early and throughout a program. Many teacher educators argue that student teachers *see and understand* both theory and practice differently if they are taking coursework concurrently with fieldwork. Research on the outcomes of teacher education efforts lends support to this idea that carefully constructed field experiences can enable new teachers to reinforce, apply, and synthesize concepts they are learning in their coursework (Denton, 1982; Denton and others, 1982; Henry, 1983; Ross and others, 1981; Baumgartner, Koerner, and Rust, 2002; Sunal, 1980).

It appears that novices who have some experience with teaching when they encounter coursework are more prepared to make sense of the ideas, theories, and concepts that are addressed in their academic work. For instance, in a study of 139 undergraduate teacher education students which compared those with thirty hours of field experiences (n = 61) and those who had no early field experiences (n = 78), Denton (1982) found that students with early field experiences performed significantly better in their methods courses than those without early field experience. The author concluded that early field experiences appear to increase learning and understanding about the principles of how to teach within a content area. It appears that when teachers have multiple opportunities to experience and study the relationship of theory with practice, their learning is enhanced.

It is not just the availability of classroom experience that enables teachers to apply what they are learning. Recent studies of learning to teach suggest that immersing teachers in the materials of practice and working on particular concepts using these materials has the potential to be particularly powerful for teachers' learning (Ball and Cohen, 1999; Lampert and Ball, 1998). As we discuss in the following section, examples of student work, artifacts from the classroom, videotapes of teaching and learning in classrooms, and cases of teaching and learning enable them to relate their coursework to classrooms and children. Ball and Cohen (1999) have termed this kind of learning "learning *in and from* practice." Although this notion emphasizes the importance of preservice teachers spending substantial time learning in real classrooms, Ball and Cohen explain that "learning in practice" does not necessarily mean that teachers need always to be in the classroom in "real time." It can also happen away from real classrooms, as long as the work being done is centered in authentic classroom materials:

> Being "centered in practice" does not necessarily imply situations in school classrooms in real time. Although the bustle of immediacy lends authenticity, it also interferes with opportunities to learn. Being situated in a classroom restricts opportunities to the sort of teaching underway in that particular class. Further, being so situated confines learning to the rush of minute-to-minute practice. Better opportunities can be created by using strategic documentation of practice. Copies of student work, videotapes of classroom lessons, curriculum materials, and teachers' notes all would be candidates. Using such things could locate the curriculum of teacher education "in practice" for they could focus professional learning in materials taken from real classrooms that represent salient problems of practice. (1999, p. 14)

Learning in practice does not just happen on its own, of course. Though the importance of teaching experience has been reinforced by much research, it is important to recognize that practice alone does not make perfect, or even good, performance. Opportunities to connect practice to expert knowledge must be built into learning experiences for teachers. For example, a recent study of experienced teachers who elected to enter a preservice teacher education program after several years of teaching found that these teachers—far from feeling that they had learned everything they needed to know about teaching from experience—reported that the teacher education program taught them for the first time how to design productive curriculum, how to support struggling students, and how to assess, reflect on, and improve their teaching (Kunzman, 2002).

Studies of teachers' learning have suggested that when opportunities to reflect on their work and to connect it to research and theory are included in teacher education, teachers are better able to identify areas needing improvement, to consider alternative strategies for the future, and to problem solve and reason through pedagogical dilemmas (Freese, 1999; Hammerness and others, 2002; Laboskey, 1992). This is consonant with research that has found that unguided experience is not nearly as effective as inquiry tied to instruction that outlines the major concepts about which experience raises questions and provides examples. There is, as Schwartz and Bransford (1998) found, a "time for telling," which is especially effective when it joins strong conceptual explanations with specific examples and opportunities for application and analysis. This study and others have found that either "telling" alone or hands-on inquiry alone is less effective than both together. That is, in a recent resolution of the long-standing debates about "direct instruction" versus "indirect instruction," learning that involves deep understanding and transfer often is a product of the skillful integration of both inquiry and explanation. This kind of conceptual learning also appears to support the application or enactment of the concepts studied.

Many studies from different lines of research on teacher learning provide examples of the importance of conceptual explanation about pedagogical approaches tied to direct opportunities for inquiry and application. In a number of experimental studies, teachers who have experienced targeted preservice preparation or professional development focused on effective teaching practices in specific content areas, including immediate opportunities to apply what they have learned, have produced student achievement gains that are significantly greater than those of comparison or control group teachers (Angrist and Lavy, 1998; Crawford and Stallings, 1978; Ebmeier and Good, 1979; Good and Grouws, 1979; Lawrenz and McCreath, 1988; Mason and Good, 1993).

One such study, aimed at improving classroom management strategies, randomly assigned experienced teachers to a group that received no training and one that received training in research-based classroom management strategies. The strategies were described in a text outlining the conceptual approach along with specific classroom-based approaches, and were taught with small-group problem-solving sessions based on classroom scenarios and supported by staff who could link the problems to concepts that had been studied. The training occurred in two sets of sessions about a month apart. The group that received the training demonstrated a significant increase in use of the management strategies and a significant decrease in student misbehavior coupled with an increase in student engagement and on-task learning, whereas no changes occurred for the control group (Evertson, Emmer, Sanford, and Clements, 1983). Experience alone had not taught teachers to enact these kinds of strategies. Key to what teachers said enabled their learning were both the increased awareness they gained from being exposed to a conceptual framework for organizing their classrooms and the concrete, specific, and practical suggestions for *how* to enact the theories, which they could immediately seek to apply in practice. They also felt they learned from sessions that allowed them to share problems and strategies with other teachers within the context of this conceptual framework as they attempted to implement the new ideas.

Situating Learning in Productive Contexts

Finally, modern learning theory makes clear that expertise is developed within specific domains and learning is situated within specific contexts where it needs to be developed and from which it must be helped to transfer. Whereas programs of teacher education have sometimes focused on generic conceptions of knowledge and skill development, it now seems clear that, to be enacted, teachers' learning should be developed in ways that derive from and connect to the content and students they teach. At the same time, teachers need to learn how to evaluate how aspects of what they have learned in one context may apply to new contexts or problems they encounter.

Treating Content as Context. Recent research in cognitive psychology suggests that expertise is developed within particular domains rather than generically. Because of this, current discussions of scope in teacher education now acknowledge the importance of content pedagogy (see, for example, Ball and Bass, 2000; Grossman and Stodolsky, 1995; Shulman, 1987). The importance and nature of content pedagogy have become better appreciated over time, especially as research on learning and teaching has focused within specific domains. This research suggests that much of what teachers must learn about teaching is particular to different content areas: prospective teachers need opportunities to wrestle with and think about how students learn concepts of ratio in mathematics or strategies for composing a persuasive essay in language arts. To help students understand the structure of the discipline, teachers need to examine what the key modes of inquiry and thinking are in the field and what key ideas are foundational in their field. To plan curriculum and address learning problems, they need to understand the common challenges and misconceptions learners often face in learning their subject.

There have also been a series of studies that suggest that professional development focused upon how students learn specific content within subject matter areas is helpful for teachers, particularly if the instruction is focused upon assisting students toward deeper conceptual understandings (Cohen and Hill, 2000; Desimone and others, 2002; Fennima and others, 1996; Ma, 1999). For instance, Cohen and Hill's study (2000), which included 595 California elementary school teachers, found that teachers who had opportunities to learn about particular mathematics curriculum in specific topic areas, and who worked together on teaching strategies for implementing this content, reported significant changes in their practice. They also found that these changes were associated with stronger student achievement.

Learning in Professional Communities. Research suggests that professional communities in which teachers share understandings about the nature of good teaching and work together to enact them provide particularly conducive settings for learning to teach. For example, in Desimone's previously cited study of teachers' learning, she and her colleagues (2002) found that a number of different elements in teachers' learning experiences had cumulative effects on changing teachers' practices. Not only did a focus on particular teaching practices—in this case, technology use, use of higher-order instructional methods, and alternative student assessments—increase teachers' use of those practices in their classrooms, the use of active learning strategies during professional development for teachers also increased use of the practices. The effects on practice were stronger when teachers from a school, grade level, or department participated as a group and when the strategy was consistent with other practices in the teachers' classroom or school, thus suggesting the importance of a coherent approach to learning to teach and the potential power of communities of practice.

The effects of working within a community of practice on specific teaching strategies were noted in other studies we have reviewed (for example, Cohen and Hill, 2000; Evertson and others, 1983). In addition, emerging research suggests that opportunities to engage in "lesson study," where groups of teachers are engaged in joint observation, analysis, and evaluation of lessons, may have particular promise as a learning environment in which teachers engage in learning with their peers (Fernandez, 2002; Lewis and Tsuchida, 1998; Stigler and Hiebert, 1999).

Cochran-Smith and Lytle (1993; see also Cochran-Smith, 1991) have emphasized the role that communities of inquiry can play in preservice teacher's learning. In their description of Program START, a fifth-year program in elementary education at the University of Pennsylvania, they explain that the intention of the program is to invite student teachers into a group of teachers who are participating in "a community of school-based and university-based learners, and essentially a way of life as teachers, by emphasizing reform and inquiry across the professional lifespan" (pp. 65, 68). Rather than acting as "experts" to be imitated, cooperating teachers' roles are to help initiate new teachers into the experience of framing questions and engaging in inquiry into questions of teaching, learning, and schooling. Documentation of graduates' thinking and practices suggests that they learn both dispositions and strategies that carry forward from this experience.

The role of inquiry is viewed as critical where the goal of teacher education is a lifelong ability to learn *from* teaching, rather than a more contained image of learning *for* teaching that is expected to be complete within a short span of time. As Cochran-Smith and Lytle (1993) argue: "Learning from teaching ought to be regarded as the primary task of teacher education across the professional life span. By 'learning from teaching' we mean that inquiry ought to be regarded as an integral part of the activity of teaching and . . . classrooms and schools ought to be treated as research sites" (pp. 63–64).

In sum, contemporary research suggests that learning about teaching develops through participation in a community of learners where content is encountered in contexts in which it can be applied. Emerging evidence suggests that teachers benefit from participating in the culture of teaching—by working with the *materials and tools of teaching practice;* examining teaching plans and student learning while immersed in theory about learning, development, and subject matter. They also benefit from *participating in practice* as they observe teaching, work closely with experienced teachers, and work with students to use what they are learning. And this learning is strengthened when it is embedded within a broad *community* of practitioners—experienced teachers, other student teachers, teacher educators, and students, so that they can gain access to the experiences, practices, theories, and knowledge of the profession.

Some programs have graduates who report significantly higher feelings of preparedness than their peers and are more highly rated by employers, who say they seek out these candidates because they are more effective in the classroom from their very first days of teaching. A recent study of seven such programs found common features among a group of large and small programs located in both public and private colleges and universities. These features include:

- A shared vision of good teaching that is consistent in courses and clinical work;

- Well-defined standards of practice and performance that are used to guide the design and assessment of coursework and clinical work;

- A common core curriculum grounded in substantial knowledge of development, learning, and subject matter pedagogy, taught in the context of practice;

- Extended clinical experiences (at least thirty weeks) that reflect the program's vision of good teaching, are interwoven with coursework, and are carefully mentored;

- Strong relationships, based on common knowledge and beliefs, between universities and reform-minded schools; and

- Extensive use of case study methods, teacher research, performance assessments, and portfolio examinations that relate teachers' learning to classroom practice (Darling-Hammond, 1999).

The same kinds of program features and pedagogical tools are noted in other studies of strong programs (see, for example, Cabello and others, 1995; Graber, 1996) that have documented outcomes on candidates' preparedness and performance.

PEDAGOGIES FOR PREPARING TEACHERS: EMERGING RESPONSES TO THE PROBLEMS OF LEARNING TO TEACH

Although research on the pedagogies of teacher education is still in the very early stages of development (Grossman, in press), researchers are beginning to accrue some evidence about particular practices that seem to help teachers develop the visions, understandings, practices, and dispositions for teaching we have discussed. In addition to the usual tools of education—carefully chosen readings and materials, well-crafted lectures, and descriptions or demonstrations of particular strategies—a number of pedagogies have emerged in response to the perennial problems of learning to teach, such as overcoming the apprenticeship of observation, supporting enactment, and managing the complexity of teaching. Many have been developed explicitly to aid in the professional problem of helping novices connect theory to practice, focusing upon learning *in* practice with the aid of both direct instruction and inquiry. This learning is increasingly lodged within communities of practice—cohorts of student teachers who learn together as well as placements with veteran colleagues within professional development schools and other collegial work settings. These communities are used as supports for learning and problem solving. Finally, some of these pedagogies appear to be especially useful for developing adaptive expertise.

None of these pedagogies is a silver bullet; each has particular strengths and limitations, and all can be implemented well or poorly and, in the execution, differentially capture key elements that are needed to make them productive. As Grossman (in press) notes, the utility teacher educators might attach to different approaches depends on how they view the goals of teaching:

> The plethora of pedagogies used in teacher education reflects, in part, the different conceptions of teaching practice that exist. Teaching has been described as a set of techniques or behaviors, as a form of clinical decision-making, as a cognitive apprenticeship based in disciplinary understanding, as a therapeutic relationship, and as a process of continuing inquiry. Each of these views of the nature of practice might lead to a different form of pedagogy in professional education. Training models such as micro-teaching, for example, are closely linked to the technical view of teaching, in which teachers are trained in the discrete skills of teaching. Case methods have been advocated to develop teachers' capacities to make informed decisions in the face of uncertainty, while others advocate the use of teacher research to prepare teachers to adopt an inquiry-stance into their teaching.

In their work on models of teaching, Joyce and Weil (2003) have noted that different approaches to teaching are associated with different models of and goals for learning; for example, information processing, social learning, personal development, or behavioral training. From this perspective, teachers can learn to choose strategies in relation to their objectives, drawing from multiple models as they balance the many goals they hold for student learning and development. Although there is quite a bit of evidence that different goals for students are best pursued through distinctive strategies, the pedagogies we discuss here are in many cases useful across different models of teaching, although the content of what is modeled, analyzed, evaluated, or attempted would change from one approach to another.

We begin with clinical experiences, including *student teaching,* as a signature pedagogy that is increasingly tied to coursework throughout the entire experience and forms the spine of most strong programs. Strategies like student teaching and its laboratory counterpart, *microteaching,* were developed to deal with the problem of enactment. We also address new ways to represent practice that include structured *performance assessments and portfolios* demonstrating particular abilities. In particular, we discuss the kinds of portfolios that ask teachers to demonstrate their practice and represent it through videotapes, commentaries, and artifacts, such as those created as part of the National Board for Professional Teaching Standards, some states' licensing portfolios, and the preservice Performance Assessment for California Teachers [PACT]. These performance assessments are even more systematic than student teaching in terms of what teachers are supposed to learn, in that they introduce certain practices that must be demonstrated, and these practices are evaluated against standards. These assessments add analytic expectations for student teachers' learning. They must learn to make sense of practice and learn from it, with a particular focus on understanding how their teaching decisions have enabled or undermined student learning.

We then turn to another way to examine one's own and others' practices and to connect theory and practice, through *analyses of teaching and learning* and *case methods,* which seek to make the process of student teaching more purposefully analytic and coursework more practice-based. Case methods are one way to analyze teaching and learning that deals explicitly with the problem of theory-practice connections. There are also other tools for analyzing teaching and learning that include videotapes and multimedia platforms (sometimes these are video "cases," sometimes demonstrations of particular techniques, sometimes sites for broader inquiry) and structured examinations of student work. The notion of "common texts" for studying teaching ties these together.

Another kind of text or narrative is the *autobiography,* used as a tool to confront the "apprenticeship of observation," to bring insight to one's own motivations and experiences, to learn from reflecting on experience, and to learn from others by sharing experiences. As discussed in Chapter Seven, Teaching Diverse Learners, this kind of experience can help teachers recognize that people learn differently and that many have had different learning experiences than they have, thus broadening their perspectives.

And finally, whereas autobiographies and cases typically look backward, we address *practitioner inquiry* that looks forward. It allows teachers to use these analytic tools to pose new questions that guide their current and future practice and that enable them to take a larger view, even beyond the classroom. Inquiry approaches deal with the problems of enactment (action), theory-practice connections (research), and personal experience or apprenticeship in one's own classroom. In each of the following sections, we briefly describe the pedagogy and its rationale, relevant research findings, and key features of the pedagogy that seem important in supporting student teachers' learning.

Construction of Clinical Experiences

Perhaps the most pervasive pedagogy in teacher education is that of supervised student teaching, which has long been acknowledged as having a profound impact on student teachers. Many teachers have claimed that the most important elements in their professional education were the school experiences found in student teaching (Guyton and McIntyre, 1990). Yet at the same time, current conceptions of the purposes of student teaching, what it should encompass, and how it should be constructed, differ markedly from institution to institution. Typically, the ideal has been a placement in which student teachers are supported by purposeful coaching from an expert cooperating teacher in the same teaching field who offers modeling, coplanning, frequent feedback, repeated opportunities to practice, and reflection upon practice while the student teacher gradually takes on more responsibility.

However, the actual experience of student teaching is highly variable both within and across programs, depending on how cooperating teachers are recruited, whether and how the process is guided, and what the expectations are for performance by both the novice and cooperating teacher. The experience can range from the most passive version of student teaching in which the prospective teacher sits in the back of a classroom and simply observes and, perhaps, grades papers, to a kind of "trial by fire" in which the student teacher takes over a more experienced teacher's classroom immediately and teaches alone, sometimes with little coaching, coplanning, or conceptual framework to guide what he or she does in the classroom. The practices of cooperating teachers may reflect the program's goals and contemporary research on learning and teaching to widely varying degrees.

Some internship models that aim for prospective teachers to become teachers of record fairly quickly are designed to offer and build on student teaching experiences, whereas others replace student teaching with independent teaching, usually with the expectation of close mentoring. Like the variability noted in student teaching, the mentoring intended for internship models has been found to materialize to varying degrees, sometimes intense and other times erratic, sometimes by teachers in the same field and other times not, sometimes with the opportunity of some modeling and demonstration and other times without novices having the chance to see modeled what they are trying to create in practice, with differing outcomes for candidate performance (Shields and others, 2001; California State University, 2002a).

Very different practices arise out of different conceptions and traditions, which frequently are unexamined. Programs have different ideas about what clinical experiences ought to accomplish, when and where they should occur and over what period of time, whether and how they should relate to coursework, and how many different settings a given student teacher should experience. Different strategies bring with them different benefits and limitations. For example, having multiple different settings for practice teaching may allow student teachers more explicitly to consider what kinds of generalizations can and cannot be made across settings and how contexts make a difference in the choice of strategies and how to use them. At the same time, multiple short placements reduce the opportunities to deeply understand a group of students and a kind of practice, and may make it difficult for student teachers to learn how what came before influences what is happening now in the classroom. Shorter placements also place burdens on schools without the compensating benefits of the contribution a more seasoned student teacher (for example, one who spends an entire semester or year) can make, thus making it more difficult to maintain strong partnerships for practicum placements.

There is no one right answer to these trade-offs, and there are many ways of resolving them appropriately. Whatever the design of student teaching chosen, it is important that prospective teachers' clinical experiences are constructed with careful consideration of *what* the experience should be like and *why*. For instance, decisions to design a program that will place students in more than one student teaching setting should take into account both the benefits (experiences with different students; exposures to a variety of approaches to teaching; opportunities for observing multiple models of good practice) and the downsides (student teachers cannot stay long enough to get to know the children well; to work through a whole cycle of practice; or to see the beginning and end of the learning cycle of a group of learners), so that the program can optimize the experiences offered.

Factors Influencing the Success of Student Teaching. Theories of learning can inform decisions about how to construct clinical experiences for teachers. Key features of cognitive apprenticeships include the importance of *clarity about the goals* of the experience, including the performances and practices to be developed; *modeling* of good practices by more expert teachers in which teachers *make their thinking visible*; frequent *opportunities for practice* with continuous *formative feedback* and *coaching;* multiple opportunities to *relate classroom work to university coursework*; *graduated responsibility* for all aspects of classroom teaching; and structured opportunities to *reflect* (Collins, Brown, and Holum, 1991). Use of these principles may help address some of the challenges inherent in the apprenticeship of observation by making expert teachers' work and thinking more "visible" to novices, while also providing multiple opportunities for novices to practice, get feedback, and gain more responsibility as they continue to develop expertise themselves.

There is some evidence that both the amount and timing of student teaching affect outcomes. Whereas student teaching has been often meager—averaging only about ten to twelve weeks for many programs—recent research suggests that more supervised experience with graduated responsibility can have positive effects on candidates' practice and self-confidence (Orland-Barak, 2002; LaBoskey and Richert, 2002; Baumgartner and others, 2002). For instance, some studies indicate that having a longer student teaching experience, especially when it is concurrent with theoretical coursework, is associated with stronger outcomes for teachers in terms of ability to apply learning to practice (Chin and Russell, 1995; Sumara and Luce-Kaplar, 1996).

A related finding is that program designs that include more practicum experiences and student teaching, integrated with coursework, appear to make a difference in teachers' practices, confidence, and long-term commitment to teaching. For example, Andrew (1990) found, in his study of a comparison sample of 144 graduates of a five-year program and 163 graduates of a four-year program within the same institution, that graduates of the five-year program, who had more extensive student teaching integrated with their coursework rather than a dollop added to the end of undergraduate courses, tended to spend more time evaluating their students, used a broader repertoire of teaching strategies, and conferred more with colleagues and parents than graduates of the four-year program. In a related study that examined the performance and leadership behaviors of a random sample of 1390 graduates from eleven universities with both four- and five-year teacher education programs, the authors found that graduates of five-year programs, which typically offered a full year of student teaching along with earlier practicum experiences, were more likely to enter and remain in teaching than those of four-year programs (Andrew and Schwab, 1995). The teachers from the five-year programs felt more confident in their teaching and were viewed by their supervisors as more competent.

Some studies have gathered data on the relationships between extended clinical experiences for new teachers and their students' learning. In a set of studies of two groups of secondary student teachers with different amounts of teacher education preparation within the same institution, the group of teachers with more extensive field experiences and more education coursework produced stronger student gains on pre- and post-tests of learning within curriculum units designed by the student teachers (Denton and Lacina, 1984; Denton, Morris, and Tooke, 1982; Denton and Smith, 1983; Denton and Tooke, 1981). Some research also suggests that student teachers who have a number of opportunities to teach in a variety of classrooms seem to start off their first years on more solid ground than those with only one limited clinical experience because they have a stronger "frame" with which to interpret important concepts in teaching and learning (Baumgartner and others, 2002).

The nature of the support during clinical work appears to be critical in enabling preservice teachers to make sense of their experience and learn from it. Just as cognitive research has found that children can learn more when supported within their "zone of proximal development" by more capable peers or adults, so it appears that teachers learn more when supported by expert practitioners. There are a series of studies that suggest that powerful learning does not usually occur from letting a teacher "sink or swim" in her practicum experience (Feiman-Nemser and Buchmann, 1985; Britzman, 1991) but that guidance and mentorship as well as peer support are important for novices to receive the modeling, coaching, and feedback they need (Rodriguez and Sjostrom, 1995; Sparks, 1986). Novices often attest to the important role that school and university supervisors play in the teaching and learning of practice, although there is little systematic research on exactly what the most effective supervisors do. The following example provides some suggestive insights from one successful mentor's experience in helping support student teachers' developing practice, and thinking about practice.

Strategic Mentoring Practices

Feiman-Nemser (2001b) examined the practice of an exemplary supervisor, Pete Frazer, and found several key strategies that characterized his work. Frazer described his role as balancing the tension between student teachers' personal expression and maintaining a sense of professional accountability that comes from understanding good practice, and he discussed several strategies:

- "Finding openings"—noticing fruitful topics that are not obvious to a novice teacher but that lead to key issues that all teachers need to think about.
- "Pinpointing problems"—helping student teachers develop language to frame and articulate problems in practice so they can get help and support. He also helps them understand the relationship between the typical problems of novices (discipline and management) and curriculum and instruction—for instance, how discipline problems can actually arise when tasks are unclear or directions to children are inadequate.
- "Probing novice's thinking" involves asking student teachers to carefully articulate their rationales and thinking. In doing this, Frazer helps novices develop an analytic stance and more precise language, so that they can explain themselves to others as well as inquire into their own practice.

Other strategies include the supervisor's effort to recognize signs of growth on the part of the student teachers and to keep focused upon the students in the teachers' classrooms, to direct discussion to students and their learning.

Sources of coaching and feedback can come from supervisors, teacher education instructors, cooperating teachers, other veteran teachers, and even fellow candidates. The availability of modeling is extremely important. For example, Rodriguez and Sjostrom (1995) found that the presence of experienced teachers who could model multicultural pedagogy was a central factor in whether new teachers enacted such pedagogy for themselves in their own classrooms. Another study found that training in a set of teaching techniques followed by peer coaching and observation was even more effective in producing changes in practice than was training alone (Sparks, 1986). This work is consistent with findings from sociocultural theory suggesting that learning from peers who provide feedback can be valuable (Vygotsky, 1978).

The integration of the student teaching experience within the institution also matters with respect to the issues of coherence. Student teaching placements that are consistent with a program's vision of teaching are more powerful learning sites, as are those where there is shared understanding among student teachers, cooperating teachers, and university supervisors about the purposes and activities of the student teaching placement (Koerner, Rust, and Baumgartner, 2002; LaBoskey and Richert, 2002). This shared understanding can be encouraged not only through the traditional means of contact and collaboration but also through on-line technologies that provide examples of teaching artifacts and videotapes of classrooms, feedback and coaching from school- and university-based faculty, and opportunities for joint inquiry. (See "Technological Innovations to Support Coaching and School–University Connections.")

Technological Innovations to Support Coaching and School–University Connections

The Teaching Tele-Apprenticeship Program (TTA) uses e-mail to go beyond the typical face-to-face apprenticeship model (Thomas, Larson, Clift, and Levin, 1996). The program offers preservice teachers an on-line network consisting of university faculty, supervisors, and mentor teachers. Preservice teachers use the network to receive timely responses to their questions and to engage in extended discussions around issues related to teaching and learning. TTA's goal is to use networking to create an interinstitutional context for teacher learning. The Inquiry Learning Forum (ILF) also aims to support communication among these different professionals, providing a variety of contexts in which participants can share ideas (Barab and others, 2001). ILF is developed around the metaphor of a school in which users enter different "rooms" to engage in activities. In the "library" for instance, participants can access lesson plans and unit materials. They can also visit "classrooms" to view video excerpts of lessons from teachers who have chosen to make these materials available to others. In the "lounge," participants take part in discussions concerning inquiry-based teaching strategies. Research on ILF has shown it to be a productive environment for developing communities of learners and for bridging the worlds of the university and the classroom (Barnett, Harwood, Keating, and Saam, 2002).

Source: Gomez, Sherin, Griesdorn, and Finn (2003).

Indeed, research has indicated that school placements that are not aligned in significant ways with the philosophy and practice of the teacher education program can be problematic for the student teacher, the cooperating teacher, and university faculty. For example, some research has documented how even teachers who already have some teaching experience, have strong content knowledge, and felt strongly about the teaching vision of the program have trouble with placements that are not consistent with the program and are often unable to apply what they are learning (LaBoskey and Richert, 2002). Similarly, in a study of student teachers in a field-based teacher education program (in which students spend four of five quarters in teaching placements), Goodman (1985) found that despite the program's emphasis on diversity, if student teachers did not experience a similar emphasis in their teaching settings they were unable to overcome their lay assumptions about knowledge, learning, and children.

Feiman-Nemser and Buchmann (1985) have termed this disjuncture the *two-worlds* pitfall. Student teachers, already in a difficult position of little authority and status in the classroom, cannot easily overcome the disconnect between the ideas about teaching and learning espoused in their program and those they encounter in the classroom—leaving them feeling confused, guilty, and discouraged about their ability to be successful teachers. Furthermore, negative examples—that is, placements in which student teachers are encouraged *not* to teach in the ways that their cooperating teacher does—appear not only to be ineffective, but they may actually interrupt student teachers' learning (Knowles and Hoefler, 1989; LaBoskey and Richert, 2002).

These studies suggest that consistency and coherence are important to learning in a community: learning to teach with faculty and peers who are all providing reinforcing messages about the nature of teaching, learning, and students provides a particularly strong experience of learning.

Professional Development Schools. One strategy that purposefully seeks to construct communities of practice and a greater degree of coherence between university coursework and student teaching experiences is the professional development school (PDS), a descendant of the laboratory schools of the early twentieth century. The intentions for such schools are consistent with learning theory that emphasizes inquiry about practice in learning communities. In these sites, new teachers learn to teach alongside more experienced teachers who plan and work together, and university- and school-based faculty work collaboratively to design and implement learning experiences for new and experienced teachers, as well as for students (Holmes Group, 1990). Ideally, the university program and the school develop a shared conception of good teaching that informs their joint work. Developing sites where state-of-the-art practice is possible has been one of the difficulties in constructing clinical experiences for prospective teachers: quite often if novices are to see and emulate high-quality practice, especially in schools serving low-income students and students of color, it is necessary not only to seek out individual cooperating teachers but to develop the quality of the schools where prospective teachers can learn productively and to create settings where advances in knowledge and practice can occur. Thus PDSs aim to develop *school practice* as well as the *individual practice* of new teacher candidates.

Key features of professional development school models include more extensive experience within the school for prospective teachers, more frequent and sustained supervision and feedback, more collective planning and decision making among teachers at the school as well as among school- and university-based faculty, and participation in research and inquiry about teaching and teacher education by novices, veteran teachers, and university faculty (Abdal-Haqq, 1998, pp. 13–14; Darling-Hammond, 1994). These features were found to be present in most of a group of "highly-developed" PDSs (Trachtman, 1996). In addition, novices in these schools had a schoolwide, rather than just an individual classroom, experience and worked with school teams on such tasks as curriculum development, school reform, and action research. In most of these sites, university faculty were teaching courses and organizing professional development at the school-site and were also involved in teaching children.

As of 1998, the American Association of Colleges for Teacher Education estimated that there were more than 1,000 professional schools in forty-seven states in operation across the country (Abdal-Haqq, 1998). However, like all reform ideas, the ideals of professional development schools have been unevenly implemented, and many sites that have adopted the label have not created the strong relationships or adopted the set of practices anticipated for such schools (Fullan, 1995; Mantle-Bromley, 2002). Thus there are competing findings about whether teachers trained in schools with this label are better prepared (see, for example, Ridley, Carlile, and Hurwitz, 2001). However, where the difficult work of creating these practices has been accomplished, there is evidence of positive consequences for teacher preparation, veteran teacher learning, teaching practice, and student learning.

In terms of preparation, studies of highly developed PDSs have suggested that teachers who graduate from such programs feel more knowledgeable and prepared to teach (Gettys, 1999; Sandholtz and Dadlez, 2000; Stallings, Bossung, and Martin, 1990; Yerian and Grossman, 1997). For instance, Yerian and Grossman (1997) compared three cohorts (thirty candidates) who learned to teach in a middle-level PDS program with forty candidates who had been in a traditional teacher education program. Surveys and interviews suggested that graduates of the PDS program felt more knowledgeable about early adolescents; more prepared to teach at the middle level; and better able to make connections between ideas in coursework and their clinical experiences. In contrast, graduates from the traditional program felt significantly less sure of their ability to support student learning by using different teaching strategies.

Similarly, in a longitudinal study of four cohorts of graduates from a PDS-based program at the University of California–Riverside, Sandholtz and Dadlez (2000) found that graduates of the PDS program rated their preparation for teaching and their sense of self-efficacy higher than graduates of traditional teacher preparation programs in the area. In a follow-up study based upon interviews with graduates of the PDS program where she worked, Freese (1999) found that the graduates felt that learning about reflective practice alongside experienced teachers and close collegial relationships with teachers and faculty were factors that helped them to implement that reflective practice in their own teaching.

There are only a few studies that have tried to evaluate outcomes of PDS participation for teaching practice and student achievement, but these few are promising. In studies polling employers and supervisors, PDS graduates were viewed as much better prepared than other new teachers (Hayes and Weatherill, 1996; Mantle-Bromley, 2002). Veteran teachers working in highly developed PDSs have reported changes in their own practice and improvements at both the classroom and school levels as a result of the professional development, action research, and mentoring that are part of the PDS (Trachtman, 1996; Crow, Stokes, Kauchak, Hobbs, and Bullough, 1996; Houston Consortium, 1996; Jett-Simpson, Pugach, and Whipp, 1992).

Although research is still limited on the relationship between teachers' experiences in PDSs and the impact on their teaching practice (Zeichner, Miller, and Lieberman, 1997), recent studies suggest some of the promise of programs that embed learning in communities of practice. Comparison group studies have found that PDS-prepared teachers have been rated stronger in various areas of teaching, ranging from classroom management and uses of technology to content area skills (Gill and Hove, 1999; Neubert and Binko, 1998; Shroyer, Wright, and Ramey-Gassert, 1996).

A small set of studies has documented gains in student performance and achievement tied directly to curriculum and teaching interventions resulting from the professional development and curriculum work professional development schools have undertaken with their university partners (see, for example, Frey, 2002; Gill and Hove, 1999; Glaeser, Karge, Smith, and Weatherill, 2002; Fischetti and Larson, 2002; Houston and others, 1995; Judge, Carriedo, and Johnson, 1995; Wiseman and Cooner, 1996). In a study of a group of PDS sites associated with a midwestern university, not all of them implemented the same kinds of PDS work and not all experienced achievement gains: those that experienced student achievement gains were the ones that implemented high quality professional development efforts at the site (Marchant, 2002).

Although research has also demonstrated how difficult these partnerships are to enact, many schools of education and some districts are moving toward preparing all of their prospective teachers in such settings, both because they allow prospective teachers to learn to teach in professional learning communities—and this concern can be addressed more consistently and systematically through PDS partnerships—and because such work is a key to changing school cultures so that they become more productive environments for the learning of all students and teachers (Abdal-Haqq, 1998).

Some universities have sought to create PDS relationships in schools that are working explicitly on an equity agenda, either in new schools designed to provide more equitable access to high-quality curriculum for diverse learners or in schools where faculty are actively confronting issues of tracking, poor teaching, inadequate or fragmented curriculum, and unresponsive systems (see, for example, Darling-Hammond, 1994; Darling-Hammond, French, and Garcia-Lopez, 2002; Guadarrama, Ramsey, and Nath, 2002). In these schools, student teachers or interns are encouraged to learn about and participate in all aspects of school functioning, ranging from special education and support services for students, to parent meetings, home visits, and community outreach, to faculty discussions and projects aimed at ongoing improvement in students' opportunities to learn. This kind of participation helps prospective teachers understand the broader institutional context for teaching and learning and begin to develop the knowledge and skills needed for effective participation in collegial work around school improvement throughout their careers.

Learning in Community Settings. Some teacher educators also point out that learning in a community of practice may actually involve multiple communities, including the local community in which students and their families live. As we describe in Chapter Seven, Teaching Diverse Learners, a number of teacher education programs have incorporated community-based internships or placements in non-school organizations to help prospective teachers gain new perspectives on local communities and an appreciation for the lives of students they will encounter in their classrooms. These kinds of placements provide important opportunities beyond those that student teaching provides for preparing all teachers to work with students who come from a variety of diverse backgrounds. As Gallego (2001) notes: "Though teacher education students may be placed in schools with large, culturally diverse student populations, many of these schools are isolated from and not responsive to their local communities and therefore do not provide the kind of contact with communities needed to overcome negative attitudes toward culturally different students and their families and communities (Zeichner, 1992). Indeed, without connections between the classroom, school, and local communities, classroom field experiences may work to strengthen preservice teachers' stereotypes of children, rather than stimulate their examination (Cochran-Smith, 1995; Haberman and Post, 1992), and ultimately compromise teachers' effectiveness in the classroom (Zeichner, 1996)" (p. 314).

Studies of experiential community-based learning opportunities for prospective teachers have noted that they can develop positive dispositions and attitudes toward children and families that carry over to teaching. For example, Stachowski and Mahan (1998) surveyed 109 participants in cultural immersion projects—the American Indian Reservation project and the Overseas Project—and found that those involved gained important insights about teaching and diverse cultures, including that community people can be sources of cultural knowledge and learning, an aspect of what Luis Moll and colleagues (1992) have described as "funds of knowledge." Bondy and Davis (2000) studied prospective teachers who tutored youth living in a local public housing neighborhood and found that these experiences challenged teachers to use forms of caring to help them develop relationships with children different from themselves. Similarly, Boyle-Baise (1998) found that, as a result of service-learning experiences, teachers expressed a willingness to adapt curriculum and instruction to meet students' needs or interests. A survey of 136 preservice teachers who participated in a service-learning project in human service agencies as part of a course in the teacher education program at the University of Nebraska–Kearney, found significant attitudinal growth in the areas of caring, empathy, willingness to serve others, and higher expectations for students (Pothoff and others, 2000).

As a group these studies suggest that clinical experiences in community settings may be valuable in the preparation of teachers to work with students from diverse backgrounds. The results of some studies caution, however, that experienced guidance is a critical element to ensuring that such forays can support learning. Without such guidance, experiences in communities different from one's own may actually reinforce stereotypical assumptions and beliefs about diverse children (Boyle-Baise, 1998; Duesterberg, 1998). As Dewey (1938) argued, "The belief that all genuine education comes about through experience does not mean that all experiences are genuinely or equally educative. Experience and education cannot be directly equated to each other. For some experiences are miseducative" (p. 25). Seminars and readings, along with regular reflections that occasion feedback from a thoughtful guide, can help make community experiences genuinely educative so that they expand rather than restrict novices' notions of what is possible in teaching diverse learners.

Gallego (2001) details another strategy with potential for occasioning useful insights about students and how they might be taught. In a program that coupled a community-based experience (in an after-school literacy development program) with a school-based practicum, candidates were given the opportunity to compare and contrast what they learned about their students and the possibilities and constraints of different settings for supporting students' growth. These contrasts, considered in reflections and discussion sessions, offered not only insights into students' capabilities and their learning contexts, but also provoked new ways of thinking about teaching strategies in both settings, strengthening teachers' repertoires in the process.

Some programs involve prospective teachers in school and community studies to help them understand the contexts for student learning and become more prepared to work both as culturally responsive teachers and change agents in those contexts. Strategies include mini-ethnographies focused around specific questions regarding practices or conditions in the community or potential curriculum connections between aspects of the community life and school (see, for example, Sleeter, 1995; Tellez and others, 1994; Moll and others, 1992), community interviews (Stachowski and Mahan, 1998), and studies that illuminate inequalities in various services available to socioeconomically different communities (see, for example, Martin, 1995) or in the school resources allocated to different students (Darling-Hammond, French, and Garcia-Lopez, 2002).

Cochran-Smith (1995) outlines an approach to school and community studies that involves teams of prospective teachers in gathering information about the school and community in which they are working (through statistical reports, photographs, community newspapers, visits to community centers, back-to-school nights, parent-teacher meetings, and interviews of school personnel, students, parents, and community members), which they pool to provide an overview of the school and community that is presented to others in the teacher education course. This helps them become cognizant of the different perspectives of members of the community, differences between and among schools and communities, and issues surrounding the relationships between schools and communities. With this broader view of the contexts of education, teachers can become more ready to think about the ways in which community contexts and school decisions influence students' opportunities and their own roles.

Performance Assessment Strategies

Although clinical experiences provide the opportunity for practice, they are often rather haphazard opportunities that may not ensure either the occasion to encounter certain kinds of teaching problems or the impetus to develop and demonstrate particular skills. More structured performance tasks can be used to afford these opportunities and provide another way to deal with the problem of enactment by enabling student teachers to demonstrate certain practices and analyze them (along with their effects).

An early attempt to create such targeted opportunities was the practice of microteaching. More recent efforts to create contexts for developing important skills have evolved under the banner of performance assessments and the related practice of developing portfolios that require the demonstration of certain practices and the analysis of those practices and their effects. These strategies operate at different "grain sizes" with respect to the elements of teaching to be worked out, demonstrated, practiced, and analyzed. For example, in the case of microteaching, the skills are typically quite specific and discrete (for example, using a specific style of questioning), whereas in the case of performance tasks, they are typically more multifaceted (for example, developing a lesson plan or giving a lecture that requires an understanding of a number of features of content pedagogy). Portfolios are even more comprehensive, integrating knowledge and skills across the multiple domains of teaching (for example, planning, teaching, assessing, evaluating student work, reflecting, and adapting plans in response to these findings). Through portfolios, teacher educators aim to help teacher candidates analyze and evaluate materials from their own teaching; they can also assist prospective teachers in collecting such materials in ways that provide grist for deeper analysis and reflection.

Microteaching. Microteaching was launched in the 1960s to help novices focus their attempts at learning teaching skills on discrete areas to be tackled one at a time. It was thought to permit greater concentration and reduce anxiety for novices. As Gage (1978) described it: "Microteaching is scaled-down teaching—teaching conducted for only five or ten minutes at a time, with only five or ten students, and focused on only one or a few aspects of the teacher's role. The teacher tries, say, reinforcing participation or making an assignment, rather than undertaking the whole of what a teacher does, in all its multifaceted complexity, with a class of 30 for a whole period of instruction" (p. 47).

Microteaching was frequently conducted with teacher education peers and sometimes with K–12 students in lab settings or classrooms. It often included modeling of practices to be learned, opportunities to plan and teach a brief lesson using these practices, videotaping and feedback, and sometimes, additional practice. A number of studies found that microteaching led to an increase in candidates' ability to demonstrate the desired behaviors or practice in the microteaching sessions, although the literature also includes some counterexamples, which are sometimes explained by the particular microteaching model or type of feedback attempted (see reviews by Copeland, 1982; MacLeod, 1987). There is some modest evidence about effects on student achievement. For example, in one recent study where microteaching produced greater implementation of teaching behaviors associated with instructional clarity, the students taught scored higher on end-of-lesson tests (Metcalf, 1989). The few studies that have evaluated whether teachers were able to transfer microteaching practices to real classroom settings and call upon them successfully in the context of other activities have produced mixed results. (See, for example, Harris, Lee, and Pigge, 1970, for evidence of successful transfer of skills developed in microteaching to an elementary science classroom lesson, and Andersen and Antes, 1971, for evidence suggesting little correlation between microteaching using classroom management skills aimed at creating a positive environment for culturally diverse children and later classroom performance as a teaching intern.) Sounding a theme that echoes throughout the microteaching literature, Andersen and Antes (1971) noted that, in their study, prospective teachers rated the opportunity to teach and receive feedback as strengths of microteaching, but the "artificial situation" afforded by microteaching as a weakness. In explaining the lack of correlation between microteaching evaluations and later teaching evaluations, the authors commented:

> Microteaching is a technique that focuses on a single aspect of teaching for a limited time with a small number of learners . . . In the classroom, the interns were called upon to use the whole complex of skills and techniques

necessary in this type of situation. Therefore, the outcomes may not stem from the lack of value of microteaching, but from the differences between the two situations. These differences lay in the number of people and the amount of time involved, and in the dissimilarity between the ability to practice on skills effectively under controlled conditions and the ability to practice a whole complex of skills in a variable situation. In this study the difficulty lay not in microteaching, but in the limited value it seemed to have for the general act of teaching. (pp. 148–149)

The complexity of teaching may be one aspect of the transfer difficulty for strategies like microteaching. Efforts to secure some of the benefits of microteaching while reducing the artificiality of the task have led to broader kinds of performance assessments, described in the following section.

Another important factor may be the extent to which students develop an analytic framework for what they are trying to accomplish that is available to them when they are trying to apply strategies in action. A number of studies have examined alternatives to microteaching that are more cognitive than behavioral in nature (see Gage, 1978, pp. 48–52). One intriguing study compared microteaching to cognitive discrimination training. Using a random assignment experimental design, Wagner (1973) examined the teaching performance of college students who had been given a brief explanation of student-centered questioning techniques and then asked to use them in microteaching, as compared to another group given the same explanation followed by discrimination training in which they were asked to watch videotapes of teachers and code the teachers' responses, with explanations integrated into the coding process. A third group received the brief explanation of the teaching goal and taught without the benefit of either discrimination training or microteaching (which provided a review of one's own videotape with feedback between teaching attempts). Contrary to the conventional wisdom that emphasizes the importance of practice, the students who were given stronger conceptual preparation and discrimination training, which also included models of practice that could be analyzed, actually performed significantly better when it was their turn to demonstrate these questioning techniques than the students who had had the opportunity to try the techniques twice through microteaching with videotaping and feedback. The microteaching group, which lacked both models and the opportunity to gain a deeper conceptual understanding of the behavior they were trying to develop, performed no differently from the control group.

This early study provided an indication that close analyses of other teachers' practices can be a potentially productive learning opportunity for teachers seeking to develop specific pedagogical skills. As we discuss later, there are a number of recent efforts to create opportunities for such close analyses of teaching and, increasingly, of learning as well.

Performance Tasks. Many teacher education programs have developed specific performance tasks they require of students (for example, planning and delivering a lesson, delivering a lecture, conducting a Socratic seminar, completing and teaching a curriculum unit) around which they organize coursework and practice opportunities. In addition, assessments for teacher licensing and certification have begun to incorporate performance elements that require teachers to complete specific tasks; for example, to perform and videotape specific tasks in the classroom (for example, conduct a whole group discussion about a work of literature), write a commentary and reflection, and, in some cases, provide evidence about student work and learning.

Performance tasks are often structured as public exhibitions of knowledge and practice that are measured against shared, public criteria, with opportunities for feedback. One of the most highly developed systems of performance assessment was created at Alverno College, which uses frequent exhibitions of performance, benchmarked against standards, as the foundation for much of its work. The tasks, which are designed to measure eight general education abilities (expected of all students in the college) and five advanced education abilities (specific to teacher education students), require candidates to apply their knowledge and skills in realistic contexts. From their very first day at Alverno when they make a videotape of themselves giving a short speech to their peers (a task which will be repeated and reevaluated later) to a much later assessment in which a group is evaluated while they collaboratively plan a lesson together, students are constantly assessed in relation to these abilities (Zeichner, 2000).

Virtually every assignment and assessment begins with reference to the criteria for the performance being developed and ends with an opportunity for candidates to evaluate their own work. The end result, as judged by cooperating teachers, college supervisors, employing principals, and candidate assessments of their preparation, is a set of graduates who are highly self-reflective and practically well prepared for sophisticated practice in the classroom (Zeichner, 2000).

In addition to specific acts of teaching, performance tasks can evaluate planning skills, such as the development of lessons or units in light of key ideas about instructional design (as discussed in Chapters Five and Eight). These kinds of planning activities can also engage student teachers in designing, choosing, implementing, and analyzing formative and summative assessments of student learning, and can evaluate how candidates revise their teaching in light of what they discover about student learning—the kinds of teaching skills that go far beyond the demonstration of specific classroom behaviors that characterized early performance assessments, such as microteaching.

As with other strategies, the benefits of performance assessments are not automatic. They depend on choosing tasks that represent important skills and abilities and on integrating such assessments into a well-developed set of learning experiences. Exhibitions also require a clear and focused set of goals that adequately reflect the complexities of the tasks to be accomplished and consider their outcomes for teaching and learning. They demand assessors who are themselves expert in the areas of work being developed. Absent these characteristics, exhibitions can be merely performances without standards, unfocused activities that provide little guidance or evaluation for developing high levels of skill. The fate of competency-based teacher education as used by many teacher education programs in the 1970s is one illustration of this potential problem. Although well developed in some institutions (Alverno's ability-based curriculum was, for example, an outgrowth of the competency movement of that time), in others the techniques of specifying and observing performances became disconnected from a well-grounded base of theory and from standards for performance. Consequently, the exhibitions of behavior often became little more than tallies of actions that were not well-assessed in terms of their appropriateness for a particular purpose or context or for their influences on students' learning. Assessments that overcome these difficulties integrate exhibitions with a well-conceptualized set of standards; analysis of teachers' goals, contexts, and intentions; and a view of the larger conceptual picture of teaching and learning for both prospective teachers and their students (Darling-Hammond and Snyder, 2000).

An example of a comprehensive approach to performance assessment for preservice teachers can be seen in the Performance Assessment for California Teachers (PACT) project's Teaching Event, described in detail in Chapter Eight, which involves student teachers in designing a unit, teaching a set of lessons within the unit, and then completing a series of performance assessments related to this segment of instruction. These include developing an assessment plan for the unit, analyzing work samples from individuals over time and for the class as a whole at one point in time, reflecting on their teaching outcomes, and revising their plans. Early evidence about this assessment, as well as the Connecticut beginning teacher assessment and the National Board for Professional teaching standards portfolio from which it was adapted, suggests that teachers feel they learn a great deal from participating in the process of developing and scoring these kinds of tasks (Athanases, 1994; Tracz, Sienty, and Mata, 1994; Tracz and others, 1995; Pecheone and Chung, 2004; Pecheone and Stansbury, 1996; Sato, 2000). (Although these assessments are called portfolios, we include them here because they require specific performances that are scored according to standardized criteria, rather than allowing for the selection of various kinds of artifacts by a candidate who assembles a more customized collection, like the portfolios we describe in the next section.)

Part of the reason these kinds of performance assessments appear to stimulate learning is that they focus teachers' reflection on professional standards in specific content areas that are used for scoring and that candidates are asked to consider when evaluating their own practice. Thus teaching practices can be reviewed, revised, and discussed in light of some shared, common language about teaching and learning, which helps ground and focus the work. Furthermore, the standards serve as public criteria by which performances can be measured.

Teaching Portfolios. Teaching portfolios represent a special case of performance assessments. Portfolios are typically collections of materials and artifacts from teachers' work, and often include statements about the teacher's educational philosophy; descriptions of the teacher's theories of classroom organization and management; curriculum materials (such as unit and lesson plans, assignments, assessments, and daily logs) and reflections; articles or papers; videotapes and commentary about instruction; and samples of student work (with or without teacher feedback). They can also include photographs, videotapes, or audiotapes of classroom activities ranging from bulletin boards and displays, to taped lessons, to conferences with students (Darling-Hammond, Wise, and Klein, 1999). Some portfolios also include documents that require additional analysis on the part of the teacher, such as teacher logs or journals, detailed descriptions or analyses of lessons or student work, and reflections on the outcomes of teaching activities. Portfolios can include documents that derive from the evaluations of others: notes by an observer of teaching, peer or administrator recommendations, student evaluations, and so on (Bird, 1990; King, 1990; Athanases, 1994; Haertel, 1991).

Proponents suggest that teacher portfolios provide opportunities for robust documentation of practice and for candidate reflection. As an assessment tool, they can provide a comprehensive look at how the various aspects of a teacher's practice—planning, instruction, assessment, curriculum design, and communications with peers and parents—come together. As a tool for learning and reflection, portfolios can alleviate what Lee Shulman (1998) has referred to as "pedagogical amnesia"—a disease endemic to teaching at all levels. Pedagogical amnesia, characterized by the inability to record and recall the fruits of teaching experience, is one symptom of the multidimensional complexity of teaching. So much happens so fast that it is a blur. Portfolios help make teaching stand still long enough to be examined, shared, and learned from. In some teacher education programs, teachers create portfolios on CD-ROMs or DVDs, including short videos of classroom teaching or of their students working together.

A growing number of teacher education programs are using portfolios to aid students toward three central purposes: in reflecting upon their growth and learning, in demonstrating their learning and development, and in seeking employment after graduation. For example, portfolios are often used to help prospective teachers document and demonstrate their growth as new teachers. To that end, prospective teachers are asked to select pieces of work that represent their learning, their growth, and their reflections about their teaching and their learning. In some cases, portfolios are also used to help new teachers demonstrate to their instructors (or others) that they are ready to teach and to demonstrate how they have met certain standards. For example, the "goal and evidence" portfolio required in the University of Southern Maine's ETEP program (described in Chapter Eight, Assessment) requires student teachers to organize their final portfolios around the five "Gorham Outcomes," and each student teacher presents evidence of the outcomes in his or her teaching practice (Whitford and others, 2000).

Some research illustrates how portfolios organized around specific goals and standards can support teachers' development of a conceptual framework about teaching, as well as the refinement of practices, by providing structured opportunities for teachers to document and describe their teaching and their learning; to articulate and demonstrate their professional knowledge and expertise; and to reflect upon what, how, and why they teach (Bird, 1990; King, 1990; Lyons, 1998). Advocates argue that the portfolio provides a structure for teachers to pull together important materials, and to reflect upon their meaning and their own learning. For instance, Richert found that the use of portfolios at Mills College, when developed and discussed with peers, helped student teachers recall classroom experiences more fully and accurately, and helped center their reflections on the context and content-specific aspects of their teaching (Richert, 1990). Lichtenstein, Rubin, and Grant (1992) found that portfolios designed to connect theory and practice enabled teachers systematically to examine and gather information about their classroom practices, students, and schools and helped connect their research-based professional coursework with the demands of the classroom.

In a study of teacher candidates who had constructed teaching portfolios as the central assignment in their master's degree program, Borko and others (1997) found that participants identified multiple benefits for the portfolio process. The most frequently cited benefit was that it enabled them to identify their strengths and limitations as new teachers, and to identify ways to improve. Some students felt that the portfolio helped them reflect upon individual students and ways to support their learning. These candidates, too, noted that the portfolio prompted them to make connections between the theories in their coursework and their classroom practices. Other researchers have found that candidates feel they learn from the process of constructing a portfolio, but that the benefits vary depending on the guidance and feedback they receive from instructors or supervisors (Borko and others, 1997; Wade and Yarbrough, 1996).

It is likely that the benefits of portfolios depend on the design of the portfolio and the learning context within which it is used. It is reasonable to expect that the benefits described earlier would not be experienced for portfolios that are just collections of random work created without standards, structured expectations, or guided opportunities for reflection. An additional challenge in using portfolios is that the three common purposes of portfolios (sharing growth and reflection; demonstrating professional competency; and seeking employment) are not always complementary, and, in many programs, one portfolio is used to serve all three purposes. However, the different purposes can create tensions for student teachers, as they imply different audiences and different criteria for selecting materials (Mosenthal, Daniels, and Hull, 1993). Furthermore, lack of clarity about purposes can also result in a portfolio that is merely a collection of everything a student teacher completed in his or her program. Such a portfolio tells evaluators "everything and nothing at the same time" about what a student teacher has learned and understood (L. Shulman, personal communication). Developing a portfolio that is rich and meaningful for both the teacher who assembles it and the assessors who review it requires careful honing of purpose, criteria, and implementation.

ANALYSIS OF TEACHING AND LEARNING

The performance assessments described earlier provide, among other things, opportunities for candidates to analyze and reflect on examples of teaching and products of student learning. Such analyses can provide structured, systematic means for closely examining the process and outcomes of teaching and learning using real classroom artifacts—student work samples, videotapes of classroom practice (and other multimedia approaches to capturing learning and teaching), video "cases," and curriculum materials. The use of these materials enables student teachers and teacher educators to jointly examine and analyze a "common text" to which all have access. The conception of a common text is a key idea that unites analyses of videotapes of teaching, analyses of student work samples, and analyses of portfolio or performance assessment entries. Typically, teacher educators engage students in examining both texts produced by *other* teachers and in analyzing and exploring their *own* materials—samples of work from learners in their own classrooms, curriculum they are developing, and videotapes of lessons, and other records of their evolving practice as new teachers.

Analysis of Teaching

During this past decade, a number of researchers and organizations have been engaged in efforts to document teaching in richer and more dynamic ways, and many of these efforts have involved the use of videotape and multimedia. These include videotapes of mathematics teaching and associated artifacts of student work; teacher plans and reflections mounted in a hypermedia platform by Deborah Ball and colleagues at the University of Michigan (Lampert and Ball, 1998); the

Carnegie Foundation's Knowledge Media Lab that documents the teaching practice of accomplished teachers through Web-based collections of materials organized around their classroom strategies and inquiries (http://www.carnegiefoundation.org/KML/index.htm); and the videotapes and analyses of teaching developed by James Stigler and coleagues as part of the TIMMS study (Stigler and Hiebert, 1999). Such efforts to document teaching have led to sets of rich materials that can now be accessed by teacher educators for joint viewing, reviewing, and analysis by students and their peers.

Teacher educators who are developing pedagogies for the analysis of teaching and learning contend that analyzing teaching artifacts has three advantages: it enables new teachers time for reflection while still using the real materials of practice; it provides new teachers with experience thinking about and approaching the complexity of the classroom; and in some cases, it can help new teachers and teacher educators develop a shared understanding and common language about teaching (Ball and Cohen, 1999; Lampert and Ball, 1998; Friel and Carboni, 2000).

First, although learning to teach must be situated within the real materials of practice, learning to teach does not necessarily need to occur solely in real time in the "crucible of the classroom." These classroom-based experiences not only focus learning upon that particular classroom but also—because of the rapid pace and complex nature of teaching—make reflection and deliberation difficult (Ball and Cohen, 1999). However, using classroom-based materials (lesson plans, videos of teaching, student and teacher work samples) enables teacher educators to represent true problems of practice under circumstances that allow for fine-grained analysis. Through repeated viewings or readings, candidates have a chance to debate, discuss, and revise initial conceptions. They address the apprenticeship of observation by providing examples of practices that candidates may not themselves have experienced and may have a hard time imagining. A shared text can also elicit different perspectives (student teachers may notice different things and interpret events in different ways), ultimately supporting discussion, argument, and reflection that can facilitate deeper understandings of the teaching and learning process. Using materials in this way helps new teachers develop skills of careful and reasoned analysis, and the ability to evaluate teaching and learning. Another use of these materials, whether print or video, is as demonstration or illustration of key ideas or principles of practice.

Second, these materials capture more of the complexity and the constantly shifting, nonroutine nature of the classroom. Because these materials are records of practice from real classrooms—either the student teachers' own classrooms or that of other teachers—they embody many of the challenges and the multilayered nature of classroom teaching and learning. In essence, because new teachers need to understand what is occurring in a classroom on multiple levels, and to make decisions based upon information from numerous sources, analyzing these artifacts gives them opportunities to evaluate teaching and learning in ways that represent and reflect its complexity. They learn to make sense of situations from a variety of perspectives—to be able to analyze an incident from a developmental point of view, an instructional point of view, a curricular point of view, and so on. Using multimedia examples and other classroom artifacts can support that kind of thoughtful and complex analysis.

Finally, using materials from real classrooms in teacher education courses provides more opportunities for prospective teachers and teacher educators to develop a common language and shared understanding about what they are examining. One key challenge teacher educators face is that sometimes language, theory, and concepts used in teacher education are understood by their students in quite different ways (as discussed in Chapter Ten; see also Kennedy, 1999). Using classroom artifacts can help give concrete instances that enable new teachers and teacher educators to point out particular and specific instances that they feel instantiate ideas or theories, and to debate, deliberate, and discuss these with common images in mind. Rather than using language and theory divorced from "real practice"—they can explore and analyze student and teacher actions in ways that surface implicit assumptions and make ideas more open to examination and probing. In this way, teacher educators can have a better understanding of what new teachers are thinking—enabling them to address the problems of misconceptions about teaching and of enactment. (See "Using Video Analysis to Reflect On and Improve Teaching," below, for an example of how video and computers are helping support such connections in a teacher education program at Northwestern University.)

Using Video Analysis to Reflect On and Improve Teaching

In NU-TEACH (Northwestern University's Alternative Certification Program), coordination between university faculty and mentor teachers in the support of new teachers is an important goal. Toward this end, interns complete a series of video-based assignments that draw on explicit feedback from mentor teachers, university faculty, and program peers. In the context of these assignments, video excerpts from the interns' summer teaching placements literally cycle between the school and the university, becoming a resource for learning about and reflecting upon teaching and for constructing multiple interpretations of classroom practices. In this way, the video technology provides an important media through which participants in teacher education become better connected, and better prepared for creating a professional discourse about teaching and learning. The NU-TEACH community uses video and computers to support analyses of teaching and to create strong connections between university and school-based experiences.

Source: Gomez, Sherin, Griesdorn, and Finn (2003).

Although the more elaborated, multimedia versions of these approaches are fairly new, research over many years has found that prospective teachers learn more about particular teaching strategies (Carlson and Falk, 1990; Overbaugh, 1995) and are more able to implement these specific strategies with students after they have seen them modeled by other teachers via videotape (Goldman and Barron, 1990; Wagner, 1973), especially when these observations are supported with discussions, readings, and frameworks to guide their analyses. Thus these new technologies offer promise for supporting both teachers' metacognitive learning about teaching and their actual practice.

Analysis of Learning

The analysis of learning is an even more recent pedagogy in teacher education than the analysis of teaching. Analysis of learning can be focused upon numerous issues that arise in the teaching and learning process, from challenges of student engagement, student understanding, and assessment to questions about the framing of subject matter curriculum. A student teacher involved in a class focused upon classroom management or teaching strategies might be asked to examine a videotape of a teachers' classroom and focus upon the ways that the teacher does and does not engages students, connect the subject matter to her students' interests and assess learning; and perhaps to make note of the students' responses to the "moves" the teacher makes to support, deepen, and develop understanding about the particular topic at hand. A student teacher involved in a course on learning or development might compare and contrast the work samples of two students, examining the work of both to ascertain the degree of understanding the students display; the misunderstandings or misconceptions; and to propose supports that might be provided to help the students develop their understandings further. Candidates might also analyze and compare and contrast the work of particular students—for instance, English language learners and native English speakers; late adolescents and preadolescents; different students with special needs—to help them focus upon the needs and strengths of different children as well as the challenges involved in each child's learning.

Because the close analysis of teaching and learning did not become widespread until the 1990s, research on the effects of this pedagogy upon teachers' learning is still in the early stages. However, there are a set of studies underway that are documenting what teachers learn from analyzing and exploring video "cases" (Sherin, 2001; Sherin and Han, 2002) and that explore what teachers learn from using multimedia (Lampert and Ball, 1998). For example, Sherin and Han (2002) examined the discourse topics of practicing mathematics teachers who were participating in a "video club" in which teachers met once monthly to discuss videotapes of the teacher members, and found changes in both *what* the teachers discussed as well as *how* they discussed it. They found that over a period of ten months, teachers became increasingly focused upon examining student thinking (as opposed to their own teaching and their own pedagogy);

and by the seventh meeting, discussions of students' conceptions of mathematics accounted for 86 percent of the time as compared to less than 15 percent in the first several meetings. Furthermore, they found that the nature of the teachers' discussion of student thinking changed over time. Participating teachers' discussions of student thinking developed from simply stating what the student said (which characterized the discussions of student thinking in the early meetings) to examining the meaning of students' comments and methods and beginning to synthesize and generalize comments about the nature of the students' learning. Finally, teachers also shifted from offering alternative teaching strategies to achieve fairly general ends that were independent of students' learning (for example, get the students to talk more) to suggesting teaching moves or strategies that would push students' understanding further.

Case Methods

Many professions, including law, medicine, and business, help candidates bridge the gap between theory and practice—as well as to develop skills of reflection and close analysis—by engaging them in the reading and writing of cases. Proponents of case methods argue that cases offer a unique form of learning that supports both systematic learning from particular contexts as well as from more generalized theory about teaching and learning. Cases can allow for the exploration of theories and dilemmas as they occur in real classrooms (Colberg, Trimble, and Desberg, 1996). Shulman (1996), for example, has argued that case pedagogies are particularly important in that they enable new teachers to connect theory with practice:

> "What is this a case of?" is a locution whose purpose is to stimulate students to initiate the intellectual work that makes cases powerful tools for professional learning. They must learn to move up and down, back and forth, between the memorable particularities of cases and the powerful generalizations and simplifications of principles and theories. Principles are powerful but cases are memorable. Only in the continued interaction between principles and cases can practitioners and their mentors avoid the inherent limitations of theory-without-practice or the equally serious restrictions of vivid practice without the mirror of principle. (1996, p. 201)

Students' case writing efforts can motivate their own learning, serve as instructional material for others, and provide "antidotes to the dangers of overgeneralization" (Shulman, 1992, p. 3).

Typically, cases are accounts of teaching and learning that pose dilemmas, provide careful descriptions of contexts, and share evidence or data about outcomes of classroom situations. In teacher education programs, student teachers can *read and analyze* cases, discerning and reasoning through dilemmas, and propose strategies to respond to problems. Students can also *write* cases, learning to represent their experiences, and analyze them through the lens of theory, so that they and others can learn from them. There are a number of perspectives that cases may take: some begin with a focus upon subject matter, probing how teachers design instruction to help students master content; some focus upon students, developing teachers' ability to observe and analyze evidence of learning and development; and still others focus upon culture, assisting teachers in examining students' lives, backgrounds, and contexts, helping prepare teachers to understand the challenges inherent in teaching students from diverse backgrounds and communities (Darling-Hammond and Snyder, 2000).

As illustrated in the chapters on Development (Chapter Three) and Teaching Diverse Learners (Chapter Seven), case studies of children and adolescents can engage new teachers in collecting and analyzing data in order to better understand student learning, developmental progress, special needs, and the influences of particular contexts. Cases can be used not only to study teaching and learning at the level of classrooms, but also at the level of the school and community. For example, case studies of children or adolescents can involve teachers in shadowing students throughout their school day, illuminating how many aspects of the school's organization, assignment policies, social context, and teaching practices affect the student. These strategies can help prospective teachers understand the broader school environment and how its policies and practices can create or undermine opportunities, or differentially meet students' needs. These kinds of cases can also involve home visits, parent interviews, and neighborhood visits to place the student in the context of the family and community, thus helping the prospective teacher gain a more holistic view of the student's experience and the ways in which many variables affect him or her (Roeser, 2002; Darling-Hammond and Snyder, 2000).

As we described in Chapter Five, Educational Goals and Purposes, case analyses of curriculum and teaching can focus upon the development of instruction and the dilemmas or "breakdowns" that can occur in teaching a particular concept or idea. These analyses can examine teachers' intentions, students' learning, and the relationship (or sometimes disconnect) between the two. Dilemma cases, such as those used by Kleinfeld at the University of Alaska (1998) (described in Chapter Seven, Teaching Diverse Learners), Levin at the University of North Carolina (2002), and Whitcomb at the University of Denver (2002), are often used to illustrate long-time teaching challenges—such as moral dilemmas, interpersonal difficulties, or cultural differences—and to engage teachers in deliberating, problem solving, and analyzing these challenges. They are also used to prepare teachers for the uncertainty and complexity of teaching in diverse classrooms.

Many gaps in the research on the case method still exist (Grossman, in press; Merseth, 1999). However, research has provided some initial evidence that cases can help students develop reasoning skills, allowing prospective teachers to more accurately identify important issues and to more thoughtfully analyze an educational dilemma (Harrington, 1995; Kleinfeld, 1992). By analyzing and coding the first and last of four case drafts for twenty-six elementary education students, Harrington found, for instance, that student teachers' pedagogical reasoning about dilemmas deepened through reading and interpreting cases about teaching; they grew more capable of framing problems, drew lessons beyond their immediate setting, and reflected upon their work from multiple perspectives. She concluded that "case-based pedagogy can be used to gain access to students' professional reasoning and may, as well, foster that reasoning" (Harrington, 1995, p. 212).

In a similar study, Hammerness and others (2002) conducted a content analysis of twenty-one curriculum cases written by student teachers, looking for the development of what Berliner (1994) has defined as "expert" thinking about teaching and learning. They found that in all cases examined, over the course of multiple drafts, students increasingly displayed a number of expert characteristics: they grew more able to generate multiple hypotheses and to look more systematically at the different influences on learning; they offered multiple connections between theory and others' practices, elaborated and expanded upon theory and research, often in relation to their own practice, understood contingencies and offered qualifications about their observations and generalizations, provided specific details about learners and learning, and analyzed evidence of student learning. Even the weaker cases demonstrated evidence of these "expert" moves by the final drafts. In addition, their analysis of multiple drafts demonstrated that students moved from an initially simplistic explanation of their case to more sophisticated, theory-based explanations of their experiences.

These and other studies suggest that learning from case writing may be a promising means to help teachers build theoretical and practical connections; to move teachers beyond simple or lay conceptions of teaching, children, and schooling; and to appreciate the complex nature of teaching (Goodwin, 2002; Kleinfeld, 1992; Levin, 1995, 2002; Roeser, 2002). However, emerging research also suggests that this kind of learning from cases does not happen without carefully designed curriculum that links research and theory about learning and teaching to the candidates' process of analysis. Some studies found disappointing progress for students writing cases without substantial connections to literature and ongoing feedback from instructors (Anderson and Bird, 1995; Copeland and Decker, 1996; Levin, 1995). They identify at least two kinds of challenges for teacher educators that case writing may not be able to overcome if the pedagogy is not fully developed. First, a case writer's limited knowledge or more narrow frame of reference may lead to a misunderstanding of the nature of the situation; a failure to appreciate all the important variables; or a lack of sufficient strategies to deal with the experience. Second, a case writer may not be able to connect the particular, personal experience related in his or her case with a broader set of principles for interpretation (Darling-Hammond and Snyder, 2000).

A few studies have described the ways in which specific teaching strategies appear to enhance stronger outcomes of case writing for students. For example, the study described earlier by Hammerness and colleagues (2002) outlines in some detail the course process used to work with cases. Students read cases written by others (education scholars, experienced teachers, as well as past teacher education students), which were paired with theoretical readings about learning and teaching. While exploring these readings and accompanying cases, students wrote several drafts analyzing a case of their own teaching in which they examined what students learned and what aspects of the context and their teaching appeared to explain what was learned. On each draft, they received extensive feedback from an instructor and a peer, based upon a publicly shared and edited rubric. Students were also paired with a partner who read the case and provided feedback, including alternative perspectives drawn from the literature and their own experiences. Finally, students participated in two "case conferences" in which they presented their case orally to a small group of classmates and a facilitator who helped them consider theories and concepts that might shed light upon the case.

In teaching with cases, it appears to be critical to help students link theoretical principles to the contextualized events they read or write about. In a sense, students need to learn cases within the "schema of the field" with a chance to see how cases represent and relate to knowledge about teaching, learning, and development, in order to make using the cases an effective and rich learning experience. Student teachers need to be supported in moving between the case and the principles. Indeed, when doctors read cases, they cannot make sense of a clinical case without considerable scientific knowledge (for example, of physiology, chemistry, and biology and of treatments and possible outcomes) that must be connected to the knowledge of particular cases of particular patients with their own medical histories. So, too, do teachers need to go "back and forth" between cases and principles, as well as have opportunities to consider "what is this a case of?" (Shulman, 1996).

Looking across several studies documenting more and less successful use of case writing in teacher education, Darling-Hammond and Hammerness (2002) identify some features of instruction that appear to help case writers overcome potential pitfalls and seem to support the learning associated with writing cases. These include:

- Connections to readings and discussion on learning, development, and teaching that provide the opportunity to link theory and practice;
- Guidance for data collection and analysis (e.g., observation and interview protocols in child cases, analytic memos, logs, and rubrics that guide analysis);
- Multiple drafts written against standards that encourage the development of important case features (e.g., details about students and context, analysis of learning as well as teaching, inclusion of multiple perspectives);

- Specific, concrete feedback that calls attention to principles of development, learning, teaching choices, moral questions, context variables, and other concerns;
- Time and timing—enough time to allow reflections on the case to unfold at a time when candidates are ready and able to consider the questions being posed. (p. 133)

As these authors point out: "Without learning opportunities that develop insights, raise other perspectives into view, and create bridges between theory and practice, cases may add up to interesting but uninstructive teaching stories that reinforce idiosyncratic or uninformed views of teaching. A key lesson . . . is that cases do not teach themselves" (p. 132).

Autobiography

As we have noted, student teachers bring very powerful lay theories about teaching and learning—many of which are based in their own personal educational histories (Crow, 1987; Holt-Reynolds, 1992). These lay theories, or beliefs developed without formal instruction (Vygotsky, 1978), often have been developed over long periods of participating in and observing classrooms (Lortie, 1975; Measor, 1985) as well as in informal experiences of teaching and learning in schools, homes, and the community (Measor, 1985). Indeed, much research has demonstrated the impact that teachers' personal educational biographies have upon their teaching, their thinking about their teaching, and their understandings about learning (Britzman, 1986, 1991; Clandinin, 1985; Cole and Knowles, 1993; Crow, 1987; Holt-Reynolds, 1992, 1994; Kagan, 1992; Knowles, 1992).

For instance, Holt-Reynolds (1992) conducted an extensive interview-based study with teacher education students in a reading class. Her findings demonstrated not only the tenacity of these teachers' personal understandings about teaching and learning, but also the ways in which they shaped how the teachers responded to, agreed with, or accepted what they were learning about in their class. Their grounds for agreeing or disagreeing were not based upon educational theory or research, professional consensus, or experiences as teachers. Instead their views were firmly rooted in their own experiences in schools as students, experiences which often were atypical. Research also demonstrates that when these firmly held personal beliefs about teaching meet with the field, difficulties can arise (Cole and Knowles, 1993).

Often teacher educators seek to confront the apprenticeship of observation and to stimulate reflection on teaching and learning through the use of autobiography. Autobiographies are nonfiction, first-person accounts of personal experiences. In teacher education programs, students can write autobiographies that focus upon the events of their education or schooling, and which may focus upon particularly formative incidents, people, or contexts that shaped them as people (and teachers) and informed the way they think about teaching and learning.

Over the years, many teacher educators have suggested that engaging preservice teachers in writing about and analyzing their own educational experiences is a fruitful pedagogy for helping address the problem of unexamined personal experience that can be overgeneralized without an opportunity for analysis and perspective (Bullough and Gitlin, 1995; Carter and Doyle, 1996; Cole and Knowles, 1993; Holt-Reynolds, 1992; Knowles and Holt-Reynolds, 1991; Baumgartner and others, 2002; Rust, 1999). Their belief is that, through autobiography, student teachers are able not only to become aware of and to articulate their own knowledge about teaching—knowledge that is often tacit and unexamined (Barclay and Wellman, 1986)—but also to bring it to the surface for examination, reflection, and even challenge (Bullough and Gitlin, 1995). In turn, making this kind of personal historical knowledge about education explicit then enables teacher educators to build upon and work with this important prior knowledge that their students bring to their coursework. The argument for autobiography rests upon psychological theory that narrative provides an important form of knowledge (Bruner, 1990) and that guided self-reflection can stimulate greater insight and perspective, especially if narratives are shared.

Autobiographies can take a variety of starting points. Some focus upon the author's past educational experiences—both formal and informal—describing in detail important educational incidents in their lives, such as key experiences of learning as well as not learning; of puzzlement or challenge; of the relationship of school and culture; and of inequities (Hoffman, 1989). These autobiographies may describe particularly influential teachers, coaches, or other influential adults in candidates' lives, or even peers from whom they learned. Sometimes these narratives also focus upon the context of the school, the peer group or a classroom, or the relationship between school and one's own culture (Chamoiseau, 1997). Yet another type of narrative may emphasize the author's school or life experiences as these relate to race, gender, ethnicity, sexual orientation, or religion, in order to discuss key formative experiences as children or young adults (Beals, 1994; Fricke, 1995; Santiago, 1993; Walker, 1991).

Autobiography at New York University

At New York University, student teachers write several autobiographical papers. As part of a strand of courses that involve students in learning about key concepts in teaching and learning called "Inquiries I, II" on the undergraduate level and "Inquiries III" on the master's level, students create a "Learning Autobiography." The Learning Autobiography takes the form of a timeline in which students identify key incidents in their experiences as learners. Students then write two separate narratives, one in which they write extensively about a selected incident in their learning, and another in which they describe a teacher who made a significant impression upon them. When they analyze their experiences with that individual or in other learning incidents, they are able to articulate what guides them as a teacher and examine their goals, motives, and models more closely.

There are two ways teacher educators tend to use autobiographies—first, in engaging students in the writing of their own autobiographies, and second, in engaging them in the reading and discussion of autobiographies of others (which sometimes also involves students in analyzing them in a reading group or other group of readers). Teacher educators frequently involve student teachers in writing autobiographies in order to explore their past and current educational experiences. (See Autobiography at New York University for a description of this practice at New York University and Chapter Seven for a description of how this practice can be embedded in a course on Multicultural Education.) Often, students are asked to construct a narrative that provides detailed descriptions of their past educational experiences—both formal and informal (Bullough and Gitlin, 1995). In other cases, they create autobiographical narratives that focus upon the exploration of a key metaphor, theme, or central image from their educational experiences—images that they may want to build upon in future teaching, such as "teaching as building community" or "creating a home" (Clandinin, 1986).

A few teacher educators have recently begun to document in small-scale studies the impact that these strategies appear to have on student teachers' thinking (Bullough and Stokes, 1994; Clarke and Medina, 2000; Florio-Ruane, 2001; Rust, 1999). They stress the insights prospective teachers report about their own learning and experiences in relation to each other and their students, broadening their perspectives and highlighting awareness that their assumptions require greater evaluation. Baumgartner and others (2002) found that autobiographical stories "provide critical insights into teachers' thinking that work to enable the group not only to understand the speaker's actions but also to provide professional support" for further growth (p. 86). The authors note that these aspects of student thinking rarely emerge in the context of most teacher education programs where the formal interactions between professors and students are not sufficient for students' stories to emerge and thus become available for them to examine. With opportunities to write and then discuss autobiographical experiences, student teachers have a chance to explore those places where their implicit theories about teaching rub up against those of other teachers or standards of practice.

Teacher educators also acknowledge some important challenges related to this pedagogy. First, autobiographical narratives can be created but remain undeveloped and unchallenged—without opportunities to revisit, explore, and compare new understandings with past understandings. Student teachers need carefully scaffolded experiences with different forms of teaching, schooling, and culture in order to productively challenge, question, and wrestle with deeply held beliefs and past experiences. In addition, if these narratives are not shared, there is no way to get a perspective on the range of experiences, learning and teaching possibilities, and school contexts that exist. Some teacher educators suggest that sharing autobiographies and revisiting personal narratives over time, in the light of new experiences of alternative practices, are particularly important.

Second, writers and readers of autobiography may come to overemphasize the role of the teacher, seeing her as a solitary actor—as both the source of and the only solution to the problems of teaching (Cazden, cited in Ballenger, 1999; and Florio-Ruane, 2001). Florio-Ruane argues that one way to avoid the solitary nature of these stories is to read them "in the company of colleagues" thus bringing multiple perspectives to bear upon the work and illustrating the importance of a community of professionals—and the knowledge located in such a community—for understanding and making sense of the challenges embedded in them.

Finally, teacher educators who work with autobiography draw attention to the deeply personal nature of this pedagogy, and to the necessity for care and respect for the intimate revelations that may emerge from writing and reading autobiography. Others have called attention to the ethics involved in asking students to disclose private, sensitive thoughts, feelings, and experiences—sometimes for public scrutiny—and sometimes for the purpose of changing and revising teachers' beliefs and conceptions about teaching (Carter and Doyle, 1996). When using such a personal form of writing, teacher educators need to think through potential problems (particularly regarding appropriate assessment of and response to personal writing) and pay special attention to the creation of a classroom atmosphere that is respectful, safe, and appropriate for personal revelations of this nature.

Inquiry and Action Research

Finally, as we noted earlier, preparing teachers to learn from teaching throughout their careers requires a set of tools that develop the skills and practices of systematic, purposeful inquiry and critical reflection. Many teacher educators have focused on developing these abilities by engaging student teachers in systematic research in their classrooms and schools (Gore and Zeichner, 1991; Price, 2001). Such experiences not only help teachers deal with the complexity of practice but also help them overcome some of the limitations of their apprenticeships of observation. Definitions and conceptions of such teacher-directed research differ considerably (Gore and Zeichner, 1991; Rearick and Feldman, 1999); and even the terms used—*teacher research, action research, practitioner research*, and *the scholarship of teaching*—come out of different intellectual traditions and carry with them different assumptions about teaching and research.[1] However, Cochran-Smith and Lytle's (1993) description of action research as "intentional, systematic and rigorous inquiry" provides a useful description of the character and nature of practitioner research in teacher education. Although not directly examining the work of preservice teachers, Cochran-Smith and Lytle (1993) have examined the impact of specific types of such research upon the knowledge base of teaching, learning, and schooling. For instance, they have demonstrated how

---

[1]See Gore and Zeichner (1991) for a discussion and critique of the breadth of definitions of practitioner inquiry, and for their argument of the necessity for conducting action research within a framework of a clearly developed educational and social philosophy.

"classroom studies" (a fairly typical genre in action research) can promote a systematic and intellectual critique of the assumptions, goals, and approaches being used in a classroom, which can lead the teacher-researchers not only to reframe questions but to revise pedagogical approaches.

The process of practitioner inquiry includes all aspects of a research or inquiry process: identifying questions of compelling interest (these may focus upon issues of teaching and learning; schooling and society; or education and social issues, such as gender, race, or equity); pursuing those questions through the collection of data (which may include observations of children, class or other observational field notes, or interviews with children, parents, or other teachers); and reflecting upon the questions through written work (journal entries, conceptual research memos) and oral discussion with peers, instructors, and master teachers. Practitioner research is not always as linear, however, as this suggests. Students often begin at different points in this process and follow a spiral of "plan-act-observe-and-reflect" (Zeichner and Noffke, 2001). Frequently these projects culminate in the writing of a formal research report that describes the nature of the inquiry, discusses the analysis, summarizes the findings, and sometimes includes reflection upon the results of the research for one's teaching—as well as discussion of the impact of the inquiry process upon the teacher's conception of teaching. However, some teacher educators note that they emphasize the inquiry process, and the development of skills of conducting classroom-based research, rather than the finished research product (Zeichner, 2003). "Action Research at the University of Maryland," below, describes one professor's pedagogy using action research.

Action Research at the University of Maryland

Jeremy Price (2001) actually begins his semester-long spring course on action research in the fall, when he introduces his students to concepts of research on teaching. In the spring, the students develop a research question that they pursue in their classrooms. Concurrently, he engages students in analyzing classroom data (such as written vignettes or videotapes of teaching) and in examining the research process by reading research articles, books, or pieces by other teacher-researchers. Students form small "research groups" to give feedback and intellectual support on one another's projects. Each teacher also keeps a research journal that becomes a source of evidence for his or her paper. Particular assignments help the students analyze and develop their research. For example, students have to describe an "engaging assignment" and to describe in detail conversations and interactions with students. This assignment is designed to encourage analysis of particular aspects of lessons and to help candidates learn to provide evidence for claims.

In research on the consequences of these practices, Price drew upon a variety of qualitative data from the course (transcripts of classroom conversations; questionnaires at the beginning and end of class; action research journals; preservice teachers' and their learners' writing; videotapes of classroom work; and informal interviews with student teachers) to examine the learning of eleven teacher— candidates, examining the process of their research, the impact on their learning, and "how they saw the relationship between classroom inquiry, teaching and educational change" (p. 43). Price found that his students were able to develop and reflect upon pedagogies that were responsive to the needs and strengths of their particular students; to better understand and evaluate the learning represented in students' work; and to appreciate teaching as not only planning and organizing instruction, but also as focusing on the learning of students. Price also found that the research project gave all eleven students an opportunity to take some risks in the classroom, and they all chose to test ideas and practices that focused upon the learning and engagement of their students—an important finding that contradicts the pervasive belief that student teachers are not developmentally ready to focus upon student learning. He concluded that the research process seemed "to be a powerful influence upon how they constructed their role as teachers and imagined their work as teachers" (p. 70).

Advocates of practitioner research build their argument upon a definition of teaching as reflective practice (Schön, 1983), contending that student teachers need to learn critical dispositions and skills that undergird reflection; the dispositions toward an open mind; a sense of responsibility and commitment; and care and respect for children, along with the skills of careful observation and reasoned analysis (Zeichner and Liston, 1987). However, the goals for practitioner research vary considerably—in part, depending upon the definition. Some teacher educators focus upon the benefit for individual teachers in helping them become more reflective and analytic about their own classroom practice and promote their individual growth as teachers (Webb, 1990). Those who emphasize the professional development that may arise from such research often focus upon the importance of teachers engaging in constructing knowledge about teaching and learning themselves, and in using this understanding to guide their practice and their future learning (see, for example, Cochran-Smith and Lytle, 1993; Hollingsworth and Sockett, 1994).

Finally, some emphasize the political insights and understandings that practitioner research may promote in teachers, by enabling them to better understand the social conditions of schooling and work toward more democratic, emancipatory education for all students through school reform and political action (Gore and Zeichner, 1991; Kemmis, 1993; Noffke and Stevenson, 1995; Price, 2001; Zeichner, 1993b). As Villegas and Lucas (2002a) note:

> By studying schools, prospective teachers can learn about the nature of the school as an institutional culture, exploring ways in which the context outside the classroom influences the lives of students and teachers. They can see the ways in which school policies and practices both support and hinder teachers' efforts to be culturally responsive. They can get a sense of the individual and frequently isolating nature of teachers' work, on the one hand, and the need and potential of collaboration, on the other. If they study schools where equity and social justice are priorities, they might learn about ways that teachers

can work collectively to bring about changes in their schools that will increase access to knowledge for all students. This can give them a sense of the possibility for teachers to play leadership roles outside the classroom. (p. 145)

Across the literature there is a view that practitioner research can support teachers in developing a disposition toward reflective, inquiry-based, and analytic thinking (what Cochran-Smith and Lytle [1999] term an *inquiry stance*) along with the important skills of data collection, observation, analysis, and reflection.

Although some researchers and educators have examined the products of teachers' inquiries (Beyer, 1996; Bissex and Bullock, 1987; Cochran-Smith and Lytle, 1993), the research on the outcomes of practitioner research for participants is quite exploratory. A small number of researchers and teacher educators have studied the learning of preservice teacher education students in action research courses (see, for example, Gore and Zeichner, 1991; Price, 2001; Tabachnik and Zeichner, 1999; Valli, 2000), often as a form of practitioner research on their own teaching and the learning of their students. As noted, Price (2001) found that the process raised candidates' confidence and caused them to pursue changes in their classrooms, which they hoped to continue as new teachers. However, this study, like others (for example, Gore and Zeichner, 1991; Valli, 2000), found that although the work candidates did in action research increased their awareness of particular classroom issues and helped them to be more student focused, relatively few were able to translate their findings into school-level considerations or organizational improvement strategies.

Highlighting some of the possibilities and challenges of this pedagogy, Gore and Zeichner (1991) analyzed the written reports of the research projects conducted by eighteen of their student teachers, and evaluated the self-assessments of learning by these students. Their students reported that the research process enabled them to become more thoughtful and purposeful about their teaching; that it helped them become more aware of their own practices and of the gaps between their beliefs and their practices; and that it helped them become aware of their learners' thinking and learning. However, these authors also expressed concerns that they found that only a small number of students emerged with a concern for moral and political issues, and few made connections between their specific topic of investigation and the larger issues or contexts within which their specific inquiry took place.

They argue that this pedagogy may be helped by some self-inquiry through autobiographies by student teachers, in order to better prepare them to later make more critical inquiry into schools and schooling, as well as to encourage more involvement of the student teachers in a "community of teachers" who are all engaged in teacher research together. There is some other evidence that placing student teachers with more experienced teacher-researchers can help prospective teachers more easily develop a perspective on teaching that is inquiry oriented (see, for example, Clift, Veal, Johnson, and Holland, 1990;

Cochran-Smith, 1991; Nath and Tellez, 1995). This work reinforces the argument that pedagogies such as practitioner research and autobiography may be most powerful and effective if combined—and also calls attention to the fact that all these pedagogies may be strengthened when supported by clinical placements and experiences that reflect and reinforce concepts, ideas, and approaches from the university coursework.

These kinds of studies, although still limited, provide some indications of the kind of learning that can emerge from practitioner research. Such inquiry can help new teachers focus upon student learning and student work, critically examine their own teaching practices in relation to their beliefs and commitments, and develop the skills of data collection, analysis, and reflection.

CONCLUSION

The pedagogies of teacher education we have described—student teaching, performance assessments and portfolios, analyses of teaching and learning, case methods, autobiography, and practitioner inquiry—are intended to support teachers' abilities to learn *in* and *from* practice. Each intends, in different ways, to build the visions, tools, practices, dispositions, and understandings of new teachers in ways that develop and make habitual the ability to reflect and the skills of close analysis. However, the interrelationship of these pedagogies to one another is also important. It is possible that these pedagogies may work more powerfully in relationship to one another, and some pedagogies (such as autobiography) may be particularly useful early on in programs whereas others (such as practitioner inquiry) may be best engaged once student teachers have had opportunities to critically examine their own experiences of schooling.

For these reasons and others, developing and enacting these pedagogies is no easy task. Teaching teachers is certainly among the most demanding kinds of professional preparation: teacher educators must constantly model practices; construct powerful learning experiences; thoughtfully support progress, understanding, and practice; carefully assess students' progress and understandings; and help link theory and practice. Skillfully enacting this kind of teaching of teachers takes time, effort, and, most important, institutional support—and cannot be easily undertaken in a context that is unsupportive or conflicting. In our final chapter, Chapter Twelve, we move to a discussion of the key factors that influence the ability of institutions to transform their practice and to teach teachers well. These broader concerns of policy and organizational change are key elements in determining how well teacher education will be able to prepare candidates who, in turn, support *their* students toward productive lives and careers.

Implementing Curriculum Renewal in Teacher Education: Managing Organizational and Policy Change

Linda Darling-Hammond, Arturo Pacheco, Nicholas Michelli,
Pamela LePage, Karen Hammerness, with Peter Youngs

Debates about quality have been part of the teacher education landscape for more than a century. Often these debates have been tied to perceptions of "crisis" in the public schools, as in the period following the launch of Sputnik in the 1950s and the reform era that was marked by the publication of *A Nation at Risk* in 1983 (National Commission of Excellence in Education, 1983). Two decades after the *A Nation at Risk* report, the reform context remains contentious, and the rhetoric of crisis remains a goad to a wide variety of policy changes. Although the state of American education may not be as sorry as is sometimes claimed (see, for example, Berliner and Biddle, 1995), there is no doubt that improvement is needed, especially in schools that serve the most disadvantaged students.

Many analysts have argued that reform efforts that have ignored the preparation of teachers have been doomed to fail, as they have assumed change could be achieved without attention to the knowledge, skills, and dispositions of the primary change agents without whom little transformation is possible (Sarason, 1990; Fullan, 1991). Sarason (1993) notes that, as in the case of medical education's overhaul, attention to professional preparation is required by a "primary prevention model." Rather than seeking to launch reforms that correct for the problems of poor practice stemming from inadequate training, the emphasis on reforming preparation acknowledges that investments in practitioners' abilities can prevent many of the problems reforms often seek, unsuccessfully, to address.

In recent years, policymakers and educational reformers have been less likely to overlook teacher education than in the past. As concerns about the quality of American education have been joined to evidence that teacher quality makes an important difference in outcomes, a variety of reforms to create more rigorous preparation, certification, and licensing have been launched. With these reforms, the quality of preparation appears to have noticeably improved in some places, as we discussed in Chapter Eleven and describe further in the sections that follow. However, the outcomes of the impetus for reform are not straightforward. For one thing, teacher education has been more heavily politicized than other areas of higher education, as it has been tied to both the public perceptions of the quality of the public schools and to the varying political interests of states, localities, and, increasingly, the federal government, as well as professional organizations and communities seeking better teachers for their children. In addition, the plethora of policies affecting programs has sometimes worked in contradictory ways. For example, state efforts to upgrade standards have resulted in more disparate testing and less reciprocity among states, which has negatively impacted the mobility of teachers from states where there are surpluses to those where there are shortages (Darling-Hammond and Sykes, 2003).

At the same time, there has been a movement to reduce the requirements for entry to teaching—sometimes viewed as important standards and other times as unnecessary hoops—especially for teachers who work in high-need urban communities that experience difficulties recruiting and retaining teachers (National Commission on Teaching and America's Future, 2003). This bimodal treatment of teaching is linked to the different levels of resources available to districts for recruiting and retaining teachers and for serving students: the schools serving the largest proportions of low-income students generally pay significantly less than those serving more affluent students, and typically also offer larger class sizes and poor working conditions (National Commission on Teaching and America's Future, 1996). Although these schools arguably need teachers with the greatest levels of knowledge and skill, they often end up hiring those with the least training and experience. Traditional and alternative preparation programs serving such districts often feel pressured to truncate both coursework and supervised clinical training in order to get candidates into their own classrooms as quickly as possible.

In addition to these competing impulses, there has historically been little coherence in the training system in education, and only haphazard professional control. For most of the twentieth century, initiatives to influence teacher preparation, licensing, accreditation, and professional development have been undertaken by a wide variety of actors and have existed in splendid isolation from one another. These actors include state legislatures, state departments of education, separate state boards for higher education and K–12 education, professional standards boards in a minority of states, local boards of education, local school district officials, accrediting bodies for schools and colleges, and a wide variety of private commercial enterprises involved in the provision of professional development and the development of texts, curriculum materials, and tests for teachers. These parties introduce into the teaching arena implicit and explicit standards for what teachers should know and be able to do that are frequently inconsistent with one another. It would be an oxymoron to call the highly fragmented U.S. teacher education enterprise that has existed for most of our history a "system." These competing impulses and the policies that attend them create a complex environment for teacher education programs seeking to improve the preparation they provide.

Furthermore, as we have noted, if the goal is to provide a high-quality education for all students, it is not enough to provide them with capable, well-prepared teachers. They also need access to strong curriculum and the materials with which to learn it; technology supports for learning and inquiry; reasonable class sizes; safe, clean facilities; and equitable opportunities to benefit from all of these. And if well-prepared teachers are to stay in teaching—and thus provide a stable teaching force for children in all communities—they need the supports that matter for their retention in the profession, including supportive administrative leadership, adequate salaries, and ongoing opportunities for learning and participation in school decision making so that they can put into practice what they have learned (Darling-Hammond and Sclan, 1996). Thus there is a set of broad social and institutional changes that are also needed to recruit and retain teachers and to provide adequate and equitable learning opportunities for students.

THE NEED FOR CURRICULUM RENEWAL IN TEACHER EDUCATION

As was true in medicine at the turn of the twentieth century, there is little guarantee in some parts of the country that *all* teachers will have access to the kinds of knowledge and skill development that can enable them to teach the diverse students in their schools in ways that respond to the increasingly challenging standards they face. Although knowledge about teaching and learning has grown, the odds that teachers will have access to this knowledge are far less than certain. This is because of wide variations in the nature and quality of teacher education programs and the fact that a substantial number of individuals enter teaching without completing teacher education. Those who enter without training or with less systematic preparation typically report feeling significantly less well prepared than those who enter having completed a preservice preparation program (California State University, 2002a; Darling-Hammond,

Chung, and Frelow, 2002). However, there is also wide variability in the preparation prospective teachers receive in different programs (Darling-Hammond, Chung, and Frelow, 2002). There are many sources of this variability, including at least the following.

Variability in Standards for Candidates

For most of the last century, there has been substantial variation in the standards to which entering teachers are held. Licensing standards have been noticeably different from state to state. As recently as the late 1990s, some high-standards states required a college major in the subject to be taught plus intensive preparation for teaching, including well-defined studies of learning and teaching, and fifteen or more weeks of student teaching. Meanwhile, some low-standards states required no coherent program of studies in the field to be taught, only a handful of education courses, and a few weeks of student teaching. In addition to differences in the standards themselves, there have been great differences in the extent to which they are enforced. Whereas some states have refused to allow districts to hire unqualified teachers, others have routinely allowed the hiring of candidates who have not met their standards, even when qualified teachers are available (Darling-Hammond, 2001a, 2004). Finally, standards for teaching candidates have varied with the wide range of licensing examinations enacted in nearly all states during the 1980s and early 1990s. These, too, set very different standards of knowledge and skill in terms of what they assess and the level of performance they require. The nature and quality of tests used across the states have varied so greatly, as have their cutoff scores, that they cannot be used to generalize about the knowledge held by prospective teachers passing examinations in different states (National Research Council, 2002).

Variability in Standards for Programs

Teaching, unlike other professions, does not require universal professional accreditation for education schools, and analysts suggest that many state procedures for approving programs have been inadequate to ensure quality. Although some states have devoted serious attention to setting and enforcing standards for teacher education programs (see, for example, Darling-Hammond and others, 1999), and most states have recently adopted or adapted a common framework for beginning teacher licensing standards developed by the thirty-state Interstate New Teacher Assessment and Support Consortium (INTASC), fewer have invested substantial resources in the enforcement of standards. Though virtually all states require programs to offer courses in subject matter and teaching methods, there is still noticeable variation in the amount of study required and whether it includes such areas as learning theory, child and adolescent development, reading or literacy development, curriculum development, assessment, or knowledge about special learning needs, such as the teaching of children with disabilities or of second language learners. Clinical requirements also vary widely. For example, in 1998, state requirements for student teaching ranged from eight weeks in some states to eighteen weeks in others (NASDTEC, 1998). A program of studies that would be approved in one state could fail to meet the standards in another. In addition, within any given state, many programs far exceed the minimal requirements imposed by their state agencies, whereas others barely meet them.

Newly enacted alternate routes to certification, introduced in more than forty states during the 1980s, also operate under widely divergent standards. These routes began as alternatives to the undergraduate program model that many states earlier required as the sole basis for program approval. Some alternative routes are one- or two-year-long postbaccalaureate models, including fifth-year master's degree programs that meet or exceed normal licensing standards. By linking key coursework to intensively supervised student teaching or internships, they provide a high-quality preparation to midcareer recruits or recent graduates who want to enter teaching. Because of their concentrated nature and tight design, many have integrated theory and skills development more productively than some traditional programs.

Others, however, are alternatives to the notion of state licensure itself in that they lower expectations for candidates' knowledge in content and pedagogical studies and sometimes shift the decision about candidate competence to employing school districts (Darling-Hammond, 1990). These models sometimes offer only a few weeks of training that may not include such fundamentals as learning theory, child development, and content pedagogy, and they place recruits in classrooms without a period of supervised practice. The same problems, however, can sometimes appear in university-based programs that are labeled as "traditional," so program categories do not distinguish programs in terms of their comprehensiveness or quality.

Aside from formal requirements, the extent to which standards are actually applied also varies. Although a few states have been able to maintain resources for program reviews, many saw great decreases in state education department funding during the 1980s and 1990s, with the staffing allocated to such functions as teacher education program approval cut so sharply that onsite program reviews by panels of experts almost never occur. In some of these states, both colleges and district providers of programs have felt free to reduce their own standards for and investments in teacher education.

Variability in Teacher Education Curriculum and Faculty

For all of the reasons just described, what teachers encounter when they try to become prepared for their future profession can be quite idiosyncratic to the state, college, and program in which they enroll, and the instructors with whom they study. Aside from the differences associated with varying state requirements, there are many opportunities for differences and disjunctures in the courses of studies available to most future teachers. Prospective teachers generally take courses in the arts and sciences and in schools of education, and they spend time in schools. What they study varies widely. Unlike other professions where the professional curriculum is reasonably common across institutions and has some substantive coherence, the curriculum of teacher education has often been idiosyncratic to the professors who teach whatever courses are required, which are different from place to place. Furthermore, relatively few colleges have strong mechanisms for coordinating the efforts of arts and sciences and education faculty, or university-based and school-based faculty (Darling-Hammond and Ball, 1997).

A number of studies in the 1980s and 1990s documented a set of long-standing problems in teacher education resulting from weaknesses in the "non-system" described earlier (Goodlad, 1990; Holmes Group, 1996; Howey and Zimpher, 1989; Zeichner, 1993b). These problems with the traditional teacher education design that predominated between 1950 and 1990 include:

Inadequate time. The confines of a four-year undergraduate degree make it hard to learn subject matter, child development, learning theory, and effective teaching strategies. Elementary preparation is considered weak in subject matter, and secondary preparation, in knowledge of learning and learners.

Fragmentation. Key elements of teacher learning are disconnected from each other. Coursework is separated from practice teaching; professional skills are segmented into separate courses; faculties in the arts and sciences are insulated from education professors. Would-be teachers are left on their own to put it all together.

Uninspired teaching methods. In order for prospective teachers to learn active, hands-on and minds-on teaching, they must have experienced it for themselves. But traditional lecture and recitation still dominate in much of higher education, including the departments in which teachers receive most of their subject matter training as well as some teacher education courses.

Superficial curriculum. "Once over lightly" describes the curriculum. Traditional programs focus on subject matter methods and a smattering of educational psychology. Candidates do not learn deeply about how to understand and handle real problems of practice.

Traditional views of schooling. Because of pressures to prepare candidates for schools as they are, most prospective teachers learn to work in isolation, rather than in teams, and to master chalkboards and textbooks instead of computers and CD-ROMs (National Commission on Teaching and America's Future, 1996, p. 32).

In addition, many have charged that **fieldwork** has had inadequate attention in program design. While it is often a core portion of student teachers' experiences and has a strong influence on teachers' thinking about teaching and learning (Guyton and McIntyre, 1990), fieldwork has often been divorced from coursework, inadequately designed, and placements have often failed to reflect standards for good teaching.

As we discuss in the following sections, important headway has been made on these problems in many places. However, the improvements have not reached all programs, and the policy contexts within which teacher education operates often work against productive reforms rather than for them. Providing all teachers with strong and effective teacher education will require both expanding access to programs and greater clarity about how to enhance quality across the enterprise. It will require greater sophistication about how to approach organizational change as *institutional development* rather than a series of single innovations that cannot survive (Fullan, 1993a). It will also require greater engagement with the policy community that exerts increasingly strong influences on teacher education programs' goals and strategies. Before we talk about the unique context of teacher education programs, it is useful to consider how other professions have faced similar challenges and have developed solutions.

PROFESSIONAL ANALOGUES

When Flexner (1910) published his landmark report on the state of medical education in the United States, he pointed out that there were important, structural weaknesses in the prevailing models of medical education that then existed. Medical education and medical practice in the early twentieth century suffered from dramatically uneven quality and differential access to knowledge, as well as an enormous divide between research in the new sciences of medicine and the state of practice. In the medical schools that had emerged in the previous decades, coursework was frequently divorced from clinical work, and curriculum was often fragmented, superficial, and didactic—the same kinds of complaints that have dogged colleges of education since they took up the charge of educating teachers in the latter half of the twentieth century.

The Reform of Medical Education

In the late nineteenth century, most medical students were educated through apprenticeships—essentially following an experienced physician on his rounds through town. This physician had often been educated in a similar fashion, if he had received any training at all. Such an experience enabled students to observe interactions with real patients, watch the course of diseases and their treatments, and be immersed in the "practice" of medicine. However, many practitioners had themselves been poorly trained and had little awareness of advances in the diagnosis and treatment of disease; thus the apprentice system passed on as much misinformation and ignorance as it did clinical wisdom. Early medical schools developed as a supplement to apprenticeships to provide a more systematic approach to the transmission of knowledge. Some of these schools entwined clinical work and bedside practice with laboratory investigations and academic work.

However, what Flexner described as the "promising early start" of these medical schools was not to last: medical schools began to spring up all over the country and, according to his research, the only apparent requirement was the existence of doctors to serve as professors and some space for classes. Flexner was strongly critical of many of the medical school models, which relied heavily upon textbooks, used didactic teaching methods, and required students to simply "parrot" back information. In such schools, students rarely were engaged in the full care and treatment of a patient—in fact, some never even had an opportunity to see a cadaver or examine a real human body. Indeed, even the most rudimentary medical equipment was not visible in many schools he visited; several long benches and textbooks were the only necessities. Students rarely accompanied doctors to visit patients. The clinical experience—the close apprenticing with an experienced practitioner that had been so central to learning to be a doctor just a few decades prior—had become lost. Flexner commented that now it seemed that "All the training a young doctor got before beginning his practice now had to be procured within the medical school. And, there was a wide range of programs that ranged from 3 weeks to 3 years. The school was no longer a supplement—it was everything" (p. 26).

Flexner could have lobbied for the prevailing argument of the time to return to the apprenticeship model—a plan that was not only less costly but also appealed to common sense. Yet, although such an experience enabled students to observe interactions with real patients, Flexner noted that such apprenticeships were also limited in that they did not enable young doctors to take advantage of much of the professional knowledge available to them (knowledge of other similar cases; texts written for the purpose of teaching general anatomy and physiology, and research on treatment of disease). In other words, an apprenticeship, though valuable in many ways, did not enable medical students to gain access to systematic theory and research.

Thus Flexner proposed that medical schools be housed at universities, where theory and practice could be intertwined. He argued for a teaching hospital under the control of medical faculty that linked *coursework*—providing access to profession-wide knowledge, recent innovations (such as the stethoscope, the self-registering thermometer, the correlation of observed symptoms with the results of chemical analysis and biological experimentation)—with *clinical and laboratory work*, which enabled students to understand what medicine looked like in practice. Flexner quotes the first clinical medical professor at

Harvard: "The student must join Examples with Study before he can be sufficiently qualified to prescribe for the sick, for Language and Books alone can never give him Adequate ideas of Diseases and the best methods of Treating them" (p. 22).

Flexner was not dissuaded by the argument that there were some successful practitioners who had done quite well without such training—he rather allowed that they had triumphed in spite of their meager education through "unusual gifts and perseverance alone" (p. 10)—and he called for faculty and students to spend equal time in the classroom and in the laboratory or clinic. The eventual widespread reform of medical education occurred as the profession set standards for medical training and infused these into the standards for accrediting professional programs and the standards for licensing and certifying medical candidates, who had to have graduated from a professionally accredited program in order to sit for licensing and Board certification examinations.

This same process, with some variations, was later followed for law, engineering, nursing, psychology, accounting, architecture, and other occupations that became professions in the twentieth century. A similar set of strategies for preparation—simultaneously strengthening and connecting scientific and clinical training—was embedded in the goals of the Holmes Group (1986), the Carnegie Task Force on Teaching as a Profession (1986), and the National Network for Education Renewal (Goodlad, 1990, 1994), among other efforts at teacher education reform. However, the connection to policy levers such as licensing, accreditation, and certification that might cause reform to spread has been much more problematic for teaching.

Issues in Teacher Education Reform

Although education struggled with many of these issues long before (and obviously after) the Flexner Report, the parallels between medical education reform and teacher education reform are striking. Just as medicine began educating young doctors by pairing them with more experienced practitioners, teachers in the mid- to late nineteenth century began to be educated in "normal schools," which focused on practice. The teaching environments of normal schools varied, however: some normal schools were quite successful at providing good pedagogical training and constructing learning experiences that drew upon the knowledge of experts as well as classroom practice (Herbst, 1989; Lucas, 1997). Yet in other normal schools, there was little attention to the practice of pedagogy and female teachers were simply required to be subservient, of "good character," and hardworking (Rury, 1989; Clifford, 1989).

Gradually, however, normal schools became obsolete as responsibility for training teachers shifted to teachers' colleges and universities. By the 1940s, few normal schools remained in existence; by the 1950s, most teachers' colleges evolved into departments within state colleges and universities. In this setting, practitioners who had been instructors were often replaced by university faculty who themselves had little or no experience teaching in K–12 settings. Many of those who have found themselves teaching teachers—faculty in English or mathematics, for example—have not thought of themselves as "teacher educators," and most have had little preparation for the task of educating teachers. They have taught their courses as they would to any college student, leaving it to the prospective teachers to integrate subject matter and pedagogical studies. Many faculty in schools of education have not thought of themselves as teacher educators, either. Instead, they are specialists in subjects like sociology, psychology, or reading. They have not always felt a mandate to figure out how what they know should apply to teaching or to coordinate their work with that of other faculty who work with prospective teachers. Although clinical work has continued to be a requirement of most programs, its relation to the work in the academy has often been attenuated by organizational barriers within the university and between the university and schools. And, unlike medicine and other developed professions, teacher education exists in a more highly politicized regulatory environment in which standards for accreditation, licensing, and certification are substantially governed by political bodies rather than by the profession itself. As a consequence, the key levers for change are more complex and difficult to manage.

Over the next ten years, the extent to which the Committee on Teacher Education's (CTE) curricular and programmatic recommendations can be implemented will be strongly influenced by the regulatory, political, and institutional contexts of teacher preparation. In this context, we examine lessons from research about the processes of curriculum reform in teacher education.

Answering the Call for Change

Teacher educators have not ignored the calls for change. Many of the teacher education reforms launched in the 1990s were developed in response to these critiques (Holmes Group, 1990; Patterson, Michelli, and Pacheco, 1999; Sockett and others, 2001; Tom, 1997; Valli, 1992). In large part because of the reform efforts of groups like the Holmes Group of education deans and the National Network for Education Renewal, a growing number of teachers are now prepared in programs of study that include a disciplinary degree at the undergraduate level; better defined and integrated education coursework, sometimes at the graduate level; and more extensive clinical practice, often in professional development schools that seek to model state-of-the-art practice. These reforms are built upon the idea that educating new teachers requires a curriculum where neither the school nor the clinical experience becomes, in Flexner's words, "everything," and where the two kinds of learning are well integrated.

Recent studies have indicated that graduates of the five-year teacher education programs created through some of these reforms are rated by principals and teaching colleagues as better prepared than graduates of traditional undergraduate programs, and they are as confident and effective in their teaching as more senior colleagues. They are also significantly more likely to enter teaching and remain in the profession after several years (Andrew, 1990; Andrew and Schwab, 1995; Baker, 1993; Denton and Peters, 1988; Shin, 1994).

Also, in contrast to past reports of teachers' negative views of teacher education, since 1990, several surveys of beginning teachers who completed teacher education have found that the great majority—more than 80 percent—felt that they were well prepared for most of the challenges of their work (Gray and others, 1993; Howey and Zimpher, 1993; Kentucky Institute for Education Research, 1997; California State University, 2002a). Veteran teachers and principals who work with current teacher preparation programs, particularly five-year programs and those that feature professional development schools, also perceive their young colleagues as much better prepared than they were some years earlier (Andrew and Schwab, 1995; Baker, 1993; Darling-Hammond, 1994; National Center for Education Statistics, 1996, tables 73 and 75).

At the same time, these surveys also suggest areas where ongoing work is needed. In general, smaller proportions of newly prepared teachers reported feeling well prepared to deal with the needs of special education students and those with limited English proficiency than they felt in other areas of teaching. (On average, surveys have suggested that about 60 to 70 percent felt prepared in these areas as compared to 80 to 90 percent in other areas.) (Darling-Hammond, Chung, and Frelow, 2002; Gray and others, 1993; Howey and Zimpher, 1993.) And graduates of some programs reported feeling much better prepared than others (California State University, 2002a; Darling-Hammond, Chung, and Frelow, 2002).

Although successful programs have been documented (see Chapter Eleven), the strategies used in these programs have sometimes been difficult to sustain and have not yet become widespread. Furthermore, it has been frequently noted by those working on these reforms that, for the results of such efforts to be lasting, schools and universities need to change in tandem, so that they are both working toward state-of-the-art practice, so that teachers can use what they know and can be prepared for schools as they should become, rather than being constrained by outmoded practices. Furthermore, a continuum of learning opportunities for entering teachers must be in place beyond preservice, so they and their colleagues can continue to develop their skills. These tasks are even more challenging than "just" changing preparation programs themselves (Darling-Hammond, 1994; Fullan, 1993a; Goodlad, 1994). In the following sections, we examine factors associated with the success of efforts to transform teacher education, focusing on the institutional contexts and strategies that support successful efforts as well as the policy contexts that influence the standards to which preparation programs are expected to respond, the resources available to them, and the change processes they can pursue.

Change Processes in Teacher Education

A number of successful traditional and alternative teacher education programs have shown that it is possible to design, develop, and maintain high-quality teacher preparation programs despite the barriers associated with program, university, and regulatory contexts (see, for example, Valli, 1992; Sockett and others, 2001; Korthagen, 2001; Novak, 1994; Pacheco, 2000; Darling-Hammond, 2000; Ross and Bondy, 1996; Snyder, 1999; Howey and Zimpher, 1989). Later we discuss what research has suggested are some of the important aspects of the *process* of change within institutions, including key elements for mobilizing and sustaining reforms.

As a prelude to this discussion, we note that there is some evidence about the causes of previous large-scale failures to reform teacher education. In his analysis of the federally sponsored Teacher Corps and Trainers of Teacher Trainers programs that existed in the 1960s and 1970s, Fullan (1993a) identified five reasons for the failures of these programs to transform preparation:

1. The programs were based on extremely vague conceptions of the desired change and the change process. "Having an ideology is not the same as having conceptions and ideas of what should be done and how it should be done," Fullan notes (1993a, p. 109).

2. The initiatives focused on individuals rather than institutions.

3. They were nonsystemic, giving little thought to changes in interinstitutional relationships, for example, between schools and universities.

4. They ignored the knowledge and skill base that would be required of teachers if they were to teach effectively a wide variety of students and transform the conditions in schools that influence what teachers can do.

5. To the extent that they worked on change, most of the effort was directed at school systems, not at universities (pp. 109–110, reprinted with permission of the publisher).

These insights suggest the importance of a systemic, institutional perspective on change that includes both universities and schools, a perspective that includes attention to clarifying the goals for knowledge and skill development, and a strategy for implementing a change process within a community focused on these goals.

Developing a Community for Preparing Teachers

In accounts that document the process of change, the importance of developing a common mission, sense of purpose, and shared locus of activity among the many actors involved in teacher education is a central theme. Although the importance of developing professional community in schools has been widely addressed in the research literature (see, for example, Dufour and Eaker, 1998; Newmann, King, and Youngs, 2000; Westheimer, 1998; Wenger, 1998), scholars and practitioners in higher education have not always paid attention to the importance of community-building in universities as well as schools.

The establishment of a strong professional community in teacher education is often dependent on strong leadership, both from faculty and from deans and department chairs. Such leadership demands energy and enthusiasm as well as administrative skill. There are lessons suggested by successful programs like those mentioned throughout this volume, many of them operating relatively small preparation programs, but we also must acknowledge that large schools often face even greater challenges as they work to develop a professional community (Goodlad, 1994). These schools must hire greater numbers of faculty who may work in balkanized structures, have little opportunity for collaboration, and perhaps have conflicting agendas, making the construction of community more difficult. Some schools also hire large numbers of adjunct faculty members who come and go, making it difficult to develop consistent and coherent curriculum across programs.

Research-focused universities that have teacher education programs also face challenges when incentive systems provide few rewards for preparing teachers. In these schools, teacher education is not always considered a priority when it comes to allocation of resources (Goodlad, 1994). Both types of universities undergo political and social upheaval when search committees, curriculum committees, and tenure committees try to balance the needs of the department, the school, and the students with the competitive and individualistic culture of traditional academia (see, Giroux and Myrsiades, 2001; Good, 2001).

District-based teacher education programs, many of them centered in urban districts, face the challenges of finding time and resources for preparing novices in the face of other pressing demands. They also need to find strong mentors who can make time available for coaching new entrants without losing their talents from classroom teaching. Both these mentors and the novice teachers need time to plan collaboratively with one another and with others in their peer groups. In some districts where there is high turnover and a steady stream of inexperienced teachers, the talent pool of experienced teachers is thin. This places pressures on both the veterans and the schools themselves to find a way to stretch expertise across the many roles of teaching, leadership, curriculum development, mentoring, evaluation, and professional learning and to create means for overstretched teachers to collaborate around both preparation and school management agendas (Shields and others, 2001).

Teacher preparation programs that support strong collaborative communities often provide incentives for collaborative planning and teaching, support and insist on the development of coherent curriculum within and across programs, and organize professional development grounded in discussions about teaching (see, for example, Ross and Bondy, 1996). School-based programs that create these conditions have typically allocated resources for collaboration and planning for all personnel, as well as for those directly engaged in instructing and mentoring new teachers (Darling-Hammond, 1994; Snyder, 1999). University programs that have a strong community find ways to evaluate teaching, research, and service that take into account the time and energy required to engage in constructive collaboration (see, for example, Miller and Silvernail, 2000). In these programs, certain types of service, like program evaluation, are rewarded and valued (see, for example, Ross and Bondy, 1996; Koppich, 2000; Howey and Zimpher, 1989). In fact, Howey and Zimpher (1989) claim that effective school-based preparation programs have been sustained at Michigan State University's large teacher education program both because the education faculty has created human-scale collaborative communities for implementing preparation—communities that connect preservice faculty within the institution and connect university and school faculty—and because it has strategically used its commitment to research and development as a means for improving teacher education. (See "Using Collaborative Communities to Create Coherence at Michigan State University.")

Using Collaborative Communities to Create Coherence at Michigan State University

One challenge for large institutions of teacher education is the challenge of offering a personalized and coherent approach to preparation to large numbers of prospective teachers. Having exerted substantial leadership in the early Holmes Group initiatives, Michigan State University (MSU) took on the challenge of transforming its large, undifferentiated teacher education program in ways that could take advantage of what it had learned from its small alternative or "boutique" programs. The faculty and department heads concluded that their existing large programs were fragmented and rested on superficial knowledge, and they decided that new efforts should reflect current research on teaching and in teacher education as well as the notion of tying program emphases to major role demands on teachers and schools. A four-year planning and development period culminated in the creation of five alternative teacher education programs. Four of the programs, Academic Learning, Heterogeneous Classrooms, Learning Community, and Multiple Perspectives, were organized around conceptual themes. The intent was to break the one-size-fits-all view of teacher education and to promote programs that were more realistic in scope and more focused in their conceptions of how to teach.

As one example, the Multiple Perspectives Program was organized to provide a systematic, coherent program of experiences that would encourage teacher candidates from diverse academic areas to come together to study and reflect on the problems of teaching and learning, and to share in their development as professionals. Working together as a cohort in both their courses and in their field experiences, teacher candidates had numerous opportunities to learn from one another, their cooperating teachers, the university faculty, and field instructors. Reflective thinking and practice were considered central to the Multiple Perspectives orientation in teacher education.

Regular evaluations have provided formative information that stimulated a number of significant changes in both structure and process. For example, a three-year study of the graduates in their first year of teaching involved interviews with program graduates and observations of their classrooms, along with debriefing sessions and interviews with each teacher's principal and selected colleagues. Findings showed that all of these respondents felt that the graduates, when compared with standard program first-year teachers, were better prepared to teach, more confident, better able to attend to student outcomes, more interactive with experienced teachers, and more capable of providing leadership in curriculum development activities during their first year of teaching. Principals agreed that these graduates were "thoughtful decision makers" (Howey and Zimpher, 1989).

Sharing Responsibility for Teacher Preparation

Reformers have increasingly realized that education faculty members are not the only professionals responsible for teacher preparation. In many cases, student teachers are faced with the challenge of integrating the seemingly disconnected experiences of the university and the school. In fact, teaching candidates often need to integrate four alien worlds: the departmentalized world of the arts and science disciplines; the pedagogical world of colleges of education; the world of school practice, where children and other teaching colleagues learn and work; and the world of children's communities, where the children and their families live. Bringing the caretakers of these worlds together to support the learning of future teachers has been another ongoing focus of reform efforts. Some would go so far as to assert that no teacher education program can succeed without the involvement of all of these: education faculty, arts and science faculty, faculty in K–12 schools, and parents and other community members.

The faculty in arts and sciences most often carry out the preparation for future teachers in undergraduate programs, but this function is rarely acknowledged and developed. These faculty introduce teachers to critical content, they demonstrate what it means to participate in a discipline, and they model teaching techniques that teachers emulate. The extent of influence of arts and sciences faculty in teacher education is especially pronounced, for example, in our two largest states, California and Texas, where education majors were abolished in earlier reforms. In California, all teacher education was moved to the postbaccalaureate level in 1970 (though prohibitions against undergraduate teacher education were removed in 2000); in Texas, students are typically limited to eighteen hours of education courses, completed late in the undergraduate program or at the graduate level. This means that for both elementary and secondary teachers, the overwhelming majority of courses are taken in arts and sciences, where students take the core courses of their bachelor's work, develop college-level reading and writing skills, learn critical thinking and analysis, and attain subject matter knowledge and understanding. Yet, it is not uncommon to find that most arts and sciences faculty feel little responsibility for the preparation of teachers through the courses they teach.

The work of national reform efforts such as the National Network for Educational Renewal (NNER), the Arts and Sciences/Teacher Education Collaborative (ASTEC), Project 30, the Renaissance Group, and the Holmes Group has focused on the need for faculty in education and the arts and sciences to work together, sharing the responsibility for the production of effective new teachers. For example, as part of the Project 30 Alliance, teams of faculty from arts and sciences and education at each institution work on the reform of the liberal arts component of teacher preparation to address five themes: subject matter understanding; general and liberal education; pedagogical content knowledge; multicultural, international, and other human perspectives; and recruitment into teaching. The Renaissance Group, like the others, has adopted operating principles that affirm the importance of the education of teachers as an all-campus responsibility, a campus culture that values and models quality teaching, the creation of partnerships with practicing professionals, the extensive use of field experiences in diverse settings, the adherence to high standards and accountability, a focus on student learning, the effective use of technology, and the development of teachers as creative and innovative leaders. The National Network for Educational Renewal and the Holmes Group subscribe to similar goals and, additionally, strongly emphasize the importance of school–university partnerships so that teachers connect theory and practice in their clinical work and so that the ongoing improvement of schools is tightly tied to the ongoing improvement of teacher education.

Schools that have sought stronger ties between arts and sciences faculty and teacher education faculty have attempted a range of strategies, including jointly taught or parallel content and content pedagogical courses that help candidates think with some immediacy about how they would teach the subject matter about which they are learning. Seminars on teaching among arts and sciences and teacher education faculty have been used as venues for comparing and developing shared ideas about the purposes of content understanding and strategies for teaching. Professional development school relationships have provided a venue for subject matter specialists to participate with teacher educators in supporting veteran teacher learning as well as student teacher practice. And pedagogical support centers on campuses have contributed to the honing of teaching skills for faculty across the campus, creating greater consciousness about the essential integration of pedagogical concerns into the teaching of content for both faculty and prospective teachers alike.

A number of universities have created a new locus of activity that allows for collaboration among all of the important actors affecting teacher education.

For example, Patterson, Michelli, and Pacheco (1999) document reform efforts at three very different institutions that prepare large numbers of teachers—Montclair State University in Newark, New Jersey, Brigham Young University in Utah, and the University of Texas at El Paso—which involved the development of partnerships with businesses, nearby school districts, other university faculty, and community members including parents. Each of these institutions took steps to institutionalize the concept that teacher education had to be shared across faculty in education, arts and science, and the schools.

Each also included a role for the community. This allowed the emergence of new questions. For example, "Are schools smooth extensions of the learning that goes on first in families and communities, or do they represent a disjuncture in the experience of children? Are schoolhouses places where parents and community members take great pride and ownership, or are they places that are alien and unwelcoming? Are teachers comfortable and familiar with the full lives of the children in their care, or are they unaware of the daily experience of children and uncomfortable and sometimes frightened by the communities from which the children come? Do parents and teachers recognize their common purpose in the achievement and well being of the children, or do they approach each other as antagonists working toward different ends?" Seeking input from parents and community members in the design and implementation of teacher education is one way to develop more productive answers to these kinds of questions.

These institutions developed a "center of pedagogy" to create new space where teacher education occurs. In surveying similar efforts across the country at more than a dozen colleges and universities, a series of "qualities" emerged that characterized such centers. These qualities include:

- A partnership among faculty in the p-12 schools, arts and sciences, and education based on a history of collaboration, mutual trust, shared vision, mutual interests, and parity.

- A common set of convictions regarding the purposes of schools in a democracy shared by faculty in education, arts and science, and the schools, and a shared vision guiding the design, implementation, and evaluation of programs in both the schools and university.

- A commitment to inquiry as central to the work of the center.

- A governance structure that permits the operations of the center in pursuit of its mission.

- Symbolic and financial support from existing leadership for the teacher education effort.

- Positive outcomes attributable to the presence of the center that are visible and considered important. (Patterson and others, 1999, pp. 206–211).

Using Collaboration and Inquiry to Support Curriculum Renewal at Montclair State University

Montclair State University's history is similar to many state universities (Patterson and others, 1999). It started as a normal school and like many universities, at various times, the function of preparing teachers was central to its purpose and at other times, the growth of additional programs and departments obscured or discredited the teacher education work. Over the last twenty years, the most important part of Montclair's renewal process has been the refinement and extension of a shared vision of the teacher education among the many stakeholders responsible for teacher education. At Montclair, the college of education is no longer solely responsible for the quality of teachers who graduate from the university. Because the college has been joined with partners from the arts and sciences and from the public schools, the school of education now has a more realistic mission, roles, and responsibility. Through discussions and retreats, stakeholders in the program developed a mission around the framework of critical thinking, access to knowledge, nurturing pedagogy, stewardship of best practice, and enculturation into a political and social democracy. A clear statement of expectations for students, the "Portrait of a Teacher," emerged as a framework for recruitment, admission, curricular planning, certification decisions, and professional development. A central activity in the renewal effort was inquiry among the faculty in education, the arts and sciences, and the public schools into pedagogy, the education of educators, and the purposes of schools. Among the many forms this activity took were the establishment of teacher study groups in partner schools and at the university, the evolution of renewal grants to support more sustained study and change in settings, and inquiry projects growing out of a local leadership associates program. Partner schools within each district were sources for recruiting clinical faculty. Schools were invited to become professional development schools when they showed a commitment to educating for a democracy.

A democratic leadership was established within the Center of Pedagogy at Montclair State University, and the University redesigned its faculty reward system. Faculty evaluations were focused on (1) teaching, (2) the scholarship of pedagogy, (3) the scholarship of discovery, (4) integration, or aesthetic creation, and (5) the scholarship of application. The success Montclair has enjoyed has been credited to the stability of leadership in the university, the establishment of networks, an emphasis on reconnecting knowledge and practice, the reconciliation of turf concerns with a sense of shared responsibility, and, most important, the development of a shared vision among all the stakeholders.

The tripartite partnership and collaboration among arts and sciences, education, and school-based faculty increases the probability of a coherent approach to preparation that is more powerful as its efforts are mutually reinforcing. Typically, education faculty must take the lead in building the consensus and shared vision necessary to bring these parties together. Agencies such as the National Council for Accreditation of Teacher Education (NCATE) encourage this effort by requiring that there be such a vision in the form of a conceptual framework that is shared among members of the teacher education community. Many schools of education have reported that the accreditation process was the stimulus for the development of a more coherent framework and more effective collaboration in the education of teachers, as well as dedication of more resources (National Commission on Teaching and America's Future, 1996, p. 71; Patterson and others, 1999; Williams, 2000).

Creating Strong School–University Partnerships

In addition to their leading roles in admission decisions, teaching foundational and pedagogical classes, setting up and monitoring student placements in internships, and monitoring the learning process, a number of schools of education are also developing preparation and ongoing professional development initiatives that strengthen partnerships with local schools. A number of new program designs, such as professional development schools, have been adopted by universities and school districts and are supported by school leaders concerned with strengthening professional learning. These allow college faculty and K–12 faculty to work together closely to develop more integrative approaches to teacher preparation.

As we describe in Chapter Eleven, more than 1,000 PDS partnerships have emerged across the nation as sites for student teaching and, sometimes, internships for beginning teachers. The sometimes-realized hope is that in these sites, novices will encounter state-of-the-art practice under intensive supervision so that they learn to teach diverse learners effectively, rather than merely to cope, or even to leave the profession, as so many do. Such schools also provide venues for developing the knowledge base for teaching by becoming places in which practice-based and practice-sensitive research can be carried out collaboratively by teachers, teacher educators, and researchers (Darling-Hammond, 1994, pp. 1–2). By creating settings that merge theoretical and practical learning, PDSs may help transmit a common set of expectations that link preparation and practice. In addition, they are a response to the age-old problem of educational change: if teacher educators prepare teachers for schools as they are, they will be unable to teach more effectively or help schools become more effective than the status quo permits. PDSs create a means to prepare teachers for schools that do not currently exist in large numbers by combining the work of preservice education, staff development, and school restructuring (Fullan, 1993a).

Although some professional development school initiatives have generated stronger outcomes for candidates and their students than traditional preparation programs (see Chapter Eleven), not all have been equally successful. Many have been projects at the margins of each institution rather than an intervention in the core of both. Among the challenges are forging a joint vision for teaching and an agenda for change, creating parity among the partners, developing joint work focused on classroom practice, and finding ways to support the work from institutional resources rather than "soft" money. Studies suggest that successful initiatives have required a long-term commitment among universities and districts that see a mutual self-interest and have worked to articulate and enact common goals based on mutual respect, a negotiated vision of practice, and a clear focus on what kind of preservice and inservice training is required to help both parties develop more powerful supports for this kind of practice (Darling-Hammond, 1994).

Fullan (1993a, pp. 121–123) describes a related kind of initiative among four school districts and two large universities in Toronto, Canada, which initiated a new field-based teacher education program linked to induction, mentoring, professional development, and school restructuring. Key to this initiative was a common focus on collaborative learning guiding the content of preparation, professional development, and school improvement. This provided a concrete, shared focus for the initial work of the consortium. In addition, each partner committed to a six-year renewable term of participation and invested $20,000 annually to generate a base budget to keep the work going. Serious work on these kinds of partnerships requires an institutionally grounded model of educational change that differs from most transitory project-oriented efforts of the past.

Strong partnerships have also been created in some successful alternative teacher certification programs. One of the benefits of such programs, when they are well designed, is that they can help to integrate the worlds of study and practice and create a more integrated preparation experience (Miller, McKenna, and McKenna, 1998; National Commission on Teaching and America's Future, 1996, p. 93). (See "Commitment to Partnership: New Haven School District's Intern Program with CSU-Hayward.")

Commitment to Partnership: New Haven School District's Intern Program with CSU-Hayward

Some of the most successful alternative routes to teacher certification are built on exceptionally strong partnerships. In 1993, for example, the New Haven Unified School District, an urban district located in Union City, California, a few miles from Oakland, joined with California State University at Hayward (CSUH) to design the Single Subject Partnership Program (SSPP). SSPP is an innovative combined preservice and internship program based in district secondary schools that simultaneously educates teachers while providing a quality education for students. Its candidates are well prepared and much sought after. As one noted: "I reluctantly looked for a credential program knowing that I just had to fulfill this requirement to become a teacher . . . In the last two months, I have radically changed my mind about the lack of opportunities for excellence in education and training for future teachers. I consider myself lucky to be part of the cohort at New Haven. Being in the program has already been a rewarding experience. Indeed, prospective employers seriously consider my candidature because I am being educated in New Haven" (Snyder, 1999, p. 45).

New Haven personnel manager Jim O'Laughlin, who was involved in the development of the program, noted that "The uniqueness of our program is based on the unique collaborative relationship we have developed with Cal. State Hayward. This is dependent upon their willingness to collaborate and truly partner with a school district in teacher preparation" (Snyder, 1999, p. 45). The curriculum is jointly planned and delivered by university professors and district faculty to provide for close articulation of district, school, and university activities. Because of the full integration of university and district in the preparation program, it is difficult to distinguish "university components" from "school components" of the program. With the exception of the content-specific pedagogy courses, SSPP teacher candidates remain in their cohort, participating in coursework and field experiences in the district. This serves both as a convenience for candidates and as a connection between theory and practice.

Potential teacher education candidates apply for admission into the CSUH program in the spring prior to their entry into the program. Candidates who note an interest in one of CSUH's local internships are interviewed by both university and school district staff. Those who are admitted begin study in June and complete several weeks of intensive workshops cotaught by New Haven and CSUH faculty. These use the California Standards for the Teaching Profession to focus on the children and their learning in relation to teaching and the design of learning environments. This introductory work reflects the strong relationships, common knowledge, and shared beliefs that exist among school- and university-based faculty. The "summer" ends with the student teachers joining New Haven's new teachers for a five-day district-sponsored orientation that includes working with veteran teachers at the school site.

The selection of part-time interns, who teach one or two periods per day under supervision, is made after at least a month of intensive work with the candidate that allows for careful screening. These interns continue student teaching during other periods and take courses with the other candidates who are engaged in student teaching and coursework. The intern's partner teacher, the SSPP district team leader, and site-based mentor teachers work with each intern in a well-supported, collaborative lesson planning process. During September, when New Haven schools are in session but CSUH is not, candidates have twice weekly after-school seminars coplanned and enacted by school and university-based educators. Once candidates begin attending CSUH methods classes, these onsite seminars occur weekly.

In addition, interns are formally observed three times each semester by the house principal, three times by the district team leader, two to four times by their partner teacher, and twice monthly by their university supervisor. The different perspectives ensure that the program does not become an idiosyncratic apprenticeship but rather professional education. In order to assure that interns can "make sense" of the different feedback (and to assure that interns receive the support they and their students require), New Haven and CSUH clearly articulate roles and responsibilities for the key support providers in their program.

Jim Zarrillo, former Chair of the CSUH Department of Teacher Education, observes of this university–district collaboration: "New Haven identifies teacher preparation as part of their reason for being, as much as teaching third graders how to write in cursive. This is the Shangri-La of partnerships" (Snyder, 1999, p. 65).

Although there are certainly differences among the roles and responsibilities of the many groups responsible for teacher learning (school faculty, education faculty, arts and sciences faculty, and community members), more institutions are finding ways for these parties to work collaboratively toward a shared vision for education in a democracy. In the following sections, we discuss further how institutional contexts and policies can support the relationships that can sustain curriculum renewal in teacher education.

FACING CHALLENGES AND OVERCOMING OBSTACLES

Although we have highlighted some successful programs, we do not suggest that change is easy. The process of renewal and transformation poses many challenges. Whereas strong programs tend to support collaboration, offer professional development for faculties, and have supportive, democratic leadership (see, for example, Zeichner, 2000; Howey and Zimpher, 1989; Patterson and others, 1999), efforts to create these conditions can run into a host of difficulties. Within school districts, these include competition for scarce time and resources that need to be devoted to the education of children; uneven knowledge and lack of shared professional norms among staff members, especially those that have the greatest difficulty recruiting and retaining teachers and principals; and lack of rewards for professional learning. Within universities, obstacles include an emphasis on individual performance rather than collaboration; lack of recognition in tenure and promotion decisions for curriculum and program development and evaluation activities; conflicting ideologies regarding the means and ends of schooling and of preparation that are not discussed or reconciled; lack of support for professional development for faculty; lack of resources for teacher education; and lack of support for innovations unless they are led from the top (Zeichner, 1983; Zeichner and Liston, 1990). In both institutional settings, leaders can sometimes find change processes problematic, viewing dissenters as disloyal or troublesome, rather than helpful.

It is useful that many successful programs that have confronted these and other obstacles have been willing to step forward and critically reflect on their challenges as well as their successes. These programs have documented the difficulties they have experienced as they endeavored to develop quality teacher preparation programs (see, for example, Delpit, 1995; Johnston, 1997; Sockett, 2001; SooHoo and Wilson, 1994; Ross and Bondy, 1996). For example, Sockett (2001) describes the resistance to change that he encountered with both university administration and education faculty in developing a nontraditional school-based professional development program. Marilyn Johnston (1997) discusses the complexity of school–university collaborations in *Contradictions in Collaboration,* written in collaboration with K–12 colleagues. Ross and Bondy

(1996) illustrate the problems of reform in an incoherent policy context, describing how their program overcame a problem the faculty faced when the state initiated an induction program that included the use of an observation instrument that was in conflict with knowledge about teacher development and effective teaching in different contexts. Challenges in creating professional development schools have been documented in several studies, along with strategies for addressing these (Darling-Hammond, 1994; Guadarrama and others, 2001).

These and other accounts describe the difficulties of maintaining a cohesive program in the face of institutional pressures and external policies that create strong centripetal forces. In the long run, it is not realistic to expect that much long-term systemic change will result from heroic efforts in hostile environments. If the preparation of teachers is to improve on a wide scale, it is critical to consider how environmental supports for strong teacher education can be strengthened within institutions and local, state, and federal policy contexts.

Institutional Supports for Collaborative Teacher Education

Successful partnerships in support of teacher preparation of the sort we described earlier typically have the support, and often a mandate, from university provosts and presidents who accept the notion that the responsibility for the production of effective new teachers is one of the entire university, not colleges of education alone (Goodlad, 1994). They often demonstrate this commitment through the quick arbitration of faculty turf wars and the thoughtful allocation of faculty resources and program funding to support collaboration within the university as well as collaboration with the field. Both incentive structures and resources are critical to this end.

Institutional Incentives

The traditional university model of rewarding scholarship, teaching, and service often is not flexible enough to reward the important work that goes on with and in K–12 schools or the collaboration needed to create a coherent curriculum. Goodlad (1994) suggests that this kind of program development is "very difficult and demanding and offers few tangible rewards. Indeed, extensive involvement is dangerous to one's career" (p. 154). This is especially true when institutions emphasize scholarship as more important, or more easily measured, than teaching and service, as is frequently the case.

One effort to reconceptualize the way universities think about scholarship was undertaken by Ernest Boyer in *Scholarship Reconsidered.* Boyer (1990) suggested that there are different kinds of scholarship that should be encouraged and honored by universities, including scholarship of discovery, of integration, of application, and of teaching. He argued that traditional scholarship usually focuses on discovery and integration rather than application. The work that faculty undertake in schools, engaging in research for program improvement, working to improve teaching, and evaluating curricula often can be conceived of as "scholarship of application." The American Association for Higher Education has engaged in a concerted effort to encourage this reconsideration of the meaning of scholarship. Where it has been applied to education, faculty members have been able to engage in work in teacher education and school renewal, write about the work (sometimes with school colleagues), and have it assessed and considered toward reappointment, tenure, and promotion. Interestingly, arts and science faculty have embraced the changed conceptions at some institutions at a higher rate than faculty in education. Faculty in anthropology have, for example, been able to gain recognition for their work in museums, and faculty in environmental sciences for their work related to the enhancement of habitats. Not every institution has a mission for which such reconsideration is appropriate, but it is possible for many institutions, and increasingly there are examples where this has occurred.

The lack of incentives applies to both university-based and school-based faculty. How does participating in teacher education bring rewards to public school faculty? Certainly there is the intrinsic reward of sustaining the profession and inducting new members into the profession. Many see that as an ethical and moral responsibility. But finding more extrinsic rewards for faculty in public schools has proved elusive. Beyond small honoraria or access to graduate courses, some institutions have made explicit the role of public school faculty in the preparation of teachers by making them "clinical faculty" of the university. With this comes access to the resources of the university, and an invitation to work as a colleague with the education and the arts and science faculty.

Schools and universities can also support faculty and encourage high standards by supporting the professional development of faculty. One of the most fully developed examples of professional development for the improvement of teacher education programs, linked to the improvement of schools, is the Leadership Associates Program of the National Network for Educational Renewal (NNER), a network of twenty-one school–university partnerships. Beginning in 1991, the Network recognized the need to establish a program to develop leaders within the settings with deep understanding of a vision for teacher education that includes the simultaneous renewal of schools and schools of education. Representatives of faculty in education, arts and sciences, and the schools, in approximately equal numbers, spent four sessions of five days each studying with facilitators in Seattle. Each participant completed an "inquiry project" with a focus on the application of the national work to a local problem. Replications of this experience produced more than 500 faculty leaders across the country, producing a valuable human resource for the work of teacher education development (Sirotnik, 2001).

Resources

Financial resources also matter. According to Howard, Hitz, and Baker (1998), "The perception held by many teacher educators is that the commitment by colleges and universities to education programs is weak and that funding for education lags behind that of other disciplines. This perception was validated by a national study in which expenditure data for education programs were compared to those of other academic disciplines." (p. 145). For each of the Carnegie classifications of universities, the average expenditures for education were below the average expenditures of other disciplines (p. 147). Like earlier studies, this one found that education programs were generally funded near the bottom ranks of departments—even many of those that do not have to manage clinical work and supervision—and well below the level of most other professional preparation programs (Howard and others, 1998; see also, Ebmeier, Twombly, and Teeter, 1991). These differentials are a function of both state funding that is allocated to state universities and to institutional allocations of resources. In addition, the National Center for Education Statistics reports that, on average, teacher educators receive lower salaries than other education faculty, who in turn, earn lower salaries than noneducation faculty (National Center for Education Statistics, 1997a, p. 31). The results of underfunding can include extremely heavy teaching and supervisory loads for faculty and staff, inadequate incentives and supports for clinical work and faculty, lack of time for collaboration and research, and a depressing influence on the overall quality of faculty who can be recruited.

Moral suasion regarding the importance of preparing teachers has been effective in securing more adequate commitments on some campuses. Increases in funding for teacher education in research universities—which now surpass the investments in teacher education of other kinds of universities (Howard and others, 1998)—occurred during the time efforts were underway by the Holmes Group and others to elevate the status and quality of preparation programs in these institutions. However, these influences appear to wax and wane with the tenures of deans and presidents, leaving the enterprise as a whole still noticeably underresourced. Policy is also implicated, as states generally provide support to public colleges and universities for programs of higher education, and they typically allocate higher reimbursement ratios for programs in other professions than they do for programs of teacher education. As we describe later, the lack of well-enforced standards for program quality—a factor that sets teaching apart from other professions with mandatory accreditation—is another depressing influence on resources.

An additional issue is the problem of collaboration between schools and universities when funding streams are targeted separately to each sector for specific purposes that do not include such innovations as professional development schools or other partnerships. Some states, however, have sought to address these disincentives. For example, North Carolina created legislation to fund professional development school partnerships launched by each university in the state. Like a few other states, it also required NCATE accreditation of all public colleges and universities and helped support the costs of acquiring accreditation, seeking to leverage change through both higher standards and explicit supports for partnerships.

Over the last twenty years, many foundations have invested funds in support of the development of more powerful schools of education. Most recently and noticeably, the Carnegie Corporation of New York has launched an initiative entitled Teachers for a New Era, which is designed to develop model teacher education programs at selected colleges and universities. Grants of up to $5 million for a period of five years are intended to support innovative reforms. Central design features include a focus on teaching as clinical practice that begins in preservice preparation and continues during a two-year residency period for graduates; the importance of formal collaboration between schools of education, traditional arts and sciences faculty, and classroom teachers; and documentation of teaching practices and pupil learning associated with teacher education.

These models are intended to inform the field in much the same way that the Johns Hopkins' medical school and teaching hospital provided a model for the reform of medical education. The availability of grants for change from foundations and places like the National Science Foundation and Department of Education have made a major difference in both the development and the improvement of teacher preparation programs by supporting infusions of technology, changes in curriculum, and the development of field-based connections. A number of thoughtful alternative programs also have been created, from the time of MAT programs in the 1970s to midcareer training programs today. Yet, studies have found that many of these programs vanish within a fairly short period (Darling-Hammond, Hudson, and Kirby, 1987; Fullan, 1991, 1993a). For successful models to be sustained in the places they have been planted and potentially useful for other institutions, the problem of ongoing resource provision must be addressed through policy that enables the maintenance of high-quality training. Such ongoing support has been built into the governmental and third-party payer systems upon which medical and nursing schools rely. Similar policies are needed for teacher education.

Policy Issues in the Improvement of Teacher Education

As adequate education is increasingly viewed as a student right rather than an option, and as the importance of teaching to student achievement is increasingly clear, students' guaranteed access to well-prepared teachers is an issue of growing concern. Critical policy issues include how to ensure that teachers get access to adequate opportunities to learn, how to encourage the spread of more productive approaches to preparing teachers, and how to support the continued advancement and use of knowledge in the field.

Policy in Support of Teacher Recruitment and Improved Preparation

In pursuing these goals, federal and state governments can play a direct role by establishing and enforcing elementary and secondary students' rights to school resources, including qualified teachers, and by investing in the education of teachers, for example, by subsidizing candidates' studies and by leveraging program improvements. The relevance of these investments to improved teacher education is twofold. First, one major reason that many candidates do not get access to adequate preparation is that they cannot afford either the tuition or the opportunity costs of being without employment for a period of time. Furthermore, these costs are harder to bear when a recruit is entering a profession that does not promise large salaries later to compensate for loans taken earlier. Whereas many countries fully subsidize an extensive program of teacher education for all candidates, the amount of preparation secured by teachers in the United States is left substantially to what they can individually afford and what programs are willing and able to offer given the resources of their respective institutions.

Second, researchers have found that institutions pressured to prepare working teachers who have entered teaching on emergency permits often have to water down the quality of preparation they provide, skipping student teaching, key areas of content, and ambitious assignments (Shields and others, 2001). Both recruits and employers find this kind of training less satisfactory than a more coherent, supportive experience that includes supervised clinical training along with more thoughtfully organized coursework (California State University, 2002a, 2002b; Shields and others, 2001). Better financial supports for teachers in training will also support the quality of training they receive.

This can be accomplished by drawing in large part on the federal experience with medical manpower programs. Since 1944, the federal government has subsidized medical training and facilities to meet the needs of underserved populations, to fill shortages in particular fields, to improve the quality of training, and to increase diversity in the medical profession. The federal government also collects data to monitor and plan for medical personnel needs. This consistent and sizable commitment has contributed significantly to America's world-renowned system of medical training and care.

Although the teacher labor market is also vital to the nation's future, federal efforts in this area have tended to be modest, fragmented, and inconsistent over time. The federal government has periodically adopted programs to enhance teacher supply, but these have not continued on the scale and with the targeting needed to address the problems noted. There has been little investment in developing a national system to monitor the teacher labor market. There have been scarce efforts to develop the capacity of training institutions to improve practice and to ensure teacher supplies in high-demand locales and fields. And there has been no serious attempt to establish comprehensive federal-state partnerships like those created to meet specific health-field shortages and to improve program quality (Darling-Hammond and Sykes, 2003).

To address these needs, Darling-Hammond and Sykes (2003) propose a comprehensive policy approach that would provide (1) a substantial, ongoing program of scholarships and forgivable loans to support individuals who prepare to teach in shortage fields and locations; (2) investments in urban and rural teacher education programs that expand the availability of high-quality training in high-need locations, including the training of candidates in professional development schools that will enable prospective teachers to learn to teach well in schools that serve diverse student populations; (3) mentoring for beginning teachers to increase their retention in teaching; and (4) efforts to reduce interstate barriers to mobility associated with patchwork licensing systems, lack of pension portability, and lack of information.

Some states, like North Carolina and Connecticut, have already developed elements of this approach with positive outcomes, supporting large-scale scholarships and forgivable loans for teacher recruitment; investments in program improvements, including financial support for professional development schools and mentoring supports for beginners; and supporting higher and more equalized teacher salaries that enable districts to compete in the labor market for well-prepared teachers (Darling-Hammond, 2000a). But teacher labor markets are now national, and state efforts must be augmented by purposeful federal action to create a national teacher supply policy that attends as well to quality.

Professional Policy

Some researchers argue that, although there are direct governmental roles in support of teacher education, like those described earlier, the most appropriate role for government is indirect (Elmore and Fuhrman, 1993; Thompson and Zeuli, 1999). These analysts suggest that development of teaching knowledge that is made widely available to teachers to support high-quality teaching is not something that can be easily mandated or bureaucratically enforced. Because knowledge is always growing and its appropriate application is contingent on many different factors, the process of developing and transmitting a complex knowledge base and ensuring its appropriate use is, many believe, better managed by members of the profession itself.

The genre of policymaking that delegates substantial authority to a profession while holding the profession more accountable for the outcomes of its actions might be called "professional policy." This kind of policy relies more on professional standard-setting than direct regulation by the state. It emphasizes the development of expertise to be used for problem solving rather than the imposition of standardized prescriptions for practice that impede teachers' ability to handle the diversity. As Richard Elmore and Susan Fuhrman (1993) note: "As equality of opportunity comes to rest more squarely on the need for quality instruction, issues of how to enhance the professional competence of educators become more important. To ensure equal opportunity in today's context means enhancing, not limiting, the professional nature of teaching, and for that task state policy as it has been conceived in the past is hardly the best instrument. We need new ways of conceiving the state role and of the strategies at the state's disposal" (p. 86).

In organized professions, the major lever for profession-wide transfer of knowledge and continual improvement is the use of standards to guide preparation and practice. Most professions set and enforce standards through (1) professional accreditation of preparation programs; (2) state licensing, which grants permission to practice and is managed through state professional standards boards; and (3) advanced certification, which is a professional recognition of high levels of competence. In virtually all professions, candidates must graduate from an accredited professional school in order to sit for state licensing examinations that test their knowledge and skill. The accreditation process is meant to ensure that all preparation programs provide a reasonably common body of knowledge and structured training experiences that are comprehensive and up-to-date. Licensing examinations are meant to ensure that candidates have acquired the knowledge they need to practice responsibly. The tests generally include both surveys of specialized information and performance components that examine aspects of applied practice in the field: lawyers must analyze cases and, in some states, develop briefs or memoranda of law to address specific issues; doctors must diagnose patients via case histories and describe the treatments they would prescribe; engineers must demonstrate that they can apply certain principles to particular design situations. These examinations are developed by members of the profession through state professional standards boards.

In addition, many professions offer additional examinations that provide recognition for advanced levels of skill, such as certification for public accountants, board certification for doctors, and registration for architects. This recognition generally takes extra years of study and practice, often in a supervised internship and/or residency, and is based on performance tests that measure greater levels of specialized knowledge and skill. Those who have met these standards are then allowed to do certain kinds of work that other practitioners cannot. The certification standards inform the other sets of standards governing accreditation, licensing, and relicensing: they are used to ensure that professional schools incorporate new knowledge into their courses and to guide professional development and evaluation throughout the career. Thus these advanced standards may be viewed as an engine that pulls along the knowledge base of the profession. Together, standards for accreditation, licensing, and certification comprise a "three-legged stool" (National Commission on Teaching and America's Future, 1996) that supports quality assurance in the mature professions.

This three-legged stool has been fairly wobbly in teaching. Until recently, there was no national body to establish a system of professional certification. Meanwhile, states have managed licensing and the approval of teacher education programs with uneven involvement of the profession itself, using widely varying standards and generally weak enforcement tools. Since the 1920s, most states have licensed teachers based primarily on their graduation from a state-approved teacher education program. Thus a critical check on quality that exists in other professions—a system for individual candidate assessment against some common standards of knowledge and skill—was missing for many decades in teaching. The program approval process, generally coordinated by the state's department of education, typically assessed "the types of learning situations to which an individual is exposed and . . . the time spent in these situations, rather than . . . what the individual actually learned" (Goertz, Ekstorm, and Coley, 1984).

Admitting individuals into practice based on their graduation from a state-approved program was a wholesale approach to licensing—one that assumed program quality could be well defined and monitored by states; that programs would be equally effective with all of their students; and that completion of the courses or experiences mandated by the state would be sufficient to produce competent practitioners. The state approval system also assumed that markets for teachers were local: that virtually all teachers for the schools in a given state would be produced by colleges within that state, a presumption that has become increasingly untrue over time. Much of the hiring of unprepared teachers in communities that claim shortages is really a function of the maldistribution of teachers between and among states and districts with surpluses and those with lower levels of supply (Darling-Hammond and Sykes, 2003).

One problem with state approval of teacher education, even as stronger standards have been developed, is that many state education agencies have inadequate budgetary resources and personpower to conduct the intensive program reviews that would support enforcement of high standards (Campbell, Sroufe, and Layton, 1967; David, 1994; Lusi, 1997). Another problem is that, even when state agencies find weak programs, political forces within states make it difficult to close them down. Teacher education programs bring substantial revenue to universities and local communities, and the availability of large numbers of teaching candidates, no matter how poorly prepared, keeps salaries relatively low. As Dennison (1992) notes, "The generally minimal state-prescribed criteria remain subject to local and state political influences, economic conditions within the state, and historical conditions which make change difficult." For various reasons, then, the traditional system of teacher licensing based upon completion of specified courses in state-approved programs of study has left most practitioners, members of the public, and policymakers unconvinced that licensing standards separate out those who can teach responsibly from those who cannot. Furthermore, this system has not provided a strong means for growing and transmitting knowledge in the field or for the widespread improvement of programs.

In contrast to other professions, teachers have traditionally had little control in creating, promulgating, and enforcing professional standards. Instead, authority for determining the nature of teacher education, the types and content of licensure tests, and the regulations that govern practice has typically been held by state legislatures, state departments of education, and state boards of higher education, as well as private commercial enterprises (Darling-Hammond, 2001a). With myriad agencies involved in teacher policy, the regulatory context for teacher preparation in which many states operate is complex and often contradictory.

For two decades, major reports calling for the professionalization of teaching have argued that teachers must engage in professional standard-setting if teaching is to make good on the promise of competence that professions make to the public (Carnegie Forum, 1986; Holmes Group, 1986). Teacher education leaders have suggested that teachers and teacher educators "must take greater control over their own destiny. A powerful place where this can be done is in standards-setting. Professionals must define high standards, set rigorous expectations, and then hold peers to these standards and expectations" (Imig, 1992).

Efforts by the profession to develop and implement more meaningful standards for teaching have been led primarily by the National Board for Professional Teaching Standards, an independent organization established in 1987 as the first professional body—composed of a majority of classroom teachers—to set standards and develop performance assessments for the advanced certification of highly accomplished teachers. Some well-designed studies have found that, indeed, the National Board's standards and assessments do distinguish more effective from less effective teachers, in terms of teachers' influences on student achievement (Goldhaber and Anthony, 2004; Bond, Jaeger, Smith, and Hattie, 2001).

The Interstate New Teacher Assessment and Support Consortium (INTASC), a consortium of more than thirty states, built upon this effort to develop "National Board-compatible" licensing standards and assessments for beginning teachers, which have been adapted by most states. The National Council for Accreditation of Teacher Education (NCATE) recently incorporated the performance standards developed by INTASC and the National Board, as well as the new student standards developed by professional associations such as the National Council of Teachers of Mathematics (NCTM).

These new standards and assessments are built around the areas of knowledge and skill we have described in this volume. They take into explicit account the teaching challenges posed by the demands of ambitious subject matter and by a student body that is multicultural, multilingual, and that includes diverse approaches to learning. By examining teaching in the light of learning, they put considerations of effectiveness at the center of practice. These standards are also performance based—that is, they describe what teachers should know, be like, and be able to do rather than listing courses that teachers should take—thus seeking to clarify the criteria for determining competence, placing more emphasis on the abilities teachers develop than the hours they spend taking classes.

Some states have incorporated this set of standards into their governance and incentive systems for teacher education as a means of bringing coherence and focus to their efforts to prepare teachers. For example, North Carolina recognized National Board Certification in its statewide salary schedule, created a professional standards board upon which Board-certified teachers sit, adopted the INTASC standards for teacher licensing and developed beginning teacher assessments based on the standards, and required all public colleges of education to be NCATE-accredited. This kind of approach is based on the belief that common standards can "clarify what the profession expects its members to get better at . . . Profession-defined standards provide the basis on which the profession can lay down its agenda and expectations for professional development and accountability" (Ingvarson, 1998, p. 1).

A number of other states have pursued similar strategies, and many colleges and universities have used these standards as the basis for organizing their curriculum efforts (Darling-Hammond, 2001a; Patterson and others, 1999). However, the development and use of professionally derived standards to govern teaching teacher education has been somewhat contentious. (For a review, see Darling-Hammond, 2001a.)

Standards for Programs. The question of accreditation has been perhaps the most controversial. Although required accreditation has been the major vehicle for transmitting knowledge and standards of practice across schools in fields like medicine, law, and engineering, professional teacher education accreditation has been voluntary in most states. Currently, forty-one states have partnerships with NCATE and fifteen require the use of NCATE standards for approval of all schools of education; however, only three require all education schools to be professionally accredited. About half of the nation's schools of education—educating about three-fourths of the nation's teachers—are in the NCATE system. Whereas advocates of accreditation are convinced that accreditation is necessary to create a more common knowledge base and to leverage the needed resources for quality preparation, opponents complain about the costs and hassle involved in undergoing accreditation. Many strained schools of education view accreditation as another bureaucratic hurdle that they do not have time to implement appropriately. Some university leaders and faculty resent the lack of autonomy suggested by the existence of external standards, especially when they consider these requirements from the vantage point of an arts and sciences department rather than that of a professional school accustomed to the unique expectations society demands of professions.

Accreditation also poses local risks: a substantial proportion of institutions that volunteer for NCATE accreditation fail fully to achieve it on their initial attempt (about 25 percent are conditionally approved or disapproved). NCATE has been criticized by some for having standards that are too difficult to achieve and by others for having standards that are too low. A paradox of the voluntary accreditation situation is that standards can never be raised beyond a level most can achieve with modest effort so long as institutions must decide whether or not to sit for accreditation. Whereas many colleges that have decided or been required to sit for accreditation have reported associated improvements in their faculty, resource base, curriculum design, and clinical work (see, for example, National Commission on Teaching and America's Future, 1996, p.71; Williams, 2000), others have felt that the process was time-consuming and did not stimulate major change in their institutions.

An alternative accrediting body, the Teacher Education Accreditation Council (TEAC), plans to accredit schools, colleges, and departments of education based on their performance in relation to their own objectives rather than common professional standards. In contrast to NCATE's governing body, which includes representatives of thirty professional associations of teachers, administrators, and teacher educators, TEAC does not include organizational representation from the teaching profession. It eschews professional standards in favor of an inquiry process in which institutions will engage to document their work and its outcomes in relation to goals that are valued by the institution. The hope of those who look to TEAC for further leverage on the improvement of teacher education is that it will, through the self-study process it champions, create a press for higher expectations and self-initiated change. Others voice concerns that a lack of external standards will allow programs to be complacent or even unaware of those elements of preparation important for teacher learning and ultimate success.

Both NCATE and TEAC have adopted an emphasis on tracking the outcomes of teacher education, although they approach the matter differently. This emphasis could prove productive, although as we describe later, the issue of how to assess teacher education outcomes is far from settled. The long-run question for the profession, with respect to these accrediting bodies as well as the state agencies also charged with approving programs, is how it will create the kind of force that operates in other professions to ensure that the programs that prepare teachers provide them with the opportunity to learn those things that their students need for them to know.

Standards for Candidates. Licensing is the legal means by which states establish the competence of members of professions, including teachers. It is meant to represent the minimum standard for responsible practice. In teaching, requirements for licensure typically include measures of basic skills and general academic ability, knowledge about teaching and learning, and subject matter knowledge, as well as some teaching experience. In many states, candidates for teaching must earn a minimum grade point average and/or achieve a minimum score on tests of basic skills, general academic ability, or general knowledge to be admitted to teacher education or gain a credential. In addition, they must take specific courses in education and complete a major or minor in the subject(s) to be taught and/or pass a subject matter test.

Although licensure requirements in many states have been strengthened during the past fifteen years, a number of states still do not require a coherent program of studies in the field to be taught, a comprehensive set of education coursework, or extended student teaching. Further, many states permit teachers to be hired without licenses or on emergency licenses without completing preparation or meeting other licensure requirements.

Standards for entry into teaching also vary based on the nature, content, and quality of the licensing examinations that candidates are required to pass. During 2001–2002, thirty-seven states required teaching candidates to pass tests of basic skills or general academic ability, thirty-three required them to pass tests of subject matter knowledge, and twenty-six required them to pass tests of pedagogical knowledge (Youngs, Odden, and Porter 2003). Whereas other professions control the content of licensure tests, teaching examinations are usually developed by testing companies or state agencies with little input from formal professional bodies. When it is solicited, input from practitioners is usually limited to reviewing test categories and items. Further, licensure tests have been criticized for oversimplifying teaching, emphasizing classroom management over the complexities of instructional decision making, and having an adverse impact on racial minorities (Haertel, 1991; Porter and others, 2001).

Although most teacher tests are multiple-choice assessments of basic skills or subject matter knowledge, some states require beginning teachers to complete subject-specific portfolios or other performance assessments in order to earn a teaching license. These assessments, modeled on those of the National Board for Professional Teaching Standards, more authentically measure candidates' ability to integrate knowledge of content, students, and context in making instructional decisions. For example, as we described in Chapter Eleven, second-year teachers in Connecticut compile portfolios that feature a description of their teaching context, a set of lesson plans, two videotapes of instruction during the unit(s), samples of student work, and written reflections on their planning, instruction, and assessment of student progress. Each completed portfolio reveals information about the logic and coherence of the teacher's curriculum, the appropriateness of their instructional decisions for students, the range of pedagogical strategies they use effectively, the quality of their assignments, their skill in assessing student learning, and their ability to reflect on their own teaching and make changes based on evidence of student learning (Wilson, Darling-Hammond, and Berry, 2001). Teacher education programs in Wisconsin and California have borrowed from this strategy to embed such portfolios in the teacher education process.

Some research suggests that the use of portfolios in licensing beginning teachers can support preparation program renewal focused on helping candidates attain important teaching abilities (Trascz and others, 1994; Wilson, Darling-Hammond, and Berry, 2001). Because the activities teachers engage in center around authentic tasks of teaching that are examined from the perspective of standards within the contexts of subject matter and students, they create a setting in which serious discourse about teaching can occur. Because evidence of the effects of teaching on student learning is at the core of the exercises, candidates and assessors are continually examining the nexus between teachers' actions and students' responses. Focusing on the outcomes of practice while making teaching public in this way creates the basis for developing shared norms of practice (Shulman, 1998).

Connecticut's process of implementing INTASC-based portfolios for beginning teacher licensing illuminates how this can occur. Connecticut's licensing system is designed equally as a professional development system and a measurement activity, and educators are involved in every aspect of its development and implementation, so that these opportunities are widespread. Each assessment is developed with the assistance of a teacher in residence in the department of education; advisory committees of teachers, teacher educators, and administrators guide the development of standards and assessments; hundreds of educators have been convened to provide feedback on drafts of the standards; and many more have been involved in the assessments themselves, as cooperating teachers and school-based mentors who work with beginning teachers on developing their practice, as assessors who are trained to score the portfolios, and as expert teachers who convene regional support seminars to help candidates learn about the standards and the portfolio development process. Individuals involved in each of these roles are engaged in preparation that is organized around the examination of cases and the development of evidence connected to the standards.

System developers Pecheone and Stansbury (1996) explain how the standards are used in professional development settings for beginning and veteran teachers:

> The state support and assessment system must be centered around standards that apply across contexts and that embrace a variety of teaching practices. Teaching is highly contextual, however, varying with the strengths and needs of students, strengths of the teacher, and the availability of resources. The support program needs to help beginning teachers see how to apply general principles in their particular teaching contexts. The design currently being implemented in the Connecticut secondary projects begins support sessions by modeling selected principles, then having teachers discuss work they have brought (e.g. a student assignment, a videotape illustrating discourse, student work samples) in light of the principles presented.
>
> For experienced teachers who will become the assessors and support providers the reverse is true. They typically understand contextual teaching practices well. Although they are acquainted with the general principles at some level because they keep abreast of developments in their teaching specialty, they do not generally have extensive experience in either articulating the principles to others or in seeing their application across multiple contexts. An intensive training program for both assessors and mentors ensures similar understandings among individuals and gives them opportunities to articulate how these principles are applied in classrooms. (pp. 172–173)

Teachers report that the process of analyzing practice in this way has transformational influences on their ongoing work. Embedded in state teacher assessment policy, these processes can have far-reaching effects. By one estimate, more than half of Connecticut's teachers have served as assessees, assessors, mentors, or cooperating teachers under either the earlier beginning teacher performance assessment or the new portfolios. By the year 2010, 80 percent of elementary teachers, and nearly as many secondary teachers, will have participated in the new assessment system as candidates, support providers, or assessors (Pecheone and Stansbury, 1996, p. 174).

In states like Indiana, North Carolina, or Maryland that have recently adopted a comprehensive approach to professional standards-based reform, a continuum for teacher development is formed by the requirement of professional accreditation for teacher education programs, the development and state funding of professional development school partnerships for the preparation of all prospective teachers, the adoption of INTASC standards and assessments for beginning teacher licensing, the establishment of financial and educational incentives for veteran teachers to pursue National Board Certification, and encouragement for school districts and colleges to use National Board standards as a basis for ongoing professional development opportunities. These steps hold promise for creating a profession-wide conversation and set of learning experiences across the continuum of lifelong learning that could dramatically transform the ways that teachers look at and develop their craft. The issue is how to marry these kinds of efforts with internal engines for change within schools and universities.

MOVING BEYOND BARRIERS: STRATEGIES FOR CURRICULUM RENEWAL

Fifteen years ago, the American Association of Colleges of Teacher Education (AACTE) published a book called *The Knowledge Base for the Beginning Teacher*. In that report, Henrietta Barnes (1989) stated that while "there is no unitary, bounded knowledge base for teaching on which everyone agrees, the body of knowledge from which teacher educators can draw in formulating an effective curriculum is substantial and growing" (p. 13). More than a decade later, teacher educators, expert practitioners, and scholars have come together in this committee to explore the elements of that evolving curriculum. In this report, we have endeavored to build on past efforts to offer teacher educators, researchers, and policymakers a set of grounded recommendations regarding central ideas and pedagogies that can inform the teacher education curriculum. These are based on what is currently understood about how students learn, the influences of teaching and schooling practices, how teachers learn and develop expertise in different contexts, and how teacher preparation practices influence teachers' learning, practice, retention in the profession, and success with students.

The field of education may be able to take some lessons from other professional fields, such as medicine, law, and engineering, that have endeavored to create a more cohesive and consistent knowledge base and enact it through the development of curriculum and pedagogy in their professional fields. However, teaching is also unique in its public purposes and status, as well as the kind of work teachers do in conjunction with students, who are primary actors themselves. Given the reciprocal and contingent nature of effective teaching, we have suggested that there are three areas of knowledge, skills, and dispositions that are critical for any teacher to acquire, including (1) knowledge of learners and how they learn and develop within social contexts, (2) conceptions of curriculum content and goals: an understanding of the subject matter and skills to be taught in light of the social purposes of education, and (3) an understanding of teaching in light of the content and learners to be taught, as informed by assessment and supported by classroom environments. We have described some of the teacher education approaches that are emerging to support this kind of teacher learning, including case methods, action research, community immersion, analysis of teaching and student learning, and portfolio development. And we have discussed some of the issues that arise when educators strive to develop and strengthen preparation programs, as well as some of the strategies that have been successfully used.

Among the factors that appear to be critical to a profession-wide change process, several seem particularly important: coherence in standards, clarity about curriculum, and commitment to act based on knowledge about what appears to be effective, as well as to add to and share such knowledge among programs as well as among teaching candidates. As we have noted, although there is a strong foundation of knowledge about how people learn and develop, and a robust base of knowledge about teaching practices that support learning, research about how teachers learn to do these things is more tentative. There is growing evidence about some of the things that teachers who are more effective know and can do, and some useful studies about preparation that is successful in promoting effective practice. However, there is much more to learn if we are to inform the ongoing development of well-grounded programs. In the future, the field needs to mount more well-controlled and larger-scale studies regarding the specific outcomes of a range of preparation strategies for different kinds of candidates and contexts.

In the long run, we suggest that those who are concerned about the ability of all teachers to teach all students well may be well advised to join their concerns about improvements within local schools and schools of education with a commitment to create policy environments that foster the development of powerful preparation for effective teaching. This will require the involvement not only of teacher educators but also of superintendents, principals, and practicing teachers who join forces to insist upon solid professional learning opportunities before and during their careers; parents and community members who understand the critical importance of investments in professional preparation for the educators of their children; university presidents, faculty, and trustees who commit to ensuring that education schools are central to the work of universities and comparable in quality to other professional schools; and policymakers who understand that, if American public education is to meet the aspirations this nation has assigned to it, the preparation of excellent teachers is the central commitment without which other reforms are unlikely to succeed.

REFERENCES

Abdal-Haqq, I. (1998). *Professional development schools: Weighing the evidence.* Thousand Oaks, CA: Corwin Press.

Adler, S. A. (1996). On case method and classroom management. *Action in Teacher Education, 18*(3), 33–43.

Agne, K. J., Greenwood, G. E., and Miller, L. D. (1994). Relationships between teacher belief systems and teacher effectiveness. *Journal of Research and Development in Education, 27*(3), 141–152.

Agnew, E. J. (1985, April). *The grading policies and practices of high school teachers.* Paper presented at the Annual Meeting of the American Educational Research Association, Chicago.

Airasian, P. W. (1996). *Assessment in the classroom.* New York: McGraw-Hill.

Aitchison, J. (1996). *The seeds of speech: Language origin and evolution.* New York: Cambridge University Press.

Akin, R. (2001). On my knees again. *Teacher Education Quarterly, 28*(3), 7–10.

Alexopoulou, E., and Driver, R. (1996). Small group discussion in physics: Peer interaction modes in pairs and fours. *Journal of Research in Science Teaching, 33*(10), 1099–1114.

Allen, J., Fabregas, V., Hankins, K. H., Hull, G., Labbo, L., Lawson, H. S., and others (2002). PhOLKS lore: Learning from photographs, families, and children. *Language Arts, 79*(4), 312–322.

Allen, J., and Labbo, L. (2001). Giving it a second thought: Making culturally engaged teaching culturally engaging. *Language Arts, 79*(1), 40–52.

Alvermann, D., and Moore, D. (1991). Secondary school reading. In R. Barr, M. Kamil, P. Mosenthal, and P. D. Pearson (Eds.), *Handbook of reading research* (Vol. II, pp. 951–983). New York: Longman.

American Association of Colleges for Teacher Education. (1997). *Selected data from the 1995 AACTE/NCATE joint data collection system.* Washington, DC: Author.

American Association of University Women. (1999). *Gender gaps: Where schools still fail our children.* New York: Marlowe and Co.

American Bar Association. (1980). *Law schools and professional education: A report and recommendations of the Special Committee for a Study of Legal Education of the American Bar Association.* Chicago: The Committee.

American Educational Research Association, American Psychological Association, National Council on Measurement in Education, and Joint Committee on Standards for Educational and Psychological Testing (U.S.). (1999). *Standards for educational and psychological testing.* Washington, DC: American Educational Research Association.

Ames, C. (1984). Competitive, cooperative, and individualistic goal structures: A cognitive-motivational analysis. In R. Ames and C. Ames (Eds.), *Research on motivation in education* (Vol. 1, pp. 177–207). Orlando, FL: Academic Press.

Ames, C. (1992). Classrooms: Goals, structures, and student motivation. *Journal of Educational Psychology, 84*(3), 261–271.

Amrein, A. L., and Berliner, D. C. (2002). High-stakes testing, uncertainty, and student learning. *Education Policy Analysis, 10*(18). Retrieved October 3, 2004, from http://epaa.asu.edu/epaa/v10n18/

Andersen, D. W., and Antes, J. M. (1971). Micro-teaching for preparing teachers of culturally diverse children. *Elementary School Journal, 72*(3), 142–149.

Anderson, J. R., Reder, K. M., and Cocking, R. C. (1996). Situated learning and education. *Educational Researcher, 25*(4), 5–11.

Anderson, L. M. (1989). Classroom instruction. In M. C. Reynolds (Ed.), *The knowledge base for the beginning teacher* (pp. 101–115). New York: Pergamon.

Anderson, R. C., and Pichert, J. W. (1978). Recall of previously unrecallable information following a shift in perspective. *Journal of Verbal Learning and Verbal Behavior, 17,* 1–12.

Andrew, M. D. (1990). Differences between graduates of 4-year and 5-year teacher preparation programs. *Journal of Teacher Education, 41*(2), 45–51.

Andrew, M. D., and Schwab, R. L. (1995). Has reform in teacher education influenced teacher performance? An outcome assessment of graduates of an eleven-university consortium. *Action in Teacher Education, 17*(3), 43–53.

Angrist, J. D., and Lavy, V. (1998). *Does teacher training affect pupil learning? Evidence from matched comparisons in Jerusalem Public Schools.* Working paper 6781. Cambridge, MA: National Bureau of Economic Research.

Anson, A., Cook, T. D., Habib, F., Grady, M. K., Haynes, N. M., and Comer, J. P. (1991). The Comer School Development Program: A theoretical analysis. *Urban Education, 26*(1), 56–82.

Anyon, J. (1980). Social class and the hidden curriculum of work. *Journal of Education, 162*(1), 67–92.

Anyon, J. (1981). Schools as agencies of social legitimation. *Journal of Curriculum Theorizing, 3*(2), 86–103.

Apple, M. W. (1990). *Ideology and curriculum* (2nd ed.). New York: Routledge.

Apple, M. W. (1993). *Official knowledge: Democratic education in a conservative age.* New York: Routledge.

Applebee, A. N. (1974). *Tradition and reform in the teaching of English: A history.* Urbana, IL: National Council of Teachers of English.

Applebee, A. N. (1993). *Literature in the secondary school.* Urbana, IL: National Council of Teachers of English.

Appleby, J. (1992). Recovering America's historic diversity: Beyond exceptionalism. *Journal of American History, 79*(2), 419–431.

ARC Center. (2002). The ARC Tri-State Student Achievement Study. Retrieved October 3, 2003, from http://www.comap.com/elementary/projects/arc/tristate%20achievement.htm

Arias, M. B., and Casanova, U. (1993). *Bilingual education: Politics, practice, and research.* Chicago: National Society for the Study of Education: Distributed by the University of Chicago Press.

Armstrong, S., and Chen, M. (2002). *Edutopia: Success stories for learning in the digital age.* San Francisco: Jossey-Bass.

Assor, A., and Connell, J. P. (1992). The validity of students' self-reports as measures of performance affecting self-appraisals. In D. H. Schunk and J. L. Meece (Eds.), *Student perceptions in the classroom.* Hillsdale, NJ: Erlbaum.

Athanases, S. Z. (1994). Teachers' reports of the effects of preparing portfolios of literacy instruction. *Elementary School Journal, 94*(4), 421–439.

Atkin, J. M., Black, P., and Coffey, J. (2001). *Classroom assessment and the National Science Education Standards.* Washington, DC: National Academies Press.

Atkinson, R. C., and Schiffrin, R. M. (1968). Human memory: A proposed system and its control processes. In K. W. Spence and J. T. Spence (Eds.), *The psychology of learning and motivation* (Vol. 2). New York: Academic Press.

Au, K. H. (1980). Participation structures in a reading lesson with Hawaiian children: Analysis of a culturally appropriate instructional event. *Anthropology and Education Quarterly, 1*(2), 91–115.

Au, K. H. (2002). Communities of practice: Engagement, imagination, and alignment in research on teacher education. *Journal of Teacher Education, 53*(3), 222–227.

August, D., and Hakuta, K. (1997). *Improving schooling for language-minority children: A research agenda.* Washington, DC: National Academies Press.

August, D., and Hakuta, K. (1998). *Educating language-minority children.* Washington, DC: National Academies Press.

Austin, J. L. (1975). *How to do things with words* (2nd ed.). Cambridge, MA: Harvard University Press.

Ayers, W. (Ed.). (1995). *To become a teacher: Making a difference in children's lives.* New York: Teachers College Press.

Baker, A. J. (1997). Improving parent involvement programs and practice: A qualitative study of teacher perceptions. *School Community Journal, 7*(2), 27–55.

Baker, L., Hitz, R., and Howard, R. D. (1998, Fall). A national study comparing the expenditures of teacher education programs by Carnegie Classification and with other disciplines. *Action in Teacher Education, 20*(3), 1–14.

Baker, T. (1993). A survey of four-year and five-year program graduates and their principals. *Southeastern Regional Association of Teacher Educators Journal, 2*(2), 28–33.

Balanced Assessment Elementary Grades Assessment Package 1 (1999). White Plains, NY: Dale Seymour Publications.

Balanced Assessment Middle Grades Assessment Package 1 (1999). White Plains, NY: Dale Seymour Publications.

Balanced Assessment High School Assessment Package 1 (1999). White Plains, NY: Dale Seymour Publications.

Balanced Assessment Advanced High School Assessment Package 1 (1999). White Plains, NY: Dale Seymour Publications.

Balanced Assessment Elementary Grades Assessment Package 2 (1999). White Plains, NY: Dale Seymour Publications.

Balanced Assessment Middle Grades Assessment Package 2 (1999). White Plains, NY: Dale Seymour Publications.

Balanced Assessment High School Assessment Package 2 (1999). White Plains, NY: Dale Seymour Publications.

Balanced Assessment Advanced High School Assessment Package 2 (1999). White Plains, NY: Dale Seymour Publications.

Ball, D. L. (1993). With an eye on the mathematical horizon: Dilemmas of teaching elementary school mathematics. *Elementary School Journal, 93*(4), 373–397.

Ball, D. L., and Bass, H. (2000). Interweaving content and pedagogy in teaching and learning to teach: Knowing and using mathematics. In J. Boaler (Ed.), *Multiple perspectives on the teaching and learning of mathematics* (pp. 83–104). Westport, CT: Ablex.

Ball, D. L., and Cohen, D. K. (1999). Developing practice, developing practitioners: Toward a practice-based theory of professional education. In L. Darling-Hammond and G. Sykes (Eds.), *Teaching as the learning profession: Handbook of policy and practice* (pp. 3–32). San Francisco: Jossey-Bass.

Ball, D. L., and Cohen, D. K. (1996). Reform by the book: What is—or might be—the role of curriculum materials in teacher learning and instructional reform? *Educational Researcher, 25*(9), 6–8.

Ball, D. L., and Feimen-Nemser, S. (1988). Using textbooks and curriculum guides: A dilemma for beginning teachers and teacher educators. *Curriculum Inquiry, 18*(4), 401–422.

Ballenger, C. (1999). *Teaching other people's children: Literacy and learning in a bilingual classroom.* New York: Teachers College Press.

Bandura, A. (1997). *Self-efficacy: The exercise of control.* New York: Freeman.

Banks, J. A. (1991). Teaching multicultural literacy to teachers. *Teaching Education, 4*(1), 135–144.

Banks, J. A. (1993). Multicultural education: Historical development, dimensions, and practice. In L. Darling-Hammond (Ed.), *Review of research in education* (vol. 19, pp. 3–49). Washington, DC: American Educational Research Association.

Banks, J. A. (1996). The canon debate, knowledge construction, and multicultural education. In J. A. Banks (Ed.), *Multicultural education, transformative knowledge, and action: Historical and contemporary perspectives* (pp. 3–29). New York: Teachers College Press.

Banks, J. A. (1997). *Educating citizens in a multicultural society.* New York: Teachers College Press.

Banks, J. A. (1998). The lives and values of researchers: Implications for educating citizens in a multicultural society. *Educational Researcher, 27*(7), 4–17.

Banks, J. A. (2001a). *Cultural diversity and education: Foundations, curriculum, and teaching* (4th ed.). Boston: Allyn & Bacon.

Banks, J. A. (2001b). Multicultural education: Historical development, dimensions, and practice. In J. A. Banks and C. A. M. Banks (Eds.), *Handbook of research on multicultural education* (pp. 3–24). San Francisco: Jossey-Bass.

Banks, J. A. (2001c). Citizenship education and diversity: Implications for teacher education. *Journal of Teacher Education, 52*(1), 5–16.

Banks, J. A. (2003). *Teaching strategies for ethnic studies* (7th ed.). Boston: Allyn & Bacon.

Banks, J. A. (Ed.). (2004). *Diversity and citizenship education: Global perspectives.* San Francisco: Jossey-Bass.

Banks, J. A., Cookson, P., Gay, G., Hawley, W. D., Irvine, J. J., Nieto, S., and others (2001). *Diversity within unity: Essential principles for teaching and learning in a multicultural society.* Seattle, WA: Center for Multicultural Education, University of Washington.

Banks, J. A., and McGee, C. A. (1996). Intellectual leadership and African American challenges to meta-narratives. In J. A. Banks (Ed.), *Multicultural education, transformative knowledge, and action: Historical and contemporary perspectives* (pp. 46–63). New York: Teachers College Press.

Baptiste, H. P., and Baptiste, M. L. (1980). Competencies toward multiculturalism. In H. P. Baptiste, M. L. Baptiste, and D. M. Gollnick (Eds.), *Multicultural teacher education: Preparing teacher educators to provide educational equity* (Vol. 1, pp. 44–72). Washington, DC: Commission on Multicultural Education, American Association of Colleges for Teacher Education.

Barab, S., MaKinster, J. G., Moore, J., Cunningham, D., and the ILF Design Team. (2001). Designing and building an online community: The struggle to support sociability in the Inquiry Learning Forum. *Educational Technology Research and Development, 49*(4), 71–96.

Barclay, C. R., and Wellman, H. M. (1986). Accuracies and inaccuracies in autobiographical memories. *Journal of Memory and Language, 25*, 93–103.

Barnes, D., Barnes, D. R., and Clarke, S. (1984). *Versions of English.* Portsmouth, NH: Heinemann.

Barnes, D. R. (1982). *Practical curriculum study.* Boston: Routledge Kegan Paul.

Barnes, H. (1989). Structuring knowledge for beginning teaching. In M. C. Reynolds and American Association of Colleges for Teacher Education (Eds.), *Knowledge base for the beginning teacher* (pp. 13–22). Elmsford, NY: Pergamon.

Barnett, M., Harwood, W., Keating, T., and Saam, J. (2002). Using emerging technologies to help bridge the gap between university theory and classroom practice: Challenges and successes. *School Science and Mathematics, 102*(6), 299–313.

Barr, R., and Dreeben, R. (1983). *How schools work.* Chicago: University of Chicago Press.

Barron, B. J. S., Schwartz, D. L., Vye, N. J., Moore, A., Petrosino, A., Zech, L., and others (1998). Doing with understanding: Lessons from research on problem- and project-based learning. *Journal of the Learning Sciences, 7*(3–4), 271–311.

Barrows, H. S. (1985). *How to design a problem-based curriculum for the preclinical years.* New York: Springer.

Bartolme, L. (1994). Beyond the methods fetish: Toward a humanizing pedagogy. *Harvard Educational Review, 64*(2), 173–194.

Bass, H. (1993). *Measuring what counts: A conceptual guide for mathematics assessment.* Washington, DC: National Academies Press.

Bateman, H. V., Bransford, J. D., Goldman, S. R., and Newbrough, J. R. (2000). *Sense of community in the classroom: Relationship to students' academic goals.* Paper presented at the Annual meeting of the American Educational Research Association, New Orleans, LA.

Bateson, D. (1990). Measurement and evaluation practices of British Columbia science teachers. *Alberta Journal of Education Research, 36*, 45–51.

Battistch, V., Solomon, D., Kim, D., Watson, M., and Schaps, E. (1995). Schools as communities, poverty levels of student populations, and students' attitudes, motives, and performance: A multilevel analysis. *American Educational Research Journal, 32*(3), 627–658.

Battistch, V., Watson, M., Solomon, D., Schaps, E., and Solomon, D. (1991). The child development project: A comprehensive program for the development of prosocial character. In W. M. Kurtines and J. L. Gerwirtz (Eds.), *Handbook of moral behavior and development: Vol. 3. Application.* New York: Erlbaum.

Bauer, L., and Trudgill, P. (1998). *Language myths.* New York: Penguin Books.

Baugh, J. (1999). *Out of the mouths of slaves: African American language and educational malpractice.* Austin: University of Texas Press.

Baugh, J. (2000). *Beyond ebonics: Linguistic pride and racial prejudice.* New York: Oxford University Press.

Baumgartner, F., Koerner, M., and Rust, F. (2002). Exploring roles in student teaching placements. *Teacher Education Quarterly, 29,* 35–58.

Beals, M. P. (1994). *Warriors don't cry.* New York: Washington Square Press.

Beauchamp, G. A. (1982). Curriculum theory: Meaning, development, and use. *Theory into Practice, 21*(1), 23–27.

Becker, H. J. (2000). Findings from the teaching, learning, and computing survey: Is Larry Cuban right? *Education Policy Analysis Archives, 8*(51). Retrieved October 3, 2004, from http://epaa.asu.edu/epaa/v8n51/

Becker, H. J. (2001, April). *How are teachers using computers in instruction?* Paper presented at the American Educational Research Association, Seattle, WA. http://www.crito.uci.edu/tlc/FINDINGS/special3/

Begle, E. G. (1979). *Critical variables in mathematics education: Findings from a survey of the empirical literature.* Washington, DC: Mathematical Association of America.

Belenky, M. F., Clinchy, B. M., Goldberger, N. R., and Tarule, J. M. (1996). *Women's ways of knowing: The development of self, voice, and mind.* New York: Basic Books.

Bell, A. (1984). Language style as audience design. *Language in Society, 13*(2), 145–204.

Bennett, C., Okinaka, A., and Xiao-yang, W. (1988, April). *The effect of a multicultural education course on preservice teachers' attitudes, knowledge, and behavior.* Paper presented at the Annual Meeting of the AERA, New Orleans, LA.

Benware, C., and Deci, E. L. (1984). Quality of learning with an active versus passive motivational set. *American Educational Research Journal, 21*(4), 755–765.

Bereiter, C., and Scardamalia, M. (1989). Intentional learning as a goal of instruction. In L. B. Resnick (Ed.), *Knowing, learning, and instruction: Essays in honor of Robert Glaser* (pp. 361–392). Hillsdale, NJ: Erlbaum.

Berk, L. E. (1996). *Infants, children, and adolescents* (2nd ed.). Boston: Allyn & Bacon.

Berk, L. E., and Winsler, A. (1995). *Scaffolding children's learning: Vygotsky and early childhood education. NAEYC Research into Practice Series. Volume 7.* Washington, DC: National Association for the Education of Young Children.

Berliner, D. C. (1986). In pursuit of the expert pedogogue. *Educational Researcher, 15*(7), 5–13.

Berliner, D. C. (1991). Educational psychology and pedagogical expertise: New findings and new opportunities for thinking about training. *Educational Psychologist, 26*(2), 145–155.

Berliner, D. C. (1994). Expertise: The wonder of exemplary performances. In J. Mangieri and C. C. Block (Eds.), *Creating powerful thinking in teachers and students: Diverse perspectives* (pp. 161–186). Fort Worth, TX: Harcourt Brace College Publishers.

Berliner, D. C. (2001). Learning about and learning from expert teachers. *International Journal of Educational Research, 35*(5), 463–483.

Berliner, D. C., and Biddle, B. J. (1995). *The manufactured crisis: Myths, fraud, and the attack on America's public schools.* Reading, MA: Addison-Wesley.

Berninger, V. W., and Richards T. L. (2002). *Brain literacy for educators and psychologists.* San Diego, CA: Academic Press.

Bernstein, B. (1972). A critique of the concept "compensatory education." In C. B. Cazden, V. John, and D. Hymes (Eds.), *Functions of language in the classroom.* New York: Teachers College Press.

Betts, J. R., Rueben, K. S., and Danenberg, A. (2000). *Equal resources, equal outcomes? The distribution of school resources and student achievement in California.* San Francisco: Public Policy Institute of California. Retrieved September 30, 2004, from http://www.ppic.org/publications/reports.html

Bex, T., and Watts, R. J. (1999). *Standard English: The widening debate.* New York: Routledge.

Beyer, L. E. (1991). Teacher education, reflective inquiry and moral action. In B. R. Tabachnick and K. M. Zeichner (Eds.), *Issues and practices in inquiry-oriented teacher education* (pp. 113–129). London: Falmer.

Beyer, L. E. (Ed.). (1996). *Creating democratic classrooms: The struggle to integrate theory and practice.* New York: Teachers College Press.

Beykont, Z. F. (Ed.). (2002). *The power of culture: Teaching across language difference.* Cambridge, MA: Harvard Education Publishing Group.

Bialystok, E. (2001). *Bilingualism in development: Language, literacy, and cognition.* Cambridge, UK: Cambridge University Press.

Biederman, I., and Shiffrar, M. M. (1987). Sexing day-old chicks: A case study and expert systems analysis of a difficult perceptual learning task. *Journal of Experimental Psychology: Learning, Memory and Cognition, 13*(4), 640–645.

Bird, T. (1990), The schoolteacher's portfolio: An essay on possibilities. In J. Millman and L. Darling-Hammond (Eds.), *The new handbook of teacher evaluation: Assessing elementary and secondary school teachers.* Thousand Oaks, CA: Sage.

Bissex, G., and Bullock, R. (Eds.). (1987). *Seeing for ourselves: Case-study research by teachers of writing.* Portsmouth, NH: Heinemann Educational Books.

Biswas, G., Leelawong, K., Beylynne, K., Viswanath, K., Vye, N., Schwartz, D. L., and Davis, J. (2004). *Incorporating self regulated techniques into learning by teaching environments.* Manuscript submitted for publication.

Biswas, G., Schwartz, D., Bransford, J., and TAGV (2001). Technology support for complex problem solving: From SAD environments to AI. In K. D. Forbus and

P. J. Feltovich (Eds.), *Smart machines in education: The coming revolution in educational technology* (pp. 71–97). Cambridge, MA: The MIT Press.

Black J. B., and Bower, G. H. (1979). Episodes as chunks in narrative memory. *Journal of Verbal Learning and Verbal Behavior*, *18*, 309–318.

Black, P., and William, D. (1998). Assessment and classroom learning. *Assessment and Education: Principles, policy and practice*, *5*(1), 7–75.

Bloom, B. S. (1956). *Taxonomy of educational objectives; the classification of educational goals.* New York: Longmans, Green.

Blumenfeld, P. C., Puro, P., and Mergendoller, J. R. (1992). Translating motivation into thoughtfulness. In H. H. Marshall (Ed.), *Redefining student learning* (pp. 207–239). Norwood, NJ: Ablex.

Boaler, J. (1997). *Experiencing school mathematics: Teaching styles, sex, and setting.* Philadelphia: Open University Press.

Boaler, J., and Greeno, J. (2000). Identity, agency, and knowing in mathematical worlds. In J. Boaler (Ed.), *Multiple perspectives on mathematics and learning* (pp. 171–200). Westport, CT: Ablex.

Boden, M. A. (1980). *Jean Piaget.* New York: Viking Press.

Bodine, R. J., and Crawford, D. K. (1998). *The handbook of conflict resolution education: A guide to building quality programs in schools.* San Francisco: Jossey-Bass.

Boix-Mansilla, V., and Gardner, H. (1997). What are the qualities of understanding? In M. S. Wiske (Ed.), *Teaching for understanding: Linking research with practice* (pp. 161–183). San Francisco: Jossey-Bass.

Boix-Mansilla, V., Miller, W. C., and Gardner, H. (2000). On disciplinary lenses and multidisciplinary work. In S. W. P. Grossman (Ed.), *Interdisciplinary curriculum: Challenges to implementation* (pp. 17–38). New York: Teachers College Press.

Bond, L., Jaeger, R., Smith, T., Hattie, J. (2001). Defrocking the National Board: The certification system of the National Board for Professional Teaching Standards. *Education Matters*, *1*(2), 79–82.

Bondy, E., and Davis, S. (2000). The caring of strangers: Insights from a field experience in a culturally unfamiliar community. *Action in Teacher Education*, *22*(2), 54–66.

Bonsangue, M. V., and Drew, D. E. (1995). Increasing minority students' success in calculus. *New Directions for Teaching and Learning*, *61*, 23–33.

Booth, W. (1988). *The company we keep: An ethics of fiction.* Berkeley: University of California Press.

Borko, H., and Mayfield, V. (1995). The roles of the cooperating teacher and university supervisor in learning to teach. *Teaching and Teacher Education*, *11*(5), 501–518.

Borko, H., Michalec, P., Timmons, M., and Siddle, J. (1997). Student teaching portfolios: A tool for promoting reflective practice. *Journal of Teacher Education*, *48*(5), 345–357.

Bourdieu, P., and Thompson, J. B. (1991). *Language and symbolic power: The economy of linguistic exchanges.* Cambridge, MA: Harvard University Press.

Boyer, E. (1990). *Scholarship reconsidered.* Princeton, NJ: Carnegie Commission for the Advancement of Teaching.

Boyle-Baise, M. (1998). Community service learning for multicultural education: An exploratory study with preservice teachers. *Equity and Excellence in Education, 31*(2), 52–60.

Boyle-Baise, M. (2002). *Multicultural service learning: Educating teachers in diverse communities.* New York: Teachers College Press.

Boyle-Baise, M., and Sleeter, C. E. (2000). Community-based service learning for multicultural teacher education. *Educational Foundations, 14*(2), 33–50.

Braddock, J., and Slavin, R. E. (1993). *Life in the slow lane: A longitudinal study of effects of ability grouping on student achievement, attitudes, and perceptions.* Baltimore: Johns Hopkins University, Center for Research on Effective Schooling for Disadvantaged Students.

Bramald, R., Hardman, F., and Leat, D. (1995). Initial teacher trainees and their views of teaching and learning. *Teaching and Teacher Education, 11*(1), 23–31.

Brandon, D. P. (1995). *Demographic factors in American education.* Arlington, VA: Educational Research Service.

Bransford, J. D., Brown, A. L., and Cocking, R. R. (1999). *How people learn: Brain, mind, experience, and school.* Washington, DC: National Academies Press.

Bransford, J. D., and Johnson, M. K. (1972). Contextual prerequisites for understanding: some investigations of comprehension and recall. *Journal of Verbal Learning and Verbal Behavior, 11*(6), 717–726.

Bransford, J. D., Nitsch, K. E., and Franks, J. J. (1977). Schooling and the facilitation of knowing. In R. C. Anderson, R. J. Spiro, and W. E. Montague (Eds.), *Schooling and the acquisition of knowledge* (pp. 31–55). Hillsdale, NJ: Erlbaum.

Bransford, J. D., and Schwartz, D. L. (1999). Rethinking transfer: A simple proposal with multiple implications. In A. Iran-Nejad and P. D. Pearson (Eds.), *Review of research in education, 24,* 61–100. Washington, DC: American Educational Research Association.

Bransford, J. D., and Stein, B. S. (1993). *The IDEAL problem solver* (2nd ed.). New York: Freeman.

Bredekamp, S. E., and Copple, C. E. (1997). *Developmentally appropriate practice in early childhood programs* (Rev. ed.). Washington, DC: National Association for the Education of Young Children.

Brenner, B. (1994). A communication framework for mathematics: Exemplary instruction for culturally and linguistically diverse students. In B. McLeod (Ed.), *Language and learning: Educating linguistically diverse students* (pp. 233–267). Albany: State University of New York Press.

Brewer, E. W., Dunn, J. O., and Olszewski, P. (1988). Extrinsic reward and intrinsic motivation: The vital link between classroom management and student performance. *Journal of Education for Teaching, 14*(2), 151–170.

Briscoe, C. (1991, April). *Making the grade: Multiple perspectives on a teacher's assessment practices.* Paper presented at the Annual Meeting of the American Educational Research Association, Chicago.

Britzman, D. (1986). Cultural myths in the making of a teacher: Biography and social structure in teacher education. *Harvard Educational Review, 56*(4), 442–456.

Britzman, D. (1991). *Practice makes practice.* Albany: State University of New York Press.

Brodkin, K. (1998). *How Jews became white folks and what that says about race in America.* New Brunswick, NJ: Rutgers University Press.

Brookhart, S. M. (1993). Teachers' grading practices: Meaning and values. *Journal of Educational Measurement, 30*(2), 123–142.

Brookhart, S. M. (1994). Teachers' grading: Practice and theory. *Applied Measurement in Education, 7*(4), 279–301.

Brophy, J. (1981). Teacher praise: A functional analysis. *Psychological Review, 88*(2), 93–134.

Brophy, J. (1987). Synthesis of research on strategies for motivating students to learn. *Educational Leadership, 45*(2), 40–48.

Brophy, J. (1988). Educating teachers about managing classrooms and students. *Teaching and Teacher Education: An International Journal of Research and Studies, 4*(1), 1–18.

Brophy, J. (1998). Classroom management as socializing students into clearly articulated roles. *Journal of Classroom Interaction, 33*(1), 1–4.

Brophy, J., and Alleman, J. (1998). Classroom management in a social studies learning community. *Social Education, 62*(1), 56–58.

Brophy, J., and Good, T. L. (1986). Teacher behavior and student achievement. In M. C. Wittrock and American Educational Research Association (Eds.), *Handbook of research on teaching* (3rd ed., pp. 328–375). New York: Collier Macmillan.

Brophy, J. E., and Good, T. L. (1974). *Teacher-student relationships.* New York: Holt, Rinehart and Winston.

Brophy, S. P. (2001). Exploring the implication of an expert blind spot on learning. Unpublished manuscript, Vanderbilt University.

Broudy, H. S. (1977). Types of knowledge and purposes of education. In R. C. Anderson, R. J. Spiro, and W. E. Montanague (Eds.), *Schooling and the acquisition of knowledge* (pp. 1–17). Hillsdale, NJ: Erlbaum.

Brouwers, A., and Tomic, W. (2000). A longitudinal study of teacher burnout and perceived self-efficacy in classroom management. *Teaching and Teacher Education, 16*(2), 239–253.

Brown, A. L. (1975). The development of memory: Knowing, knowing about knowing, and knowing how to know. In H. W. Reese (Ed.), *Advances in child development and behavior,* (Vol. 10, pp. 103–152). New York: Academic Press.

Brown, A. L. (1997a). Transforming schools into communities of thinking and learning about serious matters. *American Psychologist, 52*(4), 399–413.

Brown, A. L. (1997b). Knowing when, where, and how to remember: A problem of metacognition. In R. Glaser (Ed.), *Advances in instructional psychology* (pp. 77–165). Hillsdale, NJ: Erlbaum.

Brown, A. L., Bransford, J. D., Ferrara, R. A., and Campione, J. C. (1983). Learning, remembering, and understanding. In J. H. Flavell and E. M. Markman (Eds.), *Handbook of child psychology: Vol. 3. Cognitive development* (4th ed., pp. 78–166). New York: Wiley.

Brown, A. L., and Campione, J. (1994). Guided discovery in a community of learners. In K. McGilly (Ed.), *Classroom lessons: Integrating cognitive theory and classroom practice* (pp. 229–270). Cambridge, MA: MIT Press.

Brown, A. L., and Campione, J. (1996). Psychological theory and the design of innovative learning environments: On procedures, principles, and systems. In L. Schauble and R. Glaser (Eds.), *Innovations in learning: New environments for education* (pp. 289–325). Mahwah, NJ: Erlbaum.

Brown, A. L., Campione, J. C., and Day, J. D. (1981). Learning to learn: On training students to learn from texts. *Educational Researcher, 10,* 14–21.

Brown, A. L., Palincsar, A. S., and Armbruster, B. B. (1994). Instructing comprehension-fostering activities in interactive learning situations. In R. B. Ruddell, M. R. Ruddell, and H. Singer (Eds.), *Theoretical models and processes of reading* (4th ed., pp. 757–787). Newark, DE: International Reading Association.

Brown, A. L., and Reeve, R. A. (1987). Bandwidths of competence: The role of supportive contexts in learning and development. In L. S. Liben (Ed.), *Development and learning: Conflict or congruence?* (pp. 173–223). Hillsdale, NJ: Erlbaum.

Brown, H. D. (2001). *Teaching by principles: An interactive approach to language pedagogy* (2nd ed.). White Plains, NY: Longman.

Brown, S. J. (1999). *Knowledge for health care practice: A guide to using research evidence.* Philadelphia: Saunders.

Bruer, J. T. (1993). *Schools for thought: A science of learning in the classroom.* Cambridge, MA: MIT Press.

Bruer, J. T. (1997). Education and the brain: A bridge too far. *Educational Researcher 26*(8), 4–16.

Bruner, J. S. (1960/1977). *The process of education.* Cambridge, MA: Harvard University Press.

Bruner, J. S. (1985). Vygotsky: A historical and conceptual perspective. In J. V. Wertsch and Center for Psychosocial Studies (Eds.), *Culture, communication, and cognition: Vygotskian perspectives* (pp. 21–34). New York: Cambridge University Press.

Bruner, J. S. (1990). *Acts of meaning.* Cambridge, MA: Harvard University Press.

Bruner, J. S. (1996). *The culture of education.* Cambridge, MA: Harvard University Press.

Buchmann, M. (1986). Role over person: Morality and authenticity in teaching. *Teachers College Record, 87*(4), 527–543.

Buhler, K. (1908). Tatsachen und probleme zu einer psychologie der Denkuorgange. *Ueber Gedankenerinnerungen Arch.f.d.ges.Psychol, III.*

Bullough, R. V. (1994). Digging at the roots: Discipline, management, and metaphor. *Action in Teacher Education, 16*(1), 1–10.

Bullough, R., and Gitlin, A. (1995). *Becoming a student of teaching: Methodologies for exploring self and school context.* New York: Garland.

Bullough, R., and Stokes, D. K. (1994). Analyzing personal teaching metaphors in preservice teacher education as a means for encouraging professional development. *American Educational Research Journal, 31*(1), 197–224.

Burant, T. J., and Kirby, D. (2002). Beyond classroom-based early field experiences: Understanding an "educative practicum" in an urban school and community. *Teaching and Teacher Education, 18*(5), 561–575.

Burden, P. R. (1999) *Classroom management and discipline: Methods to facilitate cooperation and instruction.* New York: Wiley.

Burden, P. R. (2000). *Powerful classroom management strategies: Motivating students to learn.* Thousand Oaks, CA: Corwin Press.

Burnard, S. (1998). *Developing children's behaviour in the classroom: a practical guide for teachers and students.* London: Falmer Press.

Burnard, S., and Yaxley, H. (1997). *Developing children's behaviour in the classroom: A practical guide for teachers and students.* Washington, DC: Routledge/Falmer Press.

Butchart, R. E. (1998). Punishments, penalties, prizes, and procedures: A history of discipline in U.S. schools. In R. E. Butchart and B. McEwan (Eds.), *Classroom discipline in American schools: Problems and possibilities for democratic education* (pp. 19–50). Albany: State University of New York Press.

Butler, R. (1987). Task-involving and ego-involving properties of evaluation: Effects of different feedback conditions on motivational perceptions, interest, and performance. *Journal of Educational Psychology, 79*(4), 474–482.

Butler, R. (1988). Enhancing and undermining intrinsic motivation: The effects of task-involving and ego-involving evaluation of interest and performance. *British Journal of Educational Psychology, 58*(1), 1–14.

Butler, R., and Nisan, M. (1986). Effects of no feedback, task-related comments, and grades on intrinsic motivation and performance. *Journal of Educational Psychology, 78*(3), 210–216.

Byrnes, J. P. (1988). Formal operations: A systematic reformulation. *Developmental Review, 8,* 66–87.

Cabello, B., Eckmier, J., and Baghieri, H. (1995). The comprehensive teacher institute: Successes and pitfalls of an innovative teacher preparation program. *Teacher Educator, 31*(1), 43–55.

California Department of Developmental Services. (1999). *Changes in the population of persons with autism and pervasive developmental disorders in California's developmental services system: 1987 through 1998: A report to the Legislature, March 1, 1999.* Sacramento, CA: Department of Developmental Services.

California State University. (2002a). *First system wide evaluation of teacher education programs in the California State University: Summary report.* Long Beach, CA: Office of the Chancellor, California State University.

California State University. (2002b). *Preparing teachers for reading instruction (K-12): An evaluation brief by the California State University.* Long Beach, CA: Office of the Chancellor, California State University.

Calkins, L., Montgomery, K., and Santman, D. (1998). *A teacher's guide to standardized reading tests: Knowledge is power.* Portsmouth, NH: Heinemann.

Cameron, J. (2001). Negative effects of reward on intrinsic motivation—A limited phenomenon: Comment on Deci, Koestner, and Ryan (2001). *Review of Educational Research, 71*(1), 29–42.

Cameron, J., and Pierce, W. D. (1996). The debate about rewards and intrinsic motivation: Protests and accusations do not alter the results. *Review of Educational Research, 66*(1), 39–51.

Campbell, R. F., Sroufe, G. E., and Layton, D. H. (1967). *Strengthening state departments of education.* Chicago: Midwestern Administration Center, The University of Chicago.

Canter, L., and Canter, M. (2002). *Assertive discipline: Positive behavior management for today's classroom.* Los Angeles: Canter and Associates.

Carlson, H., and Falk, D. (1990). Effectiveness of interactive videodisc instructional programs in elementary teacher education. *Journal of Educational Technology Systems, 19*(2), 151–163.

Carnegie Council on Adolescent Development. (1989). *Turning points: Preparing American youth for the 21st century: The report of the task force on education of young adolescents.* Washington, DC: Author.

Carnegie Forum on Education and the Economy, Task Force on Teaching as a Profession. (1986). *A nation prepared: Teachers for the 21st century.* New York: Author.

Carnegie Task Force on Meeting the Needs of Young Children. (1994). *Starting points: Meeting the needs of our youngest children: The report of the Carnegie Task Force on Meeting the Needs of Young Children.* New York: Carnegie Corporation of New York.

Carpenter, T. P., Fennema, E., Peterson, P. L., Chiang, C.-P., and Loef, M. (1989). Using knowledge of children's mathematics thinking in classroom teaching: An experimental study. *American Educational Research Journal, 26*(4), 499–531.

Carpenter-Aeby, T., and Aeby, V. G. (2001). Family-school-community interventions for chronically disruptive students: An evaluation of outcomes in an alternative school. *School Community Journal, 11*(2), 75–92.

Carter, K. (1990). Teachers' knowledge and learning to teach. In W. R. Houston, M. Haberman, J. P. Sikula, and Association of Teacher Educators (Eds.), *Handbook of research on teacher education* (pp. 291–310). New York: Collier Macmillan.

Carter, K., and Doyle, W. (1996). Personal narrative and life history in learning to teach. In J. Sikula, T. J. Buttery, and E. Guyton (Eds.), *Handbook of Research on Teacher Education* (2nd ed., pp. 120–142). New York: Macmillan.

Carter, K., and Doyle, W. (1987). Teachers' knowledge structures and comprehension processes. In J. Calderhead (Ed.), *Exploring teacher thinking* (pp. 147–160). London: Cassell.

Carter, K., Cushing, K., Sabers, D., Stein, P. and Berliner, D. (1988). Expert-novice differences in perceiving and processing visual classroom information. *Journal of Teacher Education, 39*(3), 25–31.

Carter, P. (n.d.). *Teacher Quality Initiative, Chattanooga-Hamilton County Public Education Foundation.* Retrieved October 2003, from http://www.pefchattanooga.org/www/docs/2–110

Carter, R. T., and Goodwin, A. L. (1994). Racial identity and education. In L. Darling-Hammond (Ed.), *Review of research in education 20,* 291–336. Washington, DC: American Educational Research Association.

Case, R. (1992). *The mind's staircase: Exploring the conceptual underpinnings of children's thought and knowledge.* Hillsdale, NJ: Erlbaum.

Case, R. (1998). The development of conceptual structures. In W. Damon (Ed.), *Handbook of child psychology* (Vol. 2, pp. 851–898). New York: Wiley.

Cazden, C., and Mehan, H. (1989). Principles from sociology and anthropology. In M. C. Reynolds (Ed.), *Knowledge base for the beginning teacher* (pp. 47–57). New York: Pergamon Press.

Chamoiseau, P. (1997). *School Days.* Lincoln: University of Nebraska Press.

Chandler, W. L., Jelacic, S., Boster, D. R., Ciol, M. A., Williams, G. D., Watkins, S. L., and others (2002). Prothrombotic coagulation abnormalities preceding the hemolytic-uremic syndrome. *New English Journal of Medicine 346*(1), 23–32.

Chapman, J. W., Tunmer, W. E., and Prochnow, J. E. (2000). Early reading-related skills and performance, reading self-concept, and the development of academic self-concept: A longitudinal study. *Journal of Educational Psychology, 92*(4), 703–708.

Charles, C. M. (2001). *Building classroom discipline* (7th ed.). Boston: Pearson Allyn & Bacon.

Chase, W. G., and Simon, H. A. (1973). Perception in chess. *Cognitive Psychology, 1,* 33–81.

Chavkin, N. F. (2000). Family and community involvement policies: Teachers can lead the way. *Clearing House, 73*(5), 287–290.

Chen, J.-Q., Salahuddin, R., Horsch, P., and Wagner, S. L. (2000). Turning standardized test scores into a tool for improving teaching and learning: An assessment-based approach. *Urban Education, 35*(3), 356–384.

Chi, M. T. H. (1978). Knowledge structure and memory development. In R. S. Siegler (Ed.), *Children's thinking: What develops?* (pp. 73–96). Hillsdale, NJ: Erlbaum.

Chi, M. T. H., Bassok, M., Lewis, M., Reimann, M., and Glaser, R. (1989). Self-explanations: How students study and use examples in learning to solve problems. *Cognitive Science, 13,* 145–182.

Chi, M. T. H., deLeeuw, N., Chiu, M., and La Vancher, C. (1994). Eliciting self-explanations improves understanding. *Cognitive Science, 18,* 439–477.

Chi, M. T. H., Feltovitch, P. J., and Glasser, R. (1981). Categorizing and representation of physics problems by experts and novices. *Cognitive Science, 5,* 121–152.

Chi, M. T. H., Glaser, R., and Farr, M. (1991). *The nature of expertise.* Hillsdale, NJ: Erlbaum.

Chi, M. T. H., Glaser, R., and Rees, E. (1982). Expertise in problem solving. In R. J. Sternberg (Ed.), *Advances in the psychology of human intelligence.* (pp. 7–76). Hillsdale, NJ: Erlbaum.

Children's Defense Fund. (2000). *The state of America's children: Yearbook 2000.* Washington, DC: Author.

Chin, P., and Russell, T. (1995, June). *Structure and coherence in a teacher education program: Addressing the tension between systematics and the educative agenda.* Paper presented at the Annual Meeting of the Canadian Society for the Study of Education, Montreal, Quebec, Canada.

Christensen, C., and Hansen, A. (1987). *Teaching and the case method.* Boston: Harvard Business School.

Christensen, D. (1996). The professional knowledge-research base for teacher education. In J. P. Sikula, T. J. Buttery, E. Guyton, and Association of Teacher Educators (Eds.), *Handbook of research on teacher education* (2nd ed., pp. 38–52). New York: Macmillan.

Cizek, G. J., Fitzgerald, S. M., and Rachor, R. E. (1995/1996). Teachers' assessment practices: Preparation, isolation, and the kitchen sink. *Educational Assessment, 3*(2), 159–179.

Clandinin, D. J. (1985). Personal practical knowledge: A study of teachers' classroom images. *Curriculum Inquiry, 15*(4), 361–385.

Clandinin, D. J. (1986). *Classroom practice: Teacher images in action.* Philadelphia: Falmer Press.

Clandinin, J., and Connelly, M. (1991). Narrative, experience and the study of curriculum. *Cambridge Journal of Education, 20*(3), 241–254.

Clark, H. H. (1996). *Using language.* Cambridge, UK: Cambridge University Press.

Clarke, C., and Medina, C. (2000). How reading and writing literacy narratives affect preservice teachers' understandings of literacy, pedagogy and multiculturalism. *Journal of Teacher Education, 51*(1), 63–76.

Clarke, M., Shore, A., Rhoades, K., Abrams, L., Miao, J., and Li, J. (2003). *Perceived effects of state-mandated testing programs on teaching and learning: Findings from interviews with educators in low-, medium- and high-stakes states.* Boston: National Board on Educational Testing and Public Policy, Boston College.

Cleary, L. M., and Linn, M. D. (1993). *Linguistics for teachers.* New York: McGraw-Hill.

Clifford, G. J. (1989). Man/woman/teacher: Gender, family and career in American educational history. In D. Warren (Ed.), *American teachers: Histories of a profession at work* (pp. 293–343). New York: Macmillan.

Clift, R., Veal, M. L., Johnson, M., and Holland, P. (1990). Restructuring teacher education through collaborative action research. *Journal of Teacher Education, 41*(2), 52–62.

Cobb, P., Wood, T., and Yackel, E. (1993). Discourse, mathematical thinking, and classroom practice. In E. A. Forman, N. Minick, and C. A. Stone (Eds.), *Contexts for learning: Sociocultural dynamics in children's development* (pp. 91–119). Oxford: Oxford University Press.

Cobb, P., Yackel, E., and Wood, T. (1992). A constructivist alternative to the representational view of mind in mathematics education. *Journal for Research in Mathematics Education, 23*(1), 2–33.

Cochran-Smith, M. (1991). Learning to teach against the grain. *Harvard Educational Review, 61*(3), 279–310.

Cochran-Smith, M. (1995). Color blindness and basket making are not the answers: Confronting the dilemmas of race, culture, and language diversity in teacher education. *American Educational Research Journal, 32*(3), 493–522.

Cochran-Smith, M. (2000). Blind vision: Unlearning racism in teacher education. *Harvard Educational Review, 70*(2), 157–190.

Cochran-Smith, M. (2004). Multicultural teacher education: Research, practice, and policy. In J. A. Banks and C.A.M. Banks (Eds.), *The Handbook of research on multicultural education* (2nd ed., pp. 931–978). San Francisco: Jossey-Bass.

Cochran-Smith, M., and Lytle, S. L. (1993). *Inside/outside: Teacher research and knowledge.* New York: Teachers College Press.

Cochran-Smith, M., and Lytle, S. L. (1999a). Relationships of knowledge and practice: Teacher learning in communities. In *Review of research in education* (Vol. 24, pp. 249–306). Washington, DC: American Educational Research Association.

Cochran-Smith, M., and Lytle, S. L. (1999b). The teacher research movement: A decade later. *Educational Researcher, 28*(7), 15–25.

Codell, E. R. (1999b). *Educating Esme: Diary of a teachers' first year.* Chapel Hill: Algonquin Books.

Cognition and Technology Group at Vanderbilt (CTGV). (1997). *The Jasper project: Lessons in curriculum, instruction, assessment, and professional development.* Mahwah, NJ: Erlbaum.

Cohen, D. K., and Ball, D. L. (1999). *Instruction, capacity, and improvement. CPRE Research Report Series.* Philadelphia: Consortium for Policy Research in Education.

Cohen, D. K., and Hill, H. C. (2000). Instructional policy and classroom performance: The mathematics reform in California. *Teachers College Record, 102*(2), 294–343.

Cohen, E. G. (1994). Restructuring the classroom: Conditions for productive small groups. *Review of Educational Research, 64*(1), 1–35.

Cohen, E. G., and Lotan, R. A. (1995). Producing equal-status interaction in the heterogeneous classroom. *American Educational Research Journal, 32*(1), 99–120.

Colberg, J., Trimble, K., and Desberg, P. (1996). *The case for education: Contemporary approaches for using case methods.* Boston: Allyn & Bacon.

Cole, A. L., and Knowles, J. G. (1993). Shattered images: Understanding expectations and realities of field experiences. *Teaching and Teacher Education, 9*(5/6), 457–471.

Cole, M. (1977). An ethnographic psychology of cognition. In P. N. Johnson-Laird and P. C. Wason (Eds.), *Thinking: Readings in cognitive science* (pp. 468–482). Cambridge, UK: Cambridge University Press.

Cole, M., and Cole, S. (1993). *The development of children* (2nd ed.). New York: Scientific American Books: Distributed by W. H. Freeman.

Cole, S., Horvath, B., Chapman, C., Deschenes, C., Ebeling, D., and Sprague, J. (2000). *Adapting curriculum and instruction in inclusive classrooms: A teacher's desk reference.* (2nd ed.). Bloomington, IN: Institute for the Study of Developmental Disabilities.

Coleman, J. S., Campbell, E. Q., Hobson, C. J., McPartland, J., Mood, A. M., Weinfeld, F. D., and York, R. L. (1966). *Equality of educational opportunity.* Washington, DC: U.S. Government Printing Office.

College Board. (1985). *Equality and excellence: The educational status of black Americans.* New York: College Entrance Examination Board.

Collins, A., Brown, J. S., and Holum, A. (1991). Cognitive apprenticeship: Making things visible. *American Educator, 15*(3), 6–11, 38–46.

Collins, A., Brown, J. S., and Newman, S. E. (1987). *Cognitive apprenticeship: Teaching the craft of reading, writing, and mathematics. Technical Report No. 403.* University of Illinois, Urbana-Champaign: Center for the Study of reading.

Collins, A., Brown, J. S., and Newman, S. E. (1989). Cognitive apprenticeship: Teaching the crafts of reading, writing, and mathematics. In L. B. Resnick (Ed.), *Knowing, learning and instruction: Essays in honor of Robert Glaser* (pp. 453–494). Hillsdale, NJ: Erlbaum.

Collins, M., and Dowell, M. L. (1998). Discipline and due process. *Thrust for Educational Leadership, 28*(2), 34–36.

Comer, J., Haynes, N. M., and Joyner, E. T. (1996a). The school development program. In J. P. Comer, N. M. Haynes, E. T. Joyner, and M. Ben-Avie (Eds.), *Rallying the whole village: The Comer process for reforming education* (pp. 1–26). New York: Teachers College Press.

Comer, J. P., Haynes, N. M., Joyner, E. T., and Ben-Avie, M. (Eds.). (1996). *Rallying the whole village: The Comer process for reforming education.* New York: Teachers College Press.

Conant, J. B. (1963). *The education of American teachers.* New York: McGraw-Hill.

Confrey, J. (1990). A review of research on student conceptions in mathematics, science programming. In C. B. Cazden (Ed.), *Review of research in education, Vol. 16* (pp. 3–55). Washington, DC: American Educational Research Association.

Connelly, F., and Clandinin, D. J. (1994). Telling teaching stories. *Teacher Education Quarterly, 21*(1), 145–58.

Cooper, C. R., and Odell, L. (1977). *Evaluating writing: Describing, measuring, and judging.* Buffalo: State University of New York at Buffalo.

Copeland, W. (1982). Student teachers' preference for supervisory approach. *Journal of Teacher Education, 33*(2), 32–36.

Copeland, W. D., and Decker, D. L. (1996). Video cases and the development of meaning making in preservice teachers. *Teaching and Teacher Education, 12*(5), 467–481.

Corey, S. M. (1944). Poor scholar's soliloquy. *Childhood Education, 33,* 219–220.

Corrigan, D. (1997). The role of the university in community building. *Educational Forum, 62*(1), 14–24.

Corson, D. (1999). *Language policy in schools: A resource for teachers and administrators.* Mahwah, NJ: Erlbaum.

Crago, M. B. (1988). *Cultural context in the communicative interaction of young Inuit children.* Unpublished doctoral dissertation, McGill University.

Craik, F. I. M., and Lockhart, R. S. (1972). Levels of processing: A framework for memory research. *Journal of Verbal Learning and Verbal Behavior, 11,* 67–84.

Crawford, J., and Stallings, J. (1978). *Experimental effects of in-service teacher training derived from process-product correlations in the primary grades.* Stanford, CA: Program on Teaching Effectiveness, Center for Educational Research at Stanford.

Crespo, S. (2002). Praising and correcting: Prospective teachers investigate their teacherly talk. *Teaching and Teacher Education, 18*(6), 739–758.

Crooks, T. J. (1988). The impact of classroom evaluation practices on students. *Review of Educational Research, 58*(4), 438–481.

Crow, N. A. (1987, April). *Preservice teachers' biography: A case study.* Paper presented at the Annual Meeting of the American Educational Research Association, Washington, DC.

Crow, N., Stokes, D., Kauchak, D., Hobbs, S., and Bullough, Jr., R. V. (1996, April). *Masters cooperative program: An alternative model of teacher development in PDS sites.* Paper presented at the annual meeting of the American Educational Research Association, New York.

Cuban, L. (1992). Curriculum stability and change. In P. W. Jackson (Ed.), *Handbook of research on curriculum* (pp. 216–247). New York: Macmillan.

Cuban, L. (1993). *How teachers taught: Constancy and change in American classrooms, 1890–1990* (2nd ed.). New York: Teachers College Press.

Cummins, J. (1986). Empowering minority students: A framework for intervention. *Harvard Educational Review, 56*(1), 18–36.

Curwin, R. L., and Mendler, A. N. (2000). *Discipline with dignity.* Upper Saddle River, NJ: Pearson Education.

Cusick, P. (1973). *Inside high school: The student's world.* Austin, TX: Holt Rinehart and Winston.

Damon, W. (1990). *The moral child.* New York: Free Press.

D'Andrade, R. G. (1981). The cultural part of cognition. *Cognitive Science, 5,* 179–195.

Darling-Hammond, L. (Ed.). (1994). *Professional development schools: Schools for developing a profession.* New York: Teachers College Press.

Darling-Hammond, L. (1996). The right to learn and the advancement of teaching: Research, policy, and practice for democratic education. *Educational Researcher, 25*(6), 5–17.

Darling-Hammond, L. (1997). *The right to learn: A blueprint for creating schools that work.* San Francisco: Jossey-Bass.

Darling-Hammond, L. (1999). Educating teachers for the next century: Rethinking practice and policy. In G. A. Griffin (ed.), *The education of teachers* (pp. 221–256). Chicago: University of Chicago Press.

Darling-Hammond, L. (2000a). Teacher quality and student achievement: A review of state policy evidence. *Education Policy Analysis Archives, 8*(1). Retrieved October 3, 2004, from http://epaa.asu.edu/epaa/v8n1

Darling-Hammond, L. (Ed.). (2000b). *Studies of excellence in teacher education, (3 volumes).* Washington, DC: American Association of Colleges for Teacher Education.

Darling-Hammond, L. (2000c). How teacher education matters. *Journal of Teacher Education, 51*(3), 166–173.

Darling-Hammond, L. (2001a). Standard setting in teaching: Changes in licensing, certification, and assessment. In V. Richardson (Ed.), *Handbook of research on teaching,* (4th ed., pp. 751–776). Washington, DC: American Educational Research Association.

Darling-Hammond, L. (2001b). Inequality and access to knowledge. In J. A. Banks and C. A. M. Banks (Eds.), *Handbook of research on multicultural education* (pp. 465–483). San Francisco: Jossey-Bass.

Darling-Hammond, L. (2004). What happens to a dream deferred? The continuing quest for equal educational opportunity. In J. A. Banks and C. A. M. Banks (Eds.), *Handbook of research on multicultural education* (2nd ed., pp. 607–630). San Francisco: Jossey-Bass.

Darling-Hammond, L., Ancess, J., and Falk, B. (1995). *Authentic assessment in action: Studies of schools and students at work.* New York: Teachers College Press.

Darling-Hammond, L., Chung, R., and Frelow, F. (2002). Variation in teacher preparation: How well do different pathways prepare teachers to teach? *Journal of Teacher Education, 53*(4), 286–302.

Darling-Hammond, L., French, J., and Garcia-Lopez, S. (2002). *Learning to teach for social justice.* New York: Teachers College Press.

Darling-Hammond, L., and Hammerness, K. (2002). Toward a pedagogy of cases in teacher education. *Teaching Education, 13*(2), 125–135.

Darling-Hammond, L., Hudson, L., and Kirby, S. N. (1989). *Redesigning teacher education: Opening the door for new recruits to mathematics and science teaching.* Santa Monica, CA: Rand.

Darling-Hammond, L., and MacDonald, M. (2000). Where there is learning there is hope: The preparation of teachers at the Bank Street College of Education. In L. Darling-Hammond (Ed.), *Studies of excellence in teacher education: Preparation at the graduate level* (pp. 1–95). Washington, DC: American Association of Colleges for Teacher Education.

Darling-Hammond, L., and Sclan, E. M. (1996). Who teaches and why?: Dilemmas of building a profession for twenty-first century schools. In J. P. Sikula, T. J. Buttery, and E. Guyton (Eds.), *Handbook of research on teacher education* (2nd ed., pp. 67–101). New York: Macmillan.

Darling-Hammond, L., and Snyder, J. (2000). Authentic assessment of teaching in context. *Teaching and Teacher Education, 16*(5), 523–545.

Darling-Hammond, L., and Sykes, G. (2003). Wanted: A national teacher supply policy for education: The right way to meet the 'highly qualified teacher' challenge. *Educational Policy Analysis Archives, 11*(33). Retrieved October 3, 2004, from http://epaa.asu.edu/epaa/v11n33/

Darling-Hammond, L., Wise, A. E., and Klein, S. P. (1999). *A license to teach: Building a profession for 21st-century schools.* Boulder, CO: Jossey-Bass.

Darwin, C. (1859/1999). *The origin of species by means of natural selection.* New York: Bantam Books.

David, J. L. (1994). *Transforming state agencies to support education reform.* Washington, DC: National Governors Association.

Davidson, A. L., and Phelan, P. (1999). Students' multiple worlds: An anthropological approach to understanding students' engagement with school. In T. C. Urdan (Ed.), *Advances in motivation, 11,* (pp. 233–273). Greenwich, CT: JAI.

de Corte, E., Verschaffel, L., and Greer, B. (1996). Mathematics teaching and learning. In D. C. Berliner and R. C. Calfee (Eds.), *Handbook of educational psychology* (pp. 787–806). New York: Macmillan.

Deci, E. L. (1971). Effects of externally mediated rewards on intrinsic motivation. *Journal of Personality and Social Psychology, 18*(1), 105–115.

Deci, E. L. (1972). Intrinsic motivation, extrinsic reinforcement, and inequity. *Journal of Personality and Social Psychology, 22*(1), 113–120.

Deci, E. L. (1978). Applications of research on the effects of rewards. In M. R. Lepper and D. Greene (Eds.), *The hidden costs of reward: New perspectives on the psychology of human motivation* (pp. 149–176). Hillsdale, NJ: Erlbaum.

Deci, E. L., Koestner, R., and Ryan, R. M. (2001). Extrinsic rewards and intrinsic motivation in education: Reconsidered once again. *Review of Educational Research, 71*(1), 1–27.

Deci, E. L., and Ryan, R. M. (1985). *Intrinsic motivation and self-determination in human behavior.* New York: Plenum.

Deci, E. L., Ryan, R. M., and Koestner, R. (2001). The pervasive negative effects of rewards on intrinsic motivation: Response to Cameron (2001). *Review of Educational Research, 71*(1), 43–51.

de Groot, A. D. (1965). *Thought and choice in chess.* New York: Basic Books.

De Lisi, R., and Staudt, J. (1980). Individual differences in college students' performance on formal operations tasks. *Journal of Applied Developmental Psychology, 1,* 201–208.

Delgado-Gaitan, C. (1991). Involving parents in schools: A process of empowerment. *American Journal of Education, 100*(1), 20–46.

Delpit, L. D. (1995). *Other people's children: Cultural conflict in the classroom.* New York: New Press.

Dennison, G. M. (1992). National standards in teacher preparation: A commitment to quality. *The Chronicle of Higher Education*, A40.

Denton, J. J. (1982). Early field experience influence on performance in subsequent coursework. *Journal of Teacher Education, 33*(2), 19–23.

Denton, J. J., and Lacina, L. J. (1984). Quantity of professional education coursework linked with process measures of student teaching. *Teacher Education and Practice,* 39–64.

Denton, J. J., Morris, J. E., and Tooke, D. J. (1982). The influence of academic characteristics of student teachers on the cognitive attainment of learners. *Educational and Psychological Research, 2*(1), 15–29.

Denton, J. J., and Peters, W. H. (1988). *Program assessment report: Curriculum evaluation of a non-traditional program for certifying teachers.* Unpublished report. College Station: Texas A&M University.

Denton, J. J., and Smith, N. L. (1983). *Alternative teacher preparation programs: A cost-effectiveness comparison.* Research on Evaluation Program, Paper and Report Series No. 86. Eugene, OR: University of Oregon.

Denton, J. J., and Tooke, D. J. (1981). Examining learner cognitive attainment as a basis for assessing student teachers. *Action in Teacher Education, 3*(4), 39–45.

Derry, S. J. (1992). Beyond symbolic processing: Expanding horizons for educational psychology. *Journal of Educational Psychology, 84*(4), 413–418.

Derry, S. J., and Lesgold, A. (1996). Toward a situated social practice model of instructional design. In D. C. Berliner and R. C. Calfee (Eds.), *Handbook of educational psychology* (pp. 787–806). New York: Macmillan.

Desimone, L. M., Porter, A. C., Garet, M. S., Yoon, K. S., and Birman, B. F. (2002). Effects of professional development on teachers' instruction: Results from a three year longitudinal study. *Educational Evaluation and Policy Analysis, 24*(2), 81–112.

Deutsch, M. (1992). *The effects of training in conflict resolution and cooperative learning in an alternative high school. Summary Report.* Columbia University, New York: Teachers College International Center for Cooperation and Conflict Resolution.

DeVries, R. (1998). Implications of Piaget's constructivist theory for character education. *Action in Teacher Education, 20*(4), 39–47.

Dewey, J. (1902). *The child and the curriculum.* Chicago: University of Chicago Press.

Dewey, J. (1916/1977). *Democracy and education: An introduction to the philosophy of education.* New York: Macmillan.

Dewey, J. (1938). *Experience and education.* New York: Macmillan.

Diaz, R. M., Neal, C. J., and Amaya-Williams, M. (1990). The social origins of self-regulation. In L. C. Moll (Ed.), *Vygotsky and education: Instructional implications and applications of socio-historical psychology* (pp. 127–154). Cambridge, UK: Cambridge University Press.

Dilworth, M. E. (1992). *Diversity in teacher education: New expectations.* San Francisco: Jossey-Bass.

Doll, R. C. (1982). *Curriculum improvement: Decision making and process* (5th ed.). Boston: Allyn & Bacon.

Donaldson, M. (1978). *Children's minds.* New York: Norton.

Donovan, M. S., Bransford, J. D., and Pellegrino, J. W. (1999). *How People Learn: Bridging research and practice.* Washington, DC: National Academies Press.

Doyle, D. P., and Pimentel, S. (1999). *Raising the standard: An eight-step action guide for schools and communities* (2nd ed.). Thousand Oaks, CA: Corwin Press.

Doyle, W. (1986). Classroom organization and management. In M. C. Wittrock and American Educational Research Association (Eds.), *Handbook of research on teaching* (3rd ed., pp. 392–431). New York: Collier Macmillan.

Doyle, W. (1990). Classroom management techniques. In O. C. Moles (Ed.), *Student discipline strategies: Research and practice* (pp. 113–127). Albany: State University of New York Press.

Drachsler, J. (1920). *Democracy and assimilation, the blending of immigrant heritages in America.* New York: Macmillan.

Dreeben, R., and Barr, R. (1987, April). *Class composition and the design of instruction.* Paper presented at the annual meeting of the American Educational Research Association.

Dreeben, R., and Gamoran, A. (1986). Race, instruction, and learning. *American Sociological Review, 51*(5), 660–669.

Druckman, D., and Bjork, R. A. (1994). *Learning, remembering, believing: Enhancing human performance.* Washington, DC: National Academy Press.

Druva, C. A., and Anderson, R. D. (1983). Science teacher characteristics by teacher behavior and by student outcome: A meta-analysis of research. *Journal of Research in Science Teaching, 20*(50), 467–479.

Du Bois, W. E. B. (1903/1973). *The souls of black folk.* Millwood, NY: Kraus-Thomson Organization.

Duchastel, P. C., and Merrill, P. F. (1973). The effects of behavioral objectives on learning: A review of empirical studies. *Review of Educational Research, 43,* 1, 53–69.

Duesterberg, L. (1998). Rethinking culture in the pedagogy and practices of preservice teachers. *Teaching and Teacher Education, 14*(5), 497–512.

Duffy, G. G., and Roehler, L. R. (1987). Teaching reading skills as strategies. *Reading Teacher, 40*(4), 414–418.

Duffy, G. G., and Roehler, L. R. (1989). Why strategy instruction is so difficult and what we need to do about it. In C. B. McCormick, G. Miller, and M. Pressley (Eds.), *Cognitive strategy research: From basic research to educational applications* (pp. 133–154). New York: Springer-Verlag.

Duffy, G. G., Roehler, L. R., Meloth, M. S., Polin, R. Rackliffe, G., Tracy, A., and others (1987a). Developing and evaluating measures associated with strategic reading. *Journal of Reading Behavior, 19*(3), 223–246.

Duffy, G., Roehler, L., Sivan, E., Rackliffe, G., Book, C. K., Meloth, M., and others (1987b). Effects of explaining reasoning associated with using reading strategies. *Reading Research Quarterly, 22*(3), 347–368.

Dufour, R., and Eaker, R. (1998). *Professional learning communities at work: Best practices for enhancing student achievement.* Bloomington, IN: National Educational Service.

Dupont, H., Gardner, O. S., and Brody, D. (1974). *Toward affective development.* Circle Pines, MN: American Guidance Service.

Dweck, C. S. (1986). Motivational processes affecting learning. *American Psychologist, 41*(10), 1040–1048.

Dweck, C. S. (1989). Motivation. In A. Lesgold and R. Glaser (Eds.), *Foundations for a psychology of education* (pp. 87–136). Hillsdale, NJ: Erlbaum.

Ebmeier, H., and Good, T. L. (1979). The effects of instructing teachers about good teaching on the mathematics achievement of fourth grade students. *American Educational Research Journal, 16*(1), 1–16.

Ebmeier, H., Twombly, S., and Teeter, D. J. (1991). The comparability and adequacy of financial support for schools of education. *Journal of Teacher Education, 42*(3), 226–235.

Eccles (Parsons), J. S. (1983). Expectancies, values and academic behaviors. In J. T. Spence (Ed.), *Achievement and achievement motivation.* San Francisco: Freeman.

Eccles, J. S. (1999). The development of children ages 6 to 14. *Future of Children, 9*(2), 30–44.

Eccles, J. S., Jacobs, J., Harold-Goldsmith, R., Jayaratne, T. E., and Yee, D. (1989, April). *The relations between parents' category-based and target-based beliefs: Gender roles and biological influences.* Paper presented at the Society for Research in Child Development, Kansas City, MO.

Eccles, J. S., Midgley, C., Wigfield, A., Buchanan, C. M., Reuman, D., and MacIver, D. (1993). Development during adolescence: The impact of stage/environment fit on young adolescents' experiences in schools and in families. *American Psychologist, 48*(2), 90–101.

Eccles, J. S., Wigfield, A., and Schiefele, U. (1998). Motivation to succeed. In W. Damon (Ed.), *Handbook of child psychology* (5th ed., Vol. 3, pp. 1017–1094). New York: Wiley.

Eckert, P. (1989). *Jocks and burnouts: Social categories and identity in the high school.* New York: Teachers College Columbia University.

Eckstrom, R., and Villegas, A. M. (1991). Ability grouping in middle grade mathematics: Process and consequences. *Research in Middle Level Education, 15*(1), 1–20.

Edelson, D. C., Gordin, D. N., and Pea, R. D. (1997, March). *Creating science learning tools from experts' investigation tools: A design framework.* Paper presented at the Annual Meeting of the National Association for Research in Science Teaching, Oak Brook, IL.

Education Trust (2003). *Achievement in America.* Retrieved October 5, 2004, from http://www2.edtrust.org/NR/rdonlyres/14FB5D33-31EF-4A9C-B55F-33184998BDD8/0/1

Eisner, E. (1985). *Learning and teaching the ways of knowing.* Chicago: University of Chicago Press.

Eisner, E. (1992). Curriculum ideologies. In P. W. Jackson (Ed.), *Handbook of research on curriculum: A project of the American Educational Research Association* (pp. 302–326). New York: Macmillan.

Elawar, M. C., and Corno, L. (1985). A factorial experiment in teachers' written feedback on student homework: Changing teacher behavior a little rather than a lot. *Journal of Educational Psychology, 77*(2), 162–173.

Elbow, P. (1990). *What Is English?* New York: Modern Language Association of America.

Elkind, D. (1994). *Ties that stress: The new family imbalance.* Cambridge, MA: Harvard University Press.

Elliott, E. S., and Dweck, C. S. (1988). Goals: An approach to motivation and achievement. *Journal of Personality and Social Psychology, 54*(1), 5–12.

Ellis, R. (1997). *Second language acquisition.* Oxford: Oxford University Press.

Elmore, R., and Fuhrman, S. (1993). Opportunity to learn and the state role in education. In *The Debate on Opportunity-to-Learn Standards: Commissioned Papers.* Washington, DC: National Governors Association.

Elmore, R. F. (1996). Getting to scale with good educational practices. In S. H. Fuhrman and J. A. O'Day (Eds.), *Rewards and reform: Creating educational incentives that work* (pp. 294–329). San Francisco: Jossey-Bass.

Emmer, E. T. (1994). Towards an understanding of the primacy of classroom management and discipline. *Teaching Education, 6*(1), 65–69.

Emmer, E. T., and Aussiker, A. (1990). School and classroom discipline programs. In O. C. Moles (Ed.), *Student discipline strategies: Research and practice* (pp. 129–165). Albany: State University of New York Press.

Emmer, E. T., Evertson, C. M., and Anderson, L. M. (1980). Effective classroom management at the beginning of the school year. *Elementary School Journal, 80*(5), 219–231.

Emmer, E. T., Evertson, C. M., Sanford, J. P., Clements, B. S., and Worsham, M. E. (1984). *Classroom management for secondary teachers.* Englewood Cliffs, NJ: Prentice-Hall.

Englert, C. S. (1989). Exposition: Reading, writing, and the metacognitive knowledge of learning disabled students. *Learning Disabilities Research, 5*(1), 5–24.

Englert, C., and Raphael, T. (1989). Developing successful writers through cognitive strategy instruction. In J. Brophy (ed.), *Advances in research on teaching* (Vol. 1). Greenwich, CT: JAI.

Englert, C., Raphael, T., and Anderson, L. (1992). Socially mediated instruction: Improving students' knowledge and talk about writing. *Elementary School Journal, 92*(4), 411–449.

Epstein, J. L. (2001). *School, family, and community partnerships: Preparing educators and improving schools.* Boulder, CO: Westview Press.

Epstein, J. L., Sanders, M. G., Simon, B. S., Salinas, K. S., Jansorn, N. R., and VanVoorhis, F. L. (2002). *School, family, and community partnerships: Your handbook for action* (2nd ed.). Thousand Oaks, CA: Corwin Press.

Epstein, J. L., and Sheldon, S. B. (2002). Present and accounted for: Improving student attendance through family and community involvement. *Journal of Educational Research 95*(5), 308–318.

Ericsson, K. A., Krampe, R., and Tesch-Romer, C. (1993). The role of deliberate practice in the acquisition of expert performance. *Psychological Review, 100*(3), 363–406.

Erickson, E. (1972). Eight ages of man. In C. S. Lavatelli, F. Stendler, and W. E. Martin (Eds.), *Readings in child behavior and development* (3rd ed., pp. 19–30). New York: Harcourt Brace Jovanovich.

Erikson, E. H. (1963). *Childhood and society* (2nd ed.). New York: Norton.

Ertmer, P. (2003). Transforming teacher education: Visions and strategies. *Educational Technology Research and Development, 51*(1), 124–128.

Etzioni, A. (1996). *The new golden rule: Community and morality in a democratic society.* New York: Basic Books.

Evertson, C., Emmer, E., Sanford, J., and Clements, B. (1983). Improving classroom management: An experiment in elementary school classrooms. *Elementary School Journal, 84,* 173–188.

Evertson, C. M. (1987). Creating conditions for learning: From research to practice. *Theory into Practice, 26*(1), 44–50.

Evertson, C. M. (1989). Classroom organization and management. In M. C. Reynolds and American Association of Colleges for Teacher Education (Eds.), *Knowledge base for the beginning teacher* (pp. 59–70). New York: Pergamon Press.

Evertson, C. M. (1997). Classroom management. In H. J. Walberg and G. D. Haertel (Eds.), *Psychology and educational practice* (pp. 251–273). Berkeley, CA: McCutchan.

Ewart, O. M., and Brawn, M. (1978). *Erlebnisse und probleme vorschulischer foerderung* (Vol. 34): Modellversuch Vorklasse in NW-Abschlussbericht.

Farkas, S., Johnson, J., Duffett, A., and McHugh, J. (1998). *A lot to be thankful for: What parents want children to learn about America.* New York: Public Agenda Foundation.

Fay, J., and Funk, D. (1998). *Teaching with love and logic: Taking control of the classroom.* Golden, CO: Love and Logic Institute.

Feiman-Nemser, S. (1983). Learning to teach. In L. S. Shulman and G. Sykes (Eds.), *Handbook of teaching and policy* (pp. 150–171). New York: Longman.

Feiman-Nemser, S. (1990). Teacher preparation: Structural and conceptual analysis. In W. R. Houston, M. Haberman, and J. P. Sikula (Eds.), *Handbook of research on teacher education* (pp. 212–233). New York: Macmillan.

Feiman-Nemser, S. (2001a). From preparation to practice: Designing a continuum to strengthen and sustain teaching. *Teachers College Record, 103*(6), 1013–1055.

Feiman-Nemser, S. (2001b). Helping novices learn to teach: Lessons from an exemplary support teacher. *Journal of Teacher Education, 52*(1), 17–30.

Feiman-Nemser, S., and Buchmann, M. (1985). Pitfalls of experience in teacher preparation. *Teachers College Record, 87,* 53–65.

Feiman-Nemser, S., and Buchmann, M. (1989). Describing teacher education: A framework and illustrative findings from a longitudinal study of six students. *Elementary School Journal, 89*(3), 365–378.

Feistritzer, C. E. (1999). *The making of a teacher: A report on teacher education and certification.* Washington, DC: National Center for Education Information.

Feldman, D. H. (1980). *Beyond universals in cognitive development.* Norwood, NJ: Ablex.

Fennema, E., Carpenter, T., Franke, M., Levi, L., Jacobs, V., and Empson, S. (1996). A longitudinal study of learning to use children's thinking in mathematics instruction. *Journal for Research in Mathematics Learning, 27*(4), 403–434.

Fennema, E., Carpenter, T., and Peterson, P. (1989). Learning mathematics with understanding. In J. Brophy (Ed.), *Advances in Research on Teaching* (Vol. 1, pp. 195–221). Greenwich, CT: JAI.

Fennema, E., and Romberg, T. A. (1999). *Mathematics classrooms that promote understanding.* Mahwah, NJ: Erlbaum.

Fenwick, D. T. (1998). Managing space, energy, and self: Junior high teachers' experiences of classroom management. *Teaching and Teacher Education, 14*(6), 619–631.

Ferguson, P., and Womack, S. T. (1993). The impact of subject matter and education coursework on teaching performance. *Journal of Teacher Education, 44*(1), 55–63.

Ferguson, R. F. (1991a). Paying for public education: New evidence on how and why money matters. *Harvard Journal on Legislation, 28*(2), 465–498.

Ferguson, R. F. (1991b). Racial patterns in how school and teacher quality affect achievement and earnings. *Challenge, 2*(1), 1–35.

Ferguson, R. F., and Ladd, H. F. (1996). How and why money matters: An analysis of Alabama schools. In H. F. Ladd (Ed.), *Holding schools accountable: performance-based reform in education* (pp. 265–298). Washington, DC: Brookings Institution.

Fernandez, C. (2002). Learning from Japanese approaches to professional development: The case of lesson study. *Journal of Teacher Education, 53*(5), 393–405.

Fetler, M. (1999). High school staff characteristics and mathematics test results. *Education Policy Analysis Archives, 7*(9).

Field, D. (1987). A review of preschool conservation training: An analysis of analyses. *Developmental Review, 7,* 210–251.

Fillmore, L. W., and Snow, C. E. (2002). What teachers need to know about language. In C. T. Adger, C. E. Snow, and D. Christian (Eds.), *What teachers need to know about language* (pp. 7–53). McHenry, IL: Center for Applied Linguistics/Delta Systems.

Fine, M. (1991). *Framing dropouts: Notes on the politics of an urban public school.* Albany: State University of New York Press.

Fischetti, J., and Larson, A. (2002). How an integrated unit increased student achievement in a high school PDS. In I. N. Guadarrama, J. Ramsey, and J. L. Nath (Eds.), *Forging alliances in community and thought: Research in professional development schools* (pp. 227–258). Greenwich CT: Information Age Publishing.

Fisher, C. W., Berliner, D., Filby, N. N., Marliave, R. S., Cahen, L. S., and Dishaw M. (1980). Teaching behaviors, academic learning time, and student achievement: An overview. In C. Denham and A. Lieberman (Eds.), *Time to learn* (pp. 7–32). Washington, DC: National Institute of Education.

Flavell, J. H. (1976). Metacognitive aspects of problem solving. In L. B. Resnick (Ed.), *The nature of intelligence.* Hillsdale, NJ: Erlbaum.

Flavell, J. H. (1979) Metacognition and cognitive monitoring: A new area of cognitive-development inquiry. *American Psychologist, 34,* 906–911.

Flavell, J. H. (1994). Cognitive development: Past, present and future. In R. D. Parke, P. A. Ornstein, J. J. Rieser, and C. Zahn-Waxler (Eds.), *A century of developmental psychology.* Washington, DC: American Psychological Association.

Fleming, M., and Chambers, B. (1983). Teacher-made tests: Windows on the classroom. In W. E. Hathaway (Ed.), *Testing in the schools* (pp. 29–38). San Francisco: Jossey-Bass.

Flexner, A., and Pritchett, H. S. (1910). *Medical education in the United States and Canada: A report to the Carnegie Foundation for the Advancement of Teaching.* New York: Carnegie Foundation for the Advancement of Teaching.

Floden, R. E., McDiarmid, G. W., and Werners, N. (1989). *What are they trying to do? Perspectives on teacher educators' purposes.* East Lansing, MI: National Center for Research on Teacher Education, Michigan State University.

Florio-Ruane, S. (2001). *Teacher education and the cultural imagination.* Mahwah, NJ: Erlbaum.

Fosnot, C. T. (1996). Teachers construct constructivism: The center for constructivist teaching/teacher preparation project. In C. T. Fosnot (Ed.), *Constructivism: Theory, perspectives, and practice* (pp. 205–216). New York: Teachers College Press.

Foster, M. (2001). African American teachers and culturally relevant pedagogy. In J. A. Banks and C. A. M. Banks (Eds.), *Handbook of research on multicultural education* (pp. 570–581). San Francisco: Jossey-Bass.

Frary, R. B., Cross, L. H., and Weber, L. J. (1993). Testing and grading practices and opinions of secondary teachers of academic subjects: Implications for instruction in measurement. *Educational Measurement: Issues and Practice, 12*(3), 23–30.

Frederiksen, J. R., and Collins, A. (1989). A systems approach to educational testing. *Educational Researcher, 18*(9), 27–32.

Freese, A. R. (1999). The role of reflection on preservice teachers' development in the context of a professional development school. *Teaching and Teacher Education, 15*(8), 895–909.

Freiberg, H. J. (Ed). (1999). *Beyond behaviorism: Changing the classroom management paradigm.* Boston: Allyn & Bacon.

Frey, N. (2002). Literacy achievement in an urban middle-level professional development school: A learning community at work. *Reading Improvement, 39*(1), 3–13.

Fricke, A. (1995). *Reflections of a rock lobster: A story about growing up gay.* New York: Consortium Book Sales.

Friedman, S. J., and Manley, M. (1991, April). *Grading practices in the secondary school: Perceptions of the stakeholders.* Paper presented at the Annual Meeting of the National Council on Measurement in Education, Chicago.

Friel, S., and Carboni, L. (2000). Using video-based pedagogy in an elementary mathematics methods course. *School Science and Mathematics, 100*(3), 118–127.

Fullan, M. (1991). *The new meaning of educational change.* New York: Teachers College Press.

Fullan, M. (1993a). *Change forces: Probing the depths of educational reform.* London: Falmer.

Fullan, M. (1993b). Why teachers must become change agents. *Educational Leadership, 50*(6), 12–17.

Fullan, M. (1995). Contexts: Overview and framework. In M. J. O'Hair and S. Odell (Eds.), *Educating teachers for leadership and change. Teacher education yearbook III* (pp. 1–10). Thousand Oaks, CA: Corwin.

Fullan, M. (2001). *Leading in a culture of change.* San Francisco: Wiley.

Fuller, E. (1998). *Do properly certified teachers matter? A comparison of elementary school performance on the TAAS in 1997 between schools with high and low percentages of properly certified regular education teachers.* Austin: The Charles A. Dana Center, University of Texas at Austin.

Fuller, E. (2000, April). *Do properly certified teachers matter? Properly certified Algebra teachers and Algebra I achievement in Texas.* Paper presented at the American Educational Research Association, New Orleans, LA.

Fuller, F. F. (1969). Concerns of teachers: A developmental conceptualization. *American Educational Research Journal, 6*(2), 207–226.

Gage, N. L. (1978). *The scientific basis of the art of teaching.* New York: Teachers College Press.

Gage, N. L. (1985). *Hard gains in the soft sciences: The case of pedagogy.* Bloomington, IN: Phi Delta Kappa.

Gage, N. L., and Berliner, D. C. (1998). *Educational psychology* (6th ed.). Boston: Houghton Mifflin.

Gallavan, N. P., and Davis, J. E. (1999). Building community with young adolescents: Practical economics for the middle school classroom. *Clearing House, 72*(6), 341–344.

Gallego, M. A. (2001). Is experience the best teacher? The potential of coupling classroom and community-based field experiences. *Journal of Teacher Education, 52*(4), 312–325.

Gallimore, R., Dalton, S., and Tharp, R. G. (1986). Self-regulation and interactive teaching: The effects of teaching conditions on teachers' cognitive activity. *Elementary School Journal, 86*(5), 613–631.

Gamoran, A. (1990, April). *The consequences of track-related instructional differences for student achievement.* Paper presented at the Annual Meeting of the American Educational Research Association, Boston.

Gamoran, A. (1992). Access to excellence: Assignment to honors English classes in the transition from middle to high school. *Educational Evaluation and Policy Analysis, 14*(3), 185–204.

Gamoran, A., and Berends, M. (1987). The effects of stratification in secondary schools: Synthesis of survey and ethnographic research. *Review of Educational Research, 57,* 415–436.

Gamoran, A., and Mare, R. (1989). Secondary school tracking and educational inequality: Compensation, reinforcement or neutrality? *American Journal of Sociology, 94,* 1146–1183.

Gamoran, A., and Weinstein, M. (1995). *Differentiation and opportunity in restructured schools.* Washington, DC: U.S. Department of Education, OERI.

Gandara, P. (2002). A study of High School Puente: What we have learned about preparing Latino youths for postsecondary education. *Educational Policy Special Issue: The Puente Project—Issues and perspectives on preparing Latino youth for higher education, 16*(4), 474–495.

Garcia, E. (1993). Language, culture, and education. In L. Darling-Hammond (Ed.), *Review of research in education, Volume 19,* 51–98. Washington, DC: American Educational Research Association.

Gardner, H. (1983). *Frames of mind: The theory of multiple intelligences.* New York: Basic Books.

Garland, M. (1993). The mathematics workshop model: An interview with Uri Treisman. *Journal of Developmental Education, 16*(3), 14–16, 18, 20, 22.

Gathercoal, F. (1993). *Judicious discipline* (3rd ed.). San Francisco: Caddo Gap Press.

Gathercoal, F. (1997). *Judicious Discipline* (4th ed.). San Francisco: Caddo Gap Press.

Gay, G. (1993). Building cultural bridges: A bold proposal for teacher education. *Education and Urban Society, 25*(3), 285–299.

Gay, G. (2000). *Culturally responsive teaching: Theory, research, and practice.* New York: Teachers College Press.

Gay, G. (2002). Preparing for culturally responsive teaching. *Journal of Teacher Education, 53*(2), 106–116.

Gay, G., and Howard, T. (2000). Multicultural teacher education for the 21st century. *Teacher Educator, 36*(1), 1–16.

Gebhard, M., Austin, T., Nieto, S., and Willett, J. (2002). "You can't step on someone else's words": Preparing all teachers to teach language minority students. In Z. Beykont (Ed.), *The power of culture: Teaching across language difference.* Cambridge, MA: Harvard Publishing Group.

Gee, J. (2000–2001). Identity as an analytic lens for research in education. In W. Secada, (Ed.), *Review of Research in Education* (Vol. 25, pp. 99–126). Washington, DC: American Educational Research Association.

Gee, J. P. (1990). *Social linguistics and literacies: Ideology in discourses.* New York: Falmer Press.

Gee, J. P. (1991). What is literacy? In C. Mitchell and K. Weiler (Eds.), *Rewriting literacy: Culture and the discourse of the other* (pp. 3–12). New York: Bergin and Garvey.

Gee, J. P. (1993). *An introduction to human language: Fundamental concepts in linguistics.* Englewood Cliffs, NJ: Prentice Hall.

Gee, J. P. (1998). Forward. In L. I. Bartolomé (Ed.), *The misteaching of academic discourses: The politics of language in the classroom* (pp. ix–xvi). Oxford: Westview Press.

Gee, J. P. (2003a, April). *Decontextualized language: A problem, not a solution.* Paper presented at the 4th International Symposium on Bilingual Education, Arizona State University.

Gee, J. P. (2003b). *What video games have to teach us about learning and literacy.* New York: Palgrave Macmillan.

Gelman, R. (1979). Preschool thought. *American Psychologist, 34,* 900–905.

Genesee, F. (1999). *Program alternatives for linguistically diverse students.* Washington: Center for Research on Education, Diversity, and Excellence.

Gentner, D. (1983). Structure-mapping: A theoretical framework for analogy. *Cognitive Science, 7,* 155–170.

Gentner, D., Brem, S., Ferguson, R. W., Markman, A. B., Levidow, B. B., Wolff, P., and Forbus, K. D. (1997). Analogical reasoning and conceptual change: A case study of Johannes Kepler. *Journal of the Learning Sciences 6*(1), 3–40.

Gentry, J. R. (1982). An analysis of developmental spelling in GYNS AT WRK. *Reading Teacher, 36*(2), 192–200.

Gergen, K. J. (1995). Social construction and the educational process. In L. P. Steffe and J. E. Gale (Eds.), *Constructivism in education* (pp. 17–40). Hillsdale, NJ: Erlbaum.

Gettys, C. M., Puckett, K., Ray, B. M., Rutledge, V. C., Stepanske, J., and University of Tennessee-Chattanooga. (1999). *The professional development school experience evaluation.* Paper presented at Mid-South Educational Research Association Conference, Gatlinburg, TN.

Gibson, J. J., and Gibson, E. J. (1955). Perceptual learning: Differentiation or enrichment? *Psychological Review, 62,* 32–51.

Gick, M. L., and Holyoak, K. J. (1980). Analogical problem solving. *Cognitive Psychology, 12,* 306–355.

Gick, M. L., and Holyoak, K. J. (1983). Schema induction and analogical transfer. *Cognitive Psychology, 15,* 1–38.

Gilberts, G. H., and Lignugaris-Kraft, B. (1997). Classroom management and instruction competencies for preparing elementary and special education teachers. *Teaching and Teacher Education, 13*(6), 597–610.

Gilhool, T. K. (1982). The 1980s: Teacher preparation programs, handicapped children, and the courts. In M. C. Reynolds (Ed.), *The future of mainstreaming: Next steps in teacher education* (pp. 15–25). Reston, VA: Council for Exceptional Children.

Gill, B., and Hove, A. (1999). *The Benedum collaborative model of teacher education: A preliminary evaluation.* Report prepared for the Benedum Center for Education Reform DB-303-EDU. Santa Monica, CA: Rand.

Gilligan, C. (1982). *In a different voice: Psychological theory and women's development.* Cambridge, MA: Harvard University Press.

Girard, K. L., and Koch, S. J. (1996). *Conflict resolution in the schools: A manual for educators.* San Francisco: Jossey-Bass.

Girotto, V., and Light, P. (1993). The pragmatic bases of children's reasoning. In P. Light and G. Butterworth (Eds.), *Context and cognition: Ways of learning and knowing.* Hillsdale, NJ: Erlbaum.

Giroux, H. A., and Myrsiades, K. (2001). Beyond the corporate university: Culture and pedagogy in the new millennium. Lanham, MD: Rowman and Littlefield.

Glaeser, B. C., Karge, B. D., Smith, J., and Weatherill, C. (2002). Paradigm pioneers: A professional development school collaborative for special education teacher education candidates. In I. N. Guadarrama, J. Ramsey, and J. L. Nath (Eds.), *Forging alliances in community and thought: Research in professional development schools* (pp. 125–152). Greenwich, CT: Information Age Publishing.

Glasersfeld, E. (1995). *Radical constructivism: A way of knowing and learning.* Washington, DC: Falmer Press.

Glasser, W. (1986). *Control theory in the classroom.* New York: Harper & Row.

Glasser, W. (1990). *The quality school: Managing students without coercion.* New York: Perennial Library.

Goe, L. (2002). Legislating equity: The distribution of emergency permit teachers in California, *Education Policy Analysis Archives, 10*(42). Retrieved June 2, 2003, from http://epaa.asu.edu/epaa/v10n42/

Goertz, M. E., Ekstrom, R. B., and Coley, R. J. (1984). *The impact of state policy on entrance into the teaching profession* (Final Report under National Institute of Education Grant No. G83-0073). Princeton, NJ: Educational Testing Service.

Goffman, E. (1959). *The presentation of self in everyday life.* Garden City, NY: Doubleday.

Goldhaber, D., and Anthony, E. (2004). Can teacher quality be effectively assessed? Philadelphia: Center for Policy Research in Education.

Goldhaber, D. D., and Brewer, D. J. (1998). When should we reward degrees for teachers? *Phi Delta Kappan, 80*(2), 134, 136–138.

Goldhaber, D. D., and Brewer, D. J. (2000). Does teacher certification matter? High school teacher certification status and student achievement. *Educational Evaluation and Policy Analysis, 22*(2), 129–145.

Goldman, E., and Barron, L. (1990). Using hypermedia to improve the preparation of elementary teachers. *Journal of Teacher Education, 41*(3), 21–31.

Gollnick, D. M. (2001). National and state initiatives for multicultural education. In J. A. Banks and C. A. M. Banks (Eds.), *Handbook of research on multicultural education* (pp. 3–24). San Francisco: Jossey-Bass.

Gomez, L., Sherin, M., Griesdorn, J., and Finn, L. (2003). *Exploring the role of technology in pre-service teacher preparation.* Unpublished manuscript, Northwestern University.

Gomez, M. L., and Tabachnick, B. R. (1992). Telling teaching stories. *Teaching Education, 4*(2), 129–138.

Gonsier-Gerdin, J. (1993). Elementary school children's perspectives on peers with disabilities in the context of integrated play groups: "They're not really disabled. They're like plain kids." Position Paper, University of California, Berkeley.

Gonzalez, M. M. (1994, June). *Parental distancing strategies: Processes and outcomes in a longitudinal perspective.* Paper presented at the International Society for the Study of Behavioral Development, Amsterdam, The Netherlands.

Gonzalez, N., Moll, L. C., Floyd-Tenery, M., Ribera, A., Rendon, P., Gonzalez, C., and Amanti, C. (1995). Funds of knowledge for teaching in Latino households. *Urban Education, 29*(4), 443–470.

Good, G. (2001). *Humanism betrayed: Theory, ideology, and culture in the contemporary university.* Montreal: McGill-Queen's University Press.

Good, T. L. (1996). Teaching effects and teacher evaluation. In J. P. Sikula, T. J. Buttery, E. Guyton, and Association of Teacher Educators (Eds.), *Handbook of research on teacher education: A project of the Association of Teacher Educators* (2nd ed., pp. 617–665). New York: Macmillan Library Reference, USA.

Good, T. L., and Brophy, J. E. (1994). *Looking in classrooms* (6th ed.). New York: HarperCollins College Publishers.

Good, T. L., and Brophy, J. E. (1995). *Contemporary educational psychology* (5th ed.). White Plains, NY: Longman.

Good, T. L., and Findley, M. J. (1985). Sex role expectations and achievement. In J. B. Dusek (Ed.), *Teacher expectancies* (pp. 271–294). Hillsdale, NJ: Erlbaum.

Good T. L., and Grouws, D. A. (1979). The Missouri mathematics effectiveness project: An experiment in fourth-grade classrooms. *Journal of experimental psychology, 71*, 355–362.

Goodenow, C. (1993). Classroom belonging among early adolescent students: Relationships to motivation and achievement. *Journal of Early Adolescence, 13*(1), 21–43.

Goodlad, J. I. (1984). *A place called school: Prospects for the future.* New York: McGraw-Hill.

Goodlad, J. I. (1990). *Teachers for our nation's schools.* San Francisco: Jossey-Bass.

Goodlad, J. I. (1994). *Educational renewal: Better teachers, better schools.* San Francisco: Jossey-Bass.

Goodlad, J. I., Soder, R., and Sirotnik, K. A. (1990). *Places where teachers are taught.* San Francisco: Jossey-Bass.

Goodman, J. (1985). What students learn from early field experiences: A case study and critical analysis. *Journal of Teacher Education, 36*(6), 42–48.

Goodman, K., Goodman, Y., and Hood, W. (1989). *The whole language evaluation book.* Portsmouth, NH: Heinemann.

Goodwin, A. L. (1994). Making the transition from self to other: What do preservice teachers really think about multicultural education? *Journal of Teacher Education, 45*, 119–131.

Goodwin, A. L. (Ed.). (1997a). *Assessment for equity and inclusion.* New York: Routledge.

Goodwin, A. L. (1997b). Multicultural stories: Preservice teachers' conceptions of and responses to issues of diversity. *Urban Education, 32*(1), 117–145.

Goodwin, A. L. (2002). The case of one child: Making the shift from personal knowledge to professionally informed practice. *Teaching Education, 13*(2), 137–154.

Gordon, T. (1974). *T.E.T., teacher effectiveness training.* New York: P. H. Wyden.

Gore, J. M., and Zeichner, K. M. (1991). Action research and reflective teaching in preservice teacher education: A case study from the United States. *Teaching and Teacher Education, 7*(2), 119–136.

Graber, K. C. (1996). Influencing student beliefs: The design of a "High Impact" teacher education program. *Teaching and Teacher Education, 12*(5), 451–466.

Gragg, C. I. (1940, October 19). Because wisdom can't be told. *Harvard Alumni Bulletin*, 78–84.

Grant, C. A., and Koskella, R. A. (1986). Education that is multicultural and the relationship between preservice campus learning and field experiences. *Journal of Educational Research, 79*(4), 197–204.

Grant, S. G., Derme-Insinna, A., Gradwell, J., Lauricella, A. M., Pullano, L., and Tzetzo, K. (2002). Juggling two sets of books: A teacher responds to the New York State Global History Exam. *Journal of Curriculum and Supervision, 17*(3), 232–255.

Gray, L., Cahalan, M., Hein, S., Litman, C., Severynse, J., Warren, S., Wisan, G., and Stowe, P. (1993). *New teacher in the job market: 1991 update.* Washington, DC: U.S. Department of Education, OERI.

Greeley, K. (2000). *"Why fly that way": Linking community and academic achievement.* New York: Teachers College Press.

Greenfield, S., Nadler, M. A., Morgan, M., and Shine, K. (1977). The clinical investigation and management of chest pain in an emergency department: Quality assessment by criteria mapping. *Medical Care, 15,* 898–905.

Greeno, J. G. (1997). On claims that answer the wrong questions. *Educational Researcher, 26*(1), 5–17.

Greeno, J. G., Pearson, P. D., and Shoenfeld, A. H. (1997). Implications for the National Assessment of Educational Progress of Research on Learning and Cognition. In *Assessment in transition: Monitoring the nation's educational progress, background studies* (pp. 152–215). Stanford, CA: National Academy of Education.

Greenough, W. T., Juraska, J. M., and Volkmar, F. R. (1979). Maze training effects on dendritic branching in occipital cortex of adult rats. *Behavioral and Neural Biology, 26,* 287–297.

Greenwald, R., Hedges, L. V., and Laine, R. D. (1996). The effect of school resources on student achievement. *Review of Educational Research, 66*(3), 361–396.

Grissmer, D., Flanagan, A. Kawata, J., and Williamson, S. (2000). *Improving student achievement: What state NAEP test scores tell us.* Santa Monica, CA: Rand.

Griswold, P. A., and Griswold, M. M. (1992, April). *The grading contingency: Graders' beliefs and expectations and the assessment ingredients.* Paper presented at the Annual Meeting of the American Educational Research Association, San Francisco.

Grossman, P. (1990). *The making of a teacher: Teacher knowledge and teacher education.* New York: Teachers College Press.

Grossman, P. (1994). In pursuit of a dual agenda: Creating a middle-level professional development school. In L. Darling-Hammond (Ed.), *Professional development schools: Schools for developing a profession* (pp. 50–73). New York: Teachers College Press.

Grossman, P. (in press). Research on pedagogical approaches in teacher education. In M. Cochran-Smith and K. Zeichner (Eds.), *Report of the AERA Panel on Research and Teacher Education.* Washington, DC: American Educational Research Association Consensus Panel on Teacher Education.

Grossman, P., and McDaniel, J. E. (1990, April). *Breaking boundaries: Restructuring teacher education as a collaborative school/university venture.* Paper presented at the American Educational Research Association, Boston.

Grossman, P. L. (1992). Why models matter: An alternate view on professional growth in teaching. *Review of Educational Research, 62*(2), 171–179.

Grossman, P. L. (2001). Research on the teaching of literature: Finding a place. In V. Richardson (Ed.), *Handbook of research on teaching* (4th ed.). Washington, DC: American Educational Research Association.

Grossman, P. L. (2002, May). *Teacher knowledge and professional education: The case of pedagogical content knowledge.* Keynote address presented at the Inaugural Universiti Pendidikan Sultan Idris (UPSI) International Teacher Conference, TanjongMalim, Perak, Malaysia.

Grossman, P. L., Smagorinsky, P., and Valencia, S. (1999). Appropriating tools for teaching English: A theoretical framework for research on learning to teach. *American Journal of Education, 108*(1), 1–29.

Grossman, P. L., and Stodolsky, S. S. (1995). Content as context: The role of school subjects in secondary school teaching. *Educational Researcher, 24*(8), 5–11, 23.

Grossman, P. L., and Stodolsky, S. S. (2000). Changing students, changing teaching. *Teachers College Record, 102,* 123–172.

Grossman, P. L., Thompson, C., Valencia, S. W. (2002). Focusing the concerns of new teachers. The district as teacher educator. In A. Hightower, M. S. Knapp, J. Marsh, and M. W. McLaughlin (Eds.), *School districts and instructional renewal: Opening the conversation* (pp. 129–142). New York: Teachers College Press.

Grossman, P., Wineburg, S., and Beers, S. (2000). When theory meets practice in the world of school. In S. S. Wineburg and P. L. Grossman (Eds.), *Interdisciplinary curriculum: Challenges to implementation* (pp. 1–16). New York: Teachers College Press.

Grouws, D. (Ed.). (1992). *Handbook for research on mathematics teaching and learning.* New York: Macmillan.

Guadarrama, I. N., Ramsey, J., and Nath, J. L. (Eds.). (2002). *Forging alliances in community and thought: Research in professional development schools.* Greenwich, CT: Information Age Publishing.

Guggenheim, C. (Writer) (1995). *The shadow of hate: A history of intolerance in America* [Video]. Montgomery, AL: Teaching Tolerance.

Gullickson, A. R. (1985). Student evaluation techniques and their relationship to grade and curriculum. *Journal of Educational Research, 79*(2), 96–100.

Gumperz, J. J. (1982). *Discourse strategies.* Cambridge, UK: Cambridge University Press.

Gunstone, R. F., Slattery, M., and others (1993). A case study of development in preservice science teachers. *Science Education, 77*(1), 47–73.

Gutiérrez, K., and Rogoff, B. (2003). Cultural ways of learning: Individual traits or repertoires of practice? *Educational Researcher, 32*(5), 19–25.

Gutmann, A. (1999). *Democratic education* (Rev. ed.). Princeton, NJ: Princeton University Press.

Gutmann, A. (2004). Unity and diversity in democratic multicultural education: Creative and destructive tensions. In J. A. Banks (Ed.), *Diversity and citizenship education: Global perspectives* (pp. 71–96). San Francisco: Jossey-Bass.

Gutmann, A., and Thompson, D. F. (1996). *Democracy and disagreement.* Cambridge, MA: Belknap Press.

Guyton, E., and McIntyre, D. J. (1990). Student teaching and school experiences. In W. R. Houston (Ed.), *Handbook of research on teacher education* (pp. 514–535). New York: MacMillan.

Haberman, M. (1996). Selecting and preparing culturally competent teachers for urban schools. In J. P. Sikula, T. J. Buttery, and E. Guyton (Eds.), *Handbook of research on teacher education* (2nd ed., pp. 747–760). New York: Macmillan.

Haberman, M., and Post, L. (1992). Does direct experience change education students' perception of minority children? *Midwest Educational Researcher, 5*(2), 29–31.

Haertel, E. H. (1991). New forms of teacher assessment. *Review of Research in Education, 17,* 3–29.

Halliday, M. A. K. (1993). Towards a language-based theory of learning. *Linguistics and Education, 5,* 93–116.

Hallinan, M. (2003). Ability grouping and student learning. In D. Ravitch (Ed.), *Brookings Papers on Education Policy, 2003.* Washington, DC: Brookings Institution.

Hammerness, K. (in press). *Seeing through teachers' eyes: The role of vision in teachers' lives and work.* New York: Teachers College Press.

Hammerness, K., and Darling-Hammond, L. (2002). Meeting old challenges and new demands: The redesign of the Stanford Teacher Education Program. *Issues in Teacher Education, 11*(1), 17–30.

Hammerness, K., Darling-Hammond, L., and Shulman, L. (2002, April 10–14). *Towards expert thinking: How case-writing contributes to the development of theory-based professional knowledge in student-teachers.* Paper presented at the Annual Meeting of the American Educational Research Association, Seattle, WA.

Hanafin, J., and Lynch, A. (2002). Peripheral voices: Parental involvement, social class, and educational disadvantage. *British Journal of Sociology of Education, 50*(5), 35–49.

Haney, W., and Madaus, G. (1986). *Effects of standardized testing and the future of the national assessment of educational progress.* (Working paper prepared for the NAEP Study Group). Chestnut Hill, MA: Center for the Study of Testing, Evaluation, and Educational Policy, Boston College.

Hansen, L. S. (1977). *Project born free.* Minneapolis: University of Minnesota.

Hanson, N. R. (1970). A picture theory of theory meaning. In R. G. Colodny (Ed.), *The nature and function of scientific theories* (pp. 233–274). Pittsburgh, PA: University of Pittsburgh Press.

Hanushek, E. A., Kain, J. F., and Rivkin, S. G. (1999, January). *Do higher salaries buy better teachers?* Paper presented at the Annual Meeting of the American Economic Association, New York.

Harackiewicz, J. M., Abrahams, S., and Wageman, R. (1987). Performance evaluation and intrinsic motivation: The effects of evaluative focus, rewards, and achievement orientation. *Journal of Personality and Social Psychology, 53*(6), 1015–1023.

Harackiewicz, J. M., and Sansone, C. (2000). Rewarding competence: The importance of goals in the study of intrinsic motivation. In C. Sansone and J. M. Harackiewicz (Eds.), *Intrinsic and extrinsic motivation: The search for optimal motivation and performance* (pp. 82–103). San Diego, CA: Academic Press.

Harding, S. G. (1991). *Whose science? Whose knowledge?: Thinking from women's lives.* Ithaca, NY: Cornell University Press.

Hargreaves, A. (1994). *Changing teachers, changing times: Teacher' work and culture in the postmodern age.* New York: Teachers College Press.

Harrington, H. L. (1995). Fostering seasoned decisions: Case-based pedagogy and the professional development of teachers. *Teaching and Teacher Education, 11*(3), 203–214.

Harris, M. J., and Rosenthal, R. (1985). Mediation of interpersonal expectancy effects: 31 meta-analyses. *Psychological Bulletin, 97,* 363–386.

Harris, T. R., Bransford, J. D., and Brophy, S. P. (2002). Roles for learning sciences and learning technologies in biomedical engineering education: A review of recent advances. *Annual Review Biomedical Engineering, 4,* 29–48.

Harris, W. N., Lee, V. W., and Pigge, F. L. (1970). Effectiveness of micro-teaching experiences in elementary science methods classes. *Journal of Research in Science Teaching 7,* 31–33.

Harter, S. (1988). The construction and conservation of the self: James and Cooley revisited. In D. K. Lapsley and F. C. Power (Eds.), *Self, ego, and identity: Integrative approaches* (pp. 43–69). New York: Springer-Verlag.

Harter, S. (1990). Self and identity development. In S. S. Feldman and G. R. Elliott (Eds.), *At the threshold: The developing adolescent* (pp. 352–387). Cambridge, MA: Harvard University Press.

Harter, S. (1996). Teacher and classmate influences on scholastic motivation, self-esteem, and level of voice in adolescents. In J. Juvonen and K. R. Wentzel (Eds.), *Social motivation: Understanding children's school adjustment* (pp. 11–42). Cambridge, UK: Cambridge University Press.

Harter, S. (1997). The development of self-representations. In W. Damon (Ed.), *Handbook of child psychology* (5th ed., pp. 553–618). New York: Wiley.

Harter, S. (1998). The development of self-representations. In W. Damon (Ed.), *Handbook of child psychology* (Vol. 3, pp. 553–618). New York: Wiley.

Hartup, W. (1979). The two social worlds of childhood. *American Psychologist, 34,* 944–950.

Hartup, W. (1983). The peer relations. In E. M. Hetherington (Ed.), and P. H. Mussen (Series Ed.), *Handbook of child psychology: Vol. 4. Socialization, personality, and social development* (pp. 103–196). New York: Wiley.

Hartup, W. W. (1989). Social relationships and their developmental significance. *American Psychologist, 44*(2), 120–126.

Harvard Law School. (1936). *Report of the committee on curriculum.* Cambridge, MA: Author.

Hasher, L., and Zacks, R. T. (1979). Automatic and effortful processes in memory. *Journal of Experimental Psychology: General,* 108, 356–388.

Hatano, G., and Greeno, J. G. (1999). Commentary: Alternative perspectives on transfer and transfer studies. *International Journal of Educational Research, 31,* 645–654.

Hatano, G., and Inagaki, K. (1986). Two courses of expertise. In H. Stevenson, H. Azuma, and K. Hakuta (Eds.) *Child development and education in Japan* (pp. 262–272). New York: Freeman.

Hatano, G., and Inagaki, K. (1991). Sharing cognition through collective comprehension activity. In L. Resnick, J. M. Levine, and S. D. Teasley (Eds.), *Perspectives on socially shared cognition* (pp. 331–348). Washington, DC: American Psychological Association.

Hatano, G., and Oura, Y. (2003). Commentary: Reconceptualizing school learning using insight from expertise research. *Educational Researcher, 32*(8), 26–29.

Hawk, P. P., Coble, C. R., and Swanson, M. (1985). Certification: It does matter. *Journal of Teacher Education, 36*(3), 13–15.

Hawkins, D. (1974). *I, thou, and it, the informed vision.* Flemington, NJ: Agathon Press.

Hayes, H. A., and Wetherill, K. S. (1996, April). *A new vision for schools, supervision, and teacher education: The professional development system and Model Clinical Teacher Project.* Paper presented at the annual meeting of the American Educational Research Association, New York.

Hayes, J. R. (1990). Individuals and environments in writing instruction. In B. F. Jones and L. Idol (Eds.), *Dimensions of thinking and cognitive instruction* (pp. 241–263). Hillsdale, NJ: Erlbaum.

Haynes, N. M., Ben-Avie, M., Squires, D. A., Howley, J. P., Negron, E. N., and Corbin, J. N. (1996). It takes a whole village: The SDP school. In J. P. Comer, N. M. Haynes, E. T. Joyner, and M. Ben-Avie (Eds.), *Rallying the whole village: The Comer process for reforming education* (pp. 42–71). New York: Teachers College Press.

Heath, S. B. (1982). Questioning at home and at school: A comparative study. In G. D. Spindler (Ed.), *Doing the ethnography of schooling: Educational anthropology in action* (pp. 102–131). New York: Holt, Rinehart and Winston.

Heath, S. B. (1983). *Ways with words: Language, life, and work in communities and classrooms.* Cambridge, UK: Cambridge University Press.

Heath, S. B. (1986). What no bedtime story means: Narrative skills at home and school. In B. B. Schieffelin and E. Ochs (Eds.), *Language socialization across cultures* (pp. 97–124). Cambridge, UK: Cambridge University Press.

Heath, S. B. (1994). Shared thinking and the register of coaching. In D. B. E. Finegan (Ed.), *Sociolinguistic perspectives on register* (pp. 82–105). New York: Oxford University Press.

Heath, S. B., Soep, E., and Roach, A. (1998). Living the arts through language and learning: A report on community-based youth organizations. *Americans for the Arts Monographs, 2*(7), 1–20.

Hegarty, S. (2001, January 21). Newcomers feel toll of teaching is too high. *St. Petersburg Times*. Retrieved November 21, 2002, from http://www.sptimes.com/News/012101/TampaBay/Newcomers_find_toll_o.shtml

Hendrickson, G., and Schroeder, W. H. (1941). Transfer of training in learning to hit a submerged target. *Journal of Educational Psychology, 32*(2), 5–13.

Henry, M. (1983). The effect of increased exploratory field experiences upon the perceptions and performance of student teachers. *Action in Teacher Education, 5*(1–2), 66–70.

Herbst, J. (1989). Teacher preparation in the nineteenth century: Institutions and purposes. In D. Warren (Ed.), *American teachers: Histories of a profession at work* (pp. 213–236). New York: Macmillan.

Hernández, H. (1989). *Multicultural education: A teacher's guide to content and process.* Columbus, OH: Merrill.

Hestenes, D. (1987). Toward a modeling theory of physics instruction. *American Journal of Physics, 55,* 440–454.

Heubert, J. P., and Hauser, R. M. (1999). *High stakes: Testing for tracking, promotion, and graduation.* Washington, DC: National Academies Press.

Hiebert, E. H., and Raphael, T. (1998). *Early literacy instruction.* Fort Worth, TX: Harcourt Brace College Publishers.

Hillocks, G. (2002). *The testing trap: How state writing assessments control learning.* New York: Teachers College Press.

Hmelo-Silver, C. E. (2004). Problem-based learning: What and how do students learn? *Educational Psychology Review, 16,* 235–266.

Hodgkinson, H. (2001). Educational demographics: What teachers should know. *Educational Leadership, 58*(4), 6–11.

Hoffer, T. B. (1992). Middle school ability grouping and student achievement in science and mathematics. *Educational Evaluation and Policy Analysis, 14*(3), 205–227.

Hoffman, E. (1989). *Lost in translation: A life in a new language.* New York: Penguin.

Hogan, K., and Pressley, M. (1997). Scaffolding scientific competencies within classroom communities of inquiry. In K. E. Hogan and M. E. Pressley (Eds.), *Scaffolding student learning: Instructional approaches and issues.* (pp. 74–107). Cambridge, MA: Brookline Books.

Hollingsworth, S., and Sockett, H. T. (Eds.). (1994). *Teacher research and educational reform, 93rd yearbook, Part 1, of the National Society for the Study of Education.* Chicago: National Society for the Study of Education.

Holmes Group. (1986). *Tomorrow's teachers: A report of the Holmes group.* East Lansing, MI: Author.

Holmes Group. (1990). *Tomorrow's schools: Principles for the design of professional development schools: Executive summary.* East Lansing, MI: Author.

Holmes Group. (1996). *Tomorrow's schools of education.* East Lansing, MI: Author.

Holt-Reynolds, D. (1992). Personal history-based beliefs as relevant prior knowledge in course work. *American Educational Research Journal, 29*(2), 325–349.

Holt-Reynolds, D. (1994). When agreeing with the professor is bad news: Jeneane, her personal history and coursework. *Teacher Education Quarterly, 21*(1), 13–35.

Hooever-Dempsey, K. V., Walker, J. M. T., and Jones, K. P. (2002). Teachers involving parents (TIP): Results of an in-service teacher education program for enhancing parental involvement. *Teaching and Teacher Education, 18*, 843–867.

Hopkins, K. D. (1998). *Educational and psychological measurement and evaluation* (8th ed.). Boston: Allyn & Bacon.

Horn, I. (2003). *Learning on the job: Mathematics teachers' professional development in the contexts of high school reform.* Unpublished doctoral dissertation, University of California, Berkeley.

Houston, W. R., Clay, D., Hollis, L. Y., Ligons, C., Roff, L., and Lopez, N. (1995). *Strength through diversity: Houston Consortium for Professional Development and Technology Centers.* Houston, TX: University of Houston, College of Education.

Houston Consortium of Professional Development. (1996, April). *ATE Newsletter, 7.*

Howard, G. R. (1999). *We can't teach what we don't know: White teachers, multiracial schools.* New York: Teachers College Press.

Howard, R. D., Hitz, R., and Baker, L. (1998). A national study comparing the expenditures of teacher education programs by Carnegie classification and with other disciplines. *Action in Teacher Education, 20*(3), 1–14.

Howey, K. R. (1994). *RATE VI: The context for the reform of teacher education. 1992 data set. Research about teacher education project.* Washington, DC: American Association of Colleges for Teacher Education (AACTE) Publications.

Howey, K. R., and Zimpher, N. L. (1989). *Profiles of preservice teacher education: Inquiry into the nature of programs.* Albany: State University of New York Press.

Howley, C. B. (1989). Synthesis of the effects of school and district size: What research says about achievement in small schools and school districts. *Journal of Rural and Small Schools, 4*(1), 2–12.

Howsam, R. B. (1976). *Educating a profession: Report of the Bicentennial Commission on Education for the Profession of Teaching of the American Association of Colleges for Teacher Education.* Washington, DC: American Association of Colleges for Teacher Education.

Hrycauk, M. (2002). District weaves a safety net: Program comes to the early rescue of young readers. *Journal of Staff Development, 23*(1), 55–58.

Huberman, M. (1989). The professional life cycle of teachers. *Teachers College Record, 91*(1), 31–57.

Huberman, M., Grounauer, M. M., Marti, J., and Huberman, A. M. (1993). *The lives of teachers.* New York: Teachers College Press.

Hull, G., and Schultz, K. (2001). Literacy and learning out of school: A review of theory and research. *Review of Educational Research, 71*(4), 575–611.

Hutchins, E., and Klausen, T. (1996). Distributed cognition in an airline cockpit. In Y. Engeström and D. Middleton (Eds.), *Cognition and communication at work* (pp. 15–34). New York: Cambridge University Press.

Hyde, T. S., and Jenkins, J. J. (1969). Differential effects of incidental tasks on the organization of recall of a list of highly associated words. *Journal of Experimental Psychology, 82,* 472–481.

Ignatiev, N. (1995). *How the Irish became white.* New York: Routledge.

Imbimbo, J., and Silvernail, D. (1999). *Prepared to teach? Key findings of the New York city teacher survey. Policy and Research Series.* New York: New Visions for Public Schools.

Imig, D. G. (1992). *The professionalization of teaching: Relying on a professional knowledge base.* St. Louis, MO: AACTE Knowledge-Base Seminar.

Imig, D., and Switzer, T. (1996). Changing teacher education programs: Restructuring collegiate-based teacher education. In J. P. Sikula, T. J. Buttery, and E. Guyton (Eds.), *Handbook of research on teacher education* (2nd ed., pp. 213–226). New York: Macmillan.

Ingvarson, L. (1998). Professional development as the pursuit of professional standards: The standards-based professional development system. *Teaching and Teacher Education, 14*(1), 127–140.

Inhelder, B., and Piaget, J. (1958). *The growth of logical thinking from childhood to adolescence: An essay on the construction of formal operational structures.* New York: Basic Books.

International Reading Association International. (2003). *Prepared to make a difference: Research evidence on how some of America's best college programs prepare teachers of reading.* Newark, NJ: International Reading Association.

Irvine, J. J. (1990). *Black students and school failure: Policies, practices, and prescriptions.* New York: Greenwood Press.

Irvine, J. J. (1997). *Critical knowledge for diverse teachers and learners.* Washington, DC: American Association of Colleges for Teacher Education.

Irvine, J. J. (2003). *Educating teachers for diversity: Seeing with a cultural eye.* New York: Teachers College Press.

Irvine, J. J., and Armento, B. J. (2001). *Culturally responsive teaching: Lesson planning for elementary and middle grades.* Boston: McGraw-Hill.

Jackson, P., Boostrom, R., and Hansen, D. (1998). *The moral life of schools.* San Francisco: Jossey-Bass.

Jackson, P. W. (1974). *Life in classrooms.* New York: Holt, Rinehart and Winston.

Jackson, P. W. (1992). Conceptions of curriculum and curriculum specialists. In P. W. Jackson (Ed.), *Handbook of research on curriculum: A project of the American Educational Research Association* (pp. 216–247). New York: Macmillan.

Jackson, S., Krajcik, J., Soloway, E. (2000). Model-it: A design retrospective. In Jacobson, M., and Kozma, R. (Eds.), *Advanced Designs for the technologies of learning: Innovations in science and mathematics education.* Hillsdale, NJ: Erlbaum.

Jacobson, M. F. (1998). *Whiteness of a different color: European immigrants and the alchemy of race.* Cambridge, MA: Harvard University Press.

Jadallah, E. (1996). Reflective theory and practice: A constructivist process for curriculum and instructional decisions. *Action in Teacher Education, 18*(2), 73–85.

Jadallah, E. (2000). Constructivist learning experiences for social studies education. *Social Studies, 91*(5), 221–225.

Jennings, W. S., and Kohlberg, L. (1983). Effects of a just community programme on the moral development of youthful offenders. *Journal of Moral Education, 12*(1), 33–50.

Jensen, M., Johnson, D. W., and Johnson, R. T. (2002). Impact of positive interdependence during electronic quizzes on discourse and achievement. *Journal of Educational Research, 95*(3), 161–66.

Jett-Simpson, M., Pugach, M. C., and Whipp, J. (1992, April). *Portrait of an urban professional development school.* Paper presented at the annual meeting of the American Educational Research Association, San Francisco.

Johnson, D. W., and Johnson, R. T. (1989). *Cooperation and competition: Theory and research.* Edina, MN: Interaction Book Co.

Johnson, D. W., and Johnson, R. T. (1994). Effects of conflict resolution training on elementary school students. *Journal of Social Psychology, 134*(6), 803–817.

Johnson, R. T. (1985). Effects of single-sex and mixed-sex cooperative interaction on science achievement and attitudes and cross-handicap and cross-sex relationships. *Journal of Research in Science Teaching, 22*(3), 207–220.

Johnson, R. T., and Johnson, D. W. (1983). The effects of cooperative, competitive, and individualistic learning experiences on social development. *Exceptional Children, 49*(4), 323–329.

Johnson, V. G. (1994). Student teachers' conceptions of classroom control. *Journal of Educational Research, 88*(2), 109–117.

Johnston, M. (Ed.). (1997). *Contradictions in collaboration: New thinking on school/university partnerships.* New York: Teachers College Press.

Jones, F. H. (1987). *Positive classroom discipline.* New York: McGraw-Hill.

Jones, L. V. (1984). White-Black achievement differences: The narrowing gap. *American Psychologist, 39*(11), 1207–1213.

Jones, L. V., Burton, N. W., and Davenport, E. C. (1984). Monitoring the achievement of black students. *Journal for Research in Mathematics Education, 15,* 154–164.

Jones, M. G., and Wheatley, J. (1990). Gender differences in teacher-student interactions in science classrooms. *Journal of Research in Science Teaching, 27*(9), 861–874.

Jones, V. F., and Jones, L. S. (1990). *Comprehensive classroom management: Motivating and managing students* (3rd ed.). Boston: Allyn & Bacon.

Jones, V. F., and Jones, L. S. (2001). *Comprehensive classroom management: Creating communities of support and solving problems* (6th ed.). Boston: Allyn & Bacon.

Joughin, G., and Gardiner, D. (1996). *A framework for teaching and learning law.* Sydney, NSW: Centre for Legal Education.

Joyce, B., and Showers, B. (2002). *Student achievement though staff development.* (3rd ed.). Alexandria, VA: Association for Supervision and Curriculum Development.

Joyce, B., and Weil, M. (2003). *Models of teaching* (7th ed.). Boston: Allyn & Bacon.

Juarez, D. (1999). A question of fairness: Using writing and literature to expand ethnic identity and understand marginality. In S. Friedman, E. R. Simons, J. S. Kalnin, and A. Caserno (Eds.), *Inside city schools* (pp. 111–125). New York: Teachers College Press.

Judd, C. H. (1908). The relation of special training to general intelligence. *Educational Review, 36,* 28–42.

Judge, H., Carriedo, R., and Johnson, S. M. (1995). *Professional development schools and MSU. The report of the 1995 review.* Retrieved October 5, 2004, from http://ed-web3.educ.msu.edu/pds/pdfdocs/report.pdf

Kagan, D. M. (1992). Professional growth among preservice and beginning teachers. *Review of Educational Research, 62*(2), 129–169.

Kallen, H. M. (1924). *Culture and democracy in the United States.* New York: Boni and Liveright.

Kamii, C., and Housman, L. B. (2000). *Young children reinvent arithmetic: Implications of Piaget's theory* (2nd ed.). New York: Teachers College Press.

Kammen, M. G. (1997). *In the past lane: Historical perspectives on American culture.* New York: Oxford University Press.

Kann, M. E. (1994). Discipline, character, and education. *Teaching Education, 6*(1), 71–75.

Kaplan, A., Gheen, M., and Midgley, C. (2002). Classroom goal structure and student disruptive behaviour. *British Journal of Sociology of Education, 72*(2), 191–211.

Katz, L. G. (1993). All about me: Are we developing our children's self-esteem or their narcissism? *American Educator, 17*(2), 18–23.

Katz, P. A. (1982). Development of children's awareness and intergroup attitudes. In L. G. Katz (Ed.), *Current topics in early childhood education* (4th ed., pp. 17–54). Norwood, NJ: Ablex.

Keeney, T. J., Cannizzo, S. R., and Flavell, J. H. (1967). Spontaneous and induced verbal rehearsal in a recall task. *Child Development, 38,* 953–966.

Kemmis, S. (1993). Action research and social movement: A challenge for policy research. *Education Policy Analysis, 1*(1). Retrieved September 17, 2004, from http://epaa.asu.edu/epaa/v1n1.html

Kennedy, M. (1998). *Form and substance in inservice teacher education. Research Monograph* (No. 13). WI: National Institute for Science Education, University of Wisconsin-Madison.

Kennedy, M. (1999). The role of preservice teacher education. In L. Darling-Hammond and G. Sykes (Eds.), *Teaching as the learning profession: Handbook of policy and practice* (pp. 54–85). San Francisco: Jossey Bass.

Kentucky Institute for Education Research. (1997). *The preparation of teachers for Kentucky schools: A survey of new teachers.* Frankfort, KY: Author.

Kern, D. E., Thomas, P. A., Howard, D. M., and Bass, E. B. (1998). *Curriculum development for medical education: A six step approach.* Baltimore: Johns Hopkins University Press.

Khisty, L. L. (1995). Making inequality: Issues of language and meanings in mathematics teaching with Hispanic students. In W. G. Secada, E. Fennema, and L. Byrd Adajian (Eds.), *New directions for equity in mathematics education* (pp. 279–297). Cambridge, UK: Cambridge University Press.

Khmelkov, V. T., and Hallinan, M. (1999). Organizational effects on race relations in schools. *Journal of Social Issues, 55*(4), 627–646.

King, B. (1990). *Thinking about linking portfolios with assessment center exercises: Example from the teacher assessment project.* Stanford: Teacher Assessment Project (TAP), Stanford University.

King, J., Hollins, E., and Hayman, W. (1997). *Preparing teachers for cultural diversity.* New York: Teachers College Press.

Kinsella, K. (1998). Content literacy development for college-bound ESL/EFL students. Unpublished materials from TESOL Academy, Johns Hopkins University. Baltimore: TESOL.

Kinsella, K., and Feldman, K. (2003). Structures for active participation and learning during language arts instruction. *High School Teaching Guidebook for Universal Access.* Pearson Education, Inc.

Klein, S. P., Hamilton, L. S., McCaffrey, D. F., and Stecher, B. M. (2000). What do test scores in Texas tell us? *Education Policy Analysis Archives, 8,* 49.

Kleinfeld, J. (1990). The special virtues of the case method in preparing teachers for minority schools. *Teacher Education Quarterly, 17*(1), 43–51.

Kleinfeld, J. (1991, April 3–7). *Wrestling with the angel: What student teachers learn from writing cases.* Paper presented at the Annual Meeting of the American Educational Research Association, Chicago.

Kleinfeld, J. (1992). Learning to think like a teacher. In J. H. Shulman (Ed.), *Case methods in teacher education* (pp. 33–49). New York: Teachers College Press.

Kleinfeld, J. S. (1998). The use of case studies in preparing teachers for cultural diversity. *Theory into Practice, 37*(2), 140–147.

Kleinfeld, J. S., and Yerian, S. (1995). *Gender tales: Tensions in the schools.* New York: St. Martin's Press.

Klenowski, V. (1995). Student self-evaluation process in student-centered teaching and learning contexts of Australia and England. *Assessment in Education, 2,* 145–163.

Kliebard, H. M. (1988). Fads, fashions and rituals: The instability of curriculum change. In L. Tanner (Ed.), *Critical issues in curriculum* (pp. 16–34). Chicago: University of Chicago Press.

Kluger, A. N., and DeNisi, A. (1996). Effects of feedback intervention on performance: A historical review, a meta-analysis, and a preliminary feedback intervention theory. *Psychological Bulletin, 119*(2), 254–284.

Knapp, M. S., and Shields, P. M. (1990). Reconceiving academic instruction for the children of poverty. *Phi Delta Kappan, 71*(10), 753–758.

Knapp, M. S., and Shields, P. M. (1991). *Better schooling for the children of poverty: Alternatives to conventional wisdom. Study of academic instruction for disadvantaged students. Volume II: Commissioned papers and literature review.* Washington, DC: U.S. Department of Education, Office of Educational Research and Improvement, Educational Research and Information Center.

Knapp, M. S., and Turnbull, B. J. (1990). *Better schooling for the children of poverty: Alternatives to conventional wisdom.* (Vol. 1. Summary). Washington, DC: U.S. Department of Education, Office of Planning, Budget and Evaluation.

Knobel, M. (1999). *Everyday literacies: Students, discourse, and social practice.* New York: Peter Lang.

Knowles, J. G. (1992). Models for understanding pre-service and beginning teachers' biographies: Illustrations from case studies. In I. F. Goodson (Ed.), *Studying teachers' lives* (pp. 99–152). New York: Teachers College Press.

Knowles, J. G., and Hoefler, V. B. (1989). The student-teacher who wouldn't go away: Learning from failure. *Journal of Experiential Education, 12*(2), 14–21.

Knowles, J. G., and Holt-Reynolds, D. (1991). Shaping pedagogies through personal histories in preservice teacher education. *Teachers College Record, 93*(1), 87–113.

Koenig, L. (1995). *Smart discipline for the classroom: Respect and cooperation restored* (Rev. ed.). Thousand Oaks, CA: Corwin Press.

Koerner, M., Rust, F., and Baumgartner, F. (2002). Exploring roles in student teaching placements. *Teacher Education Quarterly, 29*(2), 35–58.

Kohlberg, L. (1981). *The philosophy of moral development: Moral stages and the idea of justice.* San Francisco: Harper & Row.

Kohlberg, L., and Hersh, R. H. (1977). Moral development: A review of the theory. *Theory into Practice, 16*(2), 53–59.

Kohn, A. (1993). *Punished by rewards: The trouble with gold stars, incentive plans, A's, praise, and other bribes.* New York: Houghton Mifflin.

Kohn, A. (1996a). By all available means: Cameron and Pierce's defense of extrinsic motivators. *Review of Educational Research, 66*(1), 1–4.

Kohn, A. (1996b). *Beyond discipline: From compliance to community.* Alexandria, VA: Association for Supervision and Curriculum Development.

Kohn, A. (1997) How not to look to teach values: A critical look at character education. *Phi Delta Kappan, 78*(6), 429–439.

Kolker, A., Alvarez, L., and Holliday, P. (Writer). (1986). *American tongues* [Film]. New York: International Production Center.

Kolodner, J. L., and Guzdial, M. (2000). Theory and practice of case-based learning aids. In D. Jonassen and S. M. Land (Eds.), *Theoretical foundations of learning environments*. Mahwah, NJ: Erlbaum.

Koppich, J. (2000). Trinity University: Preparing teachers for tomorrow's schools. In L. Darling-Hammond (Ed.), *Studies of excellence in teacher education: Preparation in a five-year program* (pp. 1–48). Washington, DC: American Association of Colleges for Teacher Education.

Koretz, D. M., Baron, M., and Stecher, B. M. (1996). *Perceived effects of the Kentucky instructional results information system (KIRIS)* (No. MR-792-PCT-FF). Santa Monica, CA: RAND.

Koretz, D. M., Linn, R. L., Dunbar, S. B., and Shepard, L. A. (1991, April 3–7). *The effects of high-stakes testing on achievement: Preliminary findings about generalization across tests.* Paper presented at the Annual Meetings of the American Educational Research Association and the National Council on Measurement in Education, Chicago.

Korthagen, F. A. J. (2001). Linking practice and theory: The pedagogy of realistic teacher education. Hillsdale, NJ: Erlbaum.

Kounin, J. S. (1977). *Discipline and group management in classrooms.* New York: Holt, Rinehart and Winston.

Kozol, J. (1991). *Savage inequalities: Children in America's schools.* New York: Crown Publishers.

Kroll, L. R., and LaBoskey, V. K. (1996). Practicing what we preach: Constructivism in a teacher education program. *Action in Teacher Education, 18*(2), 63–72.

Kuhn, D., Garcia-Mila, M., Zohar, A., and Anderson, C. (1995). Strategies of knowledge acquisition. *Monographs of the Society for Research in Child Development, 60* (Whole No. 245).

Kunzman, R. (2002). Preservice education for experienced teachers: What STEP teaches those who have already taught. *Issues in Teacher Education, 11*(1), 99–112.

Kunzman, R. (2003). From teacher to student: The value of teacher education for experienced teachers. *Journal of Teacher Education, 54*(3), 241–253.

Kymlicka, W. (1995). *Multicultural citizenship: A liberal theory of minority rights.* New York: Clarendon Press.

LaBerge, D., and Samuels, S. J. (1974). Toward a theory of automatic information processing in reading. *Cognitive Psychology, 6,* 293–323.

LaBoskey, V. K. (1992). Case investigations: Preservice teacher research as an aid to reflection. In J. Shulman (Ed.), *Case methods in teacher education* (pp. 175–193). New York: Teachers College Press.

LaBoskey, V. K., and Richert, A. E. (2002). Identifying good student teaching placements: A programmatic perspective. *Teacher Education Quarterly, 29*(2), 7–34.

Ladson-Billings, G. (1994). *The dreamkeepers: Successful teachers of African American children.* San Francisco: Jossey-Bass.

Ladson-Billings, G. (1995). Toward a theory of culturally relevant pedagogy. *American Educational Research Journal, 32*(3), 465–491.

Ladson-Billings, G. (2001). *Crossing over to Canaan: The journey of new teachers in diverse classrooms.* San Francisco: Jossey-Bass.

Ladson-Billings, G. (2002). I ain't writing nuttin: Permissions to fail and demands to succeed in urban classrooms. In L. D. Delpit and J. K. Dowdy (Eds.), *The skin that we speak: Thoughts on language and culture in the classroom* (pp. 107–120). New York: New Press.

Lagemann, E. C. (1983). *Private power for the public good: A history of the Carnegie Foundation for the Advancement of Teaching.* Middletown: Wesleyan University Press.

Lampert, M. (2001). *Teaching problems and the problems of teaching.* New Haven: Yale University Press.

Lampert, M., and Ball, D. L. (1998). *Teaching, multimedia, and mathematics: Investigations of real practice.* New York: Teachers College Press.

Larsen, Y. W. (1997). Character education month resolution. *Social Studies Review, 37*(1), 11.

Lasley, T. J. (1994). Teacher technicians: A "new" metaphor for new teachers. *Action in Teacher Education, 16*(1), 11–19.

Lasley, T. J., and Wayson, W. W. (1982). Characteristics of schools with good discipline. *Educational Leadership, 40*(3), 28–81.

Lave, J. (1988). *Cognition in practice: Mind, mathematics, and culture in everyday life.* Cambridge, UK: Cambridge University Press.

Lave, J., and Wenger, E. (1991). *Situated learning: Legitimate peripheral participation.* Cambridge, UK: Cambridge University Press.

Lawrenz, F., and McCreath, H. (1988). Integrating quantitative and qualitative evaluation methods to compare two teacher inservice training programs. *Journal of Research in Science Teaching, 25*(5), 397–407.

Lee, C. D. (1993). *Signifying as a scaffold for literary interpretation: The pedagogical implications of an African American discourse genre.* Urbana, IL: National Council of Teachers of English.

Lee, C. D. (1995). A culturally based cognitive apprenticeship: Teaching African American high school students skills in literary interpretation. *Reading Research Quarterly, 30*(4), 608–630.

Lee, C. D. (2001). Is October Brown Chinese? A cultural modeling activity system for underachieving students. *American Educational Research Journal, 38*(1), 97–141.

Lee, C. D. (in press). *Conducting our blooming in the midst of the whirlwind: Understanding culture as a lens for impacting learning and development.* New York: Teachers College Press.

Lee, S. S. (1985). Children's acquisition of conditional logic structure: Teachable? *Contemporary Educational Psychology, 10*(1), 14–27.

Lee, V. E., and Bryk, A. S. (1988). Curriculum tracking as mediating the social distribution of high school achievement. *Sociology of Education, 61*(2), 78–94.

Lee, V. E., Bryk, A. S., and Smith, J. B. (1993). The organization of effective secondary schools. In L. Darling-Hammond (Ed.), *Review of Research in Education, 19*, 171–267. Washington, DC: American Educational Research Association.

Lee, V. E., Burkam, D. T., Zimiles, H., and Ladewski, B. (1994). Family structure and its effect on behavioral and emotional problems in young adolescents. *Journal of Research on Adolescence, 43*(1), 405–437.

Lee, V. E., and Smith, J. B. (1993). Effects of school restructuring on the achievement and engagement of middle-grade students. *Sociology of Education, 42*(2), 164–187.

Lee, V. E., and Smith, J. B. (1995). *Effects of high school restructuring and size on gains in achievement and engagement for early secondary school students.* Madison, WI: Wisconsin Center for Education Research, University of Wisconsin.

Lee, V. E., Smith, J. B., and Croninger, R. G. (1995). Another look at high school restructuring: More evidence that it improves student achievement and more insight into why. *Issues in Restructuring Schools* (Newsletter, Center on Organization and Restructuring of Schools, University of Wisconsin), *9*, 1–9.

Lee, V. E., Smith, J. B., and Croninger, R. G. (1997). How high school organization influences the equitable distribution of learning in mathematics and science. *Sociology of Education, 70*(2), 128–150.

Lehman, B. A. (1991). Practicing what we preach: A personal perspective on "knowing and doing" in university teacher education classes. *Action in Teacher Education, 13*(1), 22–27.

LeMoine, N. (2002). Languages, policies, and California identities, Panel moderated by John R. Rickford, *Negotiating the new racial landscape in California.* Stanford, CA: Center for Comparative Studies in Race and Ethnicity.

Leone, P. E., Mayer, M. J., Malmbren, K., and Meisel, S. M. (2000). School violence and disruption: Rhetoric, reality, and reasonable balance. *Focus on Exceptional Children, 33*(1), 1–20.

Leopold, A. (1949/1990). *Sand county almanac.* New York: Ballentine Books.

LePage, P., and Sockett, H. (2002). *Educational controversies: Toward a discourse of reconciliation.* New York: Routledge/Falmer.

Lepper, M. R. (1983). Extrinsic reward and intrinsic motivation: Implications for the classroom. In J. M. Levine and M. C. Wang (Eds.), *Teacher and student perceptions: Implications for learning* (pp. 281–317). Hillsdale, NJ: Erlbaum.

Lepper, M. R. (1988). Motivational considerations in the study of instruction. *Educational Researcher, 17*(5), 289–309.

Lepper, M. R., and Greene, D. (1975). Turning play into work: Effects of adult surveillance and extrinsic rewards on children's extrinsic motivation. *Journal of Personality and Social Psychology, 28*, 129–137.

Lepper, M. R., and Greene, D. (Eds.). (1978). *The hidden costs of reward: New perspectives on the psychology of human motivation.* Hillsdale, NJ: Erlbaum.

Lepper, M. R., Greene, D., and Nisbett, R. E. (1973). Undermining children's intrinsic interest with extrinsic reward: A test of the "overjustification" hypothesis. *Journal of Personality and Social Psychology, 28*(1), 129–137.

Lepper, M. R., Keavney, M., and Drake, M. (1996). Intrinsic motivation and extrinsic rewards: A commentary on Cameron and Pierce's meta-analysis. *Review of Educational Research, 66*(1), 5–32.

Lerner, B. (1996). Self-esteem and excellence: The choice and the paradox. *American Educator, 20*(2), 9–13, 41–42.

Levin, B. (1995). Using the case method in teacher education: The role of discussion and experience in teachers' thinking about cases. *Teaching and Teacher Education, 11*(1), 63–79.

Levin, B. B. (2002). *Case studies of teacher development: An in-depth look at how thinking about pedagogy develops over time.* Hillsdale, NJ: Erlbaum.

Levin, E., Zigmond, N., and Birch, J. (1985). A follow-up study of 52 learning disabled adolescents. *Journal of Learning Disabilities, 18*, 2–7.

Lewis, C. C., and Tsuchida, I. (1998). A lesson is like a swiftly flowing river: How research lessons improve Japanese education. *American Educator, 22*(4), 12–17, 50–52.

Lewis, R. (2001). Classroom discipline and student responsibility: The students' view. *Teaching and Teacher Education, 17*(3), 307–319.

Lichtenstein, G., Rubin, T., and Grant, G. (April, 1992). *Portfolios as professional development.* Paper presented at the Annual Meeting of the American Educational Research Association, San Francisco.

Lieber, C. M. (2002). *Partners in learning: From conflict to collaboration.* Cambridge MA: Educators for Social Responsibility.

Lieberman, A. (Ed.). (1988). *Building professional culture in schools.* New York: Teachers College Press.

Lieberman, A., and Miller, L. (2001). *Teachers caught in the action: Professional development that matters.* New York: Teachers College Press.

Lieberman, A., and Wood, D. (2003). *Inside the national writing project: Connecting network learning and classroom teaching.* New York: Teachers College Press.

Lightbown, P. M., and Spada, N. (1999). *How languages are learned.* New York: Oxford University Press.

Limerick, P. N. (1987). *The legacy of conquest: The unbroken past of the American West.* New York: Norton.

Lin, S. S. J. (1999, March). *Looking for the prototype of teaching expertise: An initial attempt in Taiwan.* Paper presented at the Annual Meeting of the American Educational Research Association, Boston.

Lin, X., and Lehman, J. D. (1999). Supporting learning of variable control in a computer-based Biology environment: Effects of prompting college students to reflect on their own thinking. *Journal of Research in Science Teaching, 36*(7), 837–858.

Lindfors, J. W. (1987). *Children's language and learning* (2nd ed.). Englewood Cliffs, NJ: Prentice-Hall.

Lionni, L. (1970). *Fish is fish.* New York: Pantheon Books.

Lippi-Green, R. (1997). *English with an accent: Language, ideology, and discrimination.* New York: Routledge.

Logan, J. (1993). *Teaching stories.* New York: Kodansha/Oxford Press.

Lorsbach, A. W., Tobin, K., Briscoe, C., and LaMaster, S. U. (1992). An interpretation of assessment methods in middle school science. *International Journal of Science Education, 14*(3), 305–317.

Lortie, D. C. (1975). *Schoolteacher; a sociological study.* Chicago: University of Chicago Press.

Los Angeles Unified School District (LAUSD) and Lemoine, N. (1999). *English for your success: A language development program for African American children, grades pre-k-8: A handbook of successful strategies for educators.* Maywood: Peoples Publishing Group.

Louis, K., and Kruse, S. (Eds.). (1995). *Professionalism and community.* Thousand Oakes, CA: Corwin Press.

Lovell, K. (1979). Intellectual growth and the school curriculum. In F. B. Murray (Ed.), *The impact of Piagetian theory: On education, philosophy, psychiatry, and psychology.* Baltimore: University Park Press.

Lovett, M. W., Borden, S. L., DeLucan, T., Lacerenza, L., Benson, N. J., and Brackstone, D. (1994). Treating the core deficits of developmental dyslexia: Evidence of transfer of learning after phonologically- and strategically-based reading training programs. *Developmental Psychology, 30*(6), 805–822.

Lovett, M. W., and Steinbach, K. A. (1997). The effectiveness of remedial programs for reading disabled children of different ages: Does the benefit decrease for older children? *Learning Disability Quarterly, 20*(3), 189–210.

Lucas, C. (1997). *Teacher education in America: Reform agendas for the twenty-first century.* New York: St. Martin's Press.

Lucas, T., Henze, R., and Donato, R. (1990). Promoting the success of Latino language-minority students: An exploratory study of six high schools. *Harvard Educational Review, 60*(3), 315–340.

Luchins, A. S. (1942). Mechanization in problem solving. *Psychological Monographs, 54*(6), Whole No. 248.

Luczak, J. (2004). *Who will teach in the 21st Century? Beginning teacher training experiences and attrition rates.* Unpublished doctoral dissertation., Stanford University, Stanford, CA.

Lunsford, A., and Connors, R. (1989). *The St. Martin's handbook.* New York: St. Martin's Press.

Lusi, S. F. (1997). *The role of state departments of education in complex school reform.* New York: Teachers College Press.

Lynch, J. (2002). Parents' self-efficacy beliefs, parents' gender, children's reader self-perceptions, reading achievement and gender. *Journal of Research in Reading, 25*(1), 54–67.

Lyons, N. (1998). *With portfolios in hand: Validating the new teacher professionalism.* New York: Teachers College Press.

Ma, L. (1999). *Knowing and teaching elementary mathematics: Teachers' understanding of fundamental mathematics in China and the United States.* Mahwah, NJ: Erlbaum.

Ma, X., and Kishor, N. (1997). Attitude toward self, social factors, and achievement in mathematics: A meta-analytic review. *Educational Psychology, 9*(2), 89–120.

MacCallum, J. A. (1991, April). *Teacher reasoning and moral judgment in the context of student discipline situations.* Paper presented at the Annual Meeting of the American Educational Research Association, Chicago.

MacDonald, J. B., and Leeper, R. R. (1965). *Theories of instruction; papers.* Washington, DC: Association for Supervision and Curriculum Development.

MacLeod, G. (1987). Microteaching: End of a Research Era? *International Journal of Educational Research, 11*(5), 531–541.

Madaus, G. F., West, M. M., Harmon, M. C., Lomax, R. G., and Viator, K. A. (1992). *The influence of testing on teaching math and science in Grades 4–12: Executive summary.* Chestnut Hill, MA: Center for the Study of Testing, Evaluation, and Educational Policy, Boston College.

Mandin, H., and Dauphinee, W. D. (2000). Conceptual guidelines for developing and maintaining curriculum and examination objectives: The experience of the medical council of Canada. *Academic Medicine, 75*(10), 1031–1037.

Mandin, H., Harasyn, P., Eagle, C., and Watanabe, M. (1995). Developing a "clinical presentation" curriculum at the University of Calgary. *Academic Medicine, 70*(3), 186–193.

Manke, M. P., and Loyd, B. H. (1990, April). *An investigation of non-achievement related factors influencing teachers' grading practices.* Paper presented at the Annual Meeting of the National Council on Measurement in Education, Boston.

Manke, M. P., and Loyd, B. H. (1991, April). *A study of teachers' understanding of their grading practices.* Paper presented at the Annual Meeting of the National Council on Measurement in Education, Chicago.

Mantle-Bromley, C. (2002). The status of early theories of professional development school potential. In I. Guadarrama, J. Ramsey, and J. Nath (Eds.), *Forging alliances in community and thought: Research in professional development schools* (pp. 3–30). Greenwich, CT: Information Age Publishing.

Marchant, G. J. (2002). Professional development schools and indicators of student achievement. *The Teacher Educator, 38*(2), 112–125.

Margolis, W., Arnone, A., and Morgan, R. L. (2002). *Official guide to A.B.A.-approved law schools, 2002 edition.* Newtown, PA: The American Bar Association and Law School Admission Council.

Marsh, H. W. (1990). A multidimensional, hierarchical model of self-concept: Theoretical and empirical justification. *Educational Psychology Review, 2*(2), 77–175.

Marshall, H. H. (1988). Work or learning: Implications of classroom metaphors. *Educational Researcher, 17*(9), 9–16.

Marston, R. Q., and Jones, R. M. (1992). *Medical education in transition.* Princeton, NJ: Robert Wood Johnson Foundation.

Martin, A. J., Linfoot, K., and Stephenson, J. (1999). How teachers respond to concerns about misbehavior in their classroom. *Psychology in the Schools, 36*(4), 347–358.

Martin, R. (1995). Deconstructing myth, reconstructing reality: Transcending the crisis in teacher education. In R. J. Martin (Ed.), *Practicing what we teach: Confronting diversity in teacher education* (pp. 65–77). Albany: State University of New York Press.

Martin, R. J., and Van Gunten, D. M. (2002). Reflected identities: Applying positionality and multicultural social reconstructionism in teacher education. *Journal of Teacher Education, 53*(1), 44–54.

Marton, F., and Saljo, R. (1976). On qualitative differences in learning: 1—Outcome and process. *British Journal of Educational Psychology, 46* pt. 1, 4–11, Feb 76.

Maslow, A. H. (1970). *Motivation and personality* (2nd ed.). New York: Harper & Row.

Mason, D. A., and Good, T. L. (1993). Effects of two-group and whole-class teaching on regrouped elementary students' mathematics achievement. *American Educational Research Journal, 30*(2), 328–360.

Masters, G. N., and Forster, M. (1996). *Developmental assessment: Assessment resource kit.* Hawthorne, Australia: Australian Council on Educational Research Press.

Mathematical Sciences Education Board. (1993). *Measuring up: Prototypes for mathematics assessment.* Washington, DC: National Academy of Sciences—National Research Council.

Mattingly, D. J., Prislin, R., McKenzie, T. L., Rodriguez, J. L., and Kayzar, B. (2002). Evaluating evaluations: The case of parent involvement programs. *Review of Educational Research, 72*(4), 549–576.

Mayer, G. R. (1995). Preventing antisocial behavior in the school. *Journal of Applied Analysis, 28,* 467–478.

Mayer, M. J., and Leone, P. E. (1999). A structural analysis of school violence and disruptions: Implications for creating safer schools. *Education and the Treatment of Children, 22,* 333–358.

Mayer, R. E. (1992). *Thinking, problem-solving, cognition* (2nd ed.). New York: Freeman.

Mazur, E. (1997). *Peer instruction: A user's manual.* Upper Saddle River, NJ: Prentice Hall.

McAllister, G., and Irvine, J. J. (2000). Cultural competency and multicultural teacher education. *Review of Educational Research, 70*(1), 3–24.

McAllister, G., and Irvine, J. J. (2002). The role of empathy in teaching culturally diverse students: A qualitative study of teachers' beliefs. *Journal of Teacher Education, 53*(5), 433–443.

McCombs, B. L., and Pope, J. E. (1994). *Motivating hard to reach students.* Washington, DC: American Psychological Association.

McDermott, R. P. (1996). The acquisition of a child by a learning disability. In S. Chaiklin and J. Lave (Eds.), *Understanding practice: Perspectives on activity and context* (pp. 269–305). Cambridge, UK: Cambridge University Press.

McDiarmid, G. W. (1994). The arts and sciences as preparation for teaching. In K. R. Howey and N. L. Zimpher (Eds.), *Informing faculty development for teacher educators* (pp. 99–137). Norwood, NJ: Ablex.

McDiarmid, G.W., and Price, J. (1990). Prospective teachers' views of diverse learners: A study of the participants in the ABCD Project. Research Report 90–6. East Lansing MI: National Center for Research on Teacher Learning.

McDonald, J. P. (1992). *Teaching: Making sense of an uncertain craft.* New York: Teachers College Press.

McEwan, A. E. (1996). Must teachers bear the moral burden alone? *Journal for a Just and Caring Education, 2*(4), 449–459.

McEwan, B., Nimmo, V., and Gathercoal, P. (1998). *Beyond behaviorism: Changing the classroom management paradigm.* Boston: Allyn & Bacon.

McIntosh, P. (1997). White privilege: Unpacking the invisible knapsack. In V. Cyrus (Ed.), *Experiencing race, class, and gender in the United States* (pp. 194–198). Mountain View, CA: Mayfield Publishing.

McIntyre, A. (1997). *Making meaning of whiteness: Exploring racial identity with white teachers.* Albany: State University of New York Press.

McIntyre, D. J., Byrd, D. M., and Foxx, S. M. (1996). Field and laboratory experiences. In J. P. Sikula, T. J. Buttery, and E. Guyton (Eds.), *Handbook of research on teacher education* (pp. 171–193). New York: Macmillan.

McKnight, C. C., Crosswhite, F. J., Dossey, J. A., Kifer, E., Swafford, J. O., Travers, K. J., and others (1987). *The underachieving curriculum: Assessing U.S. school mathematics from an international perspective.* Champaign, IL: Stipes Publishing.

McLaughlin, H. J. (1994). From negation to negotiation: Moving away from the management metaphor. *Action in Teacher Education, 16*(1), 75–84.

McLaughlin, M. W., and Talbert, J. (2001). *Professional communities and the work of high school teaching.* Chicago: University of Chicago Press.

McMillan, J. H. (2001). *Essential assessment concepts for teachers and administrators.* Thousand Oaks, CA: Corwin Press.

McNeil, L. M. (1986). *Contradictions of control: School structure and school knowledge.* New York: Routledge.

McNeil, L. (2000). *Contradictions of school reform: Educational costs of standardized testing.* New York: Routledge.

Measor, L. (1985). Critical incidents in the classroom: Identities, choices, and careers. In S. J. Ball and I. V. Goodson (Eds.), *Teachers' lives and careers.* Lewes, England: Falmer Press.

Mehan, H., Villanueva, I., Hubbard, L., and Lintz, A. (1996). *Constructing school success: The consequences of untracking low-achieving students.* Cambridge, UK: Cambridge University Press.

Mercado, C. (2001). The learner: "Race," "ethnicity," and linguistic difference. In V. Richardson (Ed.), *Handbook of research on teaching* (4th ed., pp. 668–694). Washington, DC: American Educational Research Association.

Merrett, F., and Wheldall, K. (1993). How do teachers learn to manage classroom behavior? A study of teachers' opinions about their initial training with special reference to classroom behavior management. *Educational Studies, 19*(1), 91–106.

Merseth, K. K. (1996). Cases and case methods in teacher education. In J. P. Sikula, T. J. Buttery, and E. Guyton (Eds.), *Handbook of research on teacher education* (pp. 722–744). New York: Macmillan.

Merseth, K. K. (1999). Foreword: A rationale for case-based pedagogy in teacher education. In M. A. Lundeberg, B. B. Levin, and H. L. Harrington (Eds.), *Who learns what from cases and how?: The research base for teaching and learning with cases* (pp. ix–xv). Hillsdale, NJ: Erlbaum.

Merseth, K. K., and Koppich, J. (2000). Teacher education at the University of Virginia: A study of English and mathematics preparation. In L. Darling-Hammond (Ed.), *Studies of excellence in teacher education: Preparation in a five-year program* (pp. 49–81). Washington, DC: American Association of Colleges for Teacher Education Publications.

Merydith, S. P. (2001). Temporal stability and convergent validity of the behavior assessment system for children. *Journal of School Psychology, 39*(3), 253–265.

Mestre, J. P. (1994). Cognitive aspects of learning and teaching science. In S. J. Fitzsimmons and L. C. Kerpelman (Eds.), *Teacher enhancement for elementary and secondary science and mathematics: Status, issues and problems* (pp. 3.1–3.53). Arlington, VA: National Science Foundation.

Metcalf, K. (1989). An investigation of the efficacy of a research-based regimen of skill development on the instructional clarity of preservice teachers. Unpublished doctoral dissertation, The Ohio State University, Columbus, OH.

Metz, K. E. (1995). Reassessment of developmental constraints on children's science instruction. *Review of Educational Research, 65,* 93–127.

Michael, A. L., Klee, T., Bransford, J. D., and Warren, S. (1993). The transition from theory to therapy: Test of two instructional methods. *Applied Cognitive Psychology, 7*(2), 139–154.

Michie, G. (1999). *Holler if you hear me: The education of a teacher and his students.* New York: Teachers College Press.

Mid-Atlantic Equity Center. (1999). *Adolescent boys: Statistics and trends.* Chevy Chase, MD: Mid-Atlantic Equity Center Gender Equity Resources.

Miller, A., Ferguson, E., and Moore, E. (2002). Parents' and pupils' causal attributions for difficult classroom behaviour. *British Journal of Educational Psychology, 72*(1), 27–40.

Miller, G. (1980). Medical history. In R. L. Numbers (Ed.), *The Education of American physicians: Historical essays* (pp. 290–308). Berkeley: University of California Press.

Miller, J. W., McKenna, M. C., and McKenna, B. A. (1998). A comparison of alternatively and traditionally prepared teachers. *Journal of Teacher Education, 49*(3), 165–176.

Miller, L., and Silvernail, D. L. (2000). Learning to become a teacher: The Wheelock way. In L. Darling-Hammond (Ed.), *Studies of excellence in teacher education: Preparation in the undergraduate years* (pp. 67–107). Washington, DC: American Association of Colleges for Teacher Education Publications.

Milson, A. J., and Mehlig, L. M. (2002). Elementary school teachers' sense of efficacy for character education. *Journal of Educational Research, 96*(1), 47–53.

Minstrell, J. (1989). Teaching science for understanding. In L. Resnick and L. Klopfer (Eds.), *Toward the thinking curriculum: Current cognitive research: 1989 yearbook of the association for supervision and curriculum development* (pp. 129–149). Washington: Association for Supervision and Curriculum Development.

Mitchell, L. S. (1953). *Two lives: The story of Wesley Clair Mitchell and myself.* New York: Simon and Schuster.

Mitchell, M. (1993). Situational interest: Its multifaceted structure in the secondary school mathematics classroom. *Journal of Educational Psychology, 85*(3), 424–436.

Moles, O. C. (1987). Who wants involvement? Interest, skills, and opportunities among parents and educators. *Education and Urban Society, 19*(2), 137–145.

Moles, O. C. (1990). *Student discipline strategies: Research and practice.* Albany: State University of New York Press.

Moles, O. C. (1993). Collaboration between schools and disadvantaged parents: Obstacles and openings. In N. F. Chavkin (Ed.), *Families and schools in a pluralistic society* (pp. 21–52). Albany: State University of New York Press.

Moll, L. C. (1988). Some key issues in teaching Latino students. *Language Arts, 65*(5), 465–472.

Moll, L. C., Amanti, C., Neff, D., and Gonzalez, N. (1992). Funds of knowledge for teaching: Using a qualitative approach to connect homes and classrooms. *Theory into Practice, 31*(1), 132–141.

Moll, L. C., and Gonzalez, N. (2004). Engaging life: A funds of knowledge approach to multicultural education. In J. A. Banks and C. A. M. Banks (Eds.), *Handbook of research on multicultural education* (2nd ed., pp. 699–715). San Francisco: Jossey-Bass.

Moll, L. C., and Greenberg, J. B. (1990). Creating zones of possibilities: Combining social contexts for instruction. In L. C. Moll (Ed.), *Vygotsky and education: Instructional implications and applications of socio-historical psychology* (pp. 319–348). Cambridge, UK: Cambridge University Press.

Monk, D. H. (1994). Subject area preparation of secondary mathematics and science teachers and student achievement. *Economics of Education Review, 13*(2), 125–145.

Monk, D. H., and King, J. A. (1994). Multilevel teacher resource effects in pupil performance in secondary mathematics and science: The case of teacher subject matter preparation. In R. G. Ehrenberg (Ed.), *Choices and consequences: Contemporary policy issues in education* (pp. 29–58). Ithaca, NY: ILR Press.

Montecinos, C. (1994). Teachers of color and multiculturalism. *Equity and Excellence in Education, 27*(3), 34–42.

Moore, D., Bean, T., Birdyshaw, D., and Rycik, J. (1999). *Adolescent literacy: A position statement for the Commission on Adolescent Literacy of the International Reading Association.* Newark, DE: International Reading Association.

Moore, E. G., and Smith, A. W. (1985). Mathematics aptitude: Effects of coursework, household language, and ethnic differences. *Urban Education, 20,* 273–294.

Morgan, M. (1998). More than a mood or an attitude: Discourse and verbal genres in African American culture. In S. S. Mufwene, J. R. Rickford, G. Baily, and J. Baugh (Eds.), *African American English: Structure, history and use* (pp. 251–281). London: Routledge.

Morrell, E. (2002). Toward a critical pedagogy of popular culture: Literacy development among urban youth. *Journal of Adolescent and Adult Literacy, 46*(1), 72–77.

Morris, V. G., and Taylor, S. I. (1998). Alleviating barriers to family involvement in education: The role of teacher education. *Teaching and Teacher Education, 14*(2), 219–231.

Morris, V., Taylor, S., Knight, J., and Wasson, R. (1996). Preparing teachers to reach out to families and communities. *Action in Teacher Education, 18*(1), 10–22.

Morrison, T. (1992). *Playing in the dark: Whiteness and the literary imagination.* Cambridge, MA: Harvard University Press.

Morse, L., and Handley, H. (1985). Listening to adolescents: Gender differences in science classroom interaction. In L. C. Wilkinson, C. B. Marrett, National Institute of Education (U.S.), and Wisconsin Center for Education Research (Eds.), *Gender influences in classroom interaction* (pp. 37–56). Orlando, FL: Academic Press.

Morse, P. S., and Ivey, A. E. (1996). *Face to face: Communication and conflict resolution in the schools.* Thousand Oaks, CA: Corwin Press.

Moschkovich, J. N. (1999a). Understanding the needs of Latino students in reform-oriented mathematics classrooms. In L. Ortiz-Franco, N. Hernandez, and Y. De la Cruz (Eds.), *Changing the faces of mathematics* (pp. 5–12). Reston, VA: National Council of Teachers of Mathematics.

Moschkovich, J. (1999b). Supporting the participation of English language learners in mathematical discussions. *For the Learning of Mathematics, 19*(1), 11–19.

Moschkovich, J. (2002). A situated and sociocultural perspective on mathematic learning in bilingual classrooms. *Mathematical Thinking and Learning, 4*(2–3), 189–212.

Moses, R. P., and Cobb, C. E. (2001). *Radical equations: Math literacy and civil rights.* Boston: Beacon Press.

Mott, M. S., and Klomes, J. (2001). The synthesis of writing workshop and hyperme-dia-authoring: Grades 1–4. *Early Childhood Research and Practice, 3*(2). Retrieved February 6, 2003, from http://ecrp.uiuc.edu/v3n2/mott.html

Mueller, C. M., and Dweck, C. S. (1998). Intelligence praise can undermine motivation and performance. *Journal of Personality and Social Psychology, 75*, 33–52.

Mufwene, S. S., Rickford, J. R., Baily, G., and Baugh, J. (Eds.). (1998). *African American English.* London: Routledge.

Munby, H., Russell, T., and Martin, A. K. (2001). Teachers' knowledge and how it develops. In V. Richardson (Ed.), *Handbook of research on teaching* (4th ed., pp. 877–905). Washington, DC: American Educational Research Association.

Murnane, R., and Levy, F. (1996). *Teaching the new basic skills.* New York: Free Press.

Murrell, P. C. (2002). *African-centered pedagogy: Developing schools of achievement for African-American children.* Albany: State University of New York Press.

Nath, J. M., and Tellez, K. (1995). A room of one's own: Teaching and learning to teach through inquiry. *Action in Teacher Education, 16*(4), 1–13.

Nathan, M. J., Koedinger, K. R., and Alibali, M. W. (2001, August). Expert blind spot: when content knowledge eclipses pedagogical content knowledge. In L. Chen (Ed.), *Proceeding of the Third International Conference on Cognitive Science* (pp. 644–648). Beijing, China: USTC Press.

Nathan, M. J., and Petrosino, A. J. (2003). Expert blind spot among preservice teach-ers. *American Educational Research Journal, 40*(4), 905–928.

National Association for the Education of Young Children. (1990). *Guidelines for appropriate curriculum content and assessment in programs serving children ages 3 through 8.* Washington, DC: Author.

National Association for the Education of Young Children and International Reading Association. (1998). Learning to read and write: Developmentally appropriate prac-tices for young children. A joint position statement of the International Reading Association (IRA) and the National Association for the Education of Young Chil-dren (NAEYC). *Young Children, 53*(4), 30–46.

National Association of State Directors of Teacher Education and Certification (NASDTEC) (1998.) *The NASDTEC manual on the preparation and certification of educational personnel* (4th ed.). Dubuque, IA: Kendall/Hunt Publishing.

National Center for Education Statistics (1996). *The digest of education statistics, 1996.* Washington, DC: U.S. Department of Education.

National Center for Education Statistics (1998). *Inequalities in public school district revenues.* Washington, DC: U.S. Department of Education.

National Center for Education Statistics (2000a). *Digest of education statistics, 1999.* Washington, DC: U.S. Department of Education.

National Center for Education Statistics (2000b). *Trends in educational equity of girls and women.* Washington, DC: U.S. Department of Education.

National Center for Education Statistics (2001a). *The condition of education 2000 in brief.* Washington, DC: U.S. Department of Education.

National Center for Education Statistics (2001b). *The condition of education 2001.* Washington, DC: U.S. Department of Education.

National Center for Education Statistics (2001c). *Internet access in U.S. public schools and classrooms: 1994–2000.* Washington, DC: U.S. Department of Education.

National Center for Education Statistics (2002a). *Participation in Education—Indicator 3—Racial/ethnic distribution of public school students.* Washington, DC: U.S. Department of Education.

National Center for Education Statistics (2002b). *Contexts of elementary and secondary education—Indicator 28—Inclusion of students with disabilities in regular classrooms.* Washington, DC: U.S. Department of Education.

National Center for Education Statistics (2003). *The condition of education 2003.* Washington, DC: U.S. Department of Education.

National Commission of Excellence in Education (1983). *A nation at risk: The imperative for educational reform.* Washington, DC: U.S. Government Printing Office.

National Commission on Teaching and America's Future (1996). *What matters most: Teaching for America's future.* New York: Author.

National Commission on Teaching and America's Future (2003). *No dream denied: A pledge to America's children.* Washington, DC: Author.

National Council for the Accreditation of Teacher Education (2002). *Professional standards for the accreditation of schools, colleges and departments of teacher education.* Washington, DC: Author.

National Council of Teachers of Mathematics (1989). *Curriculum and evaluation standards for school mathematics.* Reston, VA: Author.

National Council of Teachers of Mathematics (1995). *Assessment standards for school mathematics.* Reston, VA: Author.

National Council of Teachers of Mathematics (2000). *Principles and standards for school mathematics.* Reston, VA: Author.

National Education Goals Panel (1994). *Data for the national education goals report, Vol. 1. National data.* Washington: U.S. Department of Education.

National Reading Panel (2000). *Teaching children to read: An evidence-based assessment of the scientific research literature on reading and its implications for reading instruction.* Washington, DC: National Institute of Child Health and Human Development. http://www.nichd.nih.gov/publications/nrp/findings.htm

National Research Council (1993a). *Measuring up: Prototypes for mathematics assessment.* Washington, DC: National Academies Press.

National Research Council (1995). *Learning about assessment, learning through assessment.* Washington, DC: National Academies Press.

National Research Council (1996). *National Science Education Standards.* Washington, DC: National Academies Press.

National Research Council (1998). *Preventing reading difficulties in young children.* Washington, DC: National Academies Press.

National Research Council (2000). *How people learn: Brain, mind, experience, and school* (Expanded ed.). Washington, DC: National Academies Press.

National Research Council (2001). *Testing teacher candidates: The role of licensure tests in improving teacher quality.* Washington, DC: National Academies Press.

National Research Council (in press). *How students learn: History, mathematics, and science in the classroom.* Washington, DC: National Academies Press.

Nava, F. J. G., and Loyd, B. H. (1992, April). *An investigation of achievement and nonachievement criteria in elementary and secondary school grading.* Paper presented at the Annual Meeting of the American Educational Research Association, San Francisco.

Neisser, U. (1976). General, academic, and artificial intelligence. In L. Resnick (Ed.), *The nature of intelligence* (pp. 135–144). Hillsdale, NJ: Erlbaum.

Nelson, T. (1988). Managing immense storage. *Byte, 13,* 225–238.

Neubert, G. A., and Binko, J. B. (1998). Professional development schools: The proof is in the performance. *Educational Leadership, 55* (5), 44–46.

Neufeld, V., and Norman, G. R. (1985). *Assessing clinical competence.* New York: Springer Publishing.

New London Group. (1996). A pedagogy of multiliteracies: Designing social futures. *Harvard Educational Review, 66*(1), 60–92.

Newell, A., and Simon, H. A. (1972). *Human problem solving.* Englewood Cliffs, NJ: Prentice Hall.

Newman, F. M. (1992). Higher order thinking and prospects for classroom thoughtfulness. In F. M. Newmann (Ed.), *Student engagement and achievement in American secondary schools* (pp. 62–91). New York: Teachers College Press.

Newman, F. M., King, M. B., and Youngs, P. (2000). Professional development that addresses school capacity: Lessons from urban elementary schools. *American Journal of Education, 108*(4), 259–299.

Newman, F. M., Marks, H. M., and Gamoran, A. (1995). Authentic pedagogy: Standards that boost study performance. *Issues in restructuring schools, No 8* (pp. 1–15). Madison, WI: Center on Organization and Restructuring Schools.

Newman, F. M., and Wehlange, G. G. (1995). *Successful school restructuring.* Madison: University of Wisconsin.

Nicolopoulou, A., and Cole, M. (1993). Generation and transmission of shared knowledge in the culture of collaborative learning: The fifth dimension, its play-world, and its institutional contexts. In E. A. Forman, N. Minick, and C. A. Stone (Eds.), *Contexts for learning: Sociocultural dynamics in children's development* (pp. 283–314). Oxford: Oxford University Press.

Nierenberg, G. I. (1982). *The art of creative thinking.* New York: Simon and Schuster.

Nieto, S. (1999). *The light in their eyes: Creating multicultural learning communities.* New York: Teachers College Press.

Nieto, S. (2000). *Affirming diversity: The sociopolitical context of multicultural education* (3rd ed.). Boston: Pearson, Allyn & Bacon.

Nieto, S. (2002). *Language, culture, and teaching: Critical perspectives for a new century.* Mahwah, NJ: Erlbaum.

Nieto, S., and Rolon, C. (1997). Preparation and professional development of teachers: A perspective from two Latinas. In J. J. Irvine (Ed.), *Critical knowledge for diverse teachers and learners* (pp. 89–124). District of Columbia: American Association of Colleges for Teacher Education.

Noddings, N. (1992). *The challenge to care in schools: An alternative approach to education.* New York: Teachers College Press.

Noddings, N. (1997). A morally defensible mission for the schools in the 21st century. In E. Clinchy (Ed.), *Transforming public education: A new course for America's future.* New York: Teachers College Press.

Noffke, S., and Stevenson, R. (1995). *Educational action research.* New York: Teachers College Press.

Norton, B. (2000). *Identity and language learning: Gender, ethnicity, and educational change.* New York: Pearson Education.

Novak, J. M. (Ed.). (1994). *Democratic teacher education: Programs, processes, problems, and prospects.* Albany: State University of New York Press.

Nystrand, M., Gamoran, A., Kachur, R., and Prendergast, C. (1997). *Opening dialogue.* New York: Teachers College Press.

Oakes, J. (1985). *Keeping track.* New Haven, CT: Yale University Press.

Oakes, J. (1987). Tracking in secondary schools: A contextual perspective. *Educational Psychologist, 21*(2), 129–154.

Oakes, J. (1990). *Multiplying inequalities: The effects of race, social class, and tracking on opportunities to learn mathematics and science.* Santa Monica, CA: The RAND Corporation.

Oakes, J. (1992). Can tracking research inform practice? Technical, normative, and political considerations. *Educational Researcher, 21*(4), 12–21.

Oakes, J. (1993). *Ability grouping, tracking, and within-school segregation in the San Jose unified school district.* Los Angeles: University of California at Los Angeles.

Oakes, J. (1996). Making the rhetoric real: UCLA's struggle for teacher education that is multicultural and social reconstructionist. *Multicultural Education, 4*(2), 4–10.

Oakes, J. (2000). *Becoming good American schools: The struggle for civic virtue in education reform.* San Francisco: Jossey-Bass.

Oakes, J., Franke, M. L., Quartz, K. H., and Rogers, J. (2002). Research for high-quality urban teaching: Defining it, developing it, assessing it. *Journal of Teacher Education, 53*(3), 228–234.

Oakes, J., and Saunders, M. (2002). *Access to textbooks, instructional materials, equipment, and technology: Inadequacy and inequality in California's public schools.* Los Angeles: University of California at Los Angeles.

Ogle, D. M. (1986). K-W-L: A teaching model that develops active reading of expository text. *Reading Teacher, 39*(6), 564–570.

Olsen, L., and Mullen, N. A. (1990). *Embracing diversity: Teachers' voices from California's classrooms.* San Francisco: California Tomorrow.

O'Connor, T. (1999). *Teacher perspectives of facilitated play in integrated play groups.* Unpublished master's thesis, San Francisco State University.

O'Malley, C. D. (1970). *The history of medical education: An international symposium held February 5–9, 1968.* Berkeley: University of California Press.

Omi, M., and Winant, H. (1994). *Racial formation in the United States: From the 1960s to the 1990s* (2nd ed.). New York: Routledge.

Orland-Barak, L. (2002). The impact of the assessment of practice teaching on beginning teaching: Learning to ask different questions. *Teacher Education Quarterly, 29*(2), 99–122.

Ormrod, J. E. (2003). *Educational psychology: Developing learners* (4th ed.). Upper Saddle River: Merrill/Prentice Hall.

Otto, P. B., and Schuck, R. F. (1983). The effect of a teacher questioning strategy training program on teaching behavior, student achievement, and retention. *Journal of Research in Science Teaching, 20*(6), 521–528.

Overbaugh, R. (1995). The efficacy of interactive video for teaching basic classroom management skills to pre-service teachers. *Computers in Human Behavior, 11*(3–4), 511–27.

Overton, W. F., and Byrnes, J. P. (1991). Cognitive development. In R. M. Lerner, A. C. Petersen, and J. Brooks-Gunn (Eds.), *Encyclopedia of adolescence* (pp. 151–156). New York: Garland Publishing.

Owings, W. A., and Kaplan, L. S. (2001). Standards, retention, and social promotion. *NASSP Bulletin, 85*(629), 57–66.

Pacheco, A. (2000). *Meeting the challenge of high quality teacher education: Why higher education must change.* 40th Charles W. Hunt Memorial Lecture. Washington, DC: American Association of Colleges for Teacher Education.

Paine, L. (1990). *Orientation towards diversity: What do prospective teachers bring? Research Report 89–9.* East Lansing, MI: National Center for Research on Teacher Education.

Palincsar, A. S. (1989). Less charted waters: Responses to Brown, Collins and Duguid's "Situated cognition and the culture of learning." *Educational Researcher, 18*(4), 5–7.

Palincsar, A. S., and Brown, D. A. (1987). Enhancing instructional time through attention to metacognition. *Journal of Learning Disabilities, 20*(2), 66–75.

Palincsar, A. S., and Brown, A. L. (1984). Reciprocal teaching of comprehension-fostering and comprehension-monitoring activities. *Cognition and Instruction, 1*(2), 117–175.

Palincsar, A. S., Magnusson, S. J., Collins, K. M., and Cutter, J. (2001). Making science accessible to all: Results of a design experiment in inclusive classrooms. *Learning Disabilities Quarterly, 24*(1), 15–32.

Palincsar, A. S., Ransom, K., and Derber, S. (1989). Collaborative research and development of reciprocal teaching. *Educational Leadership, 46*(4), 37–40.

Palmer, P. J. (1998). *The courage to teach: Exploring the inner landscape of a teacher's life.* San Francisco: Jossey-Bass.

Pang, V., and Sablan, V. (1998). Teacher efficacy: How do teachers feel about their ability to teach African-American children? In M. E. Dilworth (Ed.), *Being responsive to cultural differences: How teachers learn* (pp. 39–58). Thousand Oaks: Corwin Press.

Parke, R. D., Harshman, K., Roberts, B., Flyer, M., O'Neil, R., and Welsh, M. (1998). Social relationships and academic success. *Thrust for Educational Leadership, 28*(1), 32–34.

Parker, F., and Riley, K. L. (1999). *Linguistics for non linguists: A primer with exercises.* New York: Allyn & Bacon.

Parker, W. (2003). *Teaching democracy: Unity and diversity in public life.* New York: Teachers College Press.

Pascarella, E. T., and Terenzini, P. T. (1991). *How college affects students: Findings and insights from twenty years of research.* San Francisco: Jossey-Bass.

Patterson, R. S., Michelli, N. M., and Pacheco, A. (1999). *Centers of pedagogy: New structures for educational renewal.* San Francisco: Jossey-Bass.

Peale, E., and Lambert, W. (1962). The relation of bilingualism to intelligence. *Psychological Monographs, 76*(546), 1–23.

Pecheone, R., and Chung, R. (April, 2004). *Exploring validity and reliability for a performance-based assessment system: The performance assessment for California teachers.* Paper presented at the Annual Meeting of the American Education Research Association, San Diego, CA.

Pecheone, R., and Stansbury, K. (1996). Connecting teacher assessment and school reform. *Elementary School Journal, 97,* 163–177.

Pedulla, J. J., Abrams, L. M., Madaus, G. F., Russell, M. K., Ramos, M. A., and Miao, J. (2003). *Perceived effects of state-mandated testing programs on teaching and learning: Findings from a national survey of teachers.* Boston: National Board on Educational Testing and Public Policy, Boston College.

Pelavin, S. H., and Kane, M. B. (1990). *Changing the odds: Factors increasing access to college.* New York: College Entrance Examination Board.

Pellegrino, J. W., Baxter, G. P., and Glaser, R. (1999). Addressing the "two disciplines" problem: Linking theories of cognition and learning with assessment and instructional practice. In P. D. Pearson and A. Iran-Nejad (Eds.), *Review of research in education* (Vol. 24, pp. 307–354). Washington, DC: American Educational Research Association.

Pellegrino, J. W., Chudowsky, N., and Glaser, R. (2001). *Knowing what students know: The science and design of educational assessment.* Washington, DC: National Academies Press.

Perkes, V. A. (1967). *Junior high school teacher preparation, teaching behaviors, and student achievement.* Ann Arbor, MI: University Microfilms.

Perkins, D. (1992). *Smart schools: From training memories to educating minds.* New York: Free Press.

Perkins, D. N., and Salomon, G. (1989). Are cognitive skills context-bound? *Educational Researcher, 18,* 16–25.

Peterson, P. L., and Clark, C. M. (1978). Teachers' reports of their cognitive processes during teaching. *American Educational Research Journal, 15*(4), 555–565.

Peterson, P. L., Fennema, E., and Carpenter, T. (1991). Teachers' knowledge of students' mathematics problem-solving knowledge. In J. Brophy (Ed.), *Advances in research on teaching, Vol. 2: Teachers' knowledge of subject matter as it relates to their teaching practice* (pp. 49–86). Greenwich, CT: JAI.

Peterson, P. L., Marx, R. W., and Clark, C. M. (1978). Teacher planning, teacher behavior, and student achievement. *American Educational Research Journal, 15*(3), 417–432.

Phelan, P., Davidson, A. L., and Yu, H. C. (1998). *Adolescents' worlds: Negotiating family, peers, and school.* New York: Teachers College Press.

Philips, S. U. (1972). Participant structures and communicative competence: Warm Springs children in community and classroom. In C. B. Cazden, V. John-Steiner, and D. H. Hymes (Eds.), *Functions of language in the classroom* (pp. 370–394). New York: Teachers College Press.

Phillips, M. B., and Hatch, J. A. (2000). Practicing what we preach in teacher education. *Dimensions of Early Childhood, 28*(3), 24–30.

Phinney, J. S., and Rotheram, M. J. (1987). *Children's ethnic socialization: Pluralism and development.* Newbury Park, CA: Sage.

Piaget, J. (1952). *The origins of intelligence in children.* New York: International Universities Press.

Piaget, J. (1970). Piaget's theory. In L. Carmichael and P. H. Mussen (Eds.), *Carmichael's manual of child psychology* (3d ed.). New York: Wiley.

Piaget, J. (1999). *Judgment and reasoning in the child.* London: Routledge.

Piaget, J., and Inhelder, B. (1969). *The psychology of the child.* New York: Basic Books.

Pichert, J. C., and Anderson, R. C. (1977). Taking different perspectives on a story. *Journal of Educational Psychology, 69,* 309–315.

Piestrup, A. M. (1973). *Black dialect interference and accommodations of reading instruction in first grade. Monograph No. 4.* Bethesda, MD: National Institute of Mental Health.

Pilarksi, M. J. (1994). Student teachers: Underprepared for classroom management? *Teaching Education, 6*(1), 77–80.

Pilcher-Carlton, J., and Oosterhof, A. C. (1993, April). *A case study analysis of parents', teachers', and students' perceptions of the meaning of grades: Identification of discrepancies, their consequences and obstacles to their resolution.* Paper presented at the Annual Meeting of the American Educational Research Association, Atlanta, GA.

Pinar, W. (1995). *Understanding curriculum: An introduction to the study of historical and contemporary curriculum discourses.* New York: P. Lang.

Pintrich, P. R., and de Groot, E. (1990). Motivation and self-regulated learning in middle school classrooms. *Journal of Educational Psychology, 80,* 123–129.

Pintrich, P. R., and Garcia, T. (1994). Regulating motivation and cognition in the classroom: The role of self-schemas and self-regulatory strategies. In D. H. Schunk and B. J. Zimmerman (Eds.), *Self-regulation of learning and performance: Issues and educational applications* (p. 329). Hillsdale, NJ: Erlbaum.

Pintrich, P. R., and Schunk, D. H. (1996). *Motivation in education: Theory, research, and applications.* Englewood Cliffs, NJ: Merrill.

Piper, T. (2002). *Language and learning: The home and school years.* Englewood Cliffs, NJ: Merrill/Prentice-Hall.

Pittman, S. I. (1985). A cognitive ethnography and quantification of a first-grade teacher's selection routines for classroom management. *Elementary School Journal, 85*(4), 541–558.

Poest, C., Williams, J., Witt, D. D., and Atwood, M. E. (1990). Challenge me to move: Large muscle development in young children. *Young Children, 45*(5), 4–10.

Pointon, P., and Kershner, R. (2000). Making decisions about organising the primary classroom environment as a context for learning: The views of three experienced teachers and their pupils. *Teaching and Teacher Education, 16*(1), 117–127.

Posner, G. J., and Rudnitsky, A. N. (1982). *Course design: A guide to curriculum development for teachers* (2nd ed.). New York: Longman.

Pothoff, D., Dinsmore, J., Eifler, K., Stirtz, G., Walsh, T., and Ziebarth, J. (2000). Preparing for democracy and diversity: The impact of a community-based field experience on preservice teachers' knowledge, skills, and attitudes. *Action in Teacher Education, 22*(1), 79–92.

Powell, A. G., Farrar, E., and Cohen, D. K. (1985). *The shopping mall high school.* Boston: Houghton Mifflin.

Price, J. (2001). Action research, pedagogy and change: The transformative potential of action research in pre-service teacher education. *Journal of Curriculum Studies, 33*(1), 43–74.

Proctor, C. D., and Groze, V. K. (1994). Risk factors for suicide among gay, lesbian, and bisexual youths. *Social Work, 39,* 504–513.

PT3 Group at Vanderbilt (2003). Three AMIGOs: Using "anchored modular inquiry" to help prepare future teachers. *Educational Technology Research and Development, 51*(1): 105–123.

Pulos, S., and Linn, M. C. (1981). Generality of the controlling variables scheme in early adolescence. *Journal of Early Adolescence, 1*(1), 26–37.

Putnam, R. T., and Borko, H. (1997). Teacher learning: Implication of new views of cognition. In B. J. Biddle, T. L. Good, and I. T. Goodson (Eds.), *International handbook of teachers and teaching* (Vol. 2, pp. 1223–1296). Boston: Kluwer Academic Publishers.

Putnam, R. T., and Borko, H. (2000). What do new views of knowledge and thinking have to say about research on teacher learning? *Educational Researcher, 29*(1), 41–45.

Quaini, F., Urbanek, K., Beltrami, A., Finato, N. L., Beltrami, C., and Nadal-Ginard, B. (2002). Chimerism of the transplanted heart. *The New England Journal of Medicine, 346*(1), 5–15.

Quality Education for Minorities Project. (1990). *Education that works: An action plan for the education of minorities.* Cambridge, MA: Quality Education for Minorities Project, Massachusetts Institute of Technology.

Ralph, E. G. (1994). Middle and secondary L2 teachers meeting classroom management challenges via effective teaching research. *Foreign Language Annals, 27*(1), 89–103.

Ramírez, M., and Castañeda, A. (1974). *Cultural democracy, bicognitive development, and education.* New York: Academic Press.

Randolph, C. H., and Evertson, C. M. (1994). Images of management for learner-centered classrooms. *Action in Teacher Education, 16*(1), 55–64.

Rearick, M., and Feldman, A. (1999). Orientations, purposes and reflection: A framework for understanding action research. *Teaching and Teacher Education, 15*(4), 333–349.

Redish, E. F. (1996). *Discipline-specific science education and educational research: The case of physics.* Paper prepared for the Committee on Developments in the Science of Learning: An Interdisciplinary Discussion. Department of Physics, University of Maryland, College Park, MD.

Reese, C. M. (1997). *NAEP 1996 Mathematics Report Card for the Nation and the States. Findings from the National Assessment of Educational Progress* (No. NCES-97-488). Washington, DC: U.S. Government Printing Office.

Remafedi, G., French, S., Story, M., Resnick, M. D., and Blum, R. (1998). The relationship between suicide risk and sexual orientation: Results of a population-based study. *American Journal of Public Health, 88*(1), 57–60.

Render, G., Pailla, J., and Krank, H. (1989). What research really shows about assertive discipline. *Educational Leadership, 47,* 72–75.

Resnick, L. B. (1987). *Education and learning to think.* Washington, DC: National Academies Press.

Resnick, L. B., Levine, J. M., and Teasley, S. D. (Eds.). (1991). *Perspectives on socially shared cognition.* Washington, DC: American Psychological Association.

Resnick, L. B., and Nelson-LeGall, S. (1998). Socializing intelligences. In L. Smith, J. Dockrell, and P. Tomlinson (Eds.), *Piaget, Vygotsky and beyond: Future issues for developmental psychology and education* (pp. 145–158). London: Routledge.

Resnick, L. B., and Resnick, D. P. (1992). Assessing the thinking curriculum: New tools for education reform. In B. R. Gifford and M. C. O'Connor (Eds.), *Changing assessments: Alternative views of aptitude, achievement, and instruction* (pp. 37–76). Boston: Kluwer Academic Publishers with the kind permission of Spring Science and Business Media.

Resnick, M. D., Bearman, P. S., Blum, R. W., Bauman, K. E., Harris, K. M., and Jones, J. (1997). Protecting adolescents from harm. Findings from the national longitudinal study on adolescent health. *Journal of American Medical Association, 278*(10), 823–832.

Reyes de la Luz, M. (1991). Bilingual student writers: A question of fair evaluation. *English Journal, 80*(8), 16–23.

Reyes de la Luz, M. (1992). Challenging venerable assumptions: Literacy instruction for linguistically different students. *Harvard Educational Review, 62*(4), 427–446.

Reynolds, A. J., Walberg, H. J., and Weissberg, R. P., (Eds.). (1999). *Promoting positive outcomes: Issues in children's and families' lives*. Washington, DC: Child Welfare League of America.

Reynolds, A. J., Wang, M. C., and Walberg, H. J. (Eds.) (2003) *Early childhood programs for a new century*. Washington, DC: Child Welfare League of America.

Reynolds, M. C. (Ed.). (1989). *Knowledge base for the beginning teacher*. New York: Pergamon Press.

Rice, J. (2003). *Teacher quality: Understanding the effects of teacher attributes*. Washington, DC: Economic Policy Institute.

Richardson, V. (1996). The case for formal research and practical inquiry in teacher education. In F. B. Murray (Ed.), *The teacher educator's handbook* (pp. 715–737). Washington, DC: American Association of Colleges for Teacher Education.

Richardson, V., and Fallona, C. (2001). Classroom management as a method and manner. *Journal of Curriculum Studies, 33*(6), 705–728.

Richardson, V., and Placier, P. (2001). Teacher change. In V. Richardson (Ed.), *Handbook of research on teaching* (4th ed., pp. 905–947). Washington, DC: American Educational Research Association.

Richert, A. E. (1990). Teaching teachers to reflect: A consideration of programme structure. *Journal of Curriculum Studies, 22*(6), 509–527.

Richert, A. E. (2002). Narratives that teach: Learning about teaching from the stories teachers tell. In N. Lyons and V. LaBoskey (Eds.), *Narrative knowing in teaching: Exemplars of reflective teaching, research and teacher education* (48–62). New York: Teachers College Press.

Ridgway, J., Crust, R., Burkhardt, H., Wilcox, S., Fisher, L., and Foster, D. (2000). *MARS report on the 2000 tests*. San Jose, CA: Mathematics Assessment Collaborative.

Ridley, D. S., Carlile, B., and Hurwitz, S. (2001, April). *A long-term analysis of PDS and campus-based preservice teacher preparation: Are new teachers prepared at a PDS really better?* Paper presented at the annual meeting of the American Educational Research Association, Seattle, WA.

Riordan, J., and Noyce, P. (2001). The impact of two standards-based mathematics curricula on student achievement in Massachusetts. *Journal for Research in Mathematics Education, 32*(4), 368–398.

Rivkin, S. G., Hanushek, E. A., and Kain, J. F. (2000). *Teachers, schools and academic achievement*. Working Paper. Retrieved March 2001, from http://www.utdallas.edu/research/greenctr/Papers.

Roberge, J. J. (1970). A study of children's abilities to reason with basic principles of deductive reasoning. *American Educational Research Journal, 7*(4), 583–596.

Roberts, R. N., and Barnes, M. L. (1992). "Let momma show you how": Maternal-child interactions and their effects on children's cognitive performance. *Journal of Applied Developmental Psychology, 13*(3), 363–376.

Rodriguez, Y., and Sjostrom, B. (1995). Culturally responsive teacher preparation evident in classroom approaches to cultural diversity: A novice and an experienced teacher. *Journal of Teacher Education, 46,* 304–311.

Roeser, R. (2002). Bringing a "whole adolescent" perspective to secondary teacher education: A case study of the use of an adolescent case study. *Teaching Education, 13*(2), 155–178.

Roeser, R. W., Midgley, C., and Urdan, T. C. (1996). Perceptions of the school psychological environment and early adolescents' psychological and behavioral functioning in school: The mediating role of goals and belonging. *Journal of Educational Psychology, 88*(3), 408–422.

Rogoff, B. (1990). *Apprenticeship in thinking: Cognitive development in social context.* New York: Oxford University Press.

Rogoff, B. (2003). *The cultural nature of human development.* New York: Oxford University Press.

Romaine, S. (1984). *The language of children and adolescents: The acquisition of communicative competence.* New York: Blackwell.

Ronnkvist, A. M., Dexter, S. L., and Anderson, R. E. (2000). *Technology support: Its depth, breadth and impact in America's schools. Teaching, learning, and computing: 1998 National Survey Report #5.* Irvine: University of California–Irvine.

Rosaldo, R. (1997). Cultural citizenship, inequality, and multiculturalism. In W. V. Flores and R. Benmayor (Eds.), *Latino cultural citizenship: Claiming identity, space, and rights* (pp. 27–38). Boston: Beacon Press.

Roschelle, J. M., Pea, R. D., Hoadley, C. M., Gordin, D. N., and Means, B. (2000). Changing how and what children learn in school with computer-based technologies. *Future of Children, 10*(2), 76–101.

Rose, M. (1995). *Possible lives.* New York: Penguin Books.

Rosenholtz, S. J., and Simpson, C. (1984). The formation of ability conceptions: developmental trend or social construction? *Review of Educational Research, 54*(1), 31–63.

Rosenholtz, S. J., and Simpson, C. (1984). Classroom organization and student stratification. *Elementary School Journal, 85*(1), 21–37.

Rosenstein, J., and New Day Films. (Writer). (1997). *In whose honor? American Indian mascots in sports* [Film]. Ho-ho-kus: New Day Films, Harriman, N.Y.

Rosenzweig, M. R., and Bennett, E. L. (1978a). Cerebral changes in rats exposed individually to an enriched environment. *Journal of Comparative and Physiological Psychology.* 80, 304–313.

Rosenzweig, M. R., and Bennett, E. L. (1978b). Experiential influences on brain anatomy and brain chemistry in rodents. In G. Gottlieb (Ed.), *Studies on the development of behavior and the nervous system. Vol. 4. Early influences* (pp. 289–330). New York: Academic Press.

Rosiek, J. (1994). Caring, classroom management, and teacher education: The need for case study and narrative methods. *Teaching Education, 6*(1), 21–30.

Ross, D., and Bondy, E. (1996). The evolution of a college course through teacher educator action research. *Action in Teacher Education, 18*(3), 44–55.

Ross, D. D. (1989). First steps in developing a reflective approach. *Journal of Teacher Education, 40*(2), 22–30.

Ross, S. M., Hughes, T. M., and Hill, R. E. (1981). Field experiences as meaningful contexts for learning about learning. *Journal of Educational Research, 75*(2), 103–107.

Routman, R. (2000). *Conversations: Strategies for teaching, learning, and evaluating.* Portsmouth, NH: Heinemann.

Rowan, B., Correntti, R., and Miller, R. J. (2002). *What large-scale, survey research tells us about teacher effects on student achievement: Insights from the prospects study of elementary schools* (No. RR-051). Philadelphia: University of Pennsylvania Graduate School of Education.

Rubin, R. L., and Norman, J. T. (1992). Systematic modeling vs. the learning cycle: Comparative effects of integrated science process skill achievement. *Journal of Research in Science Teaching, 29,* 715–727.

Rury, J. L. (1989). Who became teachers?: The social characteristics of teachers. In D. Warren (Ed.), *American teachers: Histories of a profession at work* (pp. 9–48). New York: Macmillan.

Rust, F. (1999). Professional conversations: New teachers explore teaching through conversation, story, and narrative. *Teaching and Teacher Education, 15*(4), 367–380.

Rust, F., and Freidus, H. (2001). *Guiding school change: The role and work of change agents. The series on school reform.* New York: Teachers College Press.

Rutherford, M. E. (1995). *"We can't fight with our fists, words are our power!" Children in the middle school years learning to write academic prose.* Unpublished doctoral dissertation, University of California-Berkeley.

Ryan, R. M., and Deci, E. L. (1996). When paradigms clash: Comments on Cameron and Pierce's claim that rewards do not undermine intrinsic motivation. *Review of Educational Research, 66*(1), 33–38.

Ryan, R. M., and Deci, E. L. (2000). Self-determination theory and the facilitation of intrinsic motivation, social development, and well-being. *American Psychologist, 55*(1), 68–78.

Ryan, R. M., and Lynch, J. H. (1989). Emotional autonomy versus detachment: Revisiting the vicissitudes of adolescence and young adulthood. *Child Development, 60*(2), 340–356.

Ryan, R. M., and Powelson, C. L. (1991). Autonomy and relatedness as fundamental to motivation and education. *Journal of Experimental Education, 60*(1), 49–66.

Sabers, D., Cushing, K. S., and Berliner, D. C. (1991). Differences among teachers in a task characterized by simultaneity, multidimensionality, and immediacy. *American Educational Research Journal, 28*(1), 63–88.

Sackett, D. L., Rosenberg, W. C., Gray, J. M., Haynes, R. B., and Richardson, W. S. (1996). Evidence based medicine: What it is and what it isn't. *British Medical Journal, 312,* 71–72.

Sadker, M., and Sadker, D. M. (1995). *Failing at fairness: How America's schools cheat girls.* New York: Touchstone Press.

Sadler, D. R. (1989). Formative assessment and the design of instructional systems. *Instructional Science, 18*(2), 119–144.

Salzman, S. A., Denner, P. R., and Harris, L. B. (2002, February 23–26). *Teacher outcome measures: Special study survey.* Paper presented at the American Association of Colleges of Teacher Education, New York.

Sanders, W. L., and Horn, S. (1994). The Tennessee value-added assessment system (TVAAS): Mixed-model methodology in educational assessment. *Journal of Personnel Evaluation in Education, 8,* 299–311.

Sanders, W. L., and Rivers, J. C. (1996). *Cumulative and residual effects of teachers on future student academic achievement.* Knoxville: University of Tennessee Value-Added Research and Assessment Center.

Sandholtz, J. H., and Dadlez, S. H. (2000). Professional development school trade-offs in teacher preparation and renewal. *Teacher Education Quarterly, 27*(1), 7–27.

Saner, H., and Ellickson, P. (1196). Concurrent risk factors for adolescent violence. *Journal of Adolescent Health, 19*(2), 94–103.

Sanford, J. P., Emmer, E. T., and Clements, B. S. (1983). Improving classroom management. *Educational Leadership, 40*(7), 56–60.

Sansone, C., and Harackiewicz, J. M. (2000). *Intrinsic and extrinsic motivation: The search for optimal motivation and performance.* San Diego, CA: Academic Press.

Santiago, E. (1993). *When I was Puerto Rican.* New York: Vintage.

Sarason, S. B. (1990). *The predictable failure of educational reform: Can we change course before it's too late?* San Francisco: Jossey-Bass.

Sarason, S. B. (1993). *The case for change: Rethinking the preparation of educators.* San Francisco: Jossey-Bass.

Sato, M. (2000, April). *The National Board for Professional Teaching Standards: Teacher learning through the assessment process.* Paper presented at the Annual Meeting of the American Educational Research Association, New Orleans, LA.

Sawyer, R. K. (2004). Creative teaching: Collaborative discussion as disciplined improvisation. *Educational Researcher, 33*(2), 12–20.

Scardamalia, M., and Bereiter, C. (1985). Fostering the development of self-regulation in children's knowledge processing. In J. W. Segal, S. F. Chipman, and R. Glaser (Eds.), *Thinking and learning skills* (pp. 563–578). Hillsdale, NJ: Erlbaum.

Schalock, D. (1979). Research on teacher selection. In D. C. Berliner (Ed.), *Review of Research in Education* (Vol. 7). Washington, DC: American Educational Research Association.

Schalock, M. D. (1998). Accountability, student learning, and the preparation and licensure of teachers: Oregon's teacher work sample methodology. *Journal of Personnel Evaluation in Education, 12*(3), 269–285.

Schank, R. C., and Abelson, R. P. (1975). *Scripts, plans, goals, and understanding.* Papers of the Fourth international Joint Conference on Artificial Intelligence, Tbilisi, Georgia, USSR.

Schaps, E. (1998). Risks and rewards of community building. *Thrust for Educational Leadership, 28*(1), 6–9.

Schaps, E., Watson, M., and Lewis, C. (1997). A key condition for character development: Building a sense of community in school. *Social Studies Review, 37*(1), 85–90.

Schauble, L. (1990). Belief revision in children: The role of prior knowledge and strategies for generating evidence. *Journal of Experimental Child Psychology, 49*(1), 31–57.

Schliemann, A. D., and Carraher, D. W. (1993). Proportional reasoning in and out of school. In P. Light and G. Butterworth (Eds.), *Context and cognition: Ways of learning and knowing.* Hillsdale, NJ: Erlbaum.

Schoenfeld, A. H. (1985). *Mathematical problem solving.* Orlando, FL: Academic Press.

Schoenfeld, A. H. (1991). On mathematics as sense-making: An informal attack on the unfortunate divorce of formal and informal mathematics. In J. F. Voss, D. N. Perkins, and J. W. Segal (Eds.), *Informal reasoning and education* (pp. 311–344). Hillsdale, NJ: Erlbaum.

Schoenfeld, A. H. (2002). Making mathematics work for all children: Issues of standards, testing, and equity. *Educational Researcher, 31*(1), 13–25.

Schoenfeld, A. H. (2004). Math wars. *Educational Policy.*

Schofield, W. (2003). The colorblind perspective in school: Causes and consequences. In J. A. Banks and C. A. M. Banks (Eds.), *Multicultural education: Issues and perspectives* (Updated 4th ed., pp. 265–288). New York: Wiley.

Scholes, R. (1985). *Textual power: Literary theory and the teaching of English.* New Haven, CT: Yale University Press.

Schön, D. A. (1983). *The reflective practitioner: How professionals think in action.* New York: Basic Books.

Schraw, G., and Olafson, L. (2004). Teachers' epistemological world views and educational practices. *Issues in Educational Psychology 29*(2), 95–102.

Schultz, L. H., Barr, D. J., and Selman, R. L. (2001). The value of a developmental approach to evaluating character development programmes: An outcome study of "Facing History and Ourselves." *Journal of Moral Education, 30*(1), 3–27.

Schunk, D. H. (1991). Self-efficacy and academic motivation. *Educational Psychologist, Special Issue: Current Issues and New Directions in Motivational Theory and Research, 26*(3–4), 207–231.

Schwab, J. (1964). Structure of the disciplines: Meanings and significances. In G. W. Ford and L. Pugno (Eds.), *The structure of knowledge and the curriculum* (pp. 6–30). Chicago: Rand McNally.

Schwab, J. J. (1973). The practical 3: Translation into curriculum. *School Review, 81*(4), 501–522.

Schwab, J. J. (1978). The nature of scientific knowledge as related to liberal education. In J. J. Schwab, I. Westbury, and N. J. Wilkof (Eds.), *Science, curriculum, and liberal education: Selected essays* (pp. 68–104). Chicago: University of Chicago Press.

Schwartz, D. L., and Bransford, J. D. (1998). A time for telling. *Cognition and Instruction, 16*(4), 475–522.

Schwartz, D. L., Bransford, J. D, and Sears, D. (in press). Efficiency and innovation in transfer. To appear in J. Mestre (Ed.), *Transfer of learning: Research and perspectives.* Greenwich, CT: Information Age Publishing.

Schwartz, D. L., Lin, X., Brophy, J., and Bransford, J. D. (1999). Toward the development of flexibly adaptive instructional designs. In C. M. Reigelut (Ed.), *Instructional design theories and models: Volume II* (pp. 183–213). Hillsdale, NJ: Erlbaum.

Schwartz, D. L., and Moore, J. L. (1998). The role of mathematics in explaining the material world: Mental models for proportional reasoning. *Cognitive Science, 22,* 471–516.

Secada, W. G., Fennema, E., and Adajian, L. (1995). *New directions for equity in mathematics education.* Cambridge, UK: Cambridge University Press.

Seidl, B., and Friend, G. (2002). Leaving authority at the door: Equal-status community-based experiences and the preparation of teachers for diverse classrooms. *Teaching and Teacher Education, 18*(4), 421–433.

Selman, R. L. (1980). *The growth of interpersonal understanding: Developmental and clinical analyses.* New York: Academic Press.

Senk, S. L., and Thompson, D. R. (Eds.). (2003). *Standards-based school mathematics curricula: What are they? What do students learn?* Mahwah, NJ: Erlbaum.

Sergiovanni, T. J. (1994). *Building community in schools.* San Francisco: Jossey-Bass.

Sevcik, A., Robbins, B., and Leonard, A. (1997). The deep structure of obscene language. *Journal of Curriculum Studies, 29*(4), 455–470.

Sheets, R. H., and Gay, G. (1996). Student perceptions of disciplinary conflict in ethnically diverse classrooms. *NASSP Bulletin, 80*(580), 84–94.

Shepard, L. A. (1995). Using assessment to improve learning. *Educational Leadership, 52*(5), 38–43.

Shepard, L. A. (1996, September 19). *Measuring achievement: What does it mean to test for robust understanding? William H. Angoff Memorial Lecture Series.* Princeton, NJ: Educational Testing Services.

Shepard, L. A. (1997). *Measuring achievement: What does it mean to test for robust understanding?* Princeton, NJ: Policy Information Center, Educational Testing Service.

Shepard, L. A. (2000). The role of assessment in a learning culture. *Educational Researcher, 29*(7), 4–14.

Shepard, L. A. (2003). Reconsidering large-scale assessment to heighten its relevance to learning. In J. M. Atkin, J. Coffey, and National Science Teachers Association (Eds.), *Everyday assessment in the science classroom* (pp. 121–146). Arlington: NSTA Press.

Shepard, L. A. (in press). Classroom assessment. In R. L. Brennan (Ed.), *Educational measurement* (4th ed.). Westport, CT: Greenwood Publishing Group.

Shepard, L. A., and Bliem, C. L. (1995). Parents' thinking about standardized tests and performance assessments. *Educational Researcher, 24*(8), 25–32.

Shepard, L. A., and Dougherty, K. C. (1991, April 3–7). *Effects of high-stakes testing on instruction.* Paper presented at the Annual Meetings of the American Educational Research Association and the National Council on Measurement in Education, Chicago.

Sherin, M. (2001). Developing a professional vision of classroom events. In T. Wood, B. S. Nelson, and J. Warfield (Eds.), *Beyond classical pedagogy: Teaching elementary school mathematics* (pp. 75–94). Hillsdale, NJ: Erlbaum.

Sherin, M., and Han, S. Y. (2002). *Teacher learning in the context of a video club.* Manuscript submitted for publication.

Shields, P. M., Humphrey, D. C., Wechsler, M. E., Riel, L. M., Tiffany-Morales, J., Woodworth, K., and others (2001). *The status of the teaching profession 2001.* Santa Cruz, CA: The Center for the Future of Teaching and Learning.

Shin, H. (1994, April). *Estimating future teacher supply: An application of survival analysis.* Paper presented at the meeting of the American Educational Research Association, New Orleans, LA.

Shroyer, G., Wright, E., and Ramey-Gassert, L. (1996). An innovative model for collaborative reform in elementary school science teaching. *Journal of Science Teacher Education, 7*(3), 151–168.

Shulman, J., and Lotan, R. (1998). *Groupwork in heterogeneous classrooms: A casebook.* San Francisco: Jossey-Bass.

Shulman, L. S. (1986). Those who understand: Knowledge growth in teaching. *Educational Researcher, 15*(2), 4–14.

Shulman, L. S. (1987). Knowledge and teaching: Foundations of the new reform. *Harvard Educational Review, 57*(1), 1–22.

Shulman, L. S., (1992). Toward a pedagogy of cases. In J. H. Shulman (Ed.), *Case methods in teacher education* (pp. 1–30). New York: Teachers College Press.

Shulman, L. S. (1996). Just in case: Reflections on learning from experience. In K. T. J. Colbert and P. Desberg (Eds.), *The case for education: Contemporary approaches for using case methods.* Boston: Allyn & Bacon.

Shulman, L. S. (1998). Course anatomy: The dissection and analysis of knowledge through teaching. In P. Hutchings (Ed.), *The course portfolio: How faculty can examine their teaching to advance practice and improve student learning* (pp. 5–13). Washington, DC: American Association for Higher Education.

Shulman, L. S. (1998). Theory, practice, and the education of professionals. *Elementary School Journal, 98*(5), 511–526.

Shulman, L. S., and Shulman, J. (2004). How and what teachers learn: A shifting perspective. *Journal of Curriculum Studies, 36*(2), 257–271.

Siegler, R. S. (1998). *Children's thinking* (3rd ed.). Upper Saddle River, NJ: Prentice Hall.

Siegler, R. S., and Richards, D. D. (1982). The development of intelligence. In R. J. Sternberg (Ed.), *Handbook of human intelligence* (pp. 897–971). Cambridge, UK: Cambridge University Press.

Silvestri, L. (2001). Pre-service teachers' self-reported knowledge of classroom management. *Education, 121*(3), 575–580.

Simmons, R. G., and Blyth, D. A. (1987). *Moving into adolescence: The impact of pubertal change and school context.* New York: Aldine de Gruyter.

Simon, B. S. (2001). Family involvement in high school: Predictors and effects. *NASSP Bulletin, 85*(2), 8–19.

Simon, H. A. (1980). Problem solving and education. In D. T. Tuma and R. Reif (Eds.), *Problem solving and education: Issues in teaching and research* (pp. 81–96). Hillsdale, NJ: Erlbaum.

Singley, K., and Anderson, J. R. (1989). *The transfer of cognitive skill.* Cambridge, MA: Harvard University Press.

Sirotnik, K., and Associates. (2001). *Renewing schools and teacher education: An odyssey in educational change.* Washington DC: American Association of Colleges for Teacher Education.

Sizer, T. (1984). *Horace's compromise: The dilemma of the American high school.* Boston: Houghton Mifflin.

Skjaerven, R., Wilcox, A. J., and Lie, R. T. (2002). The interval between pregnancies and the risk of preeclampsia. *New England Journal of Medicine, 346*(1), 33–38.

Slavin, R. E. (1986). *Educational psychology: Theory into practice.* Englewood Cliffs, NJ: Prentice-Hall.

Slavin, R. E. (1990a). *Cooperative learning: Theory, research, and practice.* Englewood Cliffs, NJ: Prentice Hall.

Slavin, R. E. (1990b). Achievement effects of ability grouping in secondary schools: A best evidence synthesis. *Review of Educational Research, 60*(3), 471–500.

Slavin, R. E. (1995). Enhancing intergroup relations in schools: Cooperative learning and other strategies. In W. D. Hawley and A. W. Jackson (Eds.), *Toward a common destiny: Improving race and ethnic relations in America* (pp. 291–314). San Francisco: Jossey-Bass.

Slavin, R. E. (2003). *Educational psychology: Theory and practice* (7th ed.). Boston: Allyn & Bacon.

Sleeter, C. (1995). White preservice students and multicultural education coursework. In J. M. Larkin and C. E. Sleeter (Eds.), *Developing multicultural teacher education curricula* (pp. 17–29). Albany: State University of New York Press.

Sleeter, C. (2001). Epistemological diversity in research on preservice teacher preparation for historically underserved children. In W. Secada (Ed.), *Review of research in education* (pp. 209–250). Washington, DC: American Educational Research Association.

Sleeter, C. E., and Grant, C. A. (1988). *Making choices for multicultural education: Five approaches to race, class, and gender.* Columbus, OH: Merrill.

Sleeter, C. E., and Grant, C. A. (1999). *Making choices for multicultural education: Five approaches to race, class, and gender* (3rd ed.). Upper Saddle River, NJ: Merrill.

Smith, D. C. (1983). *Essential knowledge for beginning educators.* Washington, DC: American Association of Colleges for Teacher Education.

Smith, M. S., and O'Day, J. (1990). *Systemic school reform.* London: Taylor and Francis.

Smith, R., Moallem, M., and Sherrill, D. (1997). How preservice teachers think about cultural diversity: A closer look at factors which influence their beliefs towards equality. *Educational Foundations, 11*(2), 41–61.

Smitherman, G. (1986). *Talking and testifying: The language of Black America.* Detroit: Wayne State University Press.

Smitherman, G. (2000). *Talkin that talk: Language, culture, and education in African America.* London: Routledge.

Smithey, M. (1996). *Classroom management.* Nashville, TN: Cognition and Technology Group at Vanderbilt.

Snow, C., Griffin, P., and Burns, S. (in press). *Knowledge to support the teaching of reading: Preparing teachers for a changing world.* San Francisco: Jossey-Bass.

Snyder, J. (1999). *New Haven Unified School District: A teaching quality system for excellence and equity.* Washington DC: National Commission on Teaching and America's Future.

Snyder, J. (2000). Knowing children—understanding teaching: The developmental teacher education program at the University of California, Berkeley. In L. Darling-Hammond (Ed.), *Studies of excellence in teacher education: Preparation at the graduate level* (pp. 97–172). Washington, DC: American Association of Colleges for Teacher Education.

Snyder, T. D., Hoffman, C. M., and Geddes, C. M. (1997). *Digest of Education Statistics, 1997* (No. NCES-98-015). Washington, DC: U.S. Government Printing Office.

Sockett, H. (1993). *The moral base for teacher professionalism.* New York: Teachers College Press.

Sockett, H., DeMulder, E., LePage, P., and Wood, D. (2002). *Transforming teacher education: Lessons in professional development.* Westport, CT: Bergin and Garvey.

Sockett, H. T. (2001). Leading a transformative innovation: The acceptance of despair. In E. K. Demulder, P. C. LePage, and D. R. Wood (Eds.), *Transforming teacher education: Lessons in professional development.* Westport CT: Bergin and Garvey.

SooHoo, S., and Wilson, T. C. (1994). Control and contradiction in democratic teacher education: Classroom and curriculum approaches. In J. M. Novak (Ed.), *Democratic teacher education: Programs, processes, problems, and prospects* (pp. 163–182). Albany: State University of New York Press.

Sparks, G. M. (1986). The effectiveness of alternative training activities in changing teaching practices. *American Educational Research Journal, 23*(2), 217–225.

Spaulding, C. L. (1992). *Motivation in the classroom.* New York: McGraw-Hill.

Spencer, M. B., Dobbs, B., and Swanson, D. P. (1988). African American adolescents: Adaptational processes and socioeconomic diversity in behavioral outcomes. *Journal of Adolescence 11,* 117–137.

Spencer, M. B., and Markstrom-Adams, C. (1990). Identity processes among racial and ethnic minority children in America. *Child Development 61,* 290–310.

Sperling, M., and Freedman, S. W. (2001). Research on the teaching of writing. In V. Richardson (Ed.), *Handbook of research on teaching* (4th ed., 370–389). Washington, DC: American Educational Research Association.

Spiro, R. J., Feltovich, P. L., Jacobson, M. J., and Couslon, R. L. (1991). Cognitive flexibility, constructivism, and hypertext: Random access instruction for advanced knowledge acquisition in ill-structured domains. *Educational Technology, 31*(5), 24–33.

Spiro, R. J., Vispoel, W. L., Schmitz, J., Samarapungavan, A., and Boeger, A. (1987). *Knowledge acquisition for application: Cognitive flexibility and transfer in complex content domains. Technical Report No. 409.* University of Illinois, Urbana-Champaign: Center for the Study of reading.

Springer, L., Donovan, S. S., and Stanne, M. E. (1999). Effects of small-group learning on undergraduates in science, mathematics, engineering, and technology: A meta-analysis. *Review of Educational Research, 69*(1), 21–51.

Sprinthall, N. A. (1989). Meeting the developmental needs of pupils: Toward effective classroom guidance. In M. C. Reynolds (Ed.), *Knowledge base for the beginning teacher* (pp. 233–244). New York: Pergamon Press.

Sprinthall, N. A., Reiman, A. J., and Theis-Sprinthall, L. (1996). Teacher professional development. In J. P. Sikula, T. J. Buttery, E. Guyton, and Association of Teacher Educators (Eds.), *Handbook of research on teacher education: A project of the Association of Teacher Educators* (2nd ed., pp. 666–703). New York: Macmillan Library Reference, USA.

Sroufe, L. A., Cooper, R. G., DeHart, G., and Bronfenbrenner, U. (1992). *Child development: Its nature and course* (2nd ed.). New York: McGraw-Hill.

Stachowski, L. L., and Mahan, J. M. (1998). Cross-cultural field placements: Student teachers learning from schools and communities. *Theory into Practice, 37*(2), 155–162.

Stallings, J., Bossung, J., and Martin, A. (1990). Houston Teaching Academy: Partnership in developing teachers. *Teaching and Teacher Education, 6*(4), 355–365.

Stallion, B. K., and Zimpher, N. L. (1991). Classroom management intervention: The effects of training and mentoring on the inductee teacher's behavior. *Action in Teacher Education, 13*(1), 42–50.

Stallman, A. C., and Pearson, P. D. (1990). Formal measures of early literacy. In L. M. Morrow and J. K. Smith (Eds.), *Assessment for instruction in early literacy* (pp. 7–44). Englewood Cliffs, NJ: Prentice Hall.

Stancavage, F. B., Roeber, E. D., and Bohrnstedt, G. W. (1993). Impact of the 1992 trial state assessment program: A follow-up study. In R. Glaser, R. Linn, and G. Bohrnstedt

(Eds.), *The trial state assessment: Prospects and realities: Background studies.* Stanford, CA: National Academy of Education.

Stecher, B., and Chun, T. (2001). *School and classroom practices during two years of education reform in Washington state. CSE Technical Report* (No. CSE-TR-550). Los Angeles: University of California-Los Angeles.

Steele, F. I. (1973). *Physical settings and organization development.* Upper Saddle River, NJ: Addison-Wesley.

Sternberg, R. J. (1985a). *Beyond I. Q.: Toward a triarchic theory of intelligence.* Cambridge, MA: Cambridge University Press.

Sternberg, R. J. (1985b). Teaching critical thinking, Part 1: Are we making critical mistakes? *Phi Delta Kappan, 67,* 194–198.

Stevens, R. (2000). Divisions of labor in school and in the workplace: Comparing computer and paper-supported activities across settings. *The Journal of the Learning Sciences, 9*(4), 373–401.

Stiggins, R. J., Frisbie, D. A., and Griswold, P. A. (1989). Inside high school grading practices: Building a research agenda. *Educational Measurement: Issues and Practice, 8*(2), 5–14.

Stigler, J. W., and Hiebert, J. (1999). *The teaching gap: Best ideas from the world's teachers for improving education in the classroom.* New York: Free Press.

Stipek, D. J. (1996). Motivation and instruction. In D. C. Berliner and R. C. Calfee (Eds.), *Handbook of educational psychology* (pp. 85–113). New York: Macmillan.

Stipek, D. J. (2002). *Motivation to learn: From theory to practice* (4th ed.). Boston: Allyn & Bacon.

Stipek, D., and MacIver, D. (1989). Developmental change in children's assessment of intellectual competence. *Child Development, 60,* 521–538.

Strauss, R. P., and Sawyer, E. A. (1986). Some new evidence on teacher and student competencies. *Economics of Education Review, 5*(1), 41–48.

Strickland, D. (1995). The administration and supervision of reading programs. New York: Teachers College Press.

Strickland, D. S., Bodino, A., Buchan, K., Jones, K. M., Nelson, A., and Rosen, M. (2001). Teaching writing in a time of reform. *Elementary School Journal, 101*(4), 385–397.

Sugrue, T. (1996). *The origins of the urban crisis: Race and inequality in postwar Detroit.* Princeton: Princeton University Press.

Sumara, D. J., and Luce-Kapler, R. (1996). (Un)Becoming a teacher: Negotiating identities while learning to teach. *Canadian Journal of Education, 21*(1), 65–83.

Sunal, D. W. (1980). Effect of field experience during elementary methods courses on preservice teacher behavior. *Journal of Research in Science Teaching, 17*(1), 17–23.

Swan, M., and Ridgway, J. (2002). *Understanding teacher understanding—tools for a workshop.* Nottingham, England: University of Nottingham.

Tabachnik, B. R., and Zeichner, K. M. (1999). Idea and action: Action research and the development of conceptual change teaching science. *Science Education, 83*(3), 309–322.

Takaki, R. T. (1993). *A different mirror: A history of multicultural America.* Boston: Little, Brown.

Talbert, J. E. (1990). *Teacher tracking: Exacerbating inequalities in the high school.* Stanford, CA: Center for Research on the Context of Secondary Teaching, Stanford University.

Talbert, J. E., and McLaughlin, M. W. (1993). Understanding teaching in context. In D. K. Cohen, M. W. McLaughlin, and J. E. Talbert (Eds.), *Teaching for understanding: Challenges for policy and practice* (pp. 167–206). San Francisco: Jossey-Bass.

Tamburrini, J. (1982). Some educational implications of Piaget's theory. In S. Modgil and C. Modgil (Eds.), *Jean Piaget: Consensus and controversy.* New York: Praeger.

Tanner, D., and Tanner, L. N. (1995). *Curriculum development: Theory into practice* (3rd edition). Englewood Cliffs, NJ: Merrill.

Tatto, M. T. (1996). Examining values and beliefs about teaching diverse students: Understanding the challenges for teacher education. *Educational Evaluation and Policy Analysis, 18*(2), 155–180.

Tatum, B. D. (1997). *"Why are all the Black kids sitting together in the cafeteria?" And other conversations about race.* New York: Basic Books.

Tatum, B. D. (1999). Lighting candles in the dark: One black woman's response to white antiracist narratives. In C. Clark and J. O'Donnell (Eds.), *Becoming and unbecoming white: Owning and disowning a racial identity* (pp. 56–63). Westport, CT: Bergin and Garvey.

Taylor, G., Shepard, L. A., Kinner, F., and Rosenthal, J. (2003). *A survey of teachers' perspectives on high-stakes testing in Colorado: What gets taught, what gets lost. CSE Technical Report 588.* Los Angeles: University of California-Los Angeles.

Teale, W. H. (1988). Developmentally appropriate assessment of reading and writing in the early childhood classroom. *Elementary School Journal, 89*(2), 173–184.

Teglasi, H., and Rothman, L. (2001). STORIES: A classroom-based program to reduce aggressive behavior. *Journal of School Psychology, 39*(1), 71–94.

Tellez, K., Hlebowitch, P., Cohen, M., and Norwood, P. (1994). Social service field experiences and teacher education statistics. In J. Larkin and C. E. Sleeter (Eds.), *Developing multicultural teacher education curricula* (pp. 65–78). Albany: State University of New York Press.

Terrill, M., and Mark, D. L. H. (2000). Preservice teachers' expectations for schools with children of color and second-language learners. *Journal of Teacher Education, 51*(2), 149–155.

Terwilliger, J. S. (1987, April). *Classroom evaluation practices of secondary teachers in England and Minnesota.* Paper presented at the Annual Meeting of the National Council on Measurement in Education, Washington, DC.

Tharp, R., Estrada, P., Dalton, S. Yamauchi, L. A. (2000). *Teaching transformed: Achieving, excellence, fairness, inclusion, and harmony.* Boulder, CO: Westview Press.

Tharp, R. G. (1982). The effective instruction of comprehension: Results and description of the Kamehameha early education program. *Reading Research Quarterly, 17*(4), 503–527.

Tharp, R. G., and Gallimore, R. (1988). *Rousing minds to life: Teaching, learning, and schooling in social context.* Cambridge, UK: Cambridge University Press.

Thomas, E. R. (2000). *Culture and schooling: Building bridges between research praxis and professionalism.* West Sussex, England: Wiley.

Thomas, L., Larson, A., Clift, R., and Levin, J. (1996). Integrating technology in teacher education programs. *Action in Teacher Education, 17*(4), 1–8.

Thompson, C. L., and Zeuli, J. S. (1999). The frame and the tapestry: Standards-based reform and professional development. In L. Darling-Hammond and G. Sykes (Eds.), *Teaching as the learning profession: A handbook of policy and practice,* pp. 341–375. San Francisco: Jossey-Bass.

Thorndike, E. L. (1931/1968). *Human learning.* New York: The Century Co.

Tietze, W. (1987). A structural model for the evaluation of preschool effects. *Early Childhood Research Quarterly, 2*(2), 133–154.

Tillman, B. A. (1995). Reflections on case method teaching. *Action in Teacher Education, 17*(1), 1–8.

Tobin, J., and Johnson, R. (1994). A multicultural, multivocal, multimedia approach to teaching classroom management and preservice teachers. *Teaching Education, 6*(1), 113–122.

Tom, A. R. (1997). *Redesigning teacher education.* Albany: State University of New York Press.

Tomlinson, T. M. (1993). *Motivating students to learn: Overcoming barriers to high achievement.* Berkeley, CA: McCutchan Publishing.

Toussaint, N. (1998). A community that values learning. *Thrust for Educational Leadership, 28*(1), 26–28, 35.

Townsend, B. (2000). The disproportionate discipline of African American learners: Reducing school suspensions and expulsion. *Exceptional Children, 66,* 381–392.

Trachtman, R. (1996). *The NCATE professional development school study: A survey of 28 PDS sites.* Unpublished manuscript. (Available from Professional Development School Standards Project, National Council for Accreditation of Teacher Education, Washington, DC 20036.)

Tracz, S. M., Sienty, S., and Mata, S. (1994, February). *The self-reflection of teachers compiling portfolios for National Certification: Work in progress.* Paper presented at the Annual Meeting of the American Association of Colleges for Teacher Education, Chicago.

Tracz, S. M., Sienty, S., Todorov, K., Snyder, J., Takashima, B., Pensabene, R., and others (1995, April). *Improvement in teaching skills: Perspectives from National Board for Professional Teaching Standards field test network candidates.* Paper presented at the Annual Meeting of the American Educational Research Association, San Francisco.

Tyler, R. W. (1950). *Basic principles of curriculum and instruction: Syllabus for Education 360.* Chicago: University of Chicago Press.

Tyrrell, F., Scully, T., and Halligan, J. (1998). Building peaceful schools. *Thrust for Educational Leadership, 28*(2), 30–33.

United States Bureau of the Census (2000). *Statistical abstract of the United States.* Retrieved from http://www.census.gov/prod/www/statistical-abstract-us.html

United States Department of Education Office for Civil Rights. (1999). *Elementary and secondary school compliance reports.* Washington, DC: U.S. Government Printing Office.

United States Office of Technology Assessment. (1992). *Testing in American schools: Asking the right questions.* Washington, DC: U.S. Government Printing Office.

University of Michigan Law School. (1959, June). *The law schools look ahead: Proceedings of the 1959 Conference on Legal Education.* The Twelfth Annual Summer Institute sponsored by the University of Michigan Law School, June 15–18, 1959. Ann Arbor: University of Michigan Law School.

Vaill, P. B. (1996). *Learning as a way of being: Strategies for survival in a world of permanent white water.* San Francisco: Jossey-Bass.

Valdés, G. (1996). *Con respeto: Bridging the distances between culturally diverse families and schools: An ethnographic portrait.* New York: Teachers College Columbia University.

Valdés, G. (2001). *Learning and not learning English: Latino students in American schools.* London: Teachers College Press.

Valdés, G., and Figueroa, R. A. (1994). *Bilingualism and testing: A special case of bias.* Norwood, NJ: Ablex.

Valenzuela, A. (1999). *Subtractive schooling: U.S.-Mexican youth and the politics of caring.* Albany: State University of New York Press.

Valli, L. (1989). Assessing the reflective practice of student teachers. In J. J. Denton and D. G. Armstrong (Eds.), *Shaping policy in teacher education through program evaluation* (pp. 21–35). College Station, TX: Instructional Research Laboratory, College of Education, Texas A and M University.

Valli, L. (1992). *Reflective teacher education: Cases and critiques.* Albany: State University of New York Press.

Valli, L. (1995). The dilemma of race: Learning to be color blind and color conscious. *Journal of Teacher Education, 16*(3), 120–129.

Valli, L. (2000). Connecting teacher development and school improvement: Ironic consequences of a preservice action research course. *Teaching and Teacher Education, 16*(7), 715–730.

van Lier, L. (1995). *Introducing language awareness.* New York: Penguin.

Veenman, S. (1984). Perceived problems of beginning teachers. *Review of Educational Research, 54*(2), 143–178.

Verkuyten, M. (2002). Making teachers accountable for students' disruptive classroom behaviour. *British Journal of Sociology of Education, 50*(5), 107–122.

Villegas, A. M. (1988). School failure and cultural mismatch: Another view. *Urban Review, 20*(4), 253–265.

Villegas, A. M. (1991). *Culturally responsive pedagogy for the 1990s and beyond. Trends and Issues Paper No. 6.* Washington, DC: ERIC Clearinghouse on Teacher Education.

Villegas, A. M., and Lucas, T. (2002a). *Educating culturally responsive teachers: A coherent approach.* Albany: State University of New York Press.

Villegas, A. M., and Lucas, T. (2002b). Preparing culturally responsive teachers: Rethinking the curriculum. *Journal of Teacher Education, 53*(1), 20–32.

Vosniadou, S., and Brewer, W. F. (1989). *The concept of the earth's shape: A study of conceptual change in childhood. Technical Report No. 467.* University of Illinois, Urbana-Champaign: Center for the Study of reading.

Vygotsky, L. (1986). *Thought and language* (A. Kozulin, Trans.). Cambridge, MA: MIT Press. (Original English translation published 1962).

Vygotsky, L. S. (1978). *Mind in society: The development of higher psychological processes.* Cambridge, MA: Harvard University Press.

Wade, R., and Yarbrough, D. (1996). Portfolios: A tool for reflective thinking in teacher education. *Teaching and Teacher Education, 12*(1), 63–79.

Wagner, A. C. (1973). Changing behavior: A comparison of microteaching and cognitive discrimination training. *Journal of Educational Psychology 64*(3), 299–305.

Walker, D. F., and Soltis, J. F. (1986). *Curriculum and aims.* New York: Teachers College Press.

Walker, D. F., and Soltis, J. F. (1992). *Curriculum and aims* (2nd ed.). New York: Teachers College Press.

Walker, D. F., and Soltis, J. F. (1997). *Curriculum and aims* (3rd ed.). New York: Teachers College Press.

Walker, K. (1991). *Peter.* New York: Houghton Mifflin.

Wang, M. C., and Lindvall, C. M. (1984). Individual differences and school learning. In E. W. Gordon (Ed.), *Review of research in education, 2,* 161–225. Itasca, IL: Peacock.

Warren, B., and Rosebery, A. (1995). Equity in the future tense: Redefining relationships among teachers, students, and science in linguistic minority classrooms. In W. G. Secada, E. Fennema, and L. Adajian (Eds.), *New directions for equity in mathematics education* (pp. 279–297). Cambridge, UK: Cambridge University Press.

Watson, R. T., Suter, E., Romrell, L. J., Harman, E. M., Rooks, L. G., and Neims, A. H. (1998). Moving a graveyard: How one school prepared the way for continuous curriculum renewal. *Academic Medicine, 73*(9), 948–955.

Wayne, C., Jelacic, S., Boster, D. R., Ciol, M. A., Williams, G. D., Watkins, S. L., and others (2002). Prothrombotic coagulation abnormalities preceding the hemolytic–uremic syndrome. *New England Journal of Medicine, 346*(1), 23–32.

Weade, G., and Evertson, C. M. (1991). On what can be learned by observing teaching. *Theory into Practice, 30*(1), 37–45.

Webb, R. (1990). *Practitioner research in the primary school.* London: Falmer Press.

Weiner, L. (1999). *Urban teaching: The essentials.* New York: Teachers College Press.

Weinstein, C. S. (1988). Preservice teachers' expectations about the first year of teaching. *Teaching and Teacher Education, 4*(1), 31–41.

Weinstein, C. S. (1996). *Secondary classroom management: Lessons from research and practice.* New York: McGraw-Hill.

Weinstein, C. S. (1999). Reflections of best practices and promising programs: Beyond assertive classroom discipline. In H. J. Freiberg (Ed.), *Beyond behaviorism: Changing the classroom management paradigm* (pp. 147–163). Boston: Allyn & Bacon.

Weinstein, C. S., and Mignano, A. J. (1993). *Elementary classroom management: Lessons from research and practice.* New York: McGraw-Hill.

Weinstein, C. S., Woolfolk, A. E., Dittmeier, L., and Shanker, U. (1994). Protector or prison guard? Using metaphors and media to explore student teachers' thinking about classroom management. *Action in Teacher Education, 16*(1), 41–54.

Welsh, M., Parke, R. D., Widaman, K., and O'Neil, R. (2001). Linkages between children's social and academic competence: A longitudinal analysis. *Journal of School Psychology, 39*(6), 463–482.

Wenger, E. (1998). *Communities of practice: Learning, meaning, and identity.* London: Cambridge University Press.

Wenglinsky, H. (2002). The link between teacher classroom practices and student academic performance. *Education Policy Analysis Archives, 10*(12).

Wertime, R. (1979). Students' problems and "courage spans." In J. Lockhead and J. Clements (Eds.), *Cognitive process instruction.* Philadelphia: The Franklin Institute Press.

Wertsch, J. V. (1998). *Mind as action.* New York: Oxford University Press.

Westheimer, J. (1998). *Among school teachers: Community, autonomy and ideology in teachers' work.* New York: Teachers College Press.

Whitaker Foundation. (2004). http://www.whitaker.org. Arlington, VA: Whitaker Foundation.

Whitcomb, J. A. (2002). Composing dilemma cases: An opportunity to understand moral dimensions of teaching. *Teaching Education, 13*(2), 125–135.

White, B. Y., and Frederickson, J. R. (1998). Inquiry, modeling and metacognition: Making science accessible to all students. *Cognition and Instruction, 16*(1), 3–117.

White, B. Y., and Frederickson, J. R. (2000). Metacognitive facilitation: An approach to making scientific inquiry accessible to all. In J. Minstrell and E. van Zee (Eds.), *Inquiring into inquiry learning and teaching in science* (pp. 33–370). Washington, DC: American Association for the Advancement of Science.

Whitehead, A. N. (1929). *The aims of education and other essays.* New York: Macmillan.

Whitford, B. L., Ruscoe, G. C., and Fickel, L. (2000). Knitting it all together: Collaborative teacher education in Southern Maine. In L. Darling-Hammond (Ed.), *Studies of excellence in teacher education: Preparation at the graduate level* (pp. 173–257). Washington, DC: American Association of Colleges for Teacher Education.

Wideen, M., Mayer-Smith, J., and Moon, B. (1998). A critical analysis of the research on learning to teach: Making the case for an ecological perspective on inquiry. *Review of Educational Research, 68*(2), 130–178.

Wielkiewicz, R. M. (1995). *Behavior management in the school: Principles and procedures* (2nd ed.). Boston: Allyn & Bacon.

Wiest, L. R. (1999). Practicing what they teach: Should teachers "Do as they say"? *Clearing House, 72*(5), 264–268.

Wigfield, A., Eccles, J. S., and Rodriguez, D. (1998). The development of children's motivation in school contexts. In P. D. Pearson and A. Iran-Nejad (Eds.), *Review of research in education* (Vol. 23, pp. 51–98). Itasca, IL: Peacock.

Wiggins, G. (1992). Creating tests worth taking. *Educational Leadership, 49*(8), 26–33.

Wiggins, G. (1993). Assessment: Authenticity, context, and validity. *Phi Delta Kappan, 75*(3), 200–208, 210–214.

Wiggins, G. P. (1998). *Educative assessment: Designing assessments to inform and improve student performance.* San Francisco: Jossey-Bass.

Wiggins, G. P., and McTighe, J. (1998). *Understanding by design.* Upper Saddle River, NJ: Prentice Hall.

Williams, B. C. (2000). *Reforming teacher education through accreditation: Telling our story.* Washington, DC: National Council for the Accreditation of Teacher Education and American Association of Colleges for Teacher Education.

Williams, J. P. (1980). Teaching decoding with an emphasis on phoneme analysis and phoneme blending. *Journal of Educational Psychology, 72*(1), 1–15.

Williams, S. M. (1992). Putting case-based instruction into context: Examples from legal and medical education. *The Journal of the Learning Sciences, 2*(4), 367–427.

Willis, A. I., and Lewis, K. C. (1998). Focus on research: A conversation with Gloria Ladson-Billings. *Language Arts, 75*(1), 61–70.

Wilson, R. J. (1990). Classroom processes in evaluating student achievement. *Alberta Journal of Educational Research, 36*(1), 4–17.

Wilson, S., Darling-Hammond, L., and Berry B. (2001). *A case of successful teaching policy: Connecticut's long-term efforts to improve teaching and learning.* Seattle, WA: Center for the Study of Teaching and Policy.

Wilson, S. M., and McDiarmid, G. W. (1996). Something old, something new: What do social studies teachers need to know? In F. B. Murray (Ed.), *The teacher educator's handbook: Building a knowledge base for the preparation of teachers* (pp. 295–319). Washington DC: American Association of Colleges for Teacher Education.

Wilson, S. M., Floden, R. E., and Ferrini-Mundy, J. (2001). *Teacher preparation research: Current knowledge, gaps, and recommendations: A research report prepared for the U.S. Department of Education.* Seattle, WA: Center for the Study of Teaching and Policy.

Wilson, S. M., Shulman, L. S., and Richert, A. E. (1987). "150 different ways of knowing": Representations of knowledge in teaching. In J. Calderhead (Ed.), *Exploring teachers' thinking* (pp. 104–124). London: Cassell.

Wineburg, S. (1991). Historical problem solving: A study of the cognitive processes used in the evaluation of documentary and pictorial evidence. *Journal of Education Psychology, 83*(1), 73–87.

Wineburg, S. (1998). Reading Abraham Lincoln: An expert-expert study in the interpretation of historical texts. *Cognitive Science, 22,* 319–346.

Wineburg, S. S., and Wilson, S. M. (1988). Models of wisdom in the teaching of history. *Phi Delta Kappan, 70*(1), 50–58.

Wineburg, S. S., and Wilson, S. M. (1991). Subject matter knowledge in the teaching of history. In J. E. Brophy (Ed.), *Advances in research on teaching, Vol. 2: Teachers' knowledge of subject matter as it relates to their teaching practice.* Greenwich, CT: JAI.

Winfield, L. F. (1986). Teacher beliefs toward academically at risk students in inner urban schools. *Urban Review, 18*(4), 253–268.

Winitzky, N. (1992). Structure and process in thinking about classroom management: An exploratory study of prospective teachers. *Teaching and Teacher Education, 8*(1), 1–14.

Winitzky, N., and Kauchak, D. (1995). Learning to teach: Knowledge development in classroom management. *Teaching and Teacher Education, 11*(3), 215–227.

Winkelman, W., Hollaender, A., Schmerkotte, H., and Schmalohr, E. (1979). *Kognitive entwicklung und foerderung von kindergarten und vorklassenkindern* (Vol. 2). Kronberg, Germany: Scriptor.

Wiseman, D. L., and Cooner, D. (1996). Discovering the power of collaboration: The impact of a school-university partnership on teaching. *Teacher Education and Practice 12*(1), 18–28.

Wolfberg, P. J., (1988). *Integrated play groups for children with autism and related disorders.* Unpublished master's field study, San Francisco State University.

Wolfberg, P. J. (1994). Case illustrations of emerging social relations and symbolic activity in children with autism through supported peer play. Doctoral dissertation, University of California at Berkeley with San Francisco State University. *Dissertation Abstracts International* (UMI No.9505068).

Wolfberg, P. J. (2003). *Peer play and the autism spectrum: The art of guiding children's socialization and imagination.* Shawnee Mission, KS: Autism Asperger Publishing.

Wolfberg, P. J., and Schuler, A. L. (1992). *Integrated play groups project: Final evaluation report.* Washington, DC: Department of Education.

Wolfberg, P. J., and Schuler, A. L. (1993). Integrated play groups: A model for promoting the social and cognitive dimensions of play in children with autism. *Journal of Autism and Developmental Disorders, 23*(3), 467–489.

Wolfberg, P. J., Zercher, C., Lieber, J., Capell, K., Matias, S., Hanson, M., and others (1999). "Can I Play With You?" Peer culture in inclusive preschool programs. *Journal of the Association for Persons with Severe Handicaps, 24*(2), 69–84.

Wolfram, W., Adger, C. T., and Christian, D. (1999). *Dialects in school and communities.* Mahwah, NJ: Erlbaum.

Wood, D., Bruner, J. S., and Ross, G. (1976). The role of tutoring in problem solving. *Journal of Child Psychology and Psychiatry, 17*(2), 89–100.

Wood, P. H., Bennett, T., Wood, J., and Bennett, C. (1990, April). *Grading and evaluation practices and policies of school teachers.* Paper presented at the Annual Meetings of the National Council on Measurement in Education, Boston.

Wood, T., and Sellers, P. (1996). Assessment of a problem-centered mathematics program: Third grade. *Journal for Research in Mathematics Education, 27*(3), 337–353.

Woodson, C. G. (1933/1977). *The mis-education of the Negro* (2nd rev. ed.). New York: AMS Press.

Wright, S. P., Horn, S. P., and Sanders, W. L. (1997). Teacher and classroom context effects on student achievement: Implications for teacher evaluation. *Journal of Personnel Evaluation in Education, 11*(1), 57–67.

Yackel, E., Cobb, P., and Wood, T. (1991). Small-group interactions as a source of learning opportunities in second-grade mathematics. *Journal for Research in Mathematics Education, 22*(5), 390–408.

Yelon, S. L., and Schmidt, W. H. (1973). The effect of objectives and instructions on the learning of a complex cognitive task. *Journal of Experimental Education, 41*(3), 91–96.

Yerian, S., and Grossman, P. L. (1997). Preservice teachers' perceptions of their middle level teacher education experience: A comparison of a traditional and a PDS Model. *Teacher Education Quarterly, 24*(4), 85–101.

Youngs, P., Odden, A., and Porter, A. C. (2003). State policy related to teacher licensure. *Educational Policy, 17*(2), 217–236.

Yu, S. L., Elder, A. D., and Urdan, T. C. (1995, April). *Motivation and cognitive strategies in students with a "good student" or "poor student" self-schema.* Paper presented at the American Educational Research Association, San Francisco.

Zeichner, K. M. (1993a). *Educating Teachers for Cultural Diversity. NCRTL Special Report.* East Lansing: Michigan State University.

Zeichner, K. M. (1993b). Traditions of practice in U.S. preservice teacher education programs. *Teaching and Teacher Education, 9*(1), 1–13.

Zeichner, K. M. (2000). Ability-based teacher education: Elementary teacher education at Alverno College. In L. Darling-Hammond (Ed.), *Studies of excellence in teacher education: Preparation in the undergraduate years* (pp. 1–66). Washington, DC: American Association of Colleges for Teacher Education.

Zeichner, K. (2003). Action research as a strategy for preparing teachers to work for greater social justice: A case study from the United States. In J. Diniz-Pereira and Z. Zeichner (Eds.), *A pesquisa na formação eno trabalho docente* (Research in Teacher Education and Teacher's Work). Belo Horizonto, Brasil: Autentica.

Zeichner, K. M., and Gore, J. (1990). Teacher socialization. In W. R. Houston, M. Haberman, J. P. Sikula, and Association of Teacher Educators (Eds.), *Handbook of research on teacher education* (pp. 329–348). New York: Macmillan.

Zeichner, K. M., and Hoeft, K. (1996). Teacher socialization for cultural diversity. In J. P. Sikula, T. J. Buttery, E. Guyton, and Association of Teacher Educators (Eds.), *Handbook of research on teacher education* (2nd ed., pp. 525–547). New York: Macmillan.

Zeichner, K. M., and Liston, D. P. (1987). Teaching student teachers to reflect. *Harvard Educational Review, 57*(1), 23–48.

Zeichner, K. M., and Liston, D. P. (1996). *Reflective teaching: An introduction.* Mahwah, NJ: Erlbaum.

Zeichner, K. M., and Melnick, S. L. (1996). *The role of community field experiences in preparing teachers for cultural diversity.* New York: Teachers College Press.

Zeichner, K. M., Melnick, S., and Gomez, M. L. (Eds.). (1996). *Currents of reform in preservice teacher education.* New York: Teachers College Press.

Zeichner, K. M., and Miller, M. (Eds.). (1997). *Learning to teach in professional development schools.* New York: Teachers College Press.

Zeichner, K. M., and Noffke, S. E. (2001). Practitioner research. In V. Richardson (Ed.), *Handbook of research on teaching* (4th ed., pp. 298–332). Washington, DC: American Educational Research Association.

Zeichner, K. M., and Tabachnick, B. R. (1981). Are the effects of university teacher education "washed out" by school experience? *Journal of Teacher Education, 32*(3), 7–11.

Zercher, C., Hunt, P., Schuler, A., and Webster, J. (2001). Increasing joint attention, play and language through peer supported play. *Autism: The International Journal of Research and Practice, 5*(4), 374–398.

Zumwalt, K. (1989). The need for a curricular vision. In M. C. Reynolds (Ed.), *Knowledge base for the beginning teacher* (pp. 173–184). New York: Pergamon Press.

NAME INDEX

SUBJECT INDEX